18th Coherent Laser Radar Conference (CLRC 2016)

Boulder, Colorado, USA
27 June – 1 July 2016

ISBN: 978-1-5108-2854-4

Printed from e-media with permission by:

Curran Associates, Inc.
57 Morehouse Lane
Red Hook, NY 12571

CURRAN ASSOCIATES INC. proceedings.com

Some format issues inherent in the e-media version may also appear in this print version.

Printed by Curran Associates, Inc. (2016)

For permission requests, please contact Cooperative Institute for Research in Environmental Sciences (CIRES) at the address below.

Cooperative Institute for Research in Environmental Sciences (CIRES)
University of Colorado Boulder
216 UCB
Boulder, CO 80309
USA

Phone: 303-492-1143

cires.colorado.edu

Additional copies of this publication are available from:

Curran Associates, Inc.
57 Morehouse Lane
Red Hook, NY 12571 USA
Phone: 845-758-0400
Fax: 845-758-2633
Email: curran@proceedings.com
Web: www.proceedings.com

TABLE OF CONTENTS

WIND LIDAR FOR WIND ENERGY

DIRECT DETECTION WIND LIDAR

DIAL AND ATMOSPHERIC MONITORING

NOVEL SENSING TECHNIQUES

LASERS I

LASERS II

COHERENT DETECTION WIND LIDAR III

HARD TARGET DETECTION, RANGING AND VELOCITY ESTIMATION

SPACE BASED WIND LIDAR II

18th Coherent Laser Radar Conference and the Lidar Working Group on Space Based Winds

June 26 – July 1, 2016, Boulder Colorado

Coherent Investments
Partnering Through The Early Stage

NASA

LeoSphere
THE ATMOSPHERE IS YOURS

Discovery Semiconductors, Inc.
We Chip the Future

LOCKHEED MARTIN

NORTHROP GRUMMAN

CLRC 2016
18th Coherent Laser Radar Conference

Conference Overview

The 18th conference on coherent laser radar technology and applications is the latest in a series beginning in 1980 that provides a forum for exchange of information on recent events, current status, and future directions of coherent laser radar (coherent lidar) technology and applications.

This conference was founded by Mr. Milton Huffaker, founder and CEO of Coherent Technologies, Inc. and presently CEO of Coherent Investments Inc.

The conference serves as a biennial forum for the exchange of current and future developments within the field of coherent laser radar and wind lidar including direct detection wind lidar. It is intended that the meeting will highlight recent advancements in the field, including component technology and instrumentation, systems (surface, airborne, and space-based), measurements and processing techniques, and emerging requirements for coherent laser radar applications in studies of atmospheric, ocean, surface and target properties.

Conference Chairs

Philip Gatt - Chairman

Lockheed Martin Coherent Technologies, LM Advanced Technology Center, USA

phil.gatt@lmco.com

Shoken Ishii – Co-Chairman

Applied Electromagnetic Research Institute

National Institute of Information and Communications Technology (NICT), Japan

sishii@nict.go.jp

Conference Support

Virginia Schultz - Conference Coordinator

CU Conference Services

University of Colorado Boulder

virginia.schultz@colorado.edu

Linda Pendergrass - Technical Secretariat

Cooperative Institute for Research in Environmental Sciences (CIRES)

University of Colorado Boulder

linda.pendergrass@colorado.edu

Sponsors

- NASA Earth Science Technology Office
- Coherent Investments, Inc.
- Lockheed Martin Advanced Technology Center

Exhibitors

LEOSPHERE, http://www.leosphere.com/en/

LEOSPHERE is a world leader in LIDAR (laser radar) atmospheric remote observations. The company offers new turnkey and user-friendly remote-sensing instruments allowing wind measurement, aerosol (ice, ash, dust, smoke) characterization and localization, and clouds height and atmospheric structure (boundary layer, aerosol layers). Our range of WINDCUBE LIDARs are powerful instruments for meteorological agencies, airports and atmospheric research institutes since they provide high-resolution data on extreme weather events (eg hurricanes, cyclones ...), and wind shear on airports. They are complementary to existing classic observation instruments.

Discovery Semiconductors, www.discoverysemi.com

Discovery Semiconductors, Inc. is an industry leader in manufacturing ultrafast, high optical power handling InGaAs photodetectors, RF over fiber optical receivers, balanced optical receivers and several custom products for applications ranging from analog RF links to ultrafast digital communications. Discovery's instrumentation includes their Lab Buddy and Optical Coherent Receiver System.

Northrop Grumman, www.nothropgrumman.com/ceolaser

Northrop Grumman Cutting Edge Optronics is a leading supplier of high-power laser diodes, DPSS modules, laser diode drivers and complete DPSS laser systems. Many of our diode laser based products have become industry standards, and are used in a wide variety of commercial and military applications. The company is registered to ISO 9001:2008, and is located in St. Charles, MO.

Keynote Speakers

Milton Huffaker

Milton Huffaker has been at the forefront in the development and application of coherent lidar systems since the late 1960s. He is best known for his pioneering work in demonstrating the efficacy of coherent lidar systems for atmospheric wind measurement applications. He organized the first Coherent Laser Radar Conference in 1980 in Aspen, CO, a conference series which has been instrumental in stimulating exchange of ideas and collaboration among scientists and engineers worldwide. After leading many successful coherent lidar system development programs at NASA and NOAA, in 1984 he founded Coherent Technologies, which became a world leader in the development on novel coherent lidar systems for applications ranging from wind measurement to characterization of vehicle and other target vibration at large distances. Coherent Technologies offered the first commercially available coherent lidar system for wind measurements, the *WindTracer*®, and these systems are deployed worldwide for wind measurement applications. In 2005, Lockheed Martin acquired Coherent Technologies and Milton moved to his next venture, founding Coherent Investments which provides guidance, support, and capital in order to assist companies that are in their early stage of development. He is also very well known for his kindness and eagerness to help others, and has been involved in and has founded several non-profit charitable organizations.

John L. Hall

John Hall is best known as a preeminent laser experimentalist contributing significantly to the development of the laser from a laboratory curiosity to a fundamental tool of modern science. He has pioneered the use of stabilized lasers to accomplish measurements of unprecedented accuracy and intrinsic physical interest. He has won more than 20 prestigious awards for his work, much of which was carried out in Boulder, CO at JILA (formerly called the Joint Institute for Laboratory Astrophysics) operated by the University of Colorado and the National Institute of Standards and Technology (NIST). At JILA he has been responsible for many major innovations and developments in laser frequency stabilization, high resolution spectroscopy, laser cooling, quantum optics, and high precision measurements using laser technology. He has authored more than 230 articles in refereed journals and holds 11 US patents. He is a member of the National Academy of Sciences, and is a Fellow of the Optical Society of America and the American Physical Society. He has trained numerous graduate students, postdocs and other scientists who are also recognized leaders in laser stabilization and spectroscopy. In 2005, he was awarded a Nobel Prize in Physics for contributions to the development of laser-based precision spectroscopy, including the optical frequency comb technique. He remains active as a Senior Fellow Emeritus at NIST, a Fellow at JILA, and helps others solve difficult laser stabilization problems through his company, Hall Stable Laser. He also works with his wife bringing science experience into primary schools.

Past Conferences

	Year	Location	Chair	Co-Chair
I	1980	Aspen, CO, USA	Huffaker	Huffaker
II	1983	Aspen, CO, USA	Huffaker	Vaughn
III	1985	Great Malvern, UK	Vaughn	Huffaker
IV	1987	Aspen, CO, USA	Bilbro	Werner
V	1989	Munich, Germany	Werner	Bilbro
VI	1991	Snowmass, CO, USA	Hardesty	Flamant
VII	1993	Paris, France	Flamant	Menzies
VIII	1995	Keystone, CO, USA	Menzies	Steinvall
IX	1997	Linkoping, Sweden	Steinvall	Kavaya
X	1999	Mount Hood, OR, USA	Kavaya	Willits
XI	2001	Great Malvern, UK	Willits	Heinrichs
XII	2003	Bar Harbor, ME, USA	Heinrichs	Asai
XIII	2005	Kamakura, Japan	Asai	Henderson
XIV	2007	Snowmass, CO, USA	Henderson	Dabas
XV	2009	Toulouse, France	Dabas	Spiers
XVI	2011	Long Beach, CA, USA	Spiers	Belmonte
XVII	2013	Barcelona, Spain	Belmonte	Gatt

The next CLRC, CLRC XIX, will chaired by Shoken Ishii in Okinawa Japan, 2018.

Acknowledgements

I greatly appreciate the Sponsors, Exhibitors and many paper authors for their contribution to the 18th CLRC. Their dedication and commitment to the Coherent Laser Radar field is highly commended. I would also like to give a special thank you to Virginia Schultz, Linda Pendergrass, Mike Hardesty, Sammy Henderson, Milton Huffaker, Shoken Ishii, the Advisory and Program Committees for support and assistance in the planning and execution of this conference. To them, I am deeply indebted.

Philip Gatt

CLRC XVIII Chairman

Conference Highlights

Location

The conference is being held at the University of Colorado Boulder.

Technical Sessions

TECHNICAL SESSIONS are in Math 100 on Monday June 27 and in the University Memorial Center (UMC) Ballroom on Tuesday June 28 through Friday July 1 morning session. Afternoon Lidar meeting on Friday July 1 is in Ekeley S274.

Lunches

Lunches (Monday through Friday) are included in your conference registration and are in the Center for Community (C4C) Dining Center.

Exhibitors

Exhibits will be on display in the UMC West Ballroom on Tuesday June 28 from 9 a.m. to 5 p.m., Wednesday June 29 from 9 a.m. to 1 p.m. and Thursday June 30 from 9 a.m. to 4 p.m. Please stop by and visit with the exhibitors.

Welcome Reception

Join your colleagues at the CLRC Welcome Reception at the Millennium Harvest House Hotel, Boulder CO, Sunday Evening, June 26 from 6:00 p.m. to 9:00 p.m. Appetizers, snacks and beverages will be complementary.

Registration and Information Desk

Monday June 27	Math 100 Plaza	7:00 a.m. to 11:00 a.m.
Tuesday June 28	UMC Ballroom Foyer	7:30 a.m. to 10:30 a.m.
Wednesday June 29	UMC Ballroom Foyer	7:30 a.m. to 10:30 a.m.
Thursday June 30	UMC Ballroom Foyer	7:30 a.m. to 10:30 a.m.
Friday July 1	UMC Ballroom Foyer	7:30 a.m. to 10:30 a.m.

If you need assistance and there is no one at the registration area contact the CUCS main office at 303.492.5151 for registration questions or Virginia Schultz at 303.818.5122 for other questions.

Advisory Committee Luncheon

The CLRC Advisory Committee Planning Meeting is scheduled for Tuesday, June 28, from 11:30 a.m. to 1:00 p.m. during the lunch break in the Tree House room at the Center for Community (C4C). Select your lunch items and bring your tray to the Tree House just past the Persian station.

Poster Session

The Poster session is an intricate part of the technical program. Set-up for the poster session will be from 2 p.m. to 6 p.m. on Tuesday June 28 in the UMC South Terrace Tent. Participant's posters will be organized in relation to the agenda listed in the conference program. The poster session will be held from 6:00 p.m. to 9:00 p.m. Each author will be provided a 4' by 8' wide space to display their paper. Push pins will be provided. Appetizers and beverages will be available throughout the poster session. Please use the drink tickets that you received in your badge for this event, wear your conference badge and have official government id for proof of age.

Tours

Chautauqua Park A Buff Bus shuttle will be available from 1:30 p.m. to 4:30 p.m. on Wednesday June 29 to take participants and guests to Chautauqua Park where you can enjoy the lawn area, historic buildings and Dining Hall along with many picturesque trails. The bus will depart from the street adjacent to the UMC South Terrace. Please be aware of the weather, bring plenty of water, sunscreen and/or hat and sturdy shoes. Also, due to the elevation, hiking is more demanding than you may be accustomed to so, please plan accordingly when selecting a trail. The shuttle will continuously circulate so wait times will be less than 20 minutes. Last shuttle leaves Chautauqua Park at 5:00 p.m.

Celestial Seasonings and Leanin' Tree Museum Tour A ticket is required for this tour. Those pre-registered will have a ticket in their badge. Please see the registration desk if you would like to add this tour, limited seats are available. The coach leaves from the street adjacent to the UMC South Terrace at 1:30 p.m. on Wednesday June 29 and will return at 5:00 p.m. to the UMC. Your tour guide will point out items of interest as you travel north of Boulder to the Celestial Seasonings tea production plant. Enjoy seeing the production line, experience the always popular peppermint room along with the original tea box artwork and finish the tour in the gift shop where many unique souvenirs and teas are available for purchase. The Leanin' Tree Museum is world renowned for its collection of western art and for its distinctive and often hilarious western-themed greeting cards. You will have time to enjoy one of the nation's largest private collections of western art both inside the Museum and outside in the Sculpture Garden. Tips for the tour guide are graciously accepted.

NCAR Banquet Dinner

The views from the NCAR Mesa Lab are a highlight of any trip to Boulder, Colorado! Shuttle busses will depart at 5:30 p.m. from the street adjacent to the UMC South Terrace for the NCAR Banquet. We encourage you to ride the shuttle. Return trips will begin around 9 p.m. and return to the UMC and to conference hotels. Enjoy a southwestern themed dinner of roast buffalo, fried chicken, Portobello mushrooms and all the fixins'. A program of CLRC highlights and awards will follow the buffet dinner. Please wear your conference badge and have official government id for proof of age if you are planning on consuming beer or wine. This is a private event and any guests of CLRC participants must have a ticket. Banquet is on Wednesday June 29 from 6 p.m. to 10 p.m.

Speakers and Presiders

All speakers are requested to check in at least 30 minutes prior to beginning of their respective Technical Session. Presentations should be uploaded to the AV system and previewed at this time.

Oral Presentations

Oral presentations for contributed papers should be a maximum of 17 minutes plus 3 minutes for discussion. Invited papers the corresponding times are 22 and 3 minutes respectively. Oral presentations and 4-page summary papers will be posted on the internet after the conference.

Post Deadline Papers

Post deadline papers will be accepted and posted on the internet. They are to be submitted via email to Linda Pendergrass. Send to: linda.pendergrass@colorado.edu

Conference Advisory Committee

Kazu Asai
Tohoku Institute of Technology, Japan

Aniceto Belmonte
UPC Barcelona Tech, Spain

Alain Dabas
Météo-France, France

Pierre Flamant
École Polytechnique, France

Michael Hardesty
CIRES, USA

Richards Heinrichs
DARPA, USA

Sammy Henderson
Beyond Photonics, USA

Milton Huffaker
Coherent Investments, USA

Michael Kavaya
NASA Langley Research Center, USA

Dennis Killinger
University of South Florida, USA

Paul McManamon
Exciting Technology, USA

Robert Menzies
Jet Propulsion Laboratory, USA

Stephan Rahm
DLR, German Aerospace Establishment, Germany

Gary Spiers
Jet Propulsion Laboratory, USA

Conference Program Committee

Water Buell
Aerospace Corp, USA

Jean-Pierre Cariou
Leosphere, France

Aditya Choukulkar
NOAA, USA

Xinzhao Chu
University of Colorado Boulder/CIRES, USA

Dave Emmitt
Simpson Weather Associates, USA

Maurice Halmos
Raytheon Corp., USA

Hamaki Inokuchi
Japan Aerospace Exploration Agency, Japan

Gary Kamerman
FastMetrix, Inc., USA

Shumpei Kameyama
Mitsubishi Electric Corp., Japan

Thomas Karr
DARPA, USA

Laurent Lombard
ONERA, French Aerospace Lag, France

Nathan Newbury
NIST, USA

Joe Paranto
Applied Research Associates (ARA), USA

Guy Pearson
Halo Photonics, UK

Dave Rabb
AFRL Wright Patterson, USA

Oliver Reitebuch
DLR, German Aerospace Establishment, Germany

Upendra Singh
NASA Langley Research Center, USA
Sara Tucker
Ball Aerospace & Technologies Corp., USA
Benjamin Witschas
DLR, German Aerospace Establishment, Germany

Historical Review of CLR Wind Sensing

R. Milton Huffaker
Coherent Investments, LLC
Broomfield, CO, 80021

Historical Review of CLR Wind Sensing

- **NASA-MSFC -- 1961**
  - ✓ Re-Entry Physics
  - ✓ Study of Heat Protection Materials
  - ✓ Heat and Mass Loss from Re-Entry Vehicles
  - ✓ ALSO -- Tektites
- RADIATION DESIGN CRITERIA FOR SATURN VEHICLES
  - ✓ Liquid Kerosene-Oxygen Plumes
  - ✓ Liquid Hydrogen-Oxygen Plumes
  - ✓ Strong shock interactions producing high temperatures
  - ✓ Models developed, experiments conducted, data obtained, design values calculated

Historical Review of CLR Wind Sensing

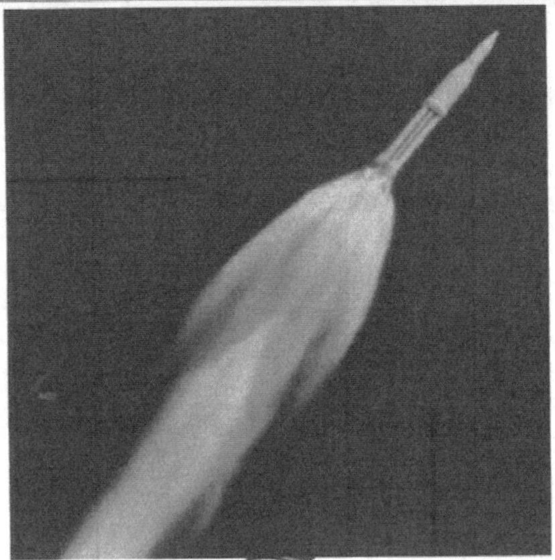

Historical Review of CLR Wind Sensing

5

Historical Review of CLR Wind Sensing

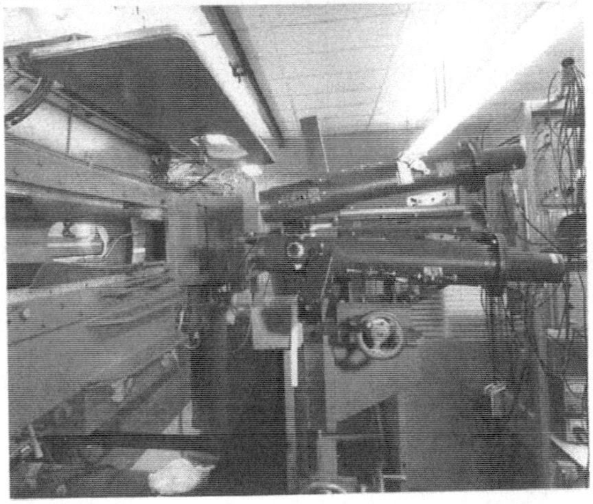

6

Historical Review of CLR Wind Sensing

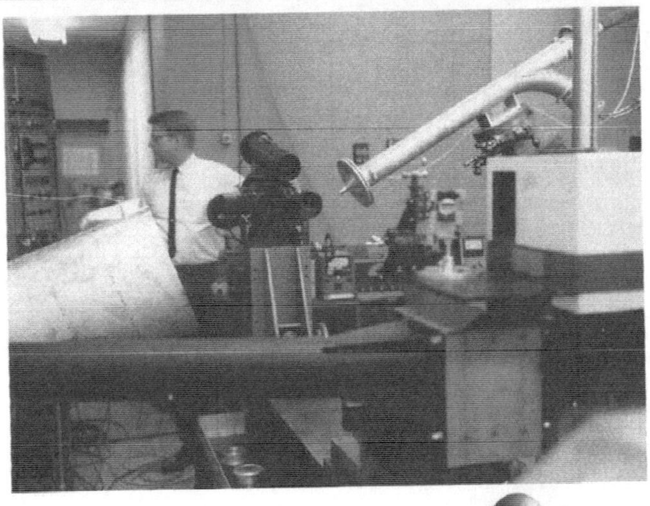

7

Historical Review of CLR Wind Sensing

- CENTER MANAGEMENT ASKED WHETHER ATMOSPHERIC WIND MEASUREMENTS WERE POSSIBLE

  - ✓ **$CO2$ laser selected**
  - ✓ **Raytheon awarded contract to develop 20 watt laser**
  - ✓ **Incorporated most simple of Doppler designs for 1st demonstration of wind-unseeded air flow measurement**
  - ✓ **Laser energy expanded thru telescope and focused, detector placed in back of laser, using appropriate internal laser mirrors, to not saturate detectors**

8

Historical Review of CLR Wind Sensing

- FIRST ATMOSPHERIC WIND COMPARISONS PERFORMED
- FIRST WAKE VORTEX VELOCITY MEASUREMENTS

HUFFAKER *ET AL.*: LASER-DOPPLER DETECTION OF TRAILING VORTICES

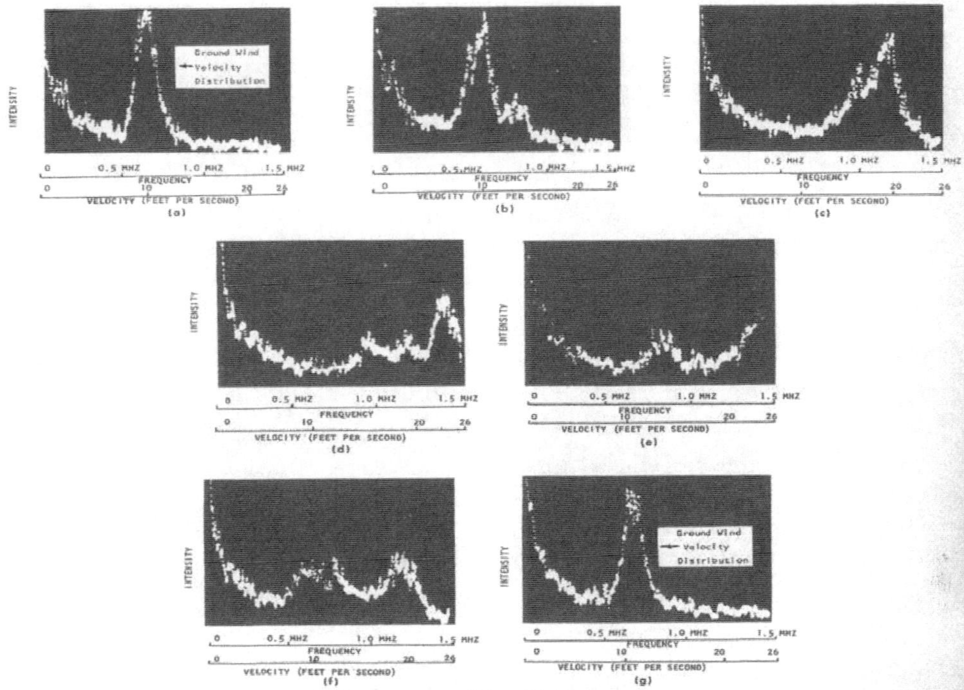

Fig. 7. Time sequence display of the velocity structure of a trailing vortex using a laser velocimeter.

CAA10057. A300. EL:90 deg LDV 75m: 3.8m/s 122 deg.

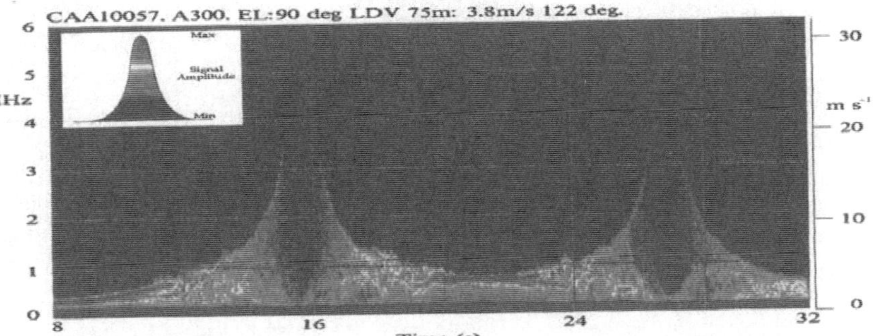

10:54am 2/12/94.
<u>Figure 3.</u> Vortices from an A300. Note the signal amplitude colour code (insert) and the Doppler frequency (MHz) and velocity (m s^{-1}) scales. Other information includes the elevation (EL-90) of the Vortex Lidar and the relevant wind (height, speed and direction) from the Wind Lidar (LDV).

CAA10056. FK10. EL: 90 deg LDV 75m: 3.0m/s 148 deg.

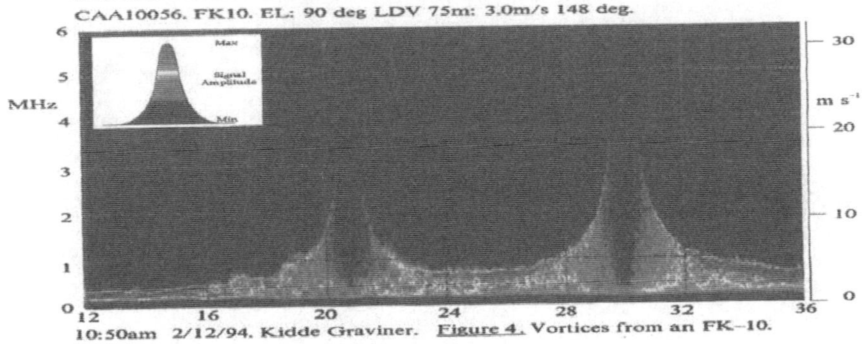

10:50am 2/12/94. Kidde Graviner. <u>Figure 4.</u> Vortices from an FK-10.

Courtesy of Michael Vaughan

Historical Review of CLR Wind Sensing

- FIRST ATMOSPHERIC WIND COMPARISONS PERFORMED
- FIRST WAKE VORTEX VELOCITY MEASUREMENTS
- SATURN DESIGN PROGRAMS WERE ENDING, FLIGHTS WERE HAPPENING. THERE WAS INTEREST IN AIRBORNE CLEAR AIR TURBULENCE DETECTION. THE CENTER ASKED WHETHER THE TECHNOLOGY COULD BE EXTENDED TO ON-BOARD AIRCRAFT MEASUREMENT-DETECTION OF 'CAT'.
- FEASIBILITY STUDY CONDUCTED. FIREPOND LIDAR DESIGN UTILIZED EXCEPT SMALLER OPTICS AND SHORT PULSE, BUT USING A MOPA DESIGN.

12

Figure 1. Pulsed CO_2 coherent lidar aboard NASA CV-990.

optically to the point of interest in the atmosphere. The aerosol particulates, present in the lower atmosphere, scatter some of the transmitted radiation in all directions and, since the particles move with the atmosphere, the frequency of the scattered light is Doppler shifted from the frequency of the transmitted beam. Receiving optics collect the backscattered radiation and direct it onto an infrared detector where it is mixed with a small portion of the original beam. The total radiation seen by the detector fluctuates at a beat frequency that is proportional to the radial component of the wind velocity at the point of interest.

The pulsed CO_2 coherent lidar system shown in figure 1 uses a small, very stable, CW, master oscillator laser. This low-power, stable laser energy is gated into variable pulse lengths by a Gallium Arsenide Modulator. The pulses then enter a power amplifier chain and are amplified from approximately 10 W per pulse to 5 kW per pulse (figure 2).

Figure 2. Schematic diagram for pulsed CO_2 coherent lidar system.

The main transmitter characteristics are: a wavelength of 10.6 μm, a pulse length of 1-10 μs, a pulse rate of 140-180 pulses per second, a peak power of 5 kW, an average power of 3 W, and an optics diameter of 30.5 cm (12 in). Figure 3 shows an exterior view of the Ames

Figure 3. Exterior view of aircraft pod for CO_2 pulsed lidar.

CV-990 with the CO_2 pulsed system on-board. The laser beam exits through the pod seen above the engine nacelle. The pod incorporates a germanium window 35.6 cm (15 in) in diameter. The telescope (see Fig. 1) is in the foreground and protrudes through the airplane into the external pod. The system was shock-mounted and the critical components insulated against noise and vibration. In figure 4, the photographs of typical display outputs taken during the flights show the intensity velocity display at a time of negligible turbulence and a range-velocity display when a wind shear was present ahead of the aircraft. For

Figure 4. Samples of output displays for CO_2 pulsed lidar.

a selected range, the intensity velocity display shows the momentary velocity distributions from the filter bank. The signal intensity distribution forms a sharp peak and is a measurement of the wind speed relative to the aircraft. When the system is directed straight ahead, this speed corresponds to the true airspeed of the aircraft at close range.

319

6/26/2016

13

Historical review of CLR wind sensing

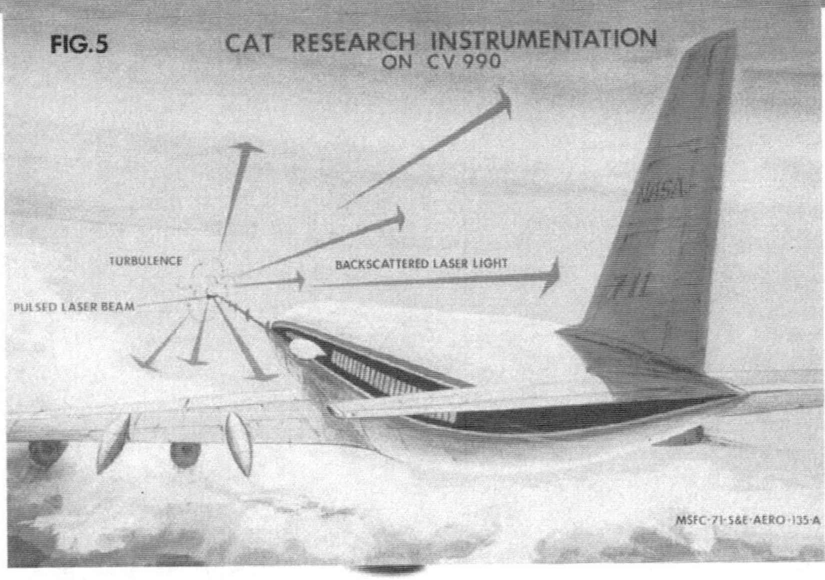

14

Historical Review of CLR Wind Sensing

- 10 MJ/PULSE CO2 SYSTEM DEVELOPED AND FLIGHT TESTED
- DEMONSTRATED OVERALL FEASIBILITY OF DETECTING CAT, BUT CONCLUDED THAT 10 MJ AT C02 WAVELENGTHS WAS NOT ENOUGH LASER ENERGY FOR ADEQUATE RANGE
- GROUND BASED CO2 SYSTEM WAS USED EXTENSIVELY FOR ATMOSPHERIC MEASUREMENTS, COMPARISONS, AND UNDERSTANDING. A 3-DIMENSIONAL WIND SYSTEM WAS DESIGNED BUT NOT DEVELOPED. AN AIRPORT WAKE VORTEX SYSTEM WAS DESIGNED BUT NOT IMPLEMENTED, UTILIZING A BI-STATIC CW APPROACH.
- CW FOCUSED CO2 SYSTEMS WERE USED AT JFK INTERNATIONAL AIRPORT FOR OBTAINING OPERATIONAL WAKE VORTEX DATA, OPERATING FOR SEVERAL MONTHS.

15

6/26/2016

16

Real Time Processing of CLR Winds

6/26/2016

17

Historical Review of CLR Wind Sensing

Many Contributors to CLR Wind Sensing

- Michael Vaughan at RSRE, Malvern, England
- Christian Werner, DFVLR, Germany
- Pierre Flamant, CNRS, France
- Mike Hardesty, NOAA, USA
- Lars Lading, RISO, Denmark
- Ove Steinvall, FOA, Sweden
- Werner K Dahm, NASA-MSFC
- Jim Bilbro, NASA-MSFC
- Bob Menzies, JPL, USA
- Sammy Henderson, CTI, USA
- Russell Targ, Lockheed, Palo Alto, USA

6/26/2016

18

Non-Mechanical Laser Beam Steering

- Have to steer on transmit and receive
- May require steering for an acquisition sensor
- Polarization birefingent gratings will make inroads
  - Can steer to random large angles high efficiency (>99% diffraction efficiency)
  - Need a stack of them, + or – 1 deg, + or – 2 deg, etc
  - Can couple with FSM, or other fine steering
  - Fast, random, efficient, steering over wide angles
  - Can steer transmit and receive

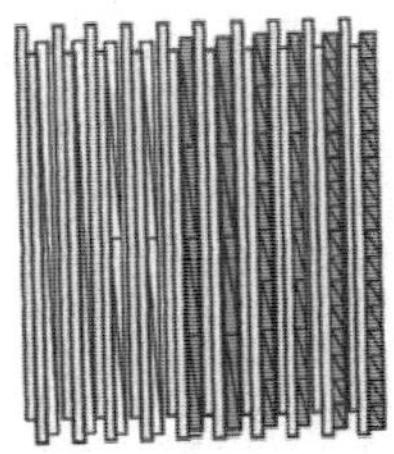

Courtesy of Boulder Non Linear Systems (BNS)

19

Polarization grating (PG) beam deflectors

BNS
BOULDER NONLINEAR SYSTEMS

- Wide-angle steering in discrete steps -

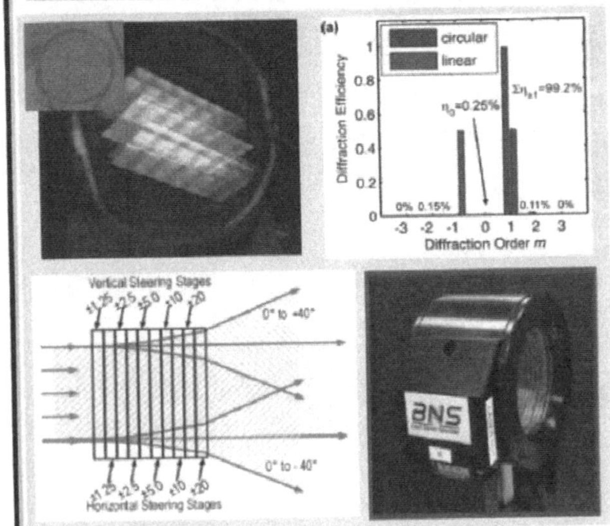

- Thin PGs with polarization control (e.g. liquid crystal (LC) switches) non-mechanically steer beams over large angles
  - 3 states per layer (+1, 0, -1)
  - >99% diffraction efficiency per layer
    - Bandwidth (±50 nm @ 1550 nm)
  - 0.25° to 20° deflection per layer
  - Small to large (>10 cm) apertures
  - Visible, NIR, SWIR & MWIR
- Geometric resolution increase
  - ~2^N steering angles for N layers
- Random-access steering
  - No slewing or overshoot
  - Digital addressing
  - Minimum number of interconnects
- Rugged, compact assembly

- Jointly developed and patented with North Carolina State University (NCSU)
  - Boulder Nonlinear Systems (BNS) has exclusive license

Courtesy of (BNS)

20

NOAA TEACO Extended Range Doppler Lidar (1985 - 2000)

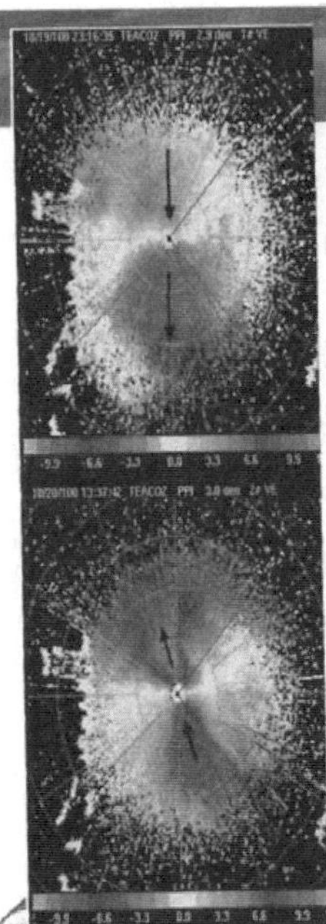

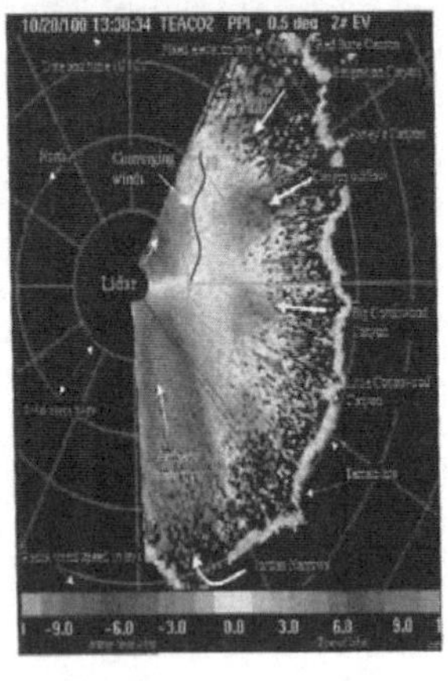

- **1 joule per pulse, 20 Hz, pulsed CO_2**
  - Injection-seeded TEA source
  - Longer range → 20-30 km
  - Moderate frequency stability (limited by chirp and pulse to pulse variability)
  - Operated on 10.59 µm CO2 lidar → absorption by atmospheric CO_2
  - 3 µs pulse duration → limited range resolution
- **Applications**
  - Air quality, extended profiling, flows in complex terrain, windstorms, thunderstorm microbursts

Courtesy of Mike Hardesty

20b

NOAA High Resolution Doppler Lidar (HRDL)

Wavelength	2.02 micron
Pulse Energy	2 mJ
PRF	200 Hz
Max Range	3-8 km
Range Res.	30 m
Beam rate	2 Hz
Scanning	Full Hemispheric
Precision	10 cm/s

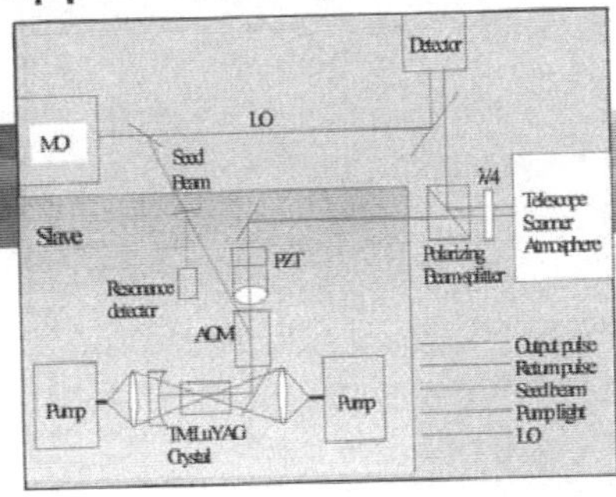

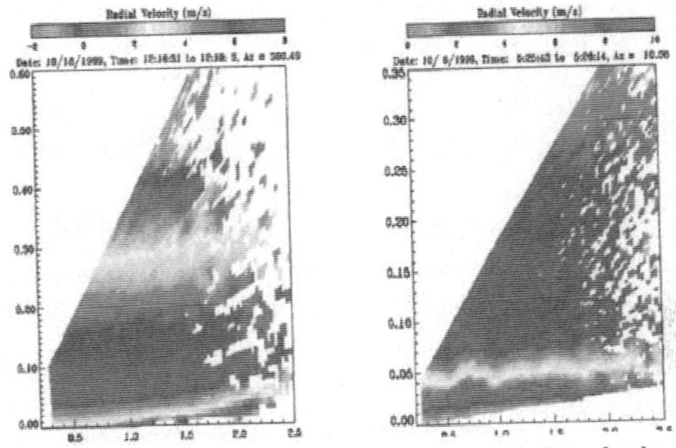

HRD observations of gravity waves and turbulence

6/26/2016

Courtesy of Mike Hardesty

21

NOAA current wind research focus

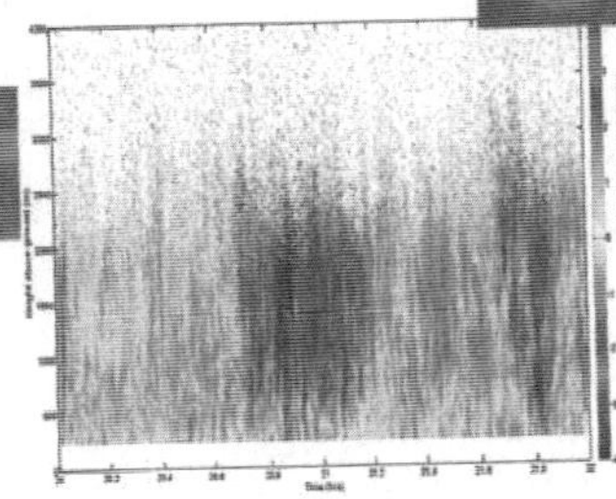

- Current NOAA efforts focused on boundary layer characterization for pollution studies, wind energy and greenhouse gas emission
- Making extensive use of small, high resolution lidars potentially deployed in arrays for 3 dimensional characterization of winds
- See talks by Brewer, Bonin, Choukulkar, Hardesty, Pichugina at this conference

Studies of sampling error in measurements of vertical velocity variance Choukulkar et al, ILRC 27, 2014

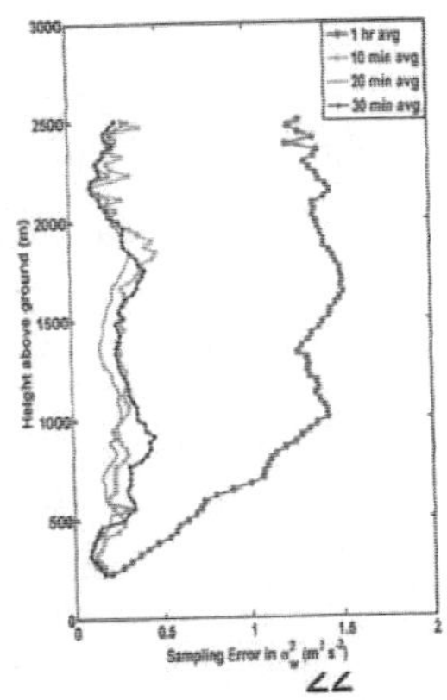

22

6/26/2016

Courtesy of Mike Hardesty

22

CLAWS MOPA Ladar Architecture

Key Specs:

- Nd:YAG at 1.06 μm
- Energy up to 1 J at 10 Hz
- 20 cm off-axis telescope
- VAD scanner mirror
- MOPA Architecture
- Variable Pulse Duration

Nd:YAG Amplifiers with Small-Signal Gain of over 100 dB seeded by pulse-sliced 50 mW MO

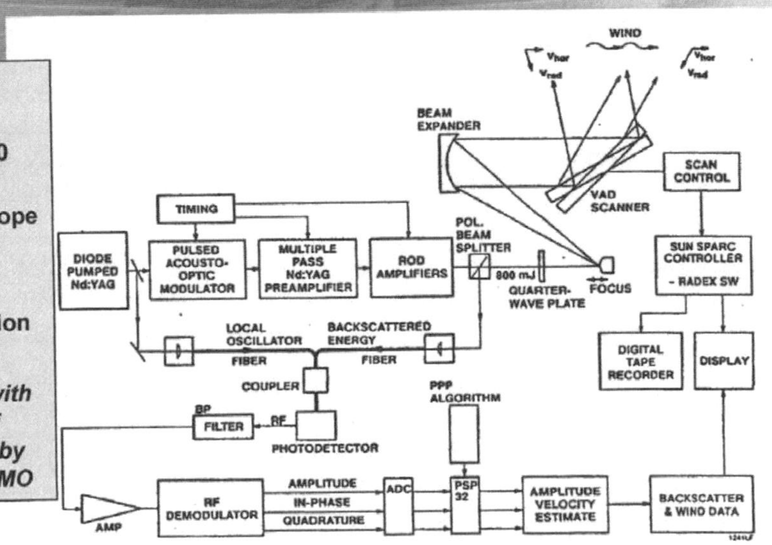

~~Not For Distribution — LMCT~~
~~Property — Not For Distribution~~

2-23

23

CLAWS

- Coherent Lidar Atmospheric Wind Sounder -

- CTI and Lockheed demonstrated a 1 J, 10 Hz, 1 m coherent laser radar in 1991
  - See *Applied Optics* 32, 4557-4568 (1993)
- Nd:YAG Master Oscillator/Power Amplifier system
  - 1 J/pulse, 0.2-5.0 μsec pulse duration (actively variable)
  - Zig-Zag slab amplifier

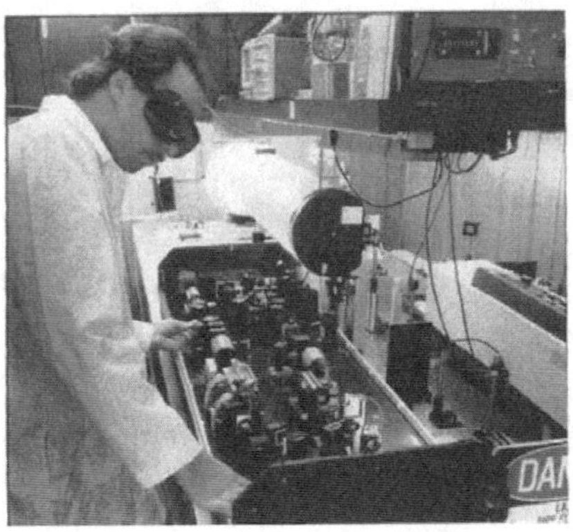

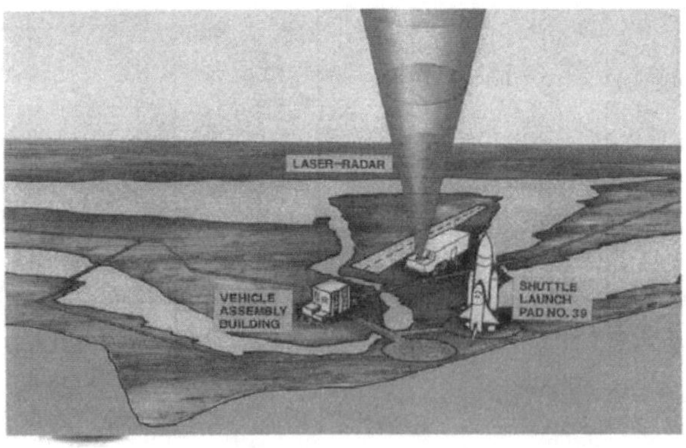

24

Winds at Kennedy Space Center

- Accurately measured to 27 km Height -

1 μm lidar and balloon borne rawinsonde data agreed well

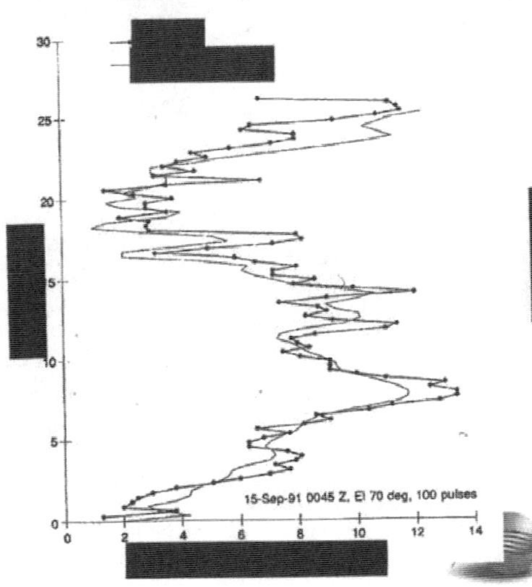

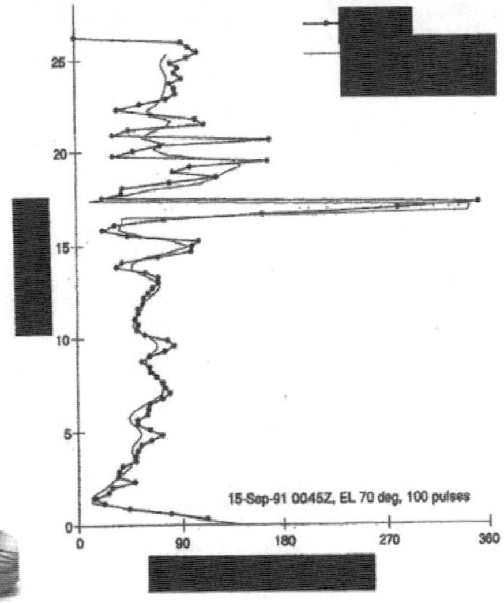

25

Key Lidar Wind Sensing Application Areas

- Precision airdrop and gunship ballistic winds
- Wind hazard alerting for aviation safety
- Wake vortex detection for aviation efficiency
- Aerosol plume detection and tracking
- Clear air turbulence (CAT) detection
- Optical air data
- Wind energy survey and management
- Boundary layer atmospheric research
- Space based winds for improved weather forecasting

26

Evolution of CTI Coherent Lidar Technology

Research Tool
Operator Required, 0.15 W
+/- 5°C; <0.5 g RMS

Air Force Ballistic Winds
Turnkey, 10 ft^3
+/- 20°C, 3g RMS

Optical Air Turbulence
Turnkey, 1W, 1.5ft^3
+/- 20°C, 3g RMS

Helicopter Air Data & Wire Det.
Turnkey, 0.5 W, 0.3ft^3
+/- 40°C, 7g RMS

1st Commercial WT Product
Turnkey 1 W
0 - 40°C, 3g RMS

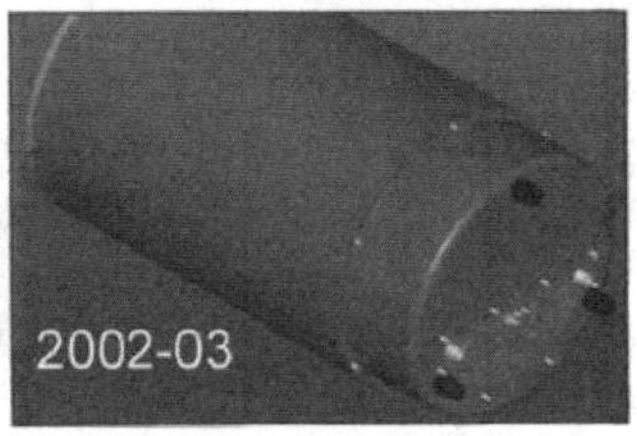

2nd Generation Product
Turnkey 1 W
Unattended Operation

courtesy of Phil Gatt (CTI)

27

Current Generation Product WindTracer® 2003-Present

WindTracer® Specifications	
Average Power	2 W
Pulse Energy	2.5 mJ ± 0.5 mJ
Pulse Repetition Frequency	750 Hz
Pulse Length (FWHM)	250 - 270 ns
Wavelength	1617 nm
Typical range	20 km (33 km max)
Velocity Accuracy	~ 0.1 m/s

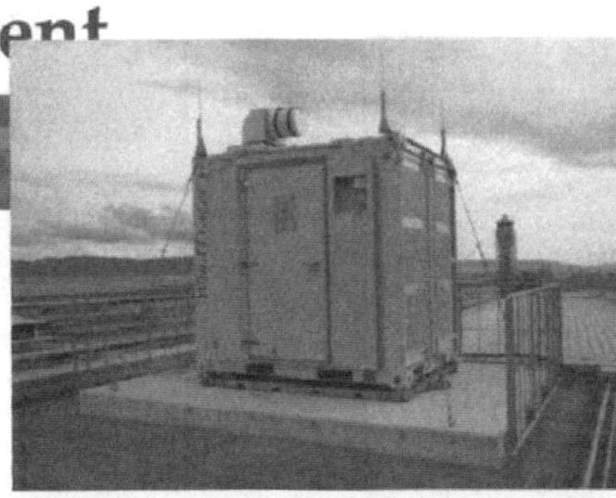

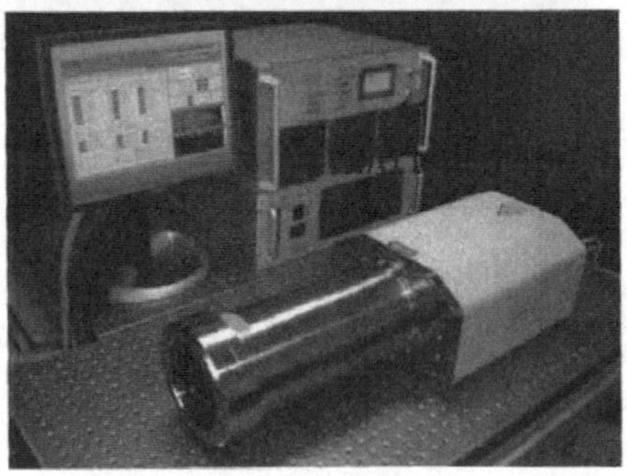

courtesy of Phil Gatt (CTI)

WindTracer® Airport Installations

- 12 Years of Operational Wind Hazard Detection and Wake Measurements for Air Traffic Management

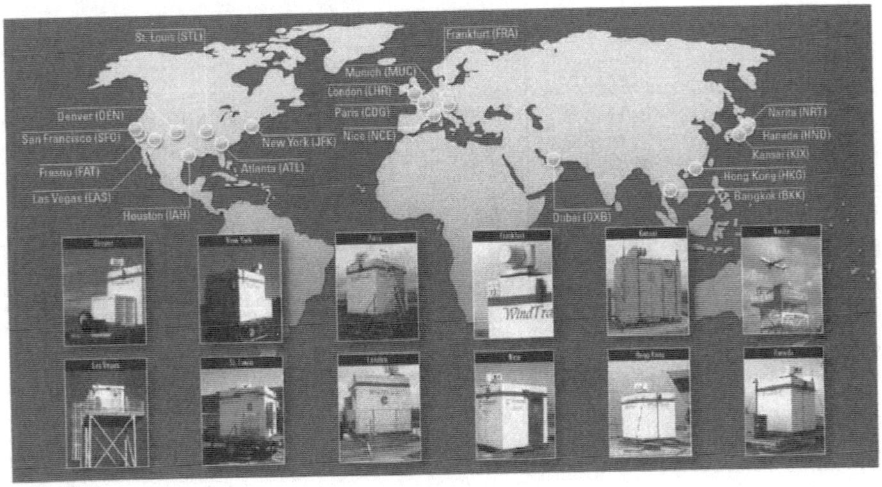

Courtesy of Phil Gatt (LMCT).

28b

WindTracer® Turbulence Measurements DFW 19Jun00, 15:11-18:25

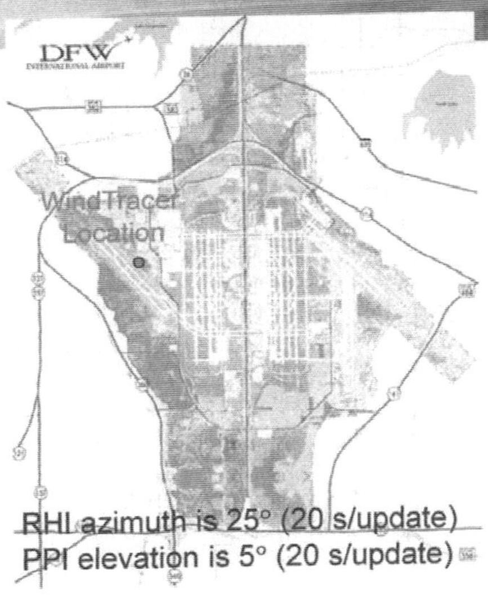

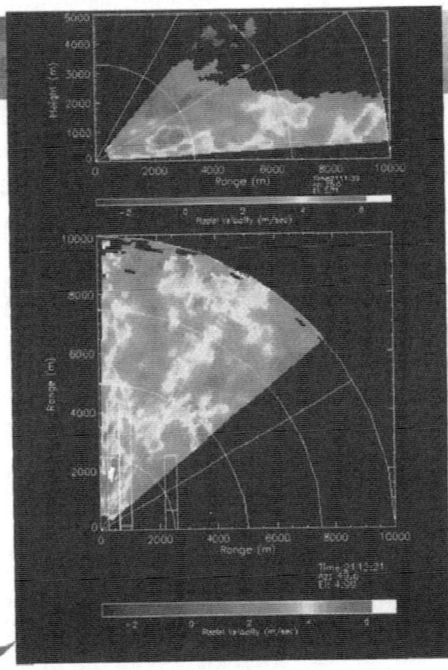

Courtesy of Phil Gatt (LMCT).

29

Summary from Paul McManamon talk at Barcelona Meeting

- CO2 Coherent ladar became wide spread in the 70's and 80's using a strong LO to suppress noise
- Solid State ladars became widespread in the 90's
- Fiber based coherent ladar is becoming widespread
- If laser diodes can solve coherence issues they will gain widespread usage in coherent ladar
- Random access, non mechanical, steering will gain traction
- Detector arrays are becoming larger and more sensitive
- Wavelengths will migrate longer as components develop
- The ability to measure field will be a significant factor in future coherent ladars
- Multi- aperture MIMO based coherent ladar will be explored for its benefits
- Coherent ladar has a strong future!
  - Both Digital Holography / Spatial heterodyne, and temporal heterodyne

courtesy of Paul McManamon. (Exciting Technologies)

Overview of the DLR 2 micron Doppler lidar campaigns with emphasis on possibilities and limits of signal processing

Stephan Rahm, Fernando Chouza, Oliver Reitebuch, Andreas Schäfler, Benjamin Witschas
Institut für Physik der Atmosphäre, Deutsches Zentrum für Luft- und Raumfahrt (DLR)
Muenchner Str. 20, D-82230 Wessling, Germany
Stephan.Rahm@dlr.de

Abstract: In the past three years several airborne campaigns all over the world with the DLR two micron Doppler lidar installed onboard the Falcon F20 research aircraft were performed. The scientific goals of these campaigns reached from the study of transport phenomena of Saharan dust over the Atlantic Ocean (SALTRACE) to gravity wave measurements in Sweden (GWLCYCLE) and New Zealand (DEEPWAVE). A comparison campaign with the ADM direct detection lidar on Iceland (WindVal) together with the NASA DC8 was also performed. This paper will give a brief overview of the campaigns and then focuses on the data processing. The accumulation of all LOS spectra of a VAD scan into one Spectrum in order to improve the coverage is presented. Furthermore the challenge of extracting a wind vector out of a set of LOS estimates of a VAD scan in the presence of gravity waves will also be addressed.

Keywords: Airborne Doppler lidar, VAD scan, GWLCYCLE, SALTRACE, DEEPWAVE, WindVal

1. Overview of campaigns

SALTRACE 2013: Saharan Aerosol Long-range Transport and Aerosol-Cloud-Interaction Experiment. Lagrange measurement of the transport of Saharan dust over the Atlantic Ocean. First time of the 2 micron Doppler lidar providing "calibrated" backscatter measurements [1, 2].
Location: Cape Verde islands and Barbados
Web: http://www.pa.op.dlr.de/saltrace/index.html

GW-LCYCLE I 2013: First Gravity wave experiment in December 2013 in Sweden with several wave events.
Location: Kiruna, Sweden
Web: http://www.pa.op.dlr.de/gwlcycle/

DEEPWAVE 2014: "Deep Propagating Gravity Wave Experiment" over New Zealand together with NOAA. At this campaign there was a constant struggle with clear air / low backscatter as there is nearly no background aerosol.
Location: Christchurch, New Zealand
Web: www.pa.op.dlr.de/deepwave/ ; https://www.eol.ucar.edu/field_projects/deepwave

WindVal 2015: Campaign together with ADM Aeolus instrument on Falcon and with DAWN Coherent Doppler Lidar [3], TWILITE direct detection Doppler lidar [4] and dropsonde unit onboard NASA DC-8.
Location: Keflavik, Iceland
Web: http://blogs.esa.int/campaignearth/2015/05/20/windval-petta-reddast/ and: http://www.dlr.de/pa/en/desktopdefault.aspx/tabid-2342/6725_read-43282/

GW-LCYCLE II 2013: Most recent gravity wave campaign. Due to very calm weather only two wave events.
Location: Kiruna / Sweden
Web: http://www.pa.op.dlr.de/gwlcycle2/news.html

2. Increased coverage by new accumulation algorithm

The DLR two micron Doppler Lidar usually applies a conical step and stare scan with 20° off nadir and 18 stare positions. Accumulation time for a single LOS is usually 1 second that is approx. 500 laser shots. Usually the processing strategy is to accumulate all shots of one stare position and then estimate the peak power spectral density PSD from the accumulated spectrum. The result are 18 Doppler shift estimates that can then be used to evaluate the 3 dimensional wind vector assuming a constant wind field across the scanning volume. In the case of poor backscatter conditions this method is suffering from low SNR because of limited accumulation time. When the peak of the backscattered Doppler signal is near the noise floor there is no reliable estimate possible anymore. Another approach is to accumulate all Doppler spectra of a scan into one resulting spectra with an accumulation time in this case of 18 s. In order to do so a wind field is assumed and the spectra of the different LOS positions are shifted according to this wind field and projected to the LOS direction before accumulation. By varying the wind field over all realistic values one gets a set of accumulated spectra. The idea is now that with the right wind field the power spectral density (PSD) of the accumulated spectra becomes maximal. This approach is already described by Smalikho [5] and the performance is assessed by Weissmann [6]. In theory the possible improvement is square root of the number of LOS positions. In practical tests it is lower due to atmospheric turbulence that causes a spectral broadening of the resultant PSD.

It was found empirically that this “accumulation algorithm” may be improved by not only looking at the maximum PSD but the quotient of PSD and vertical wind. This causes some underestimation of the vertical wind speed. To avoid this effect and to reduce processing time the approach is done in two steps. A coarse variation of the wind assumption in steps of 2 m/s followed by the above mentioned selection of the PSD and vertical wind. This first approach is followed by a fine variation of the wind assumption around the previous wind estimate with a selection of the most likely wind by using the PSD alone.

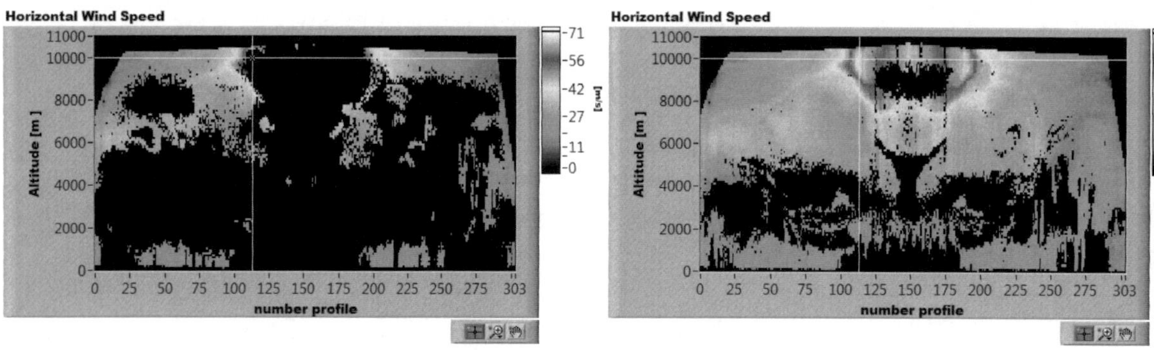

Figure 1: Example of increased coverage with the modified accumulation algorithm (right) compared to standard LOS inversion algorithm (left).

The improvement in coverage by this algorithm depends strongly on the backscatter distribution in the atmosphere. In case of a moderate reduction of the backscatter coefficient e.g. in a jet stream the coverage can be enhanced significantly like shown in Figure 1. On the other hand the r-square dependence of the lidar signal or a significant drop in backscatter cannot be compensated by this algorithm. Longer accumulation times e.g. several scans show the limits of this technique as there are some EMI peaks (e.g. from computer) buried in the noise, that make problems if the accumulation time gets too long.

3. Vertical winds causing trouble in 3D wind vector estimation

The processing step from the LOS estimates of a scan to a three dimensional wind vector seems to be straight forward. It only uses the assumption that the wind field is constant over the scanning volume. At the ADM Aeolus mission with only one LOS direction there is the even more rigid assumption, that the average vertical wind is zero over the accumulated volume. In most cases those assumptions are justified. However under special conditions like gravity waves or frontal ascend processes this may lead to dramatic errors in the estimated 3D-wind vector. The general reason for the sensitivity to a variation of the vertical wind is a small off nadir angle of the conical step and stare scan. In case of the DLR airborne 2µm Doppler lidar this off nadir angle is 20°. According to $v_{LOS} = v_{hor} \sin(20°)$ and $v_{LOS} = v_v \cos(20°)$ any error respectively variation in the vertical velocity is multiplied by up to a factor of nearly 3 and added to the horizontal wind speed! To make things even more complicated are the measurement volumes varying with altitude. Figure 2 gives an overview of the measurement volumes of the 2 µm Doppler lidar over altitude.

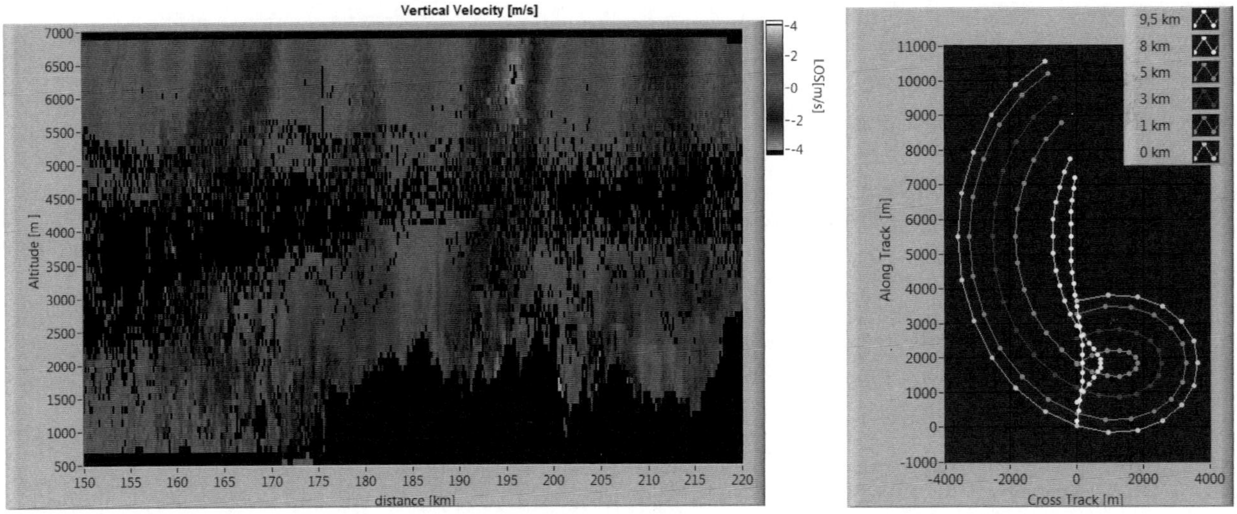

Figure 2: Example of vertical wind due to gravity waves (left) compared to the footprint of a conical scan

At the gravity wave experiments in Kiruna / Sweden and Christchurch / New Zealand several flight lags were performed two times once with conical step and stare scanning and next with fixed nadir looking LOS. The time difference between those two lags was only about 30 minutes at nearly unchanged wind situation. At those examples it was found that at areas with strong gravity waves the 3D wind estimation gets complicated and unstable. The amplitude of those gravity waves was up to 3 m/s! Consequently the observed uncertainty / variation of the estimates of the horizontal wind have been up to 9 m/s. Both the conventional "inversion" algorithm as well as the previously described "accumulation" algorithm showed similar variations. Unfortunately the geometric wavelength of the gravity waves and the scanning volume of the lidar were about the same size so that the wave had a maximum influence on the estimation of the horizontal wind estimate. However even with less LOS positions there will remain some influence from the gravity waves. With the existing scan pattern an elimination of the influence of those gravity waves seems to be impossible. For future experiments it is planned to add several nadir looking LOS directions to each scan in order to be able to subtract the vertical wind from the LOS estimate before calculating the inversion matrix. Or if this does not eliminate the gravity waves at least a warning can be generated that the resultant wind estimate may be corrupted.

4. Conclusion

Although airborne Doppler lidar measurements are well established for several decades there are still issues to be addressed at data processing. It has been shown that some improvements are still possible. On the other hand some atmospheric issues still have to be considered for an acceptable accuracy of the final wind estimates.

References

[1] Chouza, F., O. Reitebuch, S. Groß, S. Rahm, V. Freudenthaler, C. Toledano, B. Weinzierl, 2015: Retrieval of aerosol backscatter and extinction from airborne coherent Doppler wind lidar measurements, *Atmos. Meas. Tech*, **8**, 2909-2926.

[2] Chouza, F., O. Reitebuch, M. Jähn, S. Rahm, B. Weinzierl, 2016: Vertical wind retrieved by airborne lidar and analysis of island induced gravity waves in combination with numerical models and in situ particle measurements, *Atmos. Chem. Phys.*, **16**, 4675-4692.

[3] Kavaya, M. J., J. Y. Beyon, G. J. Koch, M. Petros, P. J. Petzar, U. N. Singh, B. C. Trieu, J. Yu, "The Doppler Aerosol Wind (DAWN) Airborne, Wind-Profiling Coherent-Detection Lidar System: Overview and Preliminary Flight Results." J. Atmos. Oceanic Tech., **31**, 826-842 (2014).

[4] Gentry B., H. Chen, J. Cervantes, R. Machan, D. Reed, R. Cargo, C. Marx, and P. Jordan. "Airborne Testing of the TWiLiTE Direct Detection Doppler Lidar." Proc. 16th Coherent Laser Radar Conference, Long Beach, California, USA (2011).

[5] I. Smalikho, "Techniques of Wind Vector Estimation from Data Measured with a Scanning Coherent Doppler Lidar", J ATMOS OCEAN TECHNOL **20**, 276-291 (2003).

[6] M. Weissmann, et al, "Targeted Observations with an Airborne Wind Lidar" J ATMOS OCEAN TECHNOL **22**, 1706-17191 (2005).

Airborne Coherent Doppler Wind Lidar measurements of vertical and horizontal wind speeds for the investigation of gravity waves

Benjamin Witschas, Stephan Rahm, Johannes Wagner, Andreas Dörnbrack
DLR, Institute of Atmospheric Physics, Oberpfaffenhofen, Germany
Benjamin.Witschas@dlr.de

Abstract: Gravity waves are well known phenomena in the atmosphere, but there is still a lack of knowledge of their life cycle including excitation, propagation and dissipation mechanisms. In order to investigate these topics, DLR's coherent Doppler wind lidar system was recently deployed during 3 airborne campaigns on the Falcon F20 research aircraft, namely the GW-LCYCLE I campaign (Kiruna, Sweden, December 2013), the DEEPWAVE campaign (Christchurch, New Zealand, June/July 2014) and the GW-LCYCLE II campaign (Kiruna, Sweden, January/February 2016).
In this paper, a case study based on a research flight performed during GW-LCYCLE I is discussed and a method for correcting horizontal wind contribution in the vertical wind retrieval based on ECMWF data is introduced. The remaining systematic error of the retrieved vertical wind is estimated to be less than 10 cm/s. A measurement of a flight leg across the Scandinavian mountain ridge is used to characterize gravity waves during strong forcing conditions. The measured vertical wind reaches amplitudes of larger than ± 3 m/s and horizontal wavelengths of 10 km to 20 km. A comparison with WRF-model calculations shows a quite good representation of the horizontal structure of the vertical wind. The amplitude however is obviously underestimated by a factor of 2 and shows maximum wind speeds of ± 1.5 m/s.

Keywords: Coherent Laser Radar, Vertical wind speed, GW-LCYCLE, Deepwave, Airborne Wind Lidar

1. Introduction

Gravity waves (GWs) are well known phenomena in the atmosphere and have a strong impact on vertical transport and exchange of energy and momentum the troposphere and the middle atmosphere [1]. While there is a general understanding of processes launching GWs, the nature of wave source spectra is more complex and less well-understood. Thus, a better characterization of GW sources is an outstanding issue for a proper description of the dynamical coupling of the lower and middle atmosphere.

In order to investigate the entire life cycle of GWs from their excitation towards propagation and dissipation, DLR's Institute of Atmospheric Physics recently initiated/ participated in 3 airborne campaigns namely the GW-LCYCLE I campaign (Kiruna, Sweden, December 2013), the DEEPWAVE campaign (Christchurch, New Zealand, June/July 2014) [2], and the GW-LCYCLE II campaign (Kiruna, Sweden, January/February 2016). In the frame work of these campaigns, combined ground-based and airborne observations were conducted over northern Scandinavia and southern New Zealand, respectively, where both regions in winter-time represent distinguished conditions for the generation of mountain waves which are able to propagate up to the mesosphere.

One key-instrument was DLR's airborne coherent Doppler Wind Lidar (DWL) which was operated from the Flacon F20 research aircraft. In order to carefully characterize mountain waves, both horizontal and vertical wind measurements with high horizontal and vertical resolution and a low statistical uncertainty of several 10 cm/s are desired, where all of these goals can be reached with the DWL. In particular, horizontal and vertical wind is retrieved from line-of-sight (LOS) wind measurements by applying the velocity-azimuth-display (VAD) technique [3] or by steering the beam to Nadir direction leading to a horizontal resolution of about 7 km and 0.2 km, respectively. The vertical resolution for both measurement modes is determined by the laser pulse length and is approximately 100 m.

Vertical wind measurements require an exact nadir-pointing of the laser beam which is challenging to achieve from a moving platform as an aircraft. Thus, small contributions of the horizontal wind component might contaminate the vertical wind measurement. For that reason, a method to correct for slight off-nadir pointing angles by exploiting ECMWF re-analysis wind data and the actual beam pointing direction is developed. After shortly describing the instrument itself in section 2, the vertical wind correction procedure is explained in section 3. In section 4 a few results from a research flight performed on December 13, 2013 during GW-LCYCLE I are discussed.

2. Instrument description

A schematic block diagram of the DWL is shown in Figure 1. The transceiver was developed and built by CLR Photonics (today Lockheed Martin Coherent Technologies) [4-6], the double-wedge scanner system and the data acquisition unit were built at Deutsches Zentrum für Luft und Raumfahrt (German Aerospace Center, DLR).

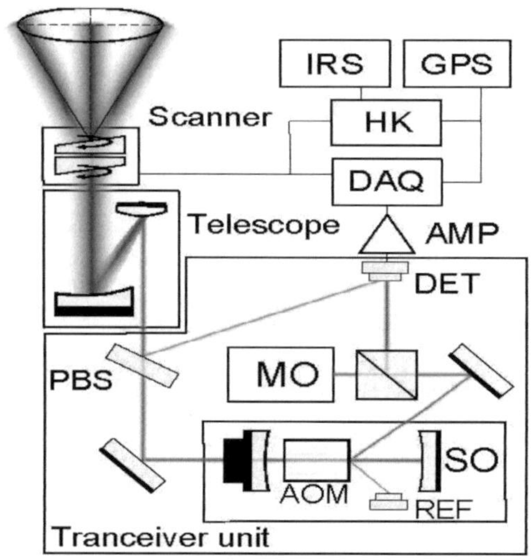

Figure 1. Simplified sketch of the wind lidar system: local oscillator (MO), slave oscillator (SO), acousto-optical modulator (AOM), reference pulse detector (REF), polarizing beam splitter (PBS), signal amplifier (AMP), data acquisition unit (DAQ), housekeeping data acquisition unit (HK), global navigation satellite system receiver (GPS), inertial reference system (IRS).

The transceiver comprises a continuous-wave master oscillator (MO) which is used as an injection seeder for the slave oscillator (SO) and additionally as local oscillator for the heterodyne detection. A part of the MO radiation is coupled into the SO via an acousto-optic modulator (AOM) which is shifting the original MO frequency by about 100 MHz, and thus, permitting determination of the magnitude and sign of the frequency difference between MO and SO which is later needed for wind measurements. The SO produces laser pulses with a wavelength of 2022.54 nm, an energy of 1.5 mJ, a length of 400 ns (~ 120 m) at a pulse repetition rate of 500 Hz. To ensure resonance between the SO cavity length and the MO radiation, the SO cavity length is controlled by the ramp and fire technique [7]. The laser beam is expanded to a diameter of about 10 cm within the telescope after it was passing a polarizing beam splitter (PBS). The expanded laser beam then enters an optical double-wedge scanner which enables to steer the laser beam to any position within a cone angle of 30°. The backscattered light is reflected on the polarizing beam splitter (PBS) and directed to the optical signal detector (DET), where it is mixed with the MO laser. The time-resolved detector signal resulting from each single laser shot is sampled and stored (Fig. 1, DAQ). This procedure leads to a data rate of about 15 Mb/s, and is applied as it gives maximum flexibility for data post-processing.

3. Measurement procedure and data processing

During the GW-LCYCLE I campaign, the DWL was operated in two different acquisition modes, namely in scanning mode or in fixed line-of-sight (LOS) mode, aiming to measure the vertical profile of the three-dimensional wind vector or vertical wind speed, respectively. While operating in scanning mode, a conical step-and-stare scan around the vertical axes with a nadir angle of 20° was performed. 24 LOS wind velocities are measured per one scanner revolution and are used to retrieve the three-dimensional wind vector. During fixed LOS mode operation, the laser beam is intentionally pointed to nadir-direction and thus the measured LOS wind equals the vertical wind speed. In the following, the retrieval of vertical wind speed and potentially needed corrections are discussed. Details about the wind vector retrieval can be found in [8].

In principle, the derived LOS wind speed equals the vertical wind speed, if the laser beam is pointing downwards in nadir direction. Although the lidar system is using an automatic flight attitude correction loop in the meantime (during DEEPWAVE and GW-LCYCLE II) that keeps the set pointing direction, such a control loop was not implemented during the GW-LCYCLE I campaign. Thus, slight off-nadir angles of up to 1° can occur during measurement. As a consequence, the LOS wind speed contains a projection of the horizontal wind speed in LOS direction which has to be corrected. For instance, considering a horizontal wind speed of 30 m/s and an off-nadir angle of 0.5° towards wind blowing direction, the projection in LOS is 0.26 m/s.

Basically, the actual beam pointing direction and the actual horizontal wind speed and direction in a certain altitude have to be known in order to calculate the LOS contribution of the horizontal wind. The beam pointing can be calculated for each measurement by considering the position of both scanner wedges and the lidar installation position which is determined in a separate procedure and which is verified to stay constant during the campaign. The wind vector information can be principally provided by the lidar itself. Though, when the lidar instrument is operating in fixed LOS mode, no information about the wind vector is available. For that reason, usually two or more legs are flown along the same geographical location giving both, the wind vector and LOS wind with a slight temporal discrepancy of about one hour. However, as the coverage of both measurements can be different, not each LOS wind measurement might correspond to a wind vector measurement that can be used for correction. Thus, in order to be able to correct all LOS measurements, ECMWF re-analysis data of wind speed and direction, interpolated to the respective flight track and time, is used. Additionally, the flight leg with the wind vector measurement is used to verify the validity of the ECMWF wind speed data.

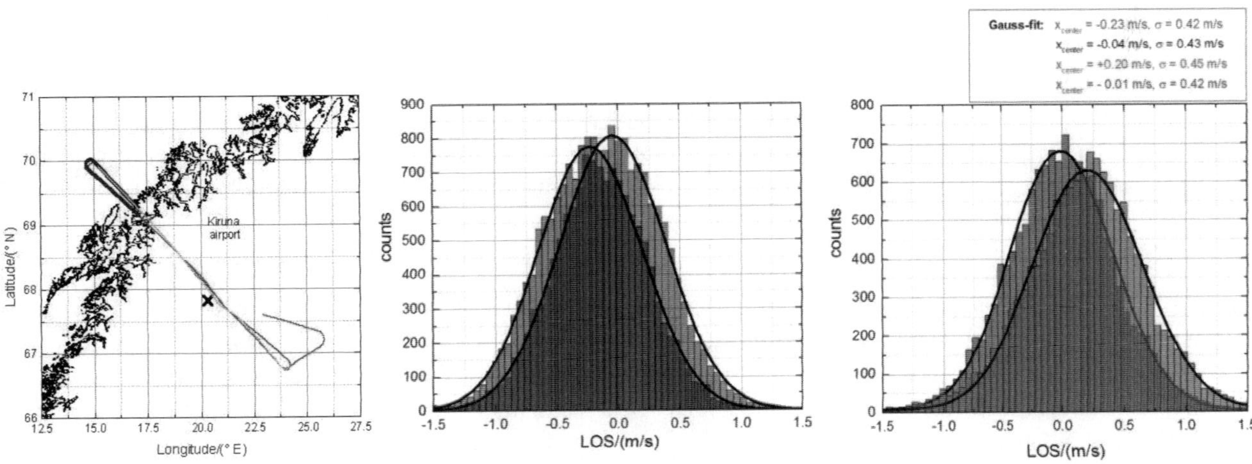

Figure 2. Left: Flight track of a research flight performed on 13. December 2013 (red line). Middle: Histogram of vertical wind speeds derived while flying westwards (left, dark blue line, before curve flight), before correction (green) and afterwards (blue). Right: Same as middle, but flying eastwards (left, dark blue line, after curve flight). Wind speeds before correction are indicated in magenta, the one after correction in red.

In the following, the wind correction procedure is described by means of a research flight performed on December 13, 2013. The corresponding flight track is indicated by the left panel of Fig. 2 (red line). The existence of slight off-nadir pointing gets obvious by plotting the vertical wind speeds measured in westward flying direction (Fig. 2, middle, green) and eastward flying direction (Fig. 2, right, magenta) separately in a histogram. It can be seen that the mean vertical wind speed has an offset of about 20 cm/s with opposite sign for opposite flying directions. This can be explained by a slight off-nadir angle perpendicular to the flying direction and crosswinds from north-west (towards to or away from the laser beam) that leads to a Doppler shift in the measured signal.

Before correcting the vertical wind measurement, the measured horizontal wind speed is used to verify the validity of the ECMWF re-analysis data. The lidar measurement, the ECMWF wind data and the direct comparison of both is shown in Fig. 3. The correlation yields an r^2 of 0.85, and the line fit a slope of 1.00 and an intercept of 0.01 m/s and thus clearly demonstrates the usability of the ECMWF data for correction purpose.

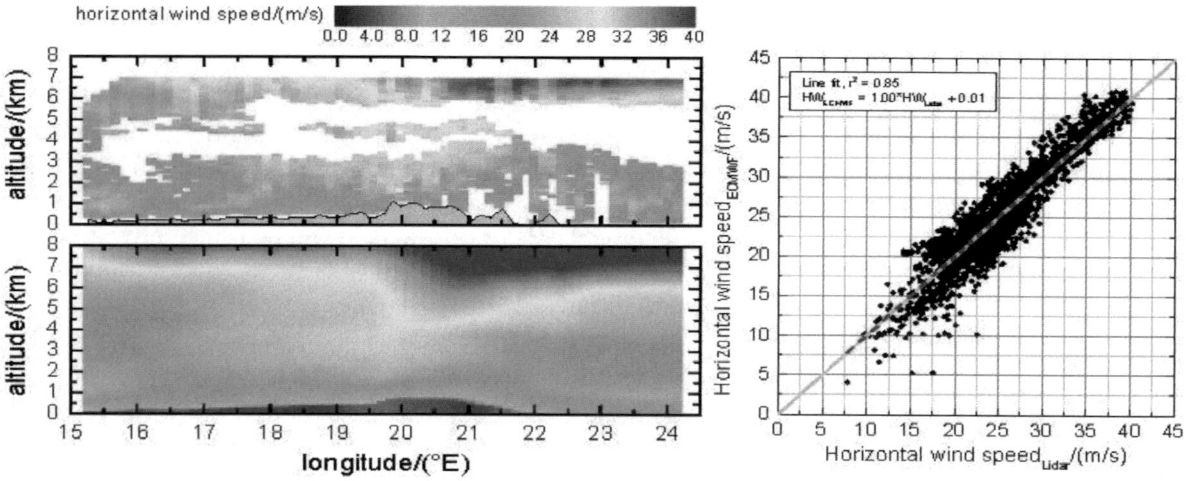

Figure 3. Left, top: Horizontal wind speed derived from lidar measurements (flight leg indicated in Fig. 2, light blue). Left, bottom: Corresponding horizontal wind from ECMWF re-analysis data. Right: Lidar data vs. ECMWF data, line fit (red) and x=y line (gray).

The vertical wind speed histograms after correction are plotted in Fig. 2, middle/blue and right/red, respectively. The mean values are - 0.01 m/s and - 0.04 m/s, which demonstrate the functionality of the correction procedure and give the possibility to estimate the systematic error to be smaller than 0.1 m/s.

4. Results

Corrected vertical wind speeds of a flight leg (13. December 2013) are shown in Fig. 4, top. Furthermore, the in-situ measured vertical wind from the aircraft is indicated at a height of 5.5 km. The data gap in-between is resulting from the pulse length of the laser which prevents to derive wind close to the aircraft. Anyway, the wind speed from the first lidar range gates and the in-situ measured wind speed show the same structure and thus additionally verify the reliability of the lidar data. From the measurement it is obvious that the vertical wind speed is varying around 0 m/s westwards of the Scandinavian mountains (up to 16.8° E). Going further eastwards, the excited gravity waves reach amplitudes of up to 3.5 m/s at the highest elevation at 19.3° E. By analyzing the wind speed in different altitudes (not shown) it can be shown that the amplitudes are decreasing with height. Thus, it is very likely that this particular wave will dissipate in the troposphere and not reach higher altitudes. Furthermore, the horizontal wavelength is determined by wavelet analysis (not shown) to be 10-20 km and thus, represents the orography structure.

A comparison with WRF model calculations (6 km and 2 km resolution, initialized with ECMWF data) as shown in Fig 4, bottom shows quite good accordance with the measurement. The wave-pattern of the vertical wind is well represented. The amplitudes however are by a factor of 2 smaller and reach values of about 1.5 m/s. Explanations for that are under investigation.

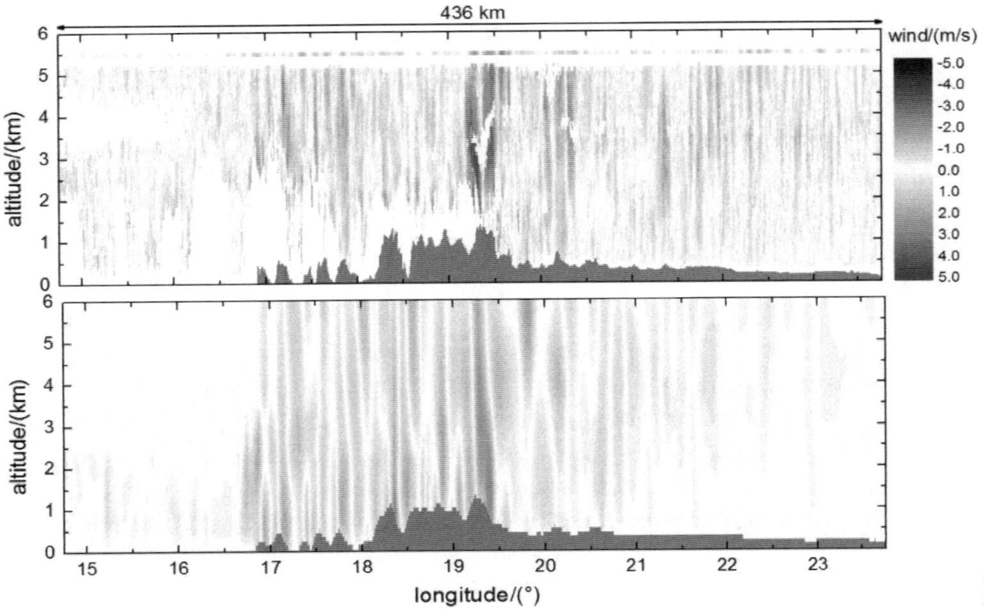

Figure 4. Top: Corrected vertical wind speed derived from lidar measurements performed on a research flight (13. December 2013). Bottom: Corresponding vertical wind speed from WRF-model.

5. Conclusion and Outlook

Recently, DLR's coherent Doppler wind lidar was deployed on three airborne campaigns related to investigate the life cycle of gravity waves. Both, the horizontal and the vertical wind measurements by the lidar are valuable for characterizing tropospheric gravity waves. In the future, in is foreseen to combine the lidar measurements other airborne and ground based instrument data in order to characterize the whole life cycle of gravity waves from excitation to dissipation.

6. References

[1] Fritts, S., and M. J. Alexander, 2003: "Gravity wave dynamics and effects in the middle atmosphere". *Reviews of Geophysics*, **41** (1).

[2] Fritts, D. C., and Coauthors, 2015: The deep propagating gravity wave experiment (Deepwave): An airborne and ground-based exploration of gravity wave propagation and effects from their sources throughout the lower and middle atmosphere. *Bulletin of the American Meteorological Society.*

[3] Browning, K., and R. Wexler, 1968: "The determination of kinematic properties of a wind field using Doppler radar". *Journal of Applied Meteorology*, **7** (1), 105–113.

[4] Henderson, S. W., C. P. Hale, J. R. Magee, M. J. Kavaya, and A. V. Huffaker, 1991: "Eye-safe coherent laser radar system at 2.1 μm using tm,ho:Yag lasers". *Optics letters*, **16** (10), 773–775.

[5] Henderson, S. W., P. J. Suni, C. P. Hale, S. Hannon, J. R. Magee, D. L. Bruns, and E. H. Yuen, 1993: "Coherent laser radar at 2 μm using solid-state lasers". *Geoscience and Remote Sensing, IEEE Transactions on*, **31** (1), 4–15.

[6] Hannon, S. M., and S. W. Henderson, 1995: "Wind measurement applications of coherent lidar". *The Review of Laser Engineering (Japan)*, **23** (2), 124–130.

[7] Henderson, S., E. Yuen, and E. Fry, 1986: "Fast resonance-detection technique for single-frequency operation of injection-seeded Nd:YAG lasers". *Opt. Lett.*, **11** (11), 715–717.

[8] Rahm, S., F. Chouza, O. Reitebuch, A. Schäfler, and B. Witschas, 2016: „Overview of the DLR 2 micron Doppler lidar campaigns with emphasis on possibilities and limits of signal processing" in papers of the 18th Coherent Laser Radar Conference CLRC, Boulder, 2016 (submitted).

Retrieval of aerosol backscatter and vertical wind from airborne coherent Doppler wind lidar measurements

F. Chouza(a), O. Reitebuch(a), S. Rahm(a), B. Weinzierl(b)

(a) Deutsches Zentrum für Luft- und Raumfahrt (DLR), Institut für Physik der Atmosphäre, Oberpfaffenhofen, Germany
(b) University of Vienna, Faculty of Physics, Wien, Austria

fernando.chouza@dlr.de

Abstract: This study presents methods for the retrieval of calibrated backscatter and vertical wind speed from an airborne Doppler wind lidar (DWL). The backscatter retrieval relies on sun photometer measurements and the simultaneous retrievals of an airborne DWL at 2 μm and a ground-based aerosol lidar at 532 nm for the retrieval of the calibration constants. A refinement of the vertical wind retrieval algorithms based on speed and distance of ground returns will also be discussed.
The derived methods were applied to a set of case studies from the SALTRACE campaign (http://www.pa.op.dlr.de/saltrace), which aimed to characterize the Saharan dust long range transport between Africa and the Caribbean. The calibrated backscatter measurements, first validated with a set of ground based lidar and CALIPSO measurements, were then used in combination with horizontal and vertical wind retrievals for the characterization of island induced gravity waves and the evaluation of an aerosol transport model.

Keywords: baskcatter retrieval, vertical wind retrieval, airborne Doppler wind lidar, SALTRACE

1. Introduction

Mineral dust is a key component of the climate system and the most mass abundant type of aerosol, accounting for about half of the total aerosol mass emissions [1], acting as cloud and ice nuclei and playing an important role in the radiation budget of the earth.

The Saharan desert has been identified as the world largest source of mineral dust [2]. Each year, large amounts of Saharan dust are transported across the Atlantic into the Caribbean region [3]. Despite the progress made during the last decades, the transport mechanisms of the Saharan dust over the Atlantic and their relative importance remain under discussion [4,5].

The Saharan Aerosol Long-range Transport and Aerosol-Cloud-Interaction Experiment (SALTRACE: http://www.pa.op.dlr.de/saltrace) conducted during June/July 2013 provided a whole new set of measurements, including in-situ, airborne and ground based observations. For the first time, an airborne coherent DWL was deployed onboard the DLR Falcon 20 research aircraft to study the Saharan dust transport over the Atlantic in combination with an extensive set of in-situ instruments to measure aerosol properties.

Usually, airborne coherent DWLs provide horizontal wind vector and qualitative aerosol backscatter measurements. In this work, quantitative aerosol backscatter and extinction profiles retrieved from the SALTRACE data set by means of a new calibration method (Sec. 3) are presented [6]. In addition the retrieval of the vertical wind from airborne wind lidar was largely refined (Sec. 4), providing new insights in the generation of island-induced gravity waves and their interaction with the Saharan dust [7]. The simultaneous retrieval of aerosol properties and, horizontal and vertical winds (Sec. 5), enhance the capabilities of the DWL for aerosol transport studies.

2. Instrumental description

The coherent DWL deployed on the DLR Falcon 20 research aircraft during SALTRACE is based on a CLR Photonics instrument [8] combined with a two wedge scanner and acquisition system developed at DLR [9]. The system operates at a wavelength of 2.02254 µm, with a pulse full width at half maximum (FWHM) of 400 ns, a pulse energy of 1-2 mJ, and a repetition frequency of 500 Hz.

3. Backscatter calibration

The DWL calibration method relies on sun-photometer measurements of the extinction coefficient wavelength dependency and the concurrent measurements of the DWL and a ground based aerosol lidar (Fig 1a). Based on these simultaneous measurements, calibration constants corresponding to different aerosol types were calculated (Fig 1b). These constants are then applied to retrieve calibrated backscatter and extinction coefficient profiles at a wavelength of 532 nm from the coherent DWL measurements during other sections of the flight. Further details of the calibration method are available in [6].

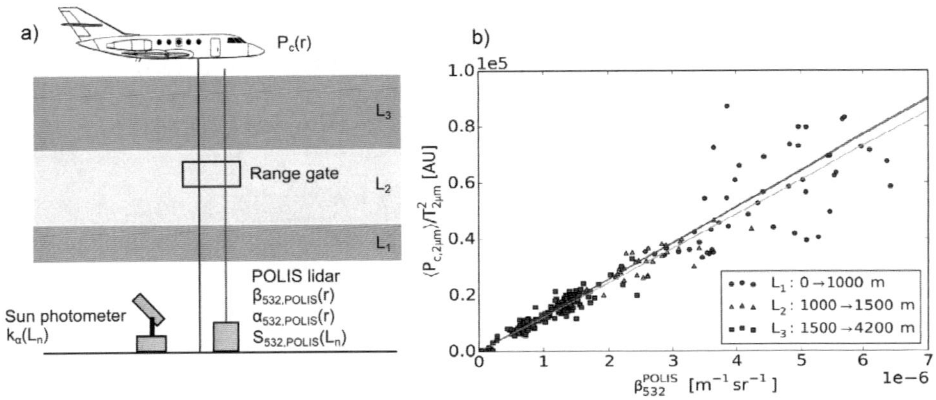

Figure 1. Scheme of the instruments and atmospheric parameters involved in the calibration and retrieval process (left). Correlation between the extinction corrected backscattered power of the DWL and the POLIS measured backscatter coefficient for 3 different aerosol layers: boundary layer (red dots), mixed layer (yellow triangles) and Saharan Air Layer (green squares) (right).

In order to validate the presented method, the calibrated backscatter coefficient corresponding to a flight carried out during SALTRACE on the west coast of Africa was retrieved. The results, compared with the measurements from a CALIPSO overpass, are presented in Fig. 2.

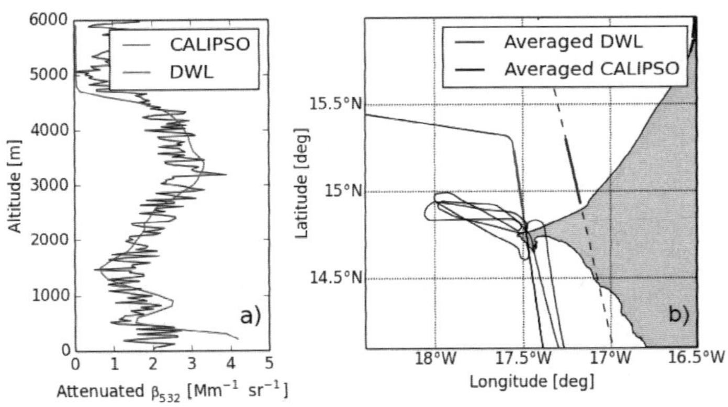

Figure 2. a) Averaged attenuated backscatter profile retrieved from the DWL (green) compared to the averaged CALIPSO measurements (blue) on the 12 June 2013. b) DLR Falcon flight track (black, solid), CALIOP overpass (black, dashed) together with the averaged flight sections.

4. Vertical wind retrieval

Due to the relatively low magnitude of the vertical winds $\vec{w}$ compared to the horizontal winds $\vec{V}$ and the Falcon flight speed $\vec{v}_{ac}$, the retrieval of the vertical wind speed require a set of instrumental corrections to be applied in order to reduce the systematic errors introduced by the uncertainties in the DWL pointing direction $\vec{L}$ and the projection of the horizontal winds (Fig. 3).

The proposed retrieval method is based on a 3-steps approach. First, an estimation of the DWL mounting angles and pointing offsets is calculated based on ground return speed $v_{DWL}(R_g)$ and distance $d_{DWL}(R_g)$ from all measurement flights. Then, the residual ground speed error, when available, is subtracted from the line-of-sight (LOS) speed $v_{DWL}(R)$ for each flight leg. Finally, if horizontal wind speed profiles are available, its projection is calculated and subtracted from the LOS speed. A detailed description of the retrieval method, the associated uncertainties and measurements performed during SALTRACE are presented in [7].

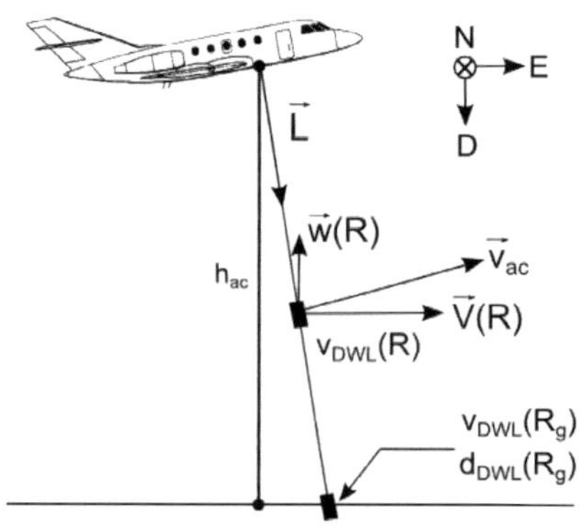

Figure 3. Sketch of the vertical wind measurements and its various contributors for correction.

Figure 4 presents a first validation of the presented vertical wind retrieval method. The DWL vertical wind measurements carried out on 20 June 2013 on the lee side of Barbados are compared with the vertical wind measurements retrieved by the Falcon in-situ sensors. Although a difference of 600 m exists between the first lidar range gate and the in-situ sensors of the aircraft, a good agreement can be observed between both measurements. The lidar retrievals show an enhanced convection over Barbados as well as the presence of island induced gravity waves on the lee side.

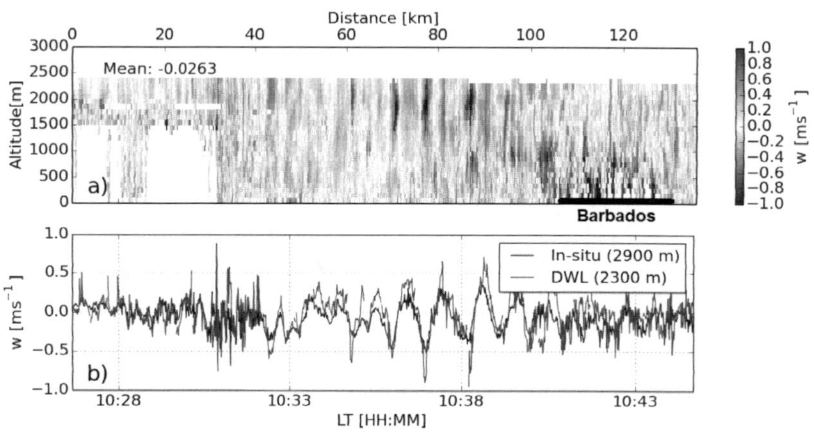

Figure 4. a) Vertical wind speed retrieved from the DWL on the lee side of Barbados. b) Vertical wind speed corresponding to the first range gate of the DWL retrieval (red) and the corresponding measurements from the Falcon in-situ sensors (blue).

5. Conclusions

Based on the methods presented in this work, the DWL capabilities were extended. The simultaneous retrievals of extinction coefficient, vertical and horizontal wind form the DWL provide a unique opportunity to evaluate different aspects of the Saharan dust transport as well as the ability of different models to reproduce them. Based on the measurements carried out during SALTRACE and the methods presented in this abstract, the capabilities of the MACC model are being evaluated [10]. The results will provide the opportunity to identify the models strengths and weaknesses.

6. References

[1] Hinds, W.C., 1999: Aerosol Technology: Properties, Behaviour and Measurement of Airborne Particles, John Wiley & Sons, Inc., New York.

[2] Mahowald, N. M., A.R. Baker, G. Bergametti, N. Brooks, R.A. Duce, T.D. Jickells, N. Kubilay, J.M. Prospero, I. Tegen, 2005: Atmospheric global dust cycle and iron inputs to the ocean, *Global Biogeochemical Cycles*, **19**, 1–15.

[3] Prospero, J. M., 1999: Long-range transport of mineral dust in the global atmosphere: Impact of African dust on the environment of the southeastern United States, *Proc. Natl. Acad. Sci. U. S. A.*, **96**, 3396-3403.

[4] Tsamalis, C., A. Chédin, J. Pelon, V. Capelle, 2013: The seasonal vertical distribution of the Saharan Air Layer and its modulation by the wind, *Atmos. Chem. Phys.*, **13**, 11235-11257.

[5] Karyampudi, V. M., S.P. Palm, J.A. Reagen, H. Fang, W.B. Grant, R.M. Hoff, C. Moulin, H.F. Pierce, O. Torres, E.V. Browell, S.H. Melfi, 1999: Validation of the Saharan dust plume conceptual model using lidar, Meteosat, and ECMWF data, *B. Am. Meteorol. Soc.*, **80**, 1045–1075.

[6] Chouza, F., O. Reitebuch, S. Groß, S. Rahm, V. Freudenthaler, C. Toledano, B. Weinzierl, 2015: Retrieval of aerosol backscatter and extinction from airborne coherent Doppler wind lidar measurements, *Atmos. Meas. Tech*, **8**, 2909-2926.

[7] Chouza, F., O. Reitebuch, M. Jähn, S. Rahm, B. Weinzierl, 2016: Vertical wind retrieved by airborne lidar and analysis of island induced gravity waves in combination with numerical models and in situ particle measurements, *Atmos. Chem. Phys.*, **16**, 4675-4692.

[8] Henderson, S.W., P. Suni, C.P. Hale, S.M. Hannon, J.R. Magee, D.L. Bruns, E.H. Yuen, 1993: Coherent laser radar at 2 µm using solid-state lasers, *IEEE Trans. Geosci. Remote Sens.*, **31(1)**, 4-15.

[9] Reitebuch, O., 2012: Wind Lidar for Atmospheric Research, in: Atmospheric Physics, Schumann, U., Springer, Berlin Heidelberg, 487-507.

[10] Chouza, F., O. Reitebuch, A. Benedetti, B. Weinzierl, 2016: Saharan dust long-range transport across the Atlantic studied by an airborne Doppler lidar and the MACC model, Atmos. Chem. Phys. Discuss., doi:10.5194/acp-2016-377, in review.

Airborne DWL in Polar Winds: Greenland and Iceland Campaigns

G. D. Emmitt[a], Steven Greco[a], Kevin Godwin[a], Michael Kavaya[b], Grady Koch[b] and Upendra Singh[b]

a – Simpson Weather Associates, 809 East Jefferson St., Charlottesville, VA 22902
b – NASA Langley Research Center, Langley, VA, 23681
gde@swa.com

During 2014 and 2015, NASA funded an airborne expedition to the Arctic called Polar Winds in order to conduct experiments focused on documenting the low level wind circulations around Greenland and validating numerical models and reanalyzes, particularly in the boundary layer transition zones between land, water and ice. The NASA/LaRC DAWN coherent 2 micron lidar was flown on the LaRC UC-12B aircraft in November, 2014 and on the NASA DC-8 in May 2015. More than 100 hours of lidar data were obtained during the two campaigns along with ~100 dropsondes launched during the May 2015 campaign. These data are being used in several studies including the perfunctory lidar dropsonde comparisons, pointing error corrections and aircraft motion projection removal. This paper will report on both the instrument related performance as well as a case study of Barrier winds off the east coast of Greenland.

Keywords: airborne Doppler wind lidar, DAWN, boundary layer

1. Introduction

During Oct-Nov 2014 and May 2015, NASA sponsored two airborne missions designed to fly the Doppler Aerosol WiNd (DAWN) and TWiLiTE lidars to take wind measurements of the Arctic atmosphere, specifically over and off the coasts of Greenland. Polar Winds Campaign I was based in Kangerlussuaq, Greenland while Polar Winds Campaign II was based in Keflavik, Iceland. This presentation will only cover the DAWN contributions to Polar Winds.

The campaigns were designed to study and document lower level atmospheric circulations and to provide validation for the numerical models and reanalyses used over the polar/arctic regions. Another goal of both campaigns was to practice underflying and validating measurements from existing satellites and sensors such as CALIPSO, MODIS (AQUA and TERRA), ASCAT (METOP-A/B) and others. In addition, much of Campaign II was planned in collaboration with ESA and DLR of Germany to conduct coordinated (with the DLR Falcon) underflights of a simulated Aeolus ADM (due to be launched in 2017) while using ADM scanning strategies and taking measurements (lidar and dropsondes) that would benefit future development.

2. DAWN

The DAWN lidar developed by NASA Langley was selected for both campaigns. DAWN, which was also previously flown on the NASA DC-8 during the 2010 Genesis and Rapid Intensification Processes (GRIP) [1], is designed to be the most powerful coherent Doppler wind lidar available today for airborne missions. A summary of the DAWN system compared to two other airborne coherent DWLs is provided in Table 1. During Campaign I, DAWN was flown on board the NASA King Air UC-12B aircraft, but was later transferred to the NASA DC-8 for the Campaign II missions.

Table 1: Specifications of DAWN

Parameter	DAWN	TODWL	P3DWL	Comments
Wavelength (microns)	2.05	2.05	1.67	Eyesafe
Energy per pulse (mJ)	250	1	2	
Pulse rate(Hz)	10	500	500	
Pulse length(m)	~37	90	90	Range resolution
Telescope diameter(m)	.15	.10	.10	
Detection type	Coherent	Coherent	Coherent	~ .05 m/s LOS precision
Weight(kg)	Varies	300	275	
Power(watts)	Varies	900	550	

Note: TODWL: Twin Otter Doppler Wind Lidar owned by Center for Interdisciplinary Remotely Piloted Aircraft Studies in Monterey, CA. P3DWL: P3 Doppler Wind Lidar owned by US Army and flown on NOAA's P3 hurricane reconnaissance aircraft.

In addition to DAWN, we also utilized the dropsonde delivery system developed by Yankee Environmental Services to drop over 100 dropsondes during Campaign II in an attempt to obtain additional high-resolution vertical wind profiles during most missions. These dropsondes would also provide wind sounding comparisons for DAWN and for validation of numerical models.

2.1 Data Processing

We continue to develop and modify algorithms to improve the processing of the DAWN raw lidar data. We are specifically focusing on algorithms that account for the projected component of the aircraft's motion as well as algorithms that provide higher sensitivity in the presence of weaker aerosols which often occurs in the arctic regions near Greenland. These algorithms still require some fine tuning but have already lead to more complete wind profiles in the vertical.

2.2 Instrument Related Performance

Although DAWN operated near the designed optical output (2.5W), there were losses associated with optical elements, alignment and other efficiencies. In spite of these losses in performance, soundings were obtained with sufficient coverage to meet the primary Polar Winds mission objective of numerical model validation.

3. *Science Objectives and Missions*

The airborne missions of the Polar Winds campaigns were designed in part to investigate the low-level and near surface winds over and off the coast of Greenland and between the open water between Greenland and Iceland. During Polar Winds Campaigns I and II, a total of 24 missions and ~ 100 flight hour was flown (Figure 1) with individual missions or parts of missions focusing on the measurement and analyses of lower tropospheric winds

Every mission was seen as a model validation experiment. The data base of 3-D wind, temperature and moisture information from DAWN and the dropsondes is being used for validation polar models and re-analyses, including the Polar WRF model run specifically for the campaign.

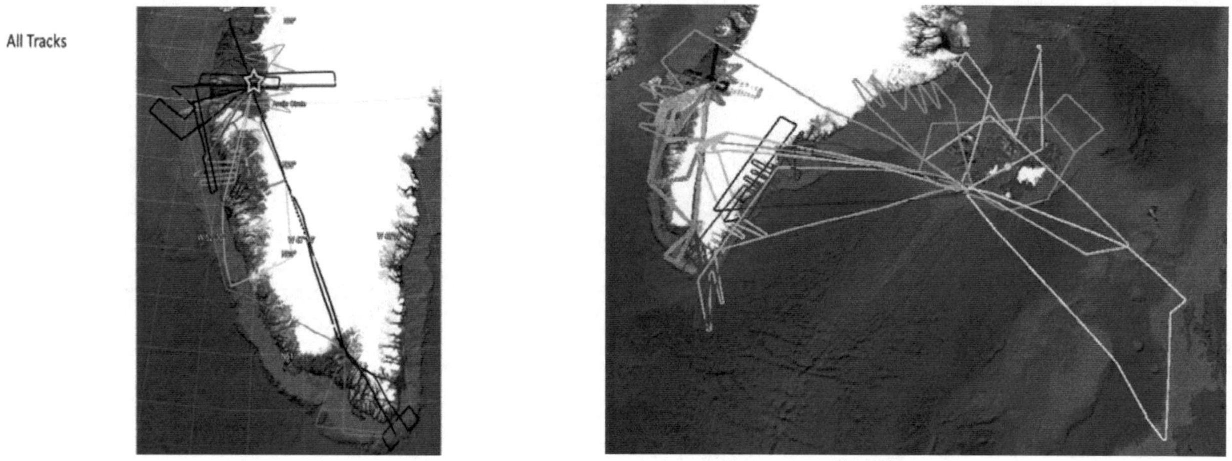

Figure 1: Composite of flight tracks of missions flown during Polar Winds Campaign I (left) and II (right).

4. Analysis and Comparisons

Although the final DAWN data set has yet to be released, we are confident enough with the existing near-final version to make comparisons with both the dropsondes dropsonde vs lidar comparisons

4.1 Comparison with Dropsondes

During Campaign II, the DC-8 and the DLR Falcon flew a coordinated flight with the DC-8 flying underneath the Falcon as both targeted the strong upper jet over the Atlantic between Iceland and Ireland. During this mission, 11 dropsondes were dropped over the Atlantic and as DAWN was in full operation. Although there were not many DAWN returns in the middle troposphere (very clean), there were strong returns in the upper and lower atmosphere. An example of dropsonde and DAWN wind profiles are provided for a mission called “The Barrier Winds”.

4.2 Barrier Winds Case Study

The region off the southern and central eastern coast of Greenland is an area noted for strong low-level Barrier winds as strong low pressure systems move eastward towards and past Iceland and the northerly/northeasterly flow is blocked and channeled by the Greenland land mass resulting in strong low level winds. May 21, 2015 was a prime example of this scenario as forecasted by the models, including the Polar WRF. A mission was flown to gather high-resolution DAWN and dropsonde wind data for this case and to compare against each other and the operational Polar WRF model [2]. The satellite image and flight track/drop location is shown in Figure 2.

Wind speed and wind direction comparisons made between the model and observed data for the May 21 case are shown (Figure 3).Between 2020 and 2100, the DC-8 was flown around 2.5 km and enabled total DAWN coverage of the boundary layer and down to the surface.

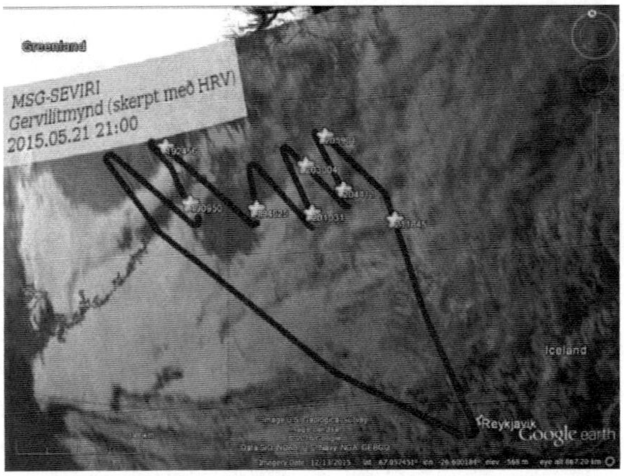

Figure 2: Satellite image on 5/21/15 21Z and location/time of flight track and drop location.

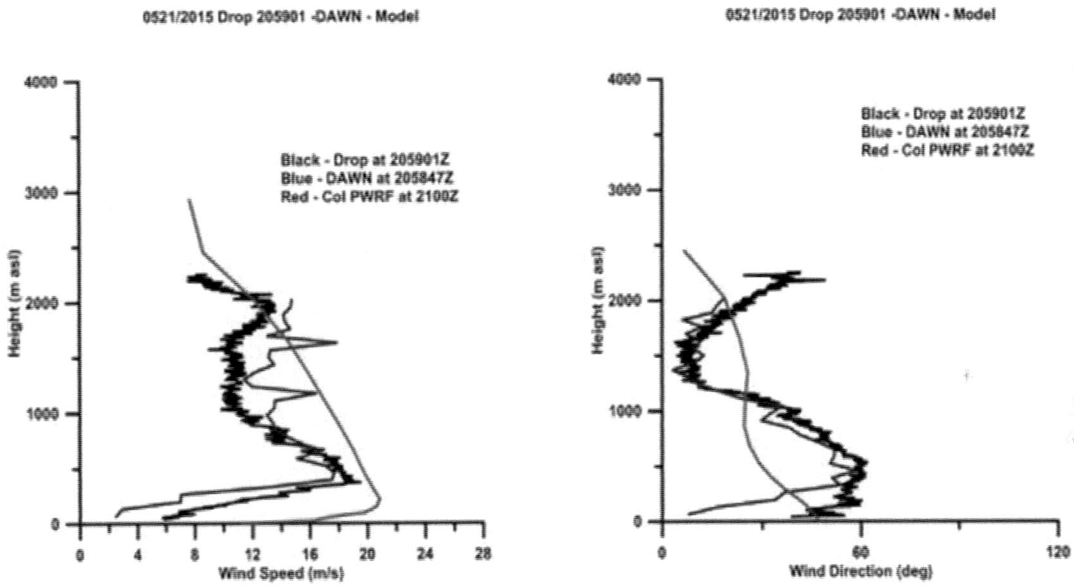

Figure 3. Wind speed and direction profiles for dropsonde (black), DAWN (blue) and Colorado Polar WRF (red) forecasts centered on the time and location of the 205901Z drop on 05/21/2015.

5. References

[1] Kavaya, M.J., , J. Y. Beyon, G. J. Koch, M. Petros, P. J. Petzar, U. N. Singh, B. C. Trieu, and J. Yu, 2014, "The Doppler Aerosol Wind Lidar (DAWN) Airborne, Wind-Profiling, Coherent-Detection Lidar System: Overview, Flight Results, and Plans," Journal of Atmospheric and Oceanic Technology (JTECH) 34 (4), 826-842 (April 2014) {http://dx.doi.org/10.1175/JTECH-D-12-00274.1}

[2] Bromwich, D. H., K. M. Hines, and L.-S. Bai, 2009, "Development and testing of Polar WRF: 2. Arctic Ocean", *J. Geophys. Res.*, 114, D08122, doi: 10.1029/2008JD010300

Development of an Onboard Safety Avionics System using a Doppler Lidar

Hamaki Inokuchi(a), Tomohiro Akiyama(a), and Shigeru Machida(a)
(a) Japan Aerospace Exploration Agency
6-13-1 Osawa, Mitaka, Tokyo, Japan, 181-0015
inokuchi.hamaki@jaxa.jp

Abstract: We are developing an airborne Doppler lidar for onboard turbulence detection. Flight experiments have shown that it is difficult for the present lidar to be used for guiding turbulence evasion maneuvers during cruise, but at low altitudes or airspeeds a lidar will enable vertical avoidance maneuvers to be provided during landing approach. It is also considered that measured wind data will be communicated directly to the aircraft's automatic flight control system during cruise. An outline of prior flight experiments and a development program of the safety avionics system are explained.

Keywords: Flight Safety, Air Turbulence, Doppler Lidar

1. Introduction

Figure 1 shows a breakdown of the causes of large airplane accidents during the 10 years between 2005 and 2014, based on an analysis of aircraft accident reports published by the Japan Transport Safety Board [1]. There were a total of 30 airliner accidents during this period, of which 16 were caused by air turbulence and 3 are judged to be due to human factors related to air turbulence. It therefore appears that more than half of the accidents were related to air turbulence. Although pilot error is sometimes identified as a factor in turbulence-related accidents, it is considered that advance warning of turbulent conditions would allow crews time to prepare and so eliminate human error as a cause. Moreover, turbulence-related accidents have been increasing in recent years according to the Federal Aviation Administration's Advisory Circular (AC) 120-88A [2]. Therefore, turbulence is the most important flight safety issue that needs to be urgently addressed by preventive measures.

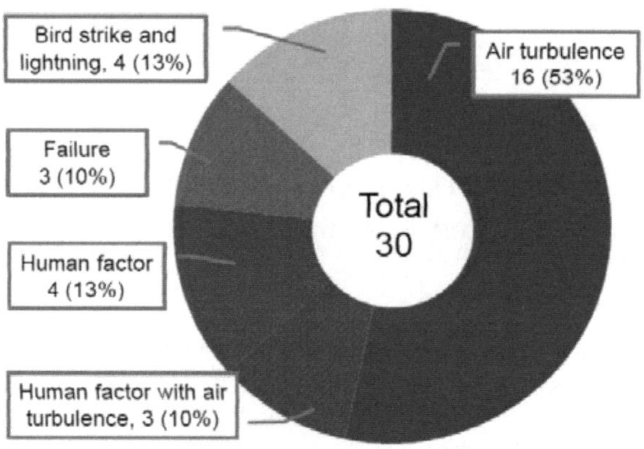

Figure 1. Aircraft Accidents to Large Civil Airplanes in Japan (2005-2014).

Conventional weather radar can detect turbulence associated with thick cloud. However, since it cannot detect turbulence in clear air, there is currently no effective means to predict Clear Air Turbulence (CAT) encounters. To reduce the number of in-flight accidents caused by CAT, we need an onboard system to detect turbulence, immediately determine its intensity, and warn the pilots if necessary. This would make flights operations safer. Based on this consideration, we are developing a lidar system to detect turbulence ahead of an aircraft even in clear air conditions and give advance warning of CAT encounters. We have developed a high-power Doppler lidar as an aircraft onboard device, and a flight demonstration successfully detected CAT ahead of an aircraft.

2. Development of the Doppler Lidar

We have been developing coherent Doppler lidars that use 1.5 μm eye-safe wavelength lasers [3]. Because aerosol densities are low at jet airliner cruising altitudes, somewhat high output power is necessary. We have therefore developed a high power optical planar waveguide amplifier (WGA) which achieved an available laser pulse energy of 1.9 mJ at a pulse repetition rate of 4 kHz [4], and applied it into our previous experimental lidar to produce a 'high altitude lidar' model shown in Figure 2. The optical transceiver includes a master laser oscillator and a heterodyne detector, and the optical antenna contains an optical telescope and optical amplifiers. A personal computer performs signal processing. A chiller provides liquid cooling of the WGA, and two amplifier drivers control the pump light for the optical amplifiers. Because this is a proof-of-concept model, no special attention was paid to miniaturizing of integrating the system components. The high altitude lidar model was installed in a Gulfstream II jet aircraft and demonstrated wind measurement capability at high speed and high altitude [5]. The system components were installed in a rack of the aircraft's cabin as shown in Figure 3, while the optical antenna was mounted in a fairing on the bottom of the fuselage. Laser light was emitted forward from the aircraft.

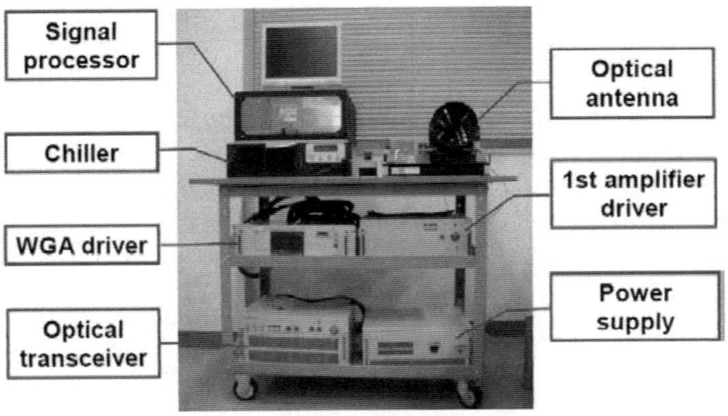

Figure 2. High Altitude Lidar Model.

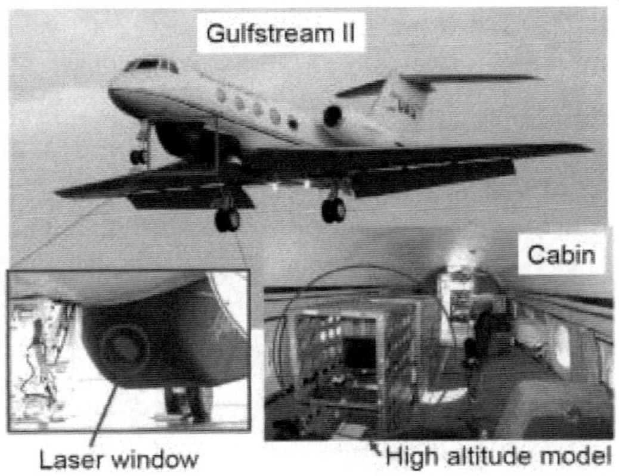

Figure 3. Experimental System Installation.

Figure 4 shows an example of CAT detected ahead of the aircraft while flying at altitude of 3,200 m [6]. The upper plot shows the wind intensities detected by the lidar, with distance ahead of the aircraft along the ordinate, so the aircraft flies along the upward direction of the graph. Time is shown along the abscissa, and vertical lines are plotted at one-second intervals. Each vertical column of blocks shows color-coded wind speed variances (Wlos) in each range bin observed each second. Wlos is used as an index of turbulence intensity. As shown in the key in the upper right corner of the figure, the color changes toward red as the Wlos value increases to indicate stronger turbulence. Since the received signal level weakens with distance, black is used to represent the absence of Wlos measurement due to insufficient received laser light. A region of turbulence detected ahead of the aircraft gets closer with time as the aircraft flies towards it. Therefore, if turbulence is detected, a downward-sloping line will appear in the graph. The upper and middle plots in Figure 4 show that a periodic change in vertical acceleration (Az) was measured and Wlos increased corresponding to the increases in Az. A periodic change of outside air temperature (OAT), shown in the bottom plot of Figure 4, was also observed that corresponded to the change of Az. Although the flight altitude fluctuated over a range of 25 m during the period of the observations shown, this is too small to account for the change in OAT. Since it is known that temperature variations are associated with CAT [7], this observation example indicates that the aircraft had encountered CAT.

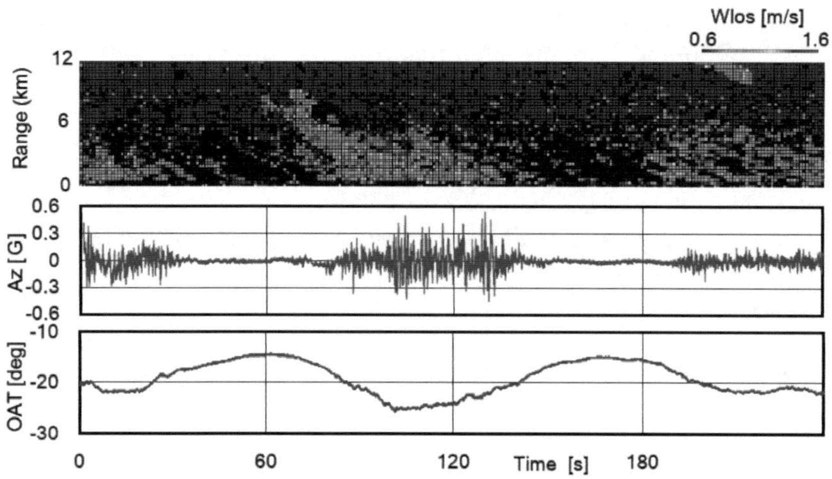

Figure 4. CAT Detection Sample.

3. R&D of Onboard Safety Avionics Technology

Although these flight experiments successfully demonstrated CAT detection in flight, at cruising speeds the present detection range means only a short warning time is available so it is difficult for the present 'high altitude lidar' model to be used to guide turbulence avoidance maneuvers during cruise. This is because high altitude CAT usually extends along horizontal layers and rapid vertical maneuvers during cruise to avoid it may have higher risk than the turbulence itself. The main aim of the lidar turbulence detection function in cruise is to therefore provide sufficient advance warning of turbulence to allow passengers and heavy cabin service items to be secured, although at lower altitudes or airspeeds a lidar will permit vertical avoidance maneuvers. Further improving the detection range of the lidar will require increases in size, weight and power consumption, with attendant higher installation cost. Consequently, now that the main components have been proven, we will now focus on reducing the size of the device and improving its reliability rather than on achieving greater detection range.

Our research and development project is moving toward achieving a system to prevent in-flight accidents caused by turbulence. The system will determine the turbulence intensity, warn the pilots if there is a risk, and automatically alleviate lurching through flight control inputs, making air travel safer for passengers and crew. An overview of operations by the system is shown in Figure 5. The system to prevent turbulence-induced in-flight accidents will have two main technical advances: reducing lurching while cruising or changing altitude, and warning pilots of turbulence encounter during landing approach.

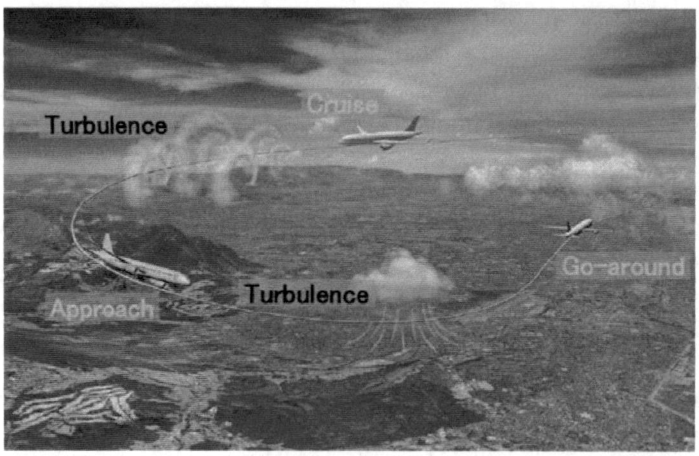

Figure 5. An Overview of Operations by Onboard Safety Avionics.

If the Doppler lidar detects distant turbulence during cruise, the seatbelt signs are turned on and the cabin is secured. Meanwhile, the lidar measures the vertical components of airflows ahead of the aircraft by two-axis observations. Based on these measurements of the airflow ahead of the aircraft, the flight control system generates control commands to suppress lurching when the aircraft enters the turbulence. Conventional automatic flight control systems use only information on the aircraft's current state, but our system utilizes data on the airflow one second ahead of the aircraft to generate control commands to counteract turbulence using the aircraft's control surfaces. If the Doppler lidar detect distant turbulence during climb or descent, the pilots can decide to level off and delay further altitude change to avoid the turbulent region.

During landing approach, the data obtained by the Doppler lidar system is used to immediately determine the risk associated with detected turbulence, and if necessary, advise the pilots to perform a go-around maneuver to avoid the hazard. The aircraft can then make another safer landing approach. Since it is unnecessary to obtain permission of air traffic control to execute a go-around, immediate action is possible. In addition, airspeed is low during landing approach and all passengers must fasten their seatbelts, so the go-around maneuver does not pose a risk of injuries. We plan to demonstrate this advisory function by flight experiments in 2016 to 2017.

4. Development of a next Doppler Lidar

In order to demonstrate an aircraft onboard safety avionics system that can improve the safety of flight operations, we are developing a prototype high-power compact Doppler lidar that integrates the components into a more suitable package for general aircraft installation. Table 1 shows the specifications of this lidar and Figure 6 shows a schematic diagram. The lidar consists of four units: an optical antenna unit, an optical transmitter and receiver (TRX) unit, a signal processor and a chiller. The optical antenna unit includes two telescopes and two optical amplifiers. A larger telescope is used by the warning function and a smaller telescope is used for measurement of the airflow vector. The optical antenna unit can switch between the telescopes by an optical polarization switch and polarized beam splitter (PBS). The lines of sight of each telescope are not parallel, and this allows the vertical component of wind speed to be obtained by measuring the wind speeds along each line-of-sight axis,. Compared with the proof-of-concept high altitude lidar model, the 1st amplifier drive, the WGA driver and the optical antenna have been downsized and integrated into the optical antenna unit. Furthermore, power supplies are integrated into each unit, and the optical antenna and the optical TRX can be operated with only a 28 VDC supply. Figure 7 shows the optical antenna of the next Doppler lidar.

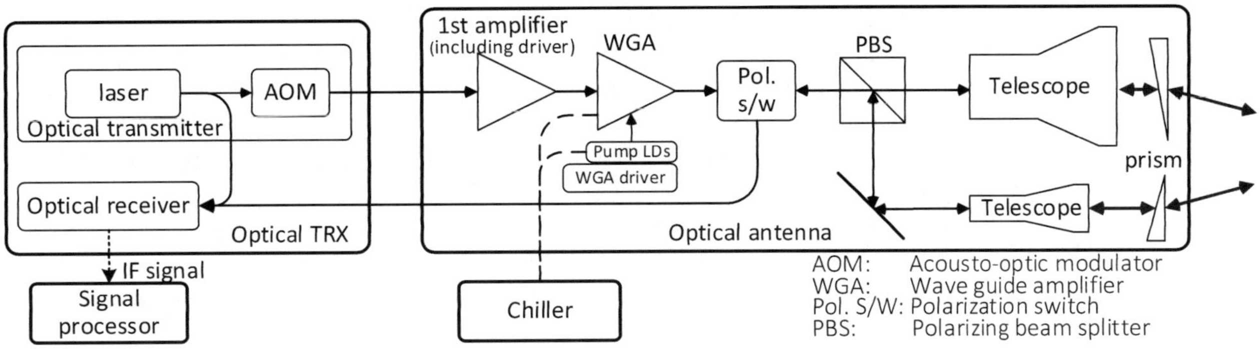

Figure 6. Schematic Diagram of the Next Doppler Lidar.

Table 1. Spec. of the Next Doppler Lidar

Wavelength	1550 nm
Pulse energy	≥3.3 mJ
Pulse repetition frequency	1 kHz
Pulse width	600 nsec
LOS switching frequency	5 Hz
Telescope diameter	150 mm 50 mm

Figure 7. Optical Antenna of the Next Doppler Lidar.

5. Concluding Remarks

We have developed a Doppler lidar for airborne turbulence detection and demonstrated CAT detection in flight. However, high aircraft cruising speeds mean that it is difficult for the present lidar to be used for guiding turbulence avoidance maneuvers during cruise. Consequently, we will focus on an advisory system, and expand its application to the landing approach phase of flight. It is also considered that measured wind data will be communicated directly to the aircraft's automatic flight control system for gust alleviation. Therefore, we have started a development program of an onboard safety avionics system using our Doppler lidar.

The Doppler lidar developed for the safety avionics system is now being tested on the ground. Compared to the proof-of-concept system, the number of components and total volume of the system have been reduced, and an airflow vector measurement function has been added.

When this system is has been proven effective and installed on passenger aircraft, we can expect a reduction in turbulence-related in-flight accidents. Flying will then be more comfortable and relaxing and passengers will be able to sleep better.

6. References

[1] Japan Transport Safety Board, Aircraft accident reports, http://www.mlit.go.jp/jtsb/, (2005-2014).

[2] Federal Aviation Administration., "Preventing injuries caused by turbulence," Advisory Circular AC 120-88A (2006).

[3] Inokuchi, H., Tanaka, H., and Ando, T. "Development of an Onboard Doppler LIDAR for Flight Safety," Journal of Aircraft, Vol. 46, No. 4, (2009), pp. 1411-1415.

[4] Sakimura, T., Watanabe, Y., Ando, T., Kameyama, S., Asaka, K., Tanaka, H., Yanagisawa, T., Hirano, Y., Inokuchi, H., "1.5-µm high-gain and high-power laser amplifier using a Er,Yb:glass planar waveguide for coherent Doppler LIDAR," Proceedings of CLEO, San Jose, (2012), pp. 114.

[5] H. Inokuchi, M. Furuta, T. Inagaki, "High Altitude Turbulence Detection using an Airborne Doppler Lidar", Proceedings of ICAS, St. Petersburg, Russia, (2014).

[6] H. Inokuchi. "Detection of the Clear Air Turbulence by an Airborne Doppler LIDAR," Proceedings of Asia-Pacific International Symposium on Aerospace Technology, Jeju, Korea, 6.4.2, (2012).

[7] D. Atras, J. I. Metcalf, J. H. Richter and E. E. Gossard. "The Birth of CAT and Microscale Turbulence," Journal of the Atmospheric Sciences, Vol. 27, (1970) , pp. 903-913.

Development of a high power Doppler Wind Lidar for measuring wind and EDR along aircraft approaches

Jean-Pierre Cariou (a), Ludovic Thobois (a), Quentin Germon (a), Agnès Dolfi-Bouteyre (b), Anne Durecu (b)

(a) LEOSPHERE, Orsay, France
(b) ONERA, Palaiseau, France
jpcariou@leosphere.com

Abstract: Air flows in the troposphere have a major impact on air traffic safety and operations. In the framework of the European UFO project (www.ufo-wind-sensors.eu), LEOSPHERE and ONERA have developed a new high powered scanning Doppler LIDAR using an innovative powerful Erbium doped fiber laser amplifier. The performances of this prototype have been evaluated through a campaign in 2014 performed at Toulouse airport, France. In addition, specific algorithms have been developed for retrieving wind and EDR quantities along aircraft approaches and in 3D around airport. The wind and EDR measurements have been then compared to reference sensors in order to assess their accuracy.

Keywords: Coherent Wind Doppler Lidar, pulsed high power EDFA, weather dependent separations, wake vortices, wind, turbulence

1. Introduction

At airports, runway operation is the limiting factor for the overall throughput; the current ICAO standards determine for three aircraft categories the minimal distance separation between aircrafts given their wake turbulence category in order to avoid the risk of wake vortex encounter whatever the weather conditions. To renew these out-of-date and conservative regulations, many studies have focused on the better understanding of vortex behaviors with weather conditions that can only be characterized accurately by scanning Doppler lidars [1][2]. They showed that wake vortex decay varies a lot with weather conditions. In case of high turbulence, wake vortices strength will for example decay quicker. To greatly optimize aircraft distance separations, weather dependent separation regulations (WDS) are under development. Such regulations require accurate and frequent observations of winds, crosswinds and eddy dissipation rate (EDR) that have a direct impact on the lifetime of wake vortices[3][4] along approach and takeoff paths.

This is why the UFO project, entitled Ultra-Fast wind sensOrs for measuring Wind and EDR for Wake Vortex mitigation has been launched [5]. The main objectives were to develop new sensor technologies, especially a 1.5 micron fiber-based high power scanning Lidar [6] developed by LEOSPHERE and ONERA and its adapted wind and EDR retrievals algorithms. The developed LIDAR has been validated during a field campaign in April/May 2014 at Toulouse-Blagnac airport in France. The complementary and combination of the scanning Doppler lidar with a 2D electronic X-band radar from THALES as well as Aircraft wind retrievals with Mode-S EHS have been evaluated. The current paper will describe the main achievements of the project with the scanning coherent Doppler LIDAR and will compare the data availability and accuracy of such a sensor. Finally the proposed combination between the different sensors for all weather wind and turbulence observing systems at airports will be presented.

2. Lidar requirements

The next table describes the operational requirements of a lidar for the different airport applications. A lidar simulation tool [7] developed by ONERA and LEOSPHERE is used to determine technical specifications compliant with the measurement requirements. The atmosphere is assumed to be standard : Aerosol Optical Depth = 0.2 and Lidar ratio =30 . Right columns of Table 1summarize the initial guess for the laser source technical specifications to be developed in UFO in order to obtain the measurement requirements. The required mean power is up to 4W for glide path measurements.

Table 1 : Synthesis of wind and EDR measurement needs and lidar solutions

Areas of interest	Needs	Horizontal range (km)	Vertical range (km)	Spatial scale (m)	Revisit time (s)	Pulse (ns) PRF (KHz)	Energy/ pulse (μJ) Integration time (s)	Mean power (W)
Glide Path	Wind measurements along glide path	10	0,5	100	10	400 10	400 <0.25	4
	EDR measurements along glide path	10	0,5	100	600	400 10	400 <0.25	4
	3D Wind measurements along glide path	10	0,5	100	30	400 10	400 <1	4
360° View	Wind shears	7-8	0,5	200	60-180	800 10	200 <1	2
	3D Wind measurements	7-8	0,5	200	300	800 10	200 <1	2
Critical area	Wake Vortices measurements on runways	1	0,2	20	<10	200 10	200 <0.1	1
	EDR measurements cross to runways	1	0,2	30	600	200 20	200 <1	1

Leosphere is developing pulsed fiber Doppler lidars for more than 10 years, based on a technology formerly developed at ONERA. The core technology is using EDFA (Erbium Doped Fiber Amplifiers) operating around 1.55μm in the telecom C band, and an all-fiber architecture.

The large-mode-area (LMA) fibers enable high peak power generation. The average power exceeds several watts and high pulse repetition frequency (PRF) efficiently compensates the relative low pulse energy. Moreover, the MOPA architecture flexibility in terms of pulse duration allows fulfilling a large variety of requirements, enabling the design of high spatial resolution or long range systems. This is particularly recommended for lidar systems addressing several ATM needs.

In fiber lasers, peak power is limited by non-linear effects. In highly coherent emission, the most limiting effect is the Stimulated Brillouin Scattering (SBS) [8]. To overcome these limitations in the UFO project, LMA fibers are used. By decreasing the power spatial density, the output peak power can be increased up to 250W.

However, this is not enough if both long range and high range resolution are required. In this case, high pulse energy and short pulse duration are needed, leading to high peak power requirement. In the frame of UFO, a new original architecture patented by ONERA is tested for the first time on a Doppler lidar, yielding a significant increase in the available peak power, around 400W. Experimental developments confirm that this technology is able to provide 4W of mean power, enough as for the performance requirements [8]. A commercial Windcube400S is used as a basis. The EDFA is replaced by the new EDFA prototype and an air conditioner is added to warranty good reliability during the Toulouse spring campaign. More than 10km range is demonstrated with 3,2W and an integration time of 0,16s.

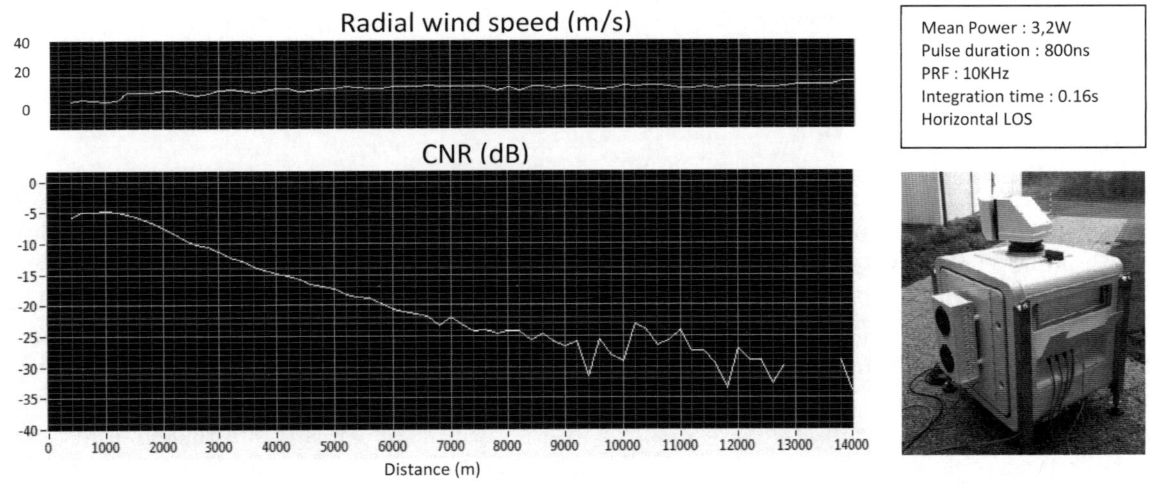

Figure 1 : Performance validation of new long range UFO lidar

3. Algorithms and methods for measuring wind and turbulence

The first objective of the scanning lidar is to provide headwinds, crosswinds and turbulence at several points along the glide path to adjust weather dependent separations. The second objective consists in providing horizontal wind speeds and directions every 500 meters horizontally and up to an altitude of 500m for being assimilated into weather forecast models and improving their forecasts. To retrieve wind speed components both along the approaches and in 3D around the airport, a specific algorithm based on the coupling of the volume velocity processing (VVP) and a single value decomposition (SVD) has been developed [8]. This algorithm has then been tested during two months to retrieve wind speeds and directions at one point 1.6km away where an anemometer is located. The retrieved wind measurements are compared to the measurements of the anemometer [10]. The accuracy of the ten minutes averaged horizontal wind computed by the algorithm compared to the anemometer is 0.06 m/s and the correlation factor is 98%.

For characterizing the atmospheric turbulence, Eddy Dissipation Rate (EDR) was chosen. An algorithm based on the estimation of the structure function [11] has been implemented based on the combination of spatial and time data averaging. In order to test the EDR algorithm, a tool has been developed in order to simulate a 2D Von Karman turbulent wind field with a given EDR level. This tool is based on Monin and Yaglom formalism [12].

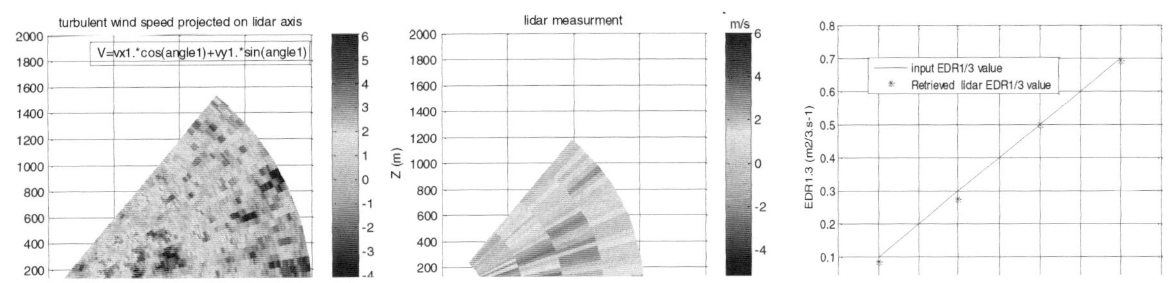

Figure 2. Left: Turbulent wind field realizations with an EDR=0.74 m2.s-3. Middle: lidar simulated measurements. Right: Correlation of EDR retrievals for different EDR values.

Figure 2 shows an example of turbulent wind field realization, over a field of 2000 m by 2000m, and its projection on the lidar axis for a given EDR level and turbulence scale L0. The EDR retrievals are in good agreement with the expected EDR values.

4. Results

The high power laser scanning WINDCUBE LIDAR has been deployed at Toulouse-Blagnac airport and configured in order to perform wind and EDR measurements every kilometer along the glide path in less than one minute and 3D wind retrievals around the airport in 5min.Typical accumulation times of 0.16s were used per line of sight. During the trial, the LIDAR has been continuously measuring up to an averaged range of 8km which could vary with weather conditions. The 3D wind retrievals were provided in order to have access to the horizontal wind fields in 3D. They have been validated against a lidar profiler located at 3km from the airport. The glide path wind retrievals provided the profiles of headwinds and crosswinds along the approaches. This information can be useful for adjusting in real time distance separation in the final approach in weather dependent separation concepts since the wind below 500m can change in direction and intensity. The accuracy of glide path winds was evaluated in comparison to the in-situ wind measurements performed by a research aircraft from TUB University. The obtained accuracy of the glide path wind retrievals with LIDAR is 0.4 m/s and its dispersion 0.5 m/s compared to the research aircraft.

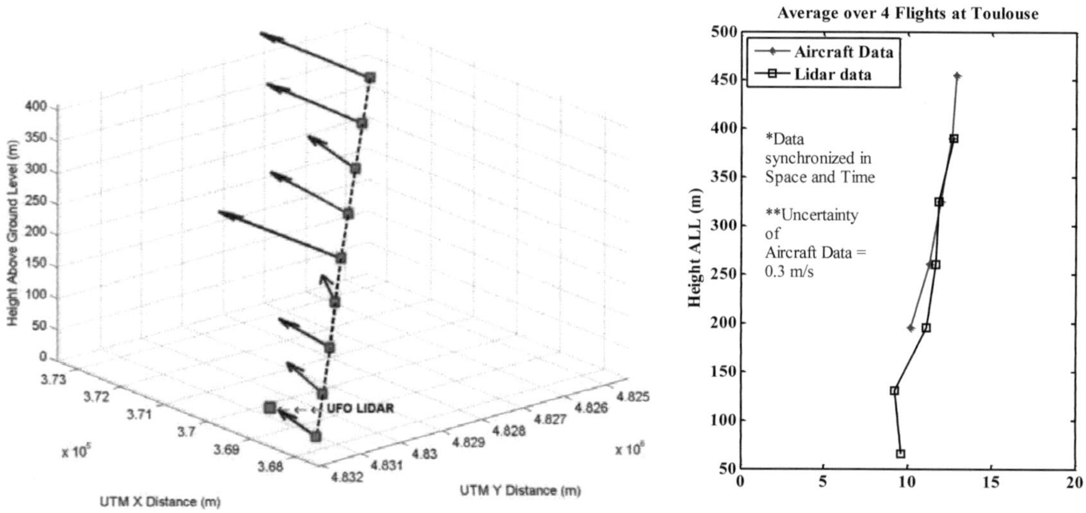

Figure 3. Headwinds and crosswinds retrievals along 10km glide path (left) and comparison of retrieved glide path winds of LIDAR with wind measurements of research aircraft (right)

The EDR retrieval algorithm has been applied on Lidar data collected at Toulouse-Blagnac airport. Examples of the 24th April 2014 are shown on Figure 3 for a set of PPI scans (PPI with elevations from 2° to 45° and azimuth 47° to 293°), as a function of time, and for different altitudes. Results show that EDR is generally higher at lowest altitudes near the surface layer as expected. Strong variations of EDR with time have also been observed within the hour of the day due to changes in cloud coverage and solar irradiance.

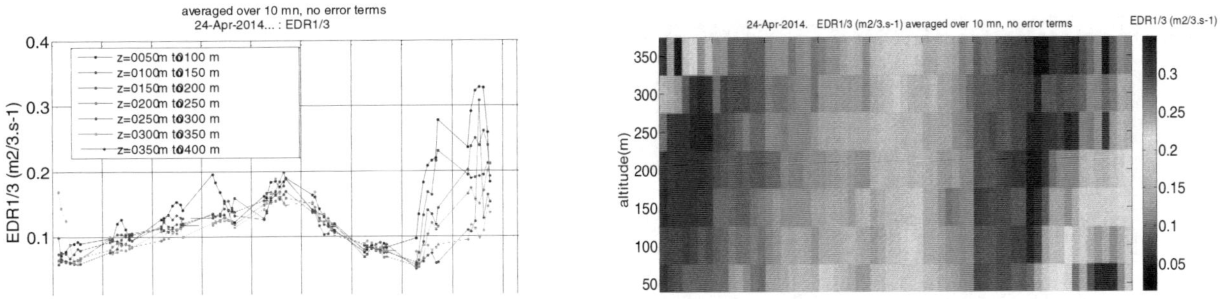

Figure 4. April 24th 2014. Left: EDR as a function of time for different altitudes – Right: evolution of EDR in color scale displayed versus time (horizontal axis) and altitude (vertical axis)

5. Conclusions and perspectives

Future concepts of weather dependent separations will require high accurate measurements of wind and turbulence (EDR) in the vicinity of airports at high resolution and frequency. A next generation high power LIDAR based on fiber technology has been developed in the UFO project to retrieve the quantities of interest respectively under clear air (visibility) and rainy (rain rate) conditions. The obtained performances of the lidar are in agreement with the requirements, ie. the capability to measure up to 10km with an accumulation time less than 0.2s and the accuracy better than 0.5m/s for retrieving glide path and 3D winds.

During the project, the combination of lidar and radar has been studied in regards to weather conditions to ensure the development of an all-weather wake vortex advisory system. On a longer term perspective, wake turbulence problematic strengthen the demands for on-board advisory systems of wake vortex or even clear air turbulence. For these applications, airborne UV LIDARs, IR LIDARs and RADARs are still under study.

6. References

[1] Dolfi-Bouteyre A. et al., "1.5µm all fiber pulsed LIDAR for wake vortex monitoring," in Conference on Lasers and Electro-Optics. Optical Society of America, 2008, p. CMQ3.

[2] Matayoshi, N. et al., Wake vortex measurement campaign towards reduced separation, WakeNet Europe Workshop, Amsterdam, 21-22 April 2015

[3] Singhal J., "From SESAR to Implementation: Completing the TBS Picture", 2014 Workshop of WakeNetEu network, 13-14 May 2014, Bretigny, France

[4] Mutuel F.(2014), "ATM Decision Support Tool for Wake Vortex Hazard Management Combining Sensors and Modeling", AIAA Paper n°2014-2332, AIAA Aviation, 6th AIAA Atmospheric and Space Environments Conference, 16 -20 June, 2014, Atlanta, Georgia, USA.

[5] UFO : UltraFast wind sensOrs for wake-vortex hazards mitigation Project reference: 314237,Funded under: FP7-TRANSPORT, From 2012-11-01 to 2015-10-31

[6] Dolfi-Bouteyre A et Al (2013) All-weather sensors (lidar + radar) for Wake-Vortex hazards mitigation on Airport., Coherent Laser RadarConference, Barcelona, June 2013

[7] Boquet, M., Royer, P., Cariou, J.-P., Machta, M., and Valla, M., "Simulation of Doppler Lidar Measurement Range and Data Availability," Journal of Atmospheric and Oceanic Technology, 33, 977-987 (1997).

[8] Long Range Wind Lidars Based On Novel High Spectral Brilliance All-Fibered Sources, L Lombard, A. Dolfi-Bouteyre, C. Besson, B. Augère, P. Bourdon, A. Durécu, D. Goular, J. Le Gouët, C. Planchat, W. Renard, M. Valla, G. Canat – SPIE Remote Sensing Toulouse 2015.

[9] Kongara S, Calhoun R, Choukulkar A, Boldi M. Velocity retrieval for coherent Doppler lidar. International Journal of Remote Sensing 2011; In Press.

[10] Wagner, R., Courtney, M., Scanning LIDAR Verification Study, DTU Report, 2014.

[11] Frehlich R, Yannick M, Michael LJ, Ben B, Sharman R. (2006). Measurements of boundary layer profiles in an urban environment. Journal of Applied Meteorology 45: 821–837.

[12] Monin A. S. & A. M. Yaglom (1975) : Statistical fluid mechanics : Mechanics of turbulence – Vol 2 » The MIT Press

Investigation of feasibilities of aircraft wake vortex measurement by a low-energy 1.5-micron pulsed coherent Doppler lidar

I.N. Smalikho, V.A. Banakh, and A.V. Falits
V.E. Zuev Institute of Atmospheric Optics SB RAS 1 Akademik Zuev Square,
Tomsk, 634021, Russia
smalikho@iao.ru

Abstract: In this work the feasibilities of the extraction of information about aircraft wake vortices from data measured by a low-energy 1.5-micron pulsed coherent Doppler lidar (PCDL) are investigated. A strategy of measurement by such lidar at airfield of an airport has been developed and the conditions of applicability of the lidar for wake vortex measurement have been determined. The applicability of the 1.5-micron Stream Line PCDL for measurements of the wake vortices generated by a landing aircraft has been demonstrated in the experiments carried out at the airfield of the Tolmachevo Airport. We estimated parameters of the wake vortices for aircrafts of various types, including Boing-747 cargo aircraft.

Keywords: Coherent Doppler lidar, aircraft wake vortex

1. Introduction

Investigation of aircraft wake vortices is important for development of the flight safety systems. A 2-μm pulsed coherent Doppler lidar [1] with the pulse energy of 2 mJ is used most widely for the measurement of aircraft wake vortices [2]. Relatively large pulse energy of this lidar provides a sufficiently high signal-to-noise ratio (SNR) at ranges up to 2-3 km. In contrast to this lidar, the energy of the probing pulse of a low-energy 1.5-micron PCDL is 100 or more times be lower.

The method of velocity envelopes for estimation of parameters of aircraft wake vortices [2] can not be applied in the case of 1.5-micron PCDL, because too low SNR that is usually realized in practice. As shown by numerical simulations and field experiment with the use of the 1.5-micron Stream Line PCDL (made by HALO Photonics, [3]) with a pulse energy of 14 μJ , the radial velocity method [4,5] allows us to obtain information about the aircraft vortices, under certain conditions. This paper is devoted to the study of feasibilities of the aircraft vortex measurement by this lidar. Results of estimation of coordinates of the wake vortex axis and the vortex circulation from raw data measured by the Stream Line lidar at airfield of the Tolmachevo airport are presented.

2. Measurement strategy and estimation of wake vortex parameters

The Stream Line lidar can be used to study the spatial dynamics and evolution of wake vortices generated by a landing aircraft at height of no more than 70 m [5]. During the measurement, the scanning by the probing beam in the vertical plane perpendicular to the runway is used, alternately increasing and decreasing the elevation angle φ within the scan sector $[0°, \varphi_{max}]$. The distance between the lidar and the runway should be about 300 m. The probing beam is focused at 300 m to increase the SNR. The most optimal are the following parameters of measurement and lidar data processing: angular speed of the scanning is $2°s^{-1}$, $\varphi_{max} = 20°$ (10 s for one scan), and number of pulses used for the data accumulation equals 1500 (for the Stream Line lidar the measurement duration is 0.1 s). From obtained array of the correlation functions of the complex lidar signal the Doppler spectra are calculated and then the radial velocities $V_r(R_k,\varphi_m;n')$ are estimated, where $R_k = R_0 + k\Delta R$ is the range; ΔR = 3 m, $0° \le \varphi_m \le \varphi_{\max}$; $k,m = 0,1,2,3,...$; and n' is the scan number.

Let from the scan number $n' = n_0 + 1$ and to $n' = n_0 + N$ the array of lidar estimates of the radial velocity contain the information about wake vortices. To avoid the influence of the background wind, we obtain the array $V_r'(R_k,\varphi_m;n) = V_r(R_k,\varphi_m;n_0+n) - V_r(R_k,\varphi_m;n_0)$, where $n = n' - n_0 = 1,2,...,N$. To obtain estimates of the distance from the lidar to the axis of i-th vortex $R_{Ci}(t_{ni})$, angular coordinate of the axis $\varphi_{Ci}(t_{ni})$, and the vortex circulation $\Gamma_i(t_{ni})$ from the array $V_r'(R_k,\varphi_m;n)$ (indexes $i=1$ for left and $i=2$ for right vortex, t_{ni} is time after over-flight or vortex age) we use the method of radial velocities. Detailed description of this method is given in [4,5].

Using numerical simulation, we calculated the error of estimation of vortex parameters at various SNR and found that acceptable accuracy is possible under the condition: $\text{SNR} \ge 0.04$. But in the simulation we did not take into account that the wind is not homogeneous, aircraft wake vortices move, and the Earth's surface can significantly influence on the spatial dynamics and evolution of wake vortices. Therefore, to fully investigate the feasibilities of lidar sensing aircraft vortices it is necessary a field experiment.

3. Experiment

We carried out first measurements of aircraft wake vortices by the Stream Line lidar at the airfield of the Tomsk Airport in 2014 and obtained results only for a few B737-8 aircrafts [4].

Figure 1. During the experiment at the airfield of the Tolmachevo Airport.

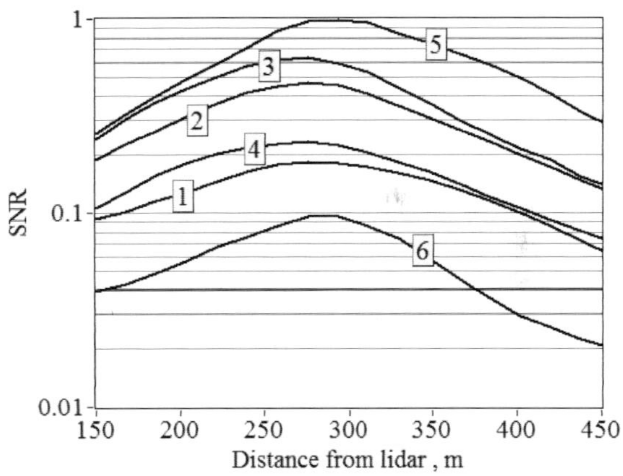

Figure 2. SNR versus range at time moments, when B747 aircrafts crossed the scanning plane.

From 4-th to 6-th May 2016, we conducted an experiment with the Stream Line PCDL at the airfield of the Tolmachevo Airport (near Novosibirsk city). Continuous lidar measurements (see Figure 1) were carried out from 18:00 to 21:00 on May 4, from 00:00 to 13:00 on May 5, and from 00:00 to 10:00 on May 6. During all measurements the weather was always clear without a single cloud. During the day the temperature varied from 12° to 18° above zero, at night and early morning temperatures dropped to 0°. The SNR and the lateral wind velocity are important factors for lidar observations. For example, if $|V| > 5$ m/s, the wake vortices can be observed not longer than 30 s (3 scans) at distances R_k from 150 to 450 m. In this experiment, the velocity $|V|$ did not exceed 4 m/s.

The minimum distance between the lidar and a line along the runway was 285 meters. Landing aircrafts crossed the scanning plane at a height of 50 m. During our measurements 44 aircrafts of different types (A319, A320, A321, B737-8, B767, B747-4, B747-8 and a few smaller aircrafts) crossed the scanning plane. Large cargo aircrafts B747 generate very powerful wake vortices.

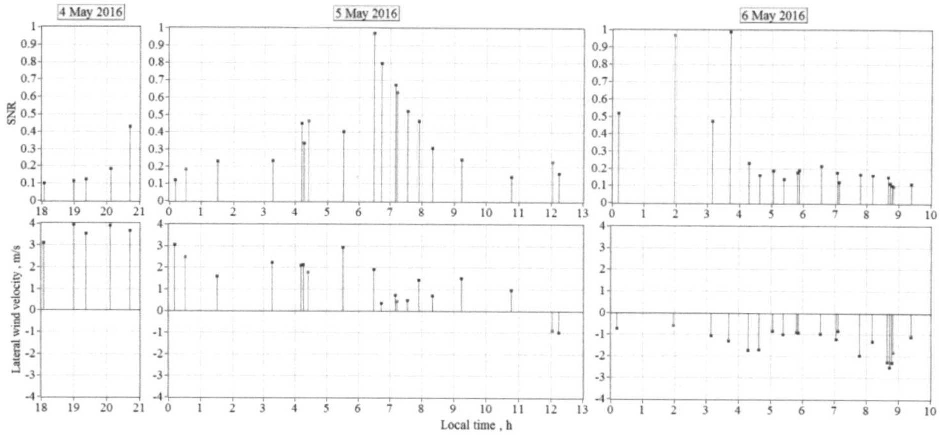

Figure 3. Maximum SNRs and lateral wind velocities at time moments of crossing the scanning plane by B747 cargo aircrafts (red squares) and other aircrafts (blue squares).

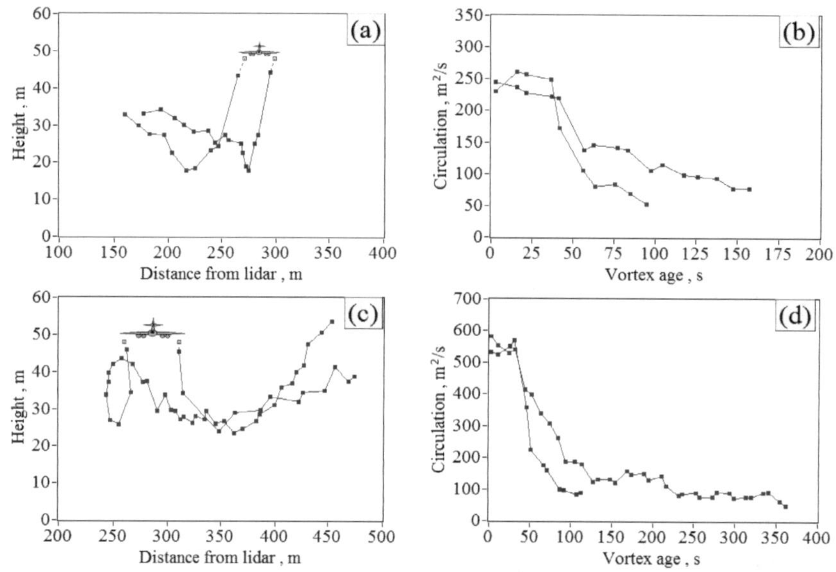

Figure 4. Trajectories of cores (a, c) and circulations (b, d) of wake vortices generated by A320 (a, b) and B747-4 (c, d) aircrafts.

Figure 2 shows 6 profiles of signal-to-noise ratio (data averaged in the interval of φ_m from 5° to 10°), which took place during the observation of vortices generated by B747 aircrafts. It is seen that the maximum signal-to-noise ratio $\mathrm{SNR}_{\max}$ varies from 0.1 to 1. Curve 6 is below the threshold level of 0.04 (red line) at ranges R_k > 370 m. Figure 3 shows $\mathrm{SNR}_{\max}$ and V (if $V > 0$, the lateral wind is directed from the lidar) during our experiment.

Figure 4 shows two examples of vortex core trajectories and vortex circulation versus time, when $\mathrm{SNR}_{\max}$ = 0.5, V = -0.8 m/s (a, b) and $\mathrm{SNR}_{\max}$ = 0.63, V = 0.4 m/s (c, d). Weak lateral wind and a rather high signal-to-noise ratio allow us to observe left wake vortex up to 6 minutes in the case of B747-4 aircraft.

According to theory [7], the initial separation between the axes of the right and left vortex b_0 is determined as $b_0 = (\pi / 4)B_A$, where B_A is the aircraft wingspan. Our comparison of experimental (for vortex age not more than 15 seconds) and theoretical values of the b_0 found them almost a full match for all types of aircraft listed above.

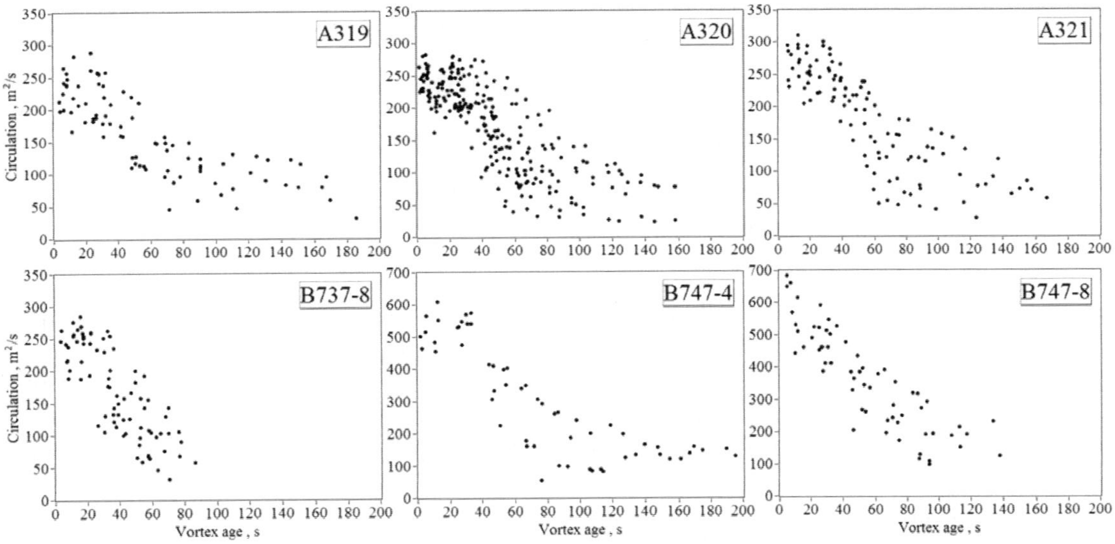

Figure 5. All lidar estimates of the circulation of wake vortices generated by airliners: A319 (5 over-flights), A320 (15 over-flights), A321 (6 over-flights), B737-8 (6 over-flights) and cargo aircrafts: B747-4 (2 over-flights), B747-8 (4 over-flights). These estimates have been obtained from data measured by the Stream Line lidar at the airfield of the Tolmachevo Airport from 4 to 6 May 2016.

Figure 5 shows all the results that we obtained from the lidar measurements in Tolmachevo, for the wake vortex circulation. Using the data of this figure we averaged estimates all circulation in the time interval from 0 to 30 s for each type of aircraft. Comparison of average values of the circulation with the results of calculations by the theoretical equation for the initial circulation [7] $\Gamma_0 = M_A g / (\rho_a b_0 V_A)$, where M_A is the aircraft mass, g is the freefall acceleration, ρ_a is the air density, and V_A is the true speed of the aircraft, yielded similar values.

This study was supported by the Russian Science Foundation, Project No. 14-17-00386.

4. References

[1] S. W. Henderson, C. P. Hale, J. R. Magee, M. J. Kavaya, and A.V. Huffaker, "Eye-safe coherent laser radar system at 2 μm using Tm. Ho: YAG lasers," Optics Letters **16**, 773–775 (1991).

[2] V. A. Banakh and I. N. Smalikho, *Coherent Doppler wind lidars in a turbulent atmosphere* (Artech House. Boston-London, 2013), 250 p.

[3] G. Pierson, F. Davies, and C. Collier, "An analysis of performance of the UFAM Pulsed Doppler lidar for the observing the boundary layer," J. Atmos. and Ocean. Technol. **26**, 240-250 (2009).

[4] I. N. Smalikho and V. A. Banakh, "Estimation of aircraft wake vortex parameters from data measured with 1.5-μm coherent Doppler lidar," Optics Letters **40**, 3408-3411 (2015).

[5] I. N. Smalikho, V. A. Banakh, F. Holzäpfel, and S. Rahm, "Method of radial velocities for the estimation of aircraft wake vortex parameters from data measured by coherent Doppler lidar," Optics Express **23**, A1194-A1207 (2015).

[6] D. C. Burnham and J. N. Hallock, "Chicago monostatic acoustic vortex sensing system," U.S. Department of Transportation, DOT-TSC-FAA-79-103, 1982, 206 pp.

[7] T. Gerz, F. Holzäpfel, and D. Darracq, "Commercial aircraft wake vortices," Progr. Aerospace Sci. **38**, 181-208 (2002).

Lidar Wind Sensing for Improved Precision AirDrop and Gunship Wind Sensing

Wesley Jones

InfoSciTex Corporation
Wesley.jones.13.ctr@us.af.mil

Abstract: To mitigate threat risk and improve fuel efficiency, Air Force operations are desired at higher altitudes. Military gunship and airdrop missions share a need for accurate and timely wind measurements to improve targeting solutions, especially from high altitudes. The Air Force Research Laboratory (AFRL) has been researching ground-based and airborne Lidar and Radar sensors to provide real-time wind profiles to improve aiming solutions for airdrop payloads and gunship munition trajectories. A systems engineering approach incorporating multiple technology demonstrations were performed using Commercial-Off-the-Shelf (COTS) systems to mature technology. Demonstration data has been used to evaluate how these systems could be used to improve Precision AirDrop (PAD) and Gunship Wind Sensing (GWS) operations. Results from these demonstrations will be presented along with analysis of wind effects on airdrop and gunship missions.

1. Introduction

The United States Air Force core missions of rapid global mobility and global strike share a need for timely and accurate wind knowledge for successful mission execution. Uncertainty in the winds between aircraft and ground can cause large errors in many of these operations. As these operations are pushed to higher altitudes for aircrew safety and fuel efficiency reasons, the error in mission accuracy from wind uncertainty only becomes more pronounced. This paper addresses improved wind knowledge through collection and application of wind data for unguided Precision AirDrop (PAD) and Gunship Wind Sensing (GWS) programs. Previous work has shown that wind sensing technology can significantly reduce the amount of error for Air Force missions [1, 2]. This work done by Air Force Research Laboratory (AFRL) is meant to build upon previous work using current Commercial-Off-the-Shelf (COTS) wind sensor systems.

2. Wind Sensing for AirDrop Missions

To support the need of Air Mobility Command (AMC) to improve airdrop precision, AFRL is exploring different technologies to measure the wind between aircraft and ground for better Computed Air Release Point (CARP) calculations. In order to assess the state of current COTS wind sensor systems and how they could improve CARP calculations, a series of demonstrations were planned and executed. A systematic approach was designed to identify and analyze system capabilities and apply wind data collection to the airdrop solution. Through the Precision AirDrop Wind Sensing (PAWS) demonstrations, COTS wind sensor systems were evaluated in a rugged mountainous terrain in an unmodified ground-based configuration. Two of the systems were selected and modified to meet AirDrop requirements and tested during a third demonstration. Three PAWS (PAWS1, PAWS2, and PAWS3) demonstrations have been executed. Each demonstration consisted of ground-based Lidar and/or Radar sensors provided by different vendors. Dugway Proving Grounds, a United States Army test range chosen for its unique terrain features and extensive meteorology instrumentation capabilities, was used as the demonstration site for the first two PAWS demonstrations. The third demonstration was held at Yuma Proving Grounds due to the large amount of parachute testing that could be leveraged during the PAWS3 demonstration. Each range was instrumented with meteorological towers and/or weather balloons. Air Force Weather Agency (AFWA) forecasts for the test locations and times were also recorded. Additionally, PAWS2 and PAWS3 demonstrations were supported by live airdrops including dropsondes, windpacks, and instrumented training bundles. Windpacks and dropsondes are small parachuted sensors that are thrown from the aircraft to measure wind from aircraft to ground by tracking its horizontal displacement while falling via Global Positioning System (GPS).

Data collected from these demonstrations were used within both the AFRL-developed Weather Integrated Stochastic Simulation (WISS) and the operational mission planner Consolidated AirDrop Tool (CAT), to perform analyses on how wind Lidar/Radar can improve PAD accuracy. CAT is an AirDrop planning system used by aircrews to produce a release point based on pre-mission information (e.g. forecast, bundle, and aircraft data) and updated winds from dropsondes when available. WISS is a physics-based model that computes an impact point for a given release point using planned and actual winds. Using these two tools allows for a complete trajectory to be modeled from CARP calculation to impact on the ground. They also provide a measure for AirDrop improvement by quantifying the difference between impact points when varying initial parameters.

Significant conclusions from these demonstrations can be summarized by the following:

- Forecast wind values perform poorly when looking at a specific time and place and should not be the sole source of wind data for any given drop.
- Forecast wind data at high altitudes are commonly accurate and can give a good overview of general winds in the area, thus forecasts should not be discarded.
- In complex terrain, winds at lower altitudes tend to be more turbulent. This turbulence creates an even larger uncertainty in the forecast wind values thus increasing the need to accurately measure and report local low altitude winds.
- A single sounding from any source (dropsonde, weather balloon, Lidar) may not be a good representation of the winds through which a payload may pass during descent. Multiple soundings should be used for a CARP calculation to increase confidence in the solution.
    - If multiple soundings are available from a single location the variance from these soundings can be used to quantify bundle dispersion and miss distance.
- No single location, by itself, regardless of distance from the drop zone (DZ), can guarantee an accurate representation of the winds over the DZ. Thus, when using an airborne sensor, winds measured along the flight path do not always represent winds at the DZ.
    - Winds measured closer to the DZ are not necessarily more representative than those measured farther away.
- Sensor range is affected by power, atmospheric conditions, and scanning geometry. Wind Lidar and Radar depend on particulates in the air to create a signal feedback. At higher altitudes the amount of particulates diminishes especially above the planetary boundary layer.
    - Higher powered Lidars tended to perform better at longer ranges, except in cases of precipitation which, at times, blacked out the Lidar, but allowed for a stronger signal and longer range for the Radar.
- Multiple scanning configurations for an airborne sensor have been studied. More testing is required to define the trade space between such configurations as it applies to PAD.

During each PAWS demonstration wind data was successfully collected from each system in a variety of weather conditions including rain, snow, high wind, clear air, and cloudy. This variety of conditions demonstrated the strengths and weaknesses of each technology. Lidar and Radar systems specifically designed for AirDrop are currently being developed for further long-term testing.

3. Wind Sensing for Gunship Missions

Similar to PAD, a series of demonstrations were performed to assess COTS systems for use in improving Gunship first-shot accuracy. This work builds upon work done in 1997 by James Hawley and George Koerner which concluded that first-shot accuracy would improve significantly when using Lidar technology [2] to provide updated wind data. The AFRL gunship demonstrations sought to verify similar improvements using today's COTS technologies.

The first Gunship Wind Sensing demonstration (GWS1) was a ground-based demonstration located at the top of Sapphire Peak in DPG. The wind sensors were aimed downward along an instrumented line of site toward a designated target on the ground approximately 20 kilometers away. The second and third demonstrations (GWS2 and GWS2A) were airborne demonstrations with a wind sensor mounted aboard a Twin Otter aircraft and a commercial C-130A aircraft respectively. The sensor during these demonstrations was pointed out of the rear port side window with a fixed downward angle toward a fixed target on the ground. Multiple flights were conducted for each demonstration where the aircraft circled in a fixed orbit to simulate a realistic gunship orbit. Since the wind sensor was mounted at a fixed angle with respect to the aircraft, the movement of the aircraft provided the necessary angular diversity to calculate vector wind profiles. Several different orbit altitudes and locations were demonstrated.

After each demonstration, aircraft motion was removed from the wind data and vector wind profiles were calculated using MATLAB® software. Wind profiles were then used in PRODAS® (Projectile Rocket Ordnance Design & Analysis System) in order to simulate how the wind would affect trajectories and impact points of munitions. PRODAS was chosen due to its high fidelity 6-Degree of Freedom (DOF) model and its ability to model how different wind profiles affect the ballistics of different munitions. For all studies, a 30mm PGU13A round was used in the simulation. For simplicity during simulation, a nominal aircraft velocity of 200 knots true and a nominal aircraft bank of 5 degrees were chosen for all simulations.

The phase 2 and 2A Gunship demonstrations showed that using a fixed scannerless Lidar during an orbit is a viable solution to measure wind profiles from the aircraft altitude to the ground. A concern with this installation method was if representative wind profiles could be measured during an unsteady aircraft orbit. If the roll in particular is not stable then the cone over which the Lidar would be measuring wind would not be well defined. During the GWS2 demonstration such a condition was experienced. A portion of the aircraft orbit with calculated Lidar Line-Of-Sight and ground impact points is presented in Figure 1. Vector wind profiles calculated from the depicted orbit are also displayed in Figure 1. The Google Earth image in Figure 1 shows that due to a variable aircraft roll angle the Lidar was not always pointed directly at the target area and frequently was pointed at a location far removed from the target. This variability can cause a large amount of change between consecutive calculated vector wind profiles (represented by the colored dots in the plots of Figure 1) since vector wind profiles are an average of the measured wind over a section of the orbit, in this case 360 degrees. As can be seen in Figure 1 the

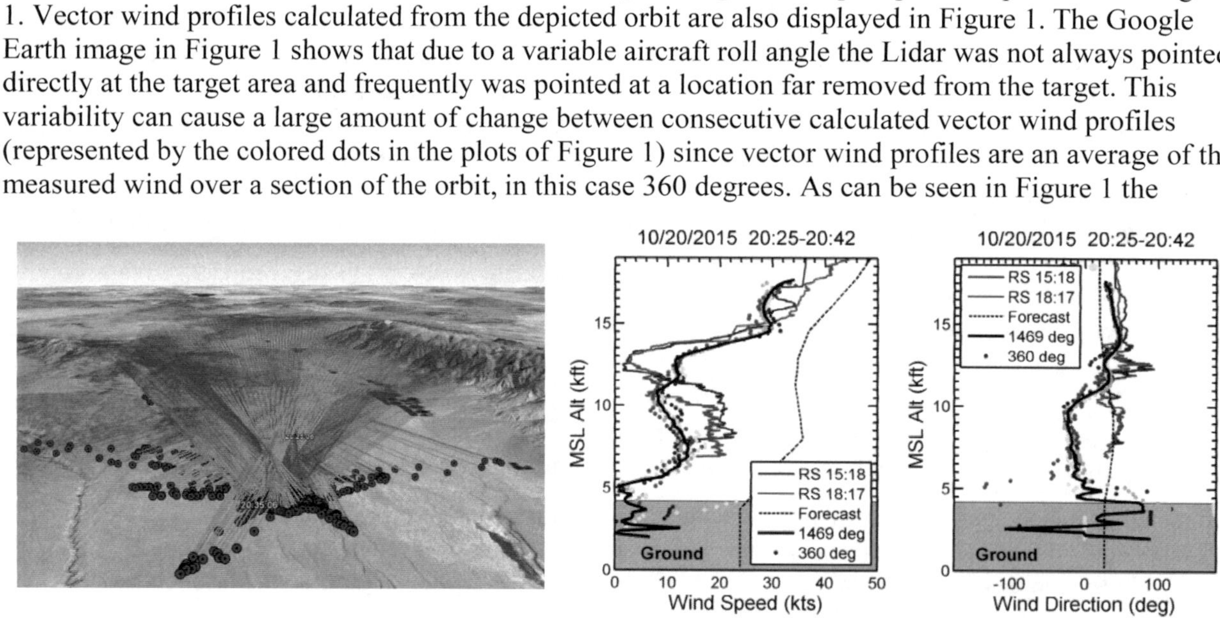

Figure 1: Example Lidar Line-Of-Sight with accompanying wind profiles

successive profiles agreed well with each other with the largest disagreements occurring at low altitudes. The solid black line in Figure 1 represents the wind profile calculated from all of the radial winds captured during the entire orbit. Points below ground level are an artifact of the inconsistent roll angles. Solid red and blue lines are wind profiles measured with weather balloons launched near the orbit site. For safety reasons balloons were launched before and after the aircraft operated in the demonstration area.

One desired objective during this demonstration was to determine how much of an orbit would be required for the aircraft to traverse before a reliable vector wind profile could be calculated. To address this question, radial wind data was divided into 30, 45, 60, 90, 180, and 360 degree sectors. Wind vectors calculated from these sectors were then compared. A sample of the vertical wind speeds calculated from the 45, 90, and 180 sector arcs are displayed in Figure 2, represented by the different colored dots. Vertical wind speeds are typically small when compared to horizontal speeds thus large vertical velocities can be attributed to errors from insufficient signal feedback or insufficient angular diversity.

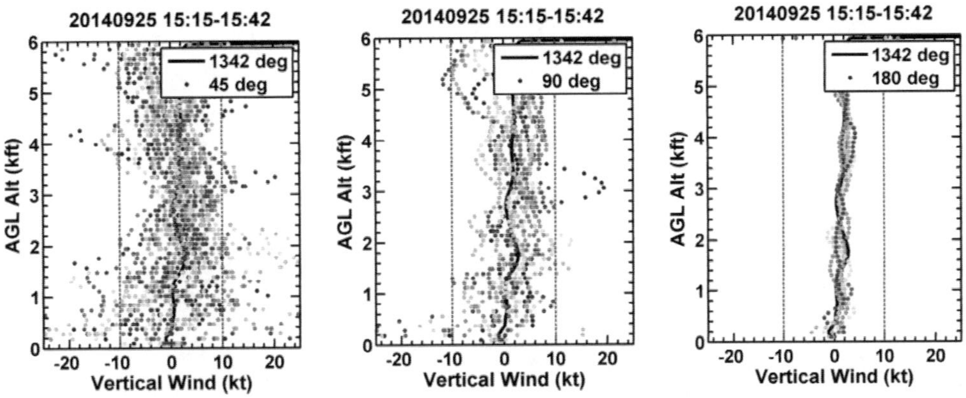

Figure 2: Vertical wind speeds calculated from different arc lengths

Sector size was inversely proportional to wind variability. Smaller sectors demonstrated a higher variability and magnitude in vertical wind speeds than did the larger sectors. Consistency between consecutive 180 and 360 degree arc profiles suggests that the wind was fairly stable over the collection time. This implies that variations in wind profiles from smaller arcs are more likely due to spatial variability or an insufficient number of particle reflections while collecting radial wind measurements. Since wind spatial variation tends to decrease with altitude and the variability from the smaller arcs tends to remain constant with altitude, the variability seen in the above plots is most likely due to low particle reflections. Because of this, smaller sector arcs are not good representations of the wind. A minimum of 180 degrees is recommended for gunship wind sensing orbit collection duration.

4. Conclusions

Multiple demonstrations have been performed for both PAD and GWS showing that Lidar and Radar can effectively measure wind between aircraft and ground and produce timely wind profiles for algorithms that calculate corrected aim points. Both ground-based and airborne sensors have been demonstrated using COTS wind profiling systems. This technology shows promise to increase accuracy of both AirDrop and Gunship missions allowing the Air Force to operate at higher altitudes thus increasing safety for the aircraft and the airmen. Work is still on-going on how best to implement this technology into current or future Air Force operations.

5. References

[1] Kathleen M. Yerdon, "The Impact of a Wind Profiling Capability on AirDrop Accuracy," in AIAA 15th Aerodynamic Decelerator Systems Technology Conference, Toulouse, France (1999).

[2] James Hawley and George Koerner, "*Gunship Ballistic Winds Remote Wind Sensor,"* Final Report WL-TR-97-1099, Wright Patterson Air Force Base (1997).

Research and development for future space-based Doppler Wind Lidar

Shoken Ishii (a), Atsushi Sato (b, a), Makoto Aoki (a), Koichi Akahane (a), Shigeo Nagano (a), Philippe Baron (a), Kohei Mizutani (a), Satoshi Ochiai (a), and Minoru Kubota (a)
(a) National Institute of Information and Communications Technology
4-2-1 Nukui-kitamachi Koganei, Tokyo, 184-8795, Japan
(b) Tohoku Institute of Technology, Sendai, Miyagi, Japan

Abstract: National Institute of Information and Communications Technology (NICT) has developed technologies for a 2-µm coherent lidar since 2001. The forth middle term research program began in April 2016 at NICT. Main objectives of the lidar project are to develop 2-µm key technologies and instruments for a future space-based coherent Doppler wind lidar (CDWL), to investigate measurement performance using a space-based coherent Doppler wind lidar simulator, and to quantitatively assess potential impacts on numerical weather prediction using results of the space-based CDWL simulator. In the paper, we introduce research and development of the 2-µm key technologies planned during the middle term research program.

1. Introduction

NICT developed a 2-µm coherent differential absorption/Doppler wind lidar for CO_2 and wind measurements [1-2] and a coherent lidar for airborne experiment during the last middle term research program. Japan Aerospace eXploration Agency (JAXA) is developing a new type of satellite for future Earth observation missions and it is looking for a candidate mission after the test flight of the satellite. NICT, Tohoku University (TU), the University of Tokyo (UT), Meteorological Research Institute (MRI), and JAXA organized a working group for a future space-based CDWL and are studying the feasibility from the technical and scientific viewpoints to realize the future space-based CDWL [3-5]. NICT started the new middle term research program to develop key technologies for the future space-based CDWL. In the paper, we present research and development for future space-based CDWL.

2. 2-µm laser system

A CDWL requires a single-frequency 2-µm Q-switched laser. A reliable single-frequency continuous-wave (CW) laser is critical for the single-frequency 2-µm Q-switched pulse laser and the heterodyne detection. The single-frequency CW laser needs to have a long coherent time, which means that it does not change the frequency during the round-trip time between the CDWL and the target atmosphere. Current technical requirements for the future single-frequency 2-µm CW laser are TEM_{00} mode, wavelength tuning, output of >30 mW, long frequency stability, long-term output power stability, linear polarization, and low frequency jitter. Figure 1 shows spectra of photoluminescence for (left) a semiconductor laser with quantum-dot structures and (right) a Tm-doped fiber amplifier (TDFA). The peak wavelengths of the semiconductor laser and the TDFA are 1980-nm and 1950-nm. The two spectra are very wide. We can confirm the photoluminescence from both the semiconductor laser and the TDFA at a target wavelength of 2.05 µm. We need to further optimize characteristics of the semiconductor laser and the TDFA.

Target pulse energy of the single-frequency Q-switched laser is 125 mJ operating at a pulse repetition frequency of 30 Hz. Two candidate laser systems are discussed for the future space-based laser: one oscillator configuration, and MOPA (MOPA: Master Oscillator Power Amplifier) configuration (Figure 2).

The laser rod of the single-frequency 2-μm Q-switched laser developed at NICT must be cooled down to -80 °C to achieve pulse energy of 80 mJ. Experiments indicated that, if a Tm,Ho:YLF laser rod were cooled lower than -100 °C, the one-oscillator-configuration 2-μm laser could achieve 125 mJ per pulse. MOPA configuration were more compact than the one-oscillator-configuration 2-μm laser, MOPA configuration 2-μm laser would be better approach. The TIT laser simulator indicates that the MOPA-configuration 2-μm laser could emit a pulse of 125 mJ at a laser rod temperature of -40 °C: a target pulse energy of the master oscillator is about 50 mJ, and a target gain of the power amplifier is about 3.

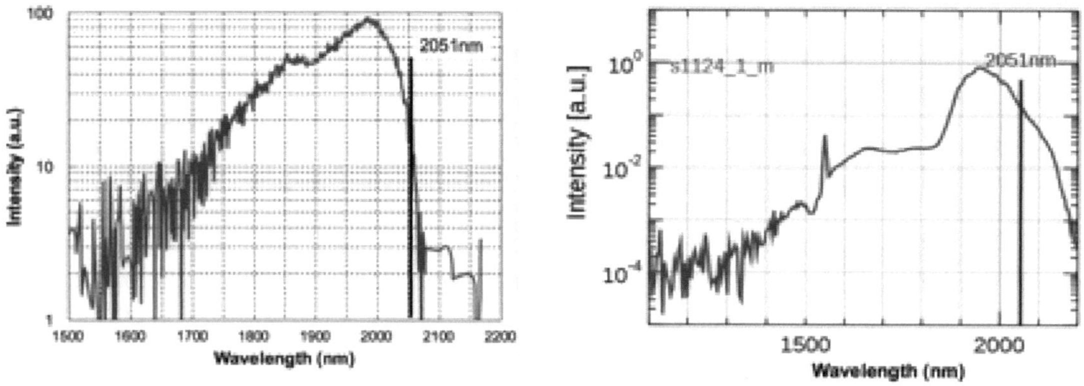

Figure 1. Photoluminescence from (left) quantum-dot laser and (right) Tm-doped fiber amplifier.

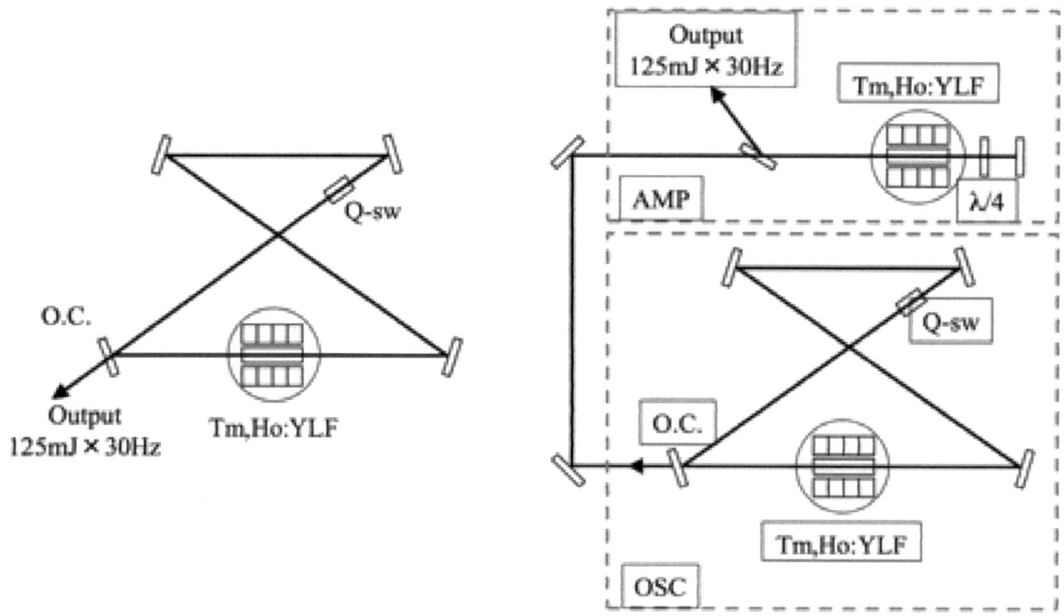

Figure 2. Tm,Ho:YLF laser: (left) one-oscillator configuration, and (right) MOPA configuration.

3. Coherent receiver

A coherent receiver requires a telescope with diffraction-limited performance. The telescope must be designed to avoid wavefront aberrations. The current concept of the afocal telescope is coaxial system with a beam-expanding collimator and a receiving telescope, and the future space-based CDWL uses two fixed off-axis telescopes in order to observe two line-of-sight wind speeds. JAXA is developing a new satellite with ion propulsion technologies developed in the past space missions. The new satellite will fry in a circular orbit at attitudes of 180-270 km at a speed of about 7.8 km/sec. We assume that the horizontal wind speed is 100 m/sec. A speed of 1 m/sec corresponds to about Doppler-shifted frequency of 1 MHz at wavelength of 2 μm. The Doppler-shifted frequency at the maximum horizontal speed at 2 μm is assumed to be 7.9 GHz (=7.8 GHz + 0.1 GHz). The laser pulse will be sent into the atmosphere at the azimuth angles of 45° and 135° and at the nadir angle of 35°. The Doppler-shifted frequency is about 3.2 GHz. A high-speed detector with a bandwidth of >3.2 GHz is required for the space-based CDWL wind measurements. The Doppler-shifted frequency due to the satellite speed must be compensated by hardware-based onboard frequency calibration. Analog-to-digital (AD) conversion from an analog signal to a discrete signal is used in data processing. Both sampling frequency and sampling points of an AD converter determine the frequency and range resolutions in the CDWL wind measurement. There are some space-qualified, high-speed, and high-resolution AD converters (e.g., Texas Instruments ADS5463-SP and ADS5474-SP). With a sampling frequency of 400 MHz, the frequency resolutions for the 4096-point FFT and the 256-point FFT are 0.10 and 1.56 MHz, respectively, and the 256-point FFT corresponds to a range resolution of 96 m. The concept of the space-based CDWL is summarized in Table 1. An InGaAs detector is one of candidate detectors. Electrical characteristics of the InGaAs detector might be affected by proton radiation. The space-qualified high-speed detector must be designed and fabricated to meet the orbital type and altitude of the new satellite.

Table 1. Concept of future space-based CDWL.

Wavelength (μm)	2.05
Pulse energy (mJ)	125
Pulse repetition frequency (Hz)	30
Effective telescope diameter (cm)	40
Number of laser directions	2
Total coherent receiver efficiency	0.07
Sampling frequency (MHz)	400
Sampling point	256
Nadir angle of observation direction (°)	35
Azimuth angle of observation direction (°)	45, 135
Target vertical resolution (km)	Altitude 0-3 km: <0.5 Altitude 3-8 km: <1 Altitude 8-20 km: <2
Target horizontal resolution (km)	<100

4. Summary

JAXA is developing a new type of satellite for future Earth observation missions and planning to launch the test satellite in FY2016. JAXA is looking for a candidate Earth observation mission after the test flight. The Japanese working group for the future space-based CDWL is studying the feasibility from the technical and scientific viewpoints to realize a future space-based CDWL. NICT started the new middle term research program and it is studying the feasibility of 2-μm key technologies for the space-based CDWL. Preliminary results of the 2-μm transmitter were presented in the paper. Approaches for development of the detector and signal processing were introduced in the paper. NICT intends to continue development of 2-μm key technologies meeting the requirements for the space-based CDWL.

5. Acknowledgements

The authors wish to thank the working group for a future Japanese space-based CDWL for supporting the research activity of the working group.

6. References

[1] Shoken Ishii et al., "Coherent 2-μm differential absorption and wind lidar with conductively cooled laser and two-axis scanning device," Appl. Opt. **49**, 1809-1817, (2010).

[2] Kohei Mizutani et al., "Diode-pumped 2-μm pulse laser with noncomposite Tm,Ho:YLF rod conduction-cooled down to -80°C," Applied Optics, 54, 7865-7869 (2015).

[3] Shoken Ishii et al., "Measurement performance assessment of future space-borne Doppler wind lidar," *SOLA* **12**, 55-59 (2016).

[4] Shoken Ishii et al., "Feasibility Study for Future Space-Borne Coherent Doppler Wind Lidar, Part I: Instrumental Overview for Global Wind Profile Observation," submitted to JMSJ (2016).

[5] Philippe Baron et al., "Feasibility Study for Future Space-Borne Coherent Doppler Wind Lidar, Part II: Measurement simulation algorithms and retrieval error characterization," submitted to JMSJ (2016).

Coherent Lidar Characterization of the Boundary Layer in Estimation of Urban-Scale Greenhouse Gas Emissions

R. Michael Hardesty (a,b), W. Alan Brewer (b), Timothy Bonin (a,b), Kenneth Davis (c), Thomas Lauvaux (c), Daniel Sarmiento (c), A. J. Deng (c), Paul Shepson (d), Alexie Heimberger (d), James Whetstone (e)

(a) Cooperative Institute for Research in Environmental Sciences
216 UCB, Boulder, Colorado 80309
(b) NOAA/ESRL Chemical Sciences Division
325 Broadway, Boulder, CO 80305
(c) Pennsylvania State University Department of Meteorology
512 Walker Building University Park, PA 16802
(d) Purdue University Department of Chemistry
560 Oval Drive, West Lafayette, Indiana 47907-2084
(e) National Institute of Standards and Technology, Special Programs Office
100 Bureau Drive, Stop 4701, Gaithersburg, MD 20899-8102
mike.hardesty@noaa.gov

Abstract: The Indianapolis Flux Experiment (INFLUX) aims to incorporate aircraft measurements, surface-based in situ and remote observations, and chemical transport models to improve greenhouse gas emissions estimates on urban scales. During INFLUX we deployed a compact, continuously-operating coherent Doppler lidar to provide information on boundary layer winds, turbulence, and aerosol structure as input for the model and aircraft-based emissions calculations and for validation of model performance. The lidar performs a repeating sequence of scans and stares to estimate the wind, horizontal and vertical velocity variance, and backscatter gradient profiles. Using these observations, a robust algorithm has been developed to estimate boundary layer depth, a key parameter in the emissions calculations, under both daytime and nighttime conditions. The presentation will discuss lidar performance, scan strategies, development and performance of the boundary layer depth algorithm, meteorological conditions observed, and use of the data for both model-based and top-down aircraft-based emissions estimates.

Keywords: Coherent Lidar. Wind Measurements, Turbulence, Boundary Layer, Greenhouse Gas Emissions Estimates

1. Introduction

Improving quantification of greenhouse gas emissions at urban scales is becoming increasingly important for establishing baselines and evaluating mitigation strategies to slow down the increase of atmospheric CO_2 and methane. Currently estimates rely primarily on "bottoms-up" techniques, in which emissions from all identified discrete sources within an area of are summed to produce an overall estimate for the area[1]. The Indianapolis flux (INFLUX) experiment incorporates aircraft and surface-based observations, as well as chemical transport models, to investigate potential improvements in regional scale emissions estimates gained by applying top-down and modeling approaches. INFLUX observational components include several-times-per-month aircraft measurements of gas concentrations and meteorological parameters, as well as a number of towers observing CO_2, CH_4, and CO augmented by a single unattended Doppler lidar to estimate wind, turbulence and aerosol structure in the boundary layer. The Doppler lidar serves a critical role for both the observational and modeling components of INFLUX by providing continuous information on mixing and transport within the urban boundary layer.

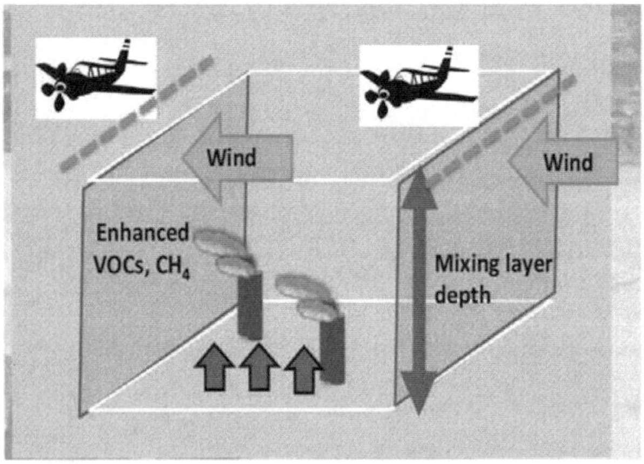

Figure 1: Schematic showing mass-balance technique for estimating emissions.

Figure 2: Commercial lidar deployed on an Ivy Tech building roof NE of Indianapolis.

2. Doppler Lidar Deployment during INFLUX

Utility of Doppler lidar for mass balance studies was initially demonstrated during the Uintah ozone study [1] where observations from the NOAA High Resolution Doppler Lidar (HRDL, [2]) were combined with aircraft measurements to assess leakage from gas wells in the Uintah basin oil and gas field. The investigation applied a mass balance technique, where the aircraft equipped with chemical sensors sampled methane gas concentrations upwind and downwind of the city, as shone in Fig. 1. By calculating the differences in the aircraft-measured upwind and downwind concentrations and incorporating lidar measured wind speed and direction profiles and boundary layer depth, the upwind and downwind methane fluxes and emission rates could be computed.

Rather than deploy our research lidar for the multi-year INFLUX study we chose to purchase and deploy a commercial, low-pulse-energy, high pulse rate Doppler lidar for the study [3]. The lidar, sold by Halo Photonics, was installed on the roof of a classroom building at Ivy Tech Community College northeast of Indianapolis in April, 2013, and operated, with the exception of a maintenance interval in summer 2013, continuously until spring, 2015, when it was sent back to the manufacturer for maintenance and performance upgrades. An upgraded version of the lidar was redeployed in January, 2016.

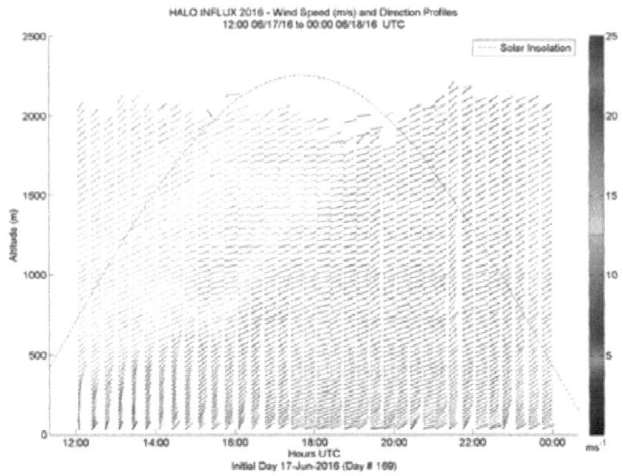

Figure 3: Time-height plot of daytime horizontal wind velocity measured on June 17, 2016.

For INFLUX, we employ a fixed scan pattern, repeated every 20-30 minutes, to measure the needed boundary layer parameters. The pattern includes several conical scans at different elevation angles for measurement of horizontal wind profiles, vertical scans at orthogonal azimuths for observations of low level winds under stable conditions, and fixed vertical stares to observe vertical turbulence and mixing. Estimates of vertical velocity variance and aerosol backscatter profiles are computed from the vertical stares to characterize atmospheric mixing. Figure 3 shows a plot of wind speed and direction measured during daytime hours on June 17, 2016, while Figure 4 shows a 1-hour

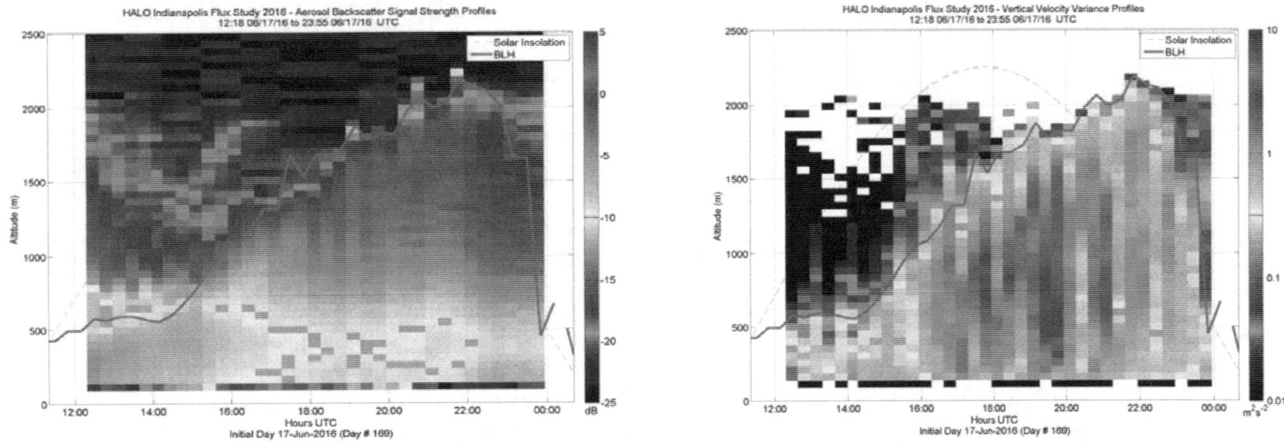

Figure 4: Twelve-hour time-height cross section of lidar SNR (proxy for backscatter, left) and vertical velocity variance (right) measured at INFLUX on June 17, 2016

time height cross-section of vertical velocity variance and aerosol backscattered signal observed on the same day. The growth of the mixing layer to about 2000 m is clearly seen in both figures. However, the presence of a residual aerosol layer extending from the surface to ~ 1.5 km above the surface between 12Z and 16Z is also observed, complicating the ability to measure mixing layer depth based on backscatter gradient during that period. For this reason, we use both aerosol and vertical velocity variance for estimation of mixing layer depth, as described in section 3.

To meet the observational requirements for the long-term INFLUX study, the lidar needed to operate continuously and reliably, and to provide profiles of wind speed and direction, vertical velocity variance, and backscatter structure from near the surface to the top of the boundary layer under all conditions. The initial instrument was quite reliable, but we identified many cases, typically under low-aerosol conditions, where the instrument did not appear to make measurements to the top of the boundary layer. To better quantify the occurrences of low sensitivity, we developed a technique where we compared the maximum range of vertical and horizontal measurements of signal-to-noise ratio (SNR) and velocity variance. We assumed that when the instrument was characterizing the full boundary the horizontal range would be significantly greater than the vertical range. Using this somewhat subjective criteria we could see that the ranges were approximately equivalent a significant portion of the time, giving some indication that the sensitivity of the original instrument was not sufficient to measure through the boundary layer under all conditions. Based on this conclusion, the instrument was returned to the manufacturer for several modifications designed to improve sensitivity.

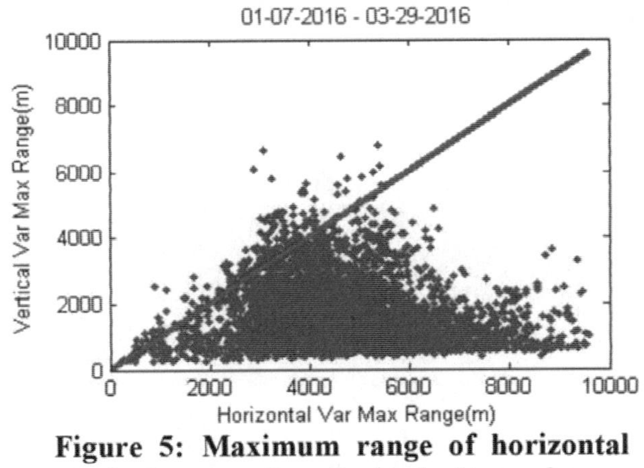

Figure 5: Maximum range of horizontal vs vertical range of vertical velocity variance.

The upgraded instrument, which featured higher pulse energy, improved processing, and slightly longer pulses, was reinstalled in Indianapolis in early 2106, and has continued to operate as part of the study. A scatter plot of horizontal versus vertical range for vertical velocity variance, measured over 3 months in early 2016, is shown in Figure 4. The figure shows that horizontal range exceeds vertical range for a large portion of the cases examined, and provides us with some confidence that the instrument is operating with sufficient sensitivity to see to the top of the boundary layer under almost all conditions. We attribute the cluster of points near the 1:1 line at 4 km range to mid-level clouds, which provide an artificial extension of the vertical range.

3. Automated Boundary Layer Height Estimation

Knowledge of boundary layer depth is essential for both mass-balance and model-based emissions estimate. Using lidar data, we have been investigating development of robust automated algorithms to detect the top of the boundary layer under a variety of daytime and nocturnal conditions. The algorithms use the lidar-based estimates of profiles of horizontal and vertical velocity variance, backscatter structure (as evidenced by signal to noise ratio, SNR), and horizontal wind velocity, which are selectively applied depending on time of day and observed atmospheric properties. Under daytime conditions vertical velocity variance and backscatter structure are generally of greatest utility, while wind velocity and horizontal velocity variance are most effective at night. In Figure 4 the red line shows an estimate of boundary layer depth for a daytime convective boundary layer overlaid on the vertical velocity and lidar SNR profiles. In this case the boundary layer is fairly obvious in both the vertical velocity variance and SNR profiles. However, our analyses have shown that no single variable can be used without caution. For example, although the reduction in vertical velocity variance is frequently a good indicator of increased stability associated with boundary layer top, in the presence of free troposphere gravity waves the unfiltered vertical velocity variance can lead to an overestimate of boundary layer thickness. We are continuing to analyze the INFLUX data set, with its variety of conditions extending over multiple seasons, to further refine and improve boundary layer height estimates.

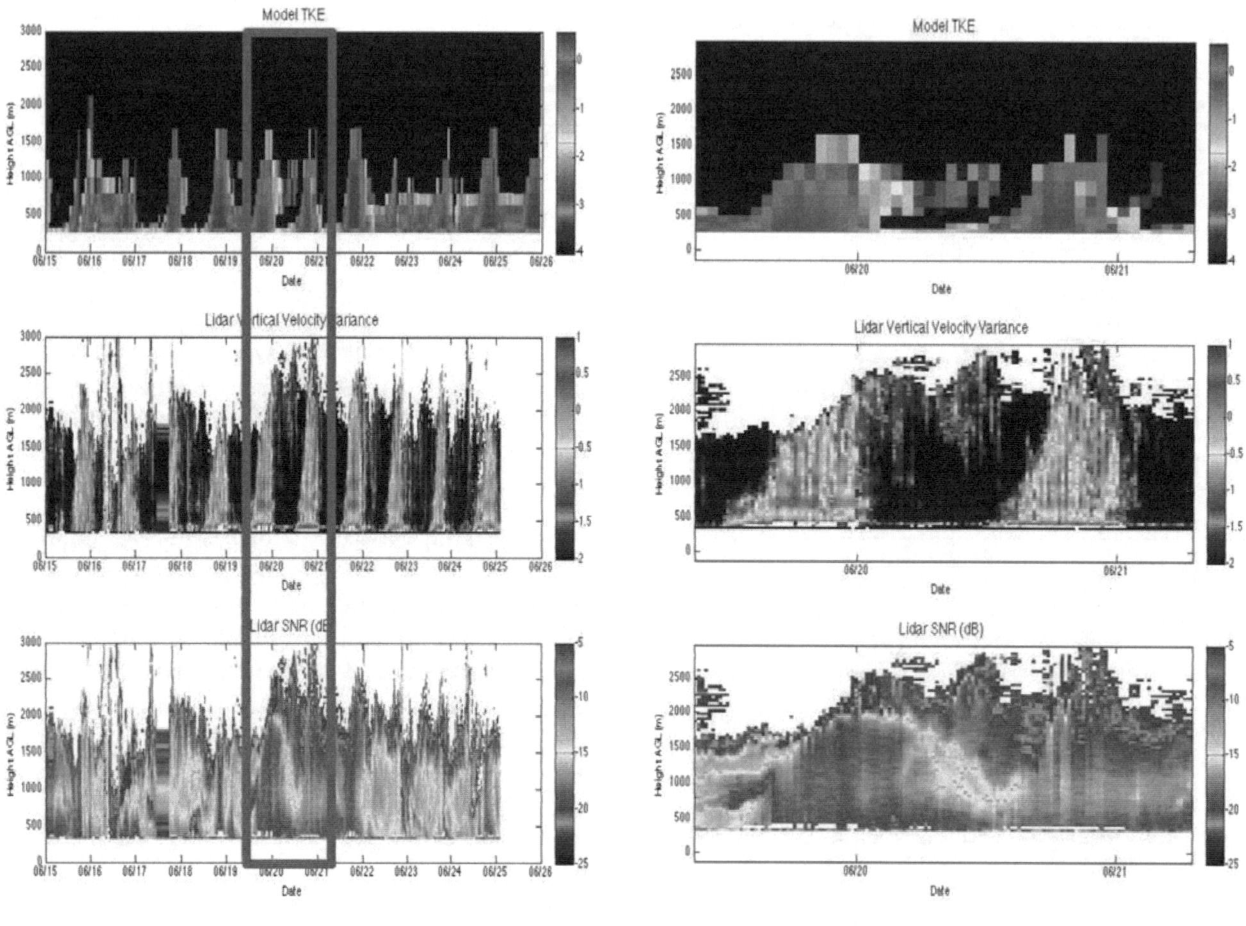

Figure 6: Lidar-measured SNR and vertical velocity variance compared with WRF model-estimated TKE for 10-day period. The right figure is a blow-up of the time period marked by the red box on the left.

4. Model validation

One component of the INFLUX study involves application and validation of numerical models that use emissions estimates from surface sites or emissions inventories in combination with meteorological data to estimate large scale emissions. The lidar wind and turbulence measurements are employed in the model studies both as input data, which are assimilated into the models, and for evaluation of model performance [5]. Figure 6 (left) shows a comparison of lidar-measured vertical velocity variance and backscatter structure (evidenced by SNR) over a 10-day period with estimates of turbulence kinetic energy (TKE) generated by a version of the Weather Research and Forecasting (WRF) model with real-time data assimilation applied at high resolution. A blowup of two days during the sequence is shown in the right figure. The similarity between the model and observational results is quite evident in this comparison, although for this model run the observational data shows a somewhat deeper boundary layer than predicted by the model.

5. Future Plans

We are continuing deployment of the Halo lidar at INFLUX. During summer 2016 plans are to deploy a micro-pulse aerosol lidar alongside the INFLUX Doppler instrument to compare aerosol and velocity variance based techniques for estimating boundary layer height. Studies are also planned to assess the need for a second Doppler lidar to the southwest of Indianapolis; the combination of the two instruments would provide upwind and downwind observations under most wind conditions, enabling investigation of issues such as urban heat island effect on emission estimation.

6. Acknowledgements

We appreciate the assistance of INFLUX colleagues Colm Sweeney, Anna Karion, Jocelyn Turnbull, and Kevin Gurney for providing insights on greenhouse gas emissions and observation of total and anthropogenic CO_2. This research was partially supported by the National Institute of Standards and Technology.

7. References

[1] Petron, G., A. Karion, C. Sweeney, et al, 2014: A new look at methane and nonmethane hydrocarbon emissions from oil and natural gas operations in the Colorado Denver-Julesburg Basin, *J. Geophys. Res., **119**, 6836-6852.*

[2] Grund, C. J.,R. M. Banta, J. L. George et al, 2001: High resolution Doppler lidar for boundary layer and cloud research, *J. Atmos. Ocean. Tech., **18**, 376-393.*

[3] Hogan, R. J., A. L. Grant, A. J. Illingworth, et al., 2009: Vertical velocity variance and skewness in clear and cloud-topped boundary layers as revealed by Doppler lidar. *Quart. J. Roy. Meteor. Soc., **135**, 635-643.*

[4] Cambaliza, M. O. L., P. B. Shepson, D. R. Caulton, et al, 2014: Assessment of uncertainties of an aircraft-based mass balance approach for quantifying urban greenhouse gas emissions, *Atmos. Chem. Phys., **14**, 9029-9050.*

[5] Deng, A., T. Lauvaux, B. Gaudet, N. Miles, K. Davis, K. Wu, D. Sarmiento, R. M. Hardesty, T. Bonin and W. A. Brewer 2016: Toward Reduced Transport Errors in a High Resolution Urban CO2 Inversion System. *In preparation.*

Wind and Spatial Variability Measurements from Single and Multiple Doppler Lidar Techniques during the XPIA Field Campaign

Single and multiple Doppler techniques can be important tools in not only visualizing complex flow, but also understanding the underlying physical processes and improve flow modeling. However, making such measurements is challenging and requires a thorough analysis of the measurement uncertainties to properly interpret the results. The XPIA (eXperimental Planetary boundary layer Instrumentation Assessment) field campaign conducted at the Boulder Atmospheric Observatory (BAO) in Erie, CO from 2 March 31 May, 2015 brought together a large suite of in-situ and remote sensing measurement platforms to evaluate complex flow measurement strategies. In this presentation, wind measurements from single and multiple Doppler lidar and dual-Doppler TTU Ka-band radars will be intercompared during periods of overlap. Estimates of spatial variability from each of these measurement techniques will be intercompared to understand the tradeoffs in terms of time/space resolution, spatial coverage and measurement uncertainty.

Investigation of vertical wavenumber and frequency spectra of gravity-wave-induced vertical wind and temperature perturbations

Cao Chen (a), Anthony Lima (a), Xinzhao Chu (a), Xian Lu (a), John Smith (a), Wentao Huang (a)
(a) Cooperative Institute for Research in Environmental Sciences, University of Colorado Boulder
216 UCB, Boulder, Colorado, USA, 80309
Cao.Chen@colorado.edu

Abstract: 233 hours of high-precision vertical wind and temperature measurements in the mesosphere and lower thermosphere (MLT) were used to study the spectra of gravity wave perturbations in the mesopause region. The temperature spectra are generally consistent with the theoretical predictions of gravity wave theory. The averaged slope of the frequency (*f*) spectra is –1.83±0.08, while the slope of the vertical wavenumber (*m*) spectra is –3.0±0.1. The observed *f* and *m* spectra of vertical winds are both very shallow. The averaged slope of the *f*-spectra is –0.4±0.1, and the averaged slope of *m*-spectra is –1.01±0.04. These spectral characteristics of gravity waves provide important insights into the mechanisms that are primarily responsible for wave damping and dissipation in the atmosphere.

Keywords: Coherent Laser Radar, etc.

1. Introduction

Gravity waves play a critical role in the middle and upper atmosphere due to their dominant influences to the residual circulation and their ability to transport energy, momentum and constituents and affecting thermal structure of the atmosphere [1]. Despite of the numerous theoretical and observational studies that aim to advance our understanding of such waves, there is still considerable disagreement about the dominant gravity wave saturation and dissipation processes. Consequently, gravity wave effects have been poorly parameterized in existing global circulation models. Currently, several proposed mechanisms that dominate gravity wave saturation and dissipation processes include: shear and convective instabilities, non-linear effects of wave-wave interaction, scale-dependent diffusion and diffusion filtering theory (see review in [2]).

Gardner [3] compared the different theories and compiled a table of predictions on the spectra of the horizontal and vertical winds. These theories can be evaluated by comparing measured spectra to the predictions. Some of the theories are founded on the assumption that the vertical wind and temporal motions (m, ω) are separable. Additionally, some of the theories require that the horizontal motions are independent of azimuth - that is: (h, ϕ) are separable. In this study, we make high resolution measurements of the vertical wind (w) and temperature (T) in the mesosphere and lower thermosphere which are used to calculate the vertical (m) and temporal (ω) spectra. With these spectra, we evaluate the accuracy of each of the theories.

2. Observations

The data used in this investigation were collected from the Student Training and Atmospheric Research (STAR) Na Doppler Lidar located at North of Boulder. This STAR lidar employs a classical dye-laser-based master oscillator power amplifier, a Newtonian telescope receiver, and modernized data acquisition and control systems, and uses the 3-requency technique to infer temperature, radial wind and Na density in the mesosphere and lower thermosphere (detailed principles can be found in [4]). Originally constructed by graduate students in summer 2010, this STAR lidar received several upgrades in the following years. In 2011, significant improvements of the receiver efficiency [5] enabled this STAR lidar to obtain very high resolution data. In 2013 the dual acoustic-optic frequency shifters were upgraded from ±480MHz to ±750MHz, making the STAR lidar more sensitive for vertical wind, temperature, and Na density measurements.

The raw photon counts were collected in the temporal and spatial resolutions of 3 s and 24 m. Temperatures and winds are then derived using the raw photon counts smoothed with a 15 min (full width) Hamming window and the window is shifted at a step of ~5 min. The raw photon counts are binned into 0.96 km to retrieve the temperature and winds in order to further increase the precision. The measurement uncertainties in the vertical wind and temperature are ~0.4 m/s and ~0.8 K respectively near the Na layer peak (~90 km). 233 hours of observations over 21 nights from August of 2013 to January of 2014 were selected for this study, which average approximately 11 hours of consecutive data each. The shortest night of data is approximately 7 hours long and subsequently the longest resolvable wave period in the frequency spectra was 14 hours. The altitude range of the data used is 85–105 km, which determines longest resolvable wavelength in the vertical wavenumber spectra to be approximately 60 km.

3. Measured Vertical Wavenumber and Frequency Spectra of Gravity Waves

Prior to spectral analysis, we removed extreme outliers caused by measurement errors from the data set and replaced them with interpolated values using a simple plate metaphor method. These data occurred at the extremes of the altitude range where the sodium density was occasionally insufficient. The perturbations of the temperatures and winds are then derived by subtracting the vertical and temporal means. In addition, to reduce the power leakage introduced by large-scale waves such as tides and planetary waves into the gravity wave spectra, we removed linear trends in both spatial and temporal domains. The linear detrend primarily affected the calculated spectra by removing power from the longer vertical wavelengths and lower frequencies essentially damping out the effect of long period waves. Following these initial processing steps, we conducted spectral analysis on the data.

We calculate the power spectral densities using a prewhitening and postcoloring method [3]. This method is employed to reduce sidelobe leakage from the finite length of the rectangular window. The 2nd order of AR model was chosen based on the final prediction error (FPE) criterion. The vertical wavenumber spectra at each time and frequency spectra at each altitude were first calculated, and then averaged to generate episode-mean wavenumber and frequency spectra, respectively. The episode-mean vertical wavenumber spectra and frequency spectra are shown in Figure 1. We also computed the average spectra over the entire 21-night dataset which are shown in Figures 2 and 3. In Figure 2 the spectra were calculated after only removing the mean while in Figure 3 the spectra were calculated after the linear detrend. We fit a power-law model to each of the spectra within the saturated regime. The estimated spectral index is the "slope" of the power-law fit and each of the indices for the four spectra are reported in Table 1. We find that the measured m-spectra fall into close agreement with the spectra measured at Starfire Optical Range using a similar technique.

Table 1. Spectral Indices of Measured Spectra

Data Set	Spectrum	Spectral Index	LIT Prediction	DFT Prediction	SCT Prediction
Temperature	m-Spectrum	-3.0 +/- 0.1	-3	-3	-3
	ω-Spectrum	-1.83 +/- 0.08	-p (p = 2)	-p (p = 2)	-2
Vertical Wind	m-Spectrum	-1.01 +/- 0.04	-3	5-2p (p = 2)	1
	ω-Spectrum	-0.4 +/- 0.1	N/A	0	0

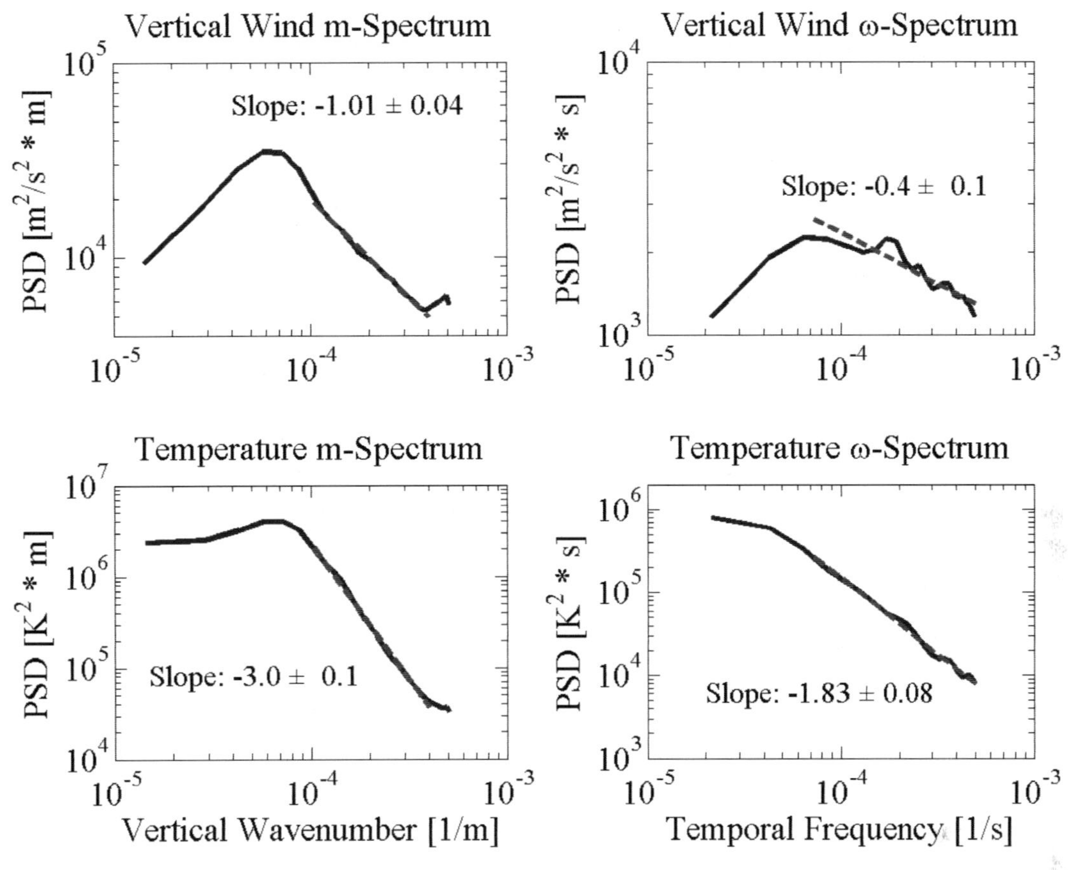

4. Discussion

Gardner 1996 [3] compares existing theories of gravity wave dissipation and their predictions. The theories considered include linear instability (LIT), saturated-cascade (SCT), diffusive filtering (DFT), diffusive damping, and Doppler spreading. The competing theories can be tested by comparing their predictions. In the table of that paper, he compares the spectral indices predicted by the different theories. Only three make predictions about the vertical wind gravity wave spectrum and those predictions are summarized in Table 1 alongside the measured spectral indices. It is apparent that the established consensus on the temperature spectrum is supported by our data. All three of the theories predict a vertical wavenumber spectral index of -3 for gravity waves in the saturated regime ($m > m_*$). In addition, they predict a temporal spectral index of -2. We measured -1.83 ± 0.08 which is slightly shallower than predicted. The agreement between our measurements and established theory reaffirms our assertion that the measured spectra are calculated accurately and that we have minimized signal pollution.

Similar to the findings in Gardner 1998 [4], we find that the spectral indices for the vertical winds are much shallower than the temperature spectra. According to Gardner [3]: "If (m, ω) separability holds, then the shapes of the horizontal and vertical wind spectra will be identical. Only the magnitudes will differ." The measured vertical wind spectra are significantly shallower than the observed temperature spectra and agree well with Gardner's findings. Therefore, we reaffirm Gardner's claim that the (m, ω) spectra are not separable. This finding challenges the fundamental assumptions of Dewan and Good's Linear Instability Theory, which is founded on the assumption that the m and ω spectra are separable. Furthermore, we see that the vertical wind m-spectrum (-1.01 ± 0.04) is in good agreement with Gardner's findings at Starfire Optical Range (-1.08 ± 0.04). We can see that the spectral index estimated from the vertical wind m-spectrum does not agree with the predictions made by any of the theories. Similarly, the observed vertical wind ω -spectrum (-0.4 ± 0.1) is much shallower than the intrinsic spectrum predicted by DFT. This discrepancy suggests that either measurement error has significantly affected the vertical wind spectra or that Doppler shifts and/or critical layer effects could alter the intrinsic spectrum.

5. Conclusions

Using the high-precision vertical wind and temperature measurements in the mesosphere and lower thermosphere (MLT), we studied the spectra of gravity wave perturbations in the mesopause region. We investigated the gravity wave spectra in the measured temperatures and found that they are generally consistent with the theoretical predictions of gravity wave theories. Such agreement reaffirms our assertion that the measured spectra are calculated accurately and that we have minimized signal pollution. We also investigated the gravity wave spectra in the measured vertical winds. The averaged slope of the frequency (f) spectra is –1.83±0.08, while the slope of the vertical wavenumber (m) spectra is –3.0±0.1. The observed f- and m- spectra of vertical winds are both very shallow, compared to the observed temperature spectra. This result suggests the f- and m-spectra are not separable and therefore challenges the fundamental assumptions of Dewan and Good's Linear Instability Theory. Although our results on the gravity wave vertical wind spectra are quite similar to Gardner's finding at Starfire Optical Range, there is significant discrepancy between the theoretical and measured spectral shapes. This discrepancy suggests that either measurement error has significantly affected the vertical wind spectra or that Doppler shifts and/or critical layer effects could alter the intrinsic spectrum.

6. References

1. D. C. Fritts and M. J. Alexander, "Gravity wave dynamics and effects in the middle atmosphere," Rev. Geophys. **41**, 1003 (2003).
2. C. S. Gardner, "Diffusive filtering theory of gravity wave spectra in the atmosphere," J. Geophys. Res. **99**, 20601–20622 (1994).
3. C. S. Gardner, "Testing theories of atmospheric gravity wave saturation and dissipation," J. Atmos. Terr. Phys. **58**, 1575–1589 (1996).
4. X. Chu and G. Papen, "Resonance Fluorescence Lidar for Measurements of the Middle and Upper Atmosphere," in *Laser Remote Sensing*, T. Fukuchi and T. Fujii, eds., Optical Science and Engineering (CRC Press, 2005), pp. 179–432.
5. J. A. Smith and X. Chu, "High-efficiency receiver architecture for resonance-fluorescence and Doppler lidars.," Appl. Opt. **54**, 3173–84 (2015).
6. C. Chen, X. Chu, J. Zhao, B. R. Roberts, Z. Yu, W. Fong, X. Lu, and J. A. Smith, "Lidar observations of persistent gravity waves with periods of 3-10 h in the Antarctic middle and upper atmosphere at McMurdo (77.83°S, 166.67°E)," J. Geophys. Res. Sp. Phys. **121**, 1483–1502 (2016).

Lidar visualization of internal gravity waves

V.A. Banakh, I.N. Smalikho
V.E. Zuev Institute of Atmospheric Optics SB RAS, Tomsk, Russia

Abstract: the results of observation of the atmospheric internal waves (AIWs) in the boundary layer of atmosphere on the coast of Lake Baikal with the use of Halo Photonics pulsed coherent Doppler wind lidar Stream Line are presented. A total of six AIW occurrences have been revealed from wind lidar measurements. This always happened in the presence of one or two (in 5 of 6 cases) narrow jet streams at heights of approximately 200 and 700 m. The parameters of the observed AIWs were determined.

Keywords: Coherent Doppler wind lidar, atmospheric internal waves

1. Introduction

Atmospheric gravity waves (AGWs) are an important feature of motions present in the atmosphere. Study of the gravity waves is carried out with the help of space images of the cloud fields in the visible and microwave regions [1, 2] and radar images of the sea surface [3, 4]. Experimental investigations of AGWs in the ionosphere from the scattering of radio waves are carried out by different methods [5]. The first results of lidar observations of the inertia gravity waves in the stratosphere and mesosphere with the use of the Doppler Rayleigh lidar are reported in [6]. However, the data of AGW observations in the lower atmosphere, in particular, in the atmospheric boundary layer (ABL) are few and far between. As a rule, they are based on the aerological data or on sodar data for the atmospheric lower 300-400 m layer.

Below we present the results of lidar observations of the coastal-mountain lee waves on the coast of Lake Baikal. Lee AIWs are one of the types of AGWs, which arise on leeward of obstacles at the stable stratification of an incoming flow.

2. Observations and analysis

Experimental investigations of AIWs in the atmospheric boundary layer of Lake Baikal were carried out with the use of the Halo Photonics CDWL Stream Line. The measurements were conducted in August 14-28 of 2015 on the western coast of Lake Baikal (52°N, 105°E), Russia. The wind in the atmospheric surface layer during the measurements was mostly directed from the north through the mountainous terrain toward Lake Baikal. The obtained lidar data have revealed several AIW occurrences. Formation of one and often simultaneously two narrow jet streams at heights of the atmospheric boundary layer were observed as well. In all the cases, AIWs were formed in the presence of low-level jet streams.

The lidar was set at a distance of 340 m from Baikal at a height of 180 m. The measurements cover heights from 280 to 1180 m above the Lake Baikal level. Conical scanning by a probing laser beam around the vertical axis allowed reconstruction of the vertical wind profile from wind velocity projections onto the axis of the probing beam estimated from the raw lidar data. During the measurements, the elevation angle of probing beam $\varphi = 60°$ was fixed, while the azimuth angle $\theta = \omega_s t$ of the beam axis position varied with time t and with the rate ω_s. The recorded lidar signal received from the distance R_k at the azimuth angle θ_n, where $k, n = 1, 2, 3, \ldots$, is then processed to reconstruct the wind vertical profile [7]. The time for one scan around the vertical axis $T_{\text{scan}} = 2\pi / \omega_s$ varied and was 2 min, 1 min, and 36 s in dependence on atmospheric conditions.

Figure 1 shows the results of lidar visualization of the wind field during the longest observations of a gravity wave for about 4 hours starting from 12:00 Local Time (LT) on August 23 of 2015. Two jet streams were observed simultaneously at heights of about 250 and 750 m.

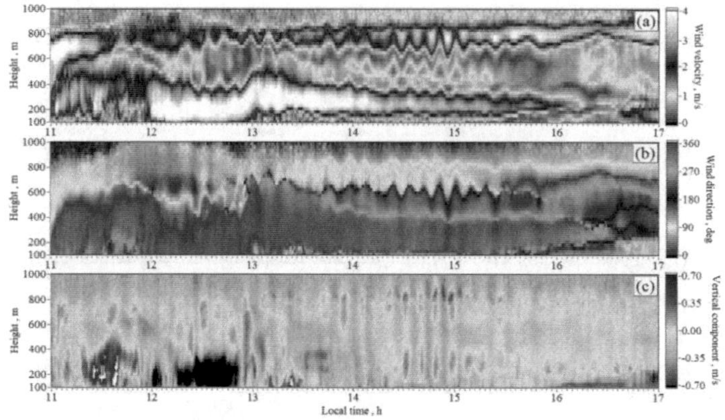

Figure 1. Spatiotemporal distributions of the wind speed (a), the wind direction angle (b), and the vertical component of the wind vector (c) obtained from measurements with the Stream Line lidar on August 23 of 2015. The height is given relatively to lidar position height.

Figures 2 and 3 show the temporal profiles at a height of 636.5 m and vertical profiles at 14:31 LT of wind taken from data in Fig. 1. From these figures, we can see oscillations of the wind parameters in both height and time. They are especially marked in the period from 13:30 to 15:30, when the amplitude of oscillations of the wind direction is approximately 45°.

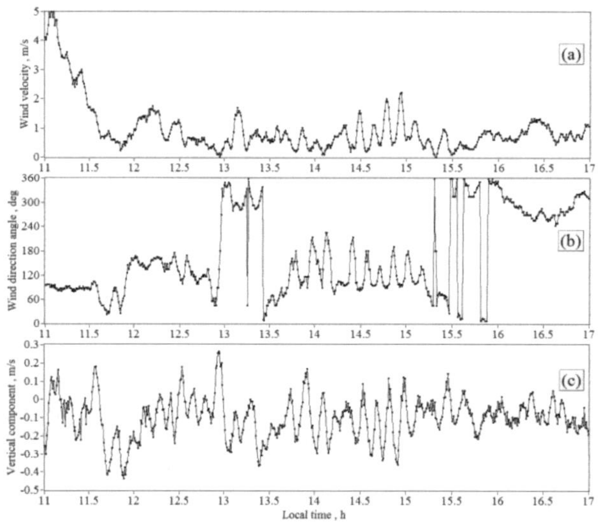

Figure 2. Temporal profiles of the wind speed (a), the wind direction angle (b), and the vertical component of the wind velocity (c). Data of Fig. 1 (measurement height of 636.5 m)

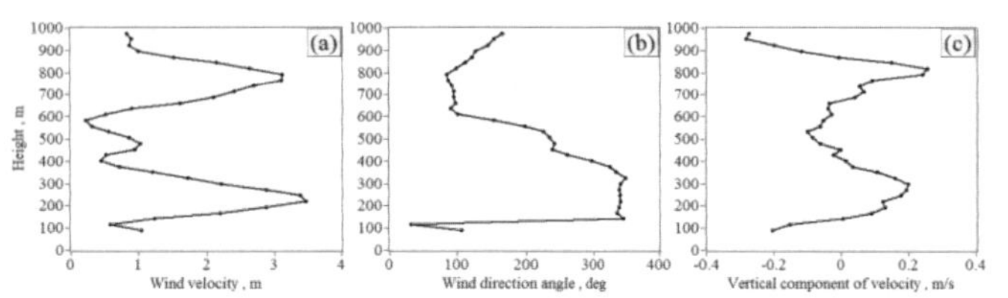

Figure 3. Vertical profiles of the wind speed (a), the wind direction angle (b), and the vertical component of the wind vector (c). Data of Fig.1 (measurement time 14:31 LT).

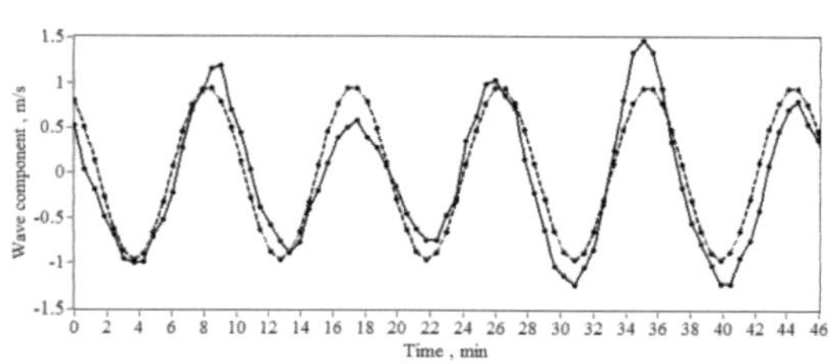

Figure 4. Time dependence of the wave addend of the longitudinal wind velocity.

Neglecting the wind turbulence, we use the model of a plane wave for the component of the wind velocity vector V_α (subscript $\alpha = z$ for the vertical component, $\alpha = x$ for the longitudinal component, and $\alpha = y$ for the transverse component) in the form [8]

$$V_\alpha(\mathbf{r},t) = <V_\alpha> + \tilde{V}_\alpha(\mathbf{r},t) . \tag{1}$$

In Eq.(1) $\mathbf{r} = \{z, x, y\}$ is the radius vector, t is time, $<V_\alpha>$ and $\tilde{V}_\alpha$ are the regular and wave addends of the α-th component of the wind velocity, respectively,

$$\tilde{V}_\alpha(\mathbf{r},t) = A_\alpha(z)\sin\left[\psi_\alpha(\mathbf{r}) - 2\pi t / T_v\right] , \tag{2}$$

A_α is the wave amplitude, ψ_α is the wave phase, and T_v is the wave period. If the wind direction coincides with the direction of propagation of the internal wave, then $A_y = 0$, $\psi_x = 2\pi x / \lambda_v$, and $\psi_z = 2\pi x / \lambda_v + \pi / 2$. Here, λ_v is the wavelength of the wave propagating with the speed $c_v = \lambda_v / T_v$.

Model (1), (2) was applied in the analysis of data in Fig.1 for a height of 766.4 m and 47-min time interval starting from 14:20. From these data, with allowance made for the linear trend, we found the wave addends $\tilde{V}_\alpha(\mathbf{r},t)$ for the three components of the wind velocity vector. In Fig. 4, the solid curve shows the dependence of $\tilde{V}_x$ on t. To determine the wave frequency $f_v = 1/T_v$, we have calculated the spectral density of experimental function $\tilde{V}_x(t)$. From the position the obtained of spectrum maximum we have determined the frequency f_v to be equal to 0.00185 Hz. Consequently, the wave period is $T_v = 9$ min. Using the least-square fitting of model (2) for $\tilde{V}_x(t)$ to the wave addend of the wind velocity component measured by the lidar (solid curve in Fig. 4), we have determined the phase ψ_x and the amplitude A_x. The amplitude of wave addend for the longitudinal component of the wind velocity vector turned out to be 0.96 m/s. The modeled temporal profile $\tilde{V}_x(t)$ calculated by Eq. (2) with the use of experimental values of A_x, ψ_x, and T_v is shown as a dashed curve in Fig. 4.

Parameters of the wave addend of the vertical wind velocity $\tilde{V}_z(t)$ were found in the same way. The estimates of periods of the internal wave for the longitudinal and vertical components coincided fully ($T_v = 9$ min), amplitude $A_z = 0.3$ m/s is approximately 3 times less than the amplitude of wave addend of the longitudinal component of the wind velocity vector, and $\psi_z - \psi_x = \pi / 2$. Since the amplitude $A_y \neq 0$ (see Fig. 1(b) and Fig. 3(b)), the direction of propagation of the internal wave did not coincide with the wind direction.

In addition to this AIW occurrence, we succeeded in observation of this phenomena five times more for the period of measurements. Thus, the period of oscillations of other AIW on August 23 at 19:24 LT was 6.5 min. The wind velocity oscillations with amplitude of 1 m/s were observed for 45 min in presence of a single jet stream at a height of about 700 m. On August 19 since 5:30 LT, the atmospheric internal wave was observed for about 40 min. The period and amplitude of the wave were, respectively, 9 min and 0.9 m/s. Two jet streams were observed simultaneously: one at a height of approximately 200 m, and another at a height of 600 m.

On August 25 in the predawn time (04:30–05:06), two jet streams and AIW with the period $T_v \approx 9$ min and the amplitude $A_x \approx 1$ m/s at a height of 402.7 m were observed in the atmospheric boundary layer. On August

26, the internal wave with the period $T_v \approx 18$ min and the amplitude $A_x \approx 0.7$ m/s at the same height 402.7 m, passed from 16:22 to 19:00 LT. In the same day, the AIW with the halved period ($T_v \approx 9$ min) and the amplitude $A_x \approx 0.4$ m/s at the height 402.7 m was observed 50 min later from 19:50 to 20:35 LT.

3. Summary

Thus, the results of the experimental campaign in the coastal zone of Lake Baikal in August of 2015 show that the raw data of measurements by the Stream Line lidar allow us to visualize the spatiotemporal structure of the wind field in the atmospheric boundary layer and reveal the presence of low-level jet streams and atmospheric internal waves.

A total of six cases of AIW formation have been revealed, which always occurred against the background of one or two (in 5 of 6 cases) narrow jet streams at heights of about 200 and 700 m. When two jet streams were formed, the period of oscillation of the wave addend of the wind vector components was 9 min. In only one case it was about 18 min. In presence of a single jet stream (at a height of 730 m), the period of oscillations of the wind vector components during AIW was about 6.5 min. The amplitude of oscillations of the horizontal wind components most often was about 1 m/s, while the amplitude of oscillations of the vertical velocity was tree times less. In the most cases, the internal waves were observed for 45 min (5 oscillations with the period $T_v = 9$ min). Only once the lifetime of the atmospheric internal wave was about 4 hours.

4. Acknowledgments

The authors are thankful to A.V. Falits and A.A. Sukharev for the measurements. The authors are grateful to the Institute of Solar-Terrestrial Physics SB RAS for the possibility of using the territory of the Baikal Observatory for the measurements.

This study was supported by the Russian Scientific Foundation for Maintenance and Development, Project No. 14-17-00386.

5. References

[1] M.A. German , *Space Methods of Investigation in Meteorology* (Leningrad: Gidrometeoizdat, 1985) [in Russian].

[2] Li Xiaofeng, Quanan Zheng, William G. Pichel, Xiao-Hai Yan, W. Timothy Liu, and Pablo Clemente-Colon, "Analysis of coastal lee waves along the coast of Texas observed in advanced very high resolution radiometer images", J. Geophys. Res. **106**(C4), 7017-7025 (2001).

[3] I. Chunchuzov, P. Vachon, and X.Li, "Analysis and modeling of atmospheric gravity waves observed in Radarsat SAR images", Remote Sens. Environ. **74**, 343-361 (2000)

[4] Yu.G. Spiridonov, A.P. Pichugin, and V.P. Shestopalov, "Space radar observation of atmospheric internal gravity waves", FEAS USSR, **296**(2), 317-320 (1987) [in Russian].

[5] E.A. Benediktov, V.V.Belikovich, N.V.Bakhmet'eva, and A.V. Tolmacheva, "Seasonal and daily variations of the velocity of vertical motions at altitudes of the mesosphere and lower thermosphere near Nizhny Novgorod", Geomagn. Aeron. **37**(5), 88-94. (1997)

[6] G. Baumgarten, J. Fiedler, J. Hildebrand, and F.-J. Lьbken, "Inertia gravity wave in the stratosphere and mesosphere observed by Doppler wind and temperature lidar Geophys", Res. Lett. **42**, 10,929–10,936, doi:10.1002/2015GL066991 (2015).

[7] V.A. Banakh and I.N. Smalikho, *Coherent Doppler wind lidars in a turbulent atmosphere* (Artech House. Boston-London, 2013), 250 p.

[8] N.K. Vinnichenko, N.Z. Pinus, S.M. Shmeter, and G.N. Shur, *Turbulence in the Rree Atmosphere. Edit by J.A.Dutton* (Consultants Bureau, 1973), 262 pp.

Innovative Fiber-Laser Architecture Based Compact Wind Lidar

Narasimha S. Prasad(a), Allen Tracy(b),Steve Vetorino(b), Rich Higgins(b), Russ Sibell(b)
(a) NASA Langley Research Center
5 N. Dryden St., MS 468, Hampton VA, 23681
(b) Sibelloptics, 1855 57th Ct S #201, Boulder, CO 80301
narasimha.s.prasad@nasa.gov

Abstract: This paper describes an innovative, all-fiber, compact, and eyesafe coherent lidar system developed for wind and wake vortex sensing applications. The all-fiber lidar, with modular architecture, incorporates an integrated 3D scanner that provides user programmable, continuous 360 degree azimuth and 180 degree elevation scan angles. Operating at 1.54 microns, the lidar allows pulsewidth agility from 50 - 400 ns with a variable PRF of up to 20 KHz. The wind lidar is air cooled with overall dimensions of 30 cm x 46 cm x 60 cm and is designed as a Class 1 system. This lidar is capable of measuring wind velocities greater than 120 +/- 0.2 m/s over ranges greater than 10 km and with a range resolution of less than 15 m. In this paper, the key features of lidar instrumentation and its functionality are discussed followed by results of recent wind forecast measurements on a wind farm.

Keywords: Coherent lidar, wind lidar, all-fiber lidar, 3D scanner

1. Introduction

The ability of coherent lidar systems to produce a continuous, real-time 3D scan of wind velocities via detection of backscatter of atmospheric aerosols in clear-air conditions and at long stand-off distances with relatively low pulse energy gives this technology a clear advantage over other atmospheric monitoring technologies. Lidar systems have proven their value in the remote measurement of spatially resolved atmospheric wind velocities in a number of applications, including the detection of clear-air turbulence, wind shear, microbursts, and aircraft wake vortices [1,2]. The technically mature and commercially proven wind lidar system in the world is the solid-state laser based WindTracer® lidar systems. WindTracer® lidar, first built in 1998 by Coherent Technologies, Inc. (CTI) (now known as Lockheed Martin Coherent Technologies, LMCT), have effectively been used worldwide for more than a decade to detect hazardous winds and aircraft wakes. However, emerging optical fiber laser and fiber amplifier in combination with 3D printing technologies are anticipated to further enhance the wind lidar architecture and expand its utility to various other applications including wind farming. These technologies have the potential to provide a versatile system by reducing overall size, weight, and power (SWaP), and significantly lowering downtime of current solid-state laser based systems. Besides cost advantage, these systems with low SWaP and long range capability could operate in demanding environments and provide a viable path for airborne and space borne applications. Accordingly, to overcome the disadvantages of current systems to a large extent, an eye-safe wind lidar with all-fiber architecture using commercial-off-the-shelf (COTS) components was developed. In this paper, the wind lidar system known as Windimager™, developed by Sibell Optics under NASA SBIR funding [3,4] with emphasis to enhancing range, sensitivity, system efficiency and reliability, while simultaneously reducing SWaP requirements, is discussed.

2. All-Fiber Wind Lidar Architecture

Figure 1 illustrates the wind lidar system architecture with optical and electrical interconnects. It can be physically separated into four modules: (1) the Scanner Head assembly, (2) the UPS unit, (3) the

Environmental Control unit, and (4) the Computer / DAQ unit. Each sub-assembly is an environmentally sealed unit and the four modules can be assembled into the full sensor system in a matter of minutes. The optical interconnects are the polarization maintaining single mode optical fibers. The Scanner Head Assembly consists of the fiber transmitter system, the telescope, and the hemispherical scanner itself, all housed within the scanner dome. The heart of a lidar sensor is the laser transmitter system and is shown in Figure 2 along with the transmit telescope (both part of the Scanner Head Sub-Assembly). Each major component of the sub-assembly is a fiber-coupled, self-contained unit that can be easily replaced, without the necessity of re-alignment if the component should fail. The Fiber Transmitter System is configured as a fiber-based Master Oscillator/Power Amplifier (MOPA) architecture. It consists of COTS components including a seed laser, a CW pre-amplifier, a pulse slicer, and a single mode CW EDFA as the first fiber preamplifier. Pulsed operation is accomplished by chopping the MO output by the acousto-optic modulator (AOM). The first preamplifier is then followed by a custom designed second fiber preamplifier and a Large Mode Area (LMA) EDFA. The fiber reels holding optical fibers are printed nylon parts. The novel fiber-amplifier network, beam-combined provides over 400 μJ of energy per pulse and the system can run between 3 kHz – 20 kHz. The MO provides an extremely narrow linewidth (3 kHz) and low RIN (-145 dB/Hz). The telescope used in this system is a Dall-Kirkham type with an aperture size of 114 mm and 25x magnification. Unlike all other scanners that use mirrors and rotating wedges to steer beams of light, the Windimager™ scanner rotates the light source itself – specifically the fiber lidar/telescope assembly. This design has several advantages. Most significantly it reduces the overall complexity of the unit, which in turn improves reliability. In addition, optical scatter and polarization losses are eliminated, thereby improving the lidar performance. The Windimager™, also features two unique components that improve the sensitivity, range and performance of the sensor. The first component is the use of a balance detector for both the monitor and the signal detection and the second one is a fiber coupled optical switch that is placed between the DFB output and the AOM to prevent a reflected acoustic pulse-generated optical signal. The "Back-Propagated Local Oscillator (BPLO)" alignment using quad cell allows performance optimization on the fly. The custom designed detector and its novel use to obtain optimum beam alignment is a significant advancement in the maintainability and manufacturability of lidar systems. The detector's frequency response is flat to within 2 dB over 250 MHz. The detector electronics is capable of detecting as few as 8 photons, which is within an order of magnitude of the theoretical limit.

The lidar system is air cooled with overall dimensions of 30" (W) x 46" (L) x 60" (H). The compact modular design allows for easy transport and rapid setup. Its features include: improved system sensitivity, continuously variable pulsewidth, compact packaging in a standard 19-inch rack, reduced complexity coupled with high-end components to maximize reliability, a unique 3D wind data display to enable easy interpretation of atmospheric conditions, and compact, rugged, modular and lightweight construction to allow for easy deployment in a variety of harsh environments. Some of the key features that separates it from the currently available free-space and fiber LIDAR systems are:

- Rapid fire rate that allows for quick and detailed atmospheric profiling
- Pulsed fiber laser technology yields excellent range and wind velocity accuracy
- Variable pulse width operation that adapts for various modes of wind measurements
- Reduced complexity coupled with high-end components maximizes reliability
- Compact, rugged, modular and lightweight construction allows for easy deployment in a variety of harsh environments
- Fiber optic, 1.55 μm architecture is easily upgradeable to higher power and greater range configurations while still remaining eye-safe
- Real-time data-processing and display update
- User GUI allows multiple application-based operating modes and scan scenarios.
- Custom 3D wind data display enables easy interpretation of atmospheric conditions
- All conduction or convection thermal control – no liquid cooling
- Significantly less expensive than systems with comparable performance

- High electrical efficiency allows the system to run on battery power up to 24 hours.

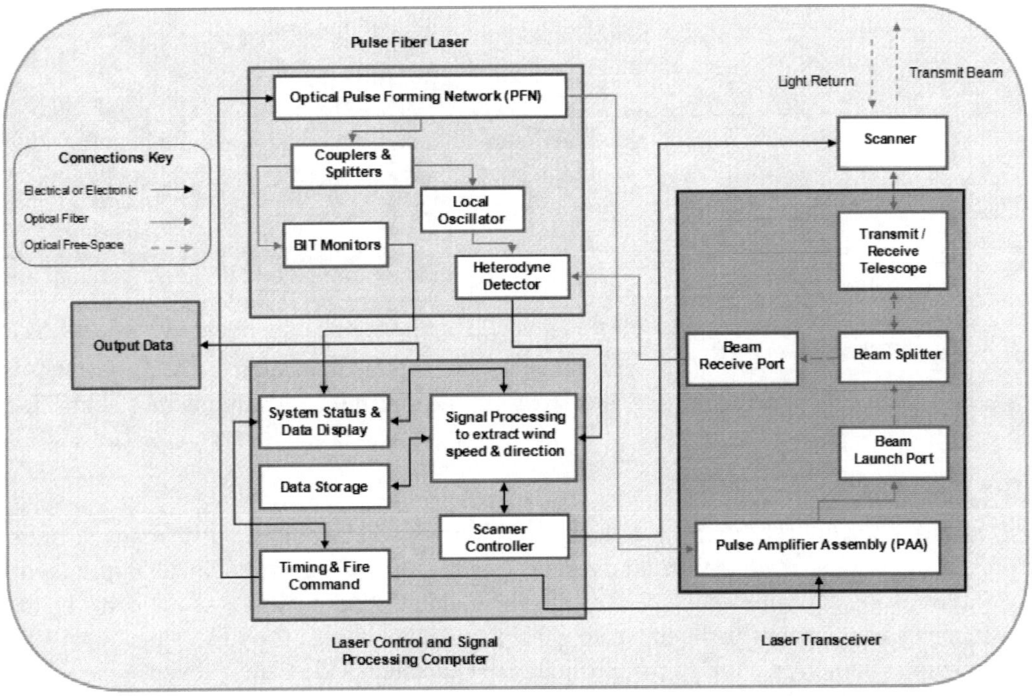

Figure 1. General system architecture of the Windimager™ lidar system.

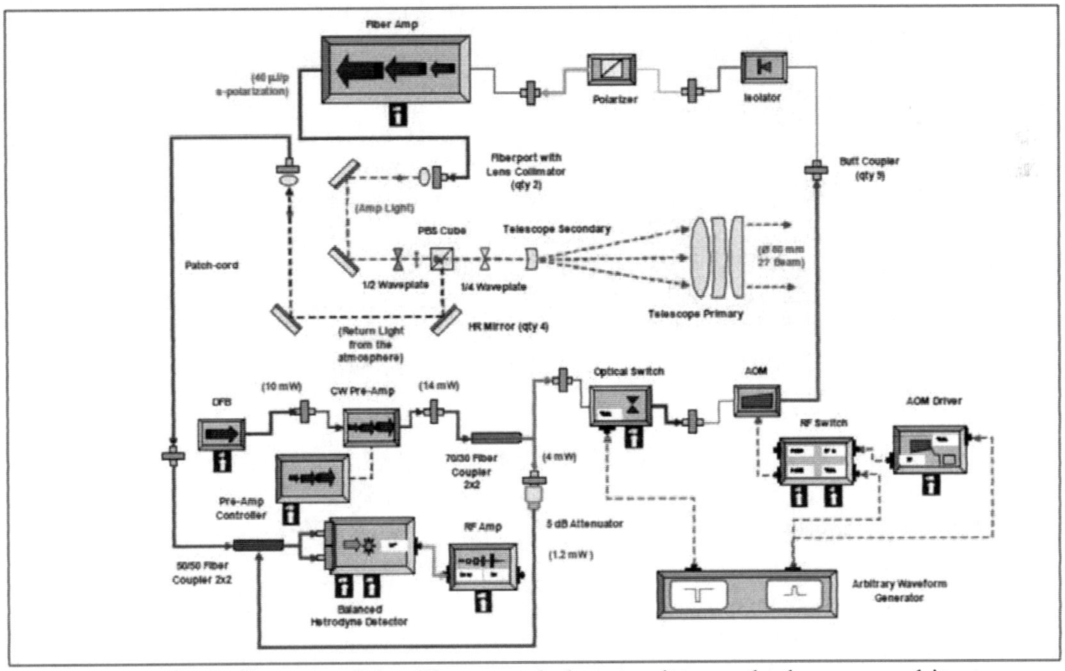

Figure 2. Block diagram of the fiber-coupled transmitter and telescope architecture.

Table 1 lists the overall specifications and Figure 3 shows the wind lidar system. Previously, heat maps (Range, km vs. Wind speed, m/s characteristics) representing horizontal single line-of-sight (LOS) returns collected by the Windimager™ lidar located facing the Rocky mountain range near Boulder, CO from a distance greater than 9 km, and BPLO alignment and other system aspects have been discussed in detail [5,6]. In the following section, the performance of the Windimager™ lidar which was successfully tested on a wind farm on the Southeast coast of Aruba for wind field forecasting purposes is discussed.

Table 1. Specifications of the all-fiber wind lidar.

Transmitter:

Typical Horizontal Detection Range:	400m to 10km
Minimum / Maximum Detection Range:	50m / 15km
Maximum Radial Velocity:	" 127m/s
Velocity Accuracy:	" 0.2m/sec
Range Resolution:	7.5m (minimum), adjustable
Wavelength:	1547nm " 3nm
Output Beam Diameter ($1/e^2$):	80mm
Laser Classification:	Class 1
Pulse Temporal Profile:	Near Gaussian
Output Pulse Options :	

Pulse Width (ns)	Pulse Energy (uJ)	Rep Rate (Hz)	Output Power (mW)
50	35	20,000	700
90	70	15,000	1050
170	115	10,000	1150
200	140	8,000	1120
330	220	5,000	1100
400	240	4,000	960

Scanner:

Elevation Scan Range / Rate:	360 *f* continuous, 40 *f* / sec (max)
Azimuth Scan Range / Rate:	360 *f* continuous, 40 *f* / sec (max)
Unidirectional Repeatability:	0.002 degrees
Min Incremental Motion:	0.001 degrees
Absolute Positional Accuracy:	" 0.01 degrees
Scan Resolution:	Up to 10,000 points / PPI scan
Scan Modes:	PPI, RHI, complex group motion, or combination
Scan Patterns	User Programmable
Rotation Stages MTBF:	20,000 hours
Optical Clear Aperture:	101 mm

Signal Processor:

Operating System:	MS Windows
Graphical User Interface:	NOTUS Data Collection System
CPU:	Intel Core i7-820QM, 1.73 GHz
Memory:	4 GB DDR3
Hard Disk Drive:	Up to 24 TB, RAID array
Digitizer Card:	750 MS/s sample rate, 16 MB RAM, 8 bits/sample
Timing:	GPS, IEEE-1588 or IRIG-B
Additional Sensors:	GPS, Compass (Optional)
Input Devices:	Ethernet
Network:	100BaseT

Size & Weight:

System Dimensions:	30-in (W) x 46-in (L) x 60-in (H)
System Weight:	800 lbs (364 kg)

Environmental:

Operating Temperature:	-40° to +55° C
Storage Temperature:	-25° to +40° C
Cooling System:	Air-cooled

Power Requirements:

Input Power:	1100 W Max, 550 W Typical
Service Circuit Req:	20 Amps
Voltage (single phase):	100-250 VAC, 50/60 Hz

Figure 3. The Windimager™ lidar unit. Left Picture: (1).Hemispherical scanner, (2). Air cooled unit. Right Picture The internal arrangement. (1).The lidar transceiver chassis. (2). The UPS unit

4. Wing Energy Harvesting

With the system running at 4000 Hz and the pulse averaging set to 1000 shots, PPI maps similar to the one shown in Figure 4 are generated. With an average wind speed of 32 km/h for example (typical for Aruba), the system gives a 17 minute advance warning of sudden drop offs in wind speed. In the event that the wind speed increases abruptly, from 32 to 80 km/h for example, then the system will give a 7 minute advance warning - which is enough time to pitch the turbine blades and prevent possible damage to the gear boxes. Further validation tests are progressing.

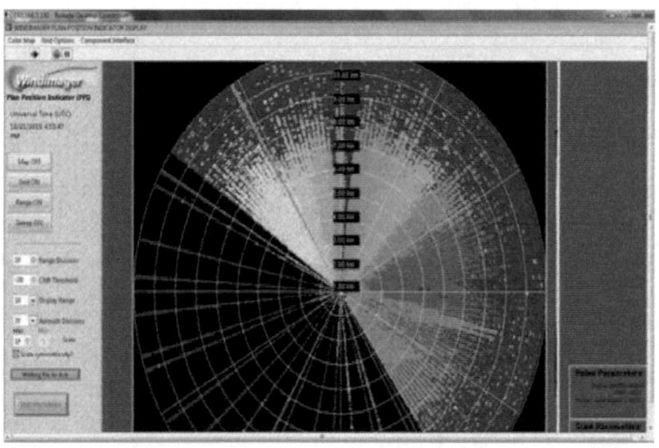

Figure 4. A wind map generated in an Aruba wind farm.

4. Summary and Conclusions

The salient features of the development of an all-fiber, modular, compact architecture based 1.55 micron wind lidar with an integrated, novel 3D hemispherical scanner for wind sensing and wake vortex applications are presented. Successful field test results carried out for wind forecasting on a wind farm in Aruba are presented. The compact all fiber, Windimager™ class of technology system has the potential to provide a developmental path for several applications including wind field forecasting for wind energy harvesting.

5. References.

[1] Huffaker, R.M. and R.M. Hardesty, "Remote sensing of atmospheric wind velocities using solid-state and CO2 coherent laser systems", Proc. of the IEEE, vol 84, No. 2, 181-204, 1996.

[2] Sammy W. Henderson and Stephen M. Hannon, "Advanced coherent lidar system for wind measurements," Proc. SPIE 5887, Lidar Remote Sensing for Environmental Monitoring VI, 58870I (16 September 2005).

[3] "Next Generation Fiber Coherent Lidar System for Wake Vortex Detection" Contract # NNX12CA74C, The NASA SBIR Phase II final report, Sibell Optics, 2014.

[4] "Novel Hemisphere Scanner for a Coherent Fiber LIDAR System", Contract # NNX12CA73C, The NASA SBIR Phase II final report, Sibell Optics, 2014.

[5] Narasimha S. Prasad, Russ Sibell, Steve Vetorino, Richard Higgins and Allen Tracy, "An all-fiber, modular, compact Wind lidar for wind sensing and wake vortex applications, Proc. SPIE 9465, Laser Radar Technology and Applications XX; and Atmospheric Propagation XII, 94650C (15 June 2015).

[6] Narasimha S. Prasad; Allen Tracy; Steve Vetorino; Richard Higgins; Russ Sibell, "Innovative fiber-laser architecture-based compact wind lidar," Proc. SPIE 9754, Photonic Instrumentation Engineering III, (28 March 2016).

Development of 1.5 μ m all-fiber pulsed coherent Doppler wind lidar

Jiqiao Liu, Weibiao Chen, Xiaolei Zhu, Xiaopeng Zhu, Xin Zhang, Yuan Liu, Wei Shi
Key Laboratory of Space Laser Communication and Detection Technology, Shanghai Institute of Optics and Fine Mechanics, CAS, No.390 Qinghe Road, Jiading, Shanghai 201800, China
X_qiao@siom.ac.cn

Abstract: A 1.54 μ m eye-safe all-fiber pulsed coherent Doppler lidar (CDL) system is developed to measure wind profiles. The laser is operated with 300μJ pulse energy and pulse width of almost 500 ns and pulse repetition rate of 10 kHz. The diameter of optical telescope is 100 mm. Spectra of 10k pulses are accumulated to increase the SNR of the signal for retrieving the Doppler shift of the light of sight (LOS) wind speeds. The profiles of wind vector are retrieved less than 20 seconds. Field experiments are implemented to validate the CDL performance. Good agreement is shown between the CDL and the balloon results with wind speed and direction errors of 0.73m/s and 5.2° . Airborne wind lidar experiments are also successfully carried out in 2015.

Keywords: Wind measurement, Pulsed Doppler lidar, coherent detection, all-fiber

1. Introduction

A coherent Doppler lidar (CDL) is proved to be an effective tool for wind profiles measurement[1] , windshear[2] and wake vortices detection [3] in clear air with high temporal and spatial resolution and high accuracy in the lower atmosphere layer. A number of groups have been developing and validating such CDL system with 10 μ m CO_2 laser[4] ,1 μ m solid laser[5], 2 μ m solid laser[6], 1.6 μ m solid laser[7] and 1.5 μ m fiber laser[8]. The 2 μ m and 1.5 μ m coherent Doppler lidar are promising measurement methods for wind remote sensing. All-fiber CDL systems at 1.5 μ m are very popular for wind measurement in the boundary layer in the last few years because of its eye safety, compact size, flexible arrangement [9]. Thanks to the cost-efficient commercially available components, this technology is much attractive and commercial all-fiber CDL systems have been developed by several companies since 2004[10]. The all-fiber CDL system is suitable for airborne platform, because the fiber laser is insensitive to vibration and temperature.

In this contribution, we demonstrate an all-fiber pulsed CDL system for wind profiles sensing. Field experiments are implemented to validate the CDL performance, and the wind profiles are compared with the results from balloon and wind profile radar. Airborne wind lidar experiments are also successfully carried out, and the wind profiles are compared with the results measured by balloon theodolite and ground based wind lidar.

2. System configuration

The system are coupled with polarization maintaining fibers with single-frequency polarized eye-safe all-fiber laser[11]. The schematic diagram of the CDL system is shown in figure 1. The CDL system consists of an all-fiber laser source based on the master oscillator power amplifier (MOPA) design, an optical transceiver with a special designed, robust fiber circulator, and a heterodyne detection unit with real-time signal pre-processor based on field programmable gate array (FPGA). The CDL system is compact with size of 450 mm×400 mm×400 mm and mass of 45 kg. A laptop is used to control the lidar system, and to calculate the line-of-speed (LOS) of the wind. After getting 8 radial wind speed in velocity azimuth display (VAD) scan mode, the wind profiles would be retrieved by the CDL through the method of Levenberg－Marquardt（LM）. The information of platform position, attitude and speed data could be also received to eliminate the effect of the moving platform.

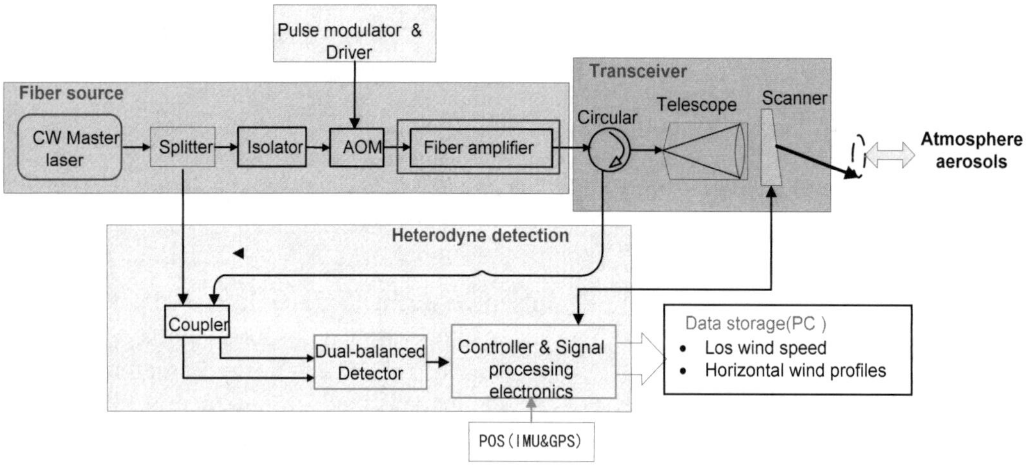

Figure 1. The block diagrams of the CDL system

An eye-safe, narrow-linewidth, polarized, pulsed, fiber laser based on master oscillator power amplifier (MOPA) configuration is acted as the source of the lidar[12]. The laser is composed of a single-frequency, narrow-linewidth external cavity diode laser, and multistage fiber amplifiers. The Distributed Feed Back Laser Diode (DFB-LD) with 10 kHz linewidth and 20mw power is used as the seeder laser. The seeder is divided into two parts by the 1×2 optical coupler. One part (about 0.8mW) is used as the local oscillator, for heterodyne detection. The other part is pulsed modulated and frequency shifted (160MHz) by the acousto-optic modulator (AOM) at repetition rate of 10 kHz, pulse duration of 470ns. Through multi-stages fiber amplifiers, fiber laser with pulse energy of 300 μ J, linewidth of 1.1MHz at wavelength of 1540nm is obtained.

The optical transceiver combines a circulator, a telescope and an optical scanner. The transceiver could separate transmitting fiber laser and signal backscattered by aerosols. The optical diameter of the telescope is 100 mm. The output beam from telescope is conically scanned by a compact refractive scanner with 20° deflection angle.

In the heterodyne detection unit the local oscillator from seeder is mixed with signal backscattered by aerosols from transceiver. The heterodyne signal from the InGaAs balanced receiver is sampled by the high speed AD converter with the sample rate of 1G bps. The range resolution is 30m (200ns). Fast Fourier Transform (FFT) of 1024 points and power spectrum accumulation with 10000 pulses are implemented in every range gate. Accumulated power spectra in every azimuth are sent to the computer through RS422 interface to process the wind profiles. The specifications of the system are summarized in the table 1.

Table1. The specifications of the CDL system

Parameter	**value**	**Parameter**	**value**	**Parameter**	**value**
Wavelength	1540nm	Aperture	Φ100mm	PRF	10 kHz
Pulse energy	300 μ J	Scanner	20° deflection angle	AD	1G/s ,10bit
Pulse width	470ns	IF	160MHz	Resolution	30m

3. Experiments

Since the equipment was complete in 2014, we have carried out a series of experiments. One verification test was taken out with the GPS balloon and wind profile radar during Sep.4th to Sep. 6th, 2014 in Hefei. The lidar worked for about 40 hours continuously. A troposphere wind profile radar was working at the same time. A GOS meteorological sounding balloon was released at the time of 17 o'clock, Sep. 5th.The measurement results of coherent Doppler lidar is shown in the figure 2. We can see that measurement range was so close because of the thick fog.

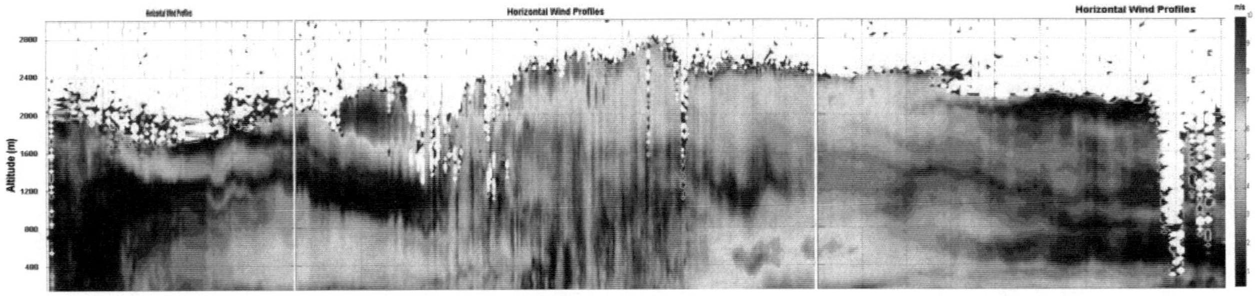

Figure 2. The wind profiles distribution with time

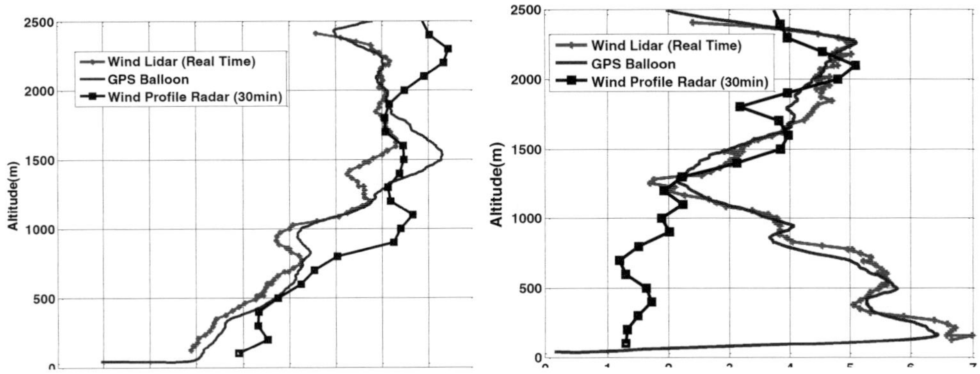

Figure 3. The comparison between the lidar, Radar, and the GPS sounding

The wind profile of the comparison between three instruments is shown in the figure 3. We can see that wind profiles from the lidar and GPS sounding balloon have better consistency. The standard deviation of the wind speed difference is about 0.73m/s, and the wind directions is about 5.2 degrees. The results of the troposphere wind profiles radar is affected by the low SNR below 1000m altitude.

Airborne CDL validation experiment is carried in Roncheng city, Shangdong province, China on Jan 19, 2015. The CDL system is installed in a propeller aircraft with the speed of 50m/s speed and flight height of 2000m. An POS system composed of Inertial Navigation System (INS) and global positioning system(GPS) is installed together with the lidar. Wind profiles measured from airborne CDL are compared with ground-based CDL and aerological theodolite in the campaign simultaneously to assess the airborne CDL performance. The whole flight time was lasted about 5 hours. Figure 4 is show the wind profiles from the airborne lidar, ground lidar and the balloon aerological theodolite on January19, 12:22, . The wind speed standard error between the three system are less 1m/s, and the wind direction differences are about 10° ,as shown in. Especially, wind speed standard error between airborne lidar and balloon aerological theodolite is less 0.4m/s, with wind speed coefficient of correlation of 0.9867.

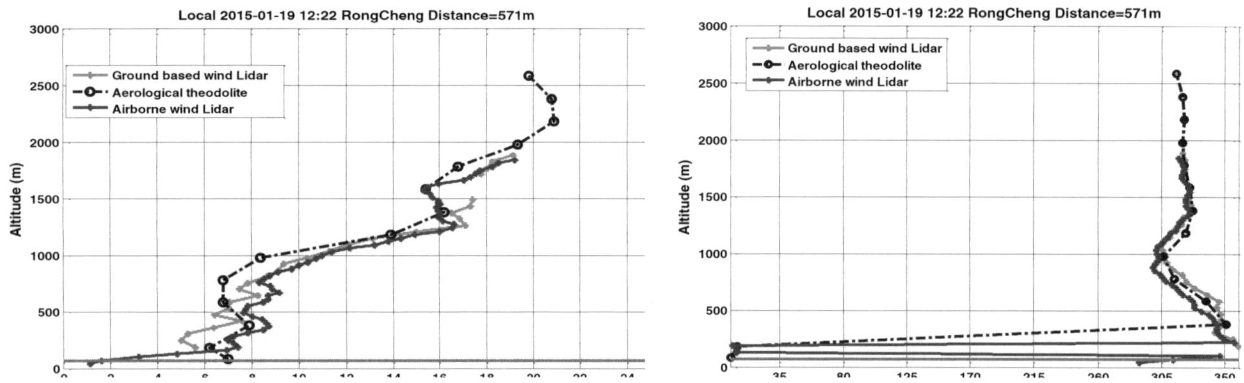

Figure 4. The wind speed profiles comparisons between the three systems.

4. CONCLUSIONS

A 1.54 μ m eye-safe al-fiber pulsed coherent Doppler lidar (CDL) system is developed for wind profiles measurement. Several experiments were carried out for performance verifications. Good agreement is shown between the CDL and the balloon results with wind speed and direction errors of 0.73m/s and 5.2° in Hefei. Airborne wind lidar experiments are also successfully carried out in 2015, and the wind profiles are compared with aerological theodolite and ground based wind lidar. The differences of the wind speed between them are less than lm/s.

5. References

[1] Asaka, K., T. Yanagisawa, and Y. Hirano, "1.5-μm eye-safe coherent lidar system for wind velocity measurement.," SPIE. 4153, 321-328 (2001).

[2] Frehlich, R., "Coherent Doppler lidar signal covariance including wind shear and wind turbulence," Appl. Opt. 33(27), 6472-6481 (1994).

[3] Dolfi-Bouteyre, A., et al., "1.5 μm all fiber pulsed lidar for wake vortex monitoring," in 14th Coherent Laser Radar Conference (2007).

[4] Huffaker, R.M. and R.M. Hardesty, "Remote sensing of atmospheric wind velocities using solid-state and CO2 coherent laser systems," Proceedings of the IEEE. 84(2), 181-204 (1996).

[5] Kane, T.J., et al., "Coherent laser radar at 1.06 um using Nd:YAG lasers," Opt. Lett. 12(4), 239-241 (1987).

[6] Jirong, Y., et al. "An all solid-state 2um laser system for space coherent wind lidar," in Aerospace Conference Proceedings, 2000 IEEE, (2000).

[7] Hannon, S.M., S.R. Vetorino, and J.V. Pelk, "Next generation Doppler lidar sensor at 1.6μm," in 14th Coherent Laser Radar Conference: Colorado (2007).

[8] Ando, T., et al., "All-fiber Coherent Doppler LIDAR for wind sensing," Materials Research Society. 1076, 1076-K04-05.

[9] Kameyama, S., et al., "Compact all-fiber pulsed coherent Doppler lidar system for wind sensing". Applied Optics. 46(11), 1953-1962 (2007).

[10]Weifeng Diao, et al., "Weibiao Chen. All fiber pulsed coherent lidar development for wind profiles measurements in boundary layers," Chinese Opitcs Letter, 12(7), 072801(2014)

[11] Ando, T., S. Kameyama, and Y. Hirano, "All-fiber Coherent Doppler LIDAR technologies at Mitsubishi Electric Corporation", in 14th International Symposium for the Advancement of Boundary Layer Remote Sensing IOP (2008).

[12] Zhang, X., et al., "Single-frequency polarized eye-safe all-fiber laser with peak power over kilowatt," Applied Physics B. 115(1),123-127 (2014).

Using multiple wavelengths for more precise detection of atmospheric wind phenomena

Albert Töws and Alfred Kurtz
Cologne University of Applied Sciences
Steinmüllerallee 1, 51643 Gummersbach, Germany
albert.toews@th-koeln.de

Abstract: An all-fiber multi-wavelength coherent Doppler lidar system in MOPA configuration with feedback controlled pulse shaping was developed and applied to wind measurements. The multi-wavelength system was designed to work with four wavelength-channels of the ITU-grid in the C-Band, which allow measurements along the same line-of-sight with different channel configurations. Those channels can be different in pulse shape, pulse length, and pulse repetition frequency (PRF). The resulting advantages and possibilities using multiple channels are: (1) All channels can be used simultaneously with the same pulse length and PRF to increase the effective PRF and therefore reduce the measurement time, enhance the detectability, or prevent ambiguity. (2) Atmospheric phenomena, such as wind shear, can be investigated with higher resolution using different pulse lengths.

Keywords: all-fiber coherent lidar, multi-wavelength, multi-channel, pulse-shape control

1. Introduction

In the past decade the 1.5 μm wavelength range has become broadly applied to pulsed coherent lidar systems due to the availability of components from the telecommunication industry. Since most of the telecommunication products are fiber based, cost effective all-fiber systems were developed. All-fiber lidar systems have successfully been commercialized, because of their compact size, mobility, low required maintenance, low cost components, and high reliability under vibrations and temperature variations [1, 2]. These systems work at lower pulse energy but at higher pulse repetition frequency (PRF) than systems based on free-space optics. However, a recently developed very large mode area (VLMA) fiber amplifier also achieves high pulse energies [3]. Thus, the peak and average power are pushed to the physical limits of such fiber amplifiers. Another possibility to enhance the performance of a lidar system is to increase the PRF. A higher PRF results in a reduced accumulation time or enhanced detectability. In single channel systems, the PRF defines the maximum range due to ambiguity of the return signal. Therefore, the effective PRF can only be increased using multiple parallel distinguishable channels. Two parallel channels can be created using two different polarization states [4]. In our lidar system, different wavelength-channels from the ITU-grid are simultaneously utilized. As already presented in [5], this system works with four independent channels.

2. Methodology

Figure 1 depicts the setup of the four-channel Doppler lidar system. Four laser diodes generate continuous-wave laser light in the master oscillator unit for each channel. The wavelengths are selected near 1.55 μm for low extinction in the atmosphere. All four channels are multiplexed and amplified by one erbium-doped fiber amplifier (EDFA). A part of that laser light is used as the local oscillator and the other part of the master oscillator laser light is guided to the pulse shaping unit. In the pulse shaping unit the laser light is demultiplexed, in order to separately shape the pulses of each channel with electro-optic modulators (EOM). Then, all pulses are frequency shifted and additionally shaped by an acousto-optic modulator (AOM). The shifted and shaped pulses are amplified with a three-stage EDFA. The output pulses to be transmitted are monitored via a coupler and a feedback control system controls the EOMs, the AOM, and the pump power of the third EDFA stage. Therefore, arbitrary pulse shapes on every channel can be created and controlled.

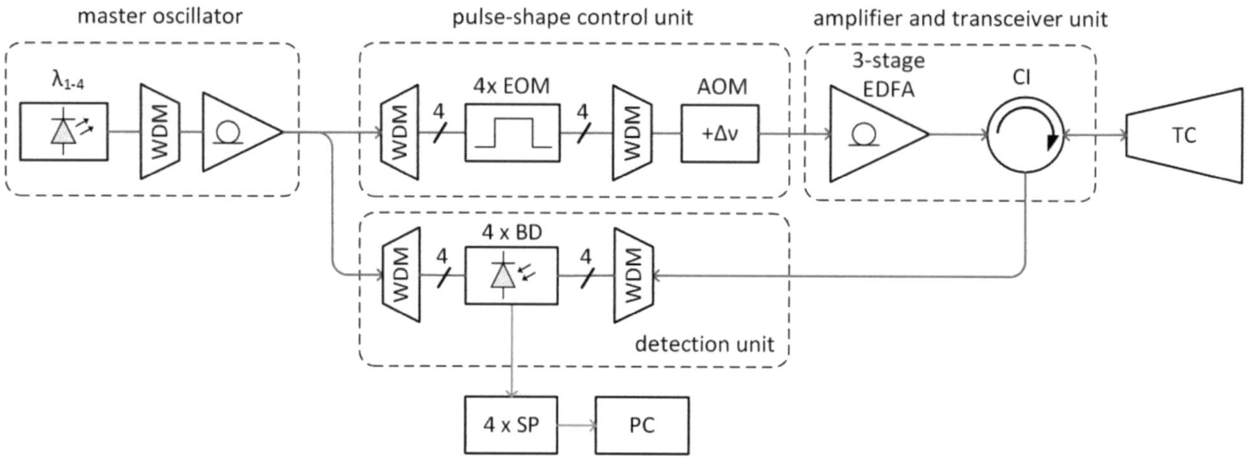

Figure 1. Overview of the multi-channel coherent Doppler lidar system.

Via a circulator (CI) the amplified and controlled pulses are directed to the telescope (TC). The backscattered light is guided to the detection unit, where the wavelengths of the local oscillator and the backscattered light are demultiplexed, thus, every channel can be mixed separately onto its balanced detector (BD). The amplified differential signal eliminates the DC and amplifies the AC component of the heterodyne signal. After analog signal processing (SP), the heterodyne signal is digitized and the raw data are sent to the personal computer (PC). An algorithm on the graphical processor extracts the information on wind velocity and signal strength in real time.

3. Multi-channel lidar system in high PRF mode

The signal-to-noise ratio (SNR) of atmospheric measurements with fiber-based lidar systems is typically below one. Hence, several pulses are transmitted successively and the measured data are averaged to enhance the detectability of the backscattered signal. The unambiguous range is $R_{max} = c/2f_{PRF}$, where f_{PRF} is the pulse repetition frequency (PRF) per channel. This is valid as long as the backscatter coefficient is constant along the line-of-sight. Under clear-air conditions the backscatter coefficient strongly decreases with height and the definition of the unambiguous range is correct. However, on cloudy days the return signal from clouds can be up to 25 dB higher [6]. If the chosen PRF is too high, those backscattered signals from clouds beyond the unambiguous range can significantly affect the measurement results.

An exemplary measurement in figure 2 shows the ambiguity due to a higher scatter intensity outside the unambiguous range. The abscissa represents the measurement time with a duration of 20 minutes, the ordinate the line-of-sight range, and the color bar in (a) the logarithmic signal amplitude and in (b) the measured radial velocity in the corresponding range gate. The depicted measurement starts with a PRF of 10 kHz and an elevation angle of 4°. With this configuration interfering signals from clouds were measured at a distance of about 3 km. The clouds were moving with ~8 m/s in the opposite direction to the wind close to the surface and are well visible in the velocity plot. After 6 minutes the elevation angle was changed to 30° for a duration of one minute. With this elevation angle the cloud ceiling was measured to be at an altitude of ~1600 m. From 8 to 16 minutes a PRF of 4 kHz and a 4° elevation angle were set to prevent ambiguity. The clouds appeared at a distance of about 18 km and no interfering signals were measured. By changing back to a PRF of 10 kHz, the backscattered signal from clouds beyond the unambiguous range appeared again at 2-3 km line-of-sight distance.

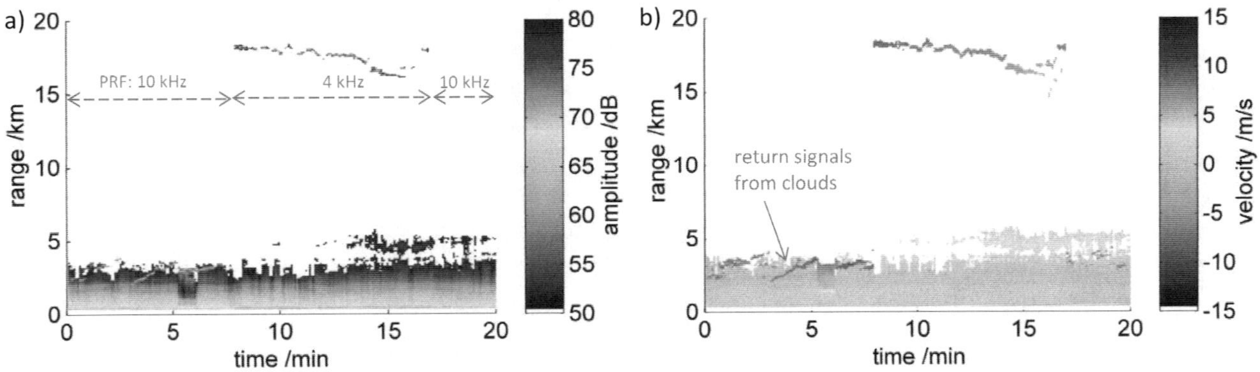

Figure 2. Measurement example of an ambiguity due to clouds.

To estimate the minimal required PRF, a constant backscatter coefficient of $1.3 \cdot 10^{-7}$ m^{-1}sr^{-1} is assumed. This value increases to $2.2 \cdot 10^{-5}$ m^{-1}sr^{-1} if clouds are the major scatterer [6]. The received SNR is predicted by the semianalytic lidar equation [7] with typical atmospheric values (one way transmittance: 0.96 km^{-1}, calm refractive turbulence parameter: $1 \cdot 10^{-16}$ m$^{-2/3}$) and shown in figure 3 as a function of range in black. The SNR of a cloud ceiling at 18 km distance is depicted in red. With an unambiguous range of 15 km the measured signal would appear at 3 km. Due to the higher SNR, the signal from outsight the unambiguous range significantly interferes with the clear-air signal in the vicinity of the lidar system. To suppress the probability of this disturbance, the PRF of single-channel coherent lidar systems has to be reduced to 4 kHz at least, which corresponds to an unambiguous range of 37.5 km. With this range the SNR of a cloud ceiling beyond the unambiguous range is >10 dB (blue) lower than the SNR of the clear-air scattering in the vicinity of the system and thus the interference would be negligible.

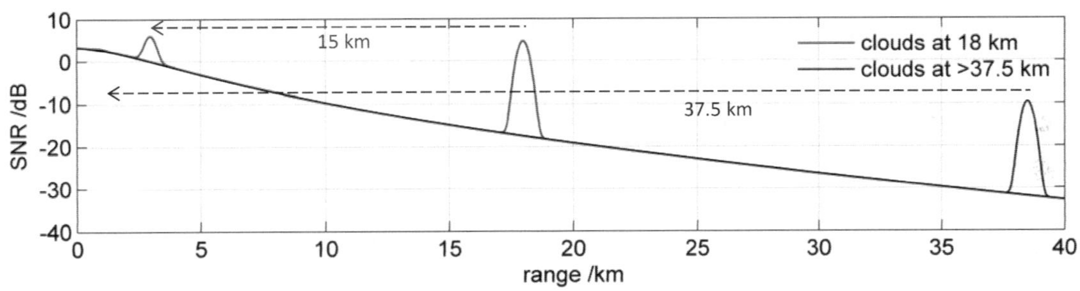

Figure 3. SNR as a function of range predicted by the lidar equation.

Due to the peak power limitation of fiber amplifiers, a lower PRF leads to lower detectability and thus to a longer required accumulation time. This downside of single-channel lidar systems is compensated by using multiple channels. With four independent channels the effective PRF is increased to 16 kHz with a corresponding unambiguous range of 37.5 km. Therefore, the multi-channel method reduces the probability of interference due to return signals from clouds outside the unambiguous range and enhances the performance of lidar systems commonly described by the basic figure-of-merit $FOM = E_P \cdot \sqrt{N \cdot f_{PRF}}$, where N is the number of channels and E_P the pulse energy per channel.

Principally, the number of channels is not limited with this multi-channel method and the PRF can be further increased. A possible limitation, using a single EDFA to amplify all channels simultaneously, is the required pump power. However, with multiple power amplifiers, for example one per channel, this limitation can be overcome.

4. Multi-channel observation with different pulse durations

This multi-channel lidar system enables atmospheric investigations with different pulse durations to be compared at the same time. For the following atmospheric measurement example, different pulse durations on two channels of the multi-wavelength system were used. The chosen full-width half-maximum (FWHM) durations were 300 ns and 600 ns. The rise- and fall-time of the controlled pulses were 30 ns. Figure 4a shows the two amplified square shaped pulses. The measured pulse energies were 2.2 µJ (300 ns) and 4.3 µJ (600 ns). The exact rectangular FFT-window (FFT: fast Fourier transformation) size is identical to the pulse durations on each channel. The resulting range gate weighting function (RWF) is the convolution of the probing pulse and the FFT-window, and the effective longitudinal size of the sensing volume is defined at $\Delta z = \mathrm{RWF}(0)^{-1}$ [8]. The calculated RWFs for both measured probing pulses are depicted in 4b, which results in $\Delta z = 46.1$ m for the shorter pulse and $\Delta z = 91.1$ m for the longer pulse.

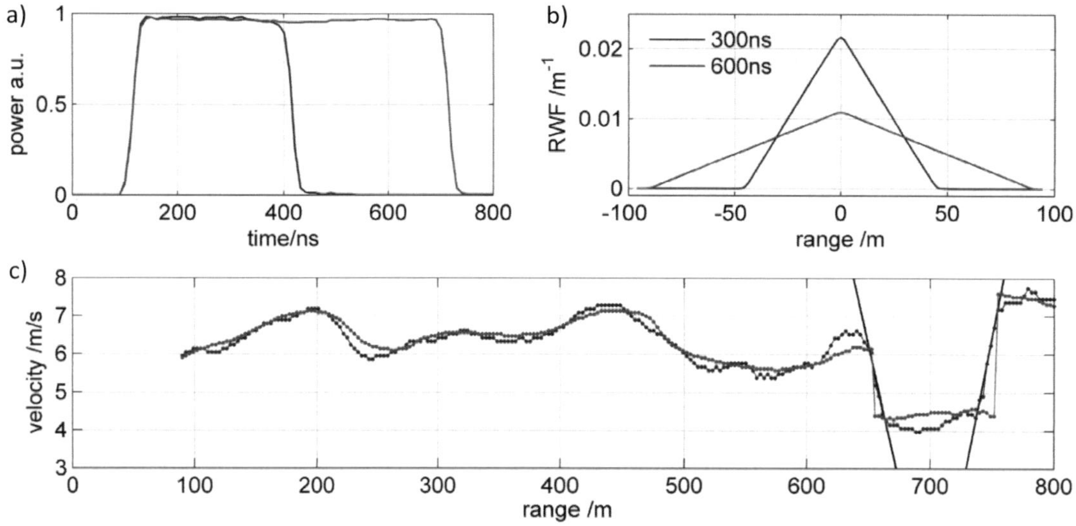

Figure 4. Atmospheric comparison measurement of different pulse durations.

The measured radial wind velocity over range is shown in figure 4c. The range gates were overlapped by 20 ns, which corresponds to a range resolution of 3 m for both channels. The shown line-of-sight velocity over range is the peak value of the averaged spectrum of 30,000 measurements. During that measurement the elevation angle was set to 5°.

As seen in 4a, the leading edges of both pulses are aligned. The measurement time for both pulses is equal to each pulse duration. Therefore, the first measurable range gate depicted in 4c corresponds to the center of both sensing volumes at 90 m. The channel with the longer pulse (red line) shows the wind structure more smoothed along the line-of-sight than the shorter pulse. A possible reason could be the influence of noise on the velocity precision. This was excluded by averaging the data for about 20 s to provide a velocity precision < 0.1 m/s over the whole range. The actual reason for the smoothing effect is the different size of the sensing volume of both channels. Due to the smaller sensing volume of the shorter pulse, the structure of the wind is determined in more detail. This can especially be seen around 650 m, where the blue channel estimates the velocity up to 0.5 m/s higher than the red channel.

In the vicinity of 700 m, strong changes of wind velocity are observed on both channels. Linear fitting to the velocity curve of the shorter pulse (black line) results in a wind shear dV/dz of -0.145 s^{-1} at 650 m and of 0.165 s^{-1} at a distance of 750 m. Despite the small depth of this shear, this change in velocity is referred to as low level wind shear in this paper, as it is defined by ICAO to 5 knots per 100 feet (0.085 s^{-1}) for moderate wind shear [9].

Using the multi-channel lidar with different pulse lengths, the longer pulses can be used to separate two existing wind velocities in one sensing volume, while with the shorter pulse the slope of those wind shears is determined more precisely. Figure 5 depicts these probing pulse properties in the frequency domain. 5a shows the wind shears measured with the longer pulse, where the velocities are well separated at 650 m and 750 m. In 5b, the spatial changes within the wind shears are measured more accurately. The center of the wind shear is at the point where the longer pulse measures both wind components with the same weighting, assuming a constant particle density within the sensing volume. Using this method, the first wind shear location is at (656 ± 3) m and the second wind shear is at a range of (752 ± 3) m.

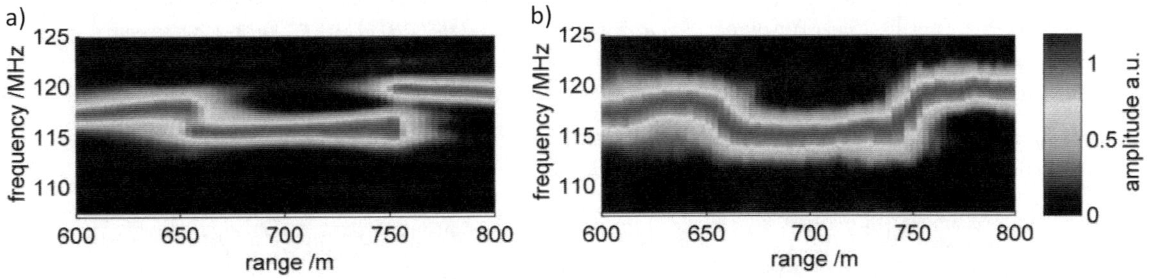

Figure 5. Measured wind shears in the frequency domain for different probing pulse lengths.

5. Conclusion

The developed multi-channel coherent Doppler lidar can be configured to work in high-PRF mode with enhanced unambiguous range and therefore performance is increased compared to conventional single-channel lidar systems. The channels of this multi-channel lidar can also be configured with different pulse lengths, allowing investigation of atmospheric phenomena with the corresponding Fourier-limited values.

6. References

[1] S. Kameyama, T. Ando, K. Asaka, Y. Hirano, and S. Wadaka, "Compact all-fiber pulsed coherent Doppler lidar system for wind sensing," Applied Optics, **46**, 1953-1962 (2007).

[2] N. S. Prasad, R. Sibell, S. Vetorino, R. Higgins, and A. Tracy, "An all-fiber, modular, compact wind lidar for wind sensing and wake vortex applications," in Laser Radar Technology and Applications XX; and Atmospheric Propagation XII, (Society of Photo-Optical Instrumentation Engineers, Baltimore, 2015), 94650C.

[3] D. Engin, B. Mathason, M. Stephen, A. Yu, H. Cao, J. Fouron, and M. Storm, "High energy, narrow linewidth 1572nm ErYb-fiber based MOPA for a multi-aperture CO_2 trace-gas laser space transmitter," in Fiber Lasers XIII: Technology, Systems, and Applications, Society of Photo-Optical Instrumentation Engineers, San Francisco, 2015), 97282S.

[4] C. F. Abari, X. Chu, R. M. Hardesty, and J. Mann, "A reconfigurable all-fiber polarization-diversity coherent Doppler lidar: principles and numerical simulations," Applied Optics, 54, 8999-9009 (2015).

[5] A. Töws and A. Kurtz, "A multi-wavelength LIDAR system based on an erbium-doped fiber MOPA-system," in Lidar Technologies, Techniques, and Measurements for Atmospheric Remote Sensing X, (Society of Photo-Optical Instrumentation Engineers, Amsterdam, 2014), 92460T.

[6] F. Boden, N. Lawson, H.W. Jentink, J. Kompenhans, *Advanced in-flight measurement techniques* (Springer, 2013), Chap. 12.

[7] S. Kameyama, T. Ando, K. Asaka, and Y. Hirano, "Semianalytic pulsed coherent laser radar equation for coaxial and apertured systems using nearest Gaussian approximation," Applied Optics, **49**, 5169-5174 (2010).

[8] V. Banakh and I. Smalikho, *Coherent Doppler wind lidars in a turbulent atmosphere* (Artech House, 2013).

[9] A. E. Richard, "Differentiating between types of wind shear in aviation forecasting," National Weather Digest, **24**(3), 39-51 (2000).

Wind Turbine Wake Characterizing using Coherent Wind Lidar

Songhua Wu, Xiaochun Zhai, Bingyi Liu, Changzhong Feng and Jintao Liu
Ocean Remote Sensing Institute, Ocean University of China
No. 238, Songling Road, Qingdao, China
wush@ouc.edu.cn

Abstract: Wind power is growing fast as one of the most promising renewable energy sources. When the wind turbine generator (WTG) extracts power from the wind, the wake evolves and leads to a considerable reduction in the efficiency of the actual power generation. The wake effect also leads to the increase of fatigue loads that reduce the life time of WTGs. In this work, a Pulsed Coherent Doppler Lidar (PCDL) is used to characterize the WTG wakes, which has high updating rate of 4 Hz and variable spatial resolution from 15 to 60 m. Field experiments were performed in the onshore and offshore wind parks from 2013 to 2015. Techniques based on a single Doppler Lidar were employed for elucidating main features of turbine wakes, including velocity deficit, wake dimension, velocity profile, 2D wind vector, turbulence dissipation rate and turbulence intensity under different conditions of surface roughness.

Keywords: Coherent Lidar, Wind turbine, Wake characteristics.

1. Introduction

Wind power generation is rapidly growing as one of the most promising renewable energy sources. When the turbine extracts power from the wind, the vortex evolves and moves downwind to form the turbine wake. Turbine wake characteristics of wind turbines have been studied since 1980s. Current industry standard for wind turbine wake measurements is the use of an in situ meteorological mast with wind cup and vane anemometers on it [1]. Because of the global growth of wind energy, techniques such as ultrasonic anemometer, profilers and SODAR (Sonic Detection and Ranging) are increasingly being used to measure wind wake [2].

As compared with the techniques mentioned above, the coherent Doppler Lidar (Light Detection and Ranging) has enabled high spatial and temporal resolution measurements of wind fields [3]. Krishnamurthy et al. presented the utilization of a commercial WindTracer Lidar to calculate spatially varying wind power density distribution in an ongoing wind assessment study [4]. The research of wind turbine wake detected by a continuous-wave CDL was done by Bingöl et al. [5] and Trujillo et al. [6]. Jungo et al [7] used scanning Lidar to analyze the velocity components over the vertical symmetry plane of the wind turbine wake. Banta et al. [8] studied the 3D structure of turbine wake using 3D volume scan patterns by a 2 μm wavelength high peak power laser system, which was a part of a field campaign generally reported by Smalikho et al. [9].

The objective of this paper is to use a PCDL with relatively high spatial resolution and sampling rate to visualize the WTGs wakes and to characterize the geometry and dynamics of wakes. The PCDL specifications and retrieval methods are described in Section 2. Field experiments to visualize and characterize WTG wakes are described in Section 3. A brief conclusion is given in Section 4.

2. Methodology

The PCDL is based on all-fiber laser technology and fast digital-signal-processing technology [10]. Because of the all-fiber structure adoption, the system is stable, reliable and high-integrated. In order to capture turbine wakes, different scan strategies are used to scan horizontal or vertical sections back and forth to track the wake. The highlights of the Lidar include the flexible range resolution from 15 to 60 m and relatively high sampling rate. The finest resolution of 15 m is useful for the detection of small scale wakes. The duration of measurement of one LOS velocity equals 0.25 s, which increases the temporal sampling rate up to 4 Hz and therefore reduces uncertainty in an averaged wind measurement.

The initial velocity deficit depends on the amount of momentum extracted by the turbine from the ambient flow, and the velocity deficit in a wake is defined as:

$$VD(z) = \frac{\bar{v}_{amb}(z) - v_{wake}(z)}{\bar{v}_{amb}(z)} \times 100\% \tag{1}$$

where $\bar{v}_{amb}(z)$ is the mean ambient wind velocity outside of the wake, and $v_{wake}(z)$ is the minimum velocity at each range gate distance z within the wake downstream, quantifying the downwind extent of the wake. The wake length is defined to be the location where the $VD(z)$ has minimum value. Figure 2 (a) shows that the location of these minimum values, plotted as black plus signs, were not necessarily located symmetrically within the wake, and the ambient wind velocity is shown in blue solid line. Figure 2 (b) shows the velocity deficit behind WTG A, and it can be seen that the maximum velocity deficit and wake length is 44.95 %, 0.63 km, respectively.

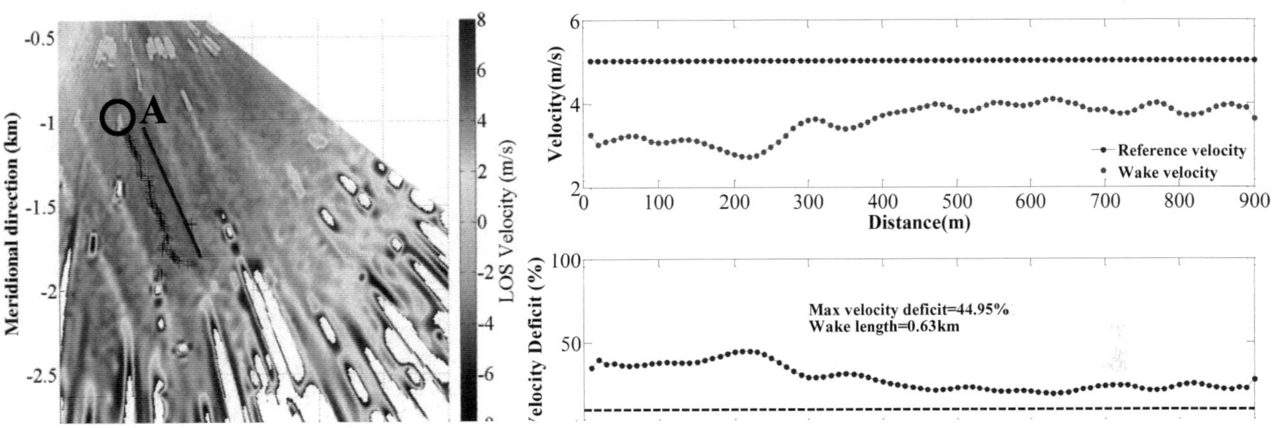

(a) **(b)**

Figure 2. (a) Conical sector scan performed at an elevation angle of 1.5° at 1930 BJT 15 Nov, 2014 in Hami gobi desert wind park, (b) Ambient wind velocity in red dot, wake area velocity in blue dot (upper), and the corresponding velocity deficit in blue dot (bottom)

To analyze the influence of atmospheric turbulence on the turbine wake using PCDL, the 2D wind field by arc PPI measurements is used. The turbulence energy dissipation rate (TEDR) is retrieved based on the structure function of 2D LOS wind velocity. Herein the transverse structure function is used to retrieve the TEDR since it has better vertical resolution and the errors, introduced by the anisotropy, is smaller than the longitudinal structure function's. This method has been described in detail by Frehlich and Cornman [11]. Figure 3 shows the structure function using different models. From the fit to the $D_{wgt-calculate}(s)$, we derived the value of $\sigma = 0.540\ m/s$ and $L_0 = 147.4\ m$, then the values for $L_i = 110.1\ m$ and $\varepsilon = 0.001\ m^2/s^3$ can be calculated from Equation.2, Equation.3, respectively.

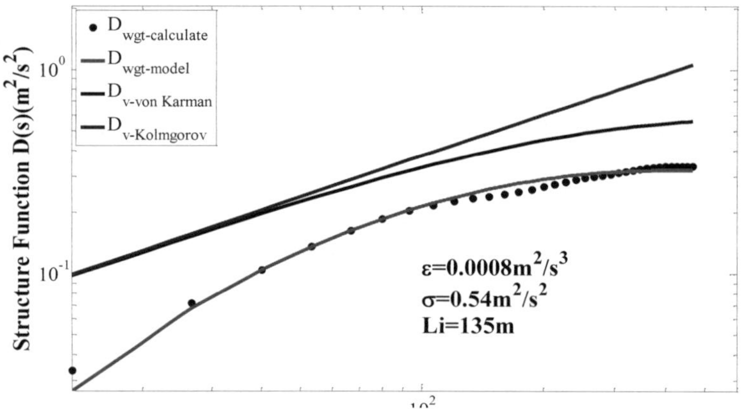

Figure 2. Transverse structure function estimates of turbulence using single PPI scanning at 1833 BJT 10 April, 2014 in Rudong tidal zone wind park with an elevation angle $\theta = 3^\circ$ range-gate distance $R = 1.275km$.

$$\varepsilon = [\frac{2^{1/3}\pi}{\sqrt{3}\Gamma(1/3)\Gamma(4/3)}]\frac{\sigma^3}{L_0} = 0.933668\frac{\sigma^3}{L_0} \tag{2}$$

$$L_i = \frac{\sqrt{\pi}\Gamma(5/6)}{\Gamma(1/3)}L_0 = 0.7468343L_0 \tag{3}$$

3. Results

In order to understand the wake characteristics in a real ambient, we performed field experiments with different topographies and surface roughness to study the turbulent wind field in the vicinity of operating WTGs in the onshore and offshore wind parks from 2013 to 2015. The first field campaign was carried out in Longgang mountain wind park shown in Figure 3 (a). The complex terrain can cause inhomogeneous flow conditions and disturb turbine wakes with more complicated behaviors. The second and third field campaign were carried out in Rudong tidal zone wind park shown in Figure 3 (b). The water covered surface and mud flat in the intertidal zone produced a more homogeneous surface with lower roughness, hence producing distinct turbine wakes with extended its longitudinal dimensions as shown in Figure 4 (b). The fourth field experiment was performed at Hami gobi desert wind park with a flat desert topography shown in Figure 3 (c). In the Lidar measurements at Gobi plain area, turbines formed wide and long wakes extending for 2 km as shown in Figure 4 (c).

Figure 3. Wind flow measurement with PCDL in (a) Longgang Mountain (b) Rudong tidal zone and (c) Hami gobi desert area.

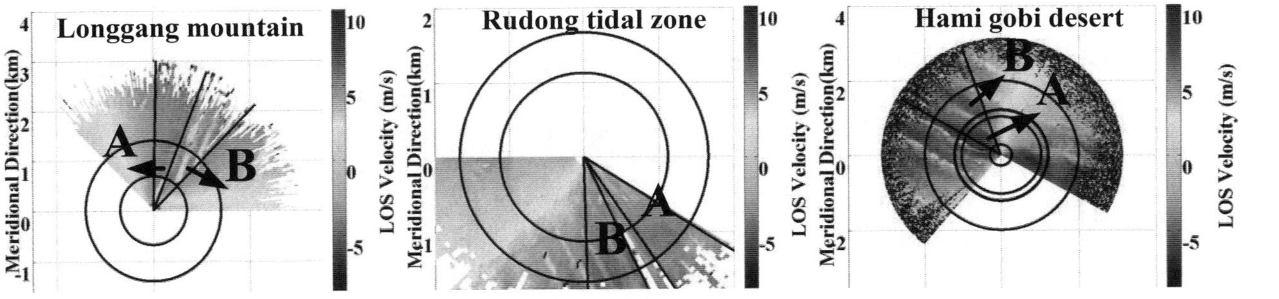

(a) (b) (c)

Figure 4. LOS wind field by PCDL PPI scanning mode at (a) Longgang Mountain, (b) Rudong tidal zone (c) Hami gobi desert area. The area A and B is the chosen ambient wind field and wake area, respectively.

In order to quantitatively compare the turbulent characteristics in the wind turbine wake area and ambient wind field in different topographies, the area with relatively distinct wake structures should be chosen as the wake area, which is marked A in Figure 4. Conversely, the ambient wind field which is seldom affected by the wind turbine is chosen marked B in Figure 4. After the determination of ambient wind area and corresponding wake area, the turbulent parameters including the TEDR ε, LOS turbulence intensity I_{LOS}, the standard deviation of transverse velocity fluctuations σ_{LOS}, turbulence integral scale L_i can be retrieved using structure function method mentioned above.

Figure 5 shows the averaged turbulence characteristics in ambient wind area A and wake area B in three wind parks, respectively. It can be seen that the experiment was mostly carried out under conditions of weak turbulence ($10^{-3} \le \varepsilon \le 10^{-2}$), and Rudong tidal zone ambient wind area has relatively higher I_{LOS} and σ_{LOS}, since during the measurements, the sea surface temperature was 14°C - 15.4 °C along the coastline and higher than the air temperature around 13°C in the nighttime. This temperature gradient may bring in surface turbulence created by thermal convection. As for the wake area, Longgang mountain area and Rudong tidal zone area have transferred into strong turbulence condition, however, although the ε in Hami gobi desert wake area is more than 10 times of its ambient wind areas', it is still in relative weak turbulence conditions. Different surface roughness may lead to obviously different turbulence characteristics in these areas.

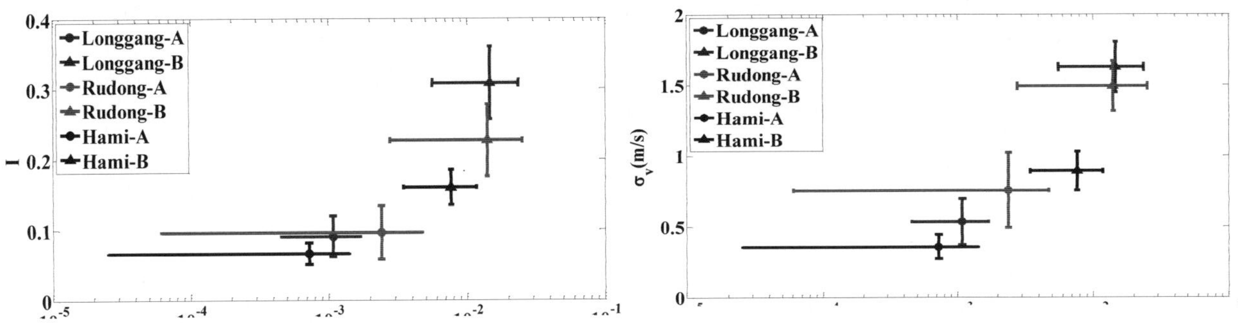

(a) (b)

Figure 5. Averaged turbulence characteristics in ambient wind area and wake area under three wind parks

4. Conclusion

In this research, four field experiments with different topographies and surface roughness have been carried out to study the turbulent wind field in the vicinity of operating WTGs in the onshore and offshore wind parks. The turbulence characteristics such as the turbulence energy dissipation rate and turbulence intensity have been retrieved and compared quantitatively in ambient wind area and wake area under different topographies in the analyzed time period. It is found that the ε, T_{LOS} and σ_{LOS} in wake area is 7.8, 2.6, 2.3 times of the ambient areas', respectively. All of these three ambient areas are in the weak turbulence conditions. On the contrary, Longgang mountain area and Rudong tidal zone area have transferred into strong turbulence condition in wake areas, but it is still in relative weak turbulence conditions in Hami gobi desert wake area, showing different surface roughness may lead to obviously different turbulence characteristics in these areas.

Acknowledgements

This work was partly supported by the National Natural Science Foundation of China (NSFC) under grant 41471309 and 41375016.

5. References

[1] F. B. Amar, M. Elamouri, and R. Dhifaoui, "Energy assessment of the first wind farm section of Sidi Daoud, Tunisia," Renew. Energy A **33**(10), 2311–2321 (2008).

[2] R. J. Barthelmie, G. C. Larsen, S. T. Frandsen, L. Folkerts, K. Rados, S. C. Pryor, B. Lange, and G. Schepers, "Comparison of wake model simulations with offshore wind turbine wake profiles measured by sodar," J. Atmos. Oceanic Technol. A **23**(7), 888–901 (2006).

[3] U. Högström, D. N. Asimakopoulos, H. Kambezidis, C. G. Helmis, and A. Smedman, "A field study of the wake behind a 2MW wind turbine," Atmos. Environ. A **22**(4), 803–820 (1988).

[4] R. Krishnamurthy, A. Choukulkar, R. Calhoun, J. Fine, A. Oliver, and K. Barr, "Coherent Doppler lidar for wind farm characterization," Wind Energy (Chichester Engl.) **16**(2), 189–206 (2013).

[5] F. Bingöl, J. Mann, and G. C. Larsen, "Light detection and ranging measurements of wake dynamics, part I: onedimensional scanning," Wind Energy A **13**(1), 51–61 (2010).

[6] J. Trujillo, F. Bingol, G. Larsen, J. Mann, and M. Kuhn, "Light detection and ranging measurements of wake dynamics. Part II: Two-dimensional scanning," Wind Energy A **14**(1), 61–75 (2011).

[7] G. Iungo, Y. Wu, and F. Porteagel, "Field Measurements of Wind Turbine Wakes with Lidars," J. Atmos. Ocean. Technol. **30**(2), 274–287 (2013).

[8] G. Iungo, Y. Wu, and F. Porteagel, "Field Measurements of Wind Turbine Wakes with Lidars," J. Atmos. Ocean. Technol. **30**(2), 274–287 (2013).

[9] I. N. Smalikho, V. A. Banakh, Y. L. Pichugina, W. A. Brewer, R. M. Banta, J. K. Lundquist, and N. D. Kelley, "Lidar investigation of atmosphere effect on a wind turbine wake," J. Atmos. Oceanic Technol. A **30**(11), 2554–2570 (2013).

[10] S. H. Wu, B. Y. Liu, J. T. Liu, X. C. Zhai, C. Z. Feng, G. N. Wang, H. W. Zhang, J. P. Yin, X. T. Wang, R. Z. Li, D. Gallacher, "Wind turbine wake visualization and characteristics analysis by Doppler lidar," Opt Express, **24**(10), A762-A780 (2016).

[11] R. Frehlich and L. Cornman, "Estimating spatial velocity statistics with coherent Doppler lidar," J. Atmos. Ocean. Technol. **19**(3), 355–366 (2002).

Long range off-shore wind assessment by high power scanning Lidars

Matthieu Boquet (a), Philippe Royer (a), Vincent Pureur (a), Jean-Pierre Cariou (a), Megan Smith (b)

(a) LEOSPHERE, Orsay, France, (b) Carbon Trust, London, UK
mboquet@leosphere-avent.com

Abstract: A specific and world-première set-up for evaluating the potential of long-range scanning Doppler Lidar to serve wind energy applications has been organized by the CarbonTrust (UK) in the Dublin bay, Ireland. In this experiment the scanning Lidars are located on the Dublin bay shore and measure over the sea. Leosphere has deployed 2 scanning Lidars: the standard WINDCUBE 400S product and a prototype that is designed to considerably increase the measurement range. Additionally 3 vertical profiler WINDCUBE Lidars are located at ranges from 6 to 14km from the scanning Lidars, offering the possibility to wind speed measurement accuracy comparison. In this paper we propose to show the different Lidars performances in term of measurement ranges and wind speed accuracy, and analyze the specific atmospheric conditions that contributes to the different performances between the standard product and the prototype scanning Lidar.

Keywords: Coherent Wind Doppler Lidar, offshore wind assessment

1. Introduction

From several years now the wind energy industry is targeting the development of offshore wind farms, in part because of the possibility to build larger wind farms with higher and more stable winds available than onshore. This ambition requires developing specific methods to harness the energy resource available offshore: for instance platforms equipped with met masts, floating buoy mounted with Lidar and long-range scanning Lidar deployed on the cost. This latter option has raised the interest of several offshore wind energy players because the solution presents several economic and operational advantages.

Therefore, the UK based consultancy Company the Carbon Trust leading the Offshore Wind Accelerator program has launched a specific project aiming at evaluating the potential of long-range scanning Lidars to accurately and safely harness the offshore wind resource from the shore. LEOSPHERE and Lockheed Martin Technology have proposed their Lidar technologies in the project, which have been deployed and operated in the Dublin Bay by the UK Wind farm developer and consultancy RES.

In this paper, the LEOSPHERE long-range scanning Lidar technology, WINDCUBE 400S, is presented along with the project set-up and initial results if the measurement campaign which started early January 2016 to finish end of May 2016.

2. WINDCUBE Lidar Technology

Leosphere is developing pulsed fiber Doppler lidars for more than 10 years, based on a technology formerly developed at ONERA ([1], [2] and [3]). The core technology is using EDFA (Erbium Doped

Fiber Amplifiers) operating around 1,55µm in the telecom C band, and an all-fiber architecture. The high pulse repetition frequency (PRF) efficiently compensates the relative low pulse energy. Moreover, the MOPA architecture flexibility in terms of pulse duration allows fulfilling a large variety of requirements, enabling the design of high spatial resolution or long range systems.

The next figure describes the architecture of LEOSPHERE pulsed fibered lidars.

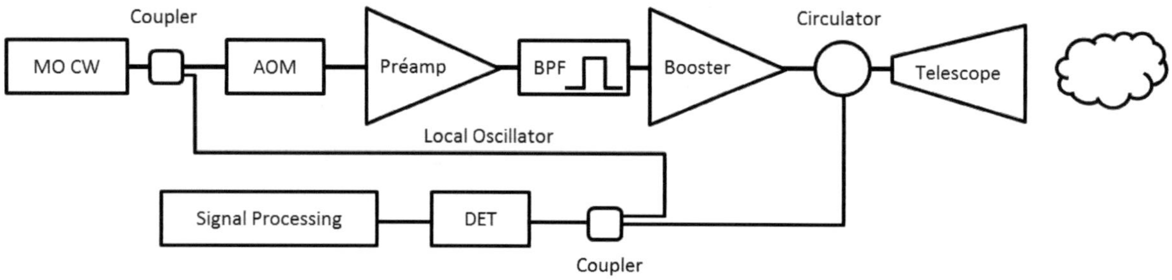

Figure 1 Architecture of fibered pulsed lidars

An endless rotation scanning head steers the beam in the full hemisphere, for either fixed line of sight, DBS, PPI, RHI, or customized scanning patterns.

Besides commercial products, Leosphere is testing new architectures to improve the Lidar performances. The RTA prototype integrates new features such as: increased energy and lower temporal ASE thanks to a larger LMA fiber, new generation circulator and optimized telescope, new fast scanning head. The max operational range is increased up to 14km, limited by the ambiguity distance associated with the high PRF.

Table 1. Lidar characteristics

Parameter	WINDCUBE400S	Proto RTA
Wavelength	1.54µm	1.54µm
PRF	10kHz	10kHz
Pulse duration	800ns	800ns
Energy	160µJ	240µJ
Telscope aperture	120mm	120mm
Recommended integration time	0.5 to 2s	0.15 to 1s
Max Acquisition Range	15km	15km
Recommended range resolution	200m	200m
Velocity range	-30m/s to +30m/s	-30m/s to +30m/s
Recommended scanning velocity	1 to 6°/s	1 to 18°/s

3. Campaign set-up

The campaign took place in the Dublin Bay, Ireland because the specific location has offered the possibility to locate several scanning Lidars on the cost as well as vertical profiler Lidars used for the validation offshore. The map below indicates the locations of the Lidars:

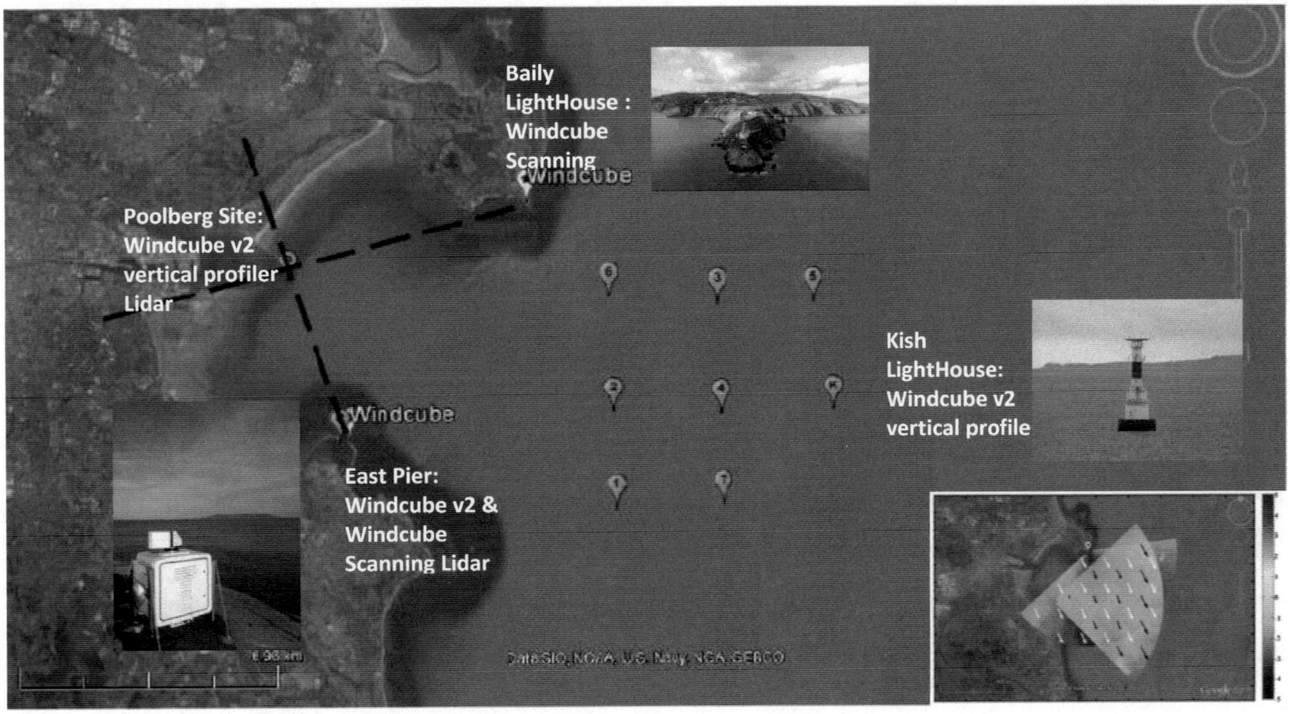

Figure 2 Measurement campaign set-up with locations of Lidars

The scanning scenarios of the Windcube 400S and prototype RTA have been defined such as horizontal wind speeds and directions could be derived from the raw measurements at selected locations and heights. Those locations comprise:

- The validation points where reference Windcube vertical profiler Lidars are deployed, ie. respectively ~10km and 13km from the scanning Lidar for the further one
- The demonstration points (indicated with red dots on the maps above)
- 2 measurement heights have been targeted: 100m and 150m above mean sea level

4. Preliminary observations

The long-range scanning Lidars have been evaluate for both their data availability at long distances (above 10km) and their capacity to accurately retrieve 10min averaged horizontal wind speeds and directions at those high distances. The graphs below respectively show the Lidars data availability over the campaign (60% of data availability at 10km is observed for the Windcube 400S, increased to 82% for the prototype scanning Lidar), and the 10min averaged wind speed and direction time series that are calculated from the raw Lidar data, using the dedicated LaserCup algorithm.

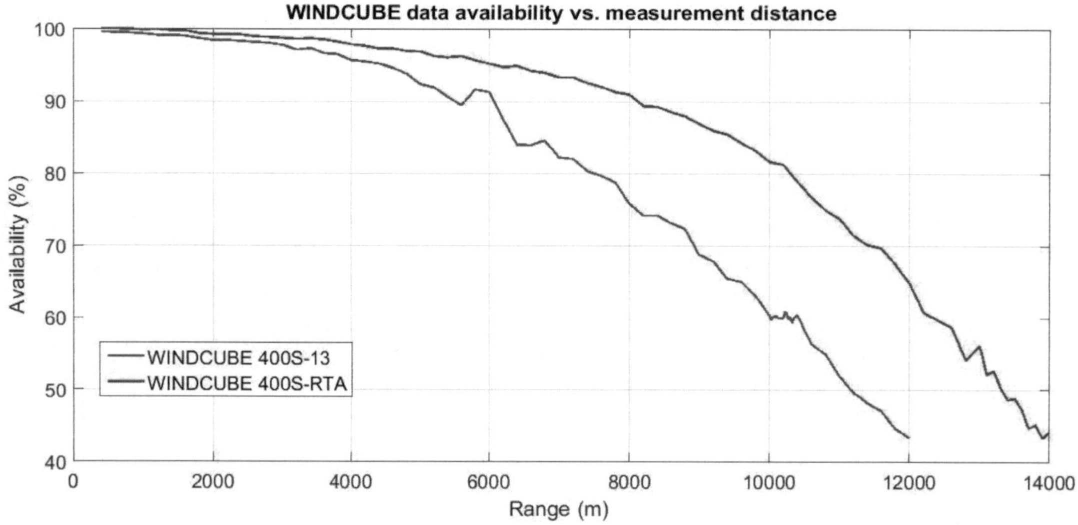

Figure 3 WINDCUBE 400S-13 data availability vs. measurement distance for the entire data set

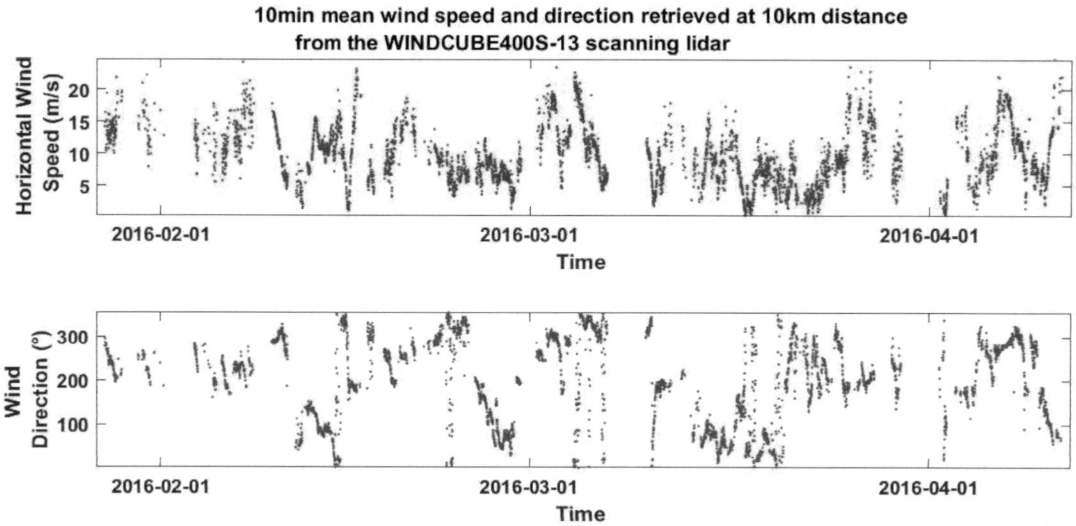

Figure 4 WINDCUBE 400S-13 calculated 10min averaged wind speed and direction at 10km distance from the Lidar

The wind data derived from the long-range scanning Lidars may then be used to evaluate the wind resource map over the sea area, covering around 200km^2 with wind speed and direction information. The evaluation of the wind variations over the area and going further from the coast into the sea is a crucial piece of information for wind farm developers.

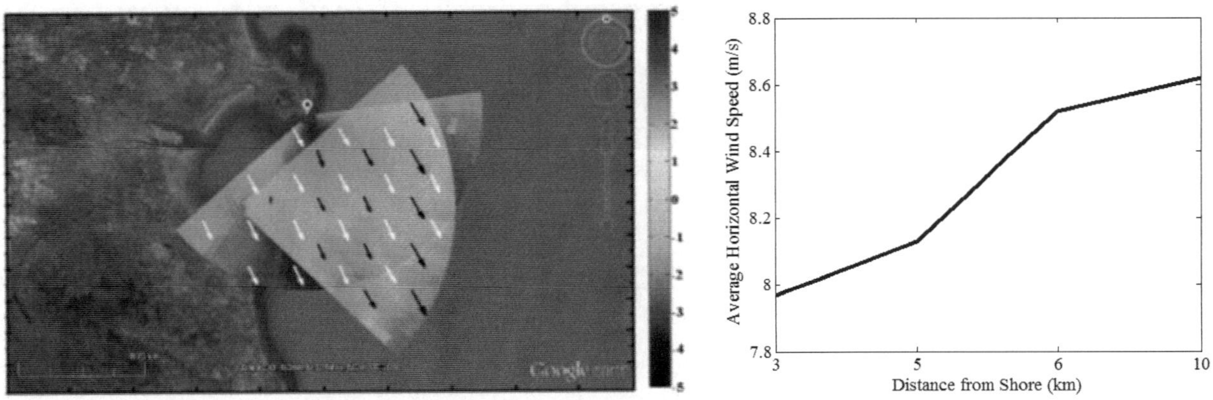

Figure 5 Wind speed map over the area and wind speed variation with distance from the shore.

5. Conclusions and perspectives

Long-range scanning wind Lidar are finding an interesting application in the wind energy industry: measuring the wind resource offshore from the shore. Although the concept is relatively new, it is gaining a lot of attraction because of the operational and economic advantages it may offer. For the industry to accept such instruments in the development of future wind farms, it is key to first validate their real capacity in terms of data availability and accuracy. This is the objective of the Carbon Trust funded project involving the Windcube 400S and its evolution prototype, for which a 5 months measurement campaign in the Dublin Bay has been performed. Up to day, the operational results are over expectations with almost 100% availability of the instruments through the entire measurement campaign, while preliminary assessment of the data availability above 10km range is looking very promising, as well as the initial verification of the retrieved wind data.

6. References

[1] Koroshetz, J. E., 2005: Fiber lasers for lidar, in Optical Fiber Communication Conference and Exposition and the National Fiber Optic Engineers Conference, Technical Digest, Optical Society of America, paper OFJ4.

[2] Targ, R., Kavaya, M. J., Huffaker, R. M., and Bowles, R. L., 1991: Coherent lidar airborne windshear sensor: performance evaluation, Applied Optics, Vol. 30, Issue 15, pp. 2013-2026, doi: 10.1364/AO.30.002013.

[3] Valla, M., 2005: Study of a pulsed doppler lidar based on an erbium fiber amplifier for wind field measurements in the boundary layer of the atmosphere, Ph.D thesis, Ecole Nationale Supérieure des Télécommunications, http://www.theses.fr/2005ENST0030.

Atmospheric features as captured by scanning Doppler lidar and predicted by NWP modelling systems in complex terrain

Pichugina Y. (a, b), A. Brewer (b), C. Clack, Banta (b), A. Choukulkar, J. Olson, M. Marquis (b), J. Kenyon, S. Baidar, T. Bonin, A. Weickmann, S. Sandberg (b) and R. Hardesty

(a) Cooperative Institute for Research in Environmental Sciences, Boulder

(b) National Oceanic and Atmospheric Administration, Boulder

Abstract: The paper presents case studies of atmospheric features, captured by scanning Doppler lidar measurements during the Wind Forecast improvement Project-2 (WFIP-2) in the complex terrain of the Columbia River Valley. This 18-month long project, sponsored by DOE and NOAA, is aiming to improve forecasting of wind flow complicated by mountainous terrain, coastal effects, and the presence of numerous wind farms in this area. In addition to the analysis of the observed meteorological events, a high-precision Doppler lidar data are being used to validate the ability of National Weather Prediction (NWP) models to forecast wind flow at the heights of wind turbine rotors and above. Preliminary results on lidar-captured wind-flow features, along with examples of model validation by lidar data, are described

Keywords: Doppler pulsed lidar, wind forecasting, complex terrain

1. Introduction

Reducing the cost of wind energy and mitigating risks associated with wind plant operations require better forecasts of overall weather conditions and particularly wind flow variability at the heights of wind turbine rotors. To improve numerical weather prediction (NWP) forecasting of winds in complex terrain the Second Wind Forecast Improvement Project (WFIP-2) is taking place in the Columbia River Basin in the states of Oregon and Washington, USA. (Fig.1a). This 18-month research experiment uses the expertise of scientists and engineers from several universities, government laboratories, and private companies to investigate atmospheric phenomena that affect model accuracy in complex terrain and improve model physics using measurements from variety of conventional and remote-sensing instruments deployed to the study area.

2. Study area and lidar locations

The Google map of the study area located east of the Cascade Mountain Range is shown on Figure 1a. Several high-elevation mountains, the Columbia River canyon, and local terrain features as well as the presence of numerous wind farms create complex wind flows. Along with other instruments, two scanning pulsed Doppler lidars were deployed by NOAA/ESRL in September 2015 to two sites about 40 km apart (Figure 1b) to provide accurate, detailed wind profiles from the surface up through the boundary layer in real-time.

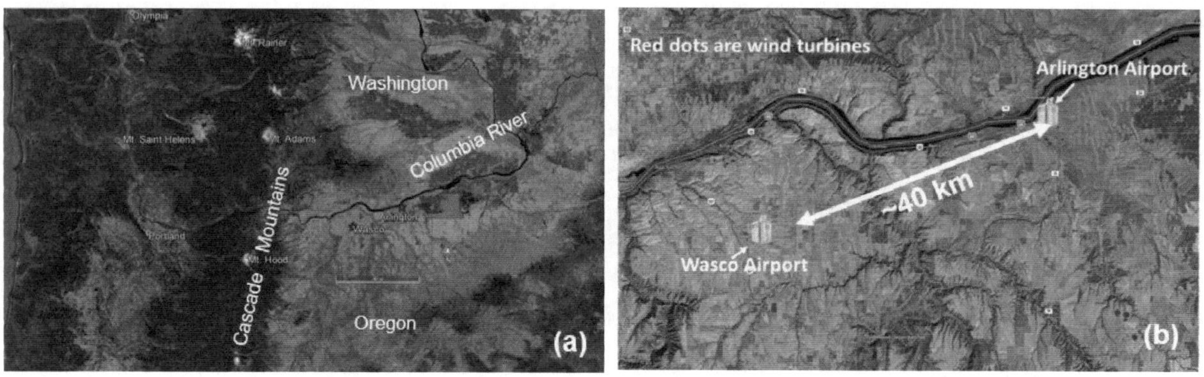

Figure 1. (a) Complex terrain of the Columbia River Basin. The WFIP 2 study areas showed by the blue rectangles. (b) Location of NOAA Doppler lidars (200S) at Wasco site at 469 m AGL and Arlington site at 179 m AGL. The surrounding wind turbines are indicated by the red symbols.

The lidar measurement routine includes a combination of multiple azimuthal scans, elevation scans, and vertical staring profiling, repeated every 15 min. Individual scan data, as well as computed, high vertical resolution profiles of wind speed, direction, and 3 wind vector components, provide critical information on wind flow variability (wakes, ramps, diurnal fluctuations), LLJs, rotor-layer shear, and turbulence. Some examples of wind flow features observed from lidar measurements are shown in the next section.

3. Capturing wind flow events

4.1 Wind turbine wakes

Deployment of two identical lidars to separate sites allows diurnal wind flow variability to be monitored at each site and between sites as illustrated in Figure 2a. The western lidar at Wasco documents an inflow profile upstream of the wind farms, whereas the eastern lidar at Arlington shows how flow changes due to distance and how wind farms affect the shape and magnitude of the wind profile, when the flow is from a westerly direction. Measurements obtained upstream and downstream of the local wind farms provide an opportunity to study turbine wake effects. An example of wakes downwind of the turbine array is shown in Figure 2b. West-south-westerly winds in the rotor layer at the Wasco site (Fig. 2a) create wakes downwind of a line of turbines, as observed by lidar at the Arlington site on October 1, 2015 during azimuthal (conical) scanning at 2.5^0 elevation angle. Velocity reductions of 3-4 ms^{-1} were detected up to ~1 km downstream of wind turbines for several hours through this day.

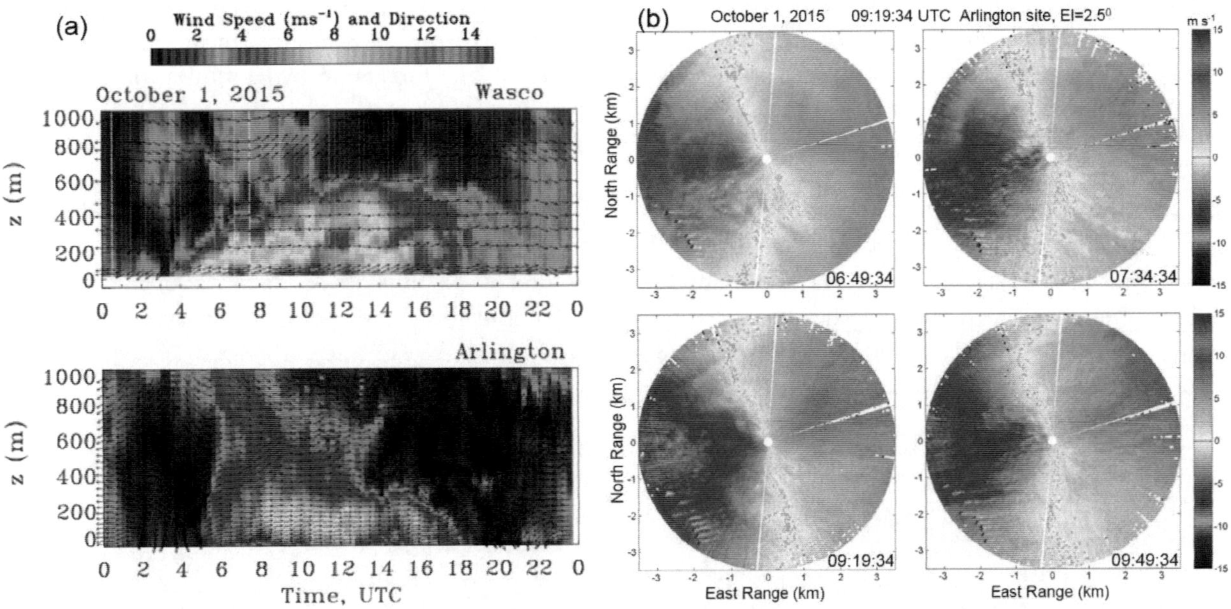

Figure 2 (a) Time height cross sections of wind speed and direction from lidar measurements at 2 sites. Wind speed is color coded from 0 to 15 m/s, black arrows show wind direction. (b) Conical azimuth scan at 2.5 elevation at the Arlington site shows a mean westerly flow over the scan disk. Several parallel streaks, representing wind turbine wakes can be seen in the southwest sector of each scan.

4.1 Wind ramps

Sudden changes in wind speed or wind direction (ramps) cause rapid changes in the power generated by the wind turbines and thus influence overall energy production. An example of an observed wind ramp event during May 7-10 at both sites is shown in Figure 3. On May 7 NE winds in the rotor layer were light at both sites. From May 8 through early morning on May 9 westerly winds increased up to ~20 ms^{-1}, as a strong

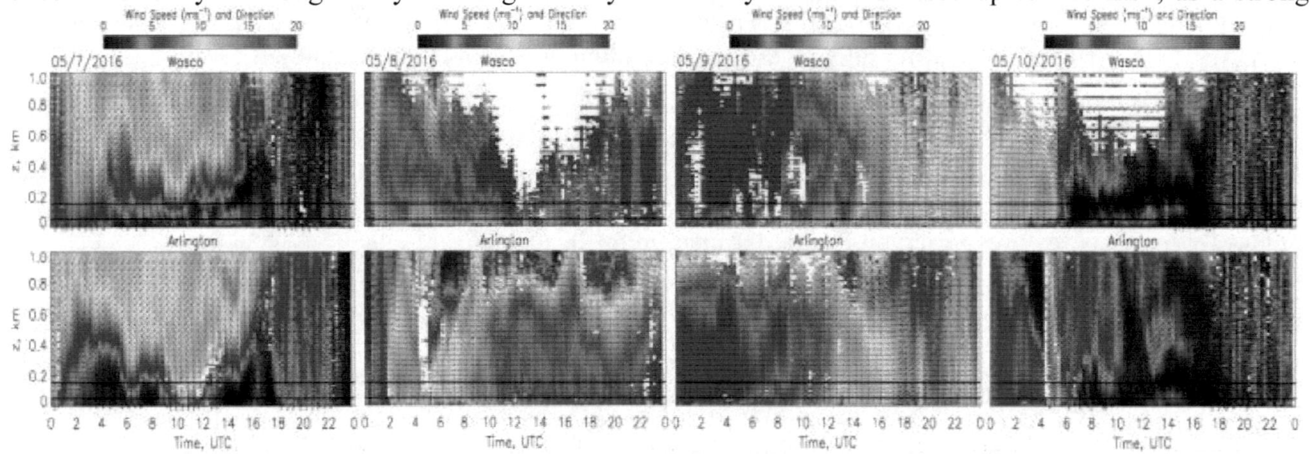

Figure 3. Time-height cross sections from lidar measurements during observed wind speed ramp event during May 7-10. Wind speed is scaled from 0 to 20 m/s. Two black horizontal lines indicate heights of the rotor layer (50-150 m).

offshore ridge pushed onto the coast. Then wind speeds abruptly decreased to 4-5 ms^{-1} during May 10, changing direction to NE. During this period the huge ramp in power production was reported by the BPA balancing authority. Note that winds at any given time at the Wasco site, compared to the Arlington site, indicate wind flow variations due to the distance, different elevations of the lidars, and the presence of wind turbines. This is an important issue for selecting a proper site for any measurement system. In addition to monitoring variability of winds, lidar data along with data from other instruments, model output, and satellite images are being used to assess meteorological conditions that may affect the accuracy of model forecasts as well as WE operations.

5 Model validation

In contrast to other instruments, lidar data are not assimilated into models, providing "independent" datasets for model verification and improvement. During WFIP 2 the high-precision Doppler lidar data are being used in real-time to validate the ability of NWP models to predict wind flow in the rotor layer and above (http://www.esrl.noaa.gov/csd/groups/csd3/measurements/wfip2/), and for post-processing analyses. Several models were validated and their domains are shown in Figure 4a.

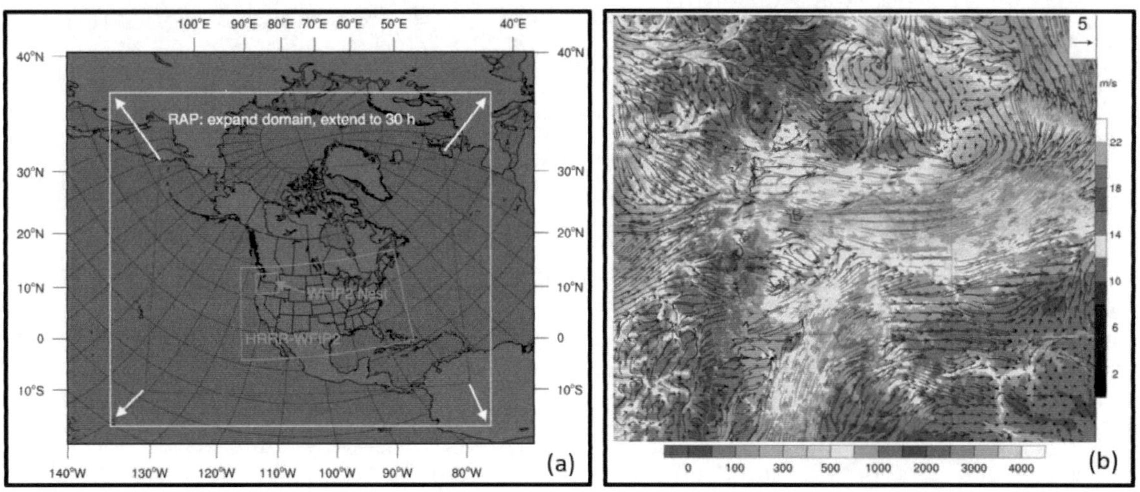

Figure 4. (a) Domains of WFIP 2 models. (b) Modeled wind flow at 80 m superimposed on area topography. (Both plots are courtesy of the NOAA Global Monitoring Division)

This paper will focus on the nested version of the High Resolution Rapid Refresh (HRRR-nest) model developed at ESRL for the WFIP2 experiment. The horizontal grid of this model is 750 m and outputs produced at 50 vertical levels. Forecasts are produced for 18 lead times. Modeled 80-m winds over HRRR-nest domain are shown in Figure 4b to illustrate the complexity of wind flow in the research area.

An example of measured and predicted wind flow at each site is illustrated in Figure 5a. Model captured major trends of wind speed and direction relatively well, but timing of wind ramps is not accurate. Details of rotor layer wind speed comparison statistics for this day are shown in Figure 5b

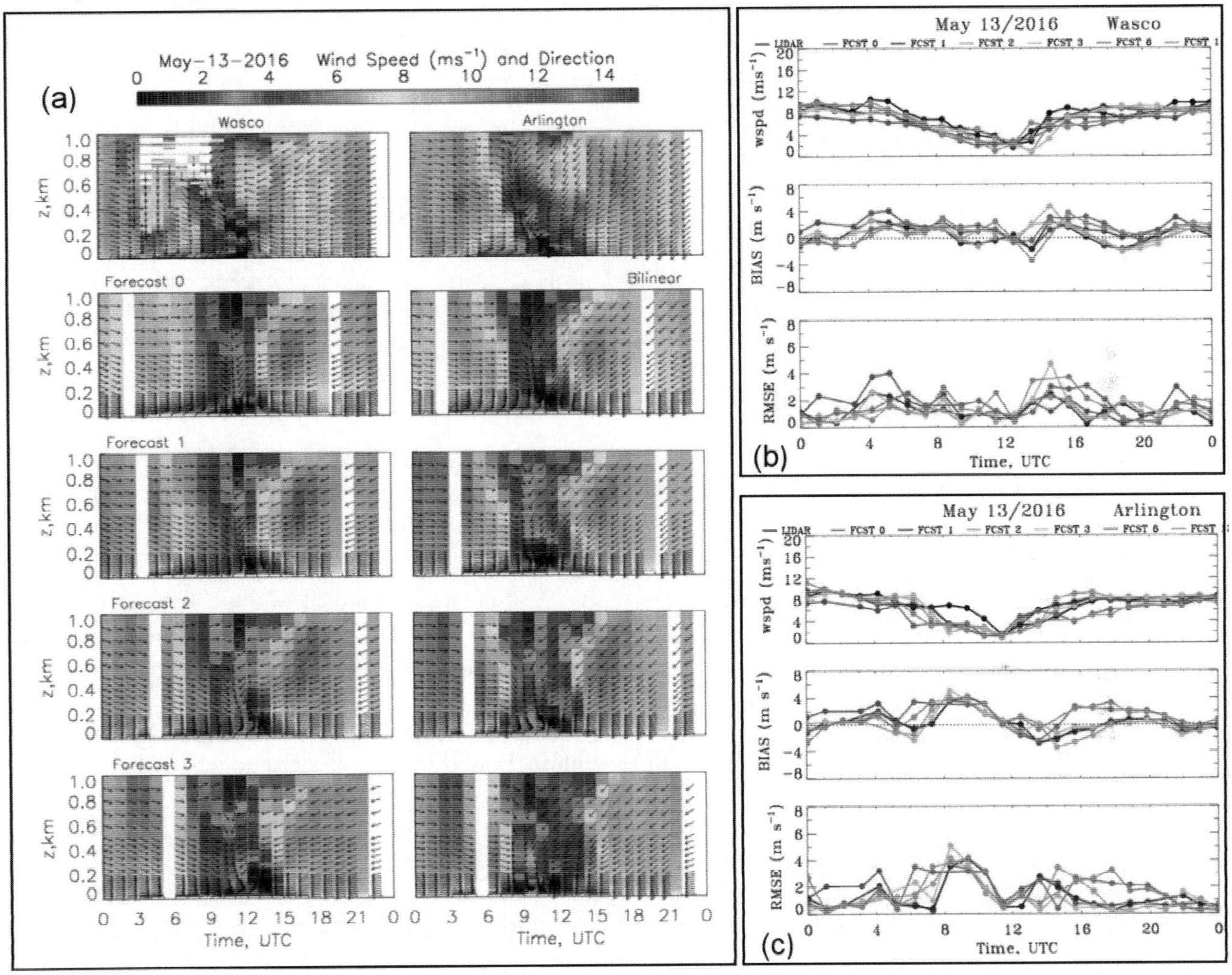

Figure 5. (a) Measured (top panels) and predicted wind flow for forecast hours 0-3 on May 13, 2016 are shown for (left panels) Wasco and (right panels) Arlington sites. (b) Time-series of the rotor-layer mean statistics between measured and modeled wind speed at (top) Wasco and (bottom) Arlington sites.

5 Conclusions

NOAA Doppler scanning lidars, along with other observing systems, provide comprehensive datasets to characterize complex terrain atmospheric phenomena that impact model accuracy, and to validate and improve model physics and wind forecasts.

Simultaneous Na and Fe Doppler Lidar Measurements of Wind and Temperature at Table Mountain

Xinzhao Chu, John A. Smith, Cao Chen, Jian Zhao, Yuli Han, Weichun Fong, Zhibin Yu, Wentao Huang, Ian F. Barry, and Muzhou Lu
Cooperative Institute for Research in Environmental Sciences
& Department of Aerospace Engineering Sciences
University of Colorado Boulder
216 UCB, CIRES, Boulder, CO 80309, USA
Lead Author e-mail address: xinzhao.chu@colorado.edu

Abstract: We present the simultaneous and common-volume Na and Fe Doppler lidar measurements of wind and temperature in the mesosphere and lower thermosphere (MLT) at Table Mountain, north of Boulder. This is the first ever measurements of the MLT region with two resonance Doppler lidars simultaneously, providing a unique opportunity to evaluate the two state-of-the-art Doppler lidar technologies. Such observations will also enable the sophisticated studies of two different meteoric metal species (Na and Fe) and how they respond to various physical and chemical processes.

Keywords: Resonance Doppler Lidar, Wind, Temperature, Meteoric Metal Layers, and MLT Region

1. Introduction

There are compelling scientific motivations to study the whole atmosphere from the ground to the thermosphere. Lying above the troposphere are the stratosphere, mesosphere and thermosphere. The natural upward extension of the Earth's atmosphere ultimately leads to its interaction with space above ~50 km altitude, where atmospheric neutral gases entwine with the dynamic plasma of space. The ionosphere, consisting of three main parts historically named as D, E, and F regions, is embedded in the mesosphere and thermosphere. This space-atmosphere interaction region is known to be essential for sustaining life on Earth by absorbing extreme radiation, ablating meteoric materials, dissipating energetic particles and fields from space, and regulating gaseous escape, while balancing the influences from the Earth itself in the form of wave energy and momentum originating from the lower atmosphere [1]. However, the properties and processes that govern the space-atmosphere interactions are not sufficiently described to fully understand their roles in atmosphere's development and evolution, largely owing to the lack of measurements with sufficient coverage, accuracy, precision, and resolution. Lidar measurements of neutral winds, temperatures, and species through the whole atmosphere certainly help address these challenges to enable explorations of the space-atmosphere interactions.

Profiling wind and temperature in the middle and upper atmosphere demands lidar technologies beyond coherent Doppler lidars, namely the direct-detection Doppler lidars for wind measurements and various techniques for temperature measurements including Rayleigh and Raman integration lidar, Fe Boltzmann lidar, and Doppler lidar [2]. Among them resonance fluorescence lidars, sensing meteoric metal layers (e.g., Fe, Na, K, Ca, Ca^+, etc.) in their main deposition regions of 80–110 km, have made significant contributions to the middle and upper atmosphere studies (see a summary in [2]). Very recently, Fe Boltzmann lidar observations have discovered neutral iron (Fe) layers in the thermosphere up to ~200 km in altitudes in Antarctica, directly measured neutral temperatures to ~170 km, and revealed close correlations of thermospheric Fe layers with geomagnetic storms [3,4]. Such discoveries have opened a new door for groundbased instruments to explore the space-atmosphere interaction region. Unfortunately, the broadband Fe Boltzmann lidar is not capable of wind measurements. Therefore, we choose narrowband resonance (Na and Fe) Doppler lidars for the development of whole atmosphere lidars.

2. Operation Principles of Resonance Doppler Lidars

Na and Fe Doppler lidars exploit the very large absorption cross-sections of Na and Fe free atoms in the mesosphere and lower thermosphere-extended region where quenching is not an issue so resonance fluorescence is achievable. The absorption lines of Na at 589 nm and Fe at 372 nm experience Doppler broadening due to thermal motion and Doppler shift due to bulk motion. By measuring the Doppler broadening and shift with narrowband lasers, temperature and wind can be derived simultaneously [2].

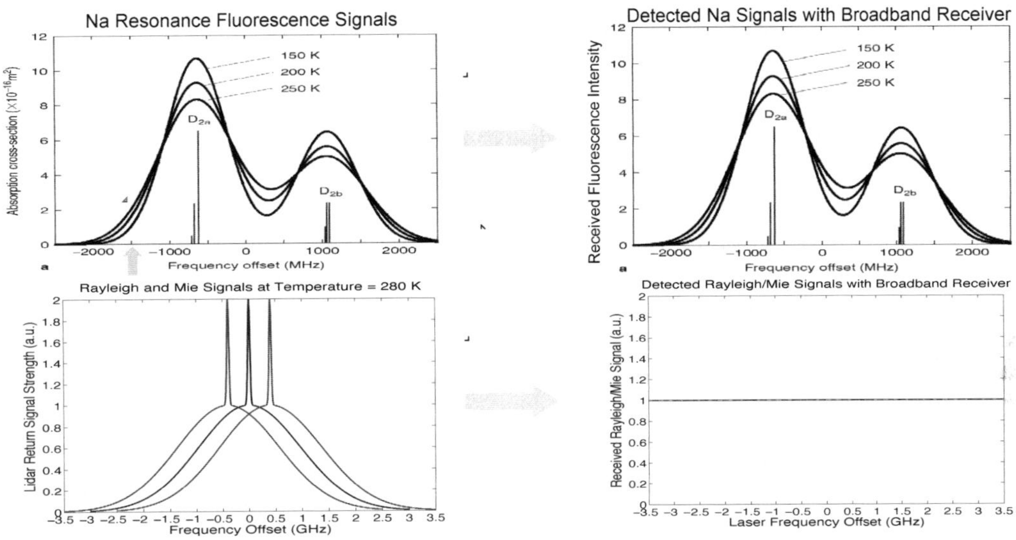

Figure 1. Resonance Doppler lidar versus other direct-detection Doppler lidars.

It is worth to note the differences between resonance Doppler and other direct-detection Doppler lidar (DDL) techniques. First, resonance absorption experiences 1 time of Doppler shift and broadening, while Rayleigh scattering experiences 2 times of Doppler shift and broadening. Second, resonance Doppler lidar has its frequency discriminator (i.e., the atomic absorption line) in the upper atmosphere and space, but other DDLs must have human-made narrowband frequency analyzers in the receivers. When scanning a narrowband laser through an absorption line, the returned fluorescence intensity exhibits the absorption lineshape along laser frequency; however, such a scan through Rayleigh scattering only results in a flat intensity over frequency if broadband receivers are employed, as demonstrated in Figure 1. Therefore, resonance Doppler lidars can employ broadband receivers to collect all fluorescence photons, thus possessing much higher optical efficiency than other DDLs equipped with very narrowband receivers.

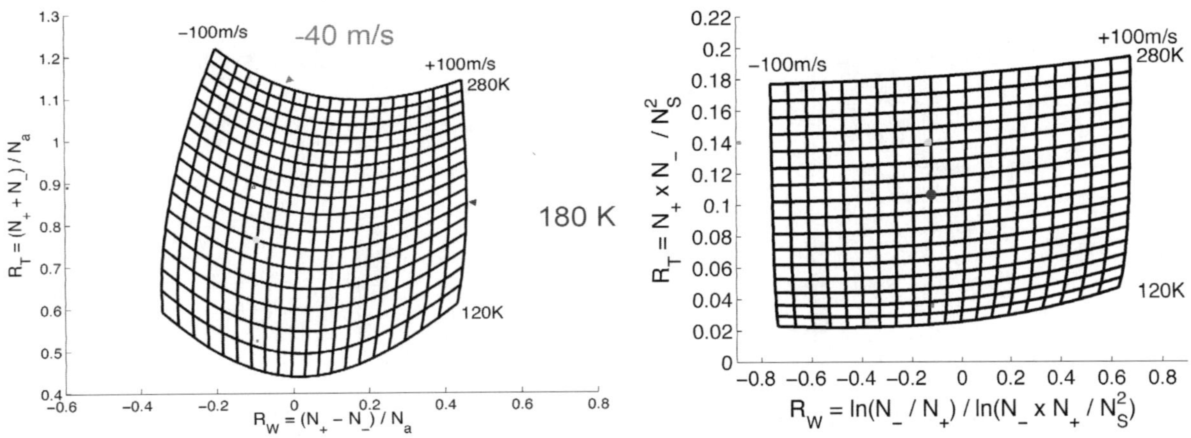

Figure 2. Calibration curves for 3-frequency Na and Fe Doppler lidars on the left and right, respectively.

To achieve the highest resolution and precision while keeping high accuracy for the upper atmosphere observations, the three-frequency ratio technique is employed in the Na and Fe Doppler lidars [2], instead of the laser frequency scanning method used in laboratory laser spectroscopy. The master laser is locked to a fixed frequency, usually a peak feature of sub-Doppler saturation-absorption spectroscopy, and acousto-optic modulators (AOMs) are used to shift laser frequency below and above the peak. By switching outgoing lidar pulses among peak, blue-shift (plus) and red-shift (minus) frequencies sequentially and repeatedly, two ratios R_T and R_W can be formed from 3-frequency Rayleigh-normalized lidar signals, which correspond to the ratios of effective backscatter cross-sections in physics, e.g.,

$$R_T = \frac{N_{Norm}(f_+,z) + N_{Norm}(f_-,z)}{N_{Norm}(f_{peak},z)} = \frac{\sigma_{eff}(f_+,z) + \sigma_{eff}(f_-,z)}{\sigma_{eff}(f_{peak},z)} \tag{1}$$

$$R_W = \frac{N_{Norm}(f_+,z) - N_{Norm}(f_-,z)}{N_{Norm}(f_{peak},z)} = \frac{\sigma_{eff}(f_+,z) - \sigma_{eff}(f_-,z)}{\sigma_{eff}(f_{peak},z)} \tag{2}$$

As illustrated in Figure 2, the calibration curves computed from atomic physics have mesh structures for both Na and Fe Doppler lidars. The measured R_T and R_W ratios will determine one cross point from the mesh, thus a pair of temperature and line of sight (LOS) wind values can be inferred simultaneously.

3. Instrumentation of Na and Fe Doppler Lidars

Both Na and Fe Doppler lidars employ the double-pass dual AOMs in transmitters to shift lidar pulse frequencies by ±750 MHz and ±742 MHz, respectively, but their laser systems are completely different. The Na Doppler laser has a "MOPA" configuration of master oscillator (CW ring dye laser) and power amplifier (pulsed dye amplifier) [2], while the Fe Doppler laser is an injection-seeded, frequency-doubled Pulsed Alexandrite Ring Laser (PARL) custom designed and made by Light Age, Inc. in collaboration with Chu Research Group at the University of Colorado Boulder [5]. Sophisticated technologies, such as Fe Doppler-free saturation-absorption spectroscopy and optical heterodyne detection at 744 and 372 nm, are applied in the Fe Doppler lidar to lock a 372-nm external cavity diode laser (ECDL) to ^{56}Fe peak frequency for providing an absolute frequency reference, and then to beat with the 372-nm lidar pulses to measure the frequency of every pulse. By tuning the frequency of a 744-nm ECDL injection seed laser, the 372-nm lidar pulses are stabilized onto the ^{56}Fe peak frequency. Owing to the high-efficiency receiver architecture [6], both Na and Fe Doppler lidars have achieved high optical efficiencies, leading to very high return signal levels, especially for the Na Doppler lidar. To obtain 3-dimensional winds, the lidar beam is split into three for west, north and zenith directions with three prime-focus Newtonian telescopes of 81-cm in diameter pointing to the same three directions. An example is shown in Figure 3 for temperature, zonal wind, and meridional wind measurements. The off-zenith angle was 20 deg.

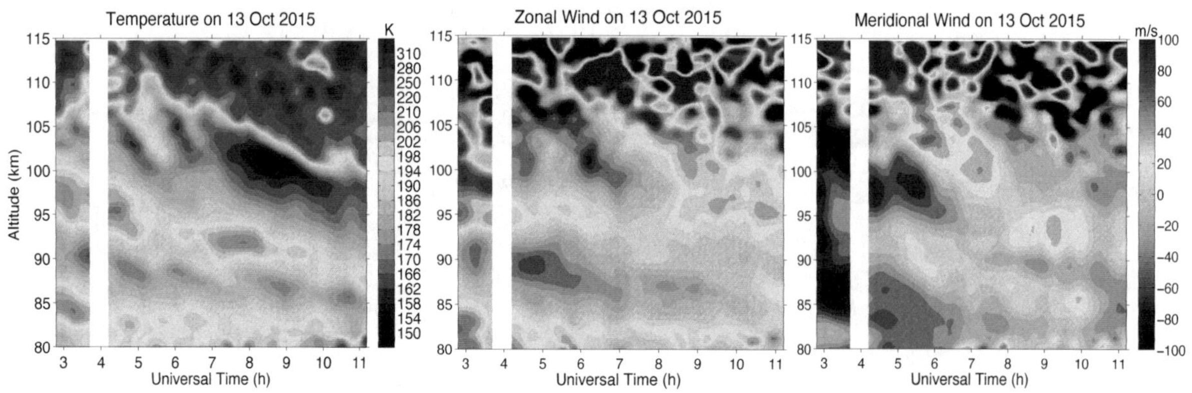

Figure 3. Temperature, zonal and meridional winds measured on 13 October 2015 at Table Mountain near Boulder. The vertical and temporal resolutions are 1 km and 15 min.

4. Simultaneous and Common-Volume Observations at Table Mountain

Illustrated in Figure 4 is an example of simultaneous and common-volume measurements of temperature and vertical winds by Fe and Na Doppler lidars at Table Mountain (40.13°N, 105.24°W) in January 2016.

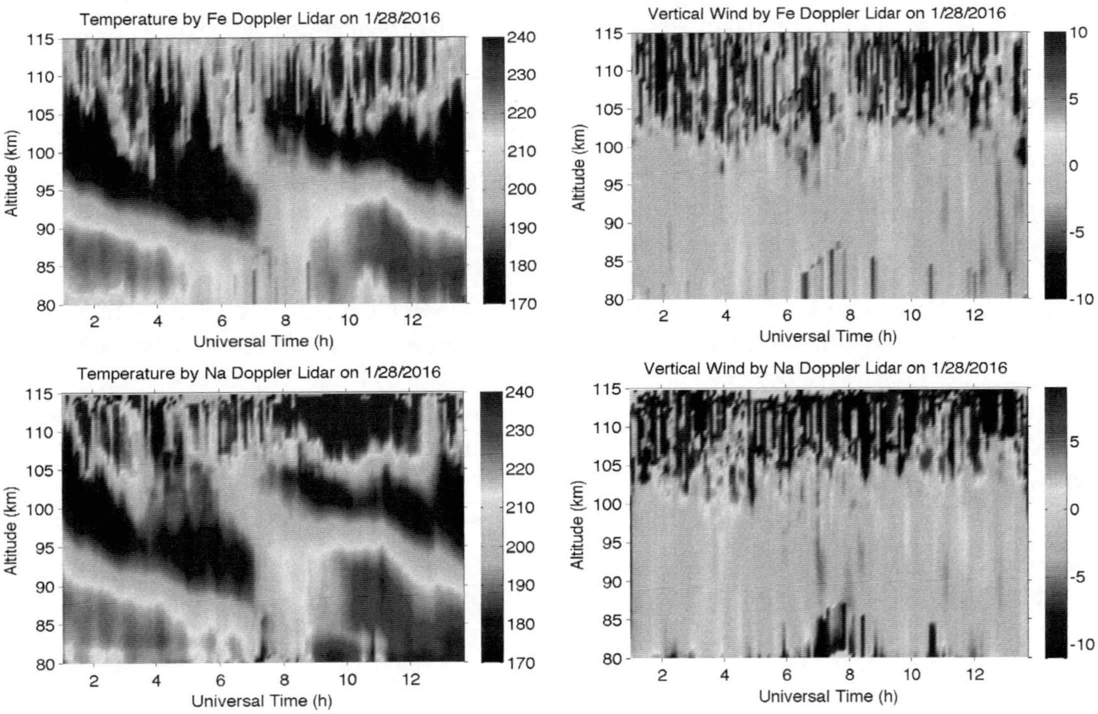

Figure 4. Temperatures and vertical winds measured simultaneously by Fe Doppler lidar (top row) and Na Doppler lidar (bottom row) on 28 January 2016 at Table Mountain Lidar Observatory, Boulder.

5. Conclusions

The simultaneous and common-volume measurements by two completely independent Fe and Na Doppler lidars show strikingly consistent temperature and vertical wind patterns with tidal and gravity waves, demonstrating the robustness of resonance Doppler lidars' measurement principles. The nearly vertical phase features occur in both lidar-measured vertical winds with similar enhancement times, which may indicate some real geophysical processes to explore. Many science endeavors will be enabled by such unprecedented measurements. For example, the cross-correlation between temperatures, vertical winds, and densities measured by two Doppler lidars will eliminate the biases induced by single lidar's error correlation, leading to accurate estimates of vertical fluxes of heat and constituents.

[1] CEDAR: *The New Dimension: Strategic Vision for the National Science Foundation Program on Coupling, Energetics and Dynamics of Atmospheric Regions* (National Science Foundation) (2011).

[2] X. Chu and G. C. Papen, "Resonance fluorescence lidar for measurements of the middle and upper atmosphere," in *Laser Remote Sensing*, T. Fujii and T. Fukuchi, eds. (CRC Press, 2005), pp. 179–432.

[3] X. Chu, Z. Yu, C. S. Gardner, C. Chen, and W. Fong, "Lidar observations of neutral Fe layers and fast gravity waves in the thermosphere (110–155 km) at McMurdo (77.8°S, 166.7°E), Antarctica," GRL **38**, L23807 (2011).

[4] X. Chu et al., "From Antarctica lidar discoveries to OASIS exploration", in *Proceeding of the 27th International Laser Radar Conference*, New York (2015), DOI: http://dx.doi.org/10.1051/epjconf/201611912001.

[5] X. Chu et al., "Progress in MRI Fe-Resonance/Rayleigh/Mie Doppler lidar," in *Proceeding of the 25th International Laser Radar Conference*, St. Petersburg, Russia (2010), pp. 947–950.

[6] J. A. Smith and X. Chu, "High-efficiency receiver architecture for resonance-fluorescence and Doppler lidars," Appl. Opt. **54**, 3173–3184 (2015).

Progress on a Whole-Atmosphere Wind and Temperature Lidar

John Smith and Xinzhao Chu
Cooperative Institute for Research in Environmental Sciences
University of Colorado Boulder, Box 216 UCB, Boulder, CO 80309, USA
Lead Author e-mail address: John.A.Smith@Colorado.EDU

Abstract: We report progress on development of a "whole atmosphere" wind and temperature lidar, which pairs an Fe Doppler lidar transmitter with a Rayleigh Doppler receiver. Significant stability improvements have been made to the original receiver, allowing us to report initial sky tests for the first time. This second iteration of the Lower Atmosphere Receiver Subsystem (LARS 2) consists of a field-widened Mach-Zehnder with an optical path length difference optimized for sensitivity to Rayleigh scattering. Use of the three available frequencies of the Fe Doppler base lidar permits a bias-free estimate of the Doppler shift. Improved mounts and a secondary chamber to further limit turbulence within the cavity of the interferometer are shown to improve the long- and short-term stability. It is hoped that this receiver architecture, by providing background wind information below the Space-Atmosphere Interaction Region (SAIR), will help us to better understand the coupling between the lower atmosphere and space.

Keywords: LARS, Mach, Zehnder, DMZ, XMZ, Fe, iron, Doppler, wind, temperature, receiver, interferometer, direct, detection, hybrid, resonance, Rayleigh

1. Introduction

The dynamics of the SAIR are heavily influenced by what occurs below. For example, the wind field below the SAIR filters the spectrum of gravity waves propagating from the surface. Gravity waves that break in the MLT region play a pivotal role in the energy and momentum budget of the SAIR. Gravity waves contribute approximately 80% to the uncertainty in the energy and momentum budget of the MLT region. The SAIR is a region important to sustaining life by serving as a barrier between the Earth and space and regulating climate. In addition, the SAIR impacts many technologies that we rely upon today, like GPS/GNSS, OTH radar, and VHF communication. Also, increasingly, the stratosphere and lower mesosphere are being exploited for commercial purposes. Understanding the coupling between the lower atmospheres and SAIR through weather and climate modeling will require extensive measurements that extend throughout these regions. What we explore in this study is a method of obtaining such measurements by marrying two mature lidar techniques- resonance-fluorescence Doppler and Rayleigh-Doppler lidar.

To profile wind and temperature from 0-105+ km, we have devised a way to combine an Fe resonance Doppler lidar with a Mach-Zehnder-based Rayleigh Doppler receiver. From the Fe resonance lidar, we derive wind and temperature from 75-105 km using the resonance technique and temperature from 30-75 km with the Rayleigh lidar technique. With the Rayleigh Doppler lidar we extend the wind measurement range of the resonance lidar down from 75 km to the surface. Both techniques are used simultaneously, and non-exclusively, to offer complete coverage of the wind field in the least understood, least monitored regions of Earth's atmosphere with virtually no trade-off in either technique's measurement precision or coverage.

2. The Fe Resonance-Fluorescence Doppler Lidar

In 2007, with the advent of suitable laser technologies, the mobile Fe Doppler lidar was funded by an NSF/MRI grant to profile wind, temperature and Fe density in the upper atmosphere with unprecedented accuracy and resolution. The measurement technique employed is identical to that for Na and K resonance Doppler lidars, whereby a narrowband transmitter is tuned to three well-defined frequencies distributed about the atomic backscatter cross-section of a strong resonance line of the metal in question. Since the spectral width of the atomic cross-section is temperature-dependent by the Maxwell-Boltzmann distribution, and the frequency offset is wind-dependent by the Doppler effect, both wind and temperature can be determined by examining the range-resolved relative backscatter strength of each of the transmitted frequencies in regions where the metal is present (typically 75-105 km). Since the strong Fe resonance lines are NUV, the Fe Doppler lidar is an effective Rayleigh lidar as well.

The Fe Doppler lidar transmitter probes the Fe a5D4 - z5D4 transition at 372.0995 nm (vac.). This wavelength is generated by doubling the output of a flashlamp-pumped, Q-switched, injection seeded Alexandrite laser tuned to 744.1990 nm (vac.). The injection seeder is stabilized by monitoring the heterodyne beat between the output of the pulsed NUV light and a CW external cavity diode laser locked to a Doppler-free feature of the Fe vapor from a hollow-cathode lamp. The wing frequencies are generated by acousto-optically shifting the NIR injection seeder alternately in time by 371 MHz to the blue and to the red, corresponding to shifts of 742 MHz in the NUV.

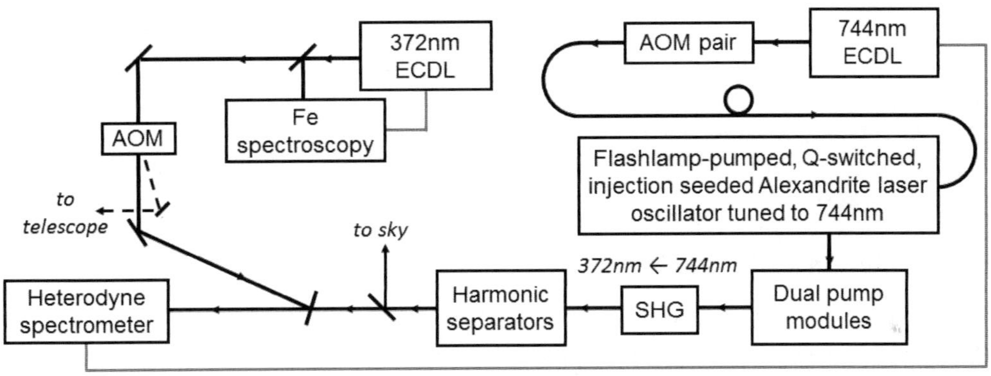

Figure1. Block diagram of MRI Fe Doppler laser transmitter system and heterodyne feedback system. Also shown is the zero-wind, CW injection AOM.

3. Lower Atmosphere Receiver Subsystem (LARS)

The LARS component is an add-on to the base Fe Doppler lidar that replaces the simple light collection receiver with a two-channel light sorting interferometer receiver. At the heart of this component is a field-widened Mach-Zehnder with an OPD of ~33 mm, optimized for sensitivity to Doppler shifts in Rayleigh backscatter of 372 nm light at stratospheric temperatures (~250 K). It is architecturally similar to the dual Mach-Zehnder, or "DMZ" design proposed and/or implemented previously [1,2], but uses the three available frequencies from the base Fe Doppler lidar to achieve a wind measurement immune from the influence of both instrumental defects and backscatter spectral width/shape, provided such modulations produce a symmetric broadening. This technique we refer to as the "XMZ" technique. A detailed description of the XMZ technique can be found in [3].

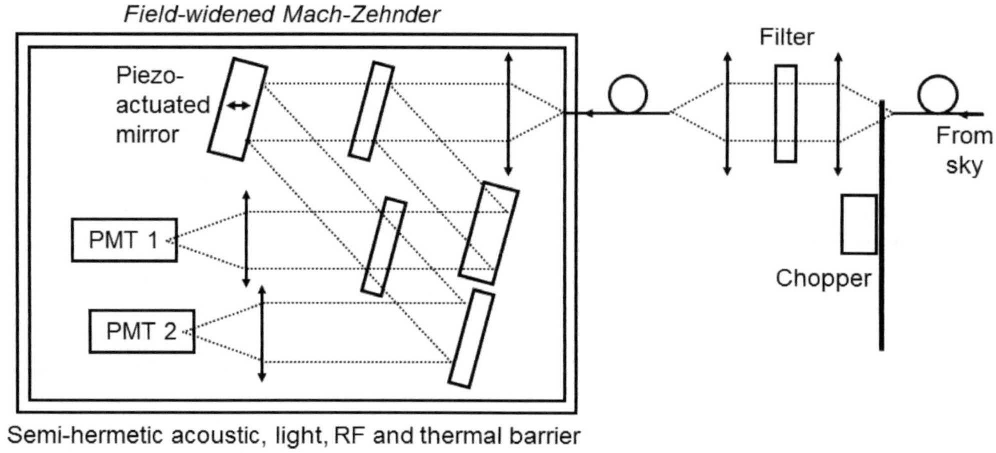

Figure 2. Sketch of the LARS 2 receiver subsystem

One leg of the interferometer is piezo-tuned to maintain the steepest slope of its sinusoidal spectral response, the cross-point of the two channels, at the zero Doppler point. In order to derive the corrections, light from the UV ECDL is "blinked" into the telescope at the end of each lidar profile to provide a zero Doppler reference. This is accomplished by a 200 MHz acousto-optic modulator, oriented to blue-shift the light, that serves as a very high-speed optical shutter. The data acquisition system sums the zero Doppler signal from both channels, then takes the difference between them and divides by their sum to derive a correction to the piezo controller.

4. Early Results and Discussion

A total of approximately 6 hours of test data were obtained at the Table Mountain Field Site 8 miles north of Boulder, Colorado between May 13th and June 13th, 2016. The 81 cm telescope was oriented to zenith to determine the zero-wind response of the receiver. A transmitter power of 1.1-1.2 W was attained using the oscillator only and the transmitter was stabilized to +80 MHz from the Fe resonance line by optical heterodyne detection and feedback. The Mach-Zehnder was stabilized to +200 MHz from the Fe resonance line by the AOM-switched light. The net shift of the MZI cross-point from the zero-wind is therefore +120 MHz.

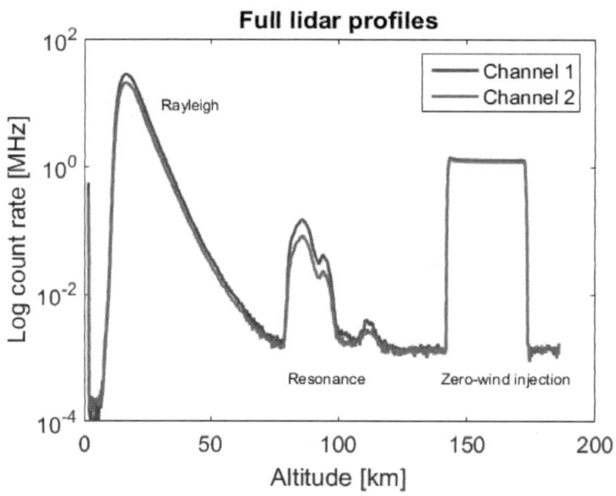

Figure 3. A full lidar profile, 30-min average, the June 13th test, un-shifted transmitter, both MZI channels, log count-rate scale, zenith direction, showing Rayleigh/Mie and resonance scattering, plus the artificial zero-wind injection near the end of the profiles.

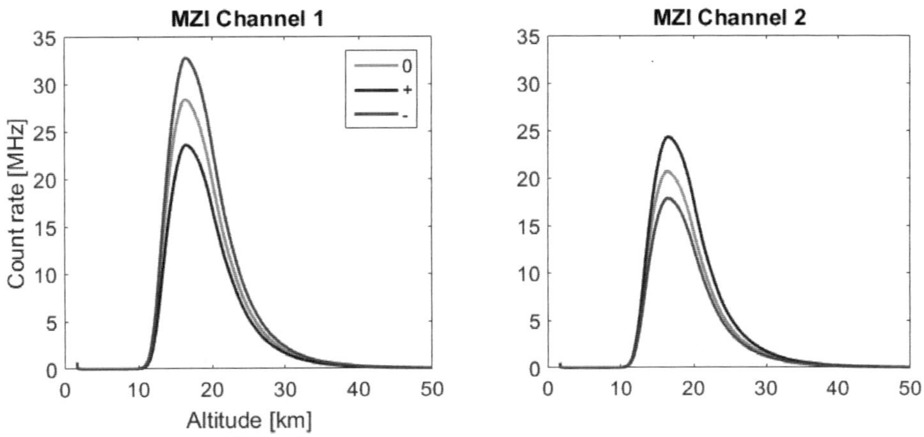

Figure 4. 30-min average lidar profiles from the same June 13th test. Un-shifted (0), blue-shifted (+) and red-shifted (-) frequencies are shown.

For each of the 3 available frequencies, we form a ratio between the difference in the channels and the sum of the channels. Defining S1, S2 and S3 as the un-shifted, blue-shifted and red-shifted signals of channel 1, respectively, and S4, S5 and S6 as the same for channel 2, the following 'Q' ratios are computed.

$$Q_1 = \frac{S_1 - S_4}{S_1 + S_4}, \quad Q_2 = \frac{S_2 - S_5}{S_2 + S_5}, \quad Q_3 = \frac{S_3 - S_6}{S_3 + S_6}$$

The Doppler shift is then, to good approximation,

$$\nu = \frac{2}{3} f_{AOM} \left(\frac{Q_1 + Q_2 + Q_3}{Q_3 - Q_2} \right) = 2\frac{v}{\lambda}$$

where f_{AOM} is the frequency between un-shifted and blue-/red-shifted profiles (+/-742 MHz). More information can be found in the literature [3]. We have discovered, in all nights of data so far, an apparent Doppler shift of approximately +500 MHz, which we have not been able to explain at this point. It could be that the interferometer is momentarily disturbed immediately following the firing of the laser in a manner that produces the observed slope in the response of the interferometer, but our preliminary tests have shown this to be a small effect. More tests are needed to identify the source of this persistent offset.

It is interesting to note that the 'Q' ratios for Rayleigh scattering are very different than the 'Q' ratios for resonance scattering due to the difference in the scattering mechanisms. Therefore, the interferometer could potentially be used as a more sensitive indicator for the presence of Fe, particularly where there is significant Rayleigh scattering contamination involved, or a high background level.

5. References

[1] Z. Liu and T. Kobayashi, "Differential Discrimination Technique for Incoherent Doppler Lidar to Measure Atmospheric Wind and Backscatter Ratio," Optical Review 3(1), 47-52 (1996).

[2] D. Bruneau, "Mach-Zehnder interferometer as a spectral analyzer for molecular Doppler wind lidar," Applied Optics 40(3), 391-399 (2001).

[3] J. Smith and X. Chu, "Investigation of a field-widened Mach-Zehnder receiver to extend Fe Doppler lidar wind measurements from the thermosphere to the ground," Applied Optics 55(6), 1366-1380 (2016).

A review of 10 years of CO2LAS flights

Gary D. Spiers, Robert T. Menzies, Joseph Jacob, Sven Geier, Santos Fregoso

Jet Propulsion Laboratory, California Institute of Technology
4800 Oak Grove Drive, Pasadena, California 91109, U.S.A.
gspiers@jpl.nasa.gov

Abstract: The CO2LAS Laser Absorption Spectrometer has been flying for 10 years measuring the weighted, column averaged carbon dioxide concentration between an aircraft and the ground using a continuous-wave heterodyne technique operating at a wavelength of 2.05 microns. Initially flying on a Twin Otter the instrument now flies on the NASA DC-8. We provide an overview of the instrument development and changes that have occurred over that time, review the results of the flights undertaken to date and discuss the practical challenges of making an accurate integrated column measurement of carbon dioxide. We conclude by looking forward to future improvements for the instrument and approach.

Keywords: Laser, Lidar, Coherent, Differential Absorption, Airborne

1. Introduction

The CO2LAS instrument was conceived and developed in the 2000-2006 time frame with the goal of demonstrating an approach to measuring CO_2 mixing ratios from Earth orbit, primarily in the lower and middle troposphere with measurement precision equivalent to 1– 2 parts per million by volume (ppmv) or better. These precisions were desired in order to define the spatial gradients of CO_2, from which sources and sinks could be estimated with much reduced uncertainty than was attainable at the time on a spatial grid scale of order 10^3 km x 10^3 km [1–3]. Atmospheric CO_2 is a long-lived gas, with sources and sinks primarily at the surface. Consequently, a remote sensing technique that could emphasize the lower tropospheric component or provide vertical profiles within the troposphere was preferred.

The laser absorption spectrometer (LAS) approach offered the potential to provide the high-accuracy CO_2 mixing ratio measurements with the vertical and horizontal spatial resolution that was desired by the carbon cycle research community. The LAS approach probes a well-characterized pressure-broadened absorption line profile with one or more laser frequencies in order to provide weighting functions suitable for retrieving vertical profile information [4]. An LAS approach to global-scale CO_2 measurement from Earth orbit utilizes differentially attenuated multi-wavelength backscatter from the Earth surface along the suborbital track, with subsequent analysis of the backscatter intensities at each wavelength to retrieve CO_2 mixing ratios. This is a form of the technique referred to as integrated path differential absorption (IPDA). An airborne LAS system utilizing the IPDA technique can obtain mixing ratio information on a regional scale with higher spatial resolution than can be obtained from low Earth orbit (LEO).

Flying the airborne CO2LAS instrument over a variety of sites offered the opportunity to demonstrate the suitability of the LAS IPDA technique, to evaluate the instrument technology, and to develop and refine the high-precision CO_2 retrieval algorithms that would be the predecessors to the LEO retrieval analogues. With an airborne platform, multiple overpasses at different altitudes provide vertical profile information in addition to the inherent weighting functions.

2. Instrument Development

The CO2LAS instrument developed jointly by the Jet Propulsion Laboratory (JPL) and Lockheed Martin Coherent Technologies consists of five key subsystems: (1) the optical assembly, (2) the control electronics unit, (3) the control software unit, (4) the thermal management assembly, and (5) the signal processing/data acquisition electronics.
The CO2LAS transceiver approach utilizes heterodyne detection, implementing a narrow bandwidth receiver, with frequency-stabilized narrow linewidth laser transmitters and local oscillators. The lasers are diode-laser-pumped rare-earth ion doped crystal lasers, specifically yttrium lithium fluoride (YLF) crystal with thulium (Tm) and holmium (Ho) dopants. These lasers are designed for efficient lasing in the 2:05 **μ**m spectral region. The transceiver consists of two separate transmit/receive channels for the on-line and off-line components of the LAS measurement. The beam expander off-axis telescopes for each channel are identical in size and configuration, with the input optics designed to optimize the truncated Gaussian beam parameters for maximum heterodyne photomixing efficiency. The transmitter frequencies are carefully stabilized with respect to a selected CO2 absorption line. Each channel has a dedicated heterodyne detector and a cw single-frequency laser, which acts both as the transmit laser and the local oscillator for heterodyne detection of the return signal. The transceiver also includes a separate low-power cw laser that provides a reference for frequency offset locking of the on-line and off-line lasers. A summary of the instrument parameters is given in Table 1 and the instrument is described in more detail in reference [5].

Parameter	Value
CO2 Line Center	4875.747 cm^{-1}
Offline Laser	4875.225 cm^{-1}
Online Laser	4875.882 cm^{-1}
Transmitted Laser Power	<100 mW/channel
Transmit/Receive Aperture	10 cm Diameter
Receiver FOV	60 μrad
Photomixer Type	InGaAs
Receiver Heterodyne Frequency Window	10-25 MHz
Signal Digitization	14 bit/ 60 MHz

Table 1 Key Instrument Parameters

Modifications to the instrument over the years have mostly been refurbishment of the lasers and upgrades to the data system throughput duty cycle which has gone from 8% in 2006 to 20% in 2007, 40% in 2009 and 100% in 2014. In 2014 the thermal control subsystem was replaced and the analog front end for the detection electronics renovated. In 2015 a 1W fiber amplifier was added to the online channel however this has yet to be tested in a field campaign.

3. Field Campaigns

Early flights of the instrument were carried out on a Twin Otter aircraft over desert dry lake beds in order to evaluate the performance characteristics of the instrument. Results from these experiments led to the CO2LAS being included as one of the instruments flown by the NASA ASCENDS Decadal Survey Study on board the NASA DC-8. A summary of the flight campaigns is given in Table 2.

Date	Aircraft	Location	Description
2006	Twin Otter	California El Mirage Dry Lake Bed and Pacific Ocean	Checkout Flights
2007	Twin Otter	Virginia	Joint flights with LaRC/ITT instrument
2009	Twin Otter	El Mirage Dry Lake Bed, California	Calibration Flights
2009	Twin Otter	ARM SGP Site	ASCENDS Joint flights with LaRC & GSFC
2010	DC-8	California, Pacific, Oklahoma	ASCENDS Joint flights with LaRC & GSFC
2011	DC-8	Multiple Flights	ASCENDS Joint flights with LaRC & GSFC
2013	DC-8	Multiple Flights	ASCENDS Joint flights with LaRC & GSFC
2014	DC-8	Multiple Flights	ASCENDS Joint flights with LaRC & GSFC

Table 2 CO2LAS Field Campaigns

The instrument has measured CO_2 drawdown over active vegetation, small scale source emissions such as individual smoke stack emissions at power plants and has demonstrated the ability to conduct retrievals over low reflectivity surfaces such as snow and ice (Figure 1).

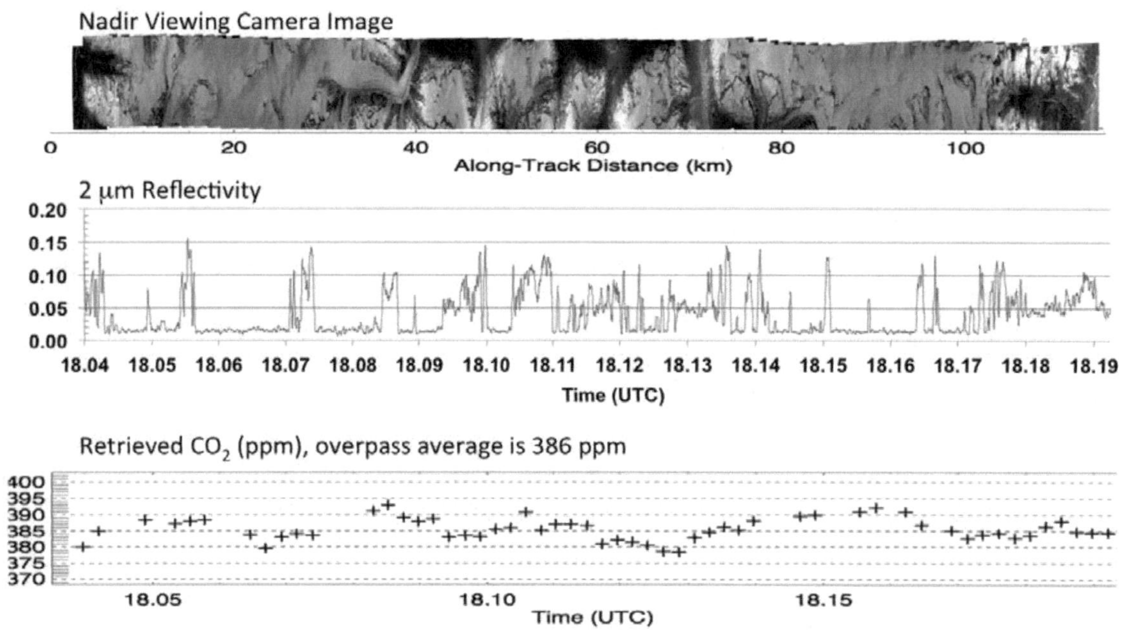

Figure 1 Simultaneous reflectivity and CO_2 retrieval during a portion of the northbound flight segment over the British Columbia Coastal Mountains, August 7, 2011. The imagery shows a mixture of snow covered areas (low backscatter), glacier segments (the blue streaks), and patches of bare rock, dirt, alpine flora. The lidar footprint track is centered in the imagery. Time duration from left to right: 9 min.

Additional results from other campaigns will be presented and details of the retrieval algorithms used will be discussed at this conference in the companion presentation by Menzies [6].

Acknowledgements

This work was carried out by the Jet Propulsion Laboratory, California Institute of Technology, under contract with the National Aeronautics and Space Administration.

4. References

1. 1. P. J. Rayner and D. M. O'Brien, "The utility of remotely sensed CO2 concentration data in surface source inversions," Geophys. Res. Lett. 28, 175–178 (2001).
2. C. E. Miller,D. Crisp, P. L. DeCola, S. C. Olsen, J. T. Randerson, A. M. Michalak, A. Alkhaled, P. Rayner, D. J. Jacob, P. Suntharalingam, D. B. A. Jones, A. S. Denning, M. E. Nicholls, S. C. Doney, S. Pawson, H. Boesch, B. J. Connor, I. Y. Fung, D. O'Brien, R. J. Salawitch, S. P. Sander, B. Sen, P. Tans, G. C. Toon, P. O. Wennberg, S. C. Wofsy, Y. L. Yung, and R. M. Law, "Precision requirements for space-based XCO2 data," J. Geophys. Res. 112 D10314, doi: 10.1029/2006JD007659 (2007).
3. "A-SCOPE—Advanced Space Carbon and Climate Observation of Planet Earth, report for assessment," ESA-SP1313/1 (European Space Agency, 2008), http://esamultimedia.esa.int/docs/SP1313-1_ASCOPE.pdf.
4. R. T. Menzies and M. T. Chahine, "Remote sensing with an airborne laser absorption spectrometer," Appl. Opt. 13, 2840–2849 (1974).
5. G.D. Spiers, R.T. Menzies, J. Jacob, L.E. Christensen, M.W. Phillips, Y. Choi, and E.V. Browell. "Atmospheric CO_2 measurements with a 2 μm airborne laser absorption spectrometer employing coherent detection", *Appl. Opt.*, **50**, 2098-2111, 2011.
6. R.T. Menzies, G.D. Spiers, J.C. Jacob, "Airborne IPDA Lidar Measurements: Factors in Optimizing Measurement Sensitivity and Precision", 18th Coherent Laser Radar Conference, Boulder (2016)

Airborne IPDA Lidar Measurements: Factors in Optimizing Measurement Sensitivity and Precision

Robert T. Menzies, Gary D. Spiers, Joseph C. Jacob

Jet Propulsion Laboratory, California Institute of Technology
4800 Oak Grove Drive, Pasadena, California 91109, U.S.A.
rmenzies@jpl.nasa.gov

Abstract: The JPL CO2LAS airborne instrument is an IPDA lidar with a coherent detection receiver that is used for atmospheric CO2 measurements. Since the objective is high accuracy retrievals of column CO2, dealing with environmental variables, along with speckle-induced fluctuations, is a major consideration. Surface reflectance is an inherent data product. In fact it is an essential dataset used in the algorithm for high accuracy retrieval of the CO2 column abundances. We discuss the use of surface reflectance and elevation datasets for tuning the differential absorption retrieval algorithm to optimize sensitivity to CO2 sources and sinks of various spatial scales. Extensions to measurement of other atmospheric constituents are included.

Keywords: Laser, Lidar, Coherent, Differential Absorption, Airborne

1. Introduction

Atmospheric CO_2 is a long-lived greenhouse gas, with sources and sinks primarily at the surface. Seeking improved capability to determine the fluxes of CO2 on various spatial scales, national space agencies have invested in Earth-orbiting passive spectrometers viewing reflected solar radiation. These instruments are providing valuable insight into the capabilities of this technique. Improved determination of CO_2 fluxes from the air and from Earth-orbit requires extraordinary high precision and low bias. Cloud and aerosol scattering, terrain complexities within the IFOV, and limited SNR (Signal to Noise Ratio) outside of daytime mid-latitudes are inherent issues that can be mitigated or eliminated using laser-based integrated path differential absorption (IPDA). An airborne laser-based approach to high-precision measurements of atmospheric CO_2 offers the potential to provide the high-accuracy mixing ratio measurements on regional scales with spatial resolution that is useful to the carbon cycle research community. The airborne environment is a good test of the component technologies and system designs. Experience with airborne IPDA lidars is also critical in assessing the instrument parameters and retrieval algorithms that are relevant to Earth-orbiting observations. Much can be learned from lidar measurements of CO_2 that applies to measurements of other greenhouse gases (e.g., CO, CH_4, H_2O) and other constituents that play important roles in atmospheric chemistry.

Assuming a nadir or near-nadir view, a weighted column dry air mixing ratio is obtained from the IPDA sounding because the absorption lines are pressure-broadened in the lower atmosphere. Thus the cross section at the probing on-line frequency is dependent on altitude. The weighting favors the lower troposphere when the on-line frequency is detuned one or more (surface pressure) halfwidths from line center. We can use this to advantage by detuning the on-line frequency to a location one to three halfwidths from line center results in selective probing of the CO2 in the lower troposphere, where the CO2 mixing ratio variability of interest is the highest. (Typical weighting functions for CO_2 sounding are found in references [1-4].)

Multiple flights of our airborne CO_2 LAS instrument have demonstrated the capability to observe various sources as well as large-scale CO_2 drawdown in the U.S. Midwest due to photosynthesis in the July/August time frame. Flights have also provided experience dealing with partially cloudy atmospheres, land surfaces with varied terrain and topography, and bodies of water with various degrees of surface roughness. These provide the opportunity to demonstrate the suitability of the LAS IPDA technique, to evaluate the instrument technology, and to develop and refine the high precision retrieval algorithms that are essential.

Minimizing measurement uncertainty and bias is extremely important. There can be many contributors to bias. Here we provide a brief instrument overview and discuss sources of uncertainty and potential bias that we have had to contend with in CO_2 retrievals. Some are inherent to the measurement from airborne or space-based platforms and apply to lidar retrievals in general.

2. Airborne CO_2 LAS Instrument Overview

The instrument was jointly developed by JPL and Lockheed Martin Coherent Technologies (LMCT) with funding from the NASA Earth Science Technology Office Instrument Incubator Program. The transceiver approach is to utilize heterodyne detection, implementing a narrow bandwidth receiver, with frequency-stabilized narrow-linewidth lasers. The transceiver consists of two separate transmit/receive channels for the on-line and off-line components of the IPDA measurement. Each channel has a dedicated heterodyne detector, and a cw single frequency compact Tm,Ho:YLF laser which acts both as the transmit laser and the local oscillator for heterodyne detection of the return signal. The transceiver includes a third laser locked to a frequency at line center of the R(30) CO_2 absorption line at 4875.749 cm^{-1} that provides an optical frequency reference for frequency offset-lock tuning of the other lasers. The instrument is described in more detail in reference [5].

The return signals from each channel are digitized followed by conversion to the frequency domain. 16K FFT's are the default in the processing scheme. The sampling duration is approximately equal to the speckle decorrelation time of the signal, τ_{decorr}, which is ~ 0.3 ms for the NASA DC-8 at nominal cruise speed. A pre-selected number of periodograms is summed, and the remainder of the signal processing steps operate on collections of these sums.

3. Speckle Noise and Environmental Effects on Measurement Precision

Attainment of CO2 measurement precision of the level of ~0.3% or 1 ppm is a very challenging endeavor. Speckle noise is a multiplicative noise that is inherent in coherent detection. The statistics are well known, and we have incorporated a one-dimensional version of a technique from the digital image enhancement and noise filtering community [6], to filter speckle noise. We continue to incorporate into our retrieval algorithms methods for minimizing environmental effects, particularly as potential sources of bias. Discussion of the effects of meteorological parameter uncertainties on the CO_2 measurement uncertainty can be found in Refs. [2-5, 7]. Here we discuss uncertainties due to the combination of topography and reflectance variability of surface and above-ground scatterers. Various means of minimizing these influences on the retrievals are discussed in Ref. [8].

The heterogeneity of surface materials and above-ground scatterers, natural and man-made, can cause sudden changes in lidar reflectance, and consideration must be given to an understanding of how this affects the column CO2 retrieval when that retrieval is an average over a portion of the ground track that includes large changes in reflectance. Sharp changes in reflectivity (e.g., water-land boundaries, or road crossings) can be problematic for IPDA systems with displacements between the on-line and off-line footprints [9], necessitating careful investigation of potential sources of misalignment. Reflectance-weighting is inherent in the lidar measurement, i.e. the high-reflectance areas are weighted preferentially in the average. When combined with elevation changes within the along-track average, this has the potential of biasing the resulting retrieval. Elevation weighting must be implemented in the retrieval algorithm to account for this inherent reflectance weighting within the ground track averaging segment, in order to mitigate biases associated with this effect. An example is shown in Figure 1, a ground track over a high elevation region of the British Columbia Coastal mountains during the August 7, 2011 flight, with snow-cover being prevalent. The low backscatter segments correspond to the snow-covered regions.

We use the SRTM database along with the aircraft INS/GPS data to determine surface elevation at the laser transmitter footprint location along the ground track, with an along-track resolution of approximately 30 m. Elevation slopes are computed, and data points over slopes above a threshold value are masked out. Co-aligned profiling laser altimetry at the same wavelength, with 3-5 m vertical resolution and high along-track resolution, would improve accuracy.

Results will be discussed.

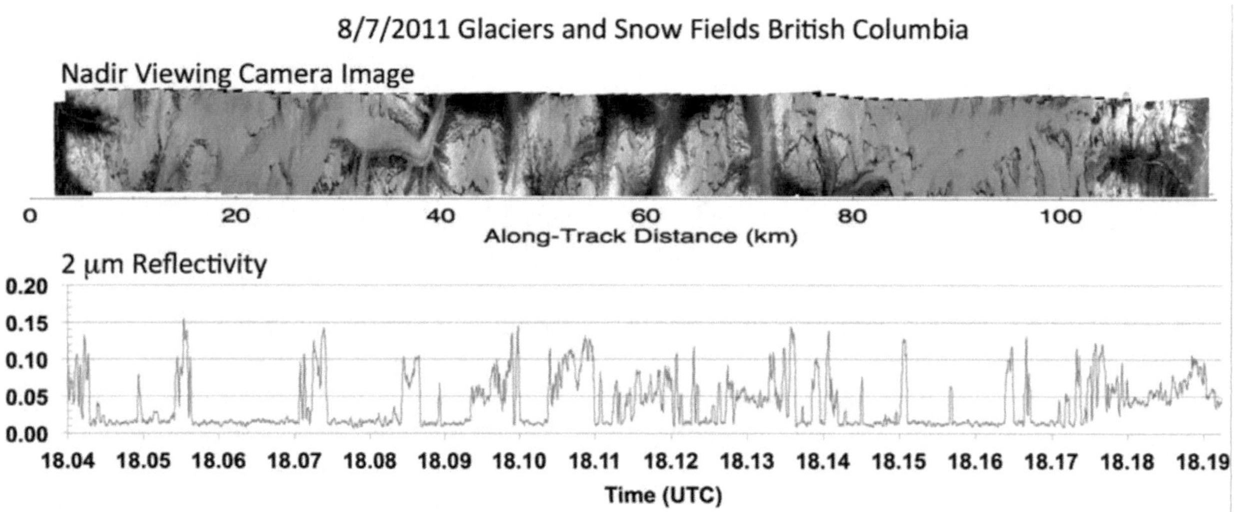

Figure 1. Surface backscatter at the airborne lidar 2.05 μm wavelength (in units of sr-1) during a portion of the northbound flight segment over the British Columbia Coastal Mountains, August 7, 2011. The imagery shows a mixture of snow covered areas (low backscatter), glacier segments (the blue streaks), and patches of bare rock, dirt, alpine flora. The lidar footprint track is centered in the imagery. Time duration from left to right: 9 min.

Acknowledgements
This work was carried out by the Jet Propulsion Laboratory, California Institute of Technology, under contract with the National Aeronautics and Space Administration.

5. References

1. R.T. Menzies and D.M. Tratt, "Differential laser absorption spectrometry for global profiling of tropospheric carbon dioxide: selection of optimum sounding frequencies for high-precision measurements", *Appl. Opt.,* **42,** 6569-6577, 2003.
2. G. Ehret, C. Kiemle, M. Wirth, A Amediek, A. Fix, and S. Houweling, "Spaceborne Remote Sensing of CO_2, CH_4, and N_2O by IPDA Lidar", *Appl. Phys. B,* **90**, 593-608, 2008.
3. F. Gibert, P.H. Flamant, J. Cuesta, D. Bruneau, "Vertical 2-μm heterodyne differential absorption lidar measurements of mean CO2 mixing ratio in the troposphere", *J. Atmos. Oceanic Technol,.* doi: 10.1175_2008JTECHA1070.1. 2008.
4. J. Caron and Y. Durand, "Operating wavelengths optimization for a spaceborne lidar measuring atmospheric CO_2 ", *Appl. Opt.***48**, 5413-5422, 2009**.**
5. G.D. Spiers, R.T. Menzies, J. Jacob, L.E. Christensen, M.W. Phillips, Y. Choi, and E.V. Browell. "Atmospheric CO_2 measurements with a 2 μm airborne laser absorption spectrometer employing coherent detection", *Appl. Opt.*, **50**, 2098-2111, 2011.
6. J.-S. Lee, "Digital Image Enhancement and Noise Filtering by Use of Local Statistics", *IEEE Trans. Pattern Analysis and Machine Intelligence*, vol. **PAMI-2**, 165-168, 1980.
7. S. Ishii and coauthors, "Partial CO_2 column-averaged dry-air mixing ratio from measurements by coherent 2-μm differential absorption and wind lidar with laser frequency offset locking", *J. Atmos. Oceanic Technol.,* **29**, 1169-1181, 2012.
8. R.T. Menzies, G.D. Spiers, and J.C. Jacob, "Airborne Laser Absorption Spectrometer Measurements of Atmospheric CO_2 Column Mole Fractions: Source and Sink Detection and Environmental Impacts on Retrievals", *J. Atmos and Oceanic Tech.* **31**, 404-421, 2014.
9. A. Amediek., A. Fix, G. Ehret, J. Caron, and Y. Durand, "Airborne lidar reflectance measurements at 1.57 μm in support of the A-SCOPE mission for atmospheric CO2", *Atmos. Meas. Tech.*, **2**, 755-772, 2009.

Development of an Airborne Triple-Pulse 2-µm Integrated Path Differential Absorption Lidar (IPDA) for Simultaneous Airborne Column Measurements of Carbon Dioxide and Water Vapor in the Atmosphere

Upendra N. Singh(a), Mulugeta Petros(b), Tamer F. Refaat(b), Jirong Yu(b), Charles W. Antill(b) and Ruben Remus(b)
(a) NASA Engineering and Safety Center,
NASA Langley Research Center, Hampton, VA 23681
(b) Remote Sensing Branch, MS 468,
NASA Langley Research Center, Hampton, VA 23681
Upendra.N.Singh@nasa.gov

Abstract: This presentation will provide status and details of an airborne 2-µm triple-pulse integrated path differential absorption (IPDA) lidar being developed at NASA Langley Research Center with support from NASA ESTO Instrument Incubator Program. The development of this active optical remote sensing IPDA instrument is targeted for measuring both atmospheric carbon dioxide and water vapor in the atmosphere from an airborne platform. This presentation will focus on the advancement of the 2-micron triple-pulse IPDA lidar development. Updates on the state-of-the-art triple-pulse laser transmitter will be presented including the status of seed laser locking, wavelength control, receiver and detector upgrades, laser packaging and lidar integration. Future plan for IPDA lidar system for ground integration, testing and flight validation will also be presented.

Keywords: Active Remote Sensing, Carbon Dioxide, Water Vapor, DIAL, IPDA Lidar, Triple-Pulse Laser

1. Introduction

Through the continual support from NASA Earth Science Technology Office (ESTO), current efforts at NASA Langley Research Center (LaRC) are focused on developing a 2-µm triple-pulse integrated path differential absorption (IPDA) lidar instrument for independent and simultaneous monitoring of carbon dioxide (CO_2) and water vapor (H_2O) in the atmosphere [1]. Triple-pulse IPDA lidar instrument design, development and integration is based on the knowledge gathered through the successful demonstration of the 2-µm double-pulse IPDA lidar for atmospheric CO_2 measurements [2]. Several enhancements and updates of the triple-pulse instrument over the double-pulse instrument included in both the transmitter and the receiver systems [3]. Transmitter updates include the ability of generating three successive pulses, instead of two, with high-energy and high-repetition rate using a single pump pulse. The wavelength control and locking scheme is extend, up to 35 GHz away from the R30 CO_2 line, to accommodate H_2O sensing. In the receiver, detection systems and data acquisition hardware are updated for better performance in terms of detection sensitivity and random error reduction. Real-time data analysis and processing implementation would expedite science data production to further extend instrument testing and validation. These enhancements are detailed in the following subsections.

2. Triple-Pulse IPDA Remote Sensing Technique

The 2 µm wavelength region offers many suitable absorption features for CO_2 as well as H_2O. For CO_2 sensing, the R30 line, located at 2050.9670 nm, provides an attractive absorption cross section with unique characteristics. These include low temperature sensitivity and low interference from higher abundant H_2O molecules. This is indicated in figure 1, which compares the composite absorption spectra for CO_2 and H_2O

derived using the HITRAN database for line parameters, assuming Voigt line profile at two altitudes. The H_2O absorption peak located at 2050.5322 nm coincides close to CO_2 absorption minima, between R30 and R32 lines and away from the R32 peak. The IPDA laser transmitter generates three successive pulses locked to three different wavelengths, as shown schematically in figure 2. A single pump pulse produces three successive 2-µm laser pulses, 150 µsec apart. Using an enhanced wavelength control scheme, each of these pulses can be tuned and locked at different wavelength, as marked in figure 1. The principle of wavelength selection for this IPDA instrument is demonstrated in the same figure. The CO_2 on and off-line wavelengths are selected around the R30 line, so that both would have similar H_2O absorption to minimizes H_2O interference on CO_2 measurements. Similarly, H_2O on- and off-line are selected around the absorption peak such that CO_2 interference is minimized on the H_2O measurement. However, both CO_2 on-line and H2O off-line measurements share the same wavelength, which achieves simultaneous measurement of both molecules with triple pulses rather than quadruple pulses almost independently while avoiding interference from each other.

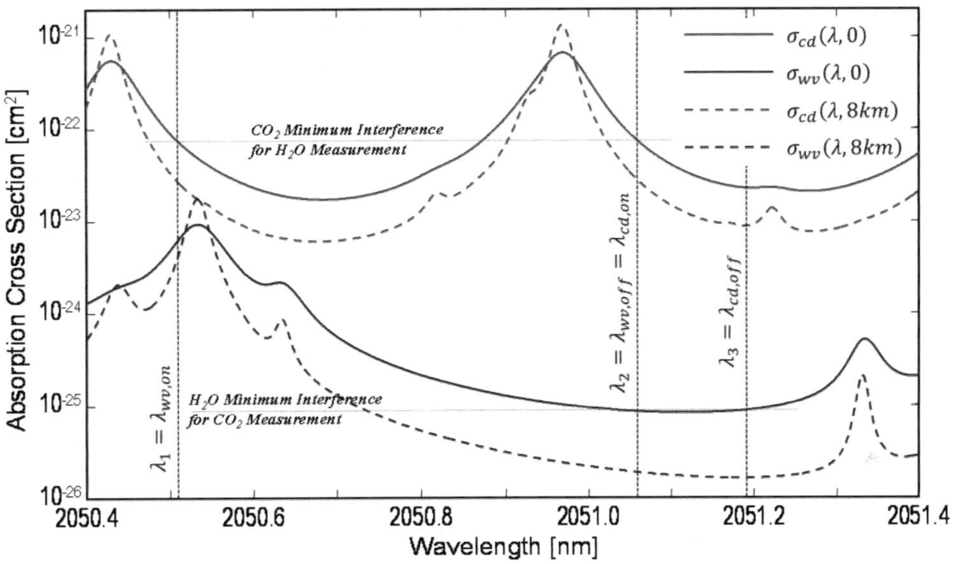

Figure 1. Absorption cross-section spectra of H_2O and CO_2, σ_{wv} and σ_{cd}, respectively at two altitudes.

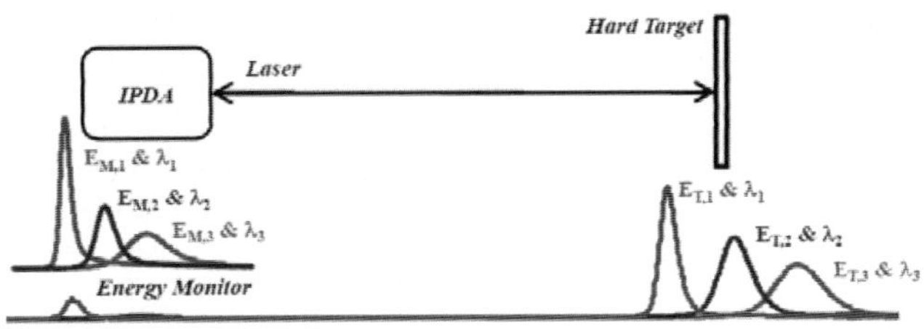

Figure 2. 2-µm triple-pulse IPDA lidar principle of operation.

3. Triple-Pulse IPDA Transmitter

The triple-pulse IPDA laser transmitters is based on the Ho:Tm:YLF high-energy 2-µm pulsed laser technology, with end pumping using 792 nm AlGaAs diode arrays [4]. Relative to the pump pulse, Q-switch triple-trigger produces three successive laser pulses with relatively controlled energies and pulse-widths are separated by approximately 200 µsec. Thermal analysis conducted for proper heat dissipation out of the laser crystal, which is a critical issue that can result in crystal damage. As a proof of concept, a prototype oscillator with triple pulsing capability was demonstrated, as shown in figure 3. Final laser configuration including thermal analysis and alignment optimization is currently on going to achieve higher energies.

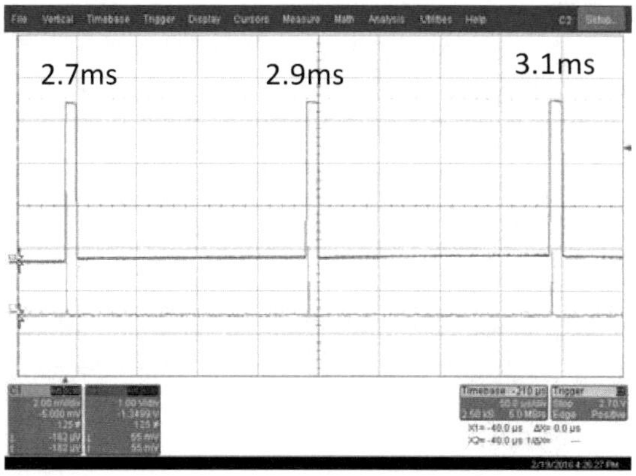

Figure 3. Oscilloscope record for the successful triple-pulse operation.

The exact wavelengths of the pulsed laser transmitter are controlled by a wavelength control unit within 1 MHz. The unique wavelength control of the triple pulses uses a single semiconductor laser (JPL) and provides three seeds of any frequency setting within 35 GHz offset from the locked CO_2 R30 line center reference. This unit includes several optical and electro-optic components which were acquired and characterized. Integration of a prototype wavelength controller demonstrated technological challenges handling high bandwidth signals which was managed by proper RF designs and implementations.

4. Triple-Pulse IPDA Receiver

Similar to the double-pulse IPDA, the 2-μm triple-pulse IPDA lidar receiver consists of a 0.4 m Newtonian telescope that focuses the radiation onto 300 μm diameter spot. The telescope secondary mirror is a two surface dichroic flat that turns the return radiation 90° to the side integrated aft-optics from one surface. The opposite surface is used to transmit the expanded laser beam coaxially with the telescope. A single automated mount is used for bore-sight alignment. The telescope focused radiation is collimated, filtered then applied to a 90%-10% beam splitter. The 90% channel is an exact replica of the double-pulsed lidar. The 10% channel is planned to be used with an e-APD detector. These e-APD devices are space-qualifiable and were validated for airborne lidar operation at 1.6-μm at NASA Goddard Space Flight Center (GSFC). In co-ordination with ESTO, LaRC is collaborating with GSFC to integrate this detector into the 2-μm IPDA. The IPDA hard target return signals are digitized and stored through a data acquisition unit. The data acquisition unit is based on two similar 2-channels, 1 GS/s high-performance digitizers (Agilent; U5303A) that are triggered from the laser Q-switch. One digitizer is dedicated to the IPDA return signals, with a variable record length of about 70k samples, while the other is dedicated to the laser energy monitors, with a fixed record length of 10k.

5. Triple-Pulse IPDA Integration

A trailer was prepared as a mobile lidar laboratory for IPDA ground testing at NASA LaRC and ground-based field validation campaigns. This trailer will be used for the triple-pulse IPDA initial integration and ground testing. Once complete, airborne integration would start by transferring the instrument to the NASA B-200 aircraft. The IPDA instrument size, weight and power consumption were restricted to the payload requirements for such small aircraft to be easily adopted in any larger airborne research platform for future missions. Other housekeeping instruments will be integrated into the B-200 aircraft as well, which will include a LiCor in-situ sensor for CO_2 and H_2O mixing ratio measurement, GPS for global timing, aircraft position, altitude and angles measurements and video recorder for target identification. Besides, aircraft built-in sensors provide altitude, pressure, temperature and relative humidity sampling at flight position.

6. Triple-Pulse IPDA Validation Plans

The 2-µm IPDA lidar validation is important to assess both CO_2 and H_2O atmospheric measurements. Instrument validation will start on ground after instrument integration in the mobile laboratory. The mobile laboratory enables IPDA lidar horizontal measurement using a set calibrated hard targets and vertical measurements using clouds as hard target. Ground validation objectives are to check IPDA operational readiness before aircraft deployment, obtain IPDA signals and noise to evaluate instrument systematic and random errors, compare instrument errors to IPDA models and compare CO_2 and H_2O measurements against correlative in-situ instruments. Other long term objectives include transferring the laboratory with the instrument to different tall tower sites, such as WLEF tall tower in Park Falls, Wisconsin, and the Southern Great Plains ARM site in Lamont, Oklahoma.

For airborne validation, initial engineering flights would focus on instrument operation and comparing airborne and ground performance. Once proven success, the objective would focus on comparing CO_2 and H_2O measurements against correlative in-situ sensors and models. The validation will rely on onboard sensors as well as coordinating and collaborate with science community for other independent sensors, such as NOAA air-sampling and Pennsylvania State University passive sensors. Airborne validation will be planned to target different conditions such as different surface reflectivity, day and night background, clear, cloudy and broken cloud conditions, variable surface elevation and urban pollution and plume detection. The validation may also cover different location such as the Upper Midwest summer, where strong vertical and horizontal spatial gradients in CO_2 occurs due to agricultural fluxes and urban deployment in winter, where flight around isolated urban centers could identify a clear atmospheric boundary layer CO_2 plume. 2-µm triple-pulse validation activities might have the potential to coordinate with ACT-America flights.

7. Conclusion

A 2-µm triple-pulse IPDA lidar instrument is being developed at NASA LaRC. This active remote sensing IPDA instrument targets and measures both atmospheric CO_2 and H_2O. Wavelength selection and laser transmitter operation allows measuring both species independently and simultaneously. This is the first demonstration of measuring two different atmospheric molecules with a single instrument. Instrument design is based on knowledge gathered through the previously successful 2-µm double-pulse IPDA. Critical transmitter and receiver enhancements were implemented in the new triple-pulse design that significantly advance the technology. In the transmitter, modifications include triple-pulse operation of the laser and wavelength control design. In the receiver, updates includes additional high performance e-APD detector and advanced data acquisition system. The e-APD detector supplied by NASA GSFC, is a state-of-art, space qualifiable device that was validated for lidar applications. Work progress of the 2-µm triple-pulse IPDA program is on schedule. Instrument validation plans are under discussions to collaborate with different institutes with similar interests.

8. References

[1] T. Refaat, U. Singh, J. Yu, M. Petros, S. Ismail, M. Kavaya, and K. Davis, "Evaluation of an airborne triple-pulsed 2-µm IPDA lidar for simultaneous and independent atmospheric water vapor and carbon dioxide measurements", Applied Optics 54, 1387-1398, 2015.

[2] T. Refaat, U. Singh, J. Yu, M. Petros, R. Remus and Syed Ismail, "Double-pulse 2-µm integrated path differential absorption lidar airborne validation for atmospheric carbon dioxide measurement", Applied Optics 55, 4232-4246, 2016.

[3] U. Singh, M. Petros, T. Refaat and J. Yu, "2-micron triple-pulse integrated path differential absorption lidar development for simultaneous airborne column measurements of carbon dioxide and water vapor in the atmosphere", Proc. of SPIE 9879, 987902, 2016.

[4] U. Singh, B. Walsh, J. Yu, M. Petros, M. Kavaya, T. Refaat, and N. Barnes, "Twenty years of Tm:Ho:YLF and LuLiF laser development for global wind and carbon dioxide active remote sensing", Optical Materials Express, 5, 827, 2015.

Preliminary study on ground based coherent differential absorption LIDAR for vertical profiling of water vapor density using 1.53 μm wavelength

Masaharu IMAKI, Ryota KOJIMA, Takayuki YANAGISAWA, and Shumpei KAMEYAMA
Mitsubishi Electric Corporation, Information Technology R&D Center,
5-1-1 Ofuna, Kamakura, Kanagawa, Japan, 247-8501
Lead Author e-mail address: Imaki.Masaharu@dc.MitsubishiElectric.co.jp

Abstract: We performed preliminary study on a ground based coherent differential absorption lidar (DIAL) for vertical profiling of water vapor density using 1.53□m laser wavelength. We assumed the atmospheric condition using the fast atmospheric signature code (FASCODE), and estimated the measurement accuracy using coherent lidar equation. Simulation results show a 10 % accuracy of water vapor density from an altitude of 0.1 km to 4.5 km with 10 minutes average.

Keywords: Water vapor, Differential absorption, Coherent

1. Introduction

Water vapor in the atmosphere affects growing cumulonimbus which causes localized heavy rainfall, therefore the measurement of water vapor density profile is required for the early prediction of this rainfall. Height profile of water vapor measurement using incoherent differential absorption lidar (DIAL) technique was reported in Ref. 1 and 2. The continuous height profile measurement was demonstrated, however, the measurement accuracy was influenced by solar background light. On the other hand, coherent DIAL technique can overcome this issue and was reported in Ref. 3 and 4. The good agreement result on water vapor density in comparison with that of radiosonde soundings was shown.

Since late 1990s, we have been developing the wind sensing coherent Doppler LIDARs with 1.5 μm wavelength. The LIDAR with 1.5 μm wavelength has advantages such as its compactness and reliability by using telecom products. Here, we consider to apply this technology to DIAL, and perform preliminary study on a ground based coherent DIAL for vertical profiling of water vapor density using 1.53 μm laser wavelength. In the followings, we discuss the concept, configuration, and simulation results of the lidar.

.

2. SYSTEM CONFIGURATION

The system configuration is shown in Fig. 1. A CW laser lights with 1.5 μm wavelength from two laser diodes are locked to the ON and OFF wavelength for water vapor. Either ON or OFF wavelength lights are selected by an optical switch. Selected laser light is modulated with a pulse waveform, is amplified, and is transmitted to the atmosphere. A part of the CW light is tapped and used for a local signal light for heterodyne detection. The received lights are converted into electrical signals by a photodetector. The received signal is analog-to-digital converted and spectral analysis and accumulation is performed in the signal processor. A coherent lidar has an advantage in daytime measurement compared with incoherent lidar because the influence of background light is greatly low. In addition, the lidar can simultaneously measure wind speed and water vapor density.

A differential absorption optical depth DAOD and water vapor density n are derived from a ratio of the normalized measured intensities of the two wavelengths, and are written by

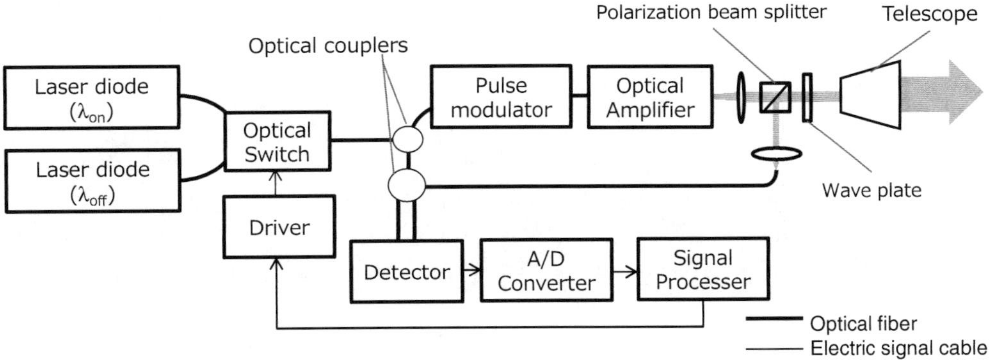

Figure 1. Schematic diagram of coherent differential absorption lidar.

$$DAOD(z_i) = \ln\left(\frac{P_{off}(z_{i+1})}{P_{on}(z_{i+1})} \cdot \frac{P_{on}(z_i)}{P_{off}(z_i)}\right), \quad \cdots(1)$$

$$n(z_i) = \frac{DAPD(z_i)}{2 \cdot \Delta z \cdot (k_{on} - k_{off})}, \quad \cdots(2)$$

where $P_{off}(z)$ is received power of OFF wavelength in electric domain and $P_{on}(z)$ is received power of ON wavelength in electric domain at range z, Δz is range resolution of the lidar, k_{on} and k_{off} are absorption coefficient of ON wavelength and OFF wavelength, respectively. If the absorption coefficient is constant, the random relative error of the water vapor density $\Delta n/n$ is expressed by

$$\frac{\Delta n}{n}(z_i) = \frac{\sqrt{\left(\frac{1}{SNR_{on}(z_i)}\right)^2 + \left(\frac{1}{SNR_{off}(z_i)}\right)^2 + \left(\frac{1}{SNR_{on}(z_{i+1})}\right)^2 + \left(\frac{1}{SNR_{off}(z_{i+1})}\right)^2}}{DAPD(z_i)}, \quad \cdots(3)$$

$$SNR_{on}(z_i) = \frac{1}{\sqrt{\left(\frac{P_{Shot}}{\sqrt{N} \cdot P_S(z_i)}\right)^2 + \left(\frac{1}{\sqrt{N}}\right)^2}}, \quad \cdots(4)$$

where P_{shot} is shot noise power in electric domain and N is number of laser shot. The first term in a denominator is the signal-to-noise ratio (SNR) depend on the shot noise, and the second term in a denominator is the *SNR* depend on the speckle noise.

3. WAVELENGTH SELECTION

The main requirements for ON wavelength selection in 1.5 μm wavelength region are (i) strong line intensity and high weighting function near the ground in the region of the band of optical amplifier, and (ii) low temperature dependence of absorption. Figure 2 shows the line intensity of water vapor absorption lines for 700 nm - 2100 nm range (upper) and 1520 nm - 1570 nm range (bottom). Although an absorption coefficient of 1.5 μm wavelength region is lower than one of 0.8 μm wavelength region which has been used widely in the past literature, it is suitable for long range measurement. In the band of optical amplifier, the strong line intensity is in shorter wavelength, and the value is 3.066×10^{-24} (cm/molecule) at 1531.374 nm wavelength.

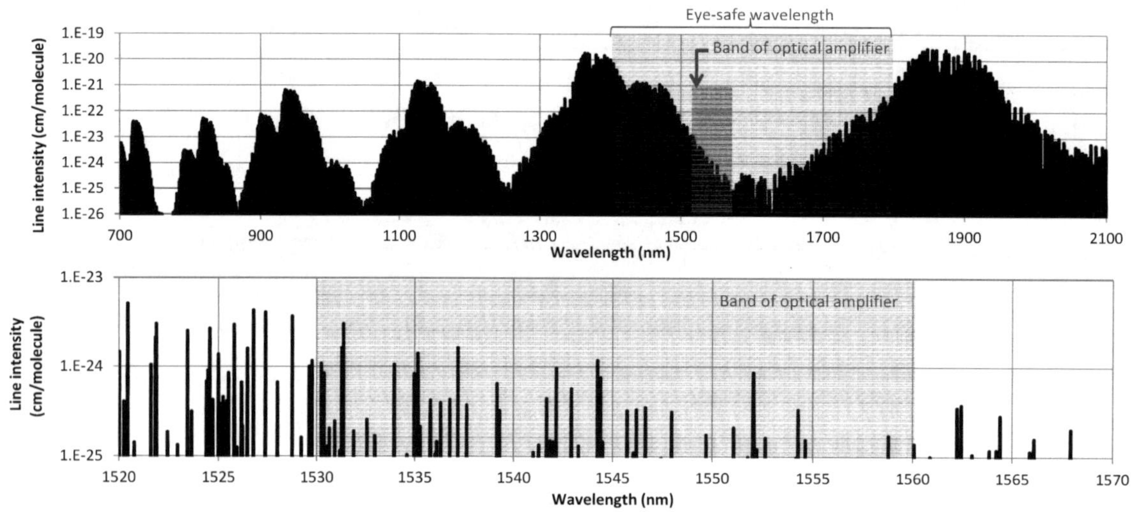

Figure 2. Line intensity of water vapor for 700-2100 nm range (upper) and 1520-1570 nm range (bottom).

Temperature dependence of the line intensity is expressed by

$$S_T(T) = S(T_{296}) \cdot \frac{Q(T_{296})}{Q(T)} \cdot \exp\left(\frac{h \cdot c \cdot E''}{k}\left(\frac{1}{T} - \frac{1}{T_0}\right)\right) \cdot \left(\frac{1 - \exp\left(\frac{h \cdot c \cdot \nu}{k \cdot T}\right)}{1 - \exp\left(\frac{h \cdot c \cdot \nu}{k \cdot T_{296}}\right)}\right), \qquad \cdots(5)$$

where *S(T296)* is line intensity at temperature of 296 K, *Q(T)* is the total internal partition sum, *h* is Plank constants, *c* is speed of light, *k* is Boltzmann constant, *E"* is the lower-state energy of the transition, and ν is the wavenumber of the spectral line transition in vacuum.

Figure 3 shows the temperature dependence of the water vapor line intensity. The line color of red, orange, yellow, green, and blue is the line intensity in 1.5 μm wavelength region. The white color line is the line intensity in 0.8 μm wavelength region which is used for the typical incoherent DIAL system [2]. The minimum temperature dependence is 1531.374 nm in the 1.5 μm wavelength region, and we selected this wavelength as the ON wavelength.

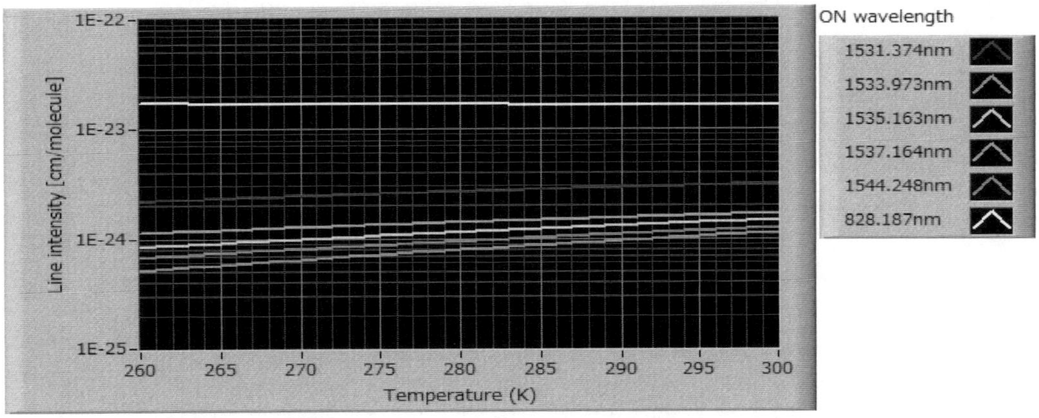

Figure 3. Temperature dependence of the water vapor line intensity.

4. CALCULATION RESULTS OF RANDOM RELATIVE ERROR IN WATER VAPOR DENSITY MEASUREMENT

We calculated the random relative error of the water vapor density by using eq. 3. The system parameters are described as follows. On and OFF wavelength are 1531.374 nm and 1531.555 nm, respectively. The output laser energy is 1.6 mJ, pulse width is 650 ns which correspond to about 100 m range resolution, and repetition frequency is 5 kHz. The receiver diameter is 150 mm, and system efficiency is -4 dB. The number of laser shot is 30,000 for each wavelength, which correspond to the 10 minutes observation time. About the atmospheric model, U.S. standard atmosphere 1976 is used, and the height profile model of aerosol backscatter coefficient from Ref. 5 and water vapor density from Ref. 6 are used. These are shown in Fig. 4 (a) and (b).

Calculation results of the received power in electrical domain and relative error of water vapor for 100 m, 300 m, and 500 m range resolution are shown in Fig. 4 (c) and (d). Simulation results show a 10 % accuracy of water vapor density from an altitude of 0.1km to 4.5km with 10 minutes averaged. These results indicate that coherent DIAL has the potential of the water vapor density measurement for weather forecast of localized heavy rainfall.

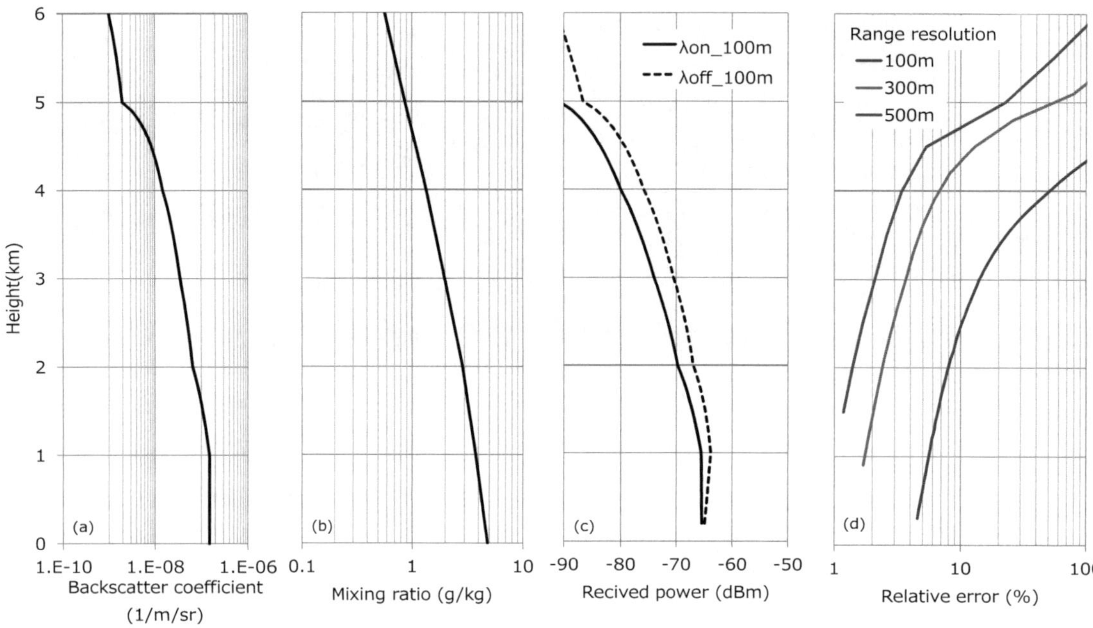

Figure 4. Height profile model of aerosol backscatter coefficient (a), water vapor mixing ratio (b), the received power for λon and λoff at 100 m range resolution (c), and the relative error of water vapor for 100 m, 300 m, and 500 m range resolution (d).

5. REFERENCES

[1] A. R. Nehrir, *et al.*, Journal of Atmospheric and Oceanic Technology **28** (2011) 131-147.

[2] S. M. Spuler, *et al.*, Atmospheric Measurement Techniques **8** (2015) 1073-1087.

[3] M. J. Kavaya, *et al.*, Appl. Opt. **28** (1989) 840-851.

[4] R. M. Hardesty, Appl. Opt. **23** (1984) 2545-2553.

[5] J. D. Spinhirne, *et al.*, Appl. Opt., **36**, (1997) 3475-3490.

[6] G. P. Anderson, *et al.*, AFGL-TR-86-0110, (1986).

Dual frequency comb spectroscopy and atmospheric modeling for the detection of methane leaks at oil and gas production sites

Sean Coburn(a), Caroline Alden(a), Robert Wright(a), Kevin Cossel(b), Garwing Truong(b), Esther Baumann(b), Subhomoy Ghosh(c), Kuldeep Prasad(c), Nathan Newbury(b), Ian Coddington(b), Gregory Rieker(a)

(a) University of Colorado Boulder
Boulder, CO, USA 80309
(b) National Institute of Standards and Technology Boulder
Boulder, CO, USA 80309
(c) National Institute of Standards and Technology Gaithersburg
Gaithersburg, MD, USA 20899
coburns@colorado.edu

Abstract: We present the development of a dual frequency comb spectrometer (DCS) system with the potential to locate and size methane leaks from oil and gas production sites over extended periods of time. The DCS system has been optimized for broadband high-precision measurements of methane over kilometer scale open paths. These measurements are coupled with an atmospheric inversion which utilizes local meteorology and a high resolution fluid dynamics simulation in order to retrieve methane leak locations and leak rates. Initial demonstrations of the instrument and techniques will be presented. In the long term, the system will be deployed at the Boulder Atmospheric Observatory (BAO) site, which is optimal for assessing the measurement and inversion methods under realistic conditions, e.g., highly variable background and high oil and gas production site density.

Keywords: Phase coherent lasers, Frequency combs, Spectroscopy, Atmospheric inversions

1. Introduction

Methane is an important greenhouse with both natural and anthropogenic sources. Uncertainty on the impact of anthropogenic methane emissions on climate change largely derives from inconsistencies in reported emission rates from many of the sources. According to the US Environmental Protection Agency (US EPA), anthropogenic methane emissions are reported to compose up to 60% of total global emissions [1], of which 33% comes from oil and natural gas (OG) production efforts [2]. Characterizing methane emissions from OG production sites is an area of increasing research interest in the US due to large increases in US methane production activity.

Dual frequency comb spectrometers (DCS) present a powerful analytical tool that are well suited for monitoring atmospheric methane and other trace gases due to their broadband nature, high spectral resolution, and fast data acquisition rate [3-10]. We have demonstrated that DCS instrumentation can operate over kilometer scale open-paths and measure multiple atmospheric trace gases with high precision [7]. Building from this work, we have a developed a DCS specifically to address the issue of monitoring OG production sites to locate and size methane leaks.

In order to derive a leak location and rate from the path integrated concentration measurements (the final data product from the DCS instrument), we are concurrently developing an atmospheric inversion that couples the DCS measurements with a high resolution fluid dynamics model and local meteorological data. Simulations with this modeling system using synthetic data have shown that we should be able to locate leaks to individual well pads and accurately determine leak rates with a fairly conservative precision (for a DCS instrument) of 4 ppb*km for methane.

Field testing of the entire system is planned to take place starting in the Summer of 2016 at the Boulder Atmospheric Observatory (BAO) located in Erie, CO (~20 km east of Boulder, CO). Currently, a majority of the inversion modeling simulations have utilized topography, meteorology, and background methane measurements from this site in order to most accurately represent measurement conditions during field testing.

2. DCS Characterization

Given the technological advances between the proof-of-concept DCS and the system presented here, a characterization of instrument performance for the newer DCS compared to the older instrument was warranted. The characterization testing has taken place at the National Institute of Standards and Technology (NIST) Boulder, which has a ~2 km open path measurement site that spans from the main NIST campus to the Koehler Mesa located directly to the west of the main campus. The 2 km link is an ideal test domain in that it enables open path measurements while allowing the DCS system to remain in a relatively controlled environment. Additionally, the proof-of-concept measurements made with an older version of the DCS instrument [8] were taken over this same path; thus allowing a reasonable comparison between instruments and quantification of improvements in the DCS instrumentation performance.

The proof-of-concept measurements showed good agreement with a Picarro multi-gas analyzer located at approximately the half-way point between the DCS launch location and the retroreflectors and was able to reach a methane precision of 6 ppb*km with 5 min averaging time [8]. Using a similar testing configuration as the proof-of-concept measurements, we were able to assess these same criteria using the newer version DCS system. We were able to reach a measurement precision of ~4 ppb*km with 90 s averaging. The precision floor reached by both of these measurement sets is determined to be limited by atmospheric variability of methane. In order to test instrument precision capability over open paths while minimizing this limitation, further tests were performed over a shorter path length (~400 m) with higher return power and under windier conditions (which results in low atmospheric trace gas concentration variability). These showed the DCS capable of reaching a precision level of ~1 ppb*km in ~100 s. Figure 1 shows Allan Deviation plots for the new DCS instrument from measurements over the full 2 km path (brown trace) and over the shorter path (red trace), as well as the data from the proof-of-concept measurements (blue trace). The grey dashed lines represent idealized curves in the absence of any atmospheric limitations; the top trace represents the proof-of-concept measurements and the bottom trace is for the newer DCS design. Better DCS performance from the new design is attributed to an optimized optical launch/receive configuration (telescope transceiver, detector, retroreflector, etc.) and the higher data acquisition rate, which is related to the lower comb tooth density of the new DCS instrument.

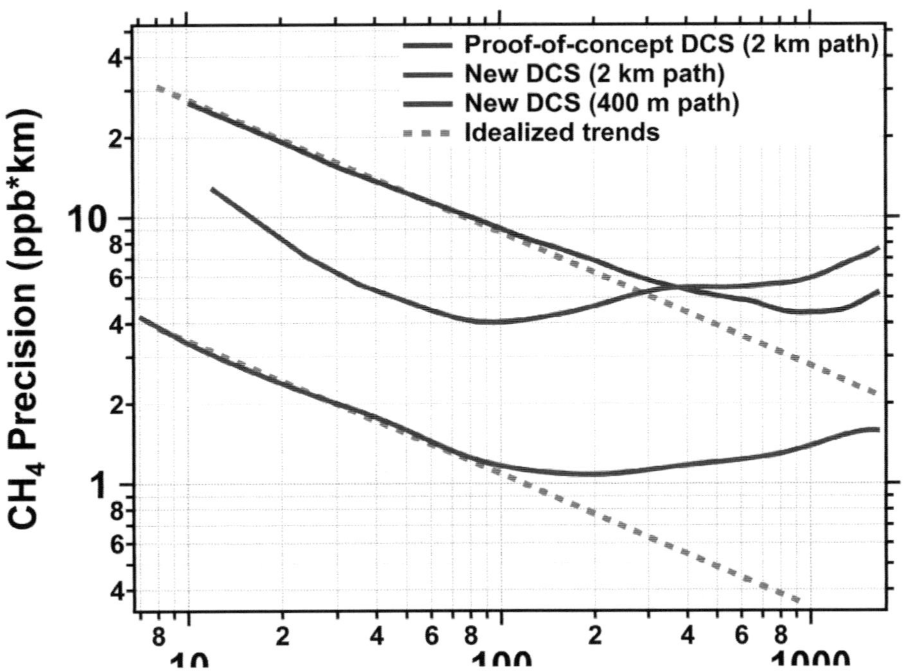

Figure 1. Allan Deviation plots for DCS system

3. Atmospheric Inversion

While the portable DCS was under development, the transport modeling and inversion schemes were developed and tested using synthetic data coupled with actual meteorological measurements taken at the field site (BAO). The synthetic data tests are able to determine the DCS system requirements and optimal measurement configurations (including site layout and measurement schemes). Methane measurements taken with a Picarro multi-gas analyzer as part of the Front Range Air Pollution and Photochemistry Experiment (FRAPPE) field campaign during the summer 2014 at the BAO tower site have been incorporated in these modeling studies to act as a way to add realistic background variability to the simulations. Additionally, wind speed and direction data taken during the same time at the BAO tower are being used to ensure the most accurate representation of the atmospheric state during the time of the methane measurements.

Several measurement site layouts, i.e. retroreflector placement relative to the DCS and wells, have been found to produce positive results in the inversion, which gives an indication that there is some flexibility when setting up the field tests. Additionally, different measurements schemes are being tested to ensure optimal and efficient sampling of the retroreflectors under varying wind conditions which is an important consideration especially when monitoring many different OG production sites.

The modeling runs have determined that an instrument precision of at least 4 ppb*km is needed in order to accurately locate and size methane leaks at the measurement site, and when using this criterion coupled with the realistic representation of atmospheric state and background methane variations described above, we find that the DCS should be fully capable of locating methane leaks to a single well-pad and estimating the leak rate. Figure 2 presents the results from one of the synthetic data modeling runs in which the simulated measurements located 2 leaks in a domain containing 52 OG production sites. In Fig. 2, blue dots show “actual” leak locations (on the x-axis and y-axis) and strengths (on the z-axis). Green dots show recovered leak locations and strengths, with error bars indicating 2 standard deviations. The recovered leak on the domain boundary shows influence of near-field outside sources and is off the z-axis scale.

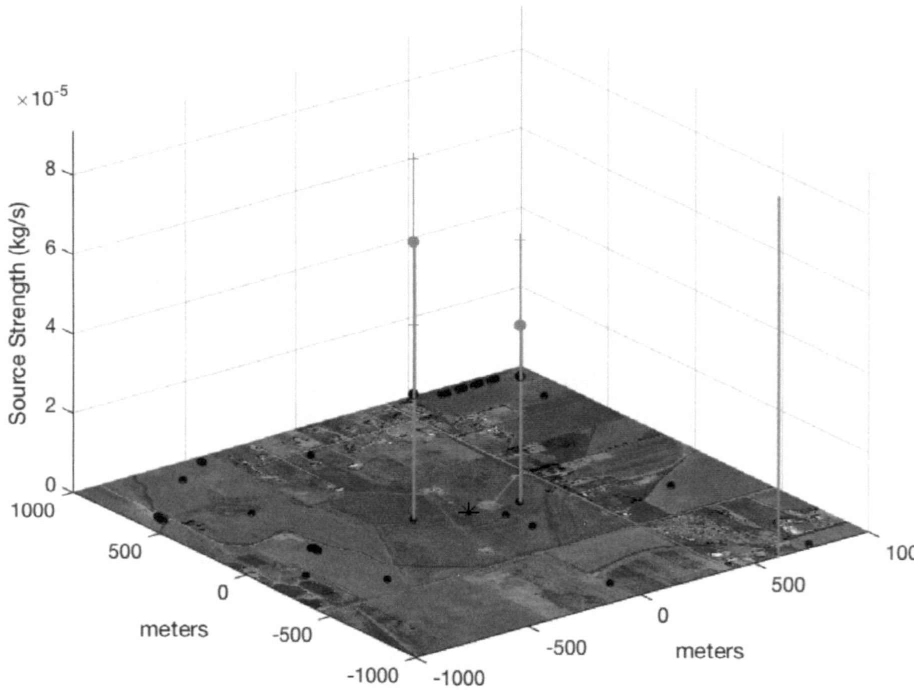

Figure 2. Inversion results using synthetic data

4. Summary

We present the development of a dual frequency comb spectrometer and atmospheric modeling/inversion technique that will facilitate the monitoring of oil and natural gas production sites for methane leaks on a regional scale. The original demonstration of the DCS proved that this instrument represents a powerful tool for monitoring multiple atmospheric trace gases over kilometer scale open paths. Building from this work, we are now able to decouple the DCS from the laboratory and operate it in a field environment at higher precision. The modeling and inversion techniques being developed allow for the derivation of leak location and rate using only path integrated concentration measurements of methane from the DCS and local meteorological data. Deploying this system in areas with high densities of OG operations would enable the simultaneous monitoring of numerous production sites and facilitate the quantification of both leak frequency and rates over extended periods of time.

5. References

[1] EPA 430-R-10-001, "Methane and Nitrous Oxide Emissions from Natural Sources", United States Environmental Protection Agency, 2010.

[2] EPA 430-R-16-002, "US Greenhouse Gas Inventory Report: 1990-2014", United States Environmental Protection Agency, 2016.

[3] A. Schliesser, M. Brehm, F. Keilmann, and D. van der Weide, "Frequency-comb infrared spectrometer for rapid, remote chemical sensing," Opt. Express **13**, 9029–9038, 2005.

[4] I. Coddington, W. C. Swann, and N. R. Newbury, "Coherent dual- comb spectroscopy at high signal-to-noise ratio," Phys. Rev. A **82**, 043817, 2010.

[5] E. Baumann, F. R. Giorgetta, W. C. Swann, A. M. Zolot, I. Coddington, and N. R. Newbury, "Spectroscopy of the methane v3 band with an accurate midinfrared coherent dual-comb spectrometer," Phys. Rev. A **84**, 062513, 2011.

[6] J. Roy, J.-D. Deschênes, S. Potvin, and J. Genest, "Continuous real-time correction and averaging for frequency comb interferom- etry," Opt. Express **20**, 21932–21939, 2012.

[7] S. Potvin and J. Genest, "Dual-comb spectroscopy using frequency-doubled combs around 775 nm," Opt. Express **21**, 30707–30715, 2013.

[8] G. B. Rieker, F. R. Giorgetta, W. C. Swann, J. Kofler, A. M. Zolot, L. C. Sinclair, E. Baumann, C. Cromer, G. Petron, C. Sweeney, P. P. Tans, I. Coddington, and N. R. Newbury, "Frequency-comb-based remote sensing of greenhouse gases over kilometer air paths," Optica **1**, 5, 290–298, 2014.

[9] T. Ideguchi, A. Poisson, G. Guelachvili, N. Picqué, and T. W. Hänsch, "Adaptive real-time dual-comb spectroscopy," Nat. Commun. **5**, 3375, 2014.

[10] D. A. Long, A. J. Fleisher, K. O. Douglass, S. E. Maxwell, K. Bielska, J. T. Hodges, and D. F. Plusquellic, "Multiheterodyne spectroscopy with optical frequency combs generated from a continuous-wave laser," Opt. Lett. **39**, 2688–2690, 2014.

A Measure of Flow Vorticity with Twisted Beams of Light

Aniceto Belmonte[1], Carmelo Rosales-Guzmán[2], and Juan P. Torres[1, 2]
(1) Technical University of Catalonia, BarcelonaTech, Dept. of Signal Theory and Communications
Campus Nord UPC, 08034 Barcelona, Spain
(2) ICFO–Institut de Ciencies Fotoniques
Mediterranean Technology Park, 08860 Castelldefels (Barcelona), Spain
belmonte@tsc.upc.edu

Abstract: The measurement of vorticity, a parameter providing local measurements of rotation at every point in a flow, would greatly assist research fields as diverse as biology microfluidics, complex motions in the oceanic and atmospheric boundary layers, and wake turbulence on fluid aerodynamics. However, the precise measurement of flow vorticity is difficult. Here, we devise an experiment in which the local vorticity of a flow can be estimated by probing the fluid with Laguerre-Gauss beams, optical beams that show an azimuthal phase variation that is the origin of its characteristic non-zero orbital angular momentum. The key point is to make use of the transversal Doppler effect of the returned signal that depends only on the azimuthal component of the flow velocity along the ring-shaped observation beam. We found from a detailed analysis of the experimental method that probing the fluid with LG beams is an effective and simple sensing technique capable to produce accurate estimates of flow vorticity [1].

Keywords: Laser Doppler velocimetry; Turbulence; Flow diagnostics; Optical sensing; Atmospheric and oceanic optics; Medical and biological imaging.

1. Introduction

Formally, vorticity $\vec{\omega} = \vec{\nabla}\times\vec{U}$ is defined as the curl of the velocity vector $\vec{U}$, which is a measure of angular rotation of a material point about a local position in a flow field and may be regarded as a measure of the local angular velocity of the fluid [2][3]. Typically, vorticity measurement systems are designed to probe one the components of the vorticity vector $\vec{\omega}$ [3]. For simplicity, and without lost of generality, we consider a two-dimensional flow in the xy–plane, where $\vec{U} = (U, V, 0)$ and vorticity $\vec{\omega} = (0,0,\omega)$ z–axis component is defined on the basis of velocity derivatives as $\omega = \partial V/\partial x - \partial U/\partial y$.

Several optical methods of vorticity measurement in a flow –Particle Image Velocimetry (PIV) [4][5] and Laser Doppler Velocimetry (LDV) [6][7], among others– attend to determine first the instantaneous velocity components U and V, and then differentiate velocity data to yield vorticity field component ω. By whatever means the velocity measurements are estimate, they must be made consecutively with high frequency to attain fine temporal resolution, and simultaneously over several closed space locations from which spatial gradients $\partial V/\partial x$ and $\partial U/\partial y$ can be evaluated using finite difference schemes. However, the fact that these techniques define vorticity in terms of the velocity gradients produces poor accuracy estimates. The accuracy of the calculate vorticity depends on the mean spatial resolution of the velocity sampling –as any real measure needs to consider the length scales dx and dy, flow measurements are always integrated over some area and a spatial average vorticity is measured– and the uncertainty error on estimates of velocity differences dU and dV affects vorticity accuracy.

To overcome the shortcomings of finite difference methods for vorticity measurements, here we consider a new optical probing technique that is not implicitly dependent upon velocity measurements and directly observes the local vorticity of fluid elements. It uses LG laser beams to illuminate the flow and obtain, by observing the transversal Doppler effect in the reflected signal [8][9], information about vorticity. It is

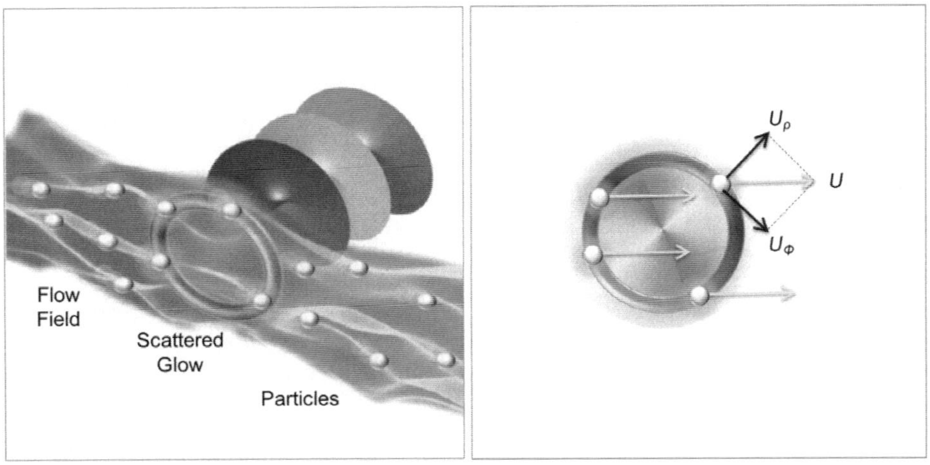

Fig. 1. Measure of vorticity in a flow.

necessary to note that other measurement methods use image techniques to directly observe local flow rotation. Vorticity Optical Probing (VOP) uses Gaussian laser beams to illuminate the passage of probe particles embedded in the flow to obtain, by image analysis, information about their trajectories [10]. Although small probe particles suspended in a flow will react to fluctuations of rotation in the flow, allowing the vorticity of the flow to be probed directly as it moves along a streamline, it is not always possible –or even convenient– to implant probe particles into the fluid whose dynamics needs to be characterized. The technique we propose is akin to laser Doppler anemometry using LG laser beams to illuminate clear flows (see Fig. 1).

The vorticity measurement technique we consider here determines the vorticity ω directly from the estimation of the transversal Doppler frequency centroid $\langle f_\perp \rangle$ of the signal backscattered by the flow when illuminated by a LG beam with mode number m [1]:

$$\omega = 4\pi/m \ \langle f_\perp \rangle$$

The frequency centroid $\langle f_\perp \rangle$ estimation is typically based on the spectrum of the observed signal. The temporal return backscattered signal –a compound of signals with different frequency Doppler shift triggered by the multiple components of velocity U_ϕ along the annular illumination beam, as shown in Fig. 1– can be Fourier transformed to define its frequency spectrum. The characteristic return Doppler spectrum is a histogram of Doppler frequency components describing the spectral content of the returned signal and it can be used to calculate the frequency centroid $\langle f_\perp \rangle$ as the average of the frequencies present in the signal.

2. Experiments on the measurement of flow vorticity

We use numerical experiments on the flow vorticity measurement to demonstrate the viability of the proposed method. The use of a realistic signal model illustrates the dependence of the results on the different experimental parameters and allows addressing the problem of vorticity estimation under the supposition of both additive (receiver) and multiplicative (speckle) noises. We assume that the Doppler measurement system uses heterodyne detection –the most straightforward to set up experimentally– where the scattered light is coherently mixed on the receiver with a more intense reference beam, which acts as a local oscillator only.

When a set of independent scatters, moving with velocity $\vec{U}$, passes the ring–like observation region, it generates a burst of optical echoes that contributes to the received optical signal. We use a superposition model for the scattering process that directly gives the complex amplitude of the return signal as the sum

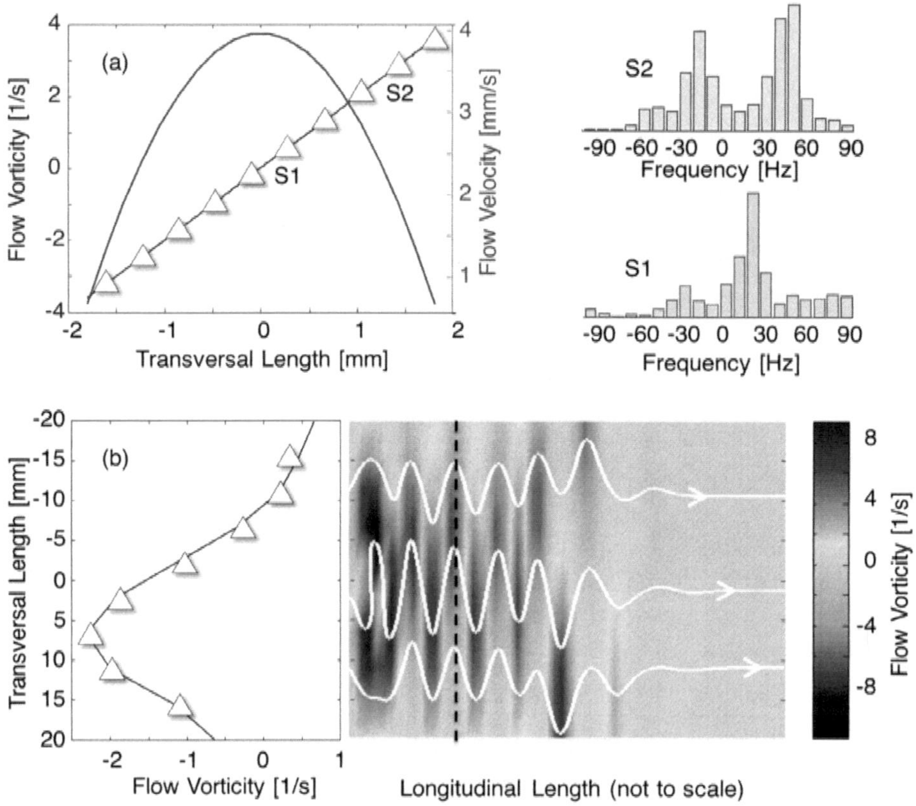

Fig. 2. Numerical experiments on the measurement of flow vorticity

of the fields scattered by all the scatters illuminated by the LG beam. After coherent detection and filtering to remove the carrier frequency and its harmonics, we obtain a detected signal (photocurrent) characterizing the optical echo from the target.

Figure 2 shows the result of our numerical experiments on two different flow patterns. The technique is tested in a steady laminar flow (Fig. 1(a)), in which the flow vorticity is known, and in a complex flow around a circular cylinder immersed in a uniform flow (Fig. 1(b)). We measure vorticity and study the effects of several flow and illumination parameters on the performance of the probing technique. In these experiments, we consider an incident LG laser beam with radial mode number $p = 0$, azimuthal mode number $m = 10$, and beam radius $\omega_0 = 45$ μm. The illuminating beam phase changes from zero to 2π ten times around the azimuth and the intensity distribution shows a bright ring of radius $\rho_0 = 100$ μm. Typical parameters for a heterodyne receiver are chosen to be signal bandwidth normalized to the sampling frequency $B/F_S = 0.5$, and number of complex samples per estimate $M = 64$. The plots consider a signal return accumulation (spectral accumulation) of $N = 250$.

Figure 2(a) shows the measure of vorticity in a laminar flow. In the numerical experiment, the fluid is flowing along the longitudinal x–axis through a closed channel of radius $R = 2$ mm. The transversal velocity $\vec{U} = (U, 0)$ of flow describes a parabolic profile of velocities along the transversal y–axis that varies from zero at the channel ends to a maximum of $U_0 = 4$ mm/s along the center of the channel. The parabolic profile of velocities $U = U_0[1 - (y/R)^2]$ gives the linear vorticity profile $\omega = 2\, U_0/R^2\, y$. The measurements with LG beams reproduce very closely these expected vorticity values.

In a different numerical experiment, Fig. 2(b) shows vorticity in a complex flow created by the unsteady separation of fluid around a cylindrical object located up stream (don't show in the graph). We estimate the velocity field $\vec{U} = (U, V)$ using a numerical tool for flow simulation. From the numerical velocity field we calculate the resultant z–component of vorticity as $\omega = \partial V/\partial x - \partial U/\partial y$. The flows on opposite sides of the cylindrical object interact in an extended region and produce a regular circulation pattern. The energy of the vortices is ultimately expended by viscosity as they move further down stream and the regular pattern disappears. The velocity field is pictured in the right graph with a set of streamlines that are tangent to the flow velocity vector. The color scale in the same graph gives an idea of the vorticity magnitude. The left plot compares a measure of flow vorticity with LG beams and the corresponding theoretical expectations. In the simulation, the measurement is realized across the flow, down stream from the cylindrical object.

The feasibility of the proposed method to measure flow vorticity was also verified through the experiments. A heterodyne receiver based on a modified Mach-Zehnder interferometer was used for experiments. Using the insight realized by numerical experiments into the problem of vorticity estimation, the operation parameters of the test system were established in order to emulate different types of flows. More details of our analysis, and results on lab experiments on the measurement of flow vorticity, will be presented at the meeting.

3. Conclusions

The problem of measuring vorticity in a flow has been confronted. We propose an optical technique that uses LG beams, characterized by ring–like intensity distributions and azimuthal phase variations, to sense rotation at every point in a flow. We develop the theoretical background behind the modeling of optical measurement of vorticity in a flow, identifying the required assumptions and input beam parameters. The spectral properties of the return signal, and the spectrum centroid integral in particular, are fundamental to interpretation of experiments used in flow vorticity monitoring. We verify the working principle of the technique with numerical and lab experiments. By using measurement data, we assess the feasibility of the sensing technique and identify the accuracy of vorticity measurements from return signals affected by target speckle and receiver noise.

4. References

[1]. A. Belmonte, C. Rosales-Guzmán, and J. P. Torres, "Measurement of flow vorticity with helical beams of light," Optica **2**, 1002-1005 (2015)

[2]. K. Batchelor, *An Introduction to Fluid Dynamics* (Cambridge University Press, 2000).

[3]. J M Wallace, and J F Foss, "The Measurement of Vorticity in Turbulent Flows," Annu. Rev. Fluid Mech. **27**, 469-514 (1995).

[4]. R. J. Adrian, "Particle-imaging techniques for experimental fluid mechanics," Annu. Rev. Fluid Mech. **23**, 261–304 (1991).

[5]. R. J. Adrian, J. Westerweel, *Particle Image Velocimetry* (Cambridge University Press, 2011).

[6]. S. Yao, P. Tong, and B. J. Ackerson, "Proposal and testing for a fiber-optic-based measurement of flow vorticity," Appl. Opt. **40**, 4022-4027 (2001).

[7]. Y. Yeh, H. Z. Cummins, "Localized Fluid Flow Measurements with an He-Ne Laser Spectrometer," Appl Phys. Lett. **4**,176-178 (1964).

[8]. A. Belmonte and J. P. Torres, "Optical Doppler shift with structured light," Opt. Lett. **36**, 4437 (2011).

[9]. C. Rosales-Guzmán, N. Hermosa, A. Belmonte, and J. P. Torres, "Experimental detection of transverse particle movement with structured light," Sci. Rep. **36**, 2815 (2013).

[10]. M. Frish and W. Webb, "Direct Measurement of Vorticity by Optical Probe," *J. Fluid Mech.* **107**, 173-200 (1981).

Photonic Integrated Circuits for Coherent Lidar

Paul J. M. Suni[(a)], John Bowers[(b)], Larry Coldren[(b)], S.J. Ben Yoo[(c)]
(a) Lockheed Martin Coherent Technologies, Louisville, CO, USA
(b) University of California Santa Barbara, California 93106, USA
(c) University of California, Davis, CA 95616, USA

Lead Author e-mail address: paul.suni@lmco.com

Abstract: A decade ago integrated photonic devices typically consisted of single components that fulfilled one specific function, such as phase modulation or splitting into *N* beams. In the intervening years, photonic integrated circuits (PICs) have undergone a revolution in terms of component functions, loss reductions, and high level functional integration. This has in part been driven by the development of device designs compatible with conventional CMOS fabrication processes. We are now at a point where component diversity, low losses, and low cost fabrication enables us to consider development of coherent laser radar systems based around PIC technology. In this talk we will highlight some of the current developments in the PIC domain, with an emphasis on technology elements applicable to coherent laser radar systems. Examples include narrowband lasers, frequency shifters, beam distribution networks, and large angle photonic beam steering.

Keywords: Photonics, Photonic Integrated Circuits, PIC, Silicon Photonics, Coherent Laser Radar, Lidar, Ladar

1. Introduction

The reduction of optical devices to microscopic dimensions has been underway for decades in the form of fiber optics, CMOS detector arrays, and components like modulators, micro-ring filters, and splitters. The past decade has seen an explosion of development that goes beyond single devices and now encompasses subsystems and systems with hundreds of components [1-4]. The technology typically falls under the name of Photonic Integrated Circuits (PICs). Silicon Photonics is a form of PIC that uses silicon substrates and silicon waveguides for the platform. .

A key enabler in the silicon photonic revolution has been the development of technologies compatible with conventional CMOS fabrication processes and foundries. In an extraordinary coincidence the multi-billion dollar investments in CMOS foundries enable the same fabrication infrastructure to produce devices that propagate light at wavelengths ideally suited for many electro-optic communications and sensing applications. Low propagation losses (<0.5 dB/cm) in waveguide dimensions smaller than the wavelength (220 nm × 300 nm cross-section for 1550 nm wavelength) have enabled integration of large numbers of components in small footprints. The large index step between silicon (n_{Si} ~ 3.5) and waveguide cladding materials like silica glass (n ~ 1.45) and silicon nitride (n ~2) enables tight mode confinement and small bend radii (<10 μm), while supporting low loss and low crosstalk between closely-spaced waveguides.

Silicon is excellent as a materials system for passive components, but is non-ideal for active components like laser sources and detectors. Fortunately heterogeneous integration techniques are maturing, whereby high-performance active components made using InP, GaAs, Ge, and other materials can be integrated with silicon.

In tandem with the development of optical devices, great progress is also being made in the integration of optics with CMOS electronics and efficient thermal management. Flip-chip bonding of PICs with CMOS chips (also known as "2.5D" integration) is routinely done today and full 3D integration of complex photonic/electronic circuitry is undergoing rapid development [3]. These advances enables us to consider construction of lidar systems on a chip.

Figure 1 shows a generic coherent lidar architecture. Aside from the signal processor, the only functional element that has not been demonstrated in PIC form is a high peak power oscillator or amplifier, because of the peak power handling limits of small waveguides. Silicon photonics offers the possibility of fabricating complete coherent lidar systems at the chip level by tailoring components to lidar needs. Until high peak power systems are developed, perhaps based on large arrays of parallel coherent amplifiers, chip-based coherent lidar systems are likely to be developed around modulated CW architectures.

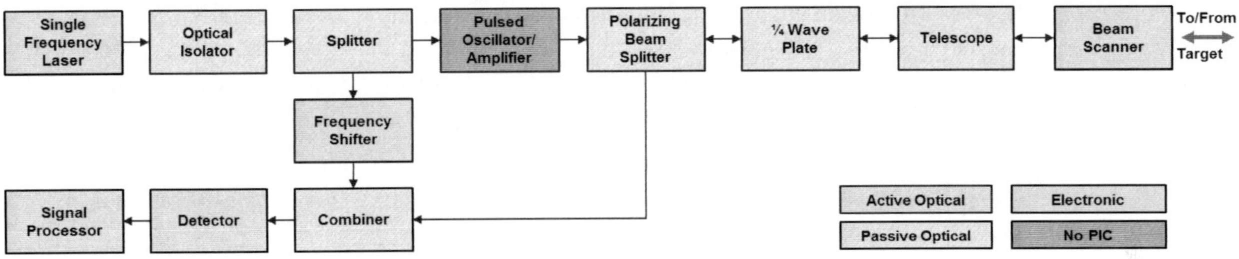

Figure 1. Generic coherent ladar architecture.

2. Device Examples

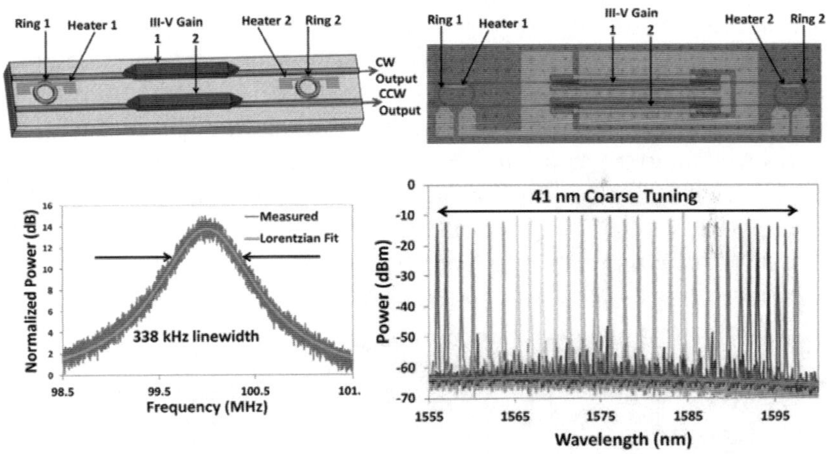

Figure 2. Laser with >40 nm tunability centered at 1575 nm [4].

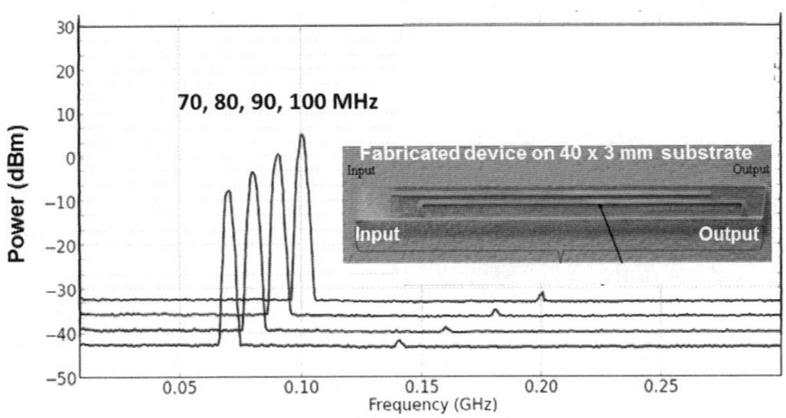

Figure 3. Frequency shifter demonstrated at UCD.

For space reasons we only provide two examples of relevant demonstrated devices. Figure **2** shows a laser developed at UC Santa Barbara comprising two gain elements [5]. Two thermally adjustable micro-rings are used in a Vernier configuration to enable >40 nm wavelength tuning with narrow linewidth and >35 dB side-mode suppression. The output power was >3 mW, which could be increased with on-chip semiconductor amplifiers (SOA) [6]. Other lasers demonstrated at UCSB include broadly tunable lasers with wavelength hopping and stabilization in 30 ns.

Frequency shifting is another important feature of coherent lidar systems as they are frequently used to generate intermediate frequencies (IF) and track out Doppler shifts. This is often accomplished using acousto-optic modulators (AOM), cascaded Mach-Zehnder interferometers, or by offset-locking two lasers. A conceptually very simple direct frequency shifter that emulates a rotating half-wave plate has recently been demonstrated [7] in $LiNbO_3$ at UC Davis – see Figure **3**. Note the absence of the carrier frequency and ~40 dB suppression of the second harmonic. This device type is predicted to enable frequency shifting in excess of 10 GHz.

Many other important components also exist, including optical isolators with >30 dB isolation and 2.3 dB insertion loss [8], low-loss PIC to fiber couplers [9], and methods for writing low-loss 3D waveguides for routing [10]. Numerous additional examples of PICs can be found in reference [11].

3. Non-Mechanical Beam Steering (NMBS)

Beam steering is frequently a SWaP limiting factor in conventional lidar systems. Many means have been devised over the years to eliminate large, heavy, and slow gimbals, Risley prisms, and other steering devices. McManamon reviewed non-mechanical beam steering (NMBS) technologies in 2009 [12]. Silicon photonics is taking beam scanning to a new level by completely eliminating the need for bulk optics. The recent DARPA SWEEPER program developed multiple PIC-based NMBS systems. Figure 4 shows approaches by researchers at UC Berkeley [13] and MIT [14]. The Berkeley approached used MEMS ribbon arrays to on-the-fly reconfigure gratings which diffract light angularly, The MIT approach uses 2D arrays of phase shifters to steer beams by imposing transverse linear phase gradients. Both of these approaches demonstrated fast and efficient beam steering, but also revealed a scalability issue. To address N far field points in two dimensions the number of required controls grows as N^2, which becomes very challenging as N becomes very large.

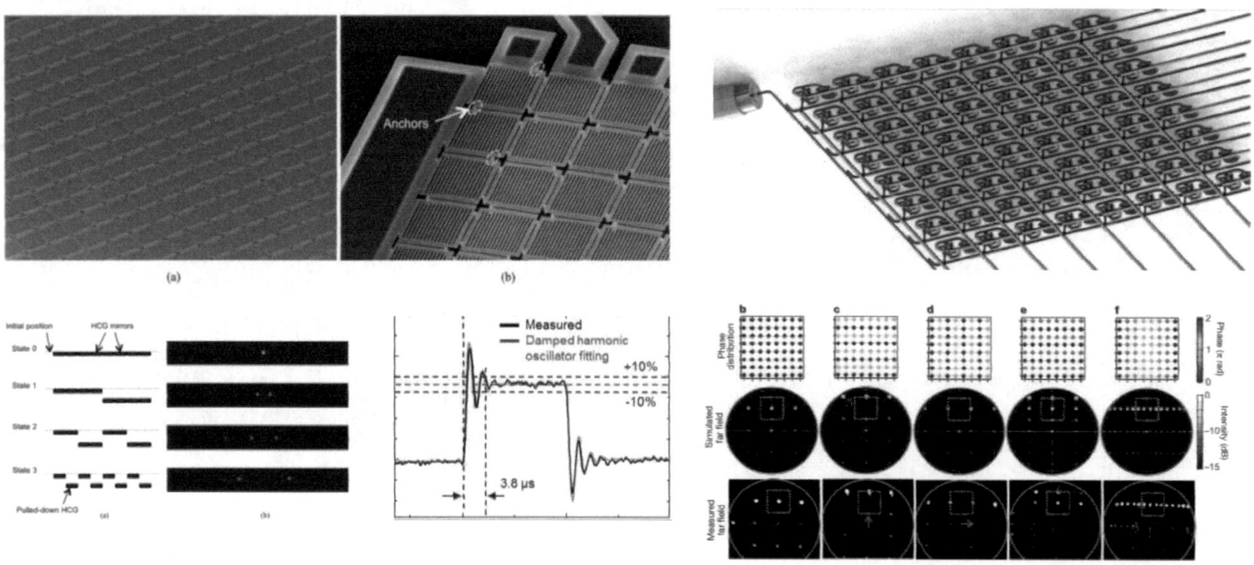

Figure 4. PIC-based NMBS demonstrated by UC Berkeley (left) [13] using MEMS ribbon arrays and by MIT (right) [14] using 2D arrays of phase shifters.

Figure 5 shows an alternative approach developed by UCSB [15,16]. In this approach laser tuning over ~43 nm combined with a fixed grating is used to steer beams in one dimension. Transverse phase gradients steer in the second dimension. This approach reduces the number of control elements to N+1, the 1 being the laser wavelength control.

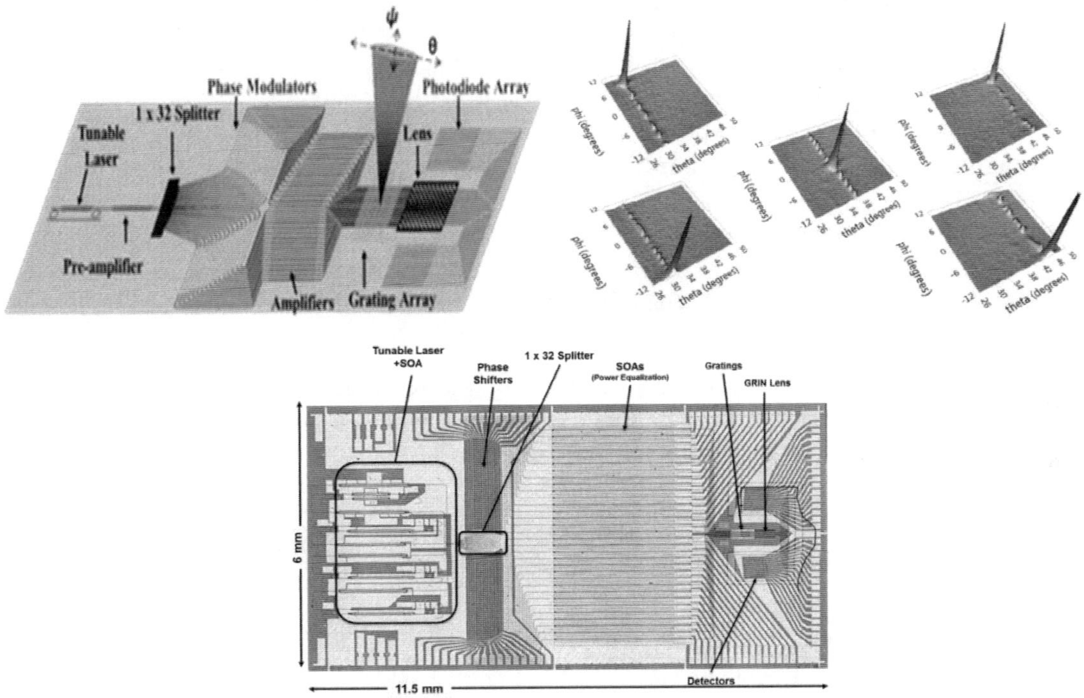

Figure 5. 2D NMBS approach developed by UCSB [15]. Top left – functional architecture. Top right – 2D beam steering demonstrated to date. Bottom – physical layout on 6 × 11.5 mm^2 chip.

4. Coherent Lidar Example

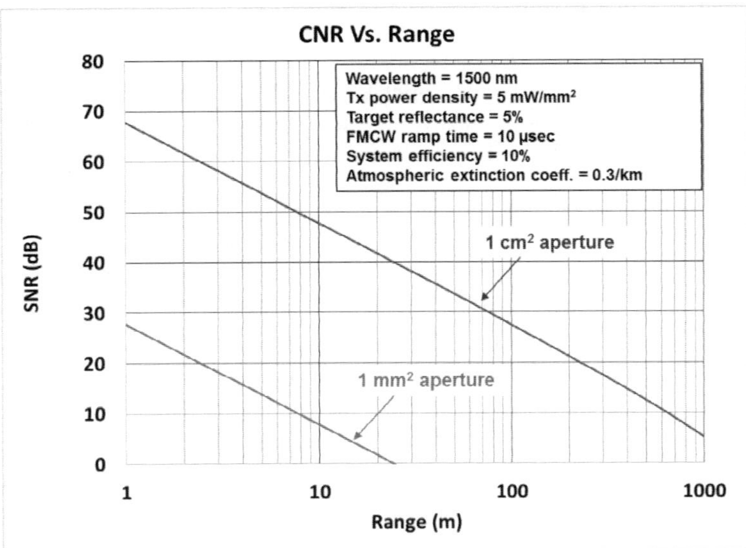

Figure 6. FMCW lidar CNR vs. range prediction for realistic sensing scenario at two aperture sizes with the same

Many versions of coherent lidar systems can be constructed as transmitted power density of 5 mW/mm^2. variations on the generic architecture shown in Figure 1. Frequency-modulated continuous wave (FMCW) operation is one approach to perform lidar functions like range finding at low peak powers and simple signal processing [17]. In this technique the laser frequency is ramped linearly in time and the time delay associated with the round-trip time to the target produces a beat signal with frequency proportional to range. Up-down frequency ramps can be used to unambiguously distinguish range and velocity. Figure 6 illustrates an example of the anticipated SNR achievable with a coherent FMCW single point sensor operating with a single shot measurement time of 10 μs, i.e. up to 100 kHz data points per second rate. The green curve corresponds to a 1 × 1 mm coherent transmit/receive aperture while the blue curve corresponds to a coherent 1 × 1 cm aperture. Multi-point simultaneous sensing similar to that used in commercial 3D lidar instruments [18] can also be incorporated into the same chip. A non-mechanical steered single-chip sensor of this type could be constructed by incorporation of the technology elements described in this paper. As seen in Figure 6 such a sensor could provide rapid 3D mapping to km ranges with a modest ~1 cm^2 coherent aperture.

Looking into the future it is not far-fetched to envision future large aperture coherent lidar systems fabricated at low cost in very small form factors. These may incorporate all photonic components, the associated signal processing, as well as efficient heat removal.

5. References

[1] M. J. Heck, et al., "Hybrid Silicon Photonic Integrated Circuit Technology", IEEE J. of Sel. Top. In Quan. Electr, **19**, pp. 6100117 (2013)

[2] Chong Zhang, et al., "2.56 Tbps (8 × 8 × 40 Gbps) Fully-Integrated Silicon Photonic Interconnection Circuit", Conference on Lasers and Electro-Optics (CLEO), San Jose, CA, USA (2016)

[3] V. Stojanovic et al., "High-Density 3D Electronic-Photonic integration," in Fourth Berkeley Symposium on Energy Efficient Electronic Systems (E3S), pp. 1-2 (2015)

[4] S. J. Ben Yoo, "Heterogeneous Photonic Integrated Circuits and Their Applications in Computing, Networking, and Imaging," Proc. SPIE 8988, Integrated Optics: Devices, Materials, and Technologies XVIII, 89881D (2014); doi:10.1117/12.2047106.

[5] J. C. Hulme et al., "Widely Tunable Vernier Ring Laser on Hybrid Silicon," Opt. Express **21**, 19718-19722 (2013)

[6] Michael L. Davenport, Sandra Skendzic, and John E. Bowers, "Heterogeneous Silicon/InP Semiconductor Optical Amplifiers with High Gain and High Saturation Power", Conference on Lasers and Electro-Optics (CLEO), San Jose, CA, USA; 5 - 10 June 2016

[7] B. Ercan et al., "Optical Frequency Shifting in Electro-Optical Waveguides by Emulating Rotating Waveplates", *J. Lightwave Technology*, **33** (to be published, 2016)

[8] D. Huang et al., "Silicon Microring Isolator With Large Optical Isolation and Low Loss", Proc. Optical Fiber Conference, OSA Publishing (2016), paper Th1K2

[9] C. Lo et al. "CMOS-compatible High Efficiency Double-Etched Apodized Waveguide Grating Coupler", Opt. Expr., **21**, pp. 7868 (2013)

[10] S. J. Ben Yoo et al., "Heterogeneous 2D/3D Photonic Integrated Microsystems" invited paper to appear in Nature Microsystems and Nanoengineering (2016)

[11] L. Chrostowski and M. Hochberg, "Silicon Photonics Design: From Devices to Systems", Cambridge University Press (2015)

[12] P.F.McManamon e al., "A Review of Phased Array Steering for Narrow-Band Electrooptical Systems", Proc. of the IEEE, **97**, PP. 1078 (2009)

[13] B. Yoo et al., "A 32x32 Optical Phased Array Using Polysilicon Sub-Wavelength High-Contrast-Grating Mirrors", Opt. Expr., **22**, DOI:10.1364/OE.22.019029

[14] J. Sun et al., "Large-Scale Nanophotonic Phased Array", Nature, **493**, pp. 195 (2013)

[15] H. Guo et al., "Two-Dimensional Optical Beam Steering with InP-based Photonic Integrated Circuits," IEEE J. Sel. Topics Quantum Electron., Special Issue on Semiconductor Lasers, **19**, pp. 6100212, (2013)

[16] J. C. Hulme, et al., "Fully Integrated Hybrid Silicon Two Dimensional Beam Scanner", Optics Express, Vol. 23, No. 5 DOI:10.1364/OE.23.005861, p. 5861-5874; 25 February 2015

[17] B. W. Krause et al., "Motion Compensated Frequency Modulated Continuous Wave 3D Coherent Imaging Ladar with Scannerless Architecture," Appl. Opt., **51**, pp. 8745-8761 (2012)

[18] www.velodynelidar.com

Coherent Detection with an Asynchronous Geiger Mode Array

Joseph C. Marron, Maurice J. Halmos and Brian F. Boland

Raytheon Space and Airborne Systems
2000 E. El Segundo Blvd
El Segundo, CA 90245
joseph.marron@raytheon.com

Abstract

Large format arrays of coherent detectors enable several advanced EO sensing modes including aperture synthesis, turbulence compensation and velocity sensing. Coherent detector arrays that operate in a linear mode are desirable; however, they are often impractical because read-out'ss offering sufficient pixel density and A/D rates are not available. Photon-counting coherent detector arrays based on Geiger-mode Avalanche Photo-Diode (GmAPD) arrays are attractive because they offer large array format, and the output is digitized via the photon arrival times. Furthermore, asynchronous GmAPD arrays offer improved blocking efficiency which in turn improves the frequency fidelity. In fact, the response time of an asynchronous GmAPD macropixel exceeds the reset time of the individual detectors. In this paper we present the results of analysis, modeling and experiments that show the performance levels attainable with asynchronous GmAPD arrays.

1 Analysis of Coherent Detection with Photon-Counting Array

For coherent detection with a photon-counting array, a sub-array of pixels (a macro-pixel) is typically used to detect the signal over a coherence cell. This improves the blocking efficiency caused by the finite pixel reset time. With a traditional coherent detector the detector size is matched to the coherence cell size, $\lambda f/D$, where f is focal length, λ is wavelength, and D is the receiver diameter. For the photon-counting case, we use an array of M x M = N_0 pixels comprising a macro-pixel to cover the coherence cell. An expression for the blocking efficiency is given by [1, 2]

$$B = 1/\left(1 + T_R\left(\frac{(N_S+N_{LO})PDE}{CPI \cdot N_0} + DCR\right)\right). \tag{1}$$

An expression for the CNR that includes the blocking efficiency is then

$$CNR = \frac{PDE \cdot B \cdot \eta_{HET} N_S N_{LO}}{N_S+N_{LO}+N_0 \cdot B \cdot CPI \cdot DCR/PDE}. \tag{2}$$

It follows that because $B < 1$ in practice, the performance of the asynchronous GmAPD is always less than that of a conventional linear mode coherent detector; however, the large formats and high-bandwidths achievable with asynchronous GmAPDs can offset this for many cases. Also note that for a linear mode detector optimal performance is obtained with N_{LO} much greater than N_s, whereas for a Geiger mode detector N_{LO} must be limited to keep the blocking efficiency high.

Figure 1 contains a plot showing the CNR dependence on the LO power and signal power from Eq. (2). We observe that the CNR peaks at LO levels comparable to the signal levels. These values are given in the table below. If we consider the case of N_s=100 with DCR= 0, we see that the asynchronous detector achieves a peak CNR value of roughly 6, whereas the peak CNR achieved with an ideal linear mode detector ($CNR = PDE \cdot \eta_{HET} N_S$) is 9. Thus CNR for the asynchronous detector is 2/3 that of the ideal detector for this specific example.

Values
$N_0 = 25$
CPI = 10 μsec
$N_S = 10^2, 10^3, 10^4$
$N_{LO} = 700, 2000, 10000$
DCR= 0, 10^5
PDE = 0.30
η_{HET} = 0.30
f = 5 MHz
T_R = 500 nsec
B = calculated

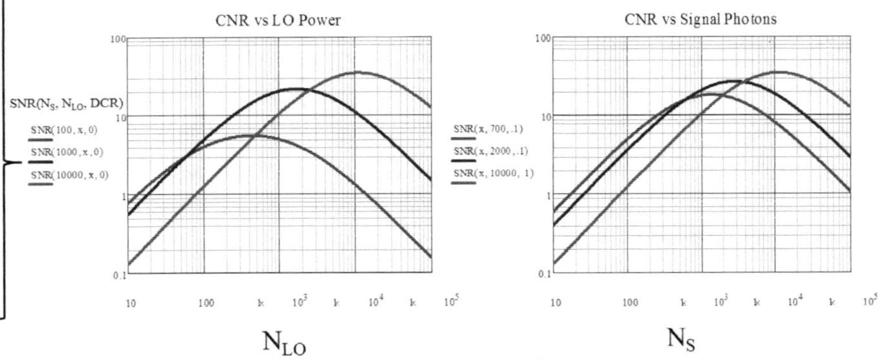

Figure 1. CNR plotted versus LO power and CNR versus signal power

2 Numerical Simulations

Here we present the results of numerical simulations performed to evaluate signal properties including the detector's frequency response and also confirm the above formulas for the blocking efficiency and CNR. We modeled the intensity of the heterodyne signal as

$$I(t) = N_S + N_{LO} + N_{DCR} + 2\sqrt{\eta_{het}}\sqrt{N_S}\sqrt{N_{LO}}cos(2\pi ft). \quad (6)$$

This intensity signal is then used as the rate parameter for a Poisson random number generator to create the macro-pixel signal which is comprised of a series of photo-events. Figure 2 shows an example of the intensity signal, photo-events recorded by a macro-pixel and the spectrum of recorded photo-events. The parameter values used in the simulation are shown in the table on the left. The intensity signal is comprised of 50 cycles within the CPI. The corresponding photo-event stream is a vector with values given by the number of photo-events recorded by the elements of the macro-pixel as a function of time. The output of each element is filtered according to the reset time of the element. The vector is created with 1 nsec time increments. The spectrum plot shows the intensity of the two-sided Fourier transform of the signal computed from DC to 15 MHz with DC removed. The peak occurs at the input frequency of 5 MHz which exceeds the inverse reset time.

Values
$N_0 = 25$
CPI = 10 μsec
$N_S = 100$
$N_{LO} = 1000$
DCR= 10^5
PDE = 0.30
η_{HET} = 0.30
f = 5 MHz
T_R = 500 nsec
B = 0.58 (calculated)
CNR = 4.78 (calculated)

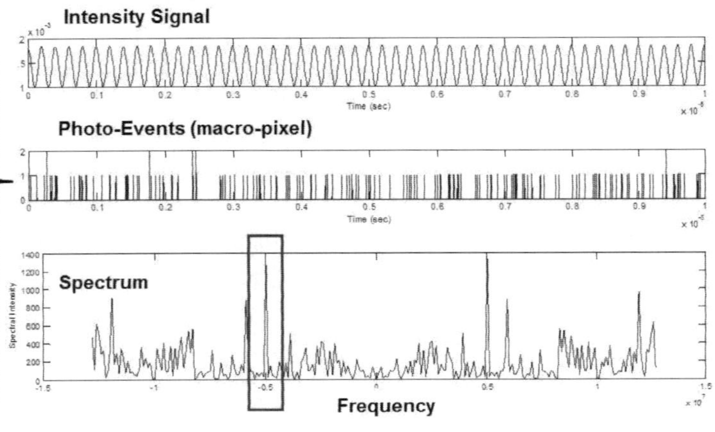

Figure 2. Example intensity signal, photo-event stream, and spectrum for the detection parameters on the left.

3 Experimental Results

The detector used in these experiments is an array of GmAPD pixels whose individual photocurrents are summed and accessible through a single connection to the array. It is a catalog part produced by SensL provided on an evaluation board with SMA connectors for bias voltage and output photocurrent.

The detector consists of 24 x 24 silicon GM pixels, and these 576 pixels comprise a single macropixel. The macropixel has a 1 x 1 mm active area with 64% fill factor, and is composed of 35 x 35 um pixels. Peak spectral response is near 440 nm.

A single source whose optical intensity was directly modulated was used to illuminate the detector. The source was a high power 405 nm LED capable of sinusoidally modulating the optical intensity between 10 and 100 MHz. The LED was collimated and it illuminated a variable aperture iris through a ground glass diffuser. The iris was then imaged onto the detector. The photocurrent was processed to produce an integer number of counts at each time sample. This data was then Fourier transformed and the spectrum was plotted. Data sets were collected at modulation frequencies of 10, 30, 50, 70, and 90 MHz. The spectrum of each data set is shown in the figure below. Modulation is clearly present in the photocurrent even at a modulation frequency of 90 MHz, although the response decreases with increasing frequency. This decrease in response may result from reduced modulation depth of the source and in future work we will monitor this with a linear mode detector. For a single pixel with a dead time of 260 ns, the fastest sampling rate possible is 3.8 MHz. This corresponds to a Nyquist frequency of 1.9 MHz (two samples per cycle). The macropixel is able to detect modulation at approximately 50 times the Nyquist frequency of a single pixel.

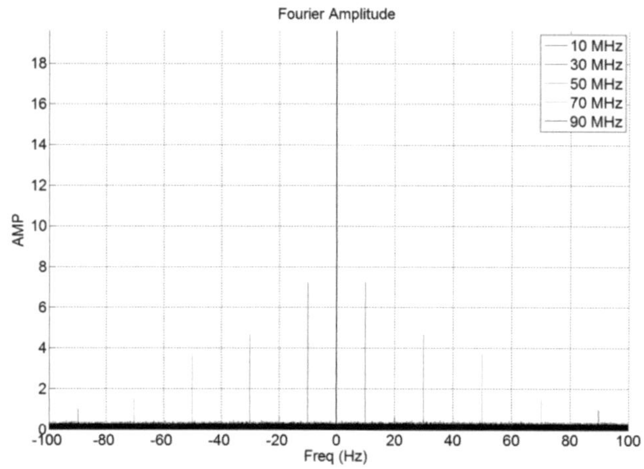

Figure 3 Several data sets overlaid. Each data set is the spectrum of detected photocurrent produced by light sinusoidally modulated at one frequency.

4 Summary

In this paper we have shown the utility of asynchronous GmAPD detector arrays for performing coherent detection in applications that require large-format, high-bandwidth detection. Results show that the performance obtained using an asynchronous GmAPD detector is always lower than that of a conventional linear mode detector. However, this loss in performance is likely offset for many applications by the large format and high sampling rates of asynchronous GmAPDs. We also performed experiments that confirm the theory and show that asynchronous GMAPDs retain frequency information well in excess of the reciprocal reset time.

References

1. J. C. Marron and M. J. Halmos, "Coherent Detection with an Asynchronous Geiger Mode Receiver," MSS Proceedings of 2014 Active E-O Systems, Springfield, VA, 2014.
2. J. X. Luu and L. A. Jiang, "Saturation effects in heterodyne detection with Geiger-mode InGaAs avalanche photodiode arrays," Appl. Opt. 45, 2006.

Pulsed serrodyning technique as applied to coherent laser transmitter for wind sensing

Eisuke HARAGUCHI(a), Hitomi ONO(a) and Toshiyuki ANDO
(a) Mitsubishi Electric Corporation, Information Technology R&D Center,
5-1-1 Ofuna, Kamakura, Kanagawa, Japan, 247-8501
Haraguchi.Eisuke@cw.MitsubishiElectric.co.jp

Abstract: We have developed a new pulsed-coherent light source for wind sensing, combining a semiconductor optical amplifier (SOA) with a phase modulator operated at serrodyning mode. The SOA-based light source has potential advantages of its small footprint, monolithic integration and gain properties, however, inevitably occurs frequency chirp, leading to the measurement error of wind velocities. We have demonstrated the correction of such frequency chirp by using phase modulation with sawtooth waveform, so called 'optical serrodyning technique'.

Keywords: Coherent Laser Transmitter, Serrpdyne Modulation, Semiconductor Optical Amplifier.

1. Introduction

All-fiber coherent Doppler LIDAR system has many advantages such as its compactness, eye-safety and reliability thanks to using commercial off the shelf components from telecom products [1]. The Semiconductor Optical Amplifier (SOA) may be well used as a multifunctional device for the compensation of optical loss [2-4]. The SOA-based light source has potential advantages of its small footprint, monolithic integration and gain properties. However, directly modulated SOA is induced frequency chirp due to gain-induced variations of the refractive index [2], [3], leading to the measurement error of wind velocities. Several studies have reported that in ns time region the frequency chirp caused by direct modulation of the SOA is about a few GHz within optical pulses [3]. Earlier studies have suggested that the frequency chirp caused by SOA is proportional to amplitude modulation rate. Therefore, the frequency chirp in the long pulse region is estimated to a few 10 MHz. Furthermore, in all-fiber CDL system the frequency chirp caused by the self - phase modulation (SPM). We have already evaluated the frequency chirp caused by SPM [5]. As a result, we have been confirmed that the frequency chirp is about a few MHz [5]. However, as far as our knowledge, there is no report about the frequency chirp caused by direct modulation of the SOA and SPM for the long pulse of a few 100ns pulses.

In this paper, at first we estimated the SOA-induced frequency chirp in the long pulse. Next, we demonstrated the correction of such frequency chirp by using phase modulation with sawtooth waveform, so called 'optical serrodyning technique'

2. EXPERIMENTAL ESTIMATION OF FREQUENCY CHIRP

At first, we have estimated the amount of frequency chirp caused by SOA in experimental. Fig. 1 shows the schematic diagrams of the loopback experimental setup for estimation of frequency chirp by using acousto optical modulator (AOM). Distributed Feed Back Laser Diode (DFB-LD) was used as a master laser with line width of 200 kHz and wavelength of 1550 nm. The output from DFB-LD was split into a local and a seed signal. The seed signal was coupled to the AOM and the SOA. The SOA was directly modulated to obtain the pulsed signal which pulses width was 500 ns and pulse repetition frequency was 4 kHz. The AOM was operated at constant frequency which is 162 MHz. This seed pulses ware amplified by an Erbium Doped Fiber Amplifier (EDFA) which output power was 20 W. The signal laser from EDFA was attenuated by the optical attenuator about 40 dB. Attenuated signal laser was propagated through the delay fiber which length is 100 m. The reflected light from fiber end were separated by the circulator and combined with a local laser. We estimated the frequency chirp caused by direct modulation of the SOA by analyzing the optical heterodyning signals between local and back – reflected light from fiber end.

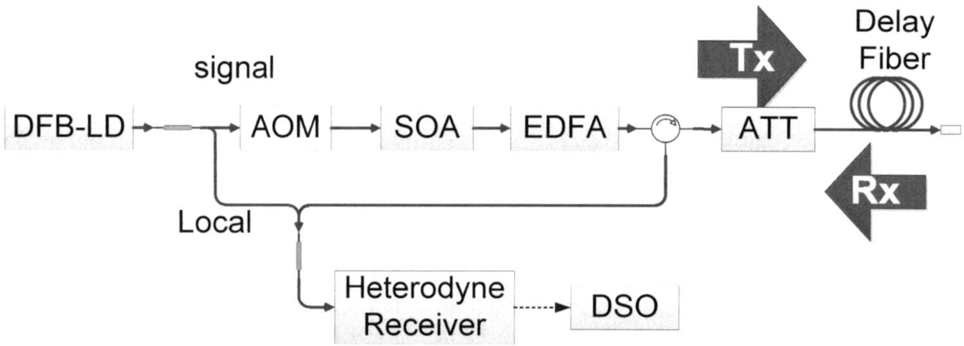

Figure 1 Scematic diagram of experimental setup

Fig. 2 shows the heterodyne signals around a signal pulse in time domain (a) and peak frequency variation of several spectral with respect to each time gate (b). As indicated in the figure, the peak frequency of spectrum in time gate of the rise time of the pulse has indicated positive deviation by 6 MHz, and in time gate of the fall time of the pulse has indicated by negative deviation by minus 4 MHz.

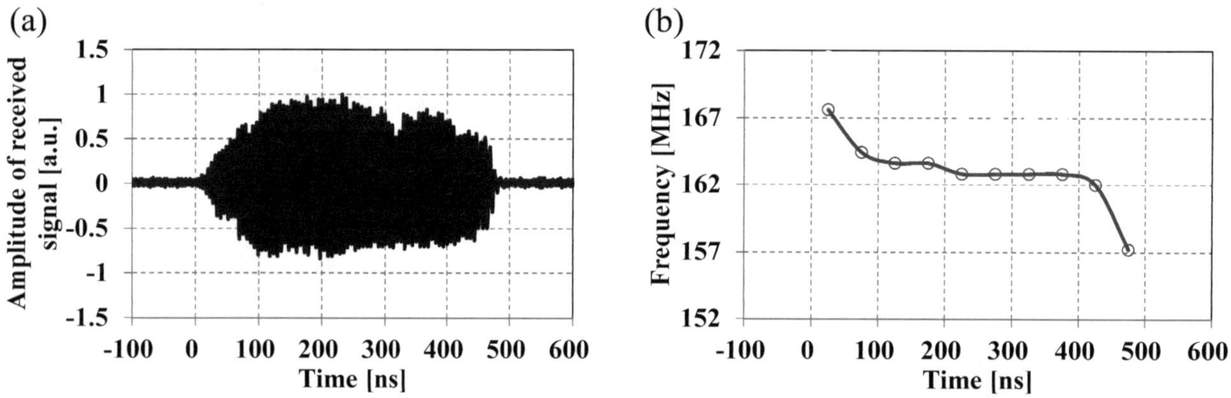

Figure 2 The heterodyne signals between local and back – reflected light
((a) : time domain data, (b) : frequency variation).

3. THE PRINCIPLE OF FREQUENCY CHIRP COMPENSATION

In the pulsed serrodyne phase modulation, a modulating signal with a pulsed sawtooth waveform is applied to the phase modulator. The optical signal of pulsed serrodyne phase modulation is shown in Eq. (1), where E_S, f_0 and Tm represent the field amplitude, the optical carrier frequency and the cycle of sawtooth waveform, respectively. From the Eq. (1), the amount of optical frequency shift depends on the cycle of the sawtooth waveform (T_m).

$$E_S(t) = E_S \exp\left[i2\pi\left(f_0 + 1/T_m\right)t\right] \tag{1}$$

Fig. 3 shows the image of the serrodyne phase modulation signal, optical pulse shape and the frequency of the heterodyne signals, respectively. Fig. 3 (a) is shown the constant frequency of serrodyne phase modulation. The frequency of heterodyne signal is chirping caused by SOA. Fig. 3 (b) shows the case of the corrected frequency chirp. Applying a serrodyne modulation signal of the inverse characteristics of the estimated frequency chirp caused by SOA, the frequency of heterodyne signal is constant.

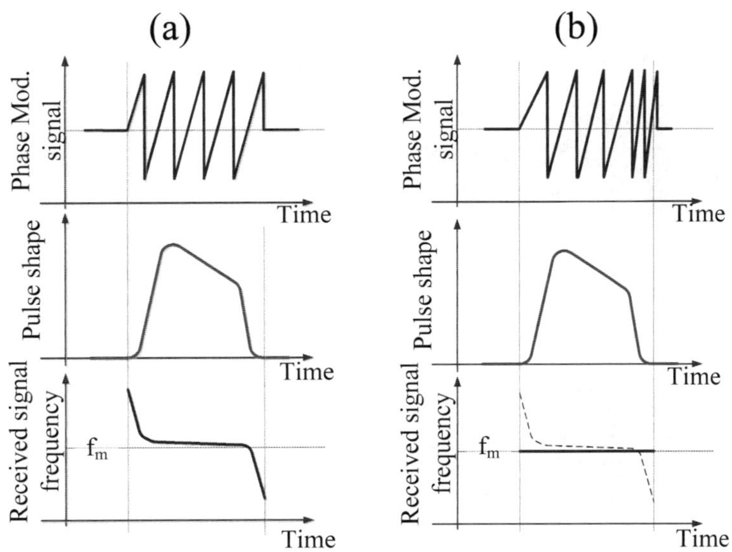

Figure 3 The image of the serrodyne modulation signal, optical pulse shape and the frequency of the heterodyne signals ((a) : no corrected frequency chirp, (b) : corrected frequency chirp).

4. CORRECTION OF FREQUENCY CHIRP

Fig. 4 shows the schematic diagrams of the experimental setup for correction of frequency chirp by using serrodyne phase modulation. The phase modulator (PM) was operated at serrodyne mode for correction of frequency chirp caused by direct modulation of the SOA. By applying a serrodyne phase modulation signal of the inverse characteristics of the estimated frequency chirp, the frequency chirp was corrected. This analysis was performed by using Digital Sampling Oscilloscope (DSO) with sampling rate of 2G samples/s. Offline Fast Fourier Transform (FFT) was executed to several data set with successive 256 sampling points around the gate time.

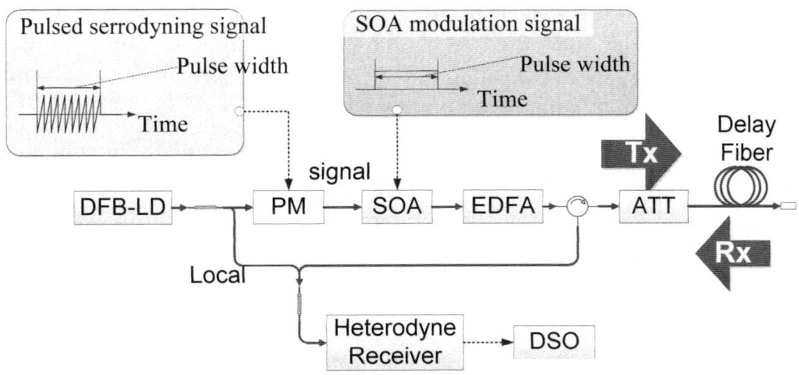

Figure 4 Scematic diagram of loopback experimental setup

Fig. 5 shows the heterodyne signals around a signal pulse in time domain (left) and peak frequency variation of several spectral with respect to each time gate (right). Fig. 5 (a) is in the case of without SOA and EDFA. It is found that the peak frequency of spectral in all time gate has indicated constant. Fig. 5 (c) shows the result in the case of a serrodyne phase modulation of the inverse characteristics of the estimated frequency chirp. It is clearly demonstrated that frequency deviation has been corrected less than 0.4 MHz compared to frequency deviation in the case of without SOA and EDFA. As for the measuring wind velocity, the frequency chirp cases the offset error. In the case of corrected frequency chirp, the average offset errors are evaluated as 0.03 MHz, which is corresponding to the offset velocity of 0.02 m/s.

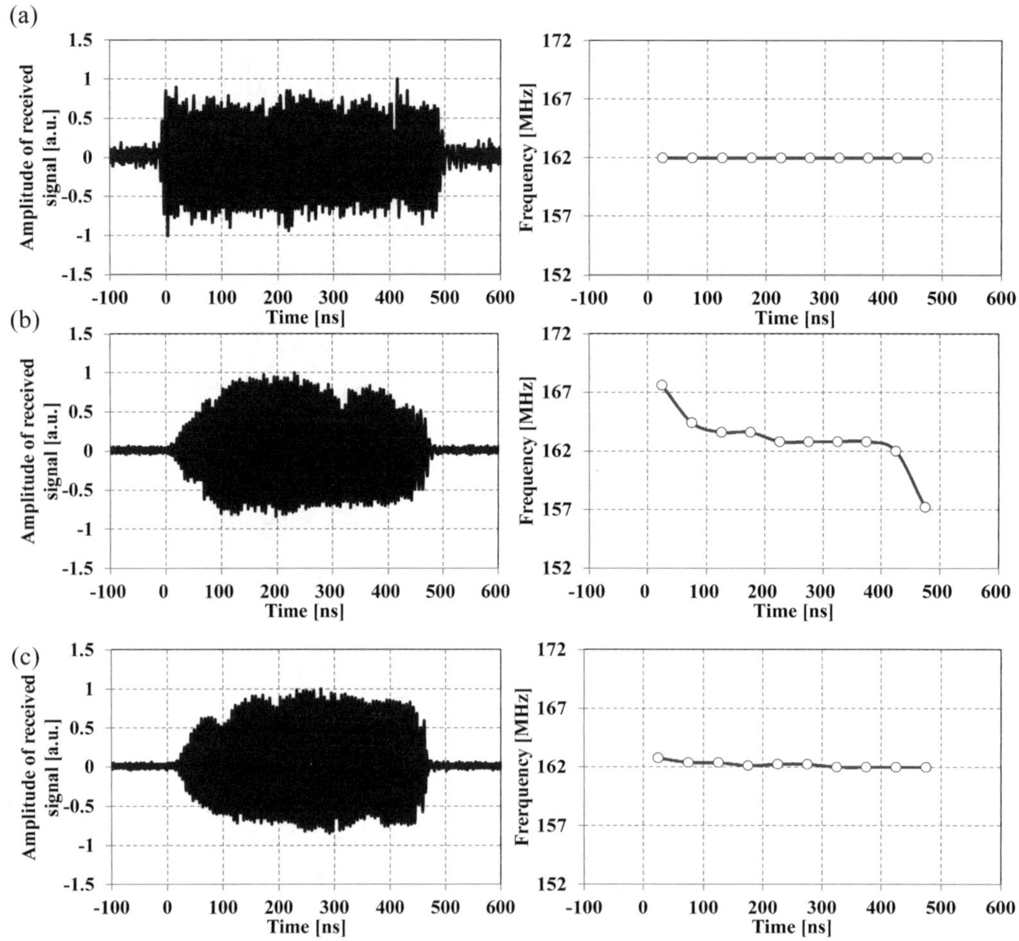

Figure 5 The heterodyne signals between local and back – reflected light (left : time domain data, right : frequency variation). (a) pulse output without SOA and EDFA, (b) pulse output with no corrected frequency chirp, and (c) pulse output with corrected frequency chirp

5. SUMMARY

We have developed a new pulsed-coherent light source for wind sensing, combining the SOA with a phase modulator operated at serrodyning mode. The SOA-based light source has potential advantages of its small footprint, monolithic integration and gain properties, however, inevitably occurs frequency chirp, leading to the measurement error of wind velocities. We have demonstrated the correction of such frequency chirp by using phase modulation with sawtooth waveform, so called 'optical serrodyning technique'. It is clearly demonstrated tha residual frequency error has been decreased less than 0.4 MHz compared to the frequency error of 6 MHz where the no corrected frequency chirp. In the case of corrected frequency chirp, the average offset errors are evaluated as 0.03 MHz, which is corresponding to the offset velocity of 0.02 m/s.

6. References

[1] S. Kameyama et al, Applied Optics, vol. 46, 1953 (2007).
[2] F. Koyama et al, Journal of Lightwave Technology, vol. 6, No.1, 87 (1988).
[3] L. Gillner, IEE Proceedings-J, vol. 139, No.5, 331, (1992).
[4] G. P. Agrawal et al, IEEE Journal of quantum electronics, vol. 25, No. 11, 2297 (1989).
[5] T. Ando et al, 13 th Coherent Laser Radar Conference Proc. p.66 (2005).

New coherent Doppler Lidar engine integrating optical transceiver with FPGA signal processor

Toshiyuki Ando(a), Eisuke Haraguchi(a) and Hitomi Ono(a)
(a) Mitsubishi Electric Corporation, Information Technology R&D Center,
5-1-1 Ofuna, Kamakura, Kanagawa, Japan, 247-8501
Ando.Toshiyuki@ap.MitsubishiElectric.co.jp

Abstract: A new coherent Doppler lidar engine has been developed for wind sensing. This new sub-system is consist of a compact optical transceiver board stacking on a FPGA based signal processor board which has small foot print of 26 x 10cm. In the optical transceiver board a pulsed serrodyning transmitter combined with a heterodyning receiver using commercial off the shelf components of the digital coherent optical communication. In the signal processor board, a system on chip embedded processors and a FPGA is used for not only controlling the optical transceiver but also executing lidar data processing without any external host computer, leading to realization of an ultra-compact wind sensing system. Preliminary experiments of line of sight wind velocities with this new lidar sub-system also presented for demonstration.

Keywords: Coherent Doppler LIDAR, Serrodyne Modulation, pulsed modulation

1. Introduction

A Coherent Doppler LIDAR (CDL) is an attractive sensor for wind sensing because it offers a method of remote wind speed measurement in clear atmospheric condition. All-fiber CDL using the wavelength of 1.5 micron has such many advantages as its eye-safety, its reliability for various environmental conditions and its flexibility for deployments [1]. Mitsubishi Electric released 1st generation commercial all-fiber CDL system in 2006[2], [3], and 2nd generation CDL, 'DIABREZZA™ compact' for wind resource assessment in 2014[4]. While the CDL deployments at a steep mountain, small islands, or disaster areas, it needed not only transportable but also battery drivable. The mobile CDL proto type has also demonstrated two-hour successive operation without exchanging batteries [5]. This CDL, however, was not enough small to be transported by one person. This paper presents a new sub-system for realizing a ultra-compact CDL.

2. Introduction

Figure 1 shows a schematic block diagram and outer view of the new coherent Doppler Lidar engine. This new sub-system is consisting of an optical transceiver board which is connected with a signal processing board via FMC connector. The optical transceiver is combined a conventional fiber-optic heterodyning receiver with a newly developed coherent optical pulse seeder based on pulse-serrodyning modulation which is described later in detail. In the signal processing board a system-on-a-chip (SoC) solutions have been adopted by using a large Field Programmable Gate Array (FPGA) with an internal processor core. Measured wind data can be displayed on a tablet PC via the WiFi after on-board signal processing for wind speed estimation. The foot prints of both boards are 26 x 10 cm, the weight is less than 600 g. The designed power consumption is less than 35VA. The power input is a single voltage of DC +12V which can be supplied with commercially available batteries. Both boards are designed with RoHS compliant optical and electrical components taking into consideration of electro-magnetic compatibility (EMC).

Note that this new coherent Doppler Lidar engine can be connected to various types of optical high power amplifiers (OHPA) via the optical fiber connecter, leading to a power-scalable design in system configurations.

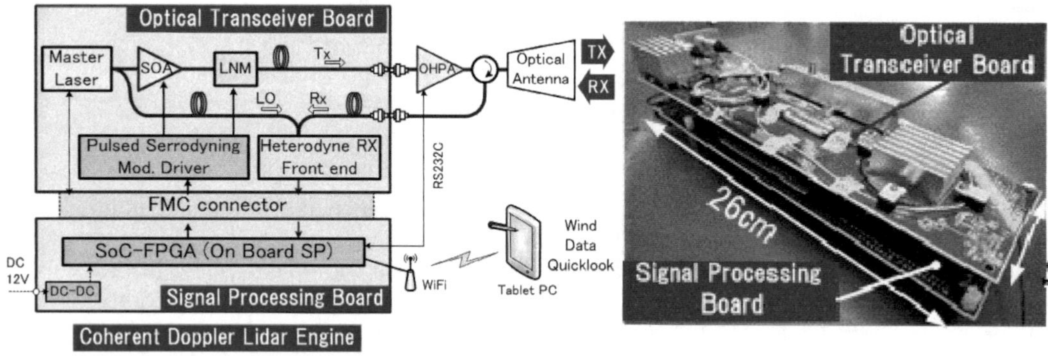

Figure 1. Schematic block diagram and outer view of the new coherent Doppler Lidar engine.

3. OPTICAL TRANSCEIVER UNIT

Figure 2 shows the block diagram and outer view of the optical transceiver unit as a coherent pulse seeder combined with a heterodyne receiver. All fiber-optic components are commercial off the shelf components in the optical communication which have enough high reliability with Telcodia GR468-core compliant. A Distributed Feed Back Laser Diode (DFB-LD) was used as a master laser with line width of 200 kHz and wavelength of 1550 nm. Then its output was split into a local oscillator (LO) and a seed light to a pulsed serrodyning modulator which is consisting of a semiconductor optical amplifier (SOA), a lithium niobate optical phase modulator (LNM) and their drivers with digital-to analog converters (DAC). The pulsed serrodyning modulation is our newly developed technique to realize both pulse modulation and frequency shift without a double-pass AO (Acousto optic) modulator currently used in our CDL system [3].

In a receiver section optical return signals (RX) are phonically mixed with a LO signal, then detected as intermediate frequency (IF) signals at balanced two photo diodes (PD). In order to accommodate a bandwidth of 100MHz corresponding to a range of Doppler frequency of +/- 35m/s, the heterodyning signal is sampled at rate of 216MSps with analog-to digital converter (ADC) and transferred to the signal processing board.

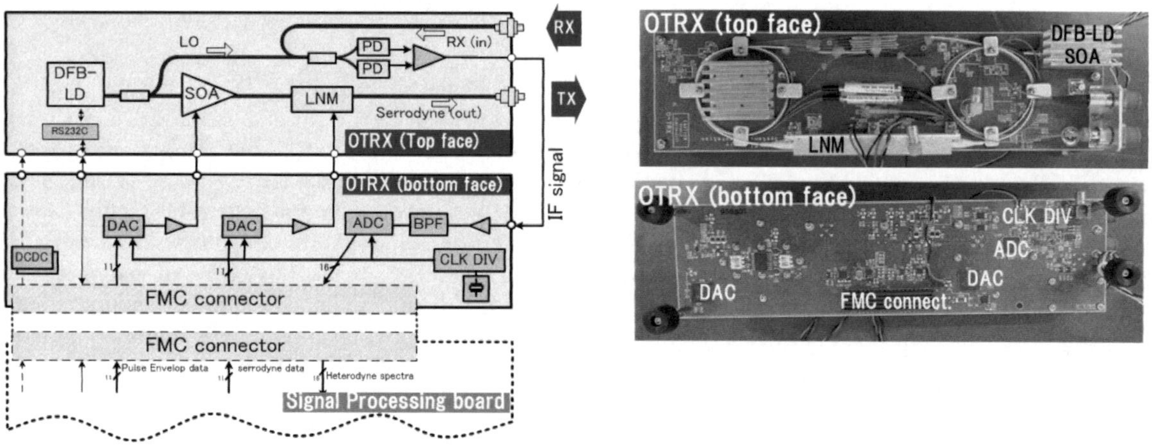

Figure 2. Schematic block diagram and outer view of the optical transceiver unit.

4. PULSED SERRODYNING MODULATOR

Serrodyine frequency shifting is realized by applying a saw-tooth phase modulation to the optical signals, which was originally used for the fiber optic gyroscope with its frequency shift up to several megahertz [6],[7]. Recently frequency shift of a few hundred megahertz as required in CDL can be obtained with a good quality by technological advances in high speed driver electronics. While, SOA is the promising to optical pulse modulator with small foot print if the issue s of frequency chirp is solved [8]. We have newly developed a pulsed serrodyning modulation which realizes both frequency shift and compensation of frequency chirp in SOA.

Figure 3 shows the temporal signals of pulsed serrodyning modulation for an optical intensity of a SOA and an optical phase of a LNM. The saw-tooth phase modulation is applied within only the pulse-on period, T1 over pulse repetition interval (PRI). If the complete saw-tooth phase modulation with cycle of Tm is applied, the output optical frequency is shifted with an offset frequency of 1/Tm.

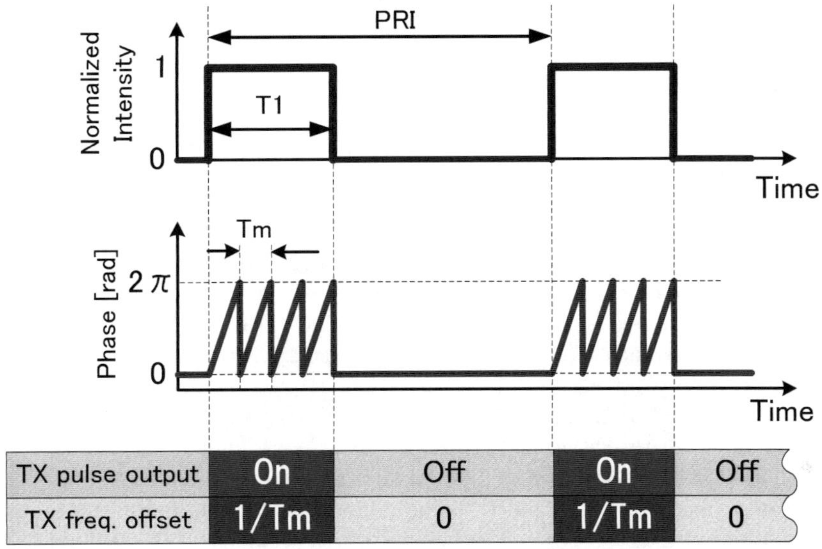

Figure 3. Temporal signals of pulsed serrodyning modulation for an optical intensity of a SOA and a optical phase of a LNM.

It is worthy to note that no frequency shift is occurred within pulse-off periods because of not applying the saw-tooth signal. This leads effective rejection performance of unwanted beat noise between optically internal reflections within pulse-off periods and the LO signal in the heterodyne receiver without such a special pulsed modulator as a double-pass AOM with a high extinction ratio. The technique for compensation of the frequency chirp in a SOA is described in the other paper of this conference [9].

5. SOC-FPGA SIGNAL PROCESSOR UNIT

Figure 4 shows the schematic diagrams and outer view of signal processor unit. In the programmable logic of the SoC-FPGA for receiver section, 256-point fast Fourier transforms (FFT) and incoherent integrations are executed with respect to 80-ranges, stored in buffer memory as raw data of Doppler spectra. In its transmitter section pulsed-serrodyning data are transfer to the DAC on the OTRX board. The processing system of the SoC-FPGA performs post processing of CDL such as subtraction of noise floor in each Doppler spectrum, estimation of wind speed. Calculated wind data are transferred through a GbE interface, which can easily connect to an external tablet PC via the WiFi. This processor can also control external components such as an OHPA, a scanner and a telescope via interfaces of RS-232C and USB.

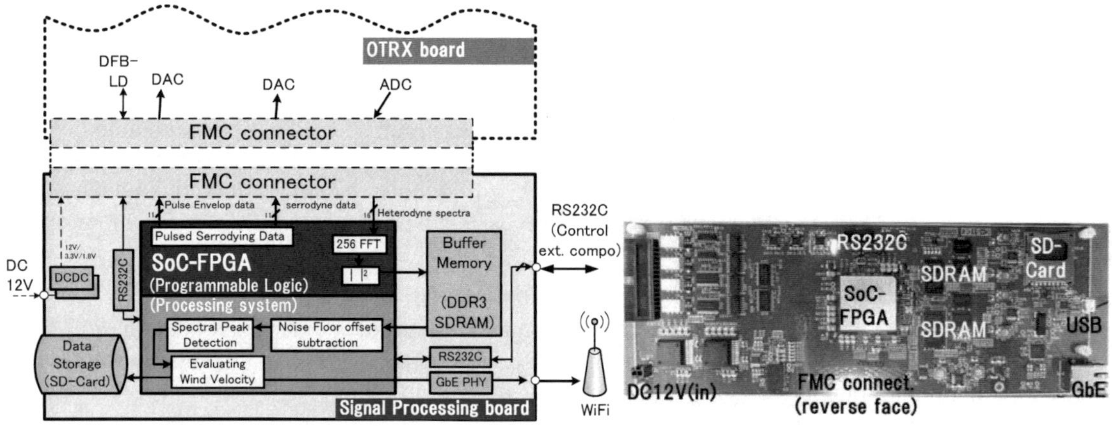

Figure 4. Schematic block diagram and outer view of the signal processor unit.

6. EXPERIMENTAL RESULTS

In order to confirm whether the pulsed-serrodyning modulation does correctly perform, line of sight (LOS) wind Doppler spectra have been evaluated in the case of pulsed-serrodyne modulation and that of single-pass AO modulation as a reference. The measuring condition as follows: the pulse-on period, T1 of 500ns corresponding to range resolution of 75m, a PRI of 250μs, the saw-tooth cycle, Tm of 6.17 ns corresponding to IF of 162MHz as shown in fig.3. Figure 5 (a) shows the LOS wind Doppler spectra at distance of 500m. In the case of single-path AO modulation the spectrum has a strong peak around zero Doppler velocity which may be caused by beat noise between a LO signal and internally reflection of leaky lights within pulse-off periods. This unwanted beat noise makes it difficult to measure wind signals near the zero-Doppler velocity. Meanwhile, the spectrum of pulsed-serrodyne modulation has a peak around -1m/s without any noise peak at zero-Doppler velocity. Figure 5 (b) shows the measurement data of the LOS wind velocity with respect to distance and that of their detectability. Theoretical calculation for detectability is also shown as a function of distance. The setting parameters are as follows: the optical peak power of 20W at a fiber end of an OHPA, the aperture diameter of 50mm, the focusing distance of 500m and the integration number of 4000. The back scattered coefficient is assumed of 8.3e-8 m-1sr-1 taking into account of measured number of aerosol using a particle counter. The measured detectability has considerably agreed with theoretical curve, which indicated the LOS wind velocities are measured up to 900m because of larger detectability than the detection limit of 7dB.

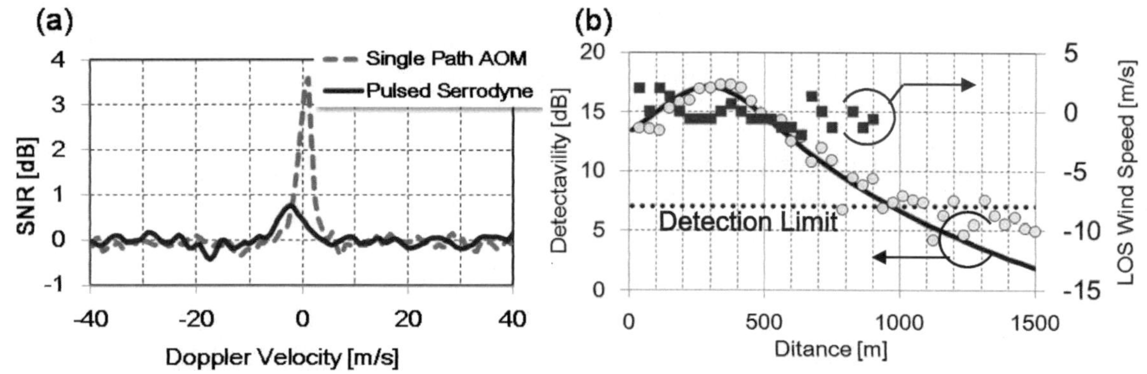

Figure 5. (a) LOS wind Doppler spectra at distance of 500m, (b) LOS wind velocity and detectability with respect to distance

7. SUMMARY

We have developed a new coherent Doppler lidar engine for wind sensing with a small foot print of 26 x 10cm. The pulsed-serrodyning modulation makes it possible to realize both frequency shift and compensation of frequency chirp within pulse-on period of the SOA as pulse modulator. The SoC-FPGA processor performed not only generating saw-tooth signal for pulsed serrodyne modulation but also estimation of wind velocity in RX section including post processing of Doppler spectra. Preliminary experiment of LOS wind velocities demonstrate this new CDL sub-system has been correctly performed.

8. References

[1] S. Kameyama et al, Applied Optics, vol.46, 1953 (2007).
[2] T. Ando et al, 13th Proc. Of Coherent Laser Radar Conference, 170 (2005).
[3] T. Ando et al, IOP Conference Series: Earth and Environmental Science, 1, 012011 (2008).
[4] http://www.mitsubishielectric .co.jp/news/2014/0528.html
[5] T. Ando et al, 17th Proc. Of Coherent Laser Radar Conference (2013).
[6] L.M. Johnson et al, J. Lightwave Technol., vol. 6, 109(1988)
[7] A. Ebbergh et al, Opt. Lett., vol. 10, 300 (1985).
[8] L. Gillner, IEE Proc.-J. Optoelectronics, vol. 139, 331 (1992).
[9] E. Haraguchi et al, 18th Proc. Of Coherent Laser Radar Conference (2016).

Single and Dual Polarization InGaAs Optical Coherent Receivers for Coherent LADARs

Abhay M Joshi and Shubhashish Datta
Discovery Semiconductors, Inc.
119 Silvia Street, Ewing, New Jersey 08628, USA
sdatta@discoverysemi.com

Abstract: We have manufactured single as well as dual polarization optical coherent receivers that comprise of InGaAs balanced receivers and an optical hybrid. The bandwidth of InGaAs balanced receivers is up to 20 GHz with a wavelength coverage of 1200 nm to 2200 nm. The single polarization coherent receiver contains two balanced receivers and a single polarization 90 degree optical hybrid; whereas the dual polarization coherent receiver contains four balanced receivers and a dual polarization 90 degree optical hybrid. The optical hybrids have limited wavelength coverage, mainly from 1530 nm to 1610 nm, and could be customized for 2000 nm operation. The InGaAs balanced receivers offer several features such as user-adjustable RF gain, bandwidth, and mode of operation (Automatic Gain Control [AGC] or Manual Gain Control). The AGC mode with a programmable differential voltage output up to 750 mV peak-to-peak compensates atmospheric fades and maximizes Effective Number of Bits (ENOBs) for backend digital signal processing.

Keywords: ultrafast photoreceiver, polarization diversity receiver, automatic gain control, coherent LADAR, extended InGaAs

1. Introduction

Laser radars (LADAR) illuminate a distant target and analyze the reflected or backscattered optical signal to ascertain its properties, such as location, velocity, and material composition. The received optical signals typically have low light levels and fluctuations induced by atmospheric fades, and are challenging to analyze with direct detection systems. Systems based on ultra-fast coherent receivers with automatic gain control, as shown in Fig. 1, enable shot noise-limited detection of amplitude, phase, and polarization of the received optical signal with a timing precision of tens of picoseconds.

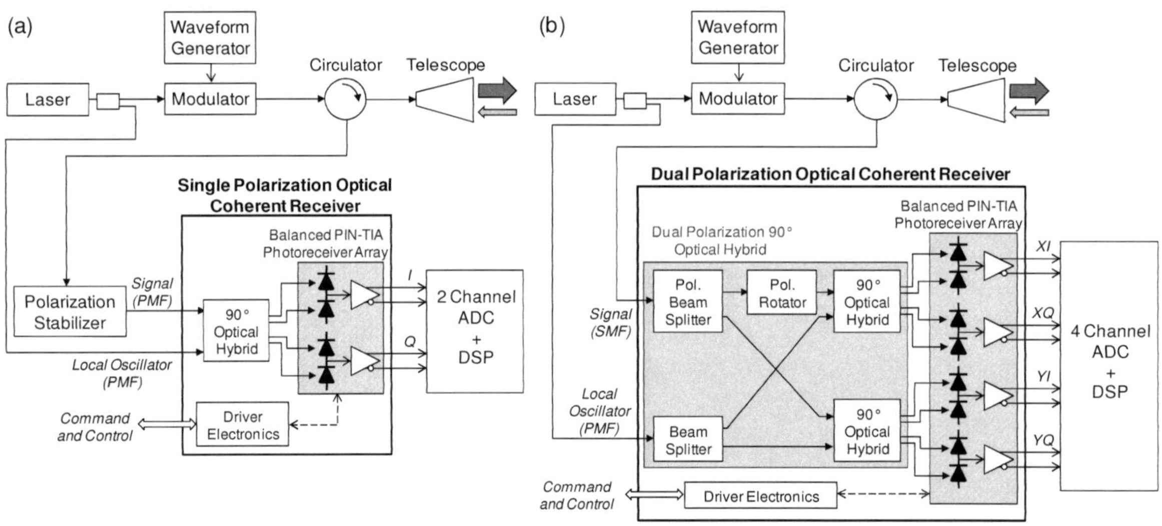

Figure 1. Block diagrams of coherent laser radar that incorporate (a) single polarization and (b) dual polarization ultra-fast coherent receivers having user-adjustable bandwidth and gain control.

The single polarization coherent receiver, which is comprised of two balanced receivers and a 90 degree optical hybrid, operates in conjunction with an external polarization stabilizer to mix the received optical signal with a local optical oscillator and demodulate it into in-phase (*I*) and quadrature phase (*Q*) components. This receiver, shown in Fig. 1a, is appropriate for applications such as Doppler LADARs that only require amplitude and phase analysis [1, 2].

In a dual polarization coherent receiver, shown in Fig. 1b, the received optical signal is first split into its orthogonal linear polarization states (*X* and *Y*) prior to demodulation into corresponding in-phase and quadrature phase components, namely *XI*, *XQ*, *YI*, and *YQ*. Such a receiver is necessary for polarization diversity LADARs that immunize the system to polarization fluctuations without requiring a polarization stabilizer. Additionally, dual polarization receiver enables polarimetry in LADARs, which is useful for material characterization [3].

Material characterization is further aided by multi-wavelength differential absorption laser radars (DIAL), which have been used for atmospheric sensing [4]. The ultra-fast InGaAs balanced receivers presented here have a broad wavelength coverage of 1200 nm to 2200 nm and are appropriate for such DIAL applications with a distance accuracy of ~1 cm. Both single and dual polarization optical hybrids currently have limited wavelength coverage, mainly from 1530 nm to 1610 nm, but have virtually unlimited bandwidth in the RF domain. These hybrids could be customized for 2000 nm operation.

We first describe the novel uncooled lattice-mismatched InP / InGaAs p-i-n photodiode technology that extends the ultra-fast operation from a traditional cut-off wavelength of 1650 nm to 2200 nm. These photodiodes enable using high-power 2 micron wavelength lasers that have been touted as a success story of NASA's Laser Risk Reduction Program for space-based atmospheric sensing [5]. We then narrate the balanced photoreceiver that combines a pair of InGaAs photodiodes with a differential transimpedance amplifier having a user-adjustable RF gain, automatic gain control with adjustable RF output amplitude, and adjustable bandwidth for matched filtering. Finally, the optical coherent receivers are described which can operate with an aggregate DC photocurrent of up to 16 mA for shot noise-limited detection.

2. Uncooled Lattice-Mismatched InP / InGaAs Photodiodes

Conventional InP / InGaAs photodiodes, commonly used in 1550 nm wavelength systems, utilize $In_{0.53}Ga_{0.47}As$ absorber layer that is lattice-matched to the InP substrate (lattice constant = 5.87 Å). The cut-off wavelength of these devices is limited to 1650 nm by the bandgap of $In_{0.53}Ga_{0.47}As$ material (Eg = 0.74 eV). In this work, we utilized a lower bandgap material, namely Indium-rich $In_{0.72}Ga_{0.28}As$ (Eg = 0.57 eV) as the absorber layer, to extend the photodiode's cut-off wavelength to 2200 nm at ambient room temperature. The epitaxial structure of the lattice-mismatched $In_{0.72}Ga_{0.28}As$ / InP photodiode is compared with the conventional lattice-matched $In_{0.53}Ga_{0.47}As$ / InP photodiode in Fig. 2.

The primary challenge in incorporating Indium-rich absorption layer is to minimize the dislocation defects that may arise from the lattice mismatch between $In_{0.72}Ga_{0.28}As$ (lattice constant = 5.94 Å) and the InP substrate. These defects act as generation-recombination centers and increase the photodiode's dark current. Also, these defects may provide interstitial sites for material impurities and elevate unintentional background doping level in intrinsic $In_{0.72}Ga_{0.28}As$ absorption layer [6]. As a result, larger reverse bias is needed in a material with higher defect density to achieve a targeted depletion width and device capacitance for ultra-fast operation. The photodiode structure shown in Fig. 2a utilizes n-doped graded $InAs_yP_{1-y}$ buffer layer that is lattice-matched to the (100) oriented, n^+-doped InP substrate in the bottom and the $In_{0.72}Ga_{0.28}As$ absorber on the top. This buffer layer contains compositionally abrupt interfaces that minimize the propagation of lattice defects into the subsequently grown intrinsic $In_{0.72}Ga_{0.28}As$ absorption layer. We have achieved uncooled 25 GHz photodiode operation with DC responsivity of ~0.9 A/W at 1550 nm wavelength and ~1.2 A/W at 2050 nm wavelength [7, 8].

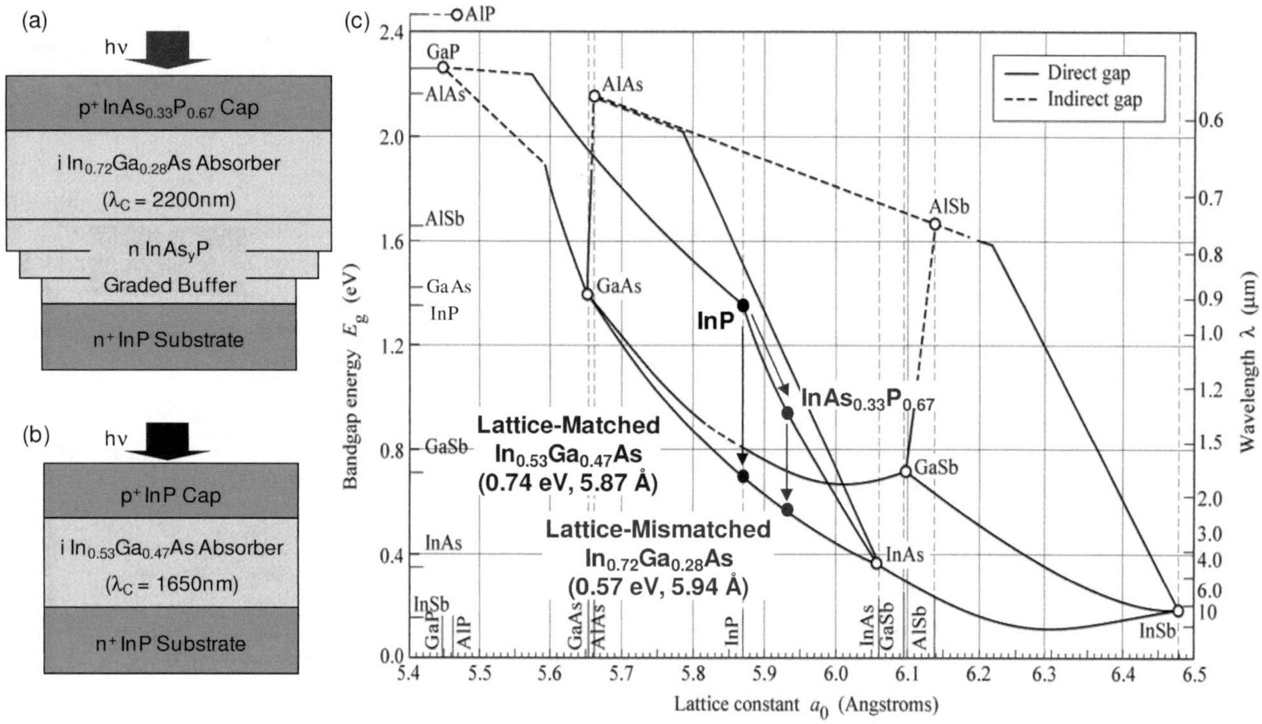

Figure 2. Epitaxial structure of (a) lattice-mismatched $In_{0.72}Ga_{0.28}As$ / InP photodiode used in this work is compared with (b) conventional lattice-matched $In_{0.53}Ga_{0.47}As$ / InP photodiode. (c) Bandgap and lattice constant of III-V semiconductors with materials of the two photodiode structures annotated.

3. Balanced Photoreceiver with Adjustable Gain and Bandwidth

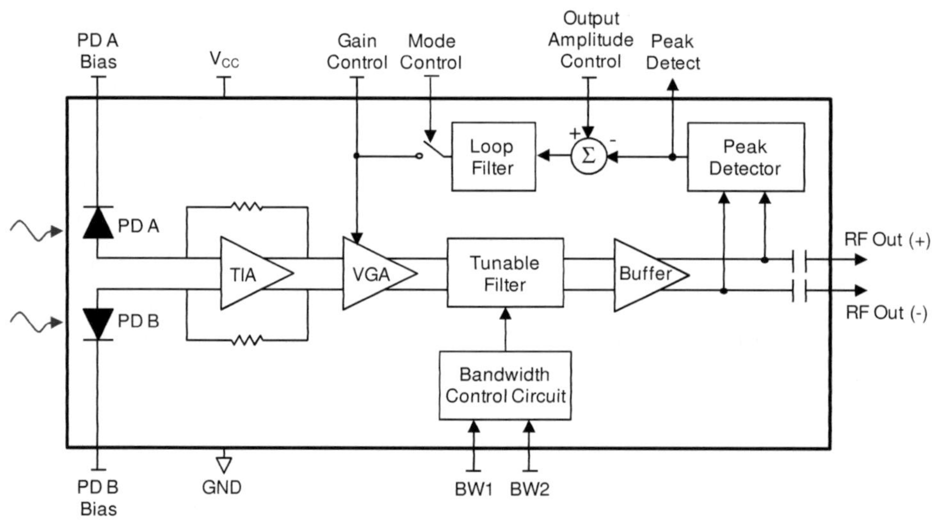

Figure 3. The block diagram of the balanced photoreceiver, incorporating two $In_{0.72}Ga_{0.28}As$ photodiodes (PD A and PD B), shows an open feedback loop for Manual Gain Control mode. The feedback loop can be closed using the "Mode Control" input for Automatic Gain Control mode.

The balanced photoreceiver is comprised of two 30 μm diameter $In_{0.72}Ga_{0.28}As$ photodiodes that are coupled to a differential amplifier, as shown in Fig 3. Beyond the usual advantages of balanced detection, such as cancellation of common-mode relative intensity noise (RIN) and suppression of second-order distortions, this device has several features to enhance its flexibility:

- The amplifier's transfer function can be chosen between seven settings by using two tri-state control signals, BW1 and BW2. As shown in Fig. 4a, the -3 dB bandwidth of the balanced photoreceiver can be optimized for specific applications. It should be noted that 18 GHz bandwidth corresponds to a time constant of 55 ps and a distance of 1.6 cm for light travelling in free space.
- The amplifier circuit incorporates a variable gain amplifier (VGA) following the input-stage trans-impedance amplifier (TIA) which allows adjusting the differential transimpedance up to 4600 Ω, as shown in Fig. 4b. Consequently, the differential conversion gain can be varied up to 5600 V/W for a photodiode responsivity of 1.2 A/W at 2050 nm wavelength. The input equivalent noise varies from 15 pA/√Hz to 38 pA/√Hz at the maximum gain setting (see Fig. 4c).
- The photoreceiver also contains a peak detection circuit that generates a voltage proportional to the peak-to-peak RF output amplitude and may be useful optimizing local oscillator power level in a coherent LADAR.
- The amplifier circuit can be operated in two modes, Manual Gain Control or Automatic Gain Control (AGC), which is determined by the "Mode Control" input. In the AGC mode, the feedback loop shown in Fig. 3 is closed and the peak detect signal is used internally to maintain a targeted peak-to-peak RF output amplitude, which can compensate for atmospheric fades. This targeted output amplitude can be chosen by the user up to 750 mV_{p-p} differential by using the "Output Amplitude Control" input and is sufficient to maximize Effective Number of Bits (ENOBs) for backend digital signal processing.

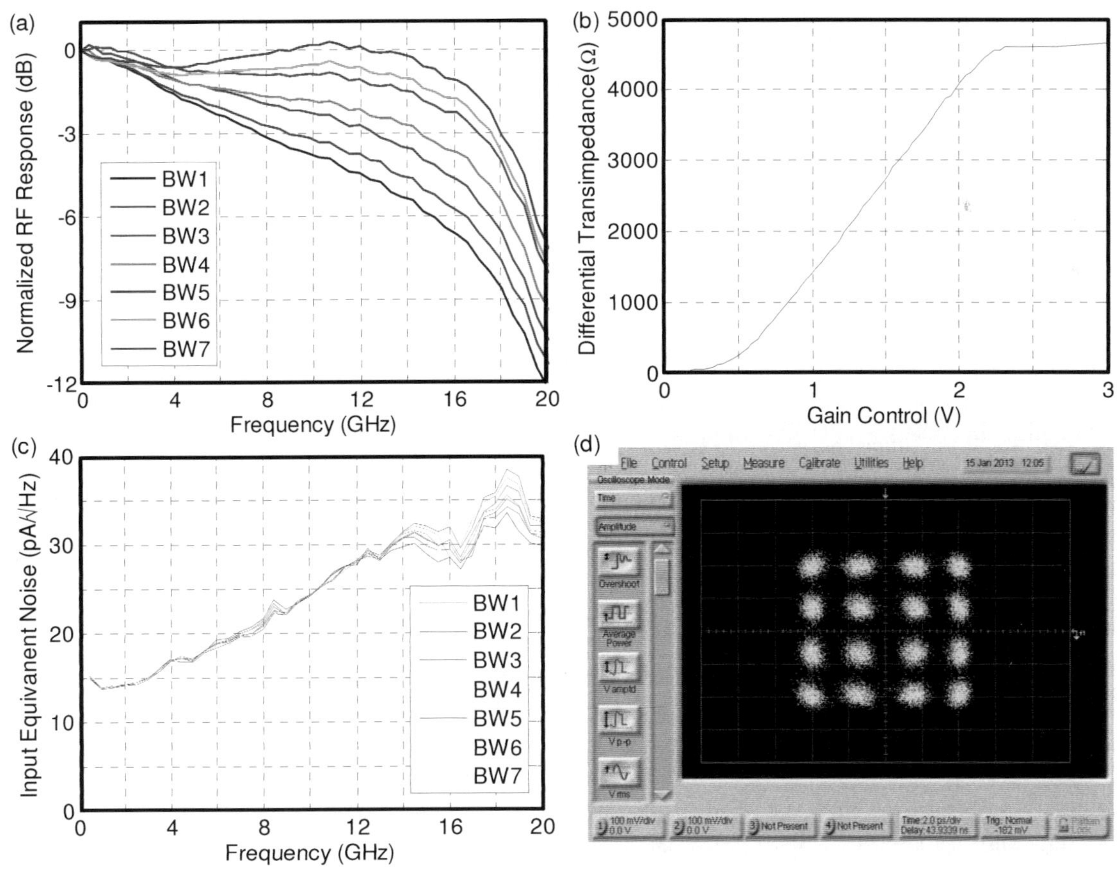

Figure 4. (a) Normalized RF response for seven user-adjustable bandwidth settings, (b) Differential transimpedance vs. gain control voltage, and (c) Input equivalent noise density at maximum gain setting of the $In_{0.72}Ga_{0.28}As$ balanced photoreceiver. (d) 16-QAM constellation having 12.5 Gbaud symbol rate for X-polarization of the dual-polarization coherent receiver shown in Fig. 1b.

4. Optical Coherent Receivers

The optical coherent receivers, shown in Fig. 1, incorporate these balanced photoreceivers integrated with single polarization and dual polarization 90 degree optical hybrids, as well as driver electronics for controlling the gain and bandwidth of the photoreceivers in an instrument format. Channel-to-channel symmetry of the optical hybrids and the balanced photoreceivers ensure a phase error within ±5° between in-phase and quadrature signals, and a maximum channel skew of 10 ps. This symmetry is exemplified by the 16-quadrature amplitude modulated (16-QAM) constellation shown in Fig. 4d, which was generated by co-plotting 4-level 12.5 Gbaud signals from *XI* and *XQ* channels of the dual-polarization coherent receiver shown in Fig. 1b. Similar 16-QAM constellation is obtained from the *YI* and *YQ* channels.

Each balanced photoreceiver can be operated at a maximum DC photocurrent of 2 mA per diode, which corresponds to an aggregate DC photocurrent of 8 mA for the single polarization device, and 16 mA for the dual polarization device. For a typical excess insertion loss of 3 dB in the optical hybrids, the coherent receivers can be operated at optical LO power levels of up to +13 dBm for the single polarization device, and +16 dBm for the dual polarization device, which is sufficient for shot noise-limited detection.

5. Conclusion

In summary, we have developed single and dual polarization ultra-fast coherent receivers that enable several key features in coherent LADARs, namely shot-noise limited detection of reflected or back-scattered optical signals with a distance accuracy of ~1 cm, polarimetry, compensation of atmospheric fades through automatic gain control, and large RF output signal to maximize the ENOBs for backend digital signal processing. These receivers are based on uncooled, lattice-mismatched InGaAs photodiode technology having wavelength coverage of 1200 nm to 2200 nm, which further enables utilizing high-power 2 micron wavelength lasers.

6. References

[1] S. Hannon, J. Alex, S. Henderson, P. Gatt, R. Stoneman, and D. Burns, "Agile multiple-pulse coherent lidar for range and micro-Doppler measurement," Proc. SPIE **3380**, 259-269 (1998).

[2] F. Amzajerdian and D. Pierrottet, "Fiber-based coherent LIDAR for target ranging, velocimetry, and atmospheric wind sensing," in Conference on Lasers and Electro-Optics/Quantum Electronics and Laser Science Conference and Photonic Applications Systems Technologies, Technical Digest (Optical Society of America, 2006), paper CPDB9.

[3] R. Neely, M. Hayman, R. Stillwell, J. Thayer, R. Hardesty, M. O'Neill, M. Shupe, and C. Alvarez, "Polarization LIDAR at Summit, Greenland, for the detection of cloud phase and particle orientation," J. Atmospheric Oceanic Tech. **30**, 1635-1655 (2013).

[4] G. Koch, B. Barnes, M. Petros, J. Beyan, F. Amzajerdian, J. Yu, R. Davis, S. Ismail, S. Vay, M. Kavaya, and U. Singh, "Coherent differential absorption lidar measurements of CO_2," Applied Optics **43**, 5092-5099 (2004).

[5] U. Singh, B. Walsh, J. Yu, M. Petros, M. Kavaya, T. Refaat, and N. Barnes, "Twenty years of Tm:Ho:YLF and LuLiF laser development for global wind and carbon dioxide active remote sensing," Optical Materials Express **5**, 828-837 (2015).

[6] A. Joshi, G. Olsen, S. Mason, M. Lange, and V. Ban, "Near-Infrared (1-3 μm) InGaAs Detectors and Arrays: Crystal Growth, Leakage Current, and Reliability," Proc. SPIE **1715**, 585-593 (1992).

[7] A. Joshi, "Developments in High Performance Photodiodes," IEEE Photonics Conf. 2012, invited paper MS1, San Francisco, CA, 23 – 27 September 2012.

[8] A. Joshi, S. Datta, and M. Lange, "2.2 micron, uncooled, InGaAs photodiodes, and balanced photoreceivers up to 25 GHz bandwidth," Proc. SPIE **8704**, 87042G1-8 (2013).

Acknowledgement

The authors thank NASA Goddard Space Flight Center for funding the development of lattice-mismatched InGaAs photodiodes, and especially Dr. Sachidananda Babu, Dr. Peter Shu, and Dr. Murzy Jhabvala for their support.

UC DAVIS COLLEGE OF ENGINEERING

Imager Based on Integrated Photonics

Samuel T. Thurman
Lockheed Martin Coherent Technologies, Louisville, CO
Alan Duncan, Richard L. Kendrick, Chad Ogden, Danielle Wuchenich
Lockheed Martin Advanced Technology Center, Palo Alto, CA
Tiehui Su, Shibnath Pathak, Wei-Cheng Lai, Mathias Prost, Roberto Proietti, Ryan P. Scott, S. J. B. Yoo
University of California Davis, Davis, CA

Coherent Laser Radar Conference
June 27 – July 1, 2016
Boulder, CO

UC DAVIS COLLEGE OF ENGINEERING

Outline

- **Size scaling of conventional imaging systems**
- **Alternative interferometric imaging approach**
  - Van Cittert-Zernike theorem
  - Michelson stellar interferometry
- **Miniaturization using integrated photonics**
- **Proof-of-concept demonstration**
- **Design principles**
  - Field of view
  - Spatial resolution
  - Spectral sampling
- **Next generation design & future concepts**
- **Summary**

Scaling of Conventional Optics

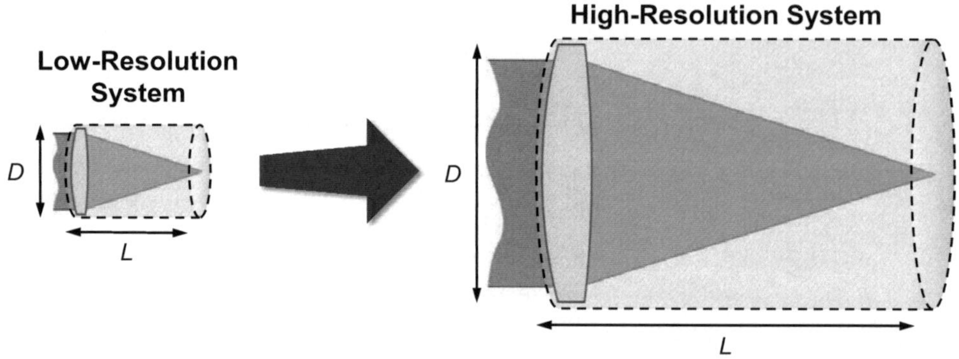

- System length L scales with aperture diameter D → volume scales with D^3
- In many applications, system volume is either minimized or constrained to fit within a predefined envelope
- A variety of approaches have been proposed for thin form-factor systems
- This talk describes a concept based on interferometric imaging

3

Van Cittert-Zernike Theorem

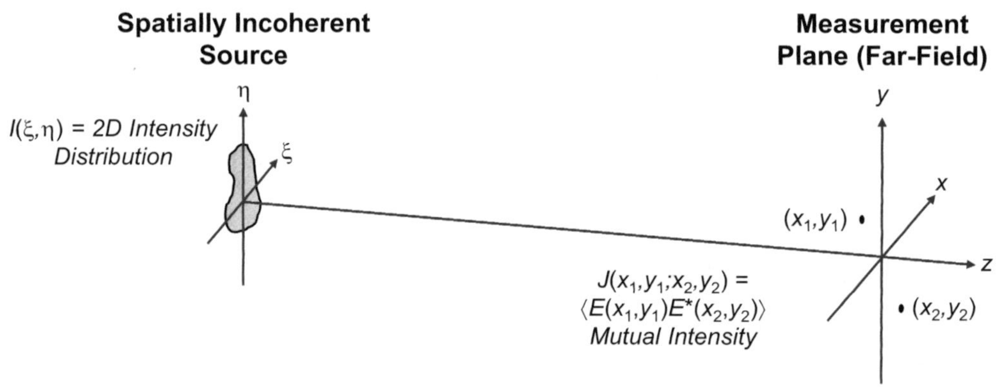

- The mutual intensity function is related to the source intensity distribution through a Fourier transform relationship [Goodman, *Statistical Optics*]

$$J(x_1,y_1;x_2,y_2)=\frac{\kappa e^{-i\psi}}{(\lambda z)^2}\iint I(\xi,\eta)\exp\left[i\frac{2\pi}{\lambda z}(\Delta x\xi+\Delta y\eta)\right]d\xi d\eta$$

4

Michelson Stellar Interferometry

- **Reconstruct an image of a source from measurements of the mutual intensity function**

(1920) Michelson & Pease used a 20 ft interferometer on the Hooker Telescope to measure the diameter of Betelgeuse (α Orionis) by finding the interferometer baseline corresponding to the first null of the mutual intensity function

By George Ellery Hale - The New Heavens, Public Domain, https://commons.wikimedia.org/w/index.php?curid=1223713

5

Astronomical Interferometers

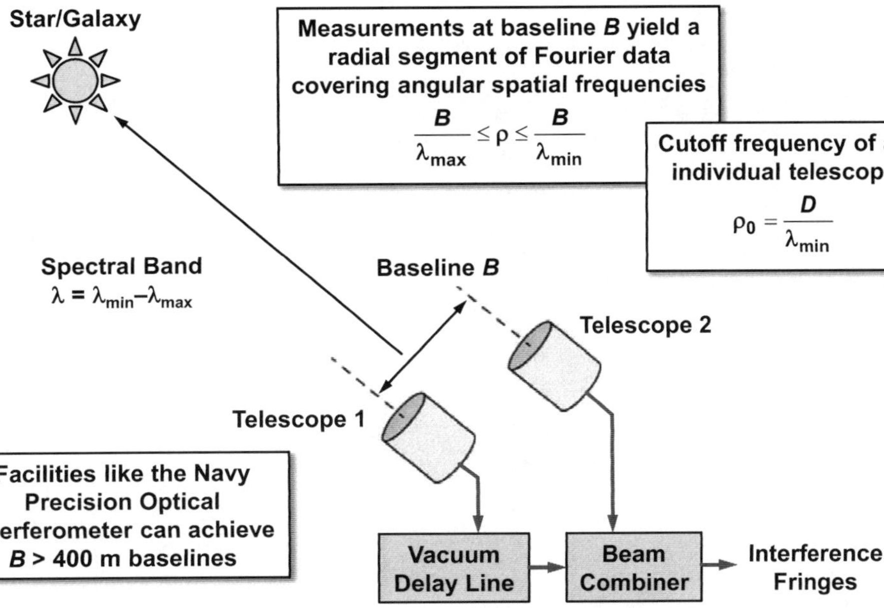

Measurements at baseline *B* yield a radial segment of Fourier data covering angular spatial frequencies

$$\frac{B}{\lambda_{max}} \leq \rho \leq \frac{B}{\lambda_{min}}$$

Cutoff frequency of an individual telescope

$$\rho_0 = \frac{D}{\lambda_{min}}$$

Facilities like the Navy Precision Optical Interferometer can achieve *B* > 400 m baselines

6

SPIDER Concept

- **Replace traditional telescope with dense interferometer array**
- **Goal is to eventually create meter-class effective apertures with system thickness of only a few centimeters**

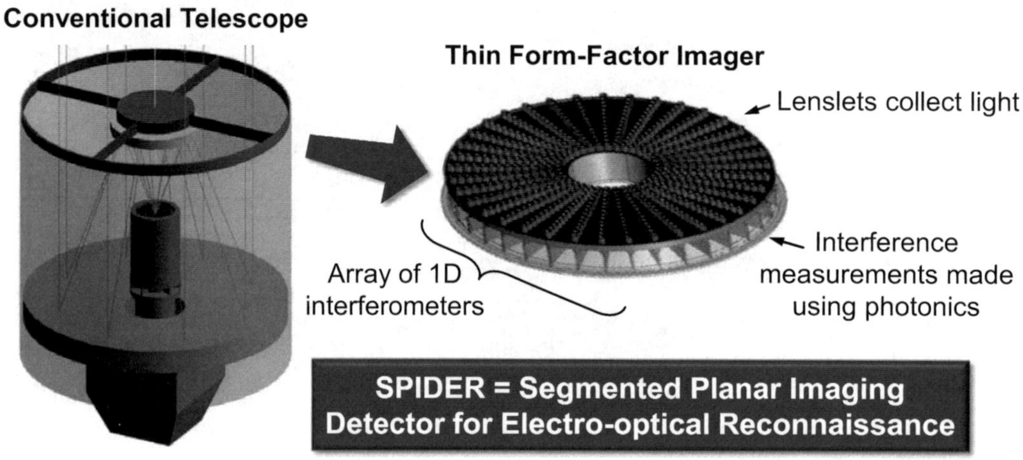

SPIDER = Segmented Planar Imaging Detector for Electro-optical Reconnaissance

7

Miniaturization Using Photonics

- **Integrated photonics design for proof-of-concept demonstration**

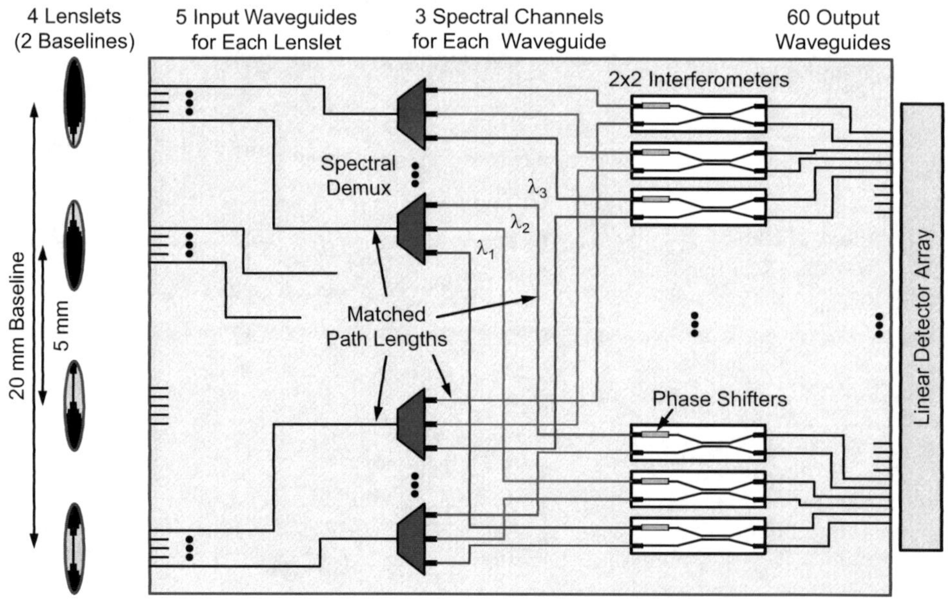

8

Fabrication/Testing

Layout | **Photonic Integrated Circuit (PIC)**

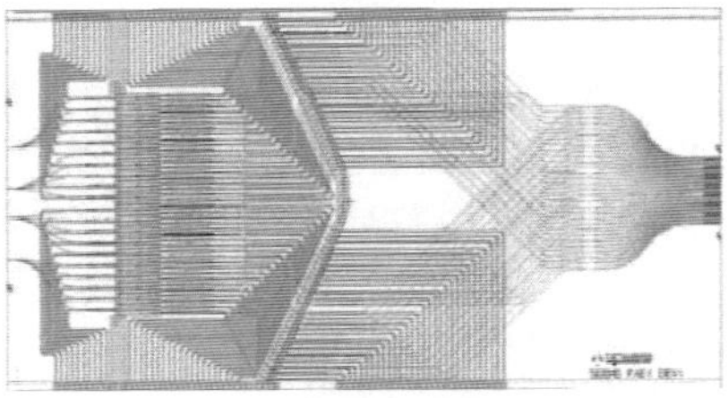

PIC in Testbed

9

Fringe Data

- **Measure**
  - Dark/background signal level
  - Light throughput from individual lenslets
  - Interference fringes (using phase shifters to scan through fringes)
- **Raw data is converted into normalized fringe signals (amplitude ≤ 1)**
  - Normalized fringe amplitude = amplitude of complex coherence factor μ

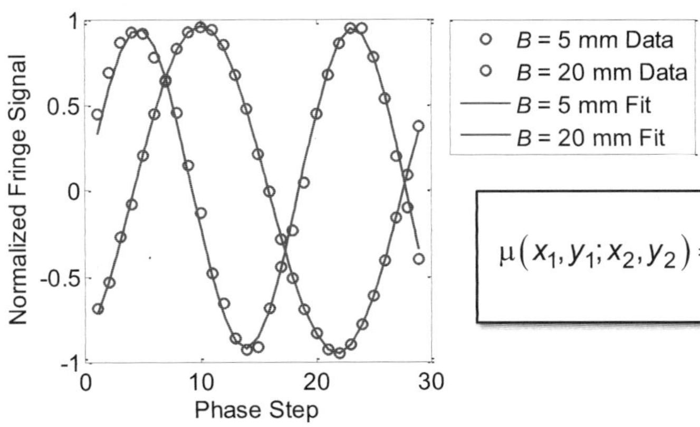

$$\mu(x_1, y_1; x_2, y_2) = \frac{J(x_1, y_1; x_2, y_2)}{\sqrt{I(x_1, y_1) I(x_2, y_2)}}$$

10

Simple Object

- **Used a variable-width slit aperture as a simple test object**
  - Two interferometer baselines only yield two spatial frequency measurements
  - If we collect data for different slit widths, the coherence estimates should follow the distribution of a sinc function (the Fourier transform of a rect)
- **Experimental results agreed well with theory**

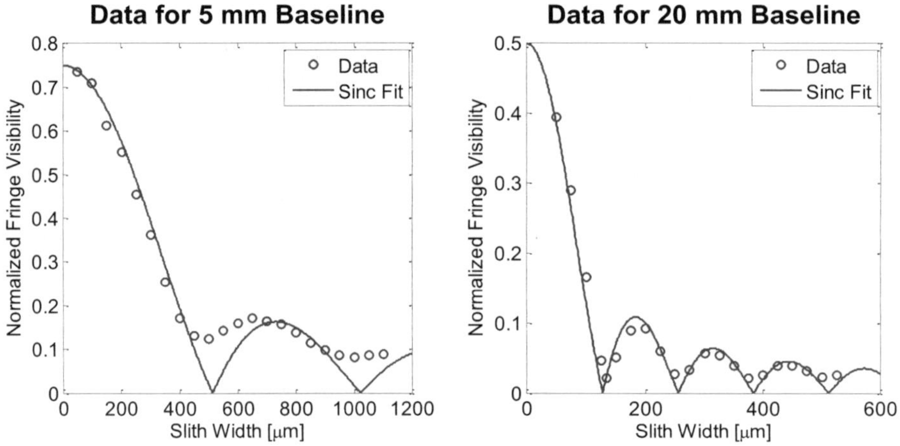

11

Design Principles - FOV

- **PIC waveguide coupling determines the imaging field-of-view**
  - Input coupling efficiency varies with field angle
  - Assume lenslet f-number is matched to waveguide numerical aperture
  - Angular field-of-view θ is determined by diffraction angle
- **Field-of-view can be reduced by lenslet alignment/pointing errors**
  - Lenslets need to collect lights from the same area of source

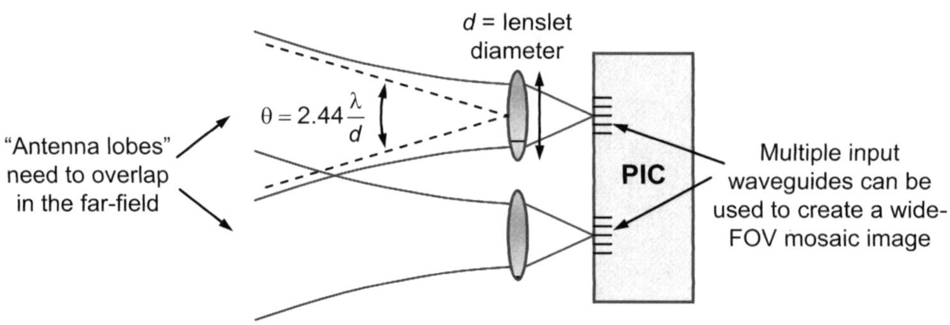

12

Spatial Resolution

- **Lenslets are paired up to form interferometer baselines of length *B***
  - Measurements for baseline B correspond to object spatial frequency $\rho = B/\lambda$
  - Image resolution is set by the cutoff spatial frequency

$$\rho_{max} = \frac{B_{max}}{\lambda_{min}}$$

- **Effective aperture size D_{eff} is equal to the longest interferometer baseline B_{max}**

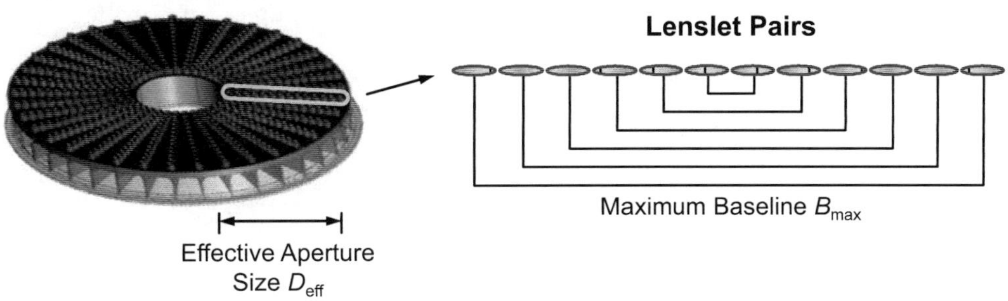

13

Spectral Sampling

- **Light from each lenslet is separated into various spectral channels before being combined**

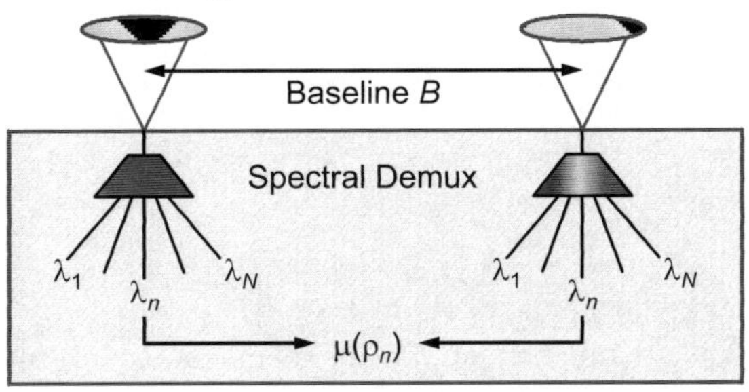

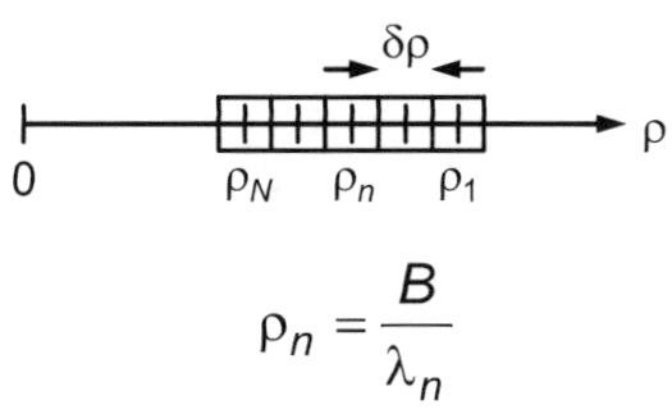

- **Nyquist sample spacing $\delta\rho$ is determined by the image FOV**

$$\delta\rho = \frac{1}{\theta} = \frac{d}{2.44\lambda}$$

- **Fractional optical bandwidth of each spectral channel needs to satisfy Nyquist criterion**

$$\frac{B}{\lambda} - \frac{B}{\lambda + \delta\lambda} \le \delta\rho \quad \Rightarrow \quad \frac{\delta\lambda}{\lambda} \le \frac{d}{2.44B}$$

$$\boxed{\frac{d}{2B_{max}} \approx \frac{1}{\text{image pixel width}}}$$

14

Next Generation Design

- Near IR wavelengths λ = 1.25-1.55 μm
- More compact PIC (Silicon Nitride)
- Similar baseline (22 mm)
- More baselines (13) & more spectral channels (12)
- Continuous radial Fourier sampling

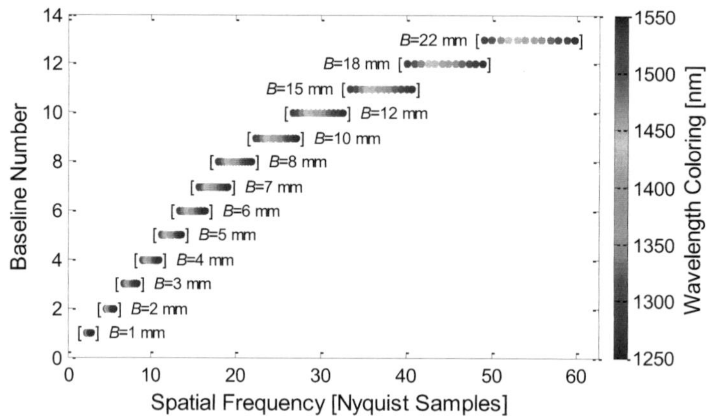

15

Miniature Camera Concept

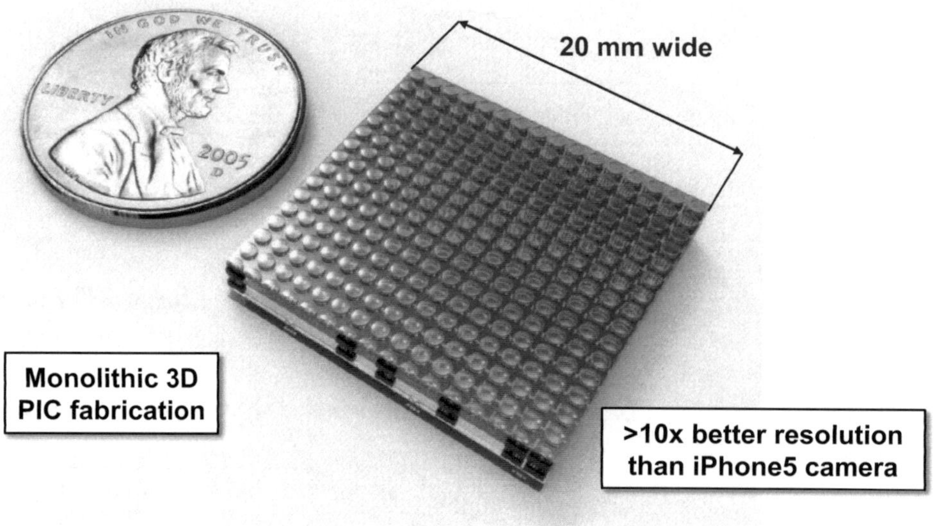

16

UC DAVIS COLLEGE OF ENGINEERING

Space Telescope Concept

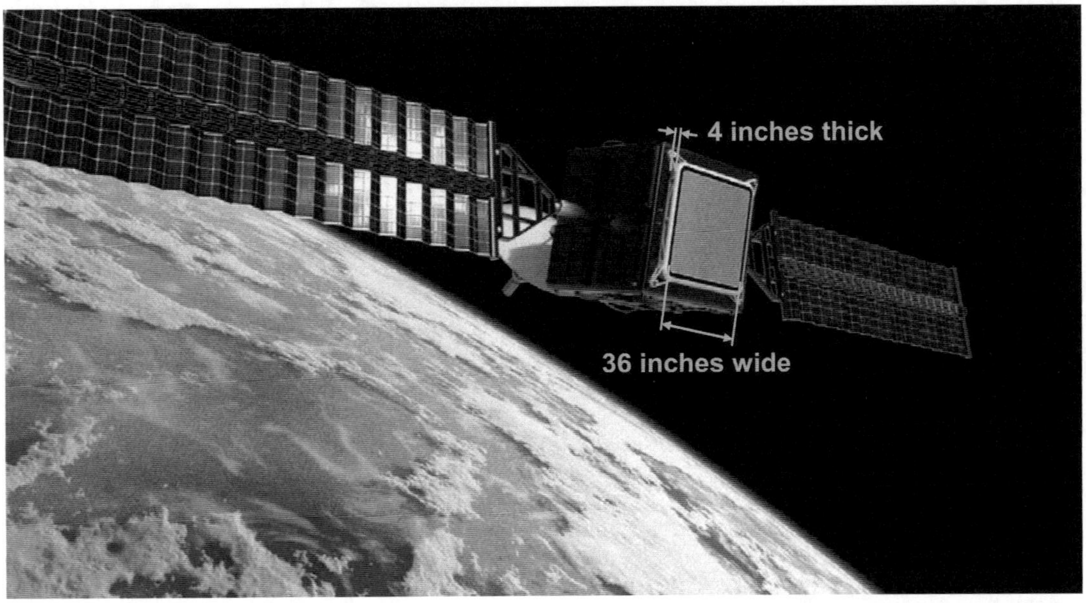

17

UC DAVIS COLLEGE OF ENGINEERING

Summary

SPIDER = Segmented Planar Imaging Detector for Electro-optical Reconnaissance

- Thin form-factor computational imager
- Based on long baseline interferometry and photonics
- Successful proof-of-concept experimental demonstration
- Design principles well understood
- Working towards future concepts

Support from DARPA for fabrication and testing of first generation device is gratefully acknowledged

18

Advances in Laser Locking -- Accuracy and S/N

☞ Locking *Accuracy* at the level of 1 E-6 Linewidths !

- Finally, 32 years after PDH, 10 orders of linewidth reduction, the Optical Comb, and all that Jazz: we can approximate the line-splitting skill of our Cesium clock colleagues!

John L Hall

JILA University of Colorado

Boulder CO 80309-0440

jhall@jila.colorado.edu

jan@HallStableLasers.com

http://jila.colorado.edu/hall

CLRC 2016
Boulder

CH_4 Saturated Absorption at 3.39 μm

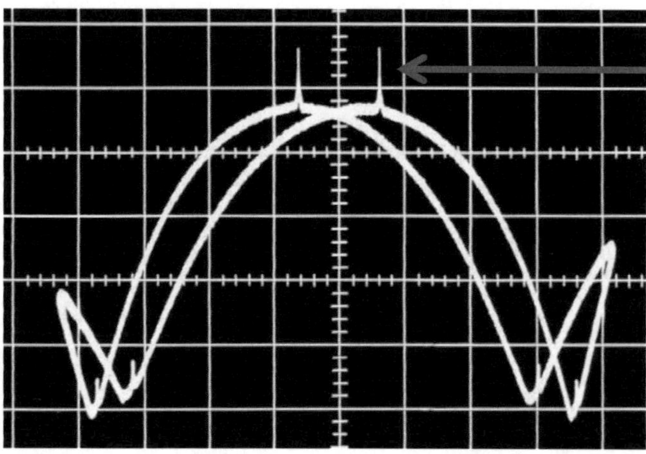

Sharp!
(Doppler/1000)
Contrast ~12 %

1968 prl

Laser Phase and Frequency Stabilization   Drever, Hall, et al. Appl. Phys. **B 31**, 97-105 (1983)   99

1715 WoS cites, 2014

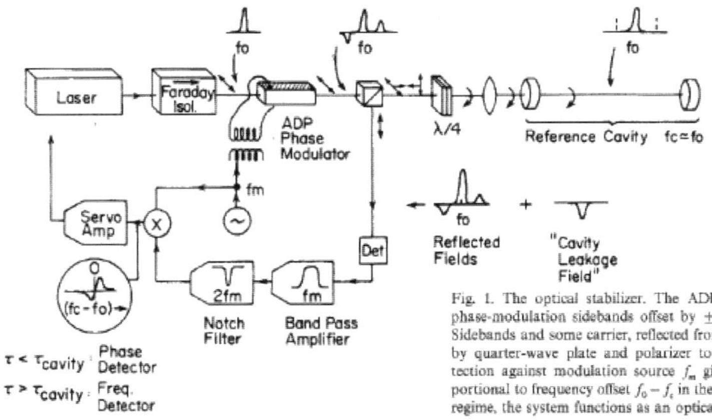

Fig. 1. The optical stabilizer. The ADP phase modulator produces phase-modulation sidebands offset by $\pm f_m$ from carrier frequency f_c. Sidebands and some carrier, reflected from reference cavity, are steered by quarter-wave plate and polarizer to detector. Phase-sensitive detection against modulation source f_m gives bipolar error signal proportional to frequency offset $f_0 - f_c$ in the adiabatic regime. In transient regime, the system functions as an optical phase detector (see text)

PDH - The *ideal* laser frequency stabilizer ! ???

Offset Issues:
1. weak reflected beams – optical isolation insufficient
2. Pure Phase modulation – contamination by AM (the RAM problem)

Noise Issues:
1. Cavity length changes – temperature and vibration
2. Thermal noise of coatings and substrates
3. Unwelcome shot-noise from image-frequency sidebands

Precision metrology in optical lattice

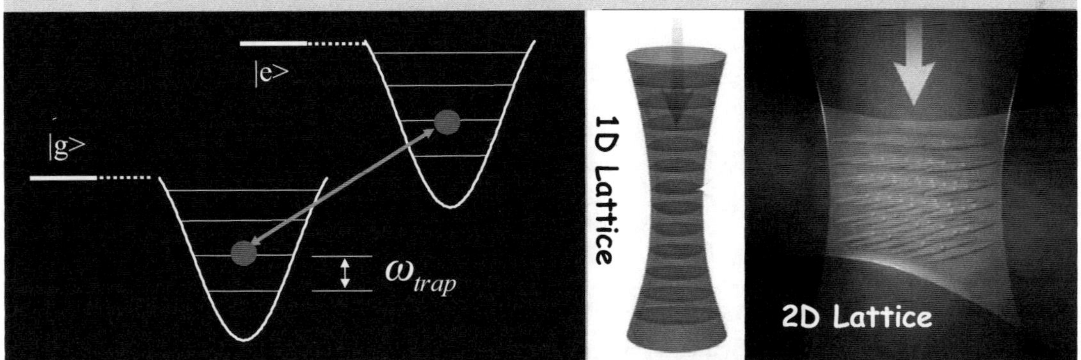

- Atomic confinement << λ ($e^{ikx} \sim 1$, $k = 2\pi/\lambda_{probe}$)
- Trap potential identical for |g> and |e>
- Precision improvement by $N^{1/2}$ $\frac{\delta\omega(\tau)}{\omega_0} = \frac{1}{Q} \times \frac{1}{\sqrt{N}} \times \sqrt{\frac{T_c}{\tau}}$
- Long coherence time; Zero Doppler shift, Zero recoil shift
- No light shift from the trap; but, interaction effects? Accuracy?

nature COMMUNICATIONS

ARTICLE

Received 14 Jan 2015 | Accepted 11 Mar 2015 | Published 21 Apr 2015 DOI: 10.1038/ncomms7896 OPEN

Systematic evaluation of an atomic clock at 2×10^{-18} total uncertainty

T.L. Nicholson[1,2], S.L. Campbell[1,2], R.B. Hutson[1,2], G.E. Marti[1,2], B.J. Bloom[1,2,†], R.L. McNally[1,2], W. Zhang[1,2], M.D. Barrett[1,3], M.S. Safronova[4,5], G.F. Strouse[6], W.L. Tew[6] & J. Ye[1,2]

The pursuit of better atomic clocks has advanced many research areas, providing better quantum state control, new insights in quantum science, tighter limits on fundamental constant variation and improved tests of relativity. The record for the best stability and accuracy is currently held by optical lattice clocks. Here we take an important step towards realizing the full potential of a many-particle clock with a state-of-the-art stable laser. Our ^{87}Sr optical lattice clock now achieves fractional stability of 2.2×10^{-16} at 1 s. With this improved stability, we perform a new accuracy evaluation of our clock, reducing many systematic uncertainties that limited our previous measurements, such as those in the lattice ac Stark shift, the atoms' thermal environment and the atomic response to room-temperature blackbody radiation. Our combined measurements have reduced the total uncertainty of the JILA Sr clock to 2.1×10^{-18} in fractional frequency units.

Evolution of atomic clocks

NPL National Physical Laboratory

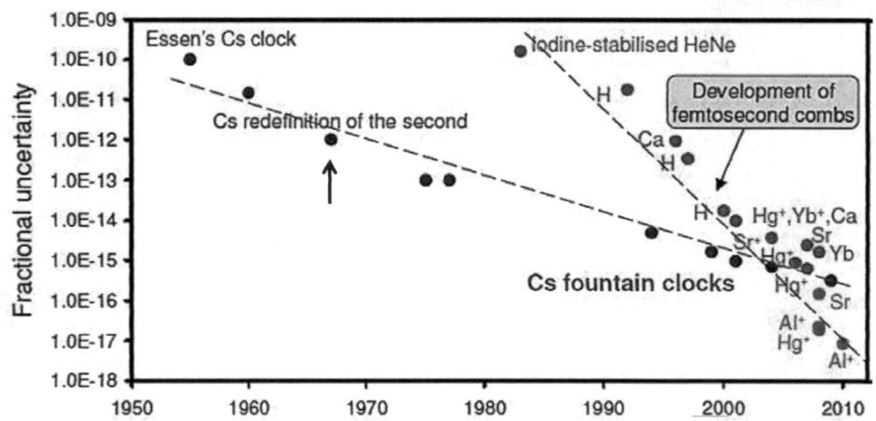

In the future, a new standard of Frequency/Time will be needed

When?

Optical Progress will have slowed down

Candidate Systems have had full & multiple Evaluations

Remote comparisons are possible/convenient

Adapted from P Gill 2013

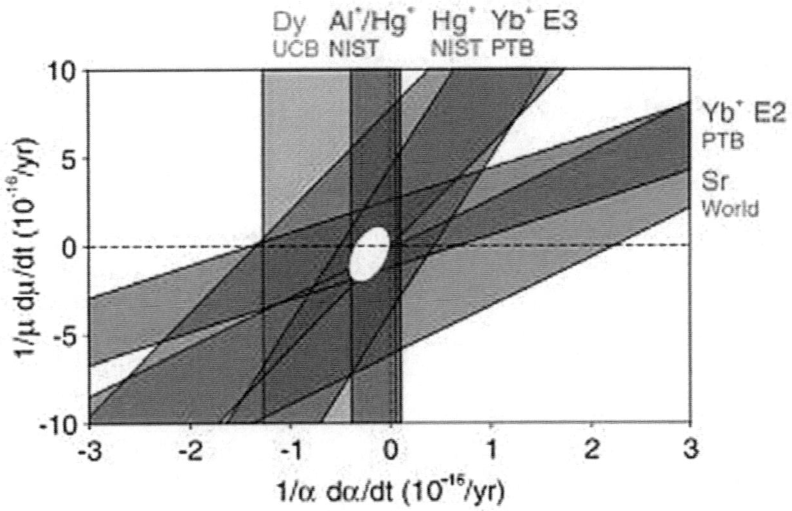

FIG. 19 (color online). Measurements between atomic clocks of different species can constrain possible variation of fundamental constants. A number of comparisons between distinct atomic-clock species are used here to constrain time variation of α and μ. From Huntemann *et al.*, 2014.

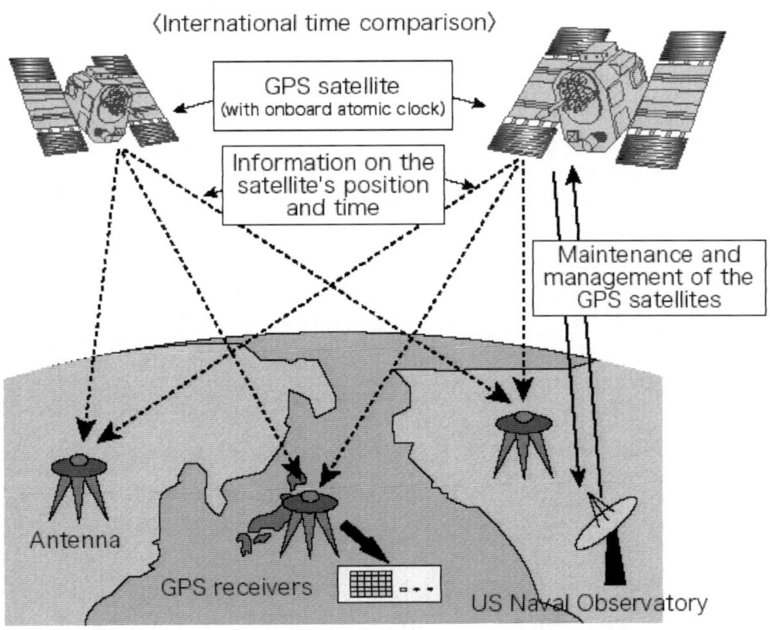

Figure Thanks to Japan's AIST

GPS allows transferring frequency to 3E-14 and time to ≈10 ns in one day

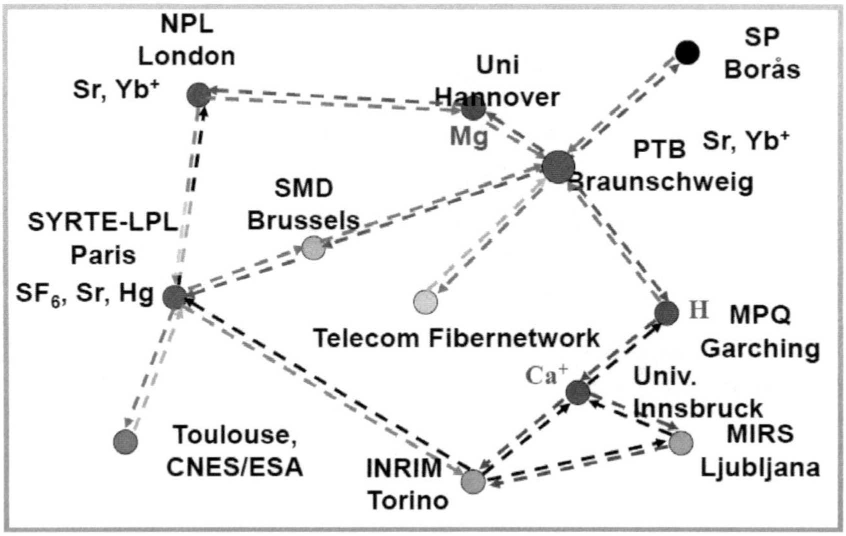

Planned European Metrology Fiber Network (2010) (planned in Paris)

First results in preprint circulation May 2016

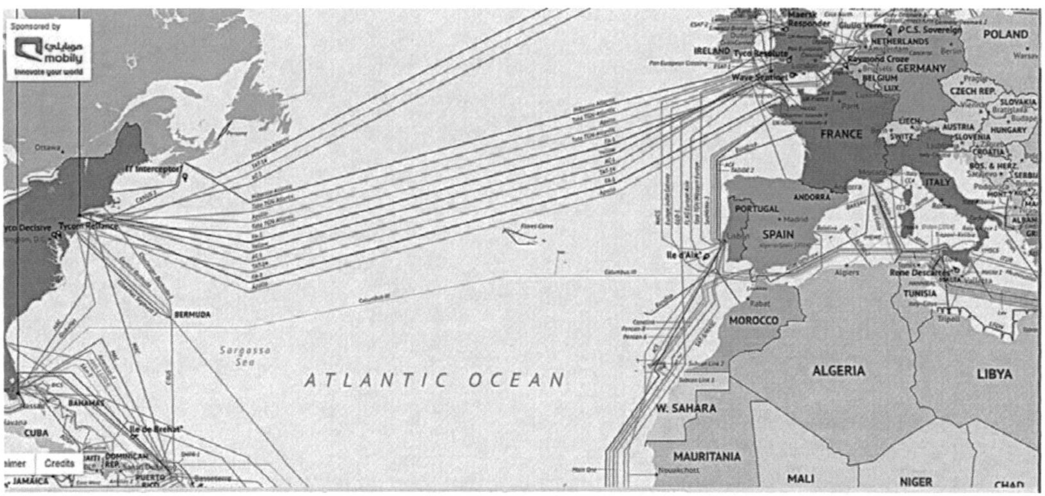

Surely there could be 1 all-optical link across?

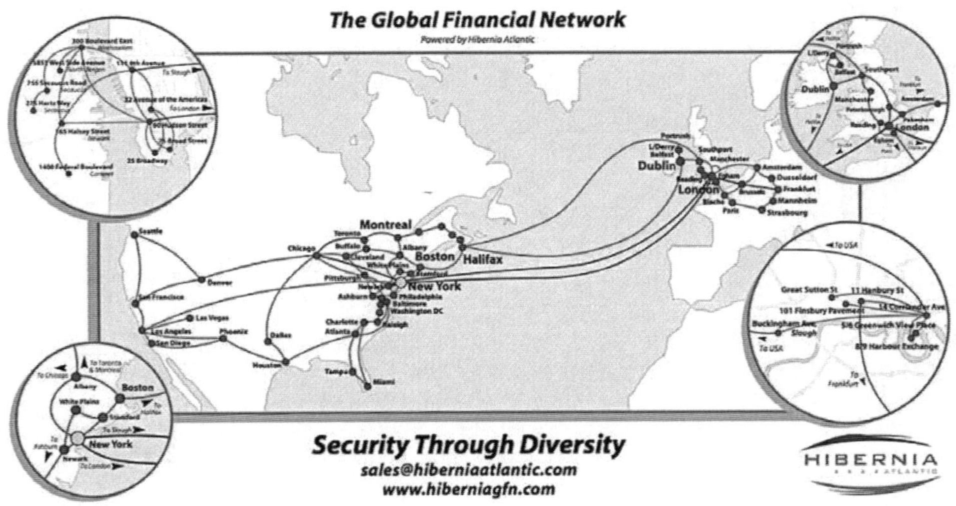

Probably these guys don't have any dark fibers we could use ....

PS: did you read "The Flash Boys" ?

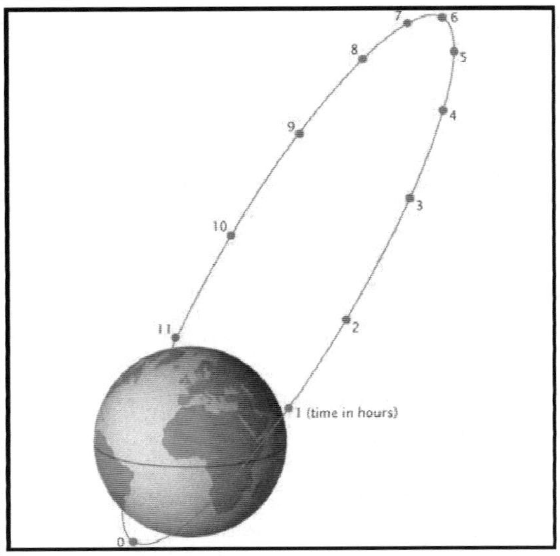

View of the Earth four hours before apogee from a Molniya orbit , if longitude of the apogee is 90° W.
The spacecraft altitude is 24,043 km over the point 87.35° W 47.04° N.

$R_{perogee}/R_e$ = 6591/6371 = 1.035 → 96.6%

R_{apogee}/R_e = 30414/6371 = 4.774 → 20.95 %

GR Shift = (0.966 – 0.2095) * 5.228 $\times 10^{-10}$ = 3.958 $\times 10^{-10}$ => 79 kHz for 1.5 μm laser

Earth's Rotation as a Distance Modulator

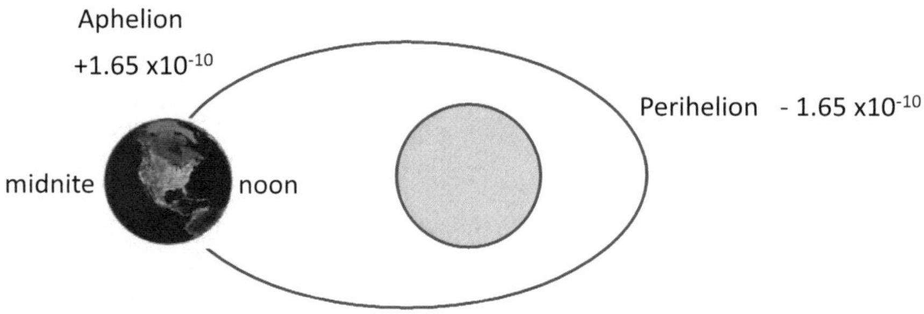

General Relativity Redshift: $\delta\omega/_{\omega} = \dfrac{GM}{Rc^2} \cong 9.8 \times 10^{-9}$

Fractional Distance Shift midnite ←→ noon ~ $\pm 4.2 \times 10^{-5}$

For Sr clock (429 THz) this is about ± 180 Hz !

Present measurement precision < 5 milli-Hz

European fiber network colleagues should compare absolute frequencies in mid-summer!

~~Universal Time?~~

After S Dali
"The Persistence
of Memory"

Home
Sweet
Home

Standard Time

The kitchen
closed
at 7:30

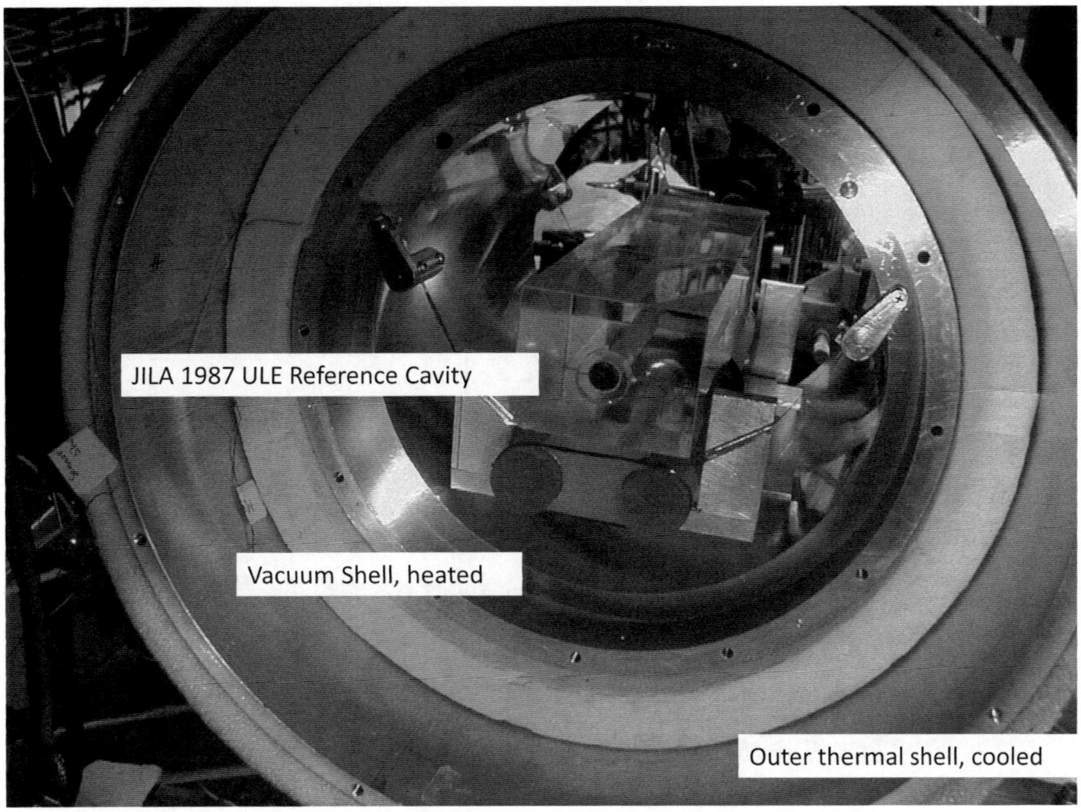

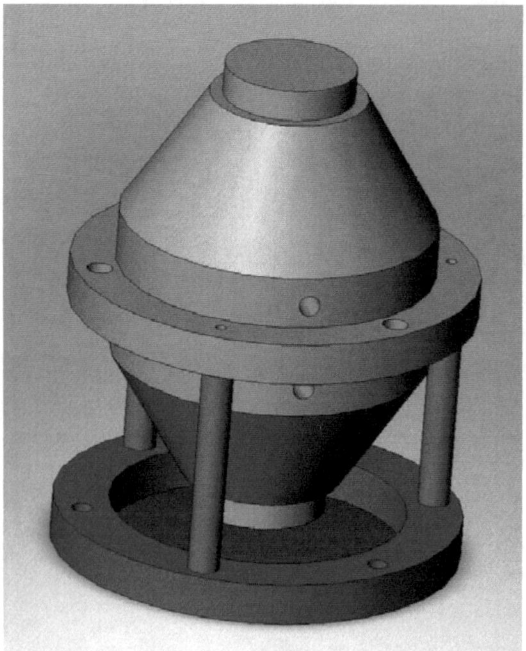

Tapered Shape

Reduces Acceleration Sensitivity

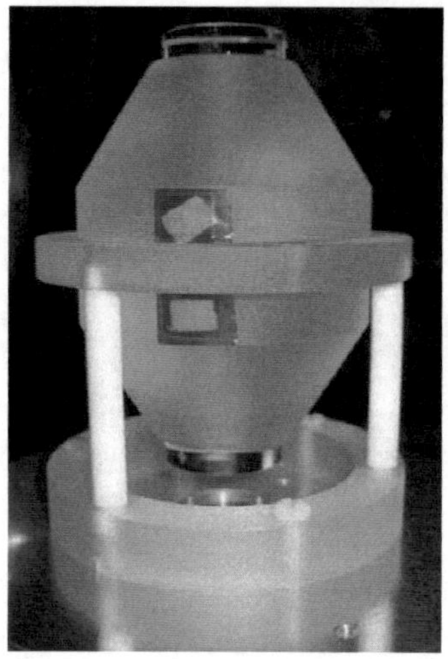

Symmetrical Mounting

Cancels

vertical acceleration sensitivity

(A. Ludlow)

NATURE PHOTONICS DOI: 10.1038/NPHOTON.2012.217

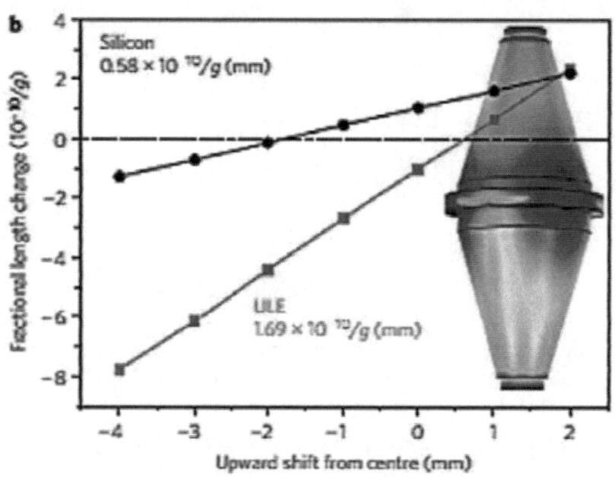

Choice of *Stiff Cavity Material* vs *Low/Zero Thermal Expansion*

ULE has zero CTE near room temperature

Silicon has zero CTE near 124 K, and near 4 K

Optical coherence & spectral resolution

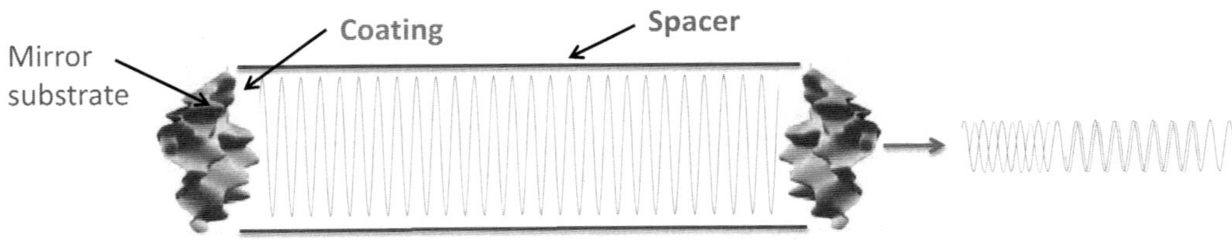

Cavity length $L \sim 1$ m → $\Delta L \sim 10^{-16}$ m (size of a nucleus: 10^{-14} m)

Mirror Thermal Noise: a fundamental process (Numata, Bergquist, ...)

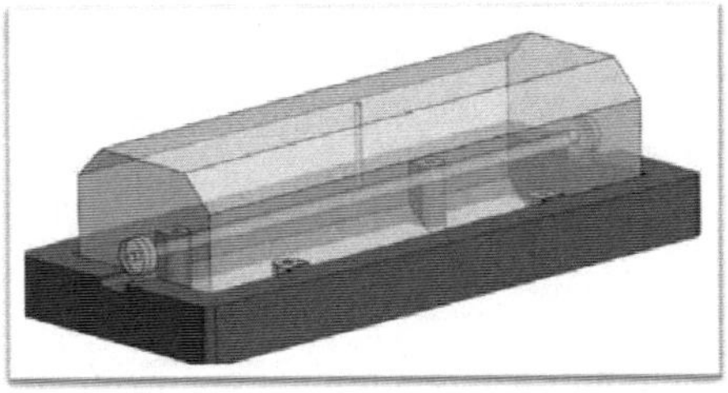

Mike Martin: Sr 40 cm ULE cavity

Bishof *et al.*, PRL **111**, 093604 (2013).

Swallows *et al.*, IEEE TUFFC **59**, 416 (2012)

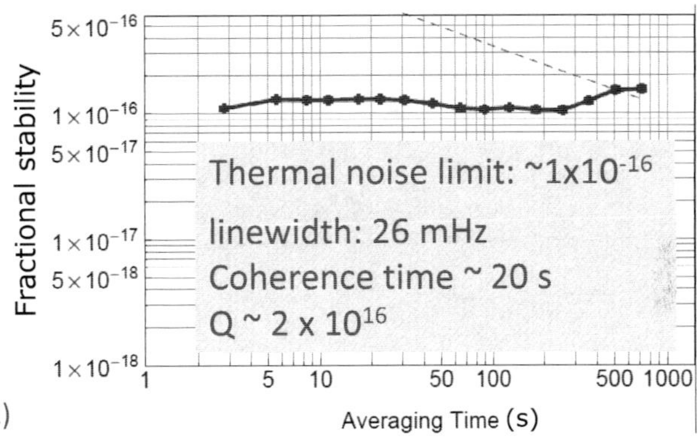

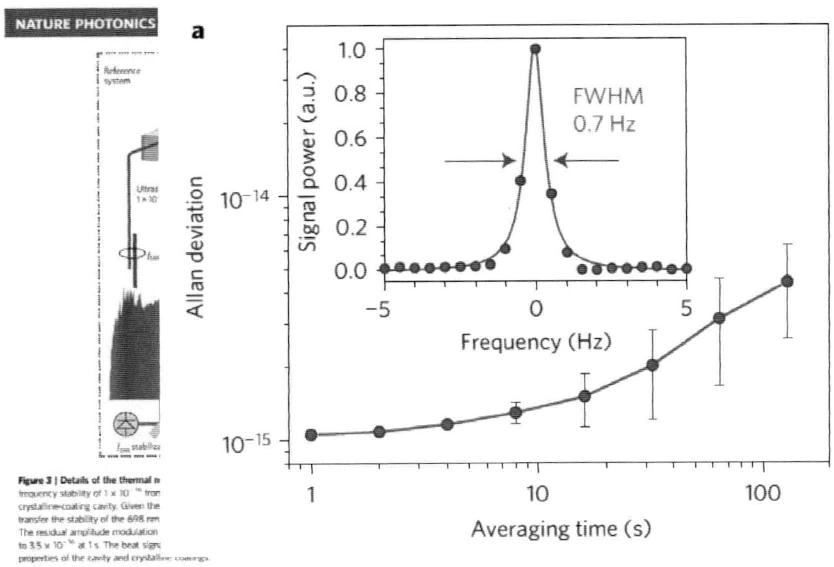

Crystal-based Mirror coatings have 10x lower thermal noise

Cole, Zhang, Martin, Ye, Aspelmeyer Nature Phot. July 2013 p. 644

Mark Notcutt (Stable Laser Systems)
will discuss cavity stability re vibrations

What about Locking the Laser to Molecular Saturated Absorption?

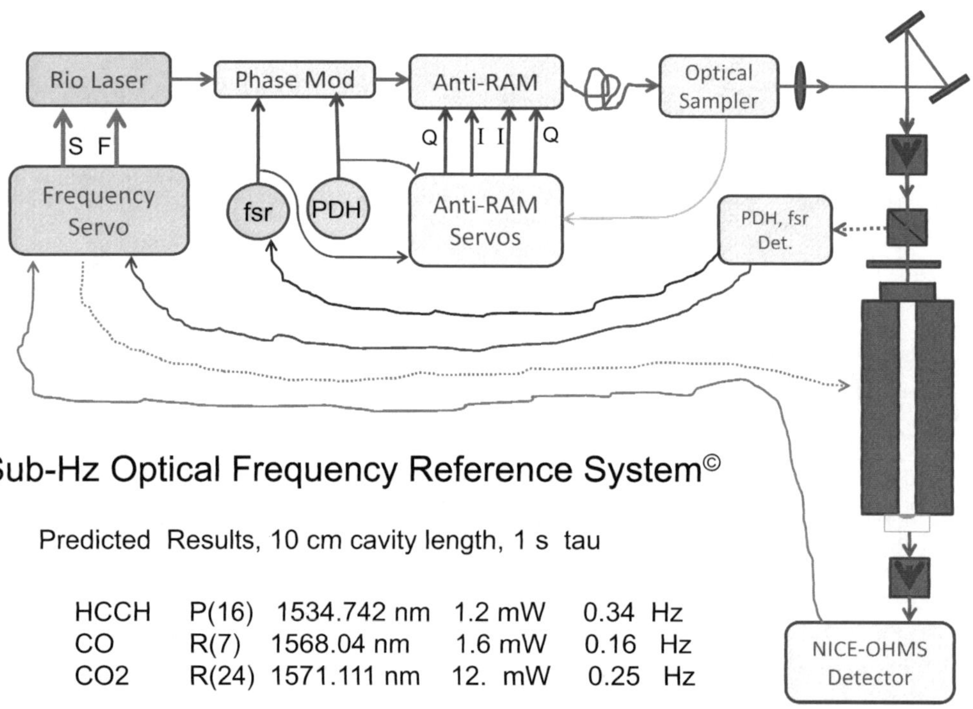

Sub-Hz Optical Frequency Reference System©

Predicted Results, 10 cm cavity length, 1 s tau

HCCH	P(16)	1534.742 nm	1.2 mW	0.34 Hz
CO	R(7)	1568.04 nm	1.6 mW	0.16 Hz
CO2	R(24)	1571.111 nm	12. mW	0.25 Hz

Sub-Hz Optical Frequency Reference System©

Let's Calculate what we could do with Saturated Molecular Absorption -1-

	A	B	C	D	E	F	G	H	I	J	K	L	M	N	O	P	Q	R	S	T
37	11/4/2010			Mirror R	Cavity	Cell Lc	zo	w0	transWidth	Gamma/P	GammaFV	Press	Pressure	Linewidth	IntegrAbs	MirrorT/	Mirror	Empty Ca	CavitAbs	Cavi
38	Scaling7						cm	cm	FWHM	kHz/mTorr	Hz/Pa	Width	Pa	Molecules		T/(L+Ab	T	Finesse	NonRes	ON
39																			1-beamSat	2-be
40		CO	3 nu R(7)	5.00E+02	10	10	49.74937	0.0499	2.12E+05	5.3	4.03E+04	1.4	2.11E+00	2.97E+05	7.16E-06	0.75	8.37E-06	2.54E+05	9.34E-06	8.4
41				5.00E+02	10	10	49.74937	0.0499	2.12E+05	5.3	4.03E+04	2	5.27E+00	4.24E+05	1.79E-05	1	2.19E-05	1.21E+05	1.72E-05	1.4
42				5.00E+02	10	10	49.74937	0.0499	2.12E+05	5.3	4.03E+04	3	1.05E+01	6.37E+05	3.58E-05	0.75	2.99E-05	9.28E+04	3.07E-05	2.6
43	c=	3.00E+10	cm/s	5.00E+02	10	10	49.74937	0.0499	2.12E+05	5.3	4.03E+04	4	1.58E+01	8.49E+05	5.37E-05	0.75	4.33E-05	6.64E+04	4.35E-05	3.6
44	pi =	3.14159		5.00E+02	28	28	82.48636	0.0642	1.65E+05	5.3	4.03E+04	2	4.09E+00	3.30E+05	3.89E-05	1	4.29E-05	6.69E+04	3.30E-05	2.8
45	Lambda=	1.57E-04	cm	5.00E+02	28	28	82.48636	0.0642	1.65E+05	5.3	4.03E+04	4	1.23E+01	6.59E+05	1.17E-04	1	1.21E-04	2.52E+04	9.11E-05	7.6
46	Lambda=	1.57E-04	cm	5.00E+02	28	28	82.48636	0.0642	1.65E+05	5.3	4.03E+04	6	2.05E+01	9.89E+05	1.95E-04	1	1.99E-04	1.55E+04	1.49E-04	1.2
47	Ttr	5291.503	kHz*cm	5.00E+02	28	28	82.48636	0.0642	1.65E+05	5.3	4.03E+04	8	2.86E+01	1.32E+06	2.73E-04	1	2.77E-04	1.12E+04	2.07E-04	1.7
48	AbsCoeff=	3.40E-07	cm^-1/Pa	1.00E+02	10	10	21.79449	0.0330	3.21E+05	5.3	4.03E+04	6	3.98E+01	1.92E+06	1.35E-04	1	1.39E-04	2.19E+04	1.05E-04	8.7
49	Mirror Loss=	4.00E-06		2.00E+02	10	10	31.22499	0.0395	2.68E+05	5.3	4.03E+04	6	3.32E+01	1.61E+06	1.13E-04	1	1.17E-04	2.60E+04	8.82E-05	7.4
50				5.00E+02	10	10	49.74937	0.0499	2.12E+05	5.3	4.03E+04	6	2.63E+01	1.27E+06	8.95E-05	1	9.35E-05	3.22E+04	7.07E-05	5.9
51	SatPower	2.063492	W	1.00E+03	10	10	70.53368	0.0594	1.78E+05	5.3	4.03E+04	6	2.21E+01	1.07E+06	7.52E-05	1	7.92E-05	3.78E+04	6.01E-05	5.0
52	PhotoDet	0.95	mA/mW	2.00E+03	30	30	172.5543	0.0929	1.14E+05	5.3	4.03E+04	4	8.48E+00	4.56E+05	8.65E-05	1	2.50E-05	1.08E+05	6.85E-05	5.7
53				2.00E+03	30	30	172.5543	0.0929	1.14E+05	5.3	4.03E+04	6	1.41E+01	6.84E+05	1.44E-04	1	2.50E-05	1.08E+05	1.12E-04	9.3
54	PressBrdn	0.067	cm-1/atm	5.00E+03	30	30	273.4502	0.1169	9.05E+04	5.3	4.03E+04	6	1.12E+01	5.43E+05	1.15E-04	1	2.50E-05	1.08E+05	8.94E-05	7.5
55	HWHM	2.644737	kHz/mTorr	2.00E+03	30	30	172.5543	0.0929	1.14E+05	5.3	4.03E+04	8	1.98E+01	9.11E+05	2.02E-04	1	2.50E-05	1.08E+05	1.55E-04	1.2
56	FWHM=	5.289474		2.00E+03	12	12	109.3801	0.0740	1.43E+05	5.3	4.03E+04	2.5	5.33E+00	3.58E+05	2.17E-05	1	2.50E-05	1.08E+05	2.02E-05	1.7
57				2.00E+03	12	12	109.3801	0.0740	1.43E+05	5.3	4.03E+04	4	1.07E+01	5.72E+05	4.35E-05	1	2.50E-05	1.08E+05	3.64E-05	3.1
58	PressShift	-1.6	kHz/Pa	2.00E+03	12	12	109.3801	0.0740	1.43E+05	5.3	4.03E+04	6	1.78E+01	8.59E+05	7.25E-05	1	2.50E-05	1.08E+05	5.80E-05	4.8
59				5.00E+03	12	12	173.1011	0.0930	1.14E+05	5.3	4.03E+04	8	1.98E+01	9.10E+05	8.06E-05	1	2.50E-05	1.08E+05	6.41E-05	5.4
60				5.00E+03	30	120	273.4502	0.1169	9.05E+04	5.3	4.03E+04	2	2.25E+00	1.81E+05	9.17E-05	1	2.50E-05	1.08E+05	7.23E-05	6.0
61				5.00E+03	30	120	273.4502	0.1169	9.05E+04	5.3	4.03E+04	2	2.25E+00	1.81E+05	9.17E-05	1	2.50E-05	1.08E+05	7.23E-05	6.0
62				5.00E+03	30	120	273.4502	0.1169	9.05E+04	5.3	4.03E+04	2	2.25E+00	1.81E+05	9.17E-05	1	2.50E-05	1.08E+05	7.23E-05	6.0
63				5.00E+03	30	120	273.4502	0.1169	9.05E+04	5.3	4.03E+04	2	2.25E+00	1.81E+05	9.17E-05	1	2.50E-05	1.08E+05	7.23E-05	6.0
64																				
65	11/4/2010			Mirror R	Cavity	Cell Lc	zo	w0	transWidth	Gamma/P	GammaFV	Press	Pressure	Linewidth	IntegrAbs	MirrorT/	Mirror	Empty Ca	CavitAbs	Cavi
66	Scaling7						cm	cm	FWHM	kHz/mTorr	Hz/Pa	Width	Pa	Molecules		T/(L+Ab	T	Finesse	NonRes	ON
67																			1-beamSat	2-be
68		CO2 - R24		5.00E+02	10	10	49.74937	0.0499	1.69E+05	7.310526	5.56E+04	4	9.14E+00	6.77E+05	7.31E-06	1	1.53E-05	1.35E+05	1.34E-05	1.2
69				5.00E+02	10	10	49.74937	0.0499	1.69E+05	5.5	4.20E+04	4	1.21E+01	6.77E+05	9.67E-06	1	1.77E-05	1.22E+05	1.52E-05	1.4
70				5.00E+02	10	10	49.74937	0.0499	1.69E+05	5.5	4.20E+04	6	2.01E+01	1.02E+06	1.61E-05	1	2.41E-05	9.78E+04	2.00E-05	1.8
71	c=	3.00E+10	cm/s	5.00E+02	10	10	49.74937	0.0499	1.69E+05	5.5	4.20E+04	8	2.82E+01	1.35E+06	2.26E-05	1	3.06E-05	8.15E+04	2.48E-05	2.2
72	pi =	3.14159		5.00E+02	28	28	82.48636	0.0642	1.31E+05	5.5	4.20E+04	2	3.13E+00	2.63E+05	7.01E-06	1	1.50E-05	1.37E+05	1.32E-05	1.2

Sheet1 / Sheet2 / Sheet3

Let's Calculate what we could do with Saturated Molecular Absorption -2-

	O	P	Q	R	S	T	U	V	W	X	Y	Z	AA	AB	AC	AD	AE	AF	AG
37	IntegrAbs	MirrorT/	Mirror	Empty Ca	CavitAbs	CavityAbs	Resonant	Cavity	BuildUp	Satura	Power	SatPower	TransCoeff	TransCoef	NonRes	ON Res	Signal	BkgNonRe	Signa
38		T/(L+Ab	T	Finesse	NonRes	ON Res	Finesse	Linewidth	on Res	param	for S=1	needed inp	offRes	ONRes	Transm	Transm	Power	Current	Curre
39					1-beamSat	2-beamSat					W				mW	mW		A	A
40	7.16E-06	0.75	8.37E-06	2.54E+05	9.34E-06	8.44E-06	1.87E+05	8.03E+03	2.96E+04	0.8	4.044444	1.09E-04	2.23E-01	0.247924	2.44E-05	2.71E-05	2.67E-06	2.57E-05	2.54
41	1.79E-05	1	2.19E-05	1.21E+05	1.72E-05	1.49E-05	8.53E+04	1.76E+04	1.62E+04	0.85	8.253968	4.34E-04	3.14E-01	0.35429	1.36E-04	1.54E-04	1.73E-05	1.46E-04	1.65
42	3.58E-05	0.75	2.99E-05	9.28E+04	3.07E-05	2.62E-05	5.60E+04	2.68E+04	9.50E+03	0.8	18.57143	1.56E-03	2.43E-01	0.283605	3.80E-04	4.44E-04	6.33E-05	4.22E-04	6.01
43	5.37E-05	0.75	4.33E-05	6.64E+04	4.35E-05	3.67E-05	3.93E+04	3.82E+04	6.77E+03	0.85	33.01587	4.15E-03	2.49E-01	0.292943	1.03E-03	1.22E-03	1.83E-04	1.15E-03	1.74
44	3.89E-05	1	4.29E-05	6.69E+04	3.30E-05	2.82E-05	4.42E+04	1.21E+04	8.50E+03	0.8	8.253968	7.77E-04	3.20E-01	0.36485	2.48E-04	2.84E-04	3.52E-05	2.69E-04	3.35
45	1.17E-04	1	1.21E-04	2.52E+04	9.11E-05	7.65E-05	1.59E+04	3.36E+04	3.10E+03	0.8	33.01587	8.51E-03	3.25E-01	0.375113	2.77E-03	3.19E-03	4.25E-04	3.03E-03	4.04
46	1.95E-04	1	1.99E-04	1.55E+04	1.49E-04	1.25E-04	9.71E+03	5.52E+04	1.90E+03	0.8	74.28571	3.13E-02	3.26E-01	0.377388	1.02E-02	1.18E-02	1.60E-03	1.12E-02	1.52
47	2.73E-04	1	2.77E-04	1.12E+04	2.07E-04	1.73E-04	6.99E+03	7.67E+04	1.37E+03	0.8	132.0635	7.72E-02	3.27E-01	0.378388	2.52E-02	2.92E-02	3.98E-03	2.78E-02	3.78
48	1.35E-04	1	1.39E-04	2.19E+04	1.05E-04	8.79E-05	1.38E+04	1.08E+05	2.70E+03	0.8	74.28571	2.20E-02	3.26E-01	0.37588	7.17E-03	8.28E-03	1.11E-03	7.86E-03	1.05
49	1.13E-04	1	1.17E-04	2.60E+04	8.82E-05	7.41E-05	1.64E+04	9.13E+04	3.20E+03	0.8	74.28571	1.85E-02	3.25E-01	0.374925	6.03E-03	6.95E-03	9.26E-04	6.61E-03	8.79
50	8.95E-05	1	9.35E-05	3.22E+04	7.07E-05	5.96E-05	2.06E+04	7.31E+04	3.99E+03	0.8	74.28571	1.49E-02	3.24E-01	0.373433	4.83E-03	5.56E-03	7.33E-04	5.28E-03	6.96
51	7.52E-05	1	7.92E-05	3.78E+04	6.01E-05	5.06E-05	2.42E+04	6.20E+04	4.70E+03	0.8	74.28571	1.26E-02	3.23E-01	0.372095	4.09E-03	4.71E-03	6.15E-04	4.47E-03	5.84
52	8.65E-05	1	2.50E-05	1.08E+05	6.85E-05	5.77E-05	3.80E+04	1.32E+04	3.66E+03	0.8	33.01587	7.22E-03	7.15E-02	0.091442	5.16E-04	6.60E-04	1.44E-04	6.27E-04	1.37
53	1.44E-04	1	2.50E-05	1.08E+05	1.12E-04	9.35E-05	2.65E+04	1.89E+04	1.78E+03	0.8	74.28571	3.34E-02	3.35E-02	0.044541	1.12E-03	1.49E-03	3.67E-04	1.41E-03	3.49
54	1.15E-04	1	2.50E-05	1.08E+05	8.94E-05	7.51E-05	3.14E+04	1.59E+04	2.50E+03	0.8	74.28571	2.38E-02	4.78E-02	0.062423	1.14E-03	1.49E-03	3.49E-04	1.41E-03	3.32
55	2.02E-04	1	2.50E-05	1.08E+05	1.55E-04	1.29E-04	2.04E+04	2.45E+04	1.05E+03	0.8	132.0635	1.01E-01	1.94E-02	0.026272	1.95E-03	2.64E-03	6.92E-04	2.51E-03	6.57
56	2.17E-05	1	2.50E-05	1.08E+05	2.02E-05	1.75E-05	7.39E+04	1.69E+04	1.39E+04	0.8	12.89683	7.45E-04	3.06E-01	0.346298	2.28E-04	2.58E-04	3.01E-05	2.45E-04	2.86
57	4.35E-05	1	2.50E-05	1.08E+05	3.64E-05	3.10E-05	5.61E+04	2.23E+04	7.98E+03	0.8	33.01587	3.31E-03	1.66E-01	0.199541	5.48E-04	6.60E-04	1.12E-04	6.27E-04	1.06
58	7.25E-05	1	2.50E-05	1.08E+05	5.80E-05	4.89E-05	4.25E+04	2.94E+04	4.57E+03	0.8	74.28571	1.30E-02	9.07E-02	0.114309	1.18E-03	1.49E-03	3.07E-04	1.41E-03	2.92
59	8.06E-05	1	2.50E-05	1.08E+05	6.41E-05	5.40E-05	3.98E+04	3.14E+04	4.00E+03	0.8	132.0635	2.64E-02	7.87E-02	0.100103	2.08E-03	2.64E-03	5.65E-04	2.51E-03	5.36
60	9.17E-05	1	2.50E-05	1.08E+05	7.23E-05	6.08E-05	3.66E+04	1.37E+04	3.39E+03	0.8	8.253968	1.95E-03	6.60E-02	0.084802	1.28E-04	1.65E-04	3.66E-05	1.57E-04	3.48
61	9.17E-05	1	2.50E-05	1.08E+05	7.23E-05	6.08E-05	3.66E+04	1.37E+04	3.39E+03	0.8	8.253968	1.95E-03	6.60E-02	0.084802	1.28E-04	1.65E-04	3.66E-05	1.57E-04	3.48
62	9.17E-05	1	2.50E-05	1.08E+05	7.23E-05	6.08E-05	3.66E+04	1.37E+04	3.39E+03	0.8	8.253968	1.95E-03	6.60E-02	0.084802	1.28E-04	1.65E-04	3.66E-05	1.57E-04	3.48
63	9.17E-05	1	2.50E-05	1.08E+05	7.23E-05	6.08E-05	3.66E+04	1.37E+04	3.39E+03	0.8	8.253968	1.95E-03	6.60E-02	0.084802	1.28E-04	1.65E-04	3.66E-05	1.57E-04	3.48
64																			
65	IntegrAbs	MirrorT/	Mirror	Empty Ca	CavitAbs	CavityAbs	Resonant	Cavity	BuildUp	Satura	Power	SatPower	TransCoeff	TransCoef	NonRes	ON Res	Signal	BkgNonRe	Signa
66		T/(L+Ab	T	Finesse	NonRes	ON Res	Finesse	Linewidth	on Res	param	for S=1	needed inp	offRes	ONRes	Transm	Transm	Power	Current	Curre
67					1-beamSat	2-beamSat					W				mW	mW		A	A
68	7.31E-06	1	1.53E-05	1.35E+05	1.34E-05	1.25E-05	1.13E+05	1.33E+04	1.97E+04	0.8	21.20646	8.59E-04	2.83E-01	0.302351	2.43E-04	2.60E-04	1.63E-05	2.47E-04	1.55
69	9.67E-06	1	1.77E-05	1.22E+05	1.52E-05	1.40E-05	9.92E+04	1.51E+04	1.76E+04	0.8	21.20646	9.63E-04	2.89E-01	0.311362	2.78E-04	3.00E-04	2.17E-05	2.85E-04	2.06
70	1.61E-05	1	2.41E-05	9.78E+04	2.00E-05	1.80E-05	7.46E+04	2.01E+04	1.36E+04	0.8	47.71453	2.81E-03	2.99E-01	0.32797	8.38E-04	9.21E-04	8.23E-05	8.75E-04	7.82
71	2.26E-05	1	3.06E-05	8.15E+04	2.48E-05	2.20E-05	5.98E+04	2.51E+04	1.11E+04	0.8	84.82583	6.13E-03	3.05E-01	0.338185	1.87E-03	2.07E-03	2.06E-04	1.97E-03	1.96
72	7.01E-06	1	1.50E-05	1.37E+05	1.32E-05	1.23E-05	1.15E+05	4.67E+03	2.01E+04	0.8	5.301614	2.11E-04	2.83E-01	0.301033	5.98E-05	6.37E-05	3.90E-06	6.05E-05	3.70

Sheet1 / Sheet2 / Sheet3

Let's Calculate what we could do with Saturated Molecular Absorption -3-

	V	W	X	Y	Z	AA	AB	AC	AD	AE	AF	AG	AH	AI	AJ	AK	AL	AM
37	Cavity	BuildUp	Satura	Power	SatPower	TransCoeff	TransCoef	NonRes	ON Res	Signal	BkgNonRe	Signal	S/N	FreqStab	Current	Axner	Press->	Temp chng
38	Linewidth	on Res	param	for S=1	needed inp	offRes	ONRes	Transm	Transm	Power	Current	Current	(1 s)	(1 s)	S/N	Stability	Shift kHz	for 1 Hz
39				W				mW	mW		A	A						
40	8.03E+03	2.96E+04	0.8	4.044444	1.09E-04	2.23E-01	0.247924	2.44E-05	2.71E-05	2.67E-06	2.57E-05	2.54E-06	8.85E+05	4.50E-01	2.82E+06	1.83E+00	-3.37E+00	-8.81E-02
41	1.76E+04	1.62E+04	0.85	8.253968	4.34E-04	3.14E-01	0.35429	1.36E-04	1.54E-04	1.73E-05	1.46E-04	1.65E-05	2.41E+06	2.40E-01	7.17E+06	9.01E-01	-8.43E+00	-3.52E-02
42	2.68E+04	9.50E+03	0.8	18.57143	1.56E-03	2.43E-01	0.283605	3.80E-04	4.44E-04	6.33E-05	4.22E-04	6.01E-05	5.18E+06	1.65E-01	1.37E+07	5.39E-01	-1.69E+01	-1.76E-02
43	3.82E+04	6.77E+03	0.85	33.01587	4.15E-03	2.49E-01	0.292943	1.03E-03	1.22E-03	1.83E-04	1.15E-03	1.74E-04	9.05E+06	1.28E-01	2.33E+07	4.02E-01	-2.53E+01	-1.17E-02
44	1.21E+04	8.50E+03	0.8	8.253968	7.77E-04	3.20E-01	0.36485	2.48E-04	2.84E-04	3.52E-05	2.69E-04	3.35E-05	3.60E+06	1.23E-01	1.02E+07	4.36E-01	-6.55E+00	-4.54E-02
45	3.36E+04	3.10E+03	0.8	33.01587	8.51E-03	3.25E-01	0.375113	2.77E-03	3.19E-03	4.25E-04	3.03E-03	4.04E-04	1.30E+07	6.82E-02	3.55E+07	2.32E-01	-1.96E+01	-1.51E-02
46	5.52E+04	1.90E+03	0.8	74.28571	3.13E-02	3.26E-01	0.377388	1.02E-02	1.18E-02	1.60E-03	1.12E-02	1.52E-03	2.53E+07	5.24E-02	6.89E+07	1.77E-01	-3.27E+01	-9.08E-03
47	7.67E+04	1.37E+03	0.8	132.0635	7.72E-02	3.27E-01	0.378388	2.52E-02	2.92E-02	3.98E-03	2.78E-02	3.78E-03	4.01E+07	4.41E-02	1.09E+08	1.48E-01	-4.58E+01	-6.48E-03
48	1.08E+05	2.70E+03	0.8	74.28571	2.20E-02	3.26E-01	0.37588	7.17E-03	8.28E-03	1.11E-03	7.86E-03	1.05E-03	2.10E+07	1.23E-01	5.74E+07	4.17E-01	-6.37E+01	-4.66E-03
49	9.13E+04	3.20E+03	0.8	74.28571	1.85E-02	3.25E-01	0.374925	6.03E-03	6.95E-03	9.26E-04	6.61E-03	8.79E-04	1.91E+07	1.13E-01	5.24E+07	3.84E-01	-5.32E+01	-5.58E-03
50	7.31E+04	3.99E+03	0.8	74.28571	1.49E-02	3.24E-01	0.373433	4.83E-03	5.56E-03	7.33E-04	5.28E-03	6.96E-04	1.69E+07	1.01E-01	4.66E+07	3.46E-01	-4.21E+01	-7.05E-03
51	6.20E+04	4.70E+03	0.8	74.28571	1.26E-02	3.23E-01	0.372095	4.09E-03	4.71E-03	6.15E-04	4.47E-03	5.84E-04	1.54E+07	9.29E-02	4.27E+07	3.20E-01	-3.54E+01	-8.39E-03
52	1.32E+04	3.66E+03	0.8	33.01587	7.22E-03	7.15E-02	0.091442	5.16E-04	6.60E-04	1.44E-04	6.27E-04	1.37E-04	9.67E+06	6.33E-02	2.07E+07	1.56E-01	-1.36E+01	-2.19E-02
53	1.89E+04	1.78E+03	0.8	74.28571	3.34E-02	3.35E-02	0.044541	1.12E-03	1.49E-03	3.67E-04	1.41E-03	3.49E-04	1.64E+07	5.59E-02	3.30E+07	1.26E-01	-2.26E+01	-1.31E-02
54	1.59E+04	2.50E+03	0.8	74.28571	2.38E-02	4.78E-02	0.062423	1.14E-03	1.49E-03	3.49E-04	1.41E-03	3.32E-04	1.56E+07	4.67E-02	3.22E+07	1.09E-01	-1.80E+01	-1.65E-02
55	2.45E+04	1.05E+03	0.8	132.0635	1.01E-01	1.94E-02	0.026272	1.95E-03	2.64E-03	6.92E-04	2.51E-03	6.57E-04	2.32E+07	5.27E-02	4.53E+07	1.14E-01	-3.17E+01	-9.38E-03
56	1.69E+04	1.39E+04	0.8	12.89683	7.45E-04	3.06E-01	0.346298	2.28E-04	2.58E-04	3.01E-05	2.45E-04	2.86E-05	3.23E+06	1.49E-01	9.46E+06	5.48E-01	-8.53E+00	-3.48E-02
57	2.23E+04	7.98E+03	0.8	33.01587	3.31E-03	1.66E-01	0.199541	5.48E-04	6.60E-04	1.12E-04	6.27E-04	1.06E-04	7.50E+06	1.02E-01	1.82E+07	2.99E-01	-1.71E+01	-1.74E-02
58	2.94E+04	4.57E+03	0.8	74.28571	1.30E-02	9.07E-02	0.114309	1.18E-03	1.49E-03	3.07E-04	1.41E-03	2.92E-04	1.37E+07	8.39E-02	3.02E+07	2.15E-01	-2.84E+01	-1.05E-02
59	3.14E+04	4.00E+03	0.8	132.0635	2.64E-02	7.87E-02	0.100103	2.08E-03	2.64E-03	5.65E-04	2.51E-03	5.36E-04	1.89E+07	6.45E-02	4.09E+07	1.61E-01	-3.16E+01	-9.39E-03
60	1.37E+04	3.39E+03	0.8	8.253968	1.95E-03	6.60E-02	0.084802	1.28E-04	1.65E-04	3.66E-05	1.57E-04	3.48E-05	4.91E+06	4.94E-02	1.04E+07	1.20E-01	-3.59E+00	-8.26E-02
61	1.37E+04	3.39E+03	0.8	8.253968	1.95E-03	6.60E-02	0.084802	1.28E-04	1.65E-04	3.66E-05	1.57E-04	3.48E-05	4.91E+06	4.94E-02	1.04E+07	1.20E-01	-3.59E+00	-8.26E-02
62	1.37E+04	3.39E+03	0.8	8.253968	1.95E-03	6.60E-02	0.084802	1.28E-04	1.65E-04	3.66E-05	1.57E-04	3.48E-05	4.91E+06	4.94E-02	1.04E+07	1.20E-01	-3.59E+00	-8.26E-02
63	1.37E+04	3.39E+03	0.8	8.253968	1.95E-03	6.60E-02	0.084802	1.28E-04	1.65E-04	3.66E-05	1.57E-04	3.48E-05	4.91E+06	4.94E-02	1.04E+07	1.20E-01	-3.59E+00	-8.26E-02
64																		
65	Cavity	BuildUp	Satura	Power	SatPower	TransCoeff	TransCoef	NonRes	ON Res	Signal	BkgNonRe	Signal	S/N	FreqStab	Current	Axner	Press->	Temp Chng
66	Linewidth	on Res	param	for S=1	needed inp	offRes	ONRes	Transm	Transm	Power	Current	Current	(1 s)	(1 s)	S/N	Stability	Shift kHz	for 1 Hz
67				W				mW	mW		A	A						
68	1.33E+04	1.97E+04	0.8	21.20646	8.59E-04	2.83E-01	0.302351	2.43E-04	2.60E-04	1.63E-05	2.47E-04	1.55E-05	1.74E+06	5.22E-01	6.95E+06	2.75E+00	-1.92E+01	-1.55E-02
69	1.51E+04	1.76E+04	0.8	21.20646	9.63E-04	2.89E-01	0.311362	2.78E-04	3.00E-04	2.17E-05	2.85E-04	2.06E-05	2.16E+06	4.21E-01	8.02E+06	2.05E+00	-2.54E+01	-1.17E-02
70	2.01E+04	1.36E+04	0.8	47.71453	2.81E-03	2.99E-01	0.32797	8.38E-04	9.21E-04	8.23E-05	8.75E-04	7.82E-05	4.67E+06	2.92E-01	1.56E+07	1.26E+00	-4.23E+01	-7.02E-03
71	2.51E+04	1.11E+04	0.8	84.82583	6.13E-03	3.05E-01	0.338185	1.87E-03	2.07E-03	2.06E-04	1.97E-03	1.96E-04	7.80E+06	2.33E-01	2.47E+07	9.44E-01	-5.92E+01	-5.01E-03
72	4.67E+03	2.01E+04	0.8	5.301614	2.11E-04	2.83E-01	0.301033	5.98E-05	6.37E-05	3.90E-06	6.05E-05	3.70E-06	8.41E+05	4.19E-01	3.40E+06	2.23E+00	-6.57E+00	-4.52E-02

Sheet1 Sheet2 Sheet3

"Detailed Model : Intracavity Saturation Absorption CO & CO2" (2009) J Hall, shared, unpubl

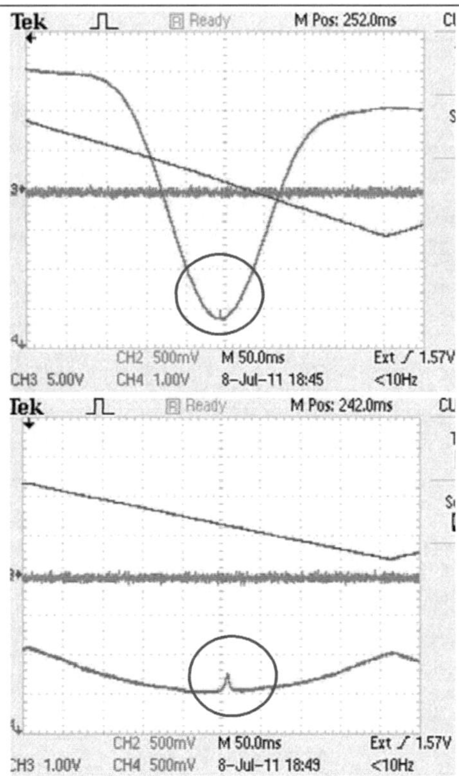

Optical Frequency Transfer Std

CO_2 Cavity-Enhanced Sat Abs

1571 nm overtone

Expt parameters: 5m vs flat, 10 cm

Calc: Cavity width ~20 kHz

Molecular resonance ~ 1.02 MHz

Contrast 9% on 840 μW

~10 mK → pressure shift → 1 Hz

Collaboration with:

Sarah Bickman

Mike Anderson

Mark Notcutt

July 2011

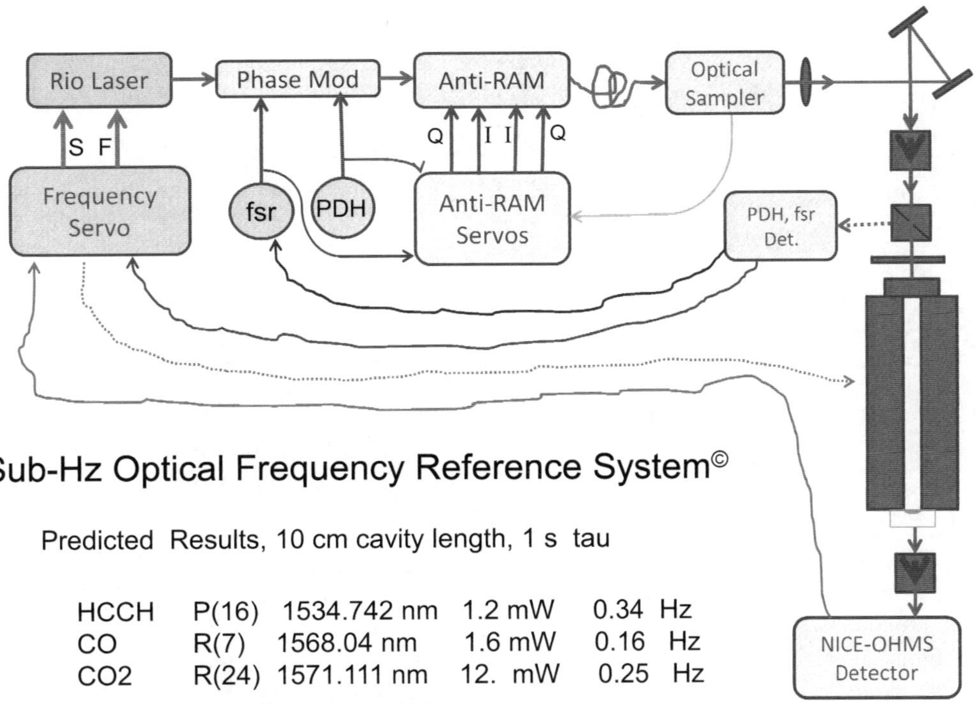

Sub-Hz Optical Frequency Reference System©

Predicted Results, 10 cm cavity length, 1 s tau

HCCH	P(16)	1534.742 nm	1.2 mW	0.34 Hz
CO	R(7)	1568.04 nm	1.6 mW	0.16 Hz
CO2	R(24)	1571.111 nm	12. mW	0.25 Hz

Sub-Hz Optical Frequency Reference System©

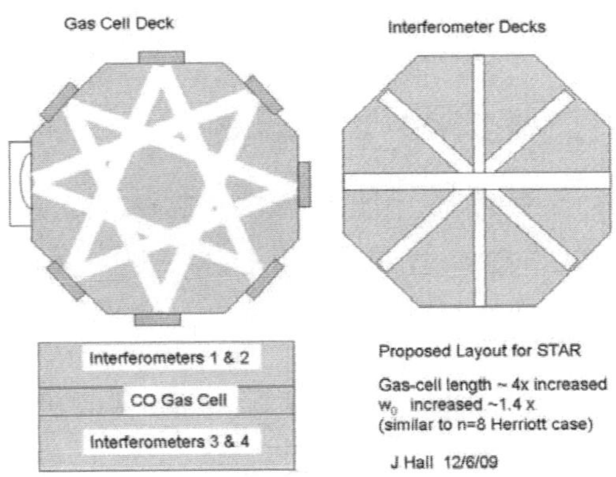

Jan's Proposed Tools

For the STAR Mission

Multiple Redundant Cavities

Duplicate Atomic Clocks

Gas-Cell Frequency Standard
CO or CO_2
1500 nm telecom optics

Ke-Xun Sun's Multipass Idea for the Gas Cell

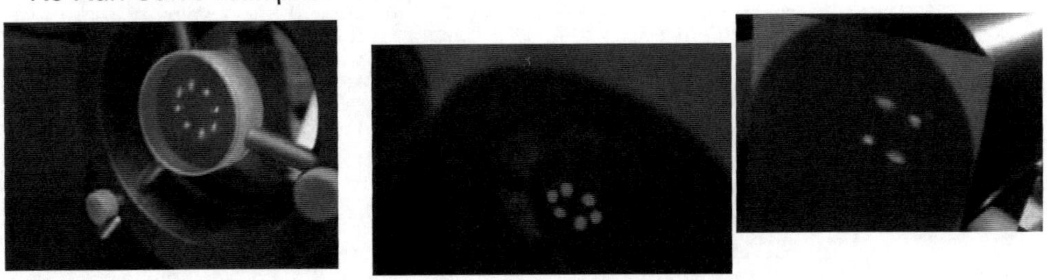

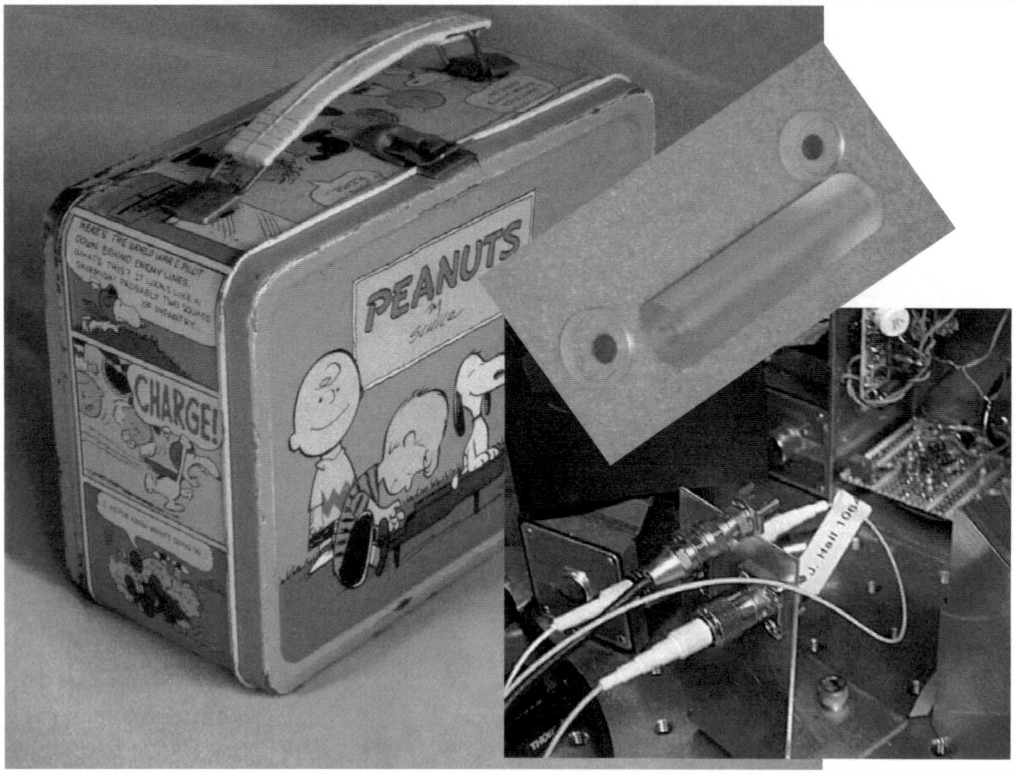

Accurate Removal of RAM from FM Beams?

☞ Locking *Accuracy* at the 1 E-6 Level !

- Finally, 32 years after PDH, 10 orders of linewidth reduction, the Optical Comb, and all that Jazz: we can approximate the line-splitting skill of our Cesium clock colleagues!

John L Hall
Wei Zhang & Jun Ye
JILA
University of Colorado
Boulder CO 80309-0440
jhall@jila.colorado.edu
http://jila.colorado.edu/hall
jan@HallStableLasers.com

Int'n'l Frequency Control Symposium April 2015 Denver CO

The RAM-Buster !

US PTO- Prov.2015/04/14/62147276

Testing: Locking at the CENTER of the resonance?

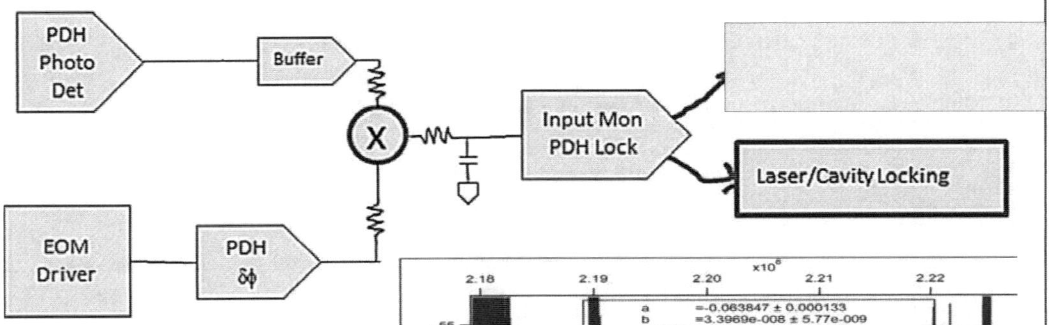

#1 "Tune off the resonance and check the baseline"

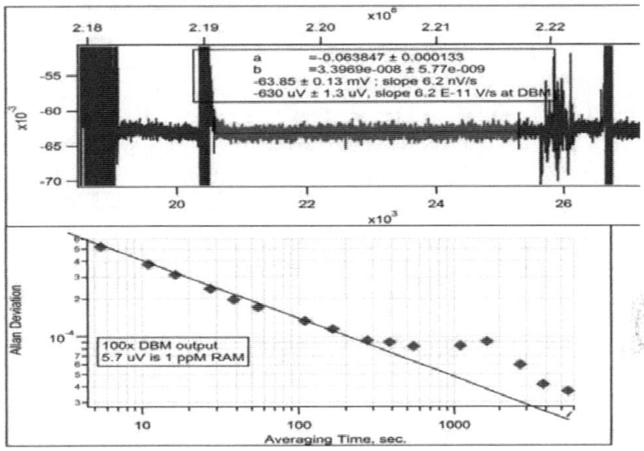

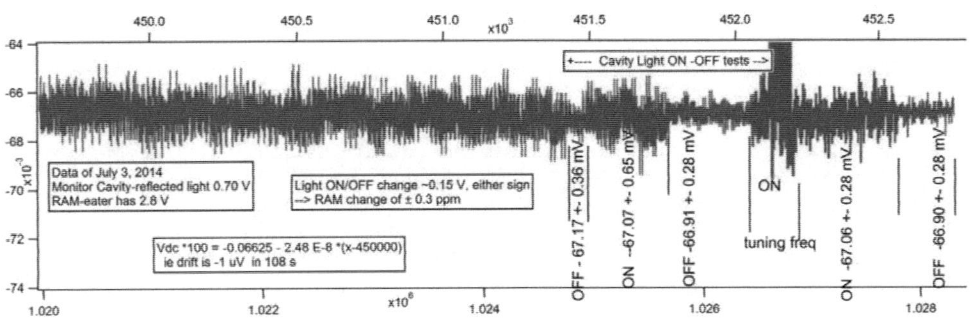

dc Offset is ~ 0.67 mV at Doubly-Balanced Mixer

HOWEVER the Offset is the same with Light ON or Light OFF ???

It is not RAM, instead it is weak non-optical pickup of the rf wave

Anti-RAM Gain seems to be ~ 1 E6 !

How is this RAM-Buster Gain even Possible?

the Big Idea: Compare two Approaches for Active Anti-RAM

1) Modulation at 1 MHz, Gain = 1E6 : → Needed BW is > 3 GHz

2) "Gas Pedal" Cancellation Servo : Gain at 1 MHz > 1E6 but BW needed is ~ 1 kHz !

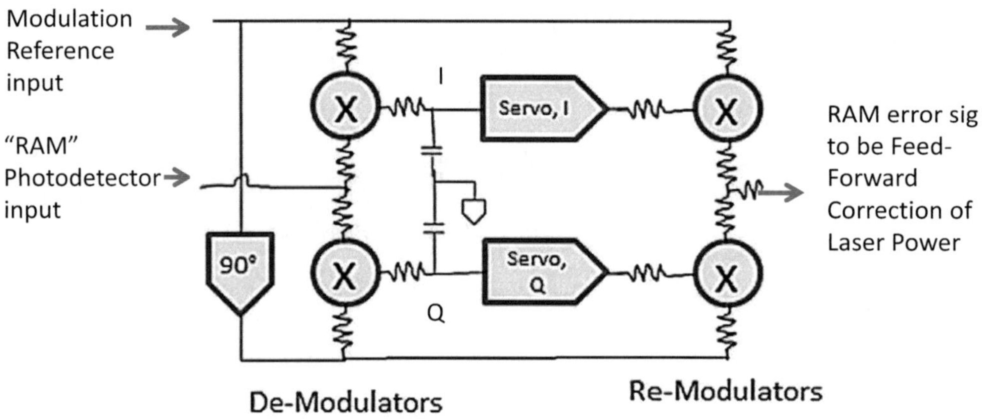

F du Burck, A Goncharev, O Lopez Metrologia 46, 599 (2009)

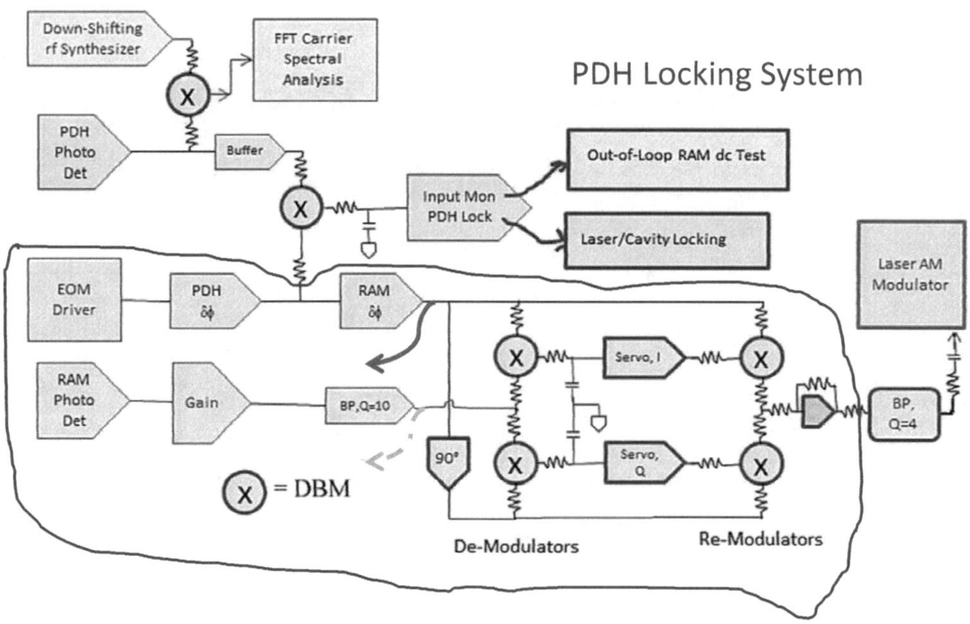

the RAM-Buster Accessory

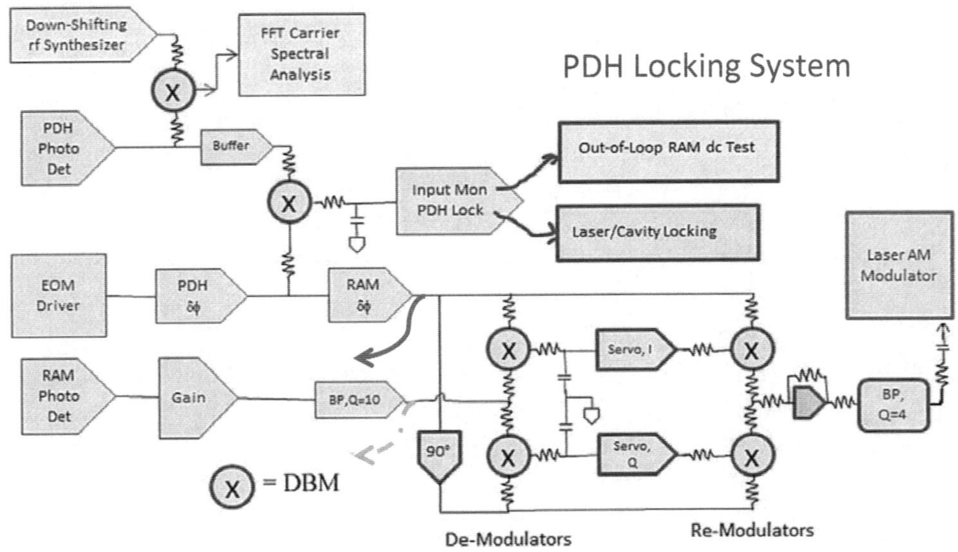

Testing the RAM-Buster - the 2nd Way

Also see Wei, Ye& Hall Opt Lett April 1, 2014 (fiber modulator)

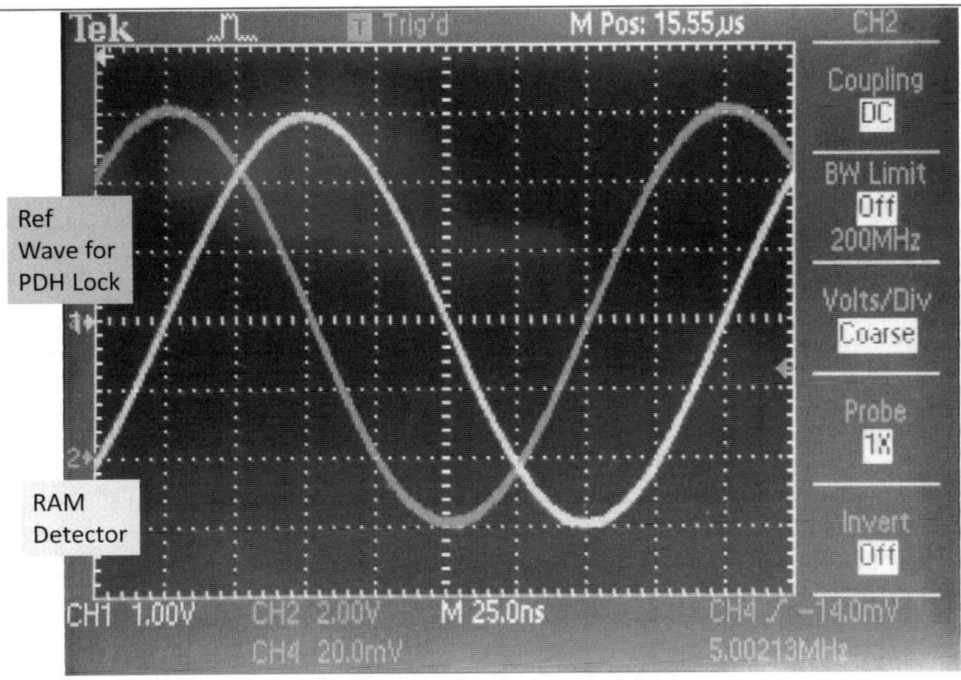

Starting Optical Alignment: ~10% RAM

EOM "prism" scans beam over fiber core - Pure Q Error

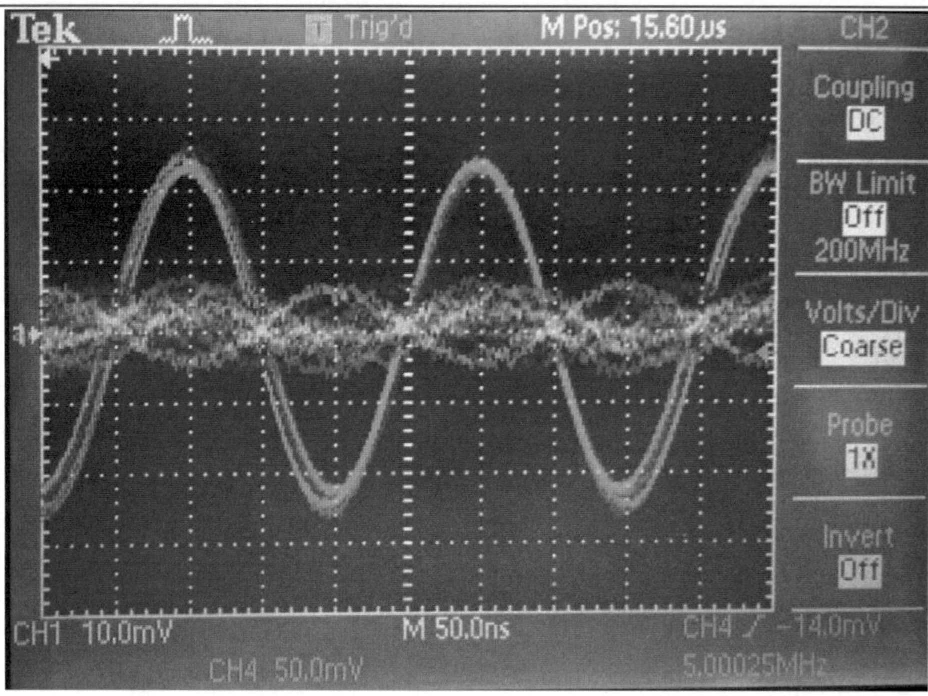

I- Gain ~0.2 Hz   Q - Gain ~10 Hz (for unity gain)

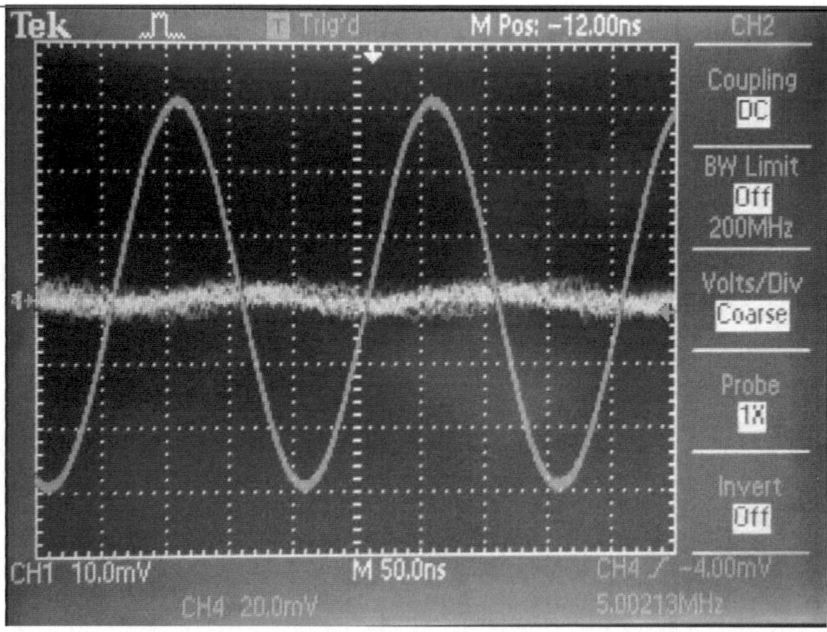

High "I" gain -- medium "Q" gain

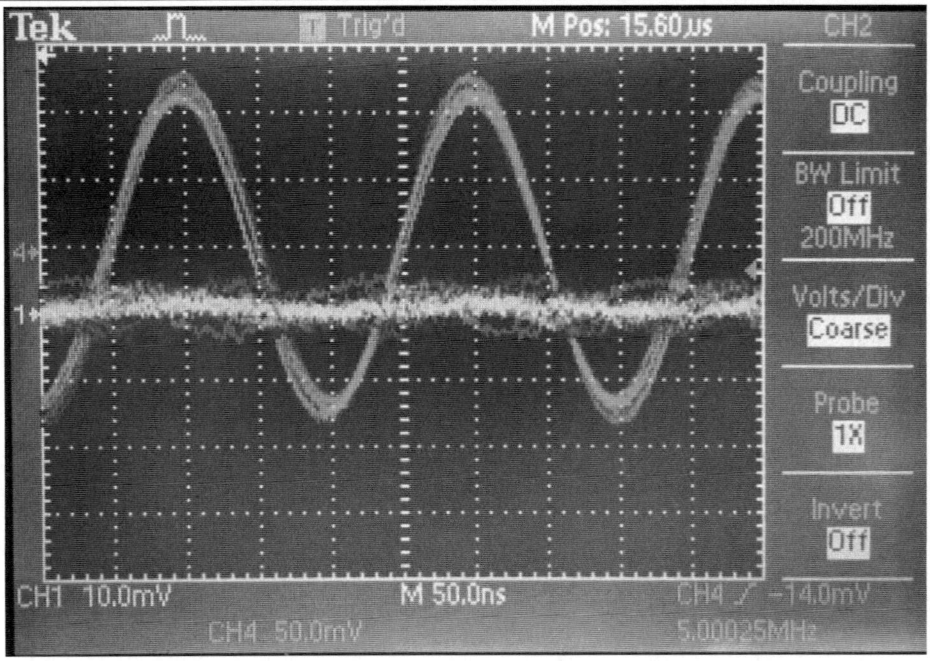

Q- and I- Gains ~ 40 Hz, for unity gain

US PTO- Prov.2015/04/14/62147276

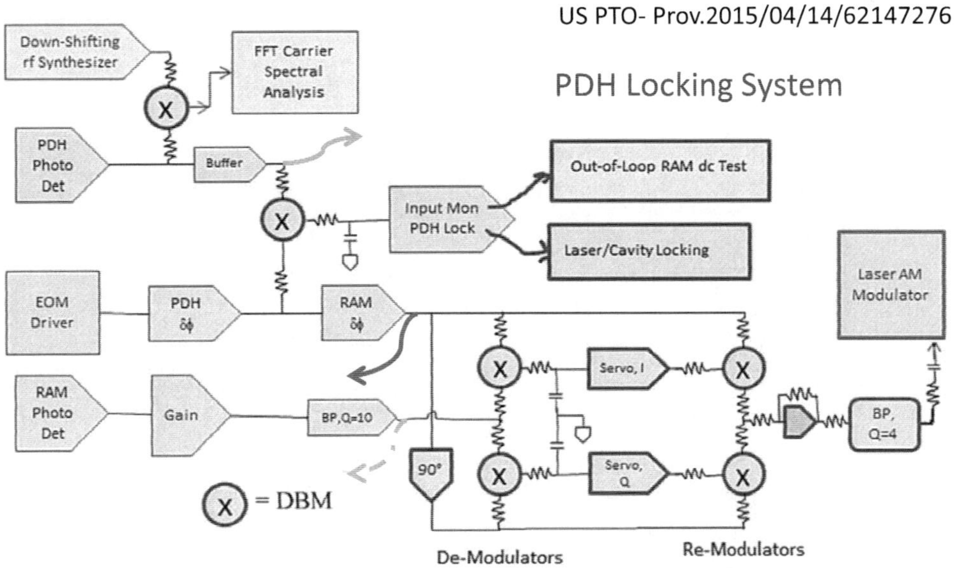

Testing the RAM-Buster

way #3 →FFT of the rf PDH-lock error signal ←

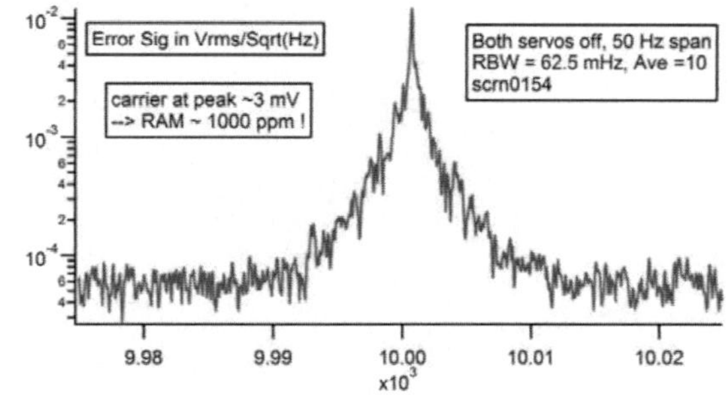

Characteristics of the
Residual Amplitude Modulation

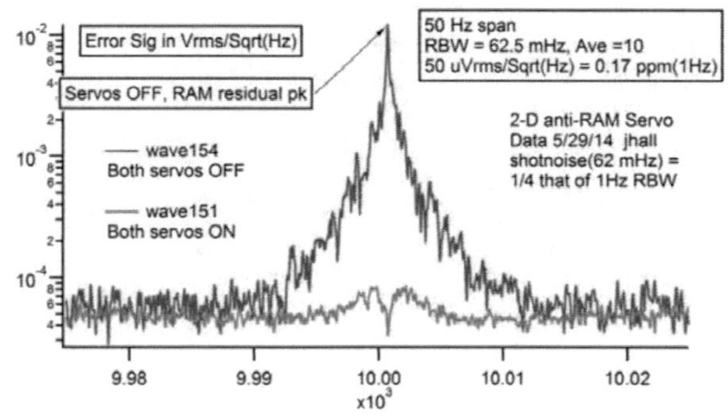

What can a PID servo do?

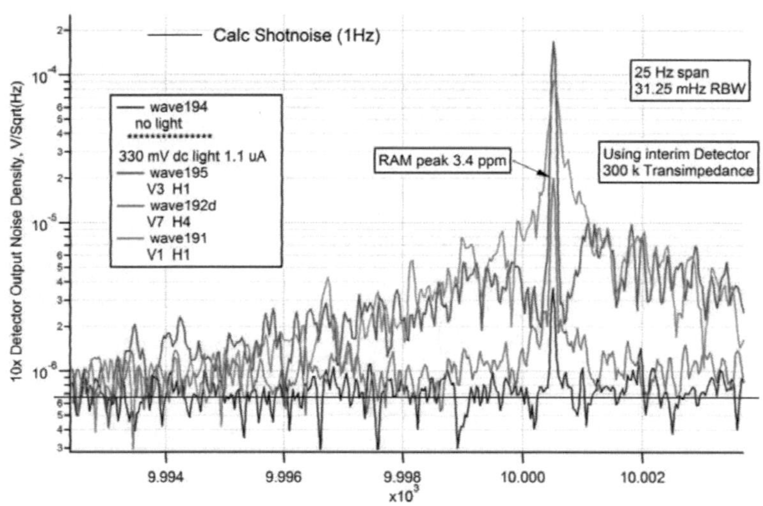

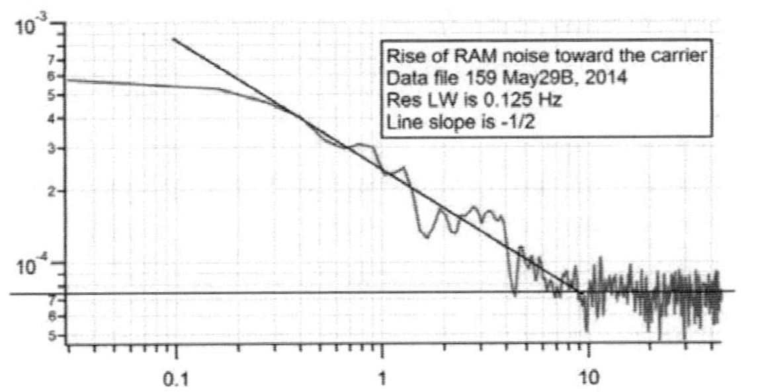

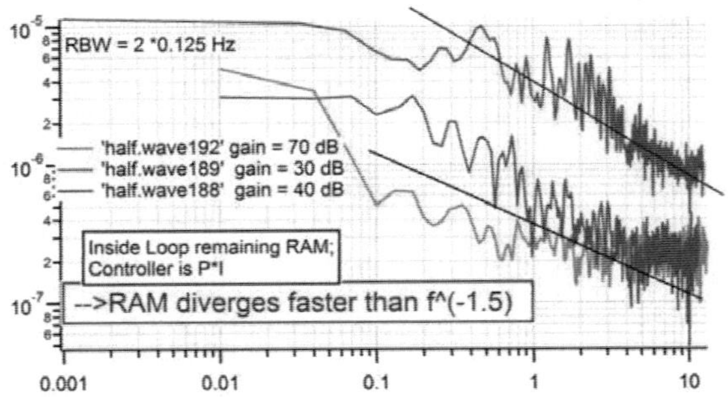

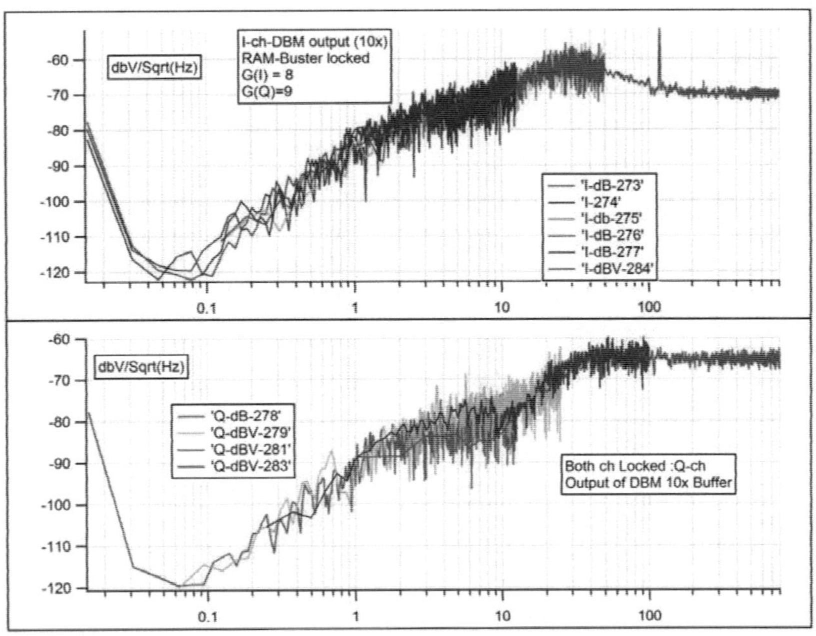

Residual Error Signals (10x DBM outputs) with RAM-Buster Locked

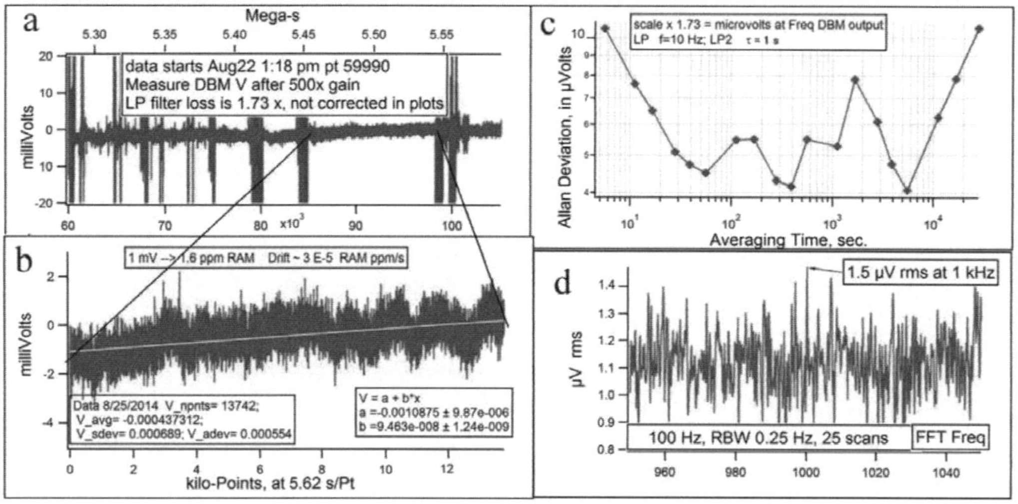

Fig.2 Two Approaches to Measuring RAM – at the ppm Level.

a) Out-of-Loop RAM via PDH signal; b). Selected 21¾ h data between noise bursts; c). Corresponding Allan Deviation; d) FFT of down-shifted cavity reflection signal. Original 1.18 MHz rf carrier is now shifted to 1 kHz, where the small residual 1.5 μV rms peak is less than shotnoise in the 0.25 Hz RBW spectrum, and is just visible in 25 coherently-added sweeps. So the effective noise BW is ~10 milliHz. - HOWEVER, this signal is 1.2 μV with the light blocked!

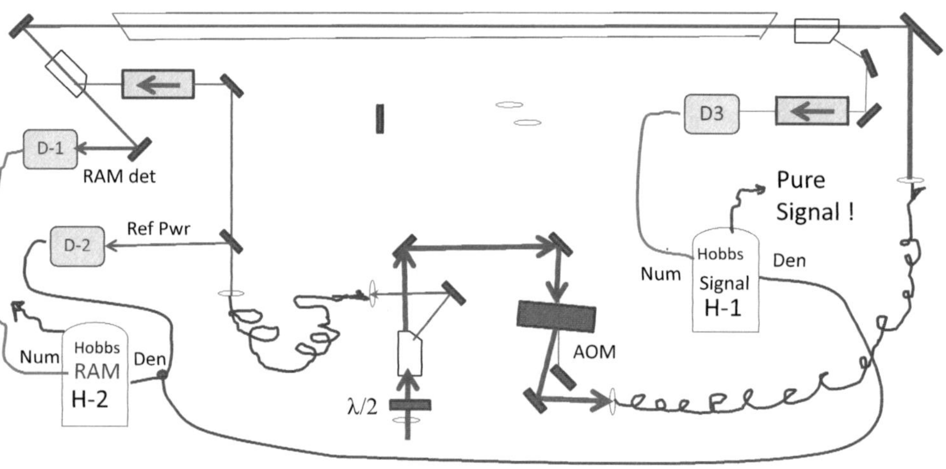

Frequency-Jump Saturated Absorption Spectroscopy

Crossed saturation and probe polarizations. Frequency to AOM jumps ±350 kHz. RAM and differential Doppler absorption cancelled by feedback to AOM power. Laser Amplitude noise is reduced to ~3 dB above signal shotnoise by Hobbs's idea.

Signals in Frequency-Jump Spectroscopy

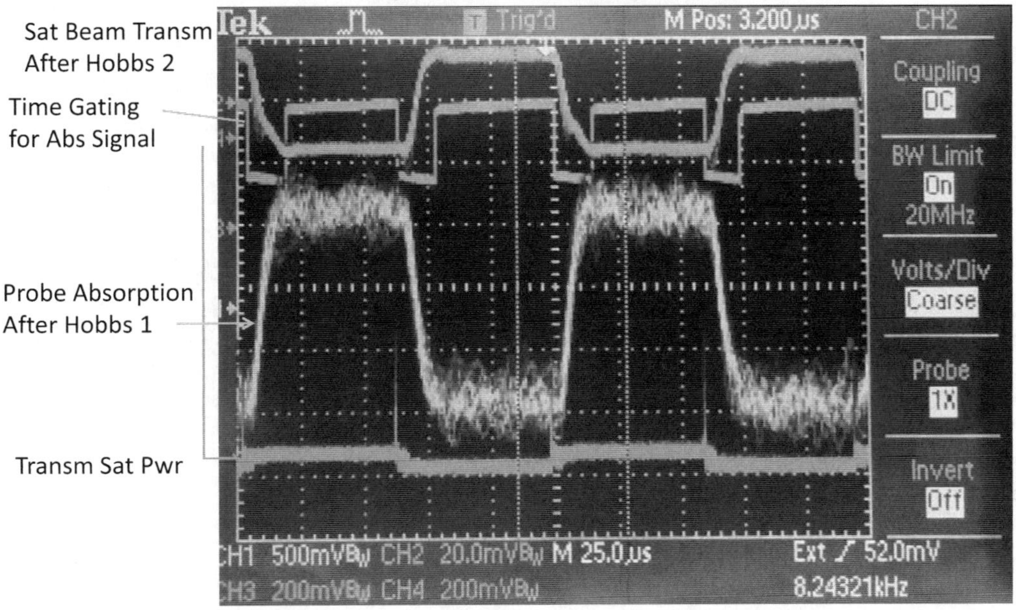

RAM Servo Locked - Freq on side of line

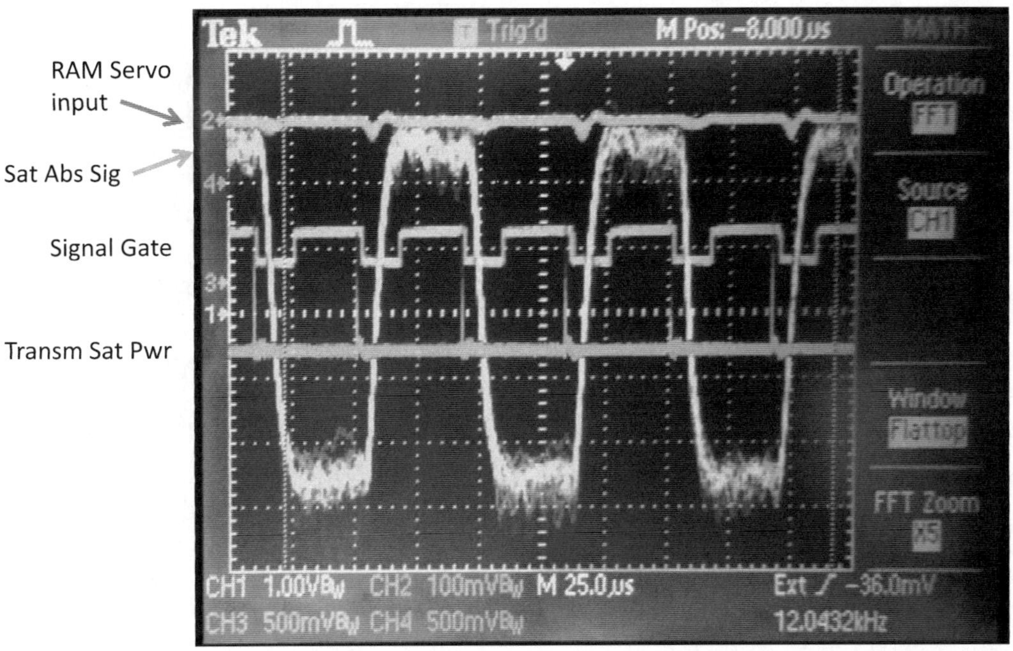

Freq Servo Locked – RAM Servo OFF

Form RAM sig
via Hobbs 2
from Sat beam,
meas. after cell

Sat Power after cell
jumps
between 2 freqs

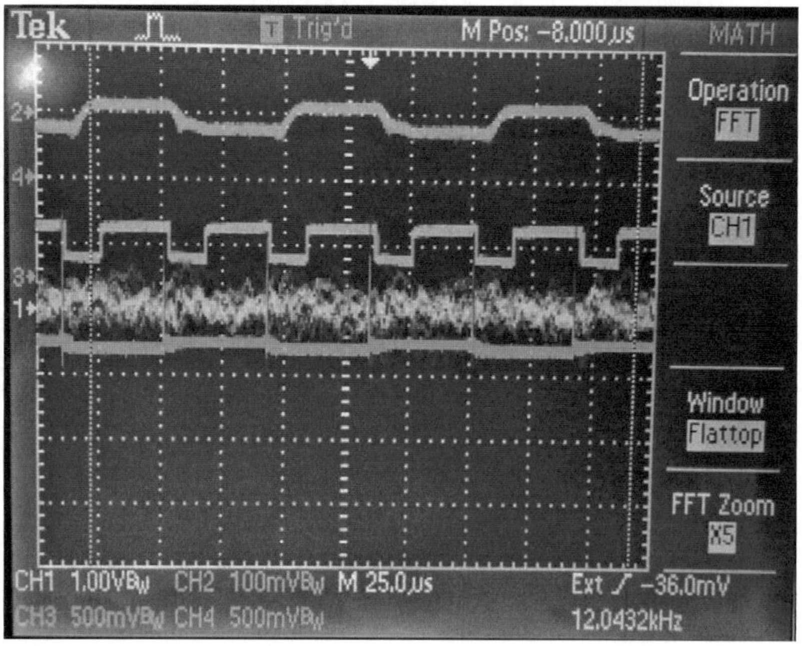

Both RAM and Freq Servos are ON

Freq noise equiv (1s) ~ 50 Hz (~1 E-13 at 1 s)

RAM input

Signal Gate

Sat Abs Signal
12 V pp => 0.6 MHz
$\delta\upsilon \approx 15$ kHz

Freq-jumping
Sat Beam,
after cell

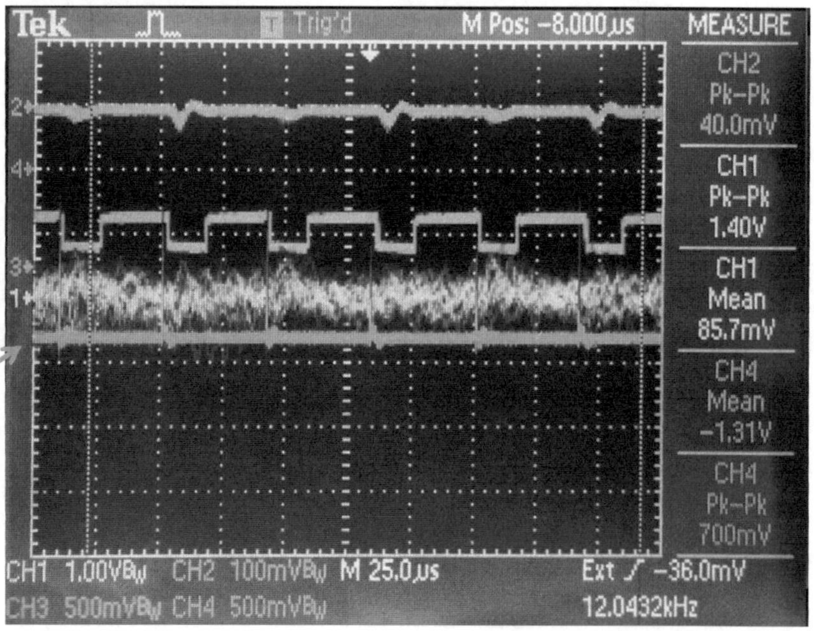

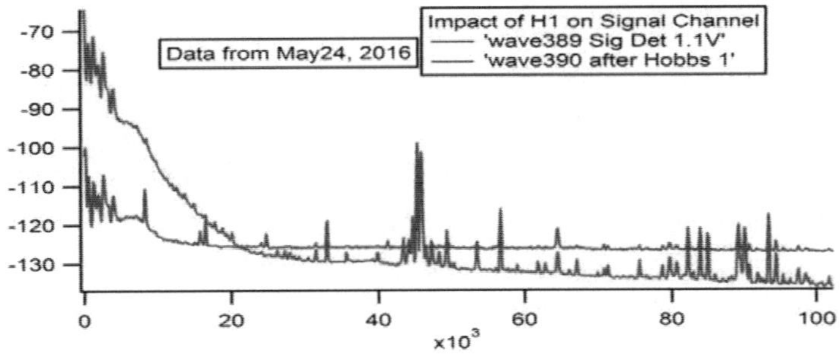

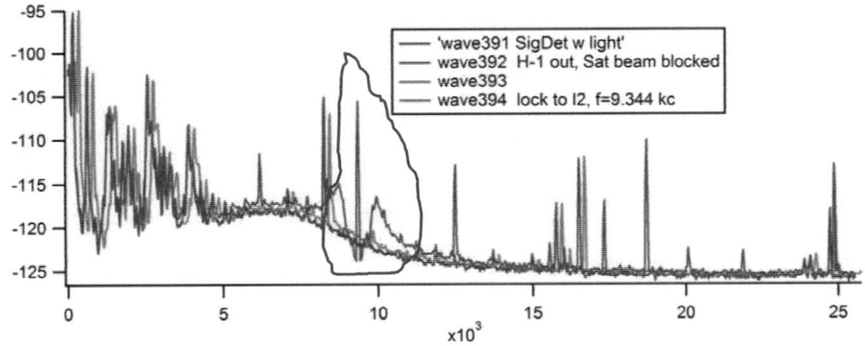

Inner Shell Temp
Drift -200 uK/60 ks

Freq Drift
+6.6 mHz/s

Iodine Resonance
w Jumper Lock
~750 kHz :
Lock instability ~1E-5 * Δυ

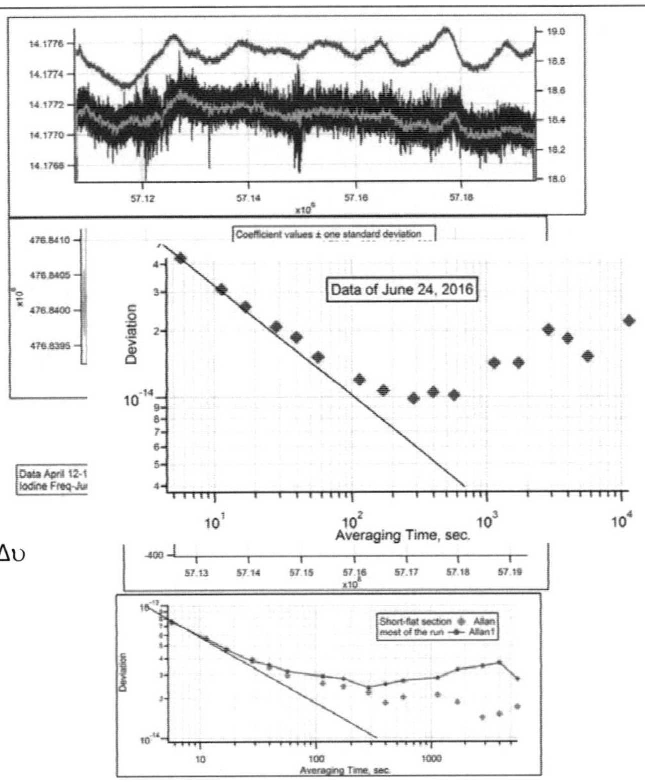

Narrow-line Lasers

87 Hz Drever, Hall, Kowalski, Hough, Ford, Munley, Ward Appl. Phys. B 31 97 (1983)

< 1 Hz Young, Cruz, Itano, Bergquist prl **82,** pp. 3799-3802 (1999)

~100 mHz Jiang, Ludlow, Lemke, Fox, Sherman, Ma, and Oates Nature Photon. **5** 158 (2011)

< 80 mHz Kessler, Hagemann, Grebing, Legero, Sterr, Riehle, Martin, Chen, Ye Nat. Phot (2012)

< 30 mHz Bishof, Zhang, Martin, Ye Phys Rev Lett 111 093604 (2013)

Thermal noise limit ~ 2 E-16 ULE spacer, SiO2 mirror blank, amorphous multilayer mirrors
Reduced thermal noise limit : expect ~10x with crystalline layer mirrors (Ye & Zhang, JILA)

Next:
Silicon crystal cavity with crystalline mirrors, at 4 degrees K !

collaboration of Ye group, PTB, and Garrett Cole

Provisional Conclusions

With present sub-optimum laser power, we lost ~10x in S/N
But
We now have $S\upsilon \cong 20$ Hz/Sqrt(Hz),
near to best from
last century's JILA work with Modulation Transfer Spectroscopy w J Ye & L-S Ma

Talking Science in Munich - 2005 Jan, Thomas Udem Ted Ron Drever

the Hall_Labs Team ~2000

Thanks for Listening

- http://jila.colorado.edu/hall/
- http://HallStableLasers.com
- http://nobelprize.org/nobel_prizes/physics/laureates/2005/hall-lecture.html

- Jun - http://jila.colorado.edu/YeLabs/
- Lindy – http://Sci-TeksDiscoveryProgramforKids.org
- NIST - http://tf.nist.gov/timefreq/
- 50th Year of Lasers - http://LaserFest.org

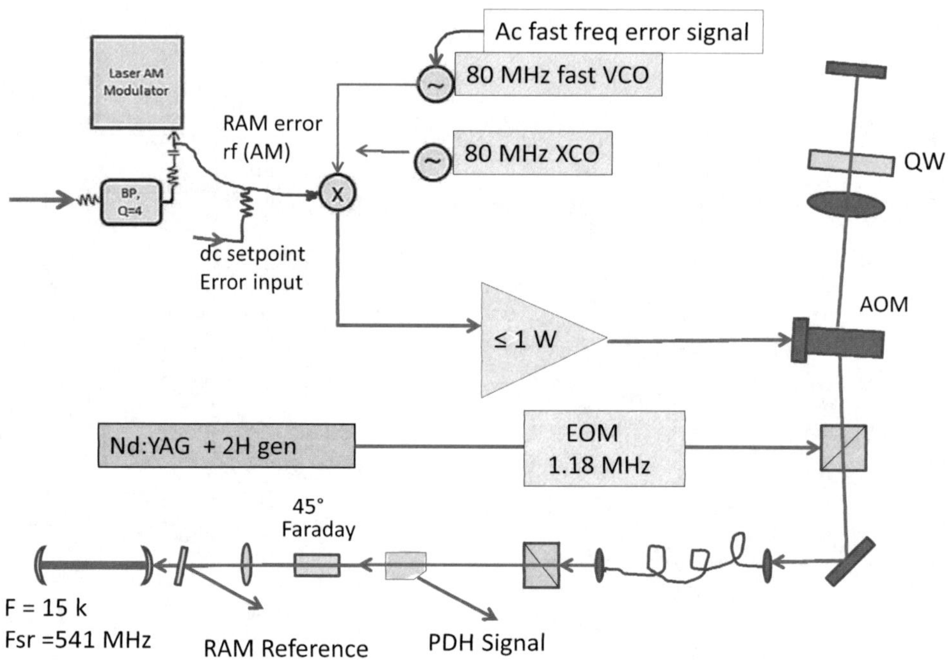

PDH Locking, with "RAM Buster" Accessory

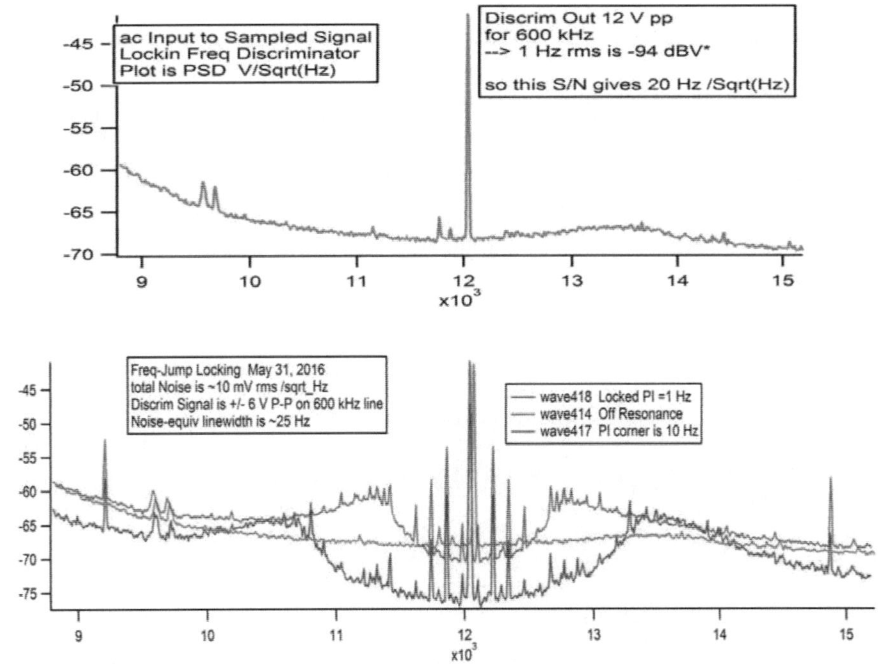

Anti-RAM Servo - digs below the (open-loop) noise level !

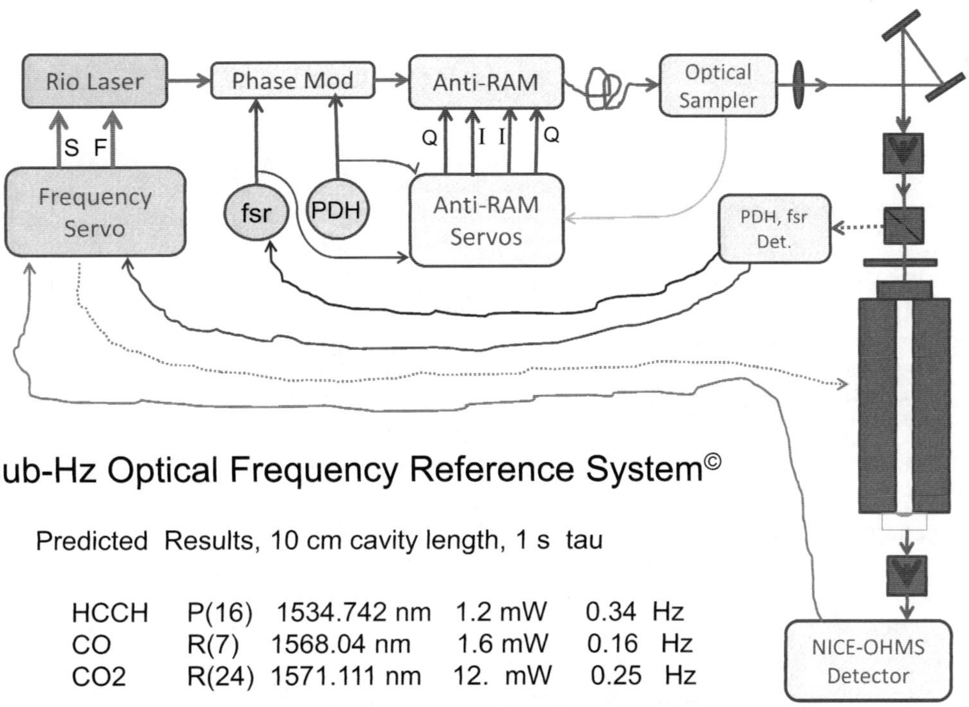

Sub-Hz Optical Frequency Reference System©

Predicted Results, 10 cm cavity length, 1 s tau

HCCH	P(16)	1534.742 nm	1.2 mW	0.34 Hz
CO	R(7)	1568.04 nm	1.6 mW	0.16 Hz
CO2	R(24)	1571.111 nm	12. mW	0.25 Hz

Sub-Hz Optical Frequency Reference System©

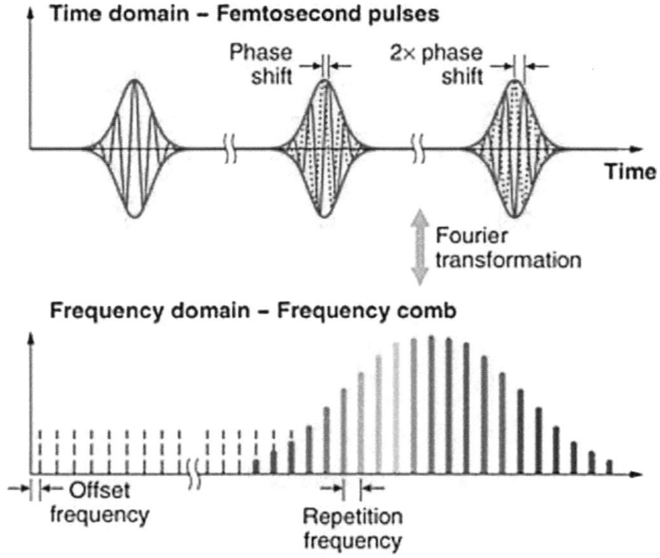

Figure is stolen from Jeff Hecht, with thanks

The offset frequency arises from:
Group velocity ≠ Phase velocity

The Comb Concept

J-B Fourier 1822; T W Hänsch, V P Chebotayev ~1979

Phase coherent distribution – at any frequency !

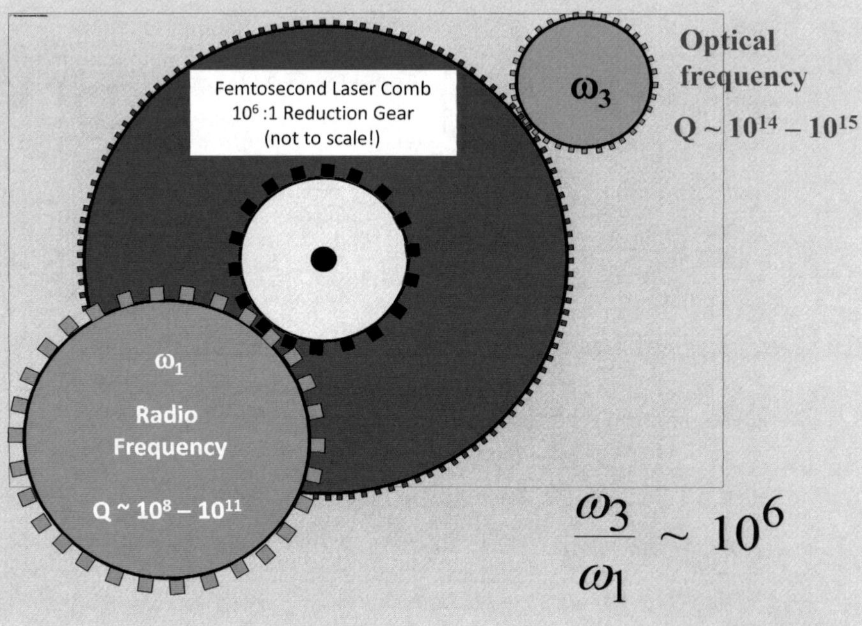

$$\frac{\omega_3}{\omega_1} \sim 10^6$$

Precise distribution of ultra-stable signals

SYRTE/PTB, NIST, …

Foreman, Holman, Hudson, Jones, and Ye,
Cover Review, Rev. Sci. Instrum. 78, 021101 (2007).

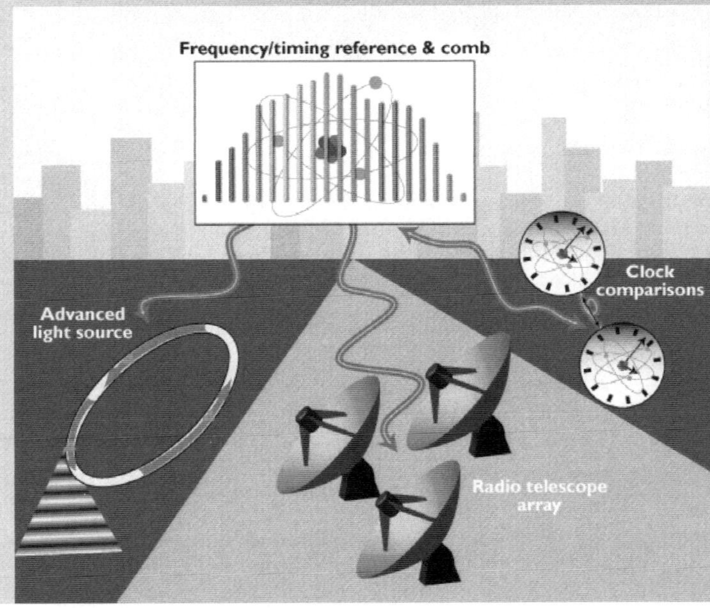

> 30 km fiber:

1×10^{-17} @ 1 s;
1 mHz optical linewidth;
0.1 fs jitter (20 MHz BW)

Squeeze-insensitive Optical Reference Cavity

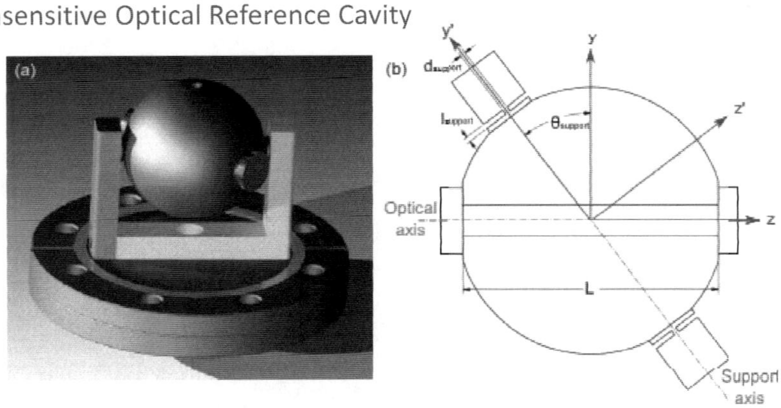

Fig. 1. (a) CAD rendering of a SC mounted at the squeeze insensitive angle with Viton o-ring contacts. Note that this is the experimental design. (b) Cross section of a SC mounted at the squeeze insensitive angle with cylindrical ULE contacts. This is the design used for the finite element analysis model. Important coordinate systems and dimensions are labeled. The sphere is 50.8 mm in diameter and has a 6 mm diameter bore drilled through it along the optical axis. The mirrors are optically contacted to the sphere on flats separated by L = 48.5 mm and are 12.7 mm in diameter and 4.2 mm thick. The two support contacts are attached to the sphere along the support axis which is oriented at $\theta_{support}$ = 37.31° with respect to the y axis and have dimensions $d_{support} = l_{support}$ = 1 mm.

Leibrandt, Thorpe, Notcutt, Drullinger, Rosenband, Bergquist Opt Exp. **19**, 3471 (2011)

A cavity-stabilized laser with acceleration sensitivity below $10^{-12}/g$

David R. Leibrandt,* James C. Bergquist, and Till Rosenband
National Institute of Standards and Technology, 325 Broadway St., Boulder, CO 80305, USA
(Dated: January 3, 2013)

We characterize the frequency-sensitivity of a cavity-stabilized laser to inertial forces and temperature fluctuations, and perform real-time feed-forward to correct for these sources of noise. We measure the sensitivity of the cavity to linear accelerations, rotational accelerations, and rotational velocities by rotating it about three axes with accelerometers and gyroscopes positioned around the cavity. The worst-direction linear acceleration sensitivity of the cavity is $2(1) \times 10^{-11}/g$ measured over 0–50 Hz, which is reduced by a factor of 50 to below $10^{-12}/g$ for low-frequency accelerations by real-time feed-forward corrections of all of the aforementioned inertial forces. A similar idea is demonstrated in which laser frequency drift due to temperature fluctuations is reduced by a factor of 70 via real-time feed-forward from a temperature sensor located on the outer wall of the cavity vacuum chamber.

PACS numbers: 42.62.Eh, 42.60.Da, 46.40.-f, 07.07.Tw

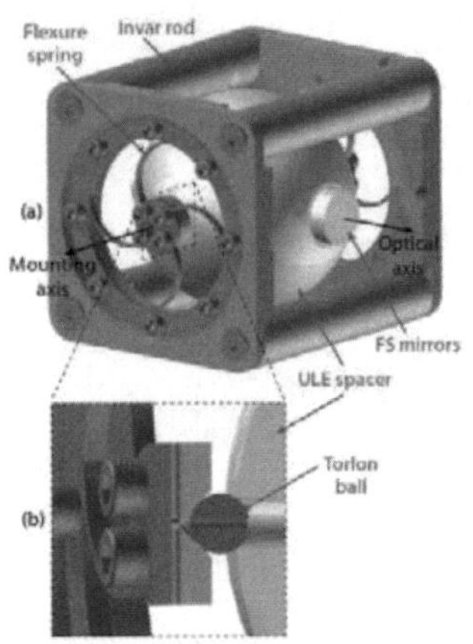

FIG. 1: (a) Computer-aided design (CAD) drawing of the mounted Fabry-Pérot cavity. The spherical cavity spacer is 50 mm in diameter. (b) Cross-sectional view showing the details of the contact between the cavity and the mount. A Torlon ball is compressed between the flexure spring and the vacuum pump-out hole in the cavity. FS: fused silica.

Accelerometers, Gyros Rotation Sensors, Thermal Sensors

Use Feed-Forward Correction:
- 50x improvement re accelerations
- 70 x improvement re temperature

Enabling Technology: phase-locked lasers in a moving automobile!

Laser Frequency and Intensity Stabilization for Advanced LIGO

Evan Hall[1, *]
(LIGO Scientific Collaboration)
[1]*Department of Physics, California Institute of Technology*

Advanced LIGO searches for gravitational wave events using two 4-km Fabry–Pérot Michelson interferometers separated by a 3000 km baseline. Each interferometer is illuminated with up to 125 W of 1064 nm light from a frequency- and intensity-stabilized Nd:YAG laser. This laser is frequency-locked to the interferometer's common-mode arm length, which acts as a 4-km-long reference cavity with a 1 Hz linewidth. This cavity stores hundreds of kilowatts of quiet light, enabling a differential strain measurement that is better than $10^{-23}/\mathrm{Hz}^{1/2}$ at 100 Hz. The interferometers' sensitivity to differential strain is designed to be limited by shot noise, radiation pressure noise, and mirror thermal noise across the astrophysical detection band (10 Hz to 7 kHz).

I. INTRODUCTION

General relativity predicts that any mass distribution with a time-varying quadrupole moment should generate ripples in the curvature of spacetime. These ripples, referred to as gravitational waves (GWs), propagate outward from the mass distribution at the speed of light and carry away energy from the system. GWs are expected to be produced by a variety of astrophysical systems, such as coalescing binary neutron stars or black holes, rotating neutron stars, and supernovae [1]. A GW induces a tidal force in any matter that it passes through: for two free masses separated by a distance L, the relative distance change ΔL induced by the GW is proportional to L. Therefore, a GW is characterized by the strain $h = (\Delta L)/L$ it produces. Additionally, GWs are tensor waves, meaning that they produce a positive strain $+h$ in one spatial direction while simultaneously producing a negative strain $-h$ in an orthogonal direction. Thus, a suitably oriented GW can be detected with a Michelson interferometer.

The Laser Interferometer Gravitational-Wave Observatory (LIGO) consists of two Michelson interferometers—one in Hanford, WA, and another in Livingston, LA—each with arm length $L = 4$ km. Installation and commissioning of the advanced versions of these interferometers started in 2010, and the first astrophysical observing run was conducted from September 2015 to January 2016. During this run, the instruments detected two GW events, each consistent with the coalescence of a binary black hole system [2, 3].

II. OPTICAL TOPOLOGY

The optical topology of the Advanced LIGO interferometers enables a differential strain measurement with an amplitude spectral density (ASD) that is a few parts in $10^{-24}/\mathrm{Hz}^{1/2}$ at 100 Hz [4], limited in large part by the shot noise and radiation pressure noise [5] of the laser light in each interferometer. The optical topology is shown on the right-hand side of fig. 1.

The beamsplitter and end test masses by themselves would form a simple Michelson interferometer with arm length $L = 4$ km. However, if this simple Michelson were illuminated with $P_0 = 125$ W of light with wavelength $\lambda_0 = 1\,\mu$m, the shot-noise-limited strain ASD would be $(hc\lambda_0/2P_0)^{1/2}/2\pi L = 1 \times 10^{-21}/\mathrm{Hz}^{1/2}$, three orders of magnitude worse than the target sensitivity [6].

To improve the Michelson sensitivity, a test mass with transmissivity $T_\mathrm{i} = 1.4\,\%$ is placed in each arm, transforming the arm into a Fabry–Pérot cavity with a finesse $\mathcal{F} = 2\pi/T_\mathrm{i}$ and cavity pole $f_\mathrm{a} = c/4L\mathcal{F}$. This enhances the shot-noise-limited strain sensitivity by $(2\mathcal{F}/\pi)/\sqrt{1+(f/f_\mathrm{a})^2}$.

The sensitivity can be further enhanced by placing a power-recycling mirror between the laser source and the beamsplitter; this increases the power circulating in the interferometer. The greatest enhancement is achieved by choosing the transmissivity to be $T_\mathrm{p} = 4\eta_\mathrm{a}/T_\mathrm{i}$, where η_a is the round-trip power loss of each arm. This has the additional benefit of narrowing the arm linewidth for common-mode signals only (e.g, laser frequency or intensity noise), so that these signals are filtered as they circulate in the interferometer.

Finally, placing a signal-recycling mirror between the beamsplitter and the GW readout changes the arm linewidth for differential signals only (e.g., from gravitational waves). The mirror may be controlled so as to either broaden or narrow this differential linewidth, allowing the shot noise and the radiation pressure noise to be optimized based on expected astrophysical waveforms [6].

For Advanced LIGO, the arm finesse is chosen to be $\mathcal{F} = 450$ (i.e., $T_\mathrm{i} = 1.4\,\%$), based on expected optical losses and displacement noise couplings from other degrees of freedom [4]. With $\eta_\mathrm{a} = 100$ ppm, this sets $T_\mathrm{p} = 3.0\,\%$, producing a common-mode cavity with finesse 3×10^4 and cavity pole $f_+ = 0.6$ Hz. The signal recycling mirror transmissivity is chosen to be $T_\mathrm{s} = 20\,\%$, and controlled so as to broaden the differential cavity pole to $f_- = 750$ Hz. For 125 W of input power, this yields a shot noise limit of $2.9 \times 10^{-24}/\mathrm{Hz}^{1/2}$ and a radiation pressure noise limit of $(6 \times 10^{-25}/\mathrm{Hz}^{1/2}) \times (100\,\mathrm{Hz}/f)^2$ for $f < f_-$ (fig. 2).

In addition to the main interferometer, several other optical cavities are employed (fig. 1). On the input side of the interferometer, two ring cavities—the pre-modecleaner and the input modecleaner—filter the laser beam's frequency noise, intensity noise, pointing noise, and shape. A two-mirror fused silica reference cavity is also used to frequency stabilize the laser. At the interferometer output, the output modecleaner filters higher-order spatial modes and rf control sidebands before the laser light is sent to the GW readout photodiodes.

* ehall@caltech.edu

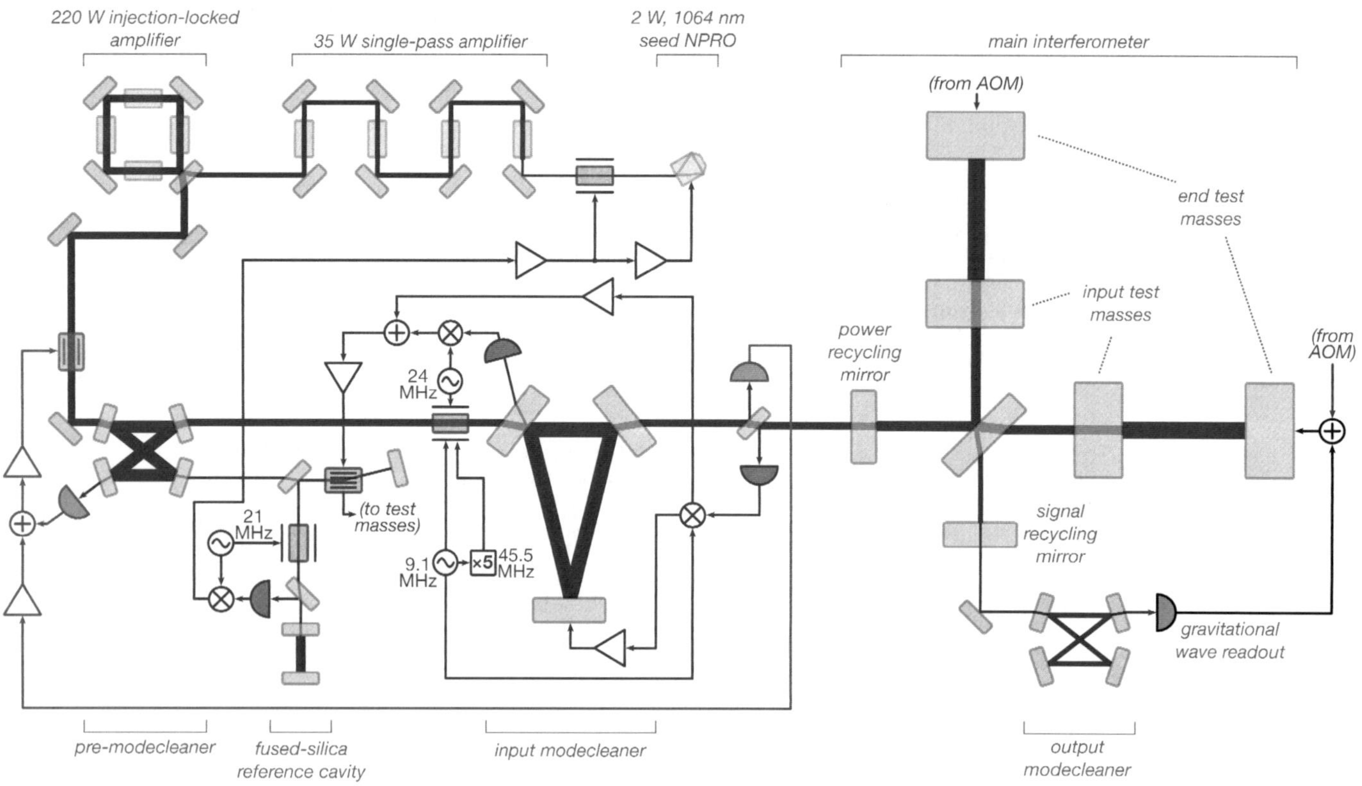

FIG. 1: Diagram of Advanced LIGO, showing the main interferometer, auxiliary optical cavities, and the high-power laser generation. Blue traces show frequency stabilization; green traces show intensity stabilization. Black traces shows the differential arm length control and strain readout. Components for sensing and control of the beamsplitter, recycling mirrors, pre-modecleaner, injection-locked amplifier, and output modecleaner have been omitted. *Key:* photodiode; mixer; electro-optic modulator; acousto-optic modulator; rf oscillator.

III. TEST MASSES, SUSPENSIONS, AND ISOLATION

Each Advanced LIGO test mass is a 40 kg cylinder of polished, low-absorption fused silica. A heavy test mass is desirable to minimize the radiation pressure noise in the interferometer. Silica (SiO_2) and titania-doped tantala (Ta_2O_5) are deposited onto the surface of the test mass via ion-beam sputtering to transform the test mass into a Bragg mirror.

The test mass transmissivity is 4 ppm for the end masses and 1.4 % for the input masses. For both types of test mass, the typical absorption is a few hundred parts per billion. The typical round-trip loss of the arm cavities is approximately 100 ppm in situ [7], suggesting a scatter of 50 ppm per test mass.

In the GW band, the dominant displacement noise arising from the test mass itself is the Brownian thermal noise of the coating [8]; this arises mostly from the modest tantala Q factor—about 4×10^3 [9]. The expected coating noise contribution to the differential strain ASD is about $(2.5 \times 10^{-24}\,/\mathrm{Hz}^{1/2}) \times (100\,\mathrm{Hz}/f)^{1/2}$ [4].

Each test mass is mounted to the bottom of a quadruple pendulum, which provides an isolation transfer function of $(10^{-15}\,\mathrm{m/m}) \times (100\,\mathrm{Hz}/f)^8$ in the GW band. To give good thermal noise performance, the penultimate mass is fabricated from fused silica, as are the fibers used to suspend the test mass from the penultimate mass [10]. Brownian noise is expected to dominate the suspension thermal noise in the GW band, with a differential strain ASD of approximately $(5 \times 10^{-25}/\mathrm{Hz}^{1/2}) \times (50\,\mathrm{Hz}/f)^{5/2}$ [4, 10], corresponding to $Q \sim 10^9$ for the pendulum longitudinal mode, which has a resonant frequency $f_0 = 0.43\,\mathrm{Hz}$.

IV. LASER

A. Generation of 220 W beam

The laser is seeded by a commercial Nd:YAG NPRO that produces 2 W of 1064 nm light. Light from this laser enters a single-pass amplifier consisting of four Nd:YVO_4 crystals, yielding 35 W of light. This light is then used to seed an injection-locked ring cavity, which contains four Nd:YAG crystals and yields 220 W of light [11, 12] (fig. 1). All crystals are pumped with 808 nm light; each ring cavity crystal receives 315 W of pump light delivered via 7 fiber-coupled diode lasers. The length of the ring cavity is locked to the seed laser frequency using the Pound–Drever–Hall (PDH) technique [13]. Higher-order mode content from the ring cavity is filtered away by the pre-modecleaner, which is also PDH-locked to the laser frequency. About 125 W of TEM_{00} light is expected to be available to illuminate the interferometer.

B. Frequency stabilization

The desired strain sensitivity of a few parts in $10^{-24}/\mathrm{Hz}^{1/2}$ sets a challenging requirement on the frequency noise of the light used to illuminate the interferometer: the common-mode frequency rejection afforded by the interferometer's Michelson topology is finite due to length, reflectivity, and loss imbalances between the two arms. To ensure that the frequency noise coupling into the GW readout is negligible, the frequency noise at the input to the interferometer must be stabilized to $1\ \mu\mathrm{Hz/Hz}^{1/2}$ at 100 Hz [14], seven orders of magnitude below the phase noise of a typical freerunning NPRO—about $(100\ \mathrm{Hz/Hz}^{1/2})\times(100\ \mathrm{Hz}/f)$. In order to achieve this frequency noise requirement, Advanced LIGO employs a multilayered frequency suppression system which exploits the frequency stability of three different optical cavities (fig. 1).

The laser is first stabilized to a 20.3-cm-long tabletop fused silica reference cavity with a 200 kHz servo loop. The PDH error signal is generated by applying 21 MHz phase sidebands and sensing the resulting beat note in reflection of the cavity. This error signal is fed back to the NPRO length (using both strain and thermal actuation), and to a broadband electro-optic modulator placed after the NPRO. Under optimal conditions, the laser's freerunning frequency noise is suppressed down to the Brownian noise level of the reference cavity coatings, about $(6\ \mathrm{mHz/Hz}^{1/2})\times(100\ \mathrm{Hz}/f)^{1/2}$ [15].

Next, the laser is stabilized to the suspended input modecleaner with a 50 kHz loop. The error signal is again generated using PDH reflection locking, here using 24 MHz sidebands. Since the modecleaner is a better length reference than the fused silica reference cavity in the GW band, the modecleaner error signal is added to the error point of the tabletop cavity in order to stabilize the laser frequency to the modecleaner. This is accomplished by actuating on a double-pass acousto-optic modulator (AOM) placed at the input to the fused silica cavity. The shot noise of the light on the photodiode limits the frequency noise performance of this loop to a few parts in $10^{-5}\ \mathrm{Hz/Hz}^{1/2}$.

Finally, the laser frequency is stabilized to the interferometer's common-mode arm length. A PDH error signal is generated in reflection of the interferometer using 9.1 MHz sidebands which resonate between the power recycling mirror and the input test masses. This common-mode error signal is fed back to the modecleaner length. Additionally, the error signal is summed directly into the electronic error point of the modecleaner loop, allowing the laser frequency to be stabilized to the interferometer common-mode length with a bandwidth of 15 kHz. The noise performance of this loop is limited by the shot noise on the PDH photodiode; with a power of 25 W into the interferometer, this amounts to a frequency noise of approximately $1\ \mu\mathrm{Hz/Hz}^{1/2}$ from 10 to 100 Hz, rising like f above 100 Hz. This input frequency noise is passively filtered above the common-mode cavity pole $f_+ \simeq 0.6$ Hz. This attenuates the frequency noise at 100 Hz to less than $10^{-8}\ \mathrm{Hz/Hz}^{1/2}$ for the light circulating inside the interferometer.

C. Intensity stabilization

The relative intensity noise (RIN) of the light exiting the injection-locked high power oscillator is typically $10^{-5}/\mathrm{Hz}^{1/2}\times(100\ \mathrm{Hz}/f)$ or better below 1 kHz. On the other hand, an input RIN of less than $1\times10^{-7}/\mathrm{Hz}^{1/2}$ at 100 Hz and $2\times10^{-9}/\mathrm{Hz}^{1/2}$ at 10 Hz is needed in order to make laser intensity fluctuations contribute negligibly to the GW signal [14]. Two dc-coupled servo loops are used to achieve the required suppression.

For the first loop, a small sample of light is picked off from the pre-modecleaner cavity; audio-band intensity fluctuations in this beam are sensed with a pair of photodiodes, producing an electronic error signal. This error signal is fed back to a single-pass AOM placed directly in the path of the main high-power beam. The loop has a bandwidth of approximately 50 kHz and stabilizes the RIN of the beam to a few parts in $10^{-8}/\mathrm{Hz}^{1/2}$ between 30 Hz and 1 kHz [11].

To provide further intensity noise suppression, a second loop is employed using a sample of the light transmitted through the input modecleaner. This loop has a bandwidth of approximately 10 kHz and is designed to produce a RIN of $2\times10^{-9}/\mathrm{Hz}^{1/2}$ at 10 Hz. Similar to the frequency noise, the intensity noise is passively filtered by the common-mode cavity above 0.6 Hz.

V. INTERFEROMETER SENSING AND CONTROL

Sensing of the interferometer's length and angle degrees of freedom is accomplished via a combination of rf (PDH-type) readout and dc signals. To facilitate rf readout, 9.1 MHz and 45.5 MHz phase sidebands are applied with an electro-optic modulator (EOM) placed before the interferometer input. The macroscopic lengths between the interferometer optics have been chosen so that the 9.1 MHz sidebands resonate between the power-recycling mirror and the input test masses, and the 45.5 MHz sidebands resonate between the signal-recycling mirror and the input test masses.

A. Lengths and angles

The interferometer's common-mode arm length is left uncontrolled in the GW band, since it serves as a length reference for the laser. Below a few hertz, common-mode length control is applied to the end test mass suspensions in order to offload low-frequency control signal accumulated on the reference cavity AOM. This low-frequency control amounts to a few hundred microns of motion per day, and arises from earth tides, static radiation pressure on the test masses, and thermally induced drifts in the tabletop reference cavity length.

Differential arm length motion is sensed with a variant of homodyne readout [16]: a small differential length offset ($\simeq 13$ pm at 25 W of input power) is applied to one of the test masses, which causes carrier light to leak out the antisymmetric port, pass through the output modecleaner, and impinge on the GW photodetectors. Differential test mass motion produces audio-frequency sidebands which beat against the dc offset light, creating intensity fluctuations on the GW photodetectors. This signal is used both as an estimate of the GW strain $h(t)$, and as an error signal for controlling the differential arm length. It is fed back to one of the end test masses, forming a control loop with a bandwidth of approximately 45 Hz.

The positions of the power- and signal-recycling mirrors and of the beamsplitter are sensed via PDH using a photodiode that monitors the light circulating in the power recycling cavity. These loop bandwidths range from 10 to 60 Hz.

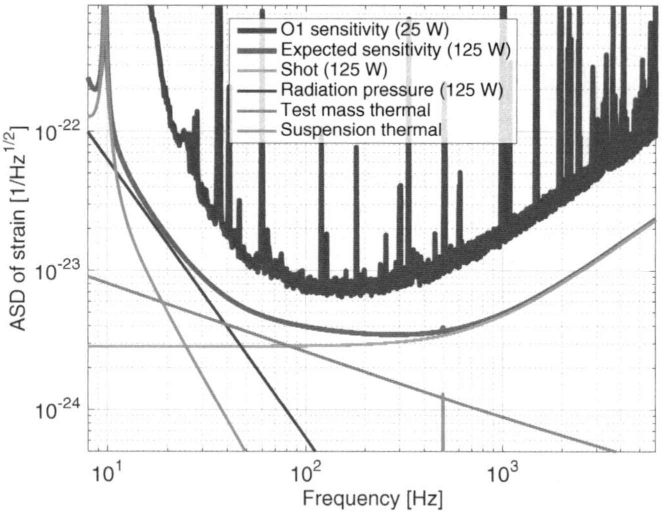

FIG. 2: Advanced LIGO differential strain sensitivity curves, showing the actual performance of the Hanford detector during the first observing run (the Livingston performance is similar), the expected performance of the detectors at full design sensitivity, and contributions to the full design sensitivity from shot noise, radiation pressure noise, and thermal noises.

The interferometer has 20 angular degrees of freedom which are sensed interferometrically [17]. The angular motion of the test masses presents a particularly challenging control problem. The light stored in the interferometer arms generates optical torques which couple the test masses, producing modes which either soften or harden the torsional modes of the test mass suspensions in a power-dependent way [18].

B. Mode shape

The interferometer's mirrors are intentionally curved, thereby keeping the spatial mode of the resonating beam well-defined. A thermal compensation system is employed in order to adjust this mode [19]. The curvature of each test mass can be fine-tuned by resistively heating a coil of nichrome wire mounted close to the test mass barrel; the thermal radiation from this wire is absorbed in the test mass substrate. This also provides a mechanism for avoiding parametric instabilities which arise from the interaction of test mass body modes with higher-order optical modes [20]. Additionally, antireflection-coated fused silica compensation plates placed between the beamsplitter and each input test mass may be heated using a CO_2 laser; a mask placed between the laser and the plate determines the geometry of the applied heating.

VI. NOISE PERFORMANCE DURING FIRST OBSERVING RUN

During the first observing run, the high-power injection-locked amplifiers were not used, and the interferometers were illuminated with about 25 W of laser light, yielding 100 kW of circulating power in each arm [21]. Additionally, a 37 % transmissive signal recycling mirror was used. The differential strain ASD was less than $10^{-23}/\mathrm{Hz}^{1/2}$ between 100 and 300 Hz (fig. 2). The strain ASD was limited by shot noise above 200 Hz, control noise from other degrees of freedom below 30 Hz [22]. The limiting noise source between 30 Hz and 200 Hz is not yet known.

VII. FUTURE PLANS

Interferometer commissioning is ongoing, with a current focus on operating with more than 25 W of input power. This requires changes to the angular control system, reconfiguration of the thermal compensation system, and new electrostatic damping infrastructure to combat the increased number of parametric instabilities. A second astrophysical observing run is planned to start before the end of 2016.

Longer-term improvements to Advanced LIGO may include frequency-dependent squeezed light to reduce the quantum noise, heavier test masses to reduce radiation pressure noise, better coating materials to reduce the test mass thermal noise, or longer suspensions to reduce suspension thermal noise [23].

ACKNOWLEDGMENTS

LIGO was constructed by the California Institute of Technology and Massachusetts Institute of Technology with funding from the National Science Foundation and operates under cooperative agreement PHY–0757058. This paper has the internal project designation LIGO–P1600132.

[1] J. D. E. Creighton *et al.*, *Gravitational-Wave Physics and Astronomy* (Wiley-VCH, 2011).
[2] B. P. Abbott *et al.*, Phys. Rev. Lett. **116**, 061102 (2016).
[3] B. P. Abbott *et al.*, Phys. Rev. Lett. **116**, 241103 (2016).
[4] J. Aasi *et al.*, Class. Quantum Grav. **32**, 074001 (2015).
[5] A. Buonanno *et al.*, Phys. Rev. D **64**, 042006 (2001).
[6] J. Mizuno, Ph.D. thesis, Universität Hannover (1995).
[7] D. V. Martynov, Ph.D. thesis, California Institute of Technology (2015).
[8] M. Evans *et al.*, Phys. Rev. D **78**, 102003 (2008).
[9] G. M. Harry *et al.*, Class. Quantum Grav. **24**, 405 (2007).
[10] A. V. Cumming *et al.*, Class. Quantum Grav. **29**, 035003 (2012).
[11] P. Kwee *et al.*, Opt. Express **20**, 10617 (2012).
[12] L. Winkelmann *et al.*, Applied Physics B **102**, 529 (2011).
[13] R. W. P. Drever *et al.*, Applied Physics B **31**, 97 (1983).
[14] R. Adhikari *et al.*, Tech. Rep. LIGO-T070236 (LIGO, 2008).
[15] T. Chalermsongsak *et al.*, Metrologia **52**, 17 (2015).
[16] T. T. Fricke *et al.*, Class. Quantum Grav. **29**, 065005 (2012).
[17] L. Barsotti *et al.*, Class. Quantum Grav. **27**, 084026 (2010).
[18] J. A. Sidles *et al.*, Physics Letters A **354**, 167 (2006).
[19] A. Brooks *et al.*, In prep. (2016).
[20] M. Evans *et al.*, Phys. Rev. Lett. **114**, 161102 (2015).
[21] B. P. Abbott *et al.*, Phys. Rev. Lett. **116**, 131103 (2016).
[22] D. V. Martynov *et al.*, Phys. Rev. D **93**, 112004 (2016).
[23] J. Miller *et al.*, Phys. Rev. D **91**, 062005 (2015).

Frequency Stabilized Lasers for LIDAR 6/29/2016
Mark Notcutt and SLS Team
Stable Laser Systems
Boulder CO

Lasers stabilized to Fabry-Perot cavities: good Signal to Noise
Compact Frequency stabilized lasers on a vibrating platform
Cavity designs that we typically use
Feedforward compensation of platform vibration

1

SLS sells frequency stable lasers ~ 1 Hz

Variety of packaging, wavelengths, and applications (defense, timekeeping, spectroscopy)

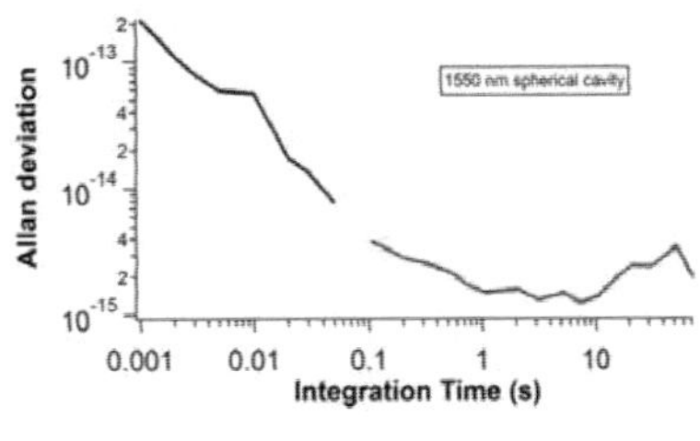

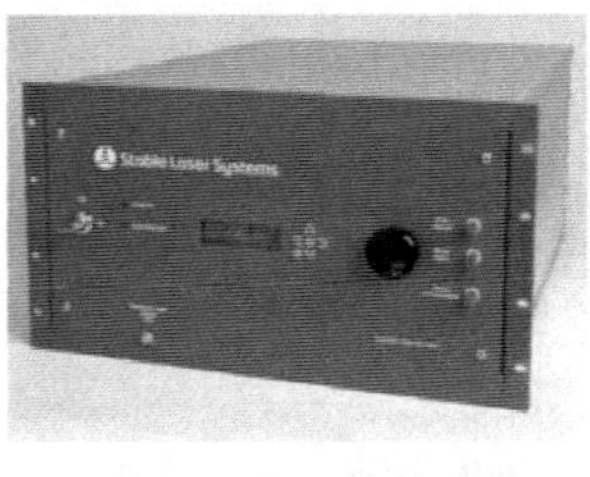

Stable Laser Systems
2

Fiber coupled filter cavities

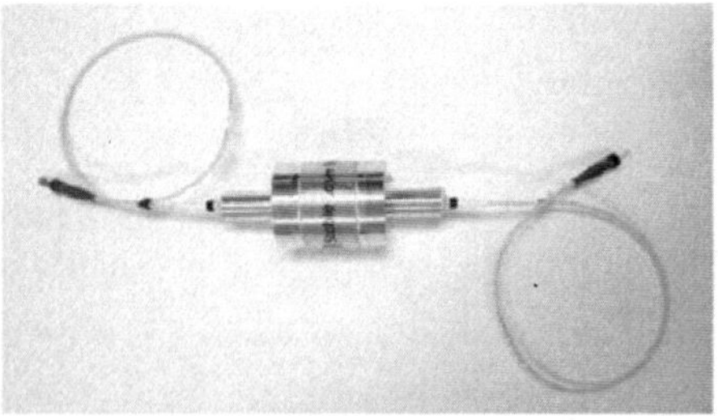

10 GHz and upwards free spectral range
Acceleration coefficient at the 10^{-9} /g level
< 1 dB loss fiber to fiber
Rugged

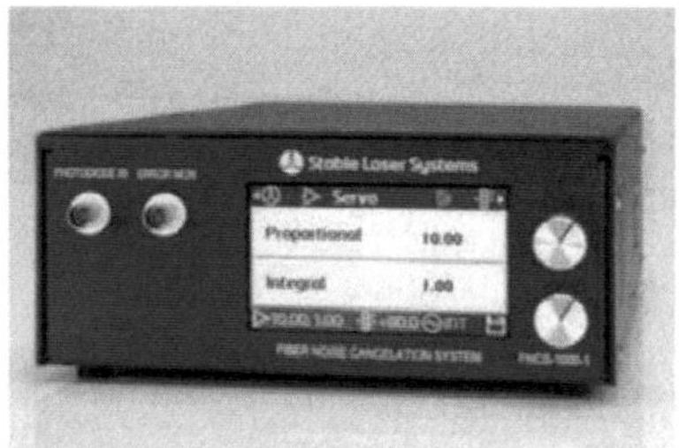

Fiber noise cancelation electronics

Stable Laser Systems 3

Laboratory-style frequency stabilized laser

Cavity in temperature controlled vacuum housing: cavity resting on springs

Pound-Drever-Hall discriminator

Vibration isolation platform underneath breadboard

Laser and fiber components

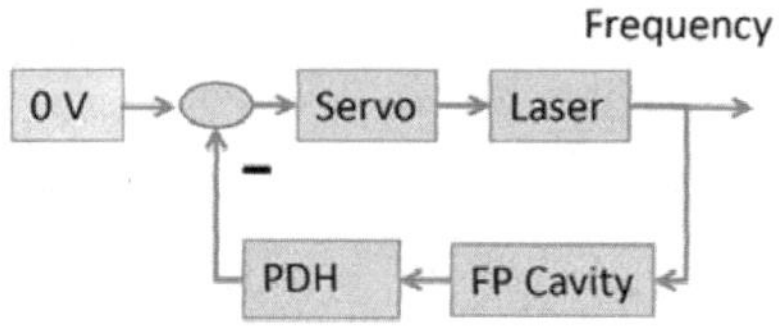

The laser is tightly servo locked to the cavity, and faithfully follows the cavity resonance
So the frequency stability properties of the stabilized laser = frequency/length stability of the reference cavity

4

Evolution to more compact packaging

Available

In development

5

Portable FP cavities with low acceleration coefficient

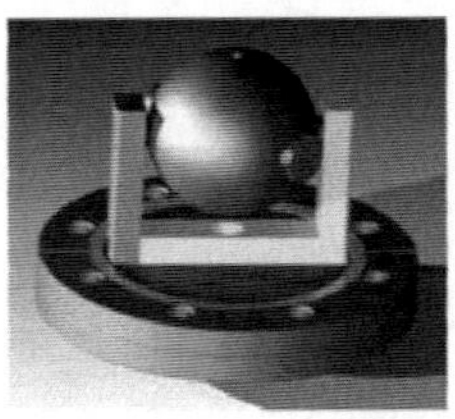

Till Rosenband and Jim Bergquist at NIST devised this squeeze insensitive cavity

Stephen Webster extended this to a cube held tetrahedrally

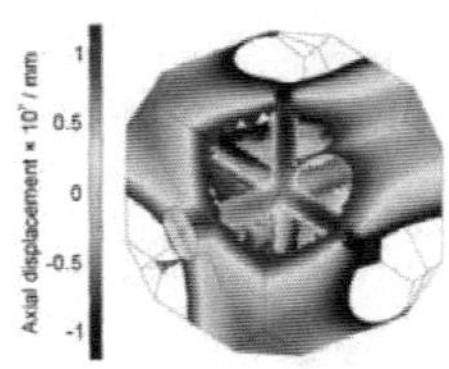

These designs are optimized using FEM

6

Portable FP cavities with low acceleration coefficient

Mirrors cause mass asymmetry **Mounting and thermal isolation take up volume**

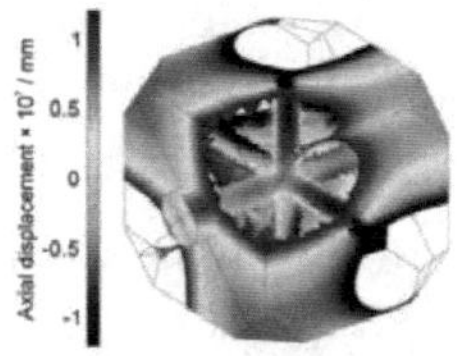

Balancing the mounting forces is difficult

Till Rosenband and Jim Bergquist at NIST devised this squeeze insensitive cavity

Stephen Webster extended this to a cube held tetrahedrally

These designs are optimized using FEM

7

SLS measurements of cavity vibration sensitivity

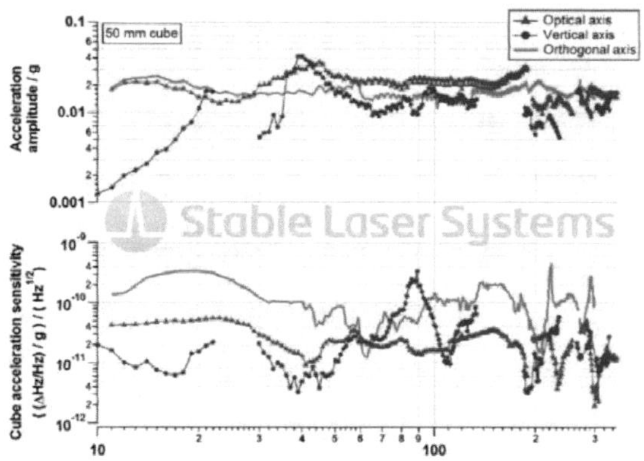

Fig. 7 Acceleration transfer function and amplitude of accelerations versus frequency for a 50 mm cube cavity (see Fig. 2 for orientation).

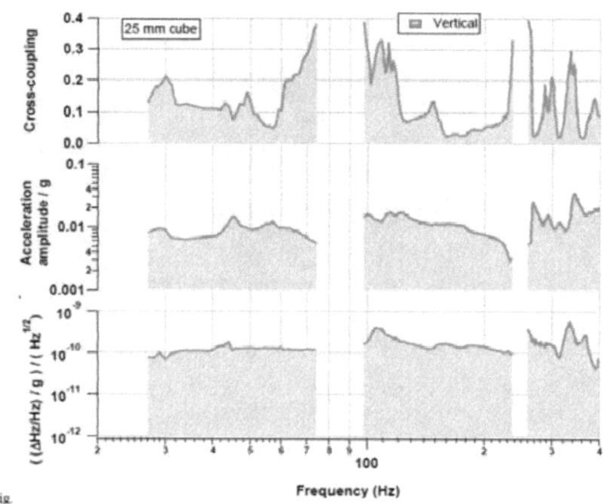

A Portable FP Cavity with df/f~ 10^{-15}

- Cavity is firmly held to be portable, 25 mm or 50 mm in length
- Low frequency drift > 1 Hz/s - improve w/ temperature feedforward
- Good acceleration coefficients in the df/f ~ 3 x 10^{-11}/g range – improve with acceleration feedforward
- NIST has done this before, in style (Rosenband, Leibrandt, et al)

+

Acceleration

- Outside the lab, accelerations can be large and low frequency, so passive filtering is not effective
- Mass asymmetry of the off-axial mirror position on the cavity (50 um) is a present limit to the acceleration coefficient
- Accelerations can easily be measured

Temperature

- Compact packaging ≠ lot of thermal insulation
- Ambient temperature and gradients are easily measured

Good Laser Frequency Stabilized Laser Drift measured wrt comb/Rb osc

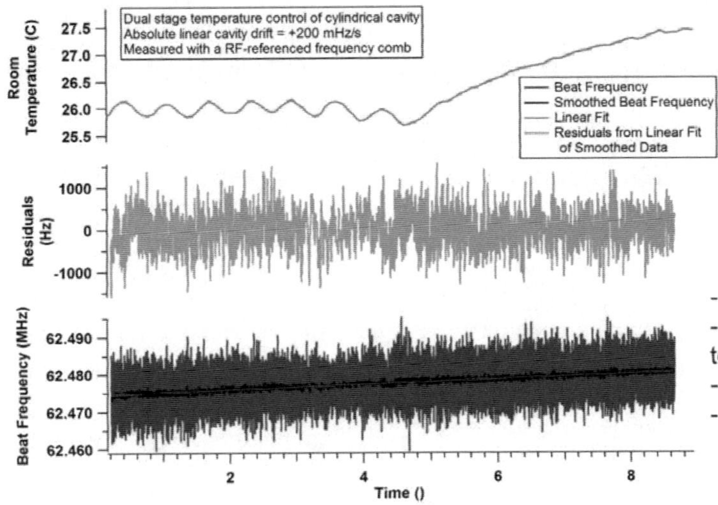

- Linear drift of ~10 kHz/day
- No visible correlation against lab temp
  - Two stages of temperature control
  - Operation at temperature at which expansion coefficient is zero

Frequency beat measurement of 2nd laser against good laser

2nd laser cavity is has low Tzc, though is controlled at ~ 30 C, so has significant expansion coefficient

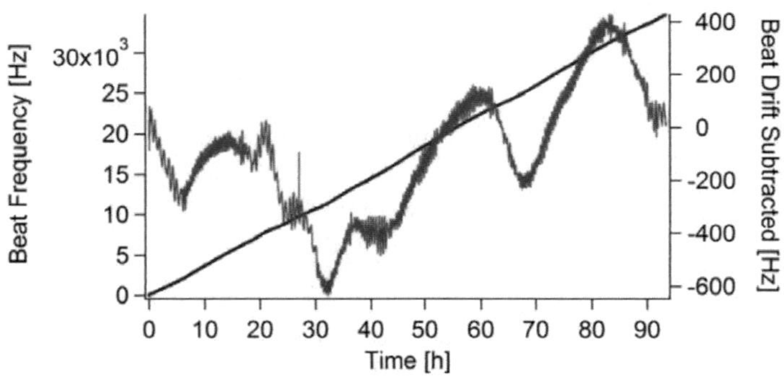

- 3 days of data here
- Significant cooling cycle at 7 am daily
- Daily variation of 600 Hz when drift subtracted
- This laser is in a different lab to the first laser

Ambient Room Temperature Change Wiener Filter Feedforward

- Step 1 Calibration: Derive the impulse response function of the plant and derive Wiener Predictive Filter
- Step 2 Operation: Input the noise to the Wiener filter predictor to calculate a frequency shift, and apply this frequency shift to an AOM on the output of the frequency stabilized laser

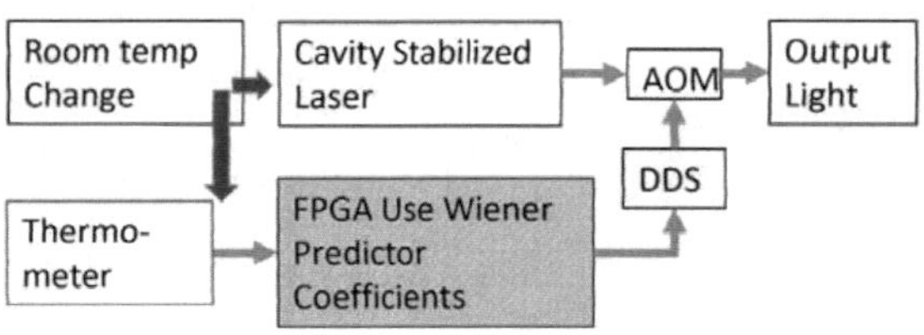

Stable Laser Systems

Correlate Frequency and Room Temperature Change

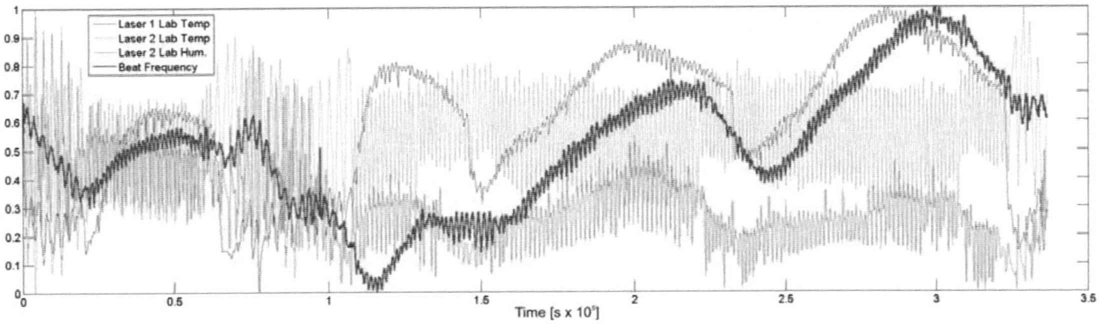

Stable Laser Systems

Results of Room Temperature Change Wiener Filter Feedforward

When good, residual is ~20 %, when not so good, residual ~ 50%

The non-convergence starts at the big morning cooldown in our lab

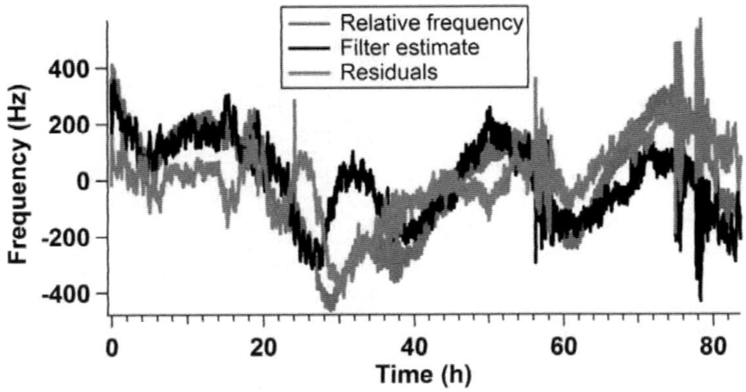

Acceleration Feedforward

With Acceleration feedforward, the Wiener filter predictions should be done to correct perturbations at ~ 300 Hz, so a microprocessor or FPGA is used for the calculation

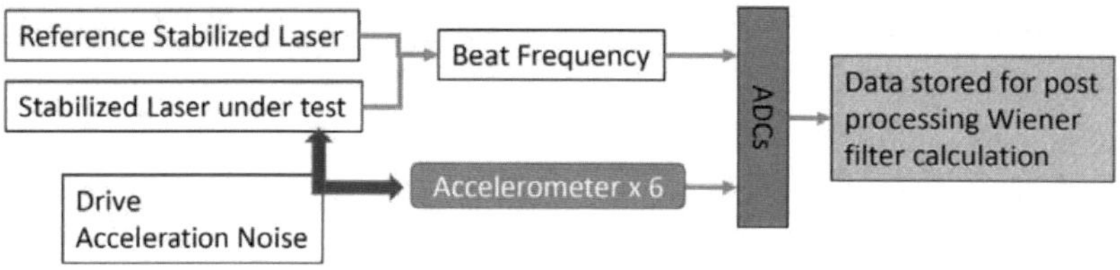

Cavity on Gimbal setup for Acceleration filter coefficients measurement

The gimbal will be used to drive translational and angular accelerations

Gimbal driven by hand for large low frequency motions, or by a voice coil for acoustic frequency drive

Six accelerometers, arranged on diagonals of faces of cube with center approx. coincident with cavity

We thank Dave Leibrandt at NIST for his help with this

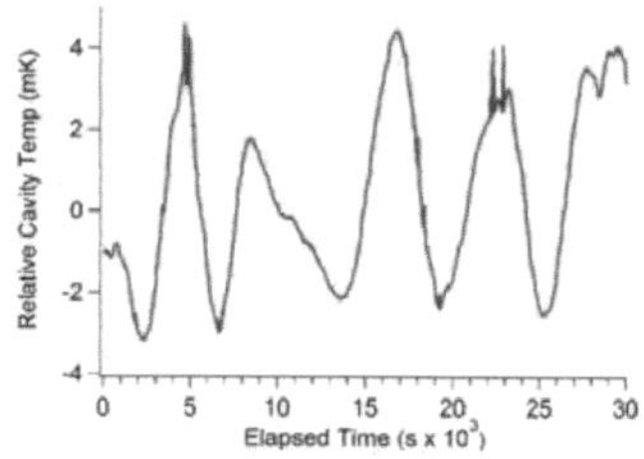

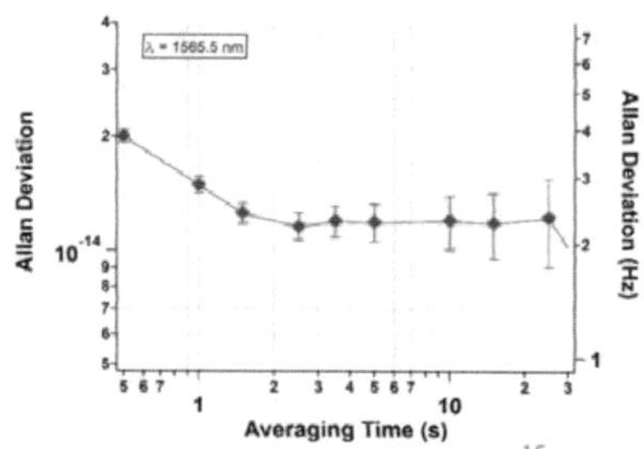

Experimental setup: Wires and Fibers

Laser coupled into fiber
Locking Electronics

Frequency Counter
Differential Amp for Accelerometers
DACs
FPGA
DDS
AOM

Out of the picture on a table to the right
Second Stabilized Laser

Vibrations applied to 25 mm cavity to simulate real-world environments

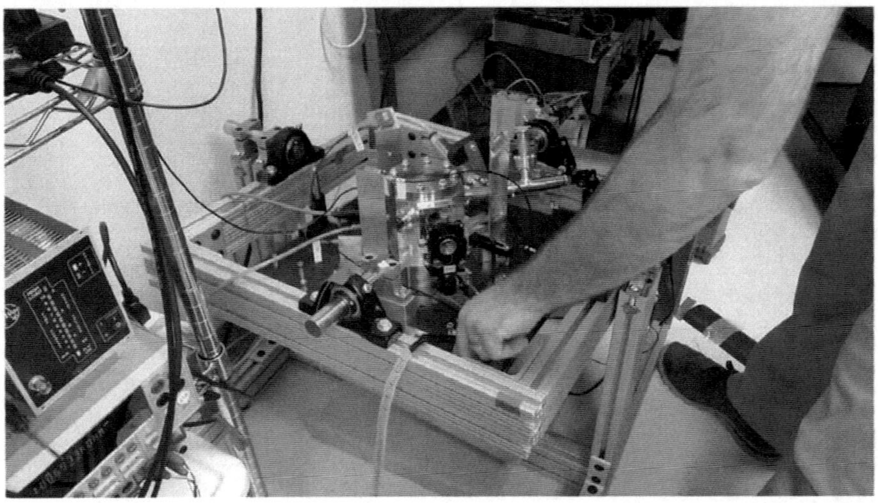

Results: Feed-forward correction of large low frequency platform motion

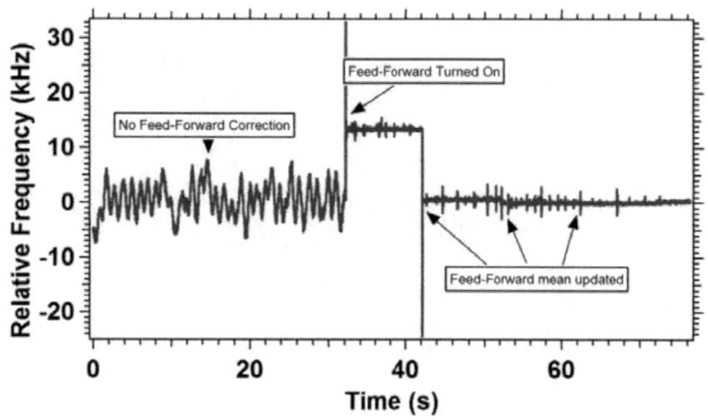

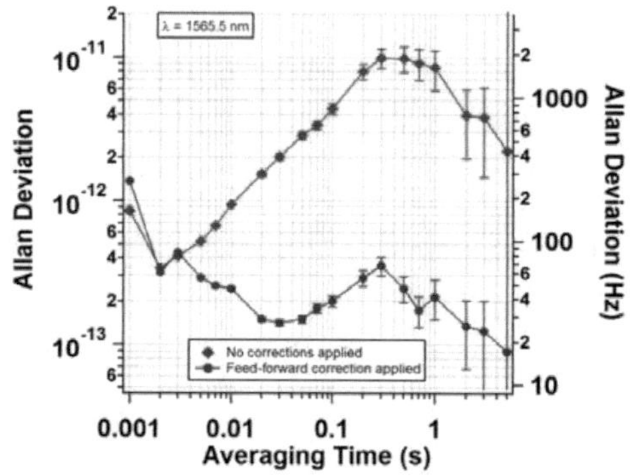

LMS minimization routine used to determine filter coefficients from 6 accelerometers. Filter length of 5 used.

Allan deviation dramatically improved when feed-forward correction applied.

Correlation between drive signal and noise of corrected signal

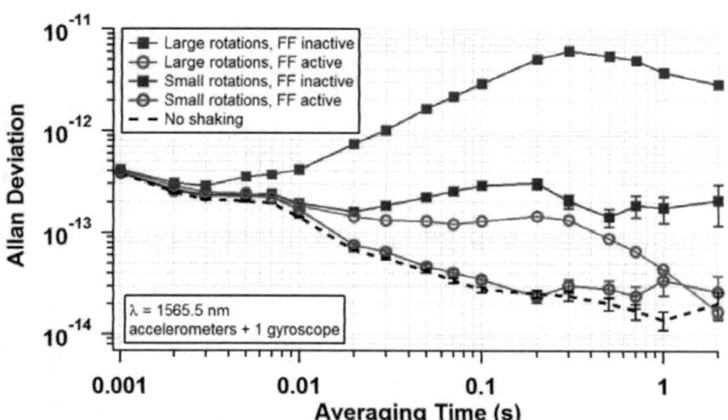

Correlation between drive signal and noise of corrected signal

A great deal of thanks to

- Nate Newbury and his group, and Scott Diddams, Frank Quinlan and Tara Fortier at NIST for their help
- Jun Ye, Wei Zhang, and Jan Hall at JILA for their help
- Jim Bergquist, Dave Leibrandt, for help with and discussions on the feedforward compensation. *A cavity-stabilized laser with acceleration sensitivity below 10−12/g* Phys. Rev. A **87**, p023829 (2013)
- DARPA for the opportunity and funding
- Colleagues at SLS

Charles Fabry

Alfred Perot

Stable Laser Systems

21

Results: Feed-forward correction of 40 Hz vibration

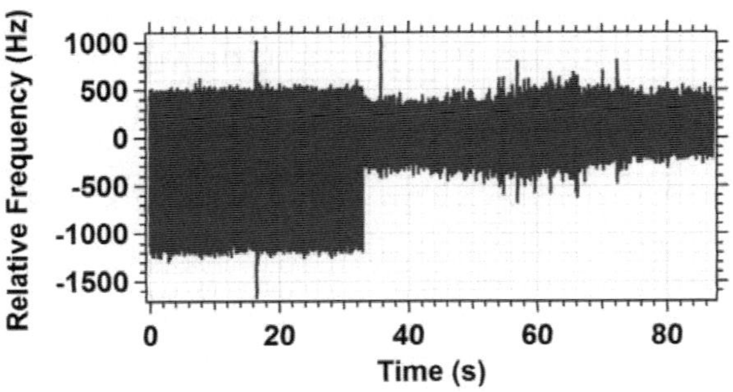

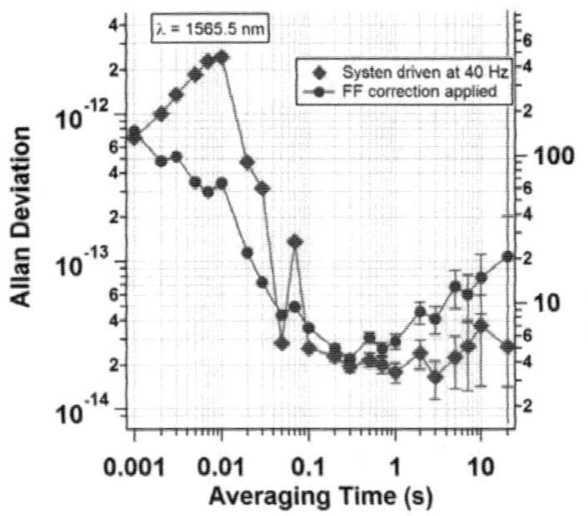

Monolithic high power semiconductor seed lasers near 2.05 μm

Mahmood Bagheri, Clifford Frez, Garry Spiers, Mathieu Fradet and Siamak Forouhar (a)
(a) Jet Propulsion Laboratory, California Institute of Technology,
4800 Oak Grove Dr., Pasadena, CA 91109;

Abstract: We report on the development and demonstration of a compact 2 μm semiconductor seed laser for CO_2 lidar instruments. Our monolithic high-power fiber pigtailed semiconductor seed laser will greatly enhance the operability and applicability of IPDA lidar systems for high spatial and temporal resolution CO_2 airborne measurements as well as future Earth-orbiting CO_2 measurement missions. The compact semiconductor transmitter has a suitably narrow linewidth (<100 KHz) and enables flexible tuning (>150 GHz) over several CO_2 absorption lines in the 2.05 μm band. The frequency agility and multi-format modulation capability of the this technology, its small size and compatibility with standard DFB lasers at the telecom band paves the way for adoption of the attractive 2.05 μm band for CO_2 profiling and measurements.

Keywords: CO_2 lidar, active sensing, semiconductor laser.

1. Introduction

The National Research Council's 2007 Earth Science decadal survey has recommended the Active Sensing of CO_2 Emissions over Nights, Days and Seasons (ASCENDS) [1] as a follow-on mission to passive CO_2 measurement missions (e.g., the current AIRS/Aqua and the near-term OCO-2/OCO-3 satellite systems) to determine the location and strength of the source and sinks of atmospheric CO_2. During the past decade, teams from JPL [2, 3] GSFC [4] and NASA LaRC [5, 6] have developed and flown airborne IPDA lidars for atmospheric CO_2 measurements. The GSFC [4] and LaRC [5] lidar systems operate in the 1.57 μm band, while the JPL [3] and the other LaRC [6] system operate in the 2.05 μm band. A great deal of useful experience and design insight has been gained as a result of the participation of these IPDA lidars in multiple flight campaigns.

The availability of fiber-pigtailed components at the 1.57 μm band allows an implementation of an all fiber-based IPDA lidars with no free-space component [4, 5, 7]. This is preferred for air-borne and space borne systems as it is more compact and robust and less susceptible to environmental fluctuations. Recently, there has been significant progress in the development of high power fiber amplifiers operating at the 2 μm wavelength [8]. However, to-date semiconductor DFB lasers operating in the 2.0 μm wavelength range have remained relatively undeveloped due to lack of telecom or wide-spread metrology applications.

A monolithic fiber-pigtailed semiconductor seed laser operating at 2 μm will greatly enhance the operability and applicability of IPDA lidar systems for high spatial and temporal resolution CO_2 airborne measurements as well as future Earth-orbiting CO_2 measurement missions.

2. Fiver-pigtailed semiconductor lasers operating at 2.05 μm

Our DFB lasers are based on InGaAsSb strained-quantum wells (QWs) with AlGaAsSb waveguide and cladding layers on GaSb substrates. InP material system, a mature laser platform due to its widespread application in the telecomm industry, has been used for making lasers emitting at 2.0 μm. However, state-of-the-art InP-based semiconductor lasers operating at the 2.0 μm band have limited output power due to increased Auger recombination rates and other loss mechanisms at longer wavelength [9, 10]. Besides, GaSb-based type-I QW diode lasers designed to operate in the spectral region from below 2 μm to above

3 μm, have shown excellent performance as compared to their InP counterpart [11, 12]; GaSb based semiconductor lasers at 2.0 μm and beyond show nearly twice the conversion efficiencies of those of InP-based lasers emitting near 1.9 - 2 μm.

After characterization and an initial reliability test, the submounts are soldered onto a temperature controlled heat sink and packaged inside a standard 14-pin butterfly package with a PM1950 Nufern output optical fiber (polarization maintain optical fiber with transmission between 1850-2200 nm). A single element optical lens is used to image the mode of the laser onto the facet of the optical fiber. An integrated single-stage optical isolator and anti-reflection (AR) coated optical elements are used to suppress and minimize optical feedback into the laser cavity and avoid potential instabilities and maintain laser spectral linewidth[13]. Figure 1(a) shows the output power and the corresponding voltage across the PN junction of a semiconductor DFB laser measured at the end of the output optical fiber measured at different heat sink temperatures. The lasers show a threshold current density of 450 Acm^{-2}, that indicates the high quality of material growth and device fabrication. The extracted slope efficiency from the end of the optical fiber is 0.055 $mWmA^{-1}$ that corresponds to a 40% fiber coupling efficiency considering a measured 0.135 $mWmA^{-1}$ slope efficiency from the emitting laser facet.

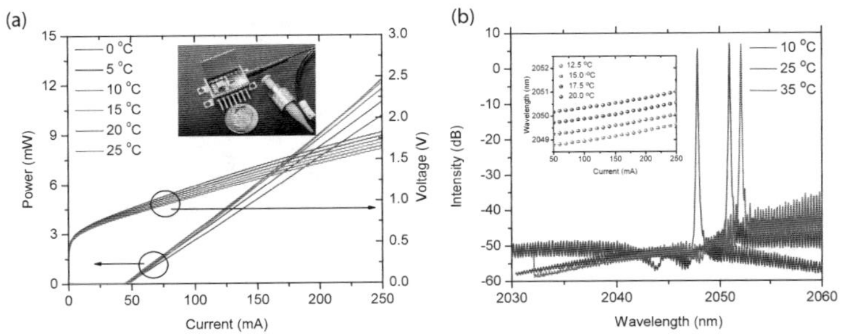

Figure 1. (a) LIV curve of the packaged module with the package layout as inset. (b) Lasing spectra of the packaged laser at different heat sink temperature at 250 mA input current, current and temperature tuning characteristics are shown as an inset showing more than 1 nm continuous tuning.

Figure 1(b) shows optical output spectra collected from the optical fiber end measured at different heat sink temperature at 250 mA input current with current and temperature tuning characteristics shown as an inset. The DFB lasers show single mode behavior with better than 50 dB of side-mode suppression ratio (SMSR). The lasers exhibit stable and constant wavelength (λ) tuning by $d\lambda dT^{-1}$ = 0.18 nmK^{-1} over a large current and temperature range with excellent side-mode suppression ratios and over 150 GHz mod hop free tuning capability.

The current tuning capability enables a variety of high-speed frequency sequencing and switching formats. This is important for high precision CO_2 lidar measurement schemes that require near-simultaneous measurements at multiple wavelengths in the vicinity of the target absorption line in order to infer column CO_2 concentration. The optical output shows a linear polarization along the slow axis of the optical fiber with better than 20 dB extinction over the operating current and temperatures.

The Schawlow-Townes linewidth of these lasers was measured using the coherent frequency discriminator technique with a fiber Mach-Zehnder interferometer [14]. The block diagram of the frequency discriminator measurement setup is depicted in Fig. 2(a). It consists of a fiber-based Mach Zehnder interferometer. By using a slow thermal phase modulator (<10 Hz bandwidth), the interferometer is locked at one of its quadrature points and the optical frequency variations are linearly converted into intensity modulations that are then detected using a fast detector [15]. Polarization drifts are suppressed by using polarization maintaining optical fibers in the interferometer.

By measuring the PSD of the Mach-Zender interferometer output photocurrent, the frequency independent part of the measured spectrum is due to the laser spontaneous emission or Schallow-Townes laser linewidth. Figure 2(a) shows three PSD spectra of the frequency fluctuations of a fiber-pigtailed 2.05 μm laser measured at 60 mA, 70 mA and 120 mA corresponding to a linewidth of 170 KHz, 70 KHz and 25 KHz, respectively. The spectra in figure 2(a) demonstrate three distinct regions. The frequency range between 3-10 MHz where the spectrum is flat is used to extract laser lineiwdth due to spontaneous emission noise. The nulls at 185 MHz correspond to a 5.4 ns delay (τ_0) between the arms of the interferometer. Figure 2(b) shows the extracted laser linewidth as a function of input current at three different laser heat-sink temperatures.

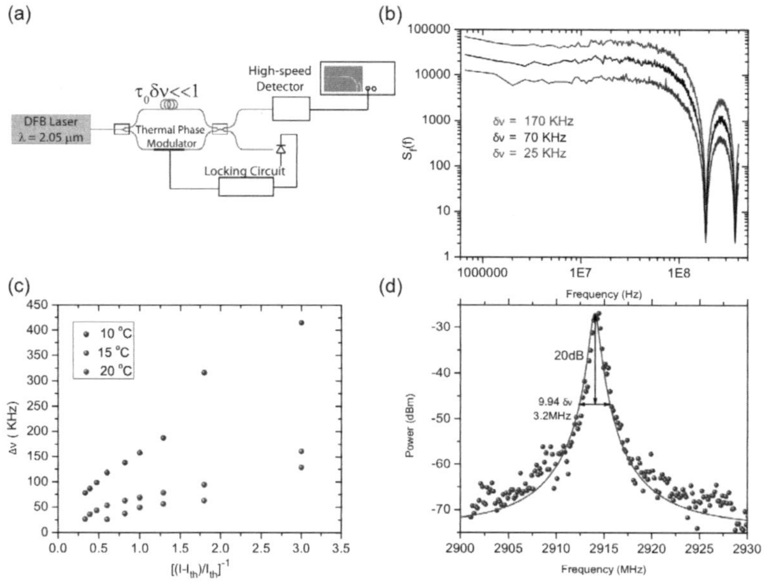

Figure 2. (a) The coherent optical frequency-discriminator setup. (b) Measured FM noise of the DFB laser at different bias levels at 15°C. (c) Extracted laser linewidth at different bias levels and heat sink temperatures. (d) Measured beat note of the free-running semiconductor laser with a solid-state laser locked to a CO_2 gas cell on an electrical spectrum analyzer.

Also, the total linewidth of the DFB laser was measured using a heterodyne beat-note measurement setup [15]. In this setup, the output of the DFB laser was mixed with the output of a fiber-coupled Tm,Ho:YLF reference laser using a fiber beam combiner. The reference laser is locked to line center of a carbon dioxide (CO_2) absorption cell [16]. The DFB laser frequency offset from the reference laser is adjusted using its temperature and input current. The beat note is detected using a high bandwidth fiber-coupled InGaAs detector and is then analyzed on an electrical spectrum analyzer. Figure 2(a) shows the measured beat note measured on an electrical spectrum analyzer with a 10 KHz resolution bandwidth. A Lorentzian fit to the line shape yielded a 321 KHz FWHM linewidth. An independent measurement of the reference laser has indicated a FWHM linewidth 150 KHz. Therefore, the total FWHM linewidth of the DFB laser was estimated to be 171 KHz.

3. Conclusion

We demonstrated a versatile 2.05 μm DFB semiconductor laser. The compact semiconductor transmitter has a suitably narrow linewidth and enables flexible tuning and versatile modulation formats that enables high precision airborne and space CO_2 measurements. The significantly stronger band strength at this wavelength, is more amenable to probing the atmosphere with weighting functions that emphasize the lowest few km above the surface, where the CO_2 sources and sinks of interest exist, while maintaining optimum differential absorption optical depth for high precision and low bias. Due to its compact size, low thermal mass, and rugged architecture, this module will significantly improve the current lidar systems performance.

4. Acknowledgements

This work was supported under the Advanced Component Technology (ACT) program of the National Aeronautics and Space Administration's (NASA) Earth and Science Technology Office (ESTO) and performed at the Jet Propulsion Laboratory (JPL), California Institute of Technology, under contract with the NASA.

5. References

[1] [National Research Council. Earth Science and Applications from Space: National Imperatives for the Next Decade and Beyond], The National Academies Press, Washington DC (2007).

[2] Menzies, R. T. and Tratt, D. M., "Differential laser absorption spectrometry for global profiling of tropospheric carbon dioxide: selection of optimum sounding frequencies for high-precision measurements," *Applied optics* 42(33), 6569-6577 (2003).

[3] Spiers, G. D., Menzies, R. T., Jacob, J., Christensen, L. E., Phillips, M. W., Choi, Y., and Browell, E. V., "Atmospheric CO_2 measurements with a 2 μm airborne laser absorption spectrometer employing coherent detection," *Applied optics* 50(14), 2098-2111 (2011).

[4] Abshire, J. B., *et al.*, "Airborne measurements of CO_2 column concentration and range using a pulsed direct-detection IPDA lidar," *Remote Sensing* 6(1), 443-469 (2013).

[5] Dobler, J. T., *et al.*, "Atmospheric CO_2 column measurements with an airborne intensity-modulated continuous wave 1.57 μm fiber laser lidar," *Applied optics* 52(12), 2874-2892 (2013).

[6] Singh, U., *et al.*, "Column CO_2 measurement from an airborne solid-state double-pulsed 2-micron integrated path differential absorption lidar," in [International Conference on Space Optics], 10 (2014).

[7] Johnson, W., Repasky, K., Nehrir, A., and Carlsten, J., "Development of an eye-safe micro-pulse differential absorption lidar (DIAL) for carbon dioxide profilings," AGU Fall Meeting Abstracts 1, 0097 (2011).

[8] Phillips, M. W., "Thulium-doped fiber amplifier development for power scaling the 2 micron coherent laser absorption instrument for ASCENDS," Lockheed Martin Coherent Technologies, Louisville, CO, Tech. Rep.

[9] Phelan, R., *et al.*, "$In_{0.75}Ga_{0.25}AsInP$ multiple quantum-well discrete-mode laser diode emitting at 2 μm," *IEEE Photon. Technol. Lett.,* 24(8), 652-654 (2012).

[10] Mitsuhara, M., Ogasawara, M., Oishi, M., Sugiura, H., and Kasaya, K., "2.05-μm wavelength InGaAs-InGaAs distributed-feedback multi-quantum-well lasers with 10-mw output power," *IEEE Photon. Technol. Lett.* ,11(1), 33-35 (1999).

[11] Forouhar, S., Briggs, R. M., Frez, C., Franz, K. J., and Ksendzov, A., "High-power laterally coupled distributed-feedback gasb-based diode lasers at 2 μm wavelength," *Applied Physics Letters* 100(3), 031107 (2012).

[12] Briggs, R. M., *et al.*, "Single-mode 2.65 μm InGaAsSb/AlInGaAsSb laterally coupled distributed-feedback diode lasers for atmospheric gas detection," *Optics express* 21(1), 1317-1323 (2013).

[13] Bagheri, M., Frez, C., Kelly, B., Gupta, J., and Forouhar, S., "High output power, fibre-coupled distributed feedback lasers operating near 2.05 μm wavelength range," *Electronics Letters* 49(24), 1552{1553 (2013).

[14] Bagheri, M., Spiers, G. D., Frez, C., Forouhar, S., and Aflatouni, F., "Linewidth measurement of distributed-feedbacksemiconductor lasers operating near 2.05 μm," *IEEE Photon. Technol. Lett.,* 27.18 (2015): 1934 1937.

[15] Baney, D. M. and V., S. W., [Fiber optic, Test and measurement], ch. High resolution optical frequency analysis, 169-218, Prentice-Hall, Inc (1998).

[16] Spiers, G. D., Menzies, R. T., Tratt, D. M., and Phillips, M., "The laser absorption spectrometer for carbon dioxide sink and source detection," in [Second Earth Science Technology Conference.], 11{13 (2002).

Fast Widely-Tunable CW Single Frequency 2-micron Laser

Charley P. Hale and Sammy W. Henderson
Beyond Photonics LLC
1650 Coal Creek Dr., Ste. B, Lafayette, CO 80026
charley@beyondphotonics.com

Abstract: We have recently developed a fast widely–tunable diode-pumped solid-state laser architecture, called the *SWIFT*, or *Super-WIde Frequency-Tunable* laser. The laser architecture is compatible with operation using many different solid state laser crystals for access of various emission lines between 1 and 2.1 micron. We initially demonstrated the laser using Tm,Ho:YLF laser crystal near 2.05 micron wavelength and achieved 100 mW of output power with 50 GHz fast PZT tuning range. The fast 50 GHz tuning range can be centered at any wavelength from 2047-2059 nm using the Tm,Ho:YLF crystal. The frequency stability and power are sufficient to serve as the local oscillator laser in long-range coherent lidar systems. The rapid and wide frequency tunablity meets the requirements for integrated-path or range-resolved differential absorption lidar or applications where multiple hard targets with significantly different line of sight velocities (Doppler shifts) must be tracked. We will describe the Tm,Ho:YLF SWIFT laser performance in detail in the presentation.

Keywords: Coherent Lidar, Single Frequency, Laser

1. Introduction

To address needs in the laser remote sensing community and for other laser-based applications requiring a small, efficient, very stable single-frequency cw Master/Local Oscillator source, Beyond Photonics has recently developed a very widely–tunable diode-pumped solid-state laser architecture, called the *SWIFT*, or *Super-WIde Frequency-Tunable* laser. These lasers have very wide mode-hop-free frequency tunability (up to as much as 50 GHz), high power (20-100 mW cw), narrow linewidth and good frequency stability (<10 kHz/ms), and can be readily adapted to different solid-state laser crystals to access wavelengths from the near IR to 2.1 micron and potentially beyond.

The frequency stability and power are sufficient to serve as the Local Oscillator (LO) laser in long-range coherent lidar systems where frequency measurement accuracy is paramount. The lasers are also rapidly frequency-tunable, meeting the requirements of many active remote sensing applications where transmitted frequencies separated by multiple GHz must be rapidly accessed for remote laser spectroscopy applications like integrated-path or range-resolved differential absorption lidar. [1, 2] Very frequency-and power-stable two-micron wavelength lasers are also being considered for use in next-generation gravitational wave detectors, to take optimal advantage of decreased thermal noise in silicon-based reference cavity optical coatings compared to shorter wavelengths. [3]

2. Laser Description and Performance

Key elements of the SWIFT laser are a diode-laser-pumped thin solid-state laser disk; a compact intracavity frequency filter element to inhibit lasing on all but a single longitudinal mode of the cavity and to permit broad frequency tunability; and an integral low-voltage piezoelectric (PZT) tuning element. To improve long term frequency stability, the entire resonator is thermally stabilized using a small thermo-electric cooler to about 1 millidegree C and housed in a hermetically sealed enclosure. Typically, the laser is isolated using a compact high-performance Faraday isolator and coupled into polarization-maintaining single mode fiber. The laser disk can be selected to be thicker for improved pump absorption and increased laser output power or alternately to be thinner for increased mode-hope free frequency tuning range at the cost of reduced pump absorption and lower laser output power.

For the prototype demonstration of this new laser architecture, we chose to initially demonstrate 50 GHz fast frequency tuning range using a thin Tm,Ho:YLF solid-state laser disk operating near 2.05 micron wavelength. The single frequency output of the *SWIFT* laser can be spectrally tuned by three different means: piezoelectrically, thermally, and with changing pump diode current. Even with the thin disk, high cw output power levels are readily achievable at moderate diode-pump levels, as shown in Figure 1 below.

We determined that the piezo tuning sensitivity of the prototype Tm,Ho:YLF *SWIFT* is 0.0114 nm/V, or ~ 800 MHz/V in terms of laser frequency change, with applied PZT voltage. We observed up to 0.70 nm of mode-hop-free SLM wavelength shift (2051.123 nm to 2051.820 nm) using a piezo DC bias voltage that ranged from 33 V to 90 V. As shown in Figure 2, this corresponds to 50 GHz in laser frequency.

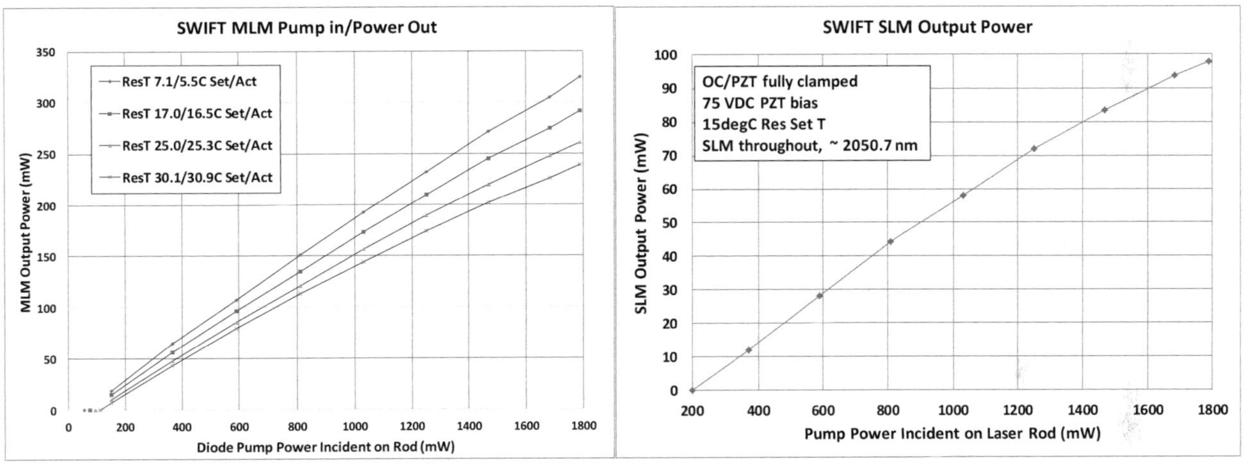

Figure 1. Prototype SWIFT multi-longitudinal mode (MLM) and SLM output power. The Tm,Ho-doped laser exhibits increasing slope efficiency with decreasing temperature due to its quasi-three-level operation. Power shown are directly from laser with no isolation or fiber coupling loss. Isolated and fiber coupled output power is typically about 70% of the power shown in the figure. Active temperature control temperature can be traded against output power performance for specific user applications.

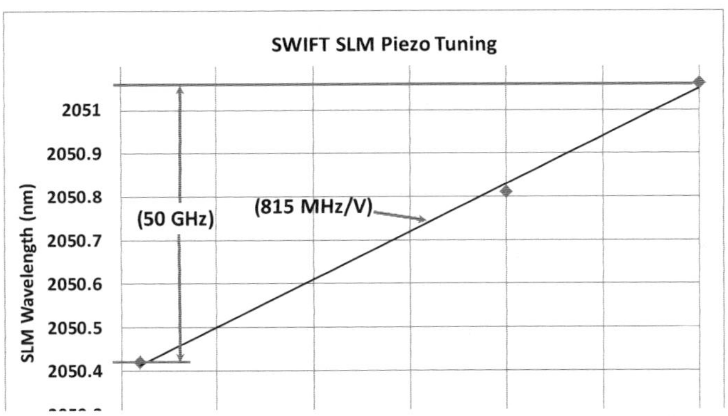

Figure 2. Prototype Tm,Ho:YLF SWIFT continuous SLM tuning; 50 GHz span.

We used an IR wavemeter to measure the piezo sensitivity of 815 MHz/V DC and the full tuning range of 50 GHz. We then used a cross-calibrated 80 GHz FSR, ~100-finesse scanning/static Fabry-Perot interferometer to provide insight into the *SWIFT*'s ability to respond to "small-signal" sinusoidal modulation of the laser cavity length. Figure 3 shows the result of driving the *SWIFT* laser's PZT actuator with a low-frequency (2.5 kHz) sine-wave drive signal (0.5 V peak-to-peak applied to the PZT actuator, corresponding to ~ 400 MHz p-p laser frequency modulation). As expected, the laser frequency modulation (Channel 2) follows the drive signal (Channel 1) perfectly at this low modulation frequency. As the sinusoidal drive frequency is increased, we eventually encounter mechanical resonances that induce phase delay and higher and lower modulation amplitude. The prototype *SWIFT* resonator assembly resulted in a first mechanical resonance at about 38 kHz. We expect to increase this first mechanical resonance frequency in the final product design by eliminating a non-optimal mechanical attachment of the laser output coupler in the prototype laser which will be corrected in the final product.

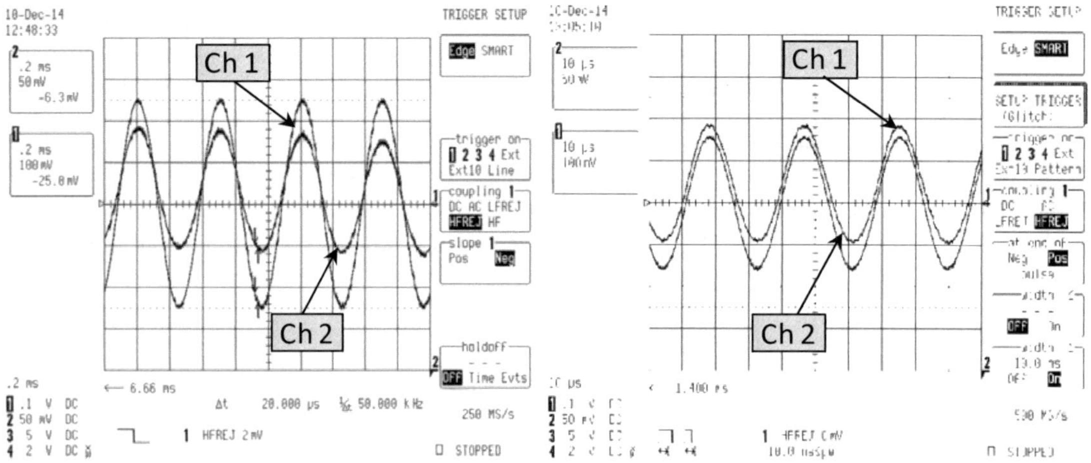

Figure 3. Prototype Tm,Ho:YLF *SWIFT* 0.5 V p-p sinusoidal drive (Ch 1) and response (Ch 2). Left: Laser frequency modulation of ~ 400 MHz p-p resulting from an initial 2.5 kHz sinewave drive signal applied to the ring actuator; no phase shift seen in response at this low drive frequency. Right: Well-behaved response is still exhibited at 35 kHz drive frequency.

Additionally, a larger-signal, 10 V p-p sine drive signal was applied at 3 kHz modulation frequency, corresponding to a peak to valley change in laser frequency of ~ 8 GHz in 167 μs. The behavior is repeatable and doesn't exhibit any significant phase delay up to even 10 kHz rates (where we stopped in the prototype due to concerns that driving at such large displacements at even higher frequencies might damage the PZT).

We also investigated the frequency jitter and found the measured frequency stability is consistent with other stable lasers we have previously developed [4] prior to the laser cavity being enclosed in its hermetic enclosure and therefore we expect that the rms frequency jitter in the hermetically enclosed device to be better than 10 kHz/ms.

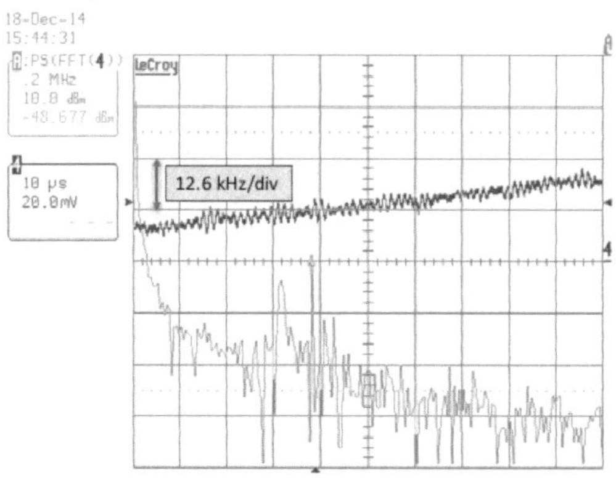

Figure 4. Prototype Tm,Ho:YLF *SWIFT* example frequency jitter and drift without hermetic enclosure and PZT shorted. Drift of ~ 12.6 kHz/100 us (see dark blue trace) dominates due to hermetic seal being removed for this sample capture time of 100 us. Lower light blue trace is FFT of the frequency vs time.

3. Conclusions

The initial SWIFT laser operating at 2.05 μm wavelength is immediately appropriate for use as a cw master/local oscillator source in current and future coherent laser radar systems. Multiple-tens of milliwatt output powers permit efficient use of the laser output for both injection-seeding higher-power pulsed transmitter lasers and as the LO source in the system's heterodyne detection circuit. The very broad and fast frequency tuning demonstrated is relevant to cw and pulsed differential absorption lidar applications where the transmitted laser frequency must be quickly switched between high- and low-transmission wavelengths relevant to measurement of molecular constituent concentrations in the atmosphere (CO_2, water vapor, methane). The basic optically-pumped SWIFT format is also applicable to very compact, high peak power pulsed lasers appropriate for use as lidar transmitter sources for coherent winds and remote spectroscopy.

Acknowledgements

A portion of this work was supported under Small Business Innovative Research funding from NASA – contract NNX14CL62P, Narasimha Prasad technical monitor. We thank Jan Hall for his advice on fast tuning PZT elements and Dale Bruns for assistance during the laboratory characterization effort.

References

[1] G. Spiers, R. Menzies, J. Jacob, L. Christensen, M. Phillips, Y. Choi, and E. Browell, "Atmospheric CO_2 Measurements with a 2-micrometer Airborne Laser Absorption Spectrometer Employing Coherent Detecton,"Applied Optics, Vol 50, Iss. 14, pp 2098-2011, 2011.

[2] J. Yu, U.N. Singh, M. Petros, and Y. Bai, "Development of a 2-micron pulsed Differential Absorption Lidar for Atmospheric CO_2 Concentration Measurement by Direct Detection," paper at American Geophysical Union Fall meeting 2011, abstract #A21D-0098.

[3] LIGO Scientific Collaboration, Instrument Science White Paper, LIGO-T15TBI-v1 (2015)

[4] S.W. Henderson, C.P. Hale, J.W. Hobbs, P. Gatt, and J.R. Magee, "Widely-Tunable 2-micron CW Local/Master Oscillator for Wind and DIAL Measurements," Proceedings of SPIE: Lidar Remote Sensing for Industry and Environmental Monitoring, SPIE 4153, paper 13, Sendai, Japan (October 9-12, 2000)

High peak power single-frequency MOPFA for lidar applications

Laurent Lombard, Guillaume Canat, Anne Durécu, Agnes Dolfi-Bouteyre, Matthieu Valla, Beatrice Augère, Didier Goular, Claudine Besson
Onera, the French Aerospace Lab, Palaiseau, France
Laurent.Lombard@onera.fr

Abstract: Long range coherent detection wind lidars have many applications in the fields of wind farms and aircraft safety. Fiber laser sources emitting around 1.5µm show key advantages such as versatility, modularity and robustness of alignments to vibrations. However, nonlinear effects such as Stimulated-Brillouin-Scattering limit achievable peak power because of strong fiber core confinement. Wind lidars based on fiber laser technologies thus operate in a regime with low energy per pulse (typically 10µJ-1mJ) and high pulse repetition frequency (typically 5-50kHz). We investigated various technologies to improve peak power in 1.5µm fiber lasers such as special large mode area (LMA) fiber designs or strain management. Integration of a high peak power source in ONERA LICORNE wind lidar enabled to achieve air speed profiles up to record ranges of 16km within 0.1s averaging time.

Keywords: Coherent Laser Radar, Laser, Pulse Fiber Amplifier, Coherent Combining

1. Introduction

A typical coherent fiber LIDAR set up is depicted on Figure 1. The master oscillator is a continuous laser diode that goes through an acousto-optic modulator (AOM) which shapes the pulse. It is then amplified through a fiber preamplification stage and a filter (BPF) and a booster stage. At the output of the booster stage, the beam is polarized, quasi-single mode and its temporal shape is optimized for efficient coherent detection. Most systems emit around 1545nm which corresponds to high gain in erbium doped fibers and a good atmospheric transmission. The assets of fiber lasers are their high efficiency enabling wall plug efficiency of 10% to 15%, their size -the volume of a coherent 2W fiber laser is the size of a thick book-and their reliability due to spliced connectors.

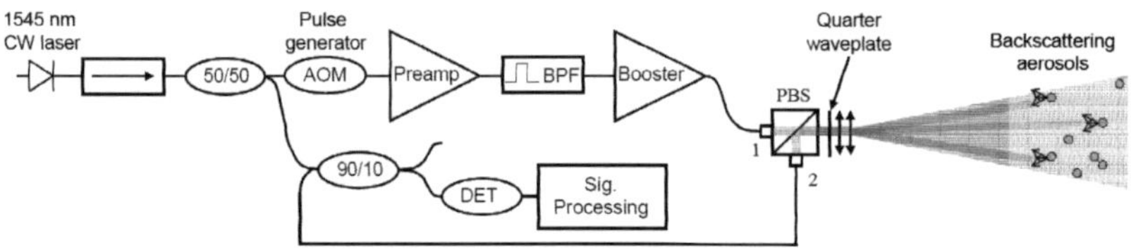

Figure 1: MOFPA coherent fiber LIDAR setup

2. High spectral brillance all fibered sources and SBS mitigation

ONERA has developed a specific know-how in high peak power, narrow linewidth pulsed fiber lasers and amplifiers. The additional laser power provides increased coherent LIDAR capability in range and scanning of large areas but also better system resistance to adverse weather conditions.

To reach long range within a short acquisition time, coherent wind LIDARs require high peak power (~kW), narrow linewidth (few MHz) pulsed laser sources with nearly Fourier transform limited pulse duration (~1µs). Eyesafe, all-fiber laser sources based on MOPFA (master oscillator, power fiber amplifier) architecture offer many advantages over bulk sources such as low sensitivity to vibrations, efficiency and versatility. In the MOFPA coherent fiber LIDAR set up shown on Figure 1, the pulses are amplified in a sequence of fiber amplifier stages with increasing pump power and core size which are separated by isolators and band-pass filters. MOFPA designers seek for fibers with low numerical aperture (NA) which is favorable to single mode guiding and low amplified spontaneous emission (ASE) in order to get high system efficiency.

Narrow linewidth pulsed MOPFA are usually limited in peak power by nonlinear effects arising in the fiber such as Stimulated Brillouin Scattering (SBS) to a few 10s-100s Watts in standard fibers [1]. In single-mode fibers, the SBS threshold is reached when the peak power time length product reaches about 80 W.m. The high power density generates acoustic waves into the fiber core which acts as a grating. The light transmitted by the fiber saturates and part of this light is backscattered by the grating. In fiber amplifiers, the backscattered light may be amplified into the active fiber generating high peak power backscattered pulses potentially harmful for beforehand components [2].

The strength of the Brillouin nonlinearities in a fiber can be quantified by the intensity length product:

$$B = g_B \frac{\int_0^L P(z)dz}{A_{eff}} = \frac{g_B P(L) L_{eff}}{A_{eff}} \qquad (1)$$

where g_B is the Brillouin gain, L is the fiber length, A_{eff} is the effective area of the fundamental mode, P(z) is the signal power distribution along the fiber, L_{eff} is the effective length. For passive fiber the effective length is equal to the fiber length and for active fiber the effective length depends on the fiber gain along the fiber [3]. From (1) it appears that there are three ways to act on the nonlinearities.

2.1. Increase of mode area

The first way is to increase the fundamental mode effective area. Large-Mode-Area (LMA) fibers, with large core diameter and low numerical aperture (NA) may be used to increase the mode area but the fiber tends to guide higher order transverse modes degrading the beam quality. A good spatial quality is crucial for many applications. For instance in a coherent detection LIDAR when the beam quality factor M^2 is increased from 1 to 1.7 we expect the Carrier-to-Noise Ratio (CNR) to decrease by 3 dB [4]. The most efficient doped fibers today are based on the Erbium-Ytterbium codoping of phosphosilicate glasses. This composition has two important limitations. First the core refractive index is quite large and special pedestal structures are needed to reduce the NA to 0.09 and limit the proportion of higher order transverse modes. A second limitation is that the core itself is usually inhomogeous with a central dip in the refractive index profile resulting in a poor beam spatial quality.

To go beyond this core diameter limit, IPHT and ONERA have built a 40 µm core diameter multifilament-core fibers (MFC) to amplify high peak power pulses [5]. In this technology the fiber core is replaced by microstructured core composed of 37 Erbium-Ytterbium doped filaments surrounded by fluorine doped silica. It was shown that this structure behaves as an effectively singlemode fiber as the light only sees an average index value for the structured core. Pulses with 940 W peak power, 1 µs duration and 1 MHz laser linewidth were achieved. The beam quality was good with M^2~1.3. However this laser setup was not all-fiber. Indeed MFC fiber manufacture and integration in all-fiber lasers systems are challenging.

Another method to increase the core size while preserving a good beam quality is to change the core composition. We have tested phosphoaluminosilicate glass fibers (PAS). It has been previously demonstrated that the simultaneous codoping by alumina and phosphorous results in the reduction of the refractive index leading to lower NA cores [6], [7]. We have tested a double cladding PAS Erbium-Ytterbium doped fiber with a 30µm diameter core with a pedestal and 300 µm inner cladding. The core NA is 0.09 with respect to the pedestal. This fiber can be highly doped and we managed to make an efficient power amplifier with a short piece of fiber only 2 m long. When the pump power is increased, the pulse peak power is increasing steadily up to 770 W peak power corresponding to a 650ns pulse energy of 450µJ (Figure 2 left). The ASE fraction in the total output power is 6% at that point and the slope efficiency is 23%. For 108ns pulses, the peak power is increased up to the SBS threshold at 1120W (Figure 2 right). The ASE fraction is then below 1%.

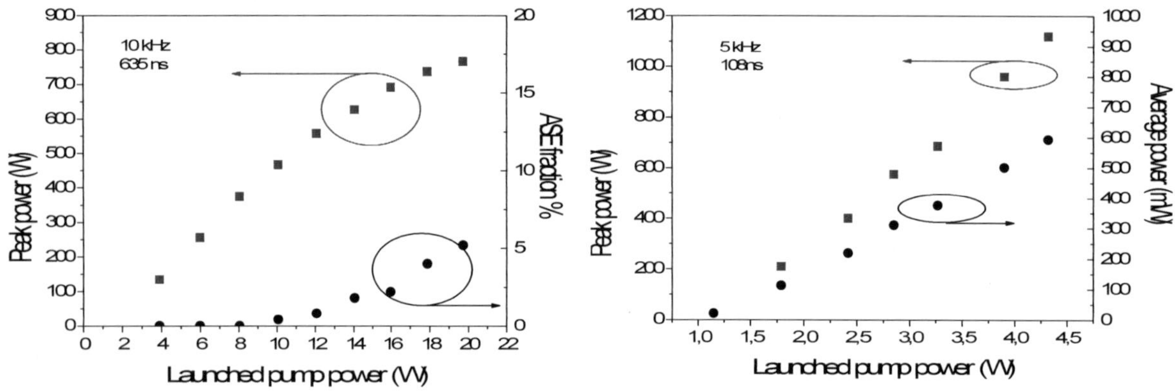

Figure 2. Pulse peak power with respect to launched pump power in the pulsed setup. Left: pulse duration = 635ns; PRF = 10 kHz. The ASE fraction in total power is shown on the right axis. Right: pulse duration =108ns; PRF = 5 kHz. The average power is shown on the right axis.

2.2. Strain distribution

A second way to decrease the Brillouin effect is to minimize the integral of the power over the fiber length. By definition, this term is also equal to the product of fiber output power times effective length L_{eff}. In a standard fiber, all the fiber length contributes to Brillouin reflectivity at the same characteristic frequency. A strain gradient applied along the fiber can be used to make each fiber segment contribute to different frequencies and spread the reflected light spectrum [8] thus allowing higher optical peak power in the fiber before reaching the Brillouin threshold.

We have recently developed a high power single-frequency all-fiber MOPFA using high reliability passive components and this strain technique. This MOPFA was used in the first experimental demonstration of a fiber laser based wind LIDAR with more than 10 km range [9]. We have been able to spread the light reflected by 25µm core fiber resulting into an increase of more than 3 dB on the SBS threshold. Without the strain gradient, SBS limits the pulse peak power to 300 W (200 µJ per 600 ns pulses). The M^2 is measured to be less than 1.3 in both axes. With the strain gradient applied to the doped fiber, peak power up to 630W was achieved (350 µJ per 550 ns pulses) (see Figure 3).

Since then, this technique has been applied to design HEPILAS a high power laser emitting at 1579nm for space application (see Figure 4). The aim of this ESA project was to study a proof of concept for monitoring CO_2 from space with a Differential Absorption LIDAR (DIAL) based on an all-fiber laser. 1.7 kW peak power was obtained for 150 ns pulses with excellent beam pointing stability. A factor of 3 gain was obtained with a modest value of strain so as to ensure that the fiber lifetime was compatible with a 5 years duration space mission. The laser was also designed so as to withstand 10 kRad radiations thanks to iXfiber radhard active fiber [10].

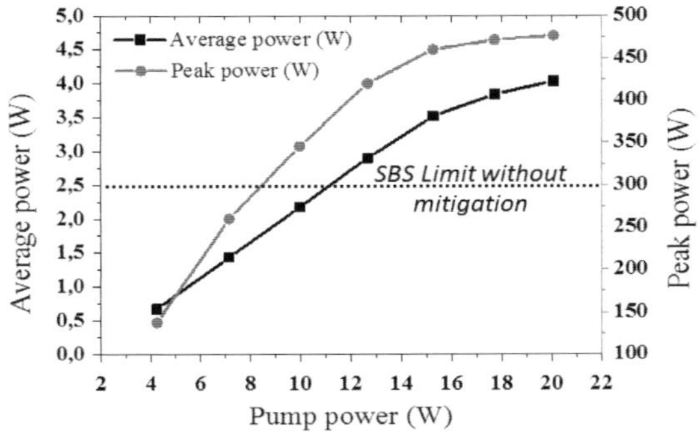

Figure 3. Evolution of the average power and peak power out of the high power amplifier with fiber straining. Dotted line: amplifier maximum peak power without strain implementation

Figure 4 : the integrated engineering model of fiber laser HEPILAS for CO2 monitoring from space.

2.3. Coherent combining

The third strategy to tune equation (1) is to coherently add up the energy emitted by several fibers limited by SBS while preserving the good beam quality. Coherent Beam Combination (CBC) allows improving the output power of MOPFA sources by adding the outputs of single amplifiers. To achieve this, two or more amplifiers seeded by the same pulsed oscillator are coherently combined into a singlemode beam. To achieve high CBC efficiency the phase differences are compensated using a controller. We have recently demonstrated CBC of two amplifiers in 100 ns-pulse regime limited to 95 and 123 W, respectively resulting in peak power of 208 W [11]. Beam quality and spectral linewidth were maintained. This source has been successfully tested in a LIDAR configuration [12]. The setup of the CBC of two pulse amplifiers is shown on Figure 5.

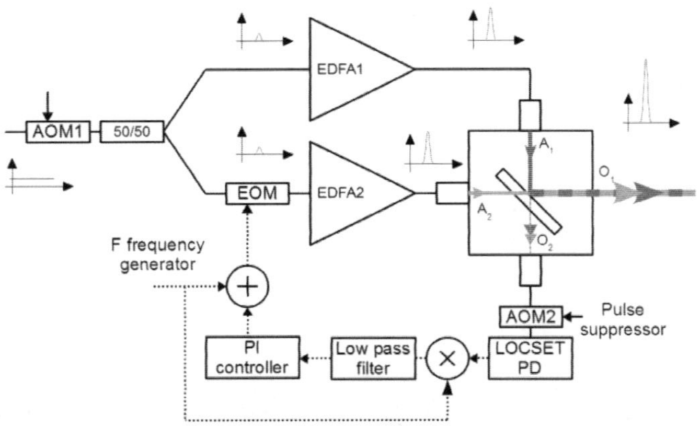

Figure 5. Coherently combined pulsed amplifier setup. Output O1 carries the total power of outputs A1 and A2.

In particular, we demonstrated that the pulse operation CBC phase controller does not impair the LIDAR performances. Indeed, the source of Figure 5 has been used as a Booster in a LIDAR Setup with 240ns pulse duration. We have compared the LIDAR performances when running (A) one amplifier at full power, (B) two amplifiers at half power and (C) two amplifiers at full power. The estimated wind speed time serie is shown on Figure 6. The Power spectral densities (PSD) of each recorded time evolutions are reported in Figure 7.

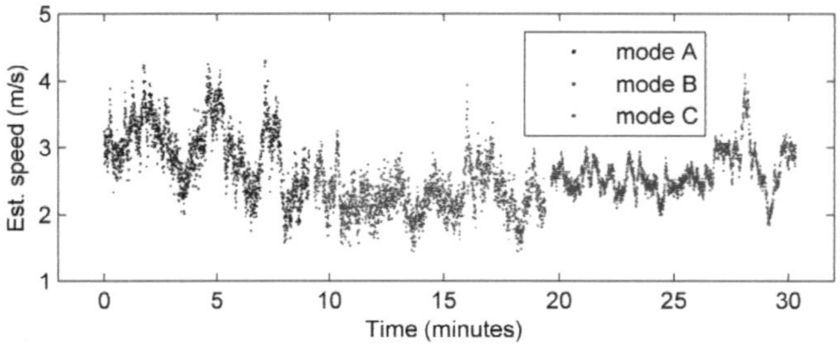

Figure 6 Estimated wind speed as recorded by the wind LIDAR in configurations A, B and C.

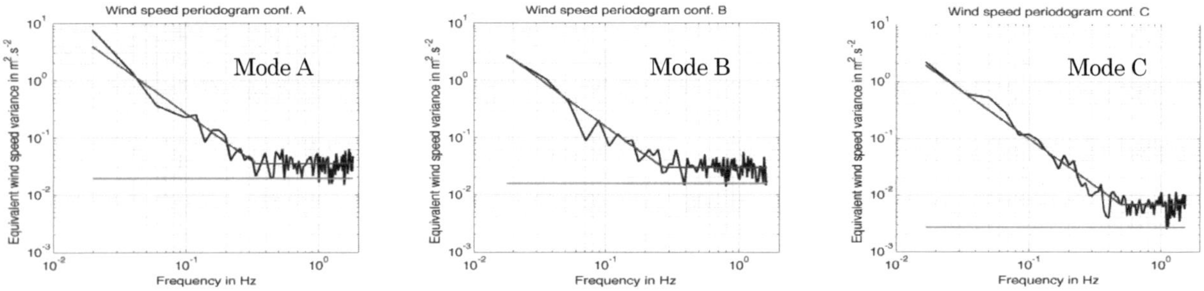

Figure 7 LIDAR performance comparison at 150m – Instrument noise floor comparison; blue: PSD of estimated wind speed from figure 6; red (low freq.): $\alpha f^{-5/3}$ Kolmogorov law (α fitted to data); red (high freq.): LIDAR noise floor fitted to data; green: LIDAR theoretical noise floor from estimated CNR (Cramer-Rao bound).

The extracted noise floors (0.21m/s for mode A, 0.19m/s for mode B and 0.08m/s for mode C) show that no performance degradation has been measured when using CBC. When both amplifiers are run at full power, the expected LIDAR performance improvement is reached. In all cases, the LIDAR performance is very close to its optimum given by the Cramer-Rao bound.

Those results show the compatibility of coherent beam combining with coherent wind LIDAR. Potentially, tens to hundreds of those amplifiers can be combined by this technique.

3. Long range Lidar measurements

Building wind Lidars based on these high power sources enabled to achieve new record ranges in 2015 [13]. Onera wind lidar system LICORNE is based on the architecture shown in figure 1 and can implement various high power sources or new components. Sample results are illustrated on figure 8 in a fixed line of sight configuration: the wind-speed spectrogram shows that ranges beyond 15 km are achieved with 0.1 s averaging time. The carrier to noise ratio and the estimated wind-speed are averaged over 1024 pulses, corresponding to 0.1 s acquisition time with a simple centroïd frequency estimation method.

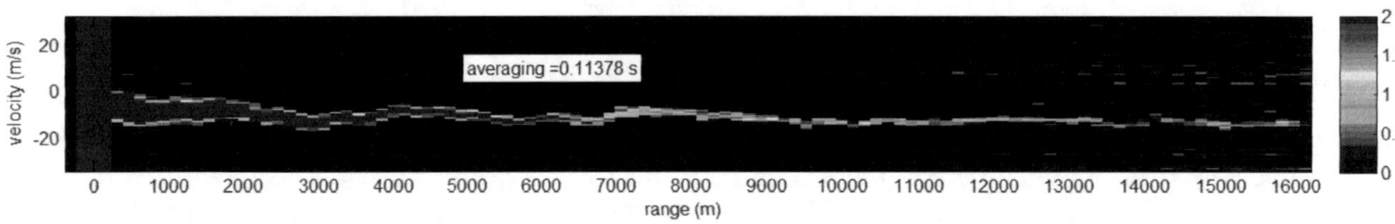

Figure 8: Wind-speed spectrograms versus range. Color scale is the power spectral density in 0.1s average time.

4. Conclusion

To improve the peak power of the lidar sources and overcome nonlinear optics limitations, we have investigated various SBS mitigation techniques and integrated them in MOFPA architectures. For example, a high power all fiber laser demonstrator for CO_2 monitoring from space has been developed.

Using PAS Erbium-Ytterbium doped fiber with 30 µm diameter, we achieved 1120 W peak power, 108ns pulses. 630W peak power, 550ns pulses were achieved using Onera strain gradient technique. Peak power can be further increased thanks to coherent beam combining of several fiber lasers and the principle of a wind lidar based on this technology has been demonstrated.

Onera wind lidars based on new high power, high spectral brightness, all-fiber sources have been used in various lidar configurations to demonstrate record ranges and EDR measurements. Indeed, horizontal air speed profiling up to 16 km in 0.1 s has been achieved, enabling to monitor large areas.

Optimized coherent lidar architectures with high power single mode fiber lasers offer new prospects for air speed and gas monitoring which should benefit to airport safety, aircraft navigation or atmosphere monitoring.

5. References

[1] G. Canat, Y. Jaouën, et J.-C. Mollier, « Performance and limitations of high brightness Er+3–Yb3+ fiber sources », *Comptes Rendus Phys.*, vol. 7, n° 2, p. 177-186, mars 2006.

[2] G. Kulcsar, Y. Jaouen, G. Canat, E. Olmedo, et G. Debarge, « Multiple-Stokes stimulated Brillouin scattering generation in pulsed high-power double-cladding Er/sup 3+/-Yb/sup 3+/-codoped fiber amplifier », *IEEE Photonics Technol. Lett.*, vol. 15, n° 6, p. 801-803, juin 2003.

[3] Y. Jaouën, G. Canat, S. Grot, et S. Bordais, « Power limitation induced by nonlinear effects in pulsed high-power fiber amplifiers », *Comptes Rendus Phys.*, vol. 7, n° 2, p. 163-169, mars 2006.

[4] J.-P. Cariou, B. Augere, et M. Valla, « Laser source requirements for coherent lidars based on fiber technology », *Comptes Rendus Phys.*, vol. 7, n° 2, p. 213-223, mars 2006.

[5] G. Canat, S. Jetschke, S. Unger, L. Lombard, P. Bourdon, J. Kirchhof, J. V., A. Dolfi, et O. Vasseur, « Multifilament-core fibers for high energy pulse amplification at 1.5 µm with excellent beam quality », *Opt. Lett.*, vol. 33, n° 22, p. 2701–2703, nov. 2008.

[6] G. G. Vienne, W. S. Brocklesby, R. S. Brown, Z. J. Chen, J. D. Minelly, J. E. Roman, et D. N. Payne, « Role of Aluminum in Ytterbium–Erbium Codoped Phosphoaluminosilicate Optical Fibers », *Opt. Fiber Technol.*, vol. 2, n° 4, p. 387-393, oct. 1996.

[7] A. N. Abramov, M. M. Bubnov, N. N. Vechkanov, A. N. Guryanov, K. V. Zotov, D. S. Lipatov, M. E. Likhachev, et M. V. Yashkov, « Fabrication of heavily Er2O3 doped aluminophosphosilicate glass fibers », *Inorg. Mater.*, vol. 46, n° 4, p. 439-444, avr. 2010.

[8] J. M. C. Boggio, J. D. Marconi, et H. L. Fragnito, « Experimental and numerical investigation of the SBS-threshold increase in an optical fiber by applying strain distributions », *J. Light. Technol.*, vol. 23, n° 11, p. 3808-3814, nov. 2005.

[9] W. Renard, D. Goular, M. Valla, C. Planchat, B. Augere, A. Dolfi-Bouteyre, C. Besson, et G. Canat, « Beyond 10 Km Range wind-speed measurement with a 1.5 µm all-fiber laser source », 2014, p. AW1P.5.

[10] G. Canat, W. Renard, T. Robin, B. Cadier, J. L. Gouët, L. Lombard, A. Durecu, et P. Bourdon, « High peak power single frequency amplifiers based on efficient Erbium-Ytterbium doped LMA fibers », in *2015 European Conference on Lasers and Electro-Optics - European Quantum Electronics Conference*, 2015, p. CJ_12_5.

[11] L. Lombard, A. Azarian, K. Cadoret, P. Bourdon, D. Goular, G. Canat, V. Jolivet, Y. Jaouen, et O. Vasseur, « Coherent beam combination of narrow-linewidth 1.5µm fiber amplifiers in a long-pulse regime », *Opt. Lett.*, vol. 36, n° 4, p. 523-525, février 2011.

[12] L. Lombard, M. Valla, C. Planchat, D. Goular, B. Augère, P. Bourdon, et G. Canat, « Eyesafe coherent detection wind lidar based on a beam-combined pulsed laser source », *Opt. Lett.*, vol. 40, n° 6, p. 1030-1033, mars 2015.

[13] C. Besson, B. Augere, G. Canat, A. Dolfi-Bouteyre, D. Fleury, D. Goular, J. Le Gouët, L. Lombard, C. Planchat, M. Valla, et W. Renard, « Recent achievements in Doppler Lidars for aircraft certification », présenté à ETTC, 2015.

Greater than 1mJ pulse energy single frequency fiber lasers at 1 micron wavelength

Single-frequency pulsed fiber lasers with high pulse energy and high peak power are needed for coherent lidar applications. Fiber-based laser sources are much more reliable and more suitable for these applications, especially for their field deployment, but the pulse energy is limited to a few hundred microjoules. In this paper we will present our recent progress of high pulse energy single frequency fiber laser at 1 micron wavelength using our proprietary Yb-doped fibers. A polarization maintaining Yb-doped fiber with a large mode field diameter was developed to effectively suppress stimulated Brillouin scattering (SBS). A singe frequency narrow linewidth laser is modulated and amplified via MOPA configuration. A pulse energy of greater than 1.4 mJ with pulse width of 31 ns was demonstrated, which represents several times increase in pulse energy and peak power. The beam quality M2 is less than 1.1. Single frequency fiber lasers with pulse width from 5 ns to 400 ns will be presented as well.

Improved Analytic Equations for Estimating the Performance of Truncated and Aberrated Gaussian-Beam Coherent Lidar

Sammy W. Henderson and Don Jacob[1]
Beyond Photonics
1650 Coal Creek Dr., Ste. B, Lafayette, CO 80026
sammy@beyondphotonics.com

Abstract: An approximate analytic equation for modeling the antenna efficiency of coherent lidar systems has been used by the lidar community for many years. This equation assumes perfect untrucated Gaussian beams and as such can lead to significant errors in performance predictions of real lidar systems. The best performance predictions are of course obtained by performing detailed numerical calculations that include all the intensity and wavefront details of the transmitted and back-propagated local oscillator beams, as well as the refractive turbulence profile in the atmosphere, but these calculations can be difficult and time consuming for trading the performance as system parameters are varied. We have developed an improved analytic approximation for calculating the antenna efficiency of Gaussian beam coherent lidar systems that includes the impact of beam quality, truncation, focus, and refractive turbulence. The development of this new equation and comparison of its predictions with those of numerical calculations and the historically used approximate analytic expression will be presented.

Keywords: Coherent Lidar, Modeling, Antenna Efficiency

1. Untruncated Gaussian Beam Lidar Antenna Efficiency

Unaberrated Gaussian beam propagation and antenna efficiency equations including misalignment have been previously described and are only briefly reviewed here due to limited space. In addition, we ignore refractive turbulence in this summary to allow room for more discussion of the impact of truncation and aberrations on antenna efficiency. Impacts of refractive turbulence will be discussed briefly in the presentation.

As described in detail in Reference 1, the untruncated Gaussian beam (UGB) antenna efficiency for arbitrary Gaussian beam sizes and overlap is given by

$$\eta_{a,UGB}(z) = \psi(z) exp\left[-2\left(\frac{\delta r(z)}{\omega_{dB}(z)}\right)^2 \psi(z)\right], \tag{1}$$

$$\text{with, } \psi(z) = \left[\frac{\omega_t^2(z)+\omega_b^2(z)}{\omega_{db}^2(z)}\right]^{-1}. \tag{2}$$

In these equations, $\omega_t(z)$ and $\omega_b(z)$ are the e^{-2} intensity radii of the transmit and back propagated local oscillator (BPLO) beams at range z, respectively, $\omega_{db}(z)$ is the diffraction limited spot size of the BPLO given by $\omega_{db}(z) = \lambda z/\pi\omega_{ob}$, where ω_{ob} is the e^{-2} beam waist intensity radius of the BPLO and $\delta r(z)$ is the offset of the two beam centers.

This can also be written as,

$$\psi(z) = \left[\frac{1}{S_t(z)} + \frac{1}{S_b(z)}\right]^{-1}. \tag{3}$$

[1] Coherent Research Group, Key West Florida

where, $S_t(z)$ and $S_b(z)$ are the Strehl ratios of the transmit and BPLO beams, defined as the peak on-axis intensity of the beams relative to that of the untruncated diffraction-limited BPLO beam focused at range z. In other words,

$$S_i(z) = \frac{I_{o,i}(z)}{I_{o,dB}(z)} = \frac{2P}{\pi\omega_i^2(z)} \Big/ \frac{2P}{\pi\omega_{db}^2(z)} = \frac{\omega_{db}^2(z)}{\omega_i^2(z)}. \quad (4)$$

The above equations are valid for unmatched Gaussian beam sizes and arbitrary misalignments, but in order to simplify the following discussion on truncated and aberrated beams we assume the beams are co-aligned and matched in size. In this case the above equations simplify to

$$\eta_{a,UGB}(z) = \frac{1}{A_u}\frac{\lambda^2 z^2}{\pi\omega^2(z)} = \frac{S(z)}{2}. \quad (5)$$

where $A_u = 2\pi\omega_o^2$ is the effective aperture area of an UGB lidar [1] and where ω_o is the e^{-2} beam waist intensity radius of the transmit beam. Although we assume matched transmit and BPLO beams for simplicity in the rest of this summary, it is straightforward to follow the same development and derive approximate analytic equations for unmatched beam lidar systems.

2. Truncated Gaussian Beam Antenna Efficiency

We next investigate the antenna efficiency of truncated Gaussian beams (TGB). We assume a circular aperture with the incident Gaussian beam centered on the aperture and the truncation level defined by the truncation ratio, $\rho_T = \omega_o/a$, with a being the aperture radius. The far field irradiance profiles of TGBs at moderate truncation ratios have a significant fraction of the diffracted energy in the central diffraction lobe – for example, if $\rho_T = 0.8$, 95.6% of the energy is transmitted through the aperture and 98.3% of that transmitted energy is in the central diffraction lobe. It is therefore reasonable to expect that the UGB antenna efficiency equations can be used to provide a first order estimate for the antenna efficiency of a TGB lidar, especially in the far field at moderate truncation ratios.

For an UGB, the antenna efficiency is a function of the Strehl ratio as shown in Equation 5. Therefore, as a first attempt at deriving a suitable analytic expression for the TGB antenna efficiency, we use what we name the Strehl-based antenna efficiency (SAE) approximation.

The on-axis intensity of a TGB with arbitrary focus and truncation ratio, found by solving the Fresnel integral equation, is

$$I(0,z) = \frac{\frac{2P}{\pi\omega_0^2}}{\left(1-\frac{z}{F}\right)^2 + \left(\frac{\lambda z}{\pi\omega_0^2}\right)^2}\left[\left(1 + e^{-\frac{2}{\rho_t^2}}\right) - 2e^{-\frac{1}{\rho_t^2}}\cos\left[\pi\frac{a^2}{\lambda}\left(\frac{1}{z} - \frac{1}{F}\right)\right]\right]. \quad (6)$$

In terms of the effective Fresnel distance, $\frac{1}{z_{Fe}} = \left|\frac{1}{z} - \frac{1}{F}\right|$, the effective Fresnel number, $N_{Fe} = \frac{a^2}{\lambda z_{Fe}}$, and the magnification, $m = \frac{z}{z_{Fe}}$, this can be written as

$$I(0,z) = \frac{1}{m^2}\frac{I(0,0)}{1+\left(\frac{1}{\rho_t}\right)^4\left(\frac{1}{\pi N_{Fe}}\right)^2}\left[\left(1 + e^{-2\left(\frac{1}{\rho_t}\right)^2}\right) - 2e^{-\left(\frac{1}{\rho_t}\right)^2}\cos[\pi N_{Fe}]\right]. \quad (7)$$

Thus, the on-axis intensity is only a function of the truncation ratio, the effective Fresnel number, and a magnification factor, which depends on the focus conditions. In general, the 2-dimensional intensity patterns of the diffracted beam at any range are also only a function these parameters. Example, radial intensity profiles as a function of effective Fresnel number are shown in Figure 1 for a truncation ratio of 0.8. Also shown is the intensity profile of the untruncated Gaussian beam, and the Gaussian beam fit determined using our CSAE model, with proper irradiance scaling for reference.

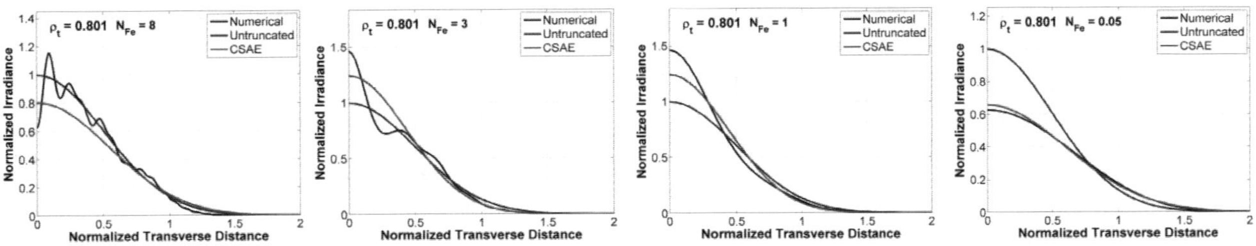

Figure 1. Example normalized irradiance profiles for a TGB vs. Fresnel number. The UGB and the CSAE Guassian beam (described later) are also shown with correct relative irradiance for reference.

The truncated and aberrated irradiance profiles presented throughout this paper are numerically calculated using a diverging grid FFT beam propagator algorithm based on the Sziklas-Siegman algorithm [2,3]. The diverging grid approach permits one to propagate finite and phase modulated beams over long distances while maintaining sufficient grid sampling.

The numerically calculated antenna efficiencies shown later in this paper are computed from the target plane normalized irradiance overlap integral of the transmit and BPLO fields as

$$\eta_a(z) = \eta_{Tx}\eta_{Tb}\frac{\lambda^2 z^2}{A_r}\iint I_{nx}(x,y,z)\, I_{nb}(x,y,z)dxdy\,, \tag{8}$$

where η_{Tx} and η_{Tb} are the truncation efficiencies of the transmit and BPLO beams, respectively, and I_{nx} and I_{nb} are, respectively, the normalized to unit power two dimensional target plane irradiance distributions of the transmit and BPLO fields. As noted above, for this paper, we assumes matched transmit and BPLO beams, so $\eta_{Tx} = \eta_{Tb} = \eta_T$.

Using Equation 6, we find that the Strehl ratio is

$$S(z) = \frac{I(0,z)}{2P/\pi\omega_d^2(z)} = \frac{\omega_d^2(z)}{\omega^2(z)}\left[\left(1 + e^{-\frac{2}{\rho_t^2}}\right) - 2e^{-\frac{1}{\rho_t^2}}\cos\left[\pi\frac{a^2}{\lambda}\left(\frac{1}{z} - \frac{1}{F}\right)\right]\right], \tag{9}$$

$$\text{with,}\ \ \omega^2(z) = \omega_o^2\left[\left(1 - \frac{z}{F}\right)^2 + \left(\frac{\lambda z}{\pi\omega_o^2}\right)^2\right]. \tag{10}$$

To convert from the UGB beam antenna efficiency expression to the TGB SAE approximation we account for the different effective aperture areas and the truncation losses using

$$\eta_{a,S}(z) \approx f_c\frac{A_u}{A_r}\eta_T^2\eta_{a,UGB}(z) \approx \eta_T\rho_T^2 f_c S(z) = \eta_T^2\frac{(\lambda z)^2}{A_r}\frac{1}{\pi\omega_{eff,S}^2(z)}, \tag{11}$$

where $\frac{A_u}{A_r} = \frac{2\pi(\rho_T a)^2}{\pi a^2} = 2\rho_T^2$, $\omega_{eff,S}^2(z) = \frac{\eta_T}{f_c S(z)}\omega_d^2(z)$ is the effective Gaussian beam size, $\eta_T = 1 - \exp(-\frac{2}{\rho_t^2})$ is the truncation efficiency, and f_c is a correction factor to allow an improved fit to the numerically calculated far-field antenna efficiency.

In the far field, when $N_{Fe} \ll 1$, the SAE model works well, but a small correction factor, f_c, is needed to account for the fact that the far field beams are not exact Gaussians. The antenna efficiency vs truncation ratio for a matched beam coherent lidar is shown in the left panel of Figure 2. Note the good agreement with the numerical prediction over most truncation ratio values.

The required correction factor as a function of the truncation ratio is shown in the right panel of Figure 2. The correction factor is small varying between 0.95 and 1.05 over truncation ratios from 0 to 2. Below truncation ratio of 0.5 the beams are UGBs, and SAE model is exact.

Upon careful comparison of the antenna efficiency predicted by the SAE model with numerically calculated values, we found that the SEA model overestimates the antenna efficiency in the intermediate field (with N_{Fe} between approximately 0.25 and 1.5). Upon examination of the diffraction patterns in this

Fresnel number range, this is understood as due to the on-axis irradiance peak occurring over this range (near $N_{Fe} = 1$) resulting in a Gaussian beam fit with a waist size, $\omega_{eff,S}$, that is too small, which in turn results in a predicted antenna efficiency that is too high.

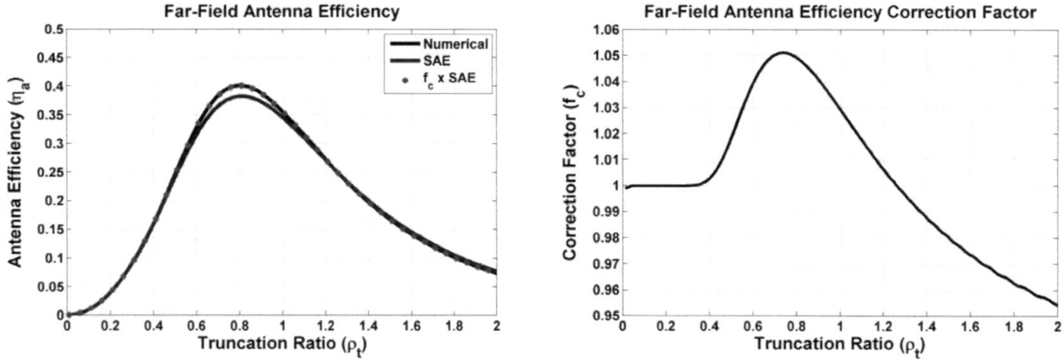

Figure 2. Left Panel: Blue curve - predicted antenna efficiency using the SAE model. Black curve-numerical calculation. Red dashed – SAE model using correction factor shown in the right panel. Right Panel: Required correction factor, f_c, with truncation ratio.

This is illustrated in Figure 3 for two focus conditions of 500 m (top row) and infinity (bottom row)) and 4 truncation ratios, 0.55, 0.8, 1.2, and 2.0. The antenna efficiency of three different models is compared to the numerically calculated antenna efficiency (see Figure caption). At a truncation ratio of 0.55 all the models are good since the beams are essentially untruncated. Note that the scaled (to the far field antenna efficiency) UGB model significantly underestimates the antenna efficiency over much of the range and underestimates the depth of focus, especially at higher truncation ratios. The SAE model (which now includes the f_c factor) does better than the scaled UGB model, but as discussed above it overestimates the antenna efficiency in the intermediate field. The corrected Strehl antenna efficiency (CSAE) analytic model, which we describe below, fits the antenna efficiency very well.

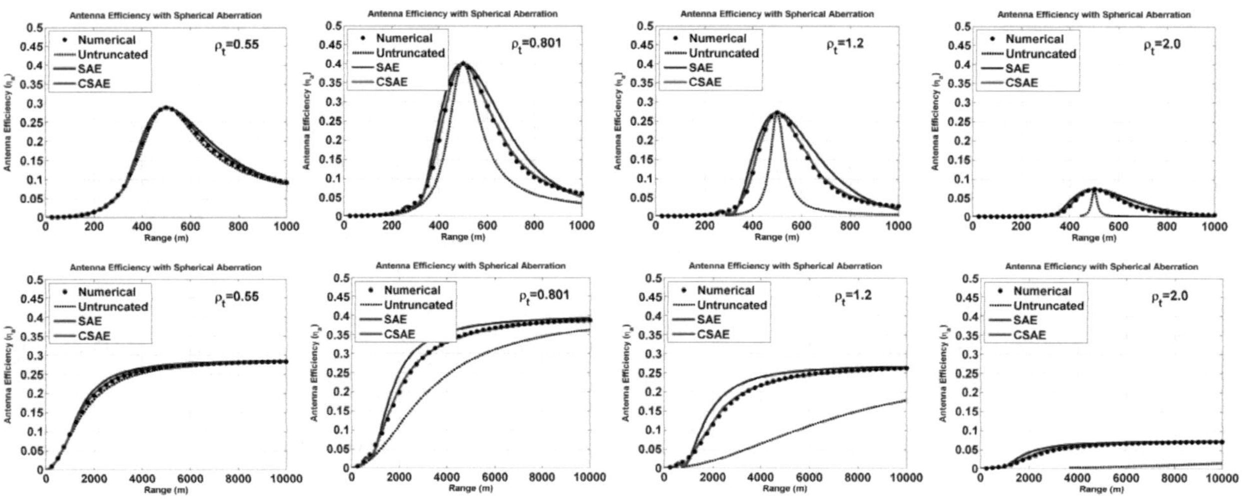

Figure 3. Comparison of numerically calculated antenna efficiency (dots) with: Black Dashed - the UGB model scaled to match the numerically calculated far-field antenna efficiency. Blue- the SAE model with the correction factor shown in Figure 3 applied. Red – Red the CSAE model.

We took into account the above noted behavior in the different effective Fresnel number ranges and constructed the CSAE analytic model to better optimize the performance across the entire range of Fresnel numbers.

First, we define two regimes in terms of the effective Fresnel distance which meet at $z_{Fe} = z_b$, given by

$$z_b = z_R \sqrt{\frac{b - 1/{M^2}^2}{{M^2}^2 - b}}\,, \qquad (12)$$

where $z_R = \frac{\pi\omega_0^2}{\lambda}$, $b = \frac{1 - exp\left(-\frac{2}{\rho_T^2}\right)}{1 + exp\left(-\frac{2}{\rho_T^2}\right)}$, and M^2 is the beam spreading factor given by

$$M^2 = \sqrt{\frac{\eta_{Tx}}{f_c S(F)}}\,. \qquad (13)$$

where $S(F) = \left(1 - e^{-\frac{1}{\rho_t^2}}\right)^2$ is the far field Strehl ratio (at the focus),

In the regime $z_{Fe} \leq z_b$

$$\omega_{eff,l}^2 = b\omega_d^2\,. \qquad (14)$$

In the regime $z_{Fe} \geq z_b$

$$\omega_{eff,g}^2 = \omega_0^2\left[\frac{1}{{M^2}^2}\left(1 - \frac{z}{f}\right)^2 + {M^2}^2\left(\frac{z}{z_R}\right)^2\right]. \qquad (15)$$

The refined effective beam size to use in Eq. 11 is then given by the average of the squares as

$$\omega_{eff}^2 = \frac{\omega_{eff,s}^2 + \omega_{eff,l}^2}{2} \qquad for \quad z_{Fe} \leq z_b \qquad (16)$$

and

$$\omega_{eff}^2 = \frac{\omega_{eff,s}^2 + \omega_{eff,l}^2}{2} \qquad for \quad z_{Fe} \leq z_b \qquad (17)$$

3. Aberrated and Truncated Beams

We have also developed an analytic expression that approximates the loss due to aberrations. The analytic Strehl expression is used to find the impact of the defocus aberration, which in terms of the rms aberration over the full aperture is

$$\eta_{a,ATGB} \approx f_c \eta_T \rho_t^2 S = \frac{f_c \rho_t^2\left(1 - e^{-\frac{2}{\rho_t^2}}\right)}{\left[1 + \left(2\pi\sqrt{12}\,\rho_t^2 \sigma_{df}\right)^2\right]}\left[\left(1 + e^{-\frac{2}{\rho_t^2}}\right) - 2e^{-\frac{1}{\rho_t^2}} cos\left[2\pi\sqrt{12}\,\sigma_{df}\right]\right] \qquad (18)$$

We find that with a slight modification to this expression we can approximate the far field antenna efficiency for specific primary aberrations. In each case we replace $\sqrt{12}$ in the numerator and denominator of the above expression with the following: for defocus $\sqrt{18\sqrt{\rho_t}}$, for spherical less defocus $\sqrt{\frac{24}{\rho_t}}$, and for astigmatism less defocus $\sqrt{12\rho_t}$. The numerical calculated antenna efficiency as a function of the rms wavefront aberration for these primary aberration types as well as coma less tilt, and for random aberrations, is shown in Figure 4. This is similar to past work [5,6] but with the primary difference that we remove defocus and tilt to minimize the rms phase over the full aperture.

For truncation ratios of 0.801 and larger (i.e., for fairly well filled aperture conditions) the degradation of the antenna efficiency with wavefront aberration predicted by these analytic expressions agrees relatively well with the simple Strehl expression given in Wyant [7] for a uniformly filled aperture, $S \approx e^{-(2\pi\sigma)^2}$, scaled to the maximum far field antenna efficiency. At lower truncation ratios, where the aperture is less well filled, the beams see less of the aberration of the full aperture and the degradation is less.

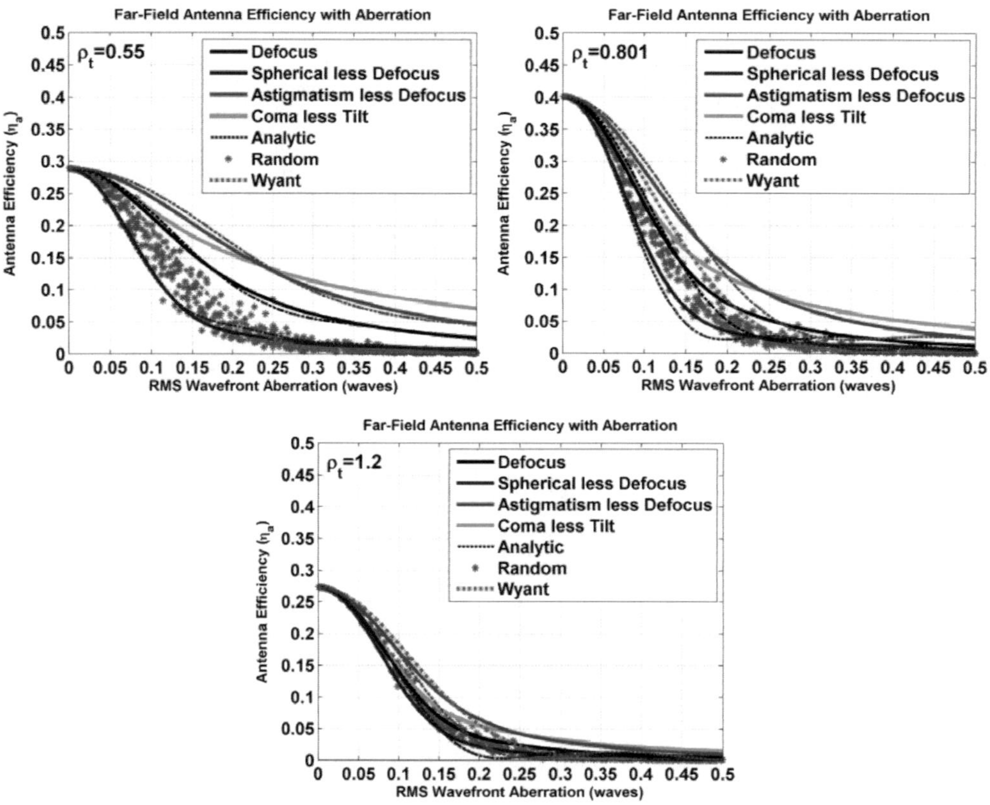

Figure 4. Comparison of antenna efficiency vs. rms wavefront aberration level for: solid curves - numerically calculated using primary aberrations, light dots –numerically calculated using random aberrations, dashed - analytic model prediction.

4. Conclusions

An improved analytic model for estimating the antenna efficiency of truncated and aberrated Gaussian beam coherent lidar systems has been developed. We are continuing to improve the model and more details will be given in the presentation.

References

[1] S.W. Henderson, P. Gatt, D. Rees, and R.M. Huffaker, **Wind Lidar**, book chapter in Laser Remote Sensing, Eds. Fujii and Fukuchi, CRC Press, Taylor and Francis Group, Boca Raton, FL, p 469-722, (2005) – see Sections 7.4.1.4.2.1 and 7.4.1.5.

[2] E. A. Sziklas and A. E. Siegman, "Mode calculations in unstable resonators with flowing saturable gain: Fast Fourier transform method," Appl. Opt. 14, 1874-1889 (1975).

[3] P. Hello, J. Y. Vinet, "Simulation of beam propagation in off-axis optical systems," J. Optics (Paris), 27, 265-276 (1996).

[5] G. Spiers, "Effect of Optical Aberrations on the Performance of Coherent Doppler Lidar", Proc. Of the 10th Coherent Laser Radar Conf., Mount Hood, Oregon, June 28 – July 2, 1999, pages 170 – 174.

[6] Barry Rye, "Primary aberration contribution to incoherent backscatter heterodyne lidar returns" Appl Opt 21, 839 (1982)

[7] J.C., Wyant and K., Creath, "Basic Wavefront Aberration Theory for Optical Metrology" Applied Optics and Optical Engineering, vol. 11, Chap., 1 (1992)

Evaluation of Simulated and Observed Wind Profile Measurements from an Airborne Doppler Lidar

Timothy A. Bonin, A. Choukulkar, W. A. Brewer, R. M. Hardesty, and S. Baidar

CIRES, NOAA ESRL Atmospheric Remote Sensing

Motivation for Airborne Doppler lidar

- Ability to capture a snapshot of the 2-D flow field over a short period of time
- Understand flows over complex terrain, surface boundaries, coastal areas, etc
- Paired with measurements of trace gases, can evaluate how pollutants are dispersed and transported

Ozone profiles from
Tunable Optical Profiler for Aerosol and oZone lidar (TOPAZ)

Key challenges and limitations

- Need to compensate for aircraft motion in determining radial velocities
- Beam azimuthal and elevation angles need to be corrected for the pitch/roll/yaw of aircraft
- Large elevation angle is typically used
  - Radial velocities are particularly sensitive to vertical winds, reducing accuracy of horizontal wind measurements
  - Particularly apparent within the planetary boundary layer

Airborne Doppler lidar simulator using Large Eddy Simulation

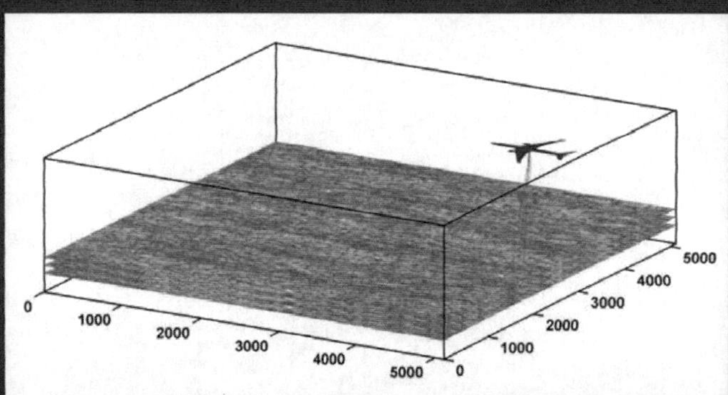

Parameters:
Aircraft speed: 60 m s^{-1}
Profile config: 4, 6, 8 beams
PRF: 10,000 Hz
Pulse averaging: 10,000
Scanner delay: 1 s
Scanner angle: 11°, 22°, and 45° degrees off nadir
Beam positioning: Centered, offset

Beam positioning

Offset

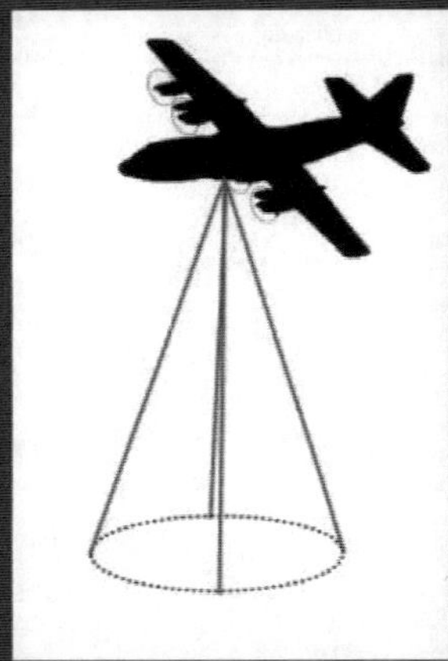

Centered

Use of Large Eddy Simulation (LES) output

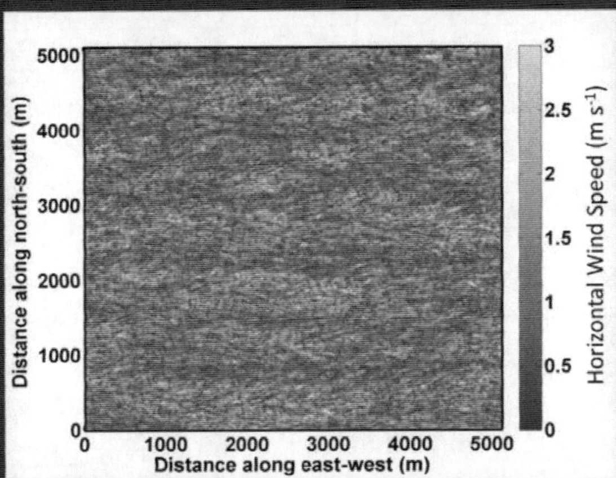

LES flow simulation over forest canopy (Patton et al., 2012; 2016)

Domain size: 5120m X 5120m

Horizontal Resolution: 2.5 m

4 levels: 10m, 20m, 40m, 80m

Stability conditions: Weakly unstable, moderately unstable and strongly unstable

Significant spatial variability in vertical motion

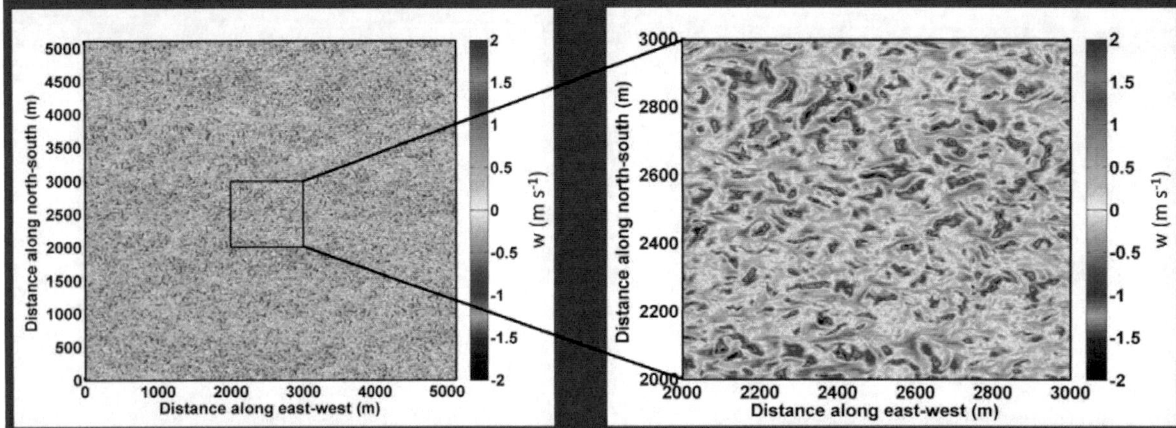

Sample scanning strategy: 4-beams

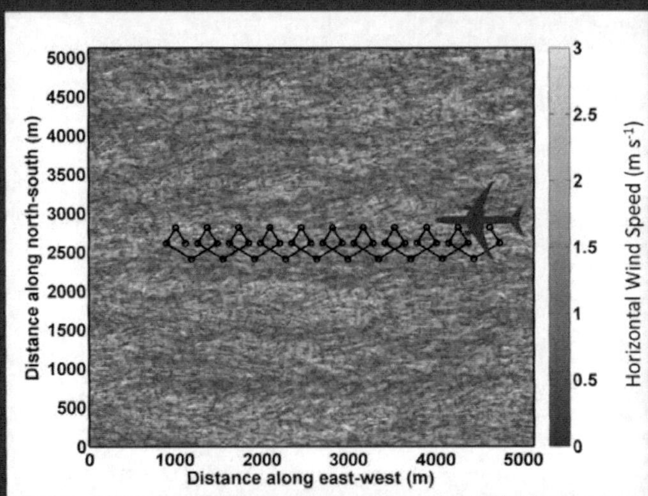

Sample scanning strategy: 6-beams

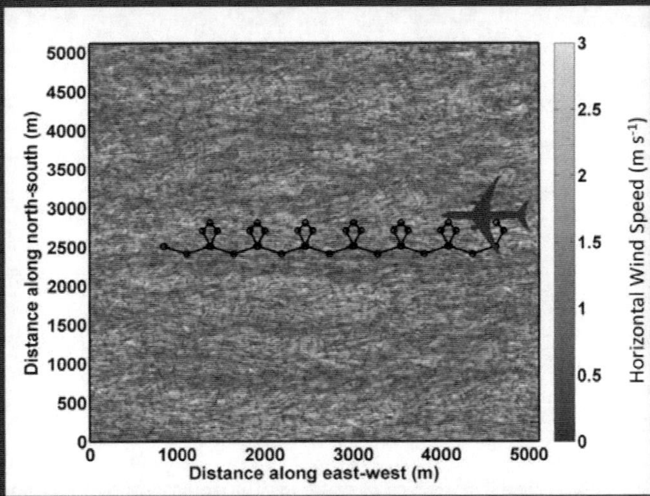

Sample scanning strategy: 8-beams

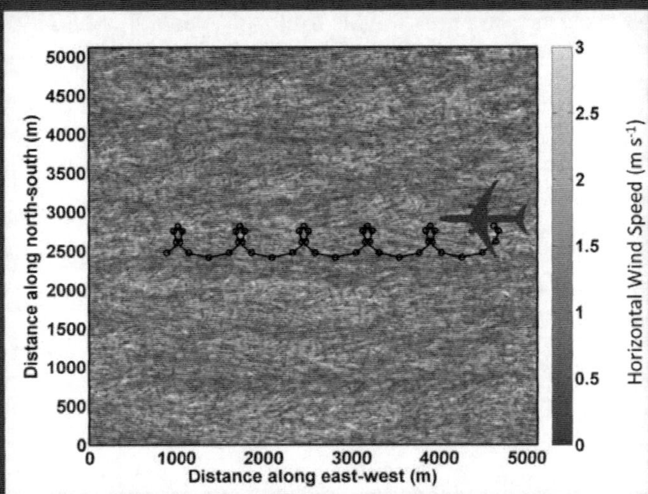

Simulated errors as a function of elevation & number of beams

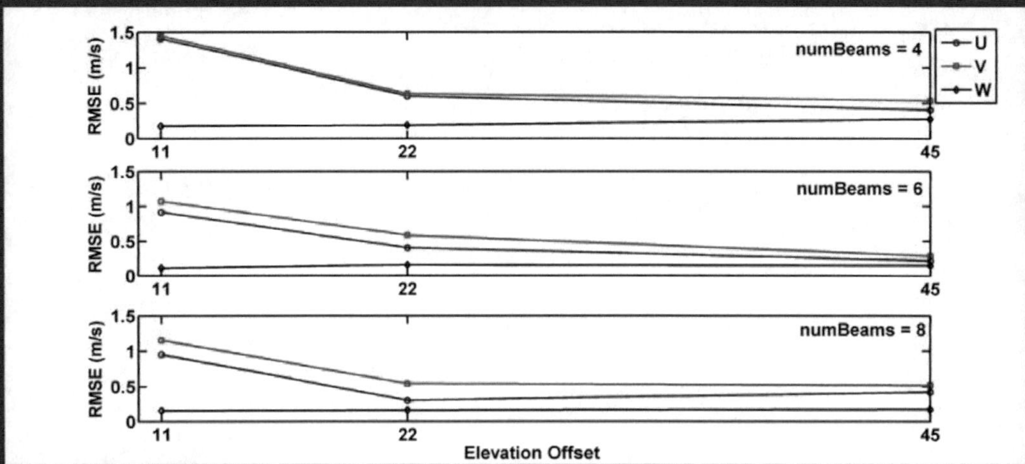

Simulated errors based on accumulation time

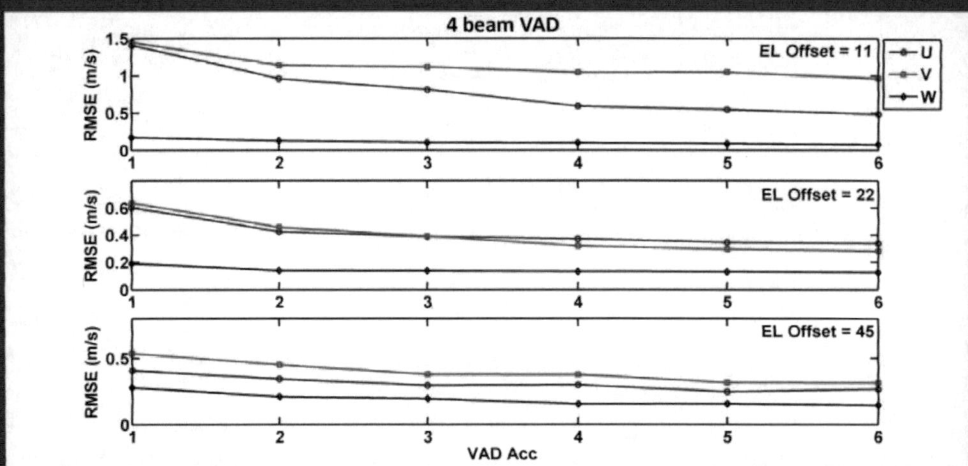

California Research at the Nexus of Air Quality and Climate Change (CalNex 2010)

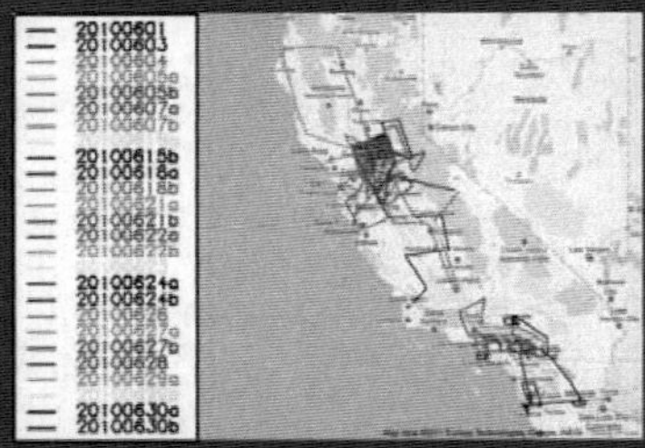

- Large collaborative experiment aimed at studying emissions and transport of pollutants and greenhouse gasses across California
    - May – July 2010
    - Multiple aircraft, surface measurements, ground-based remote sensors, and research vessel
- Data collected from a Halo Doppler lidar installed on a Twin Otter
    - 45 flights
    - 4 beam DBS used (spaced 90° in azimuth, 10.5° elevation off nadir)
    - Typical airspeed of 70 m/s

Effect of Averaging Time

- VAD profiles were made using a moving time window of radial velocities (10 sec per 4 beam VAD)
    - By including more v_r values in each VAD fit, impacts of noise and vertical velocity are reduced/averaged
    - Improvement most noticeable closer to surface in PBL

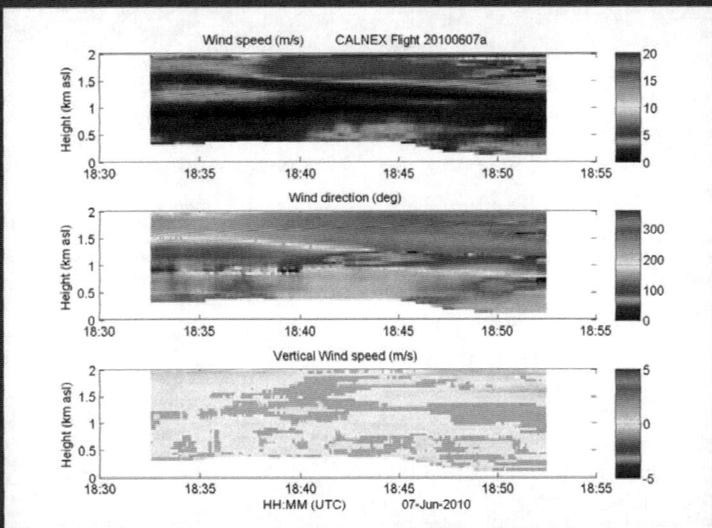

Comparisons with wind profiling radars

- 14 wind profilers operational during CalNex provided many opportunities to validate wind measurements
- Differences in averaging times (1-hr vs. sec-min), and heterogenous flows over complex terrain make direct comparison difficult

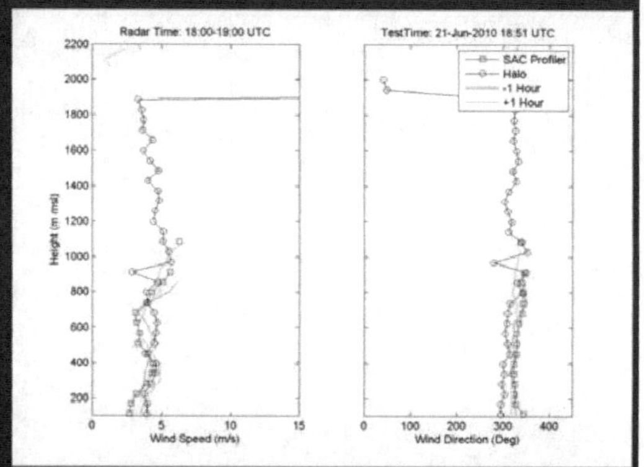

10 min avg

Statistical Validation with Wind Profilers

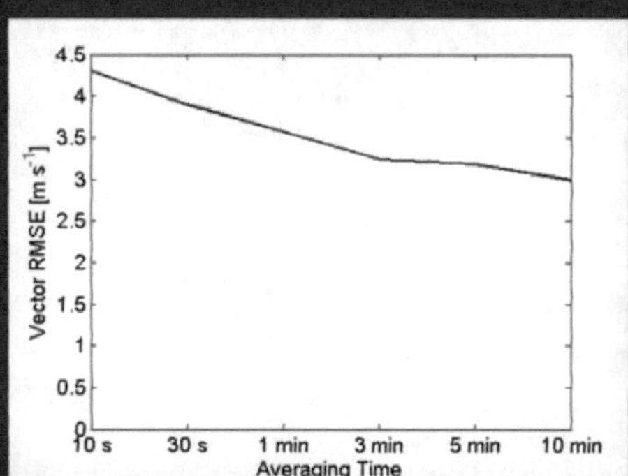

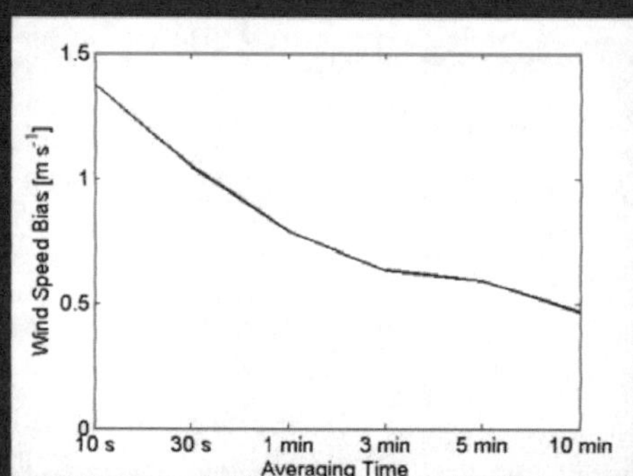

Vector RMSE = $\langle (U_{DL} - UWP)^2 + (V_{DL} - VWP)^2 \rangle^{0.5}$

brackets denote averaging

Large errors likely result of significant differences in sampling volumes and averaging times

Relationship of error with height

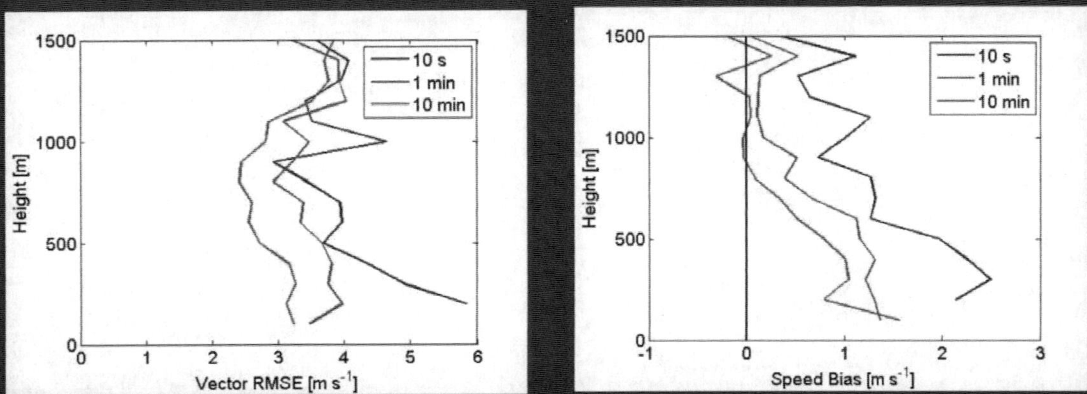

Wind measurements at higher altitudes require less averaging likely due to smaller vertical velocities near/above the boundary layer top

By combining lidar ozone and wind profiles, ozone flux can be calculated

Second transect 2 hr later shows clearly shows evolution and transport of ozone plume out of LA basin

Summary

- Developed airborne Doppler lidar simulator within Large Eddy Simulation output to quantify errors associated with different scanning techniques
- Accuracy of horizontal wind measurements within the planetary boundary layer are particularly sensitive to turbulent vertical motions
- Effects of non-uniform vertical wind can be mitigated with a longer averaging time, using more points in VAD fit
- During CALNEX, complex flows over mountainous terrain were resolved using the airborne Doppler lidar
  - Help in understanding where plumes of ozone originate, and how they are transported

Adaptive Lidar Signal Processing to Study the Diurnal Cycles of Atmospheric Boundary Layer Dynamics, Wind and Turbulence in Urban Environments

Mark Arend(a), Morann Dagan(a), Ivan Valerio(a), Sameh Abdelazim(b)
Fred Moshary(a)

(a) Department of Electrical Engineering City College of New York and NOAA CREST CUNY
New York, NY 10031
(b) School of Computer Sciences and Engineering, Fairleigh Dickinson University
Lead Author e-mail address: marend@ccny.cuny.edu

Abstract: Fiber optic based (1.5 micron) lidar technologies have been used to produce both a coherent Doppler lidar (CDL) system and a direct detection lidar (DDL) system. Special attention has been afforded in the design of the CDL system to allow for adaptive signal processing of both the accumulated correlograms and the power spectra. Both the CDL and the DDL systems require adaptive signal processing in order to account for baseline drifts that are due to both systematic changes in the operating conditions as well as dynamic changes in atmospheric boundary layer. Co-operating these two systems together (along with other meteorological profilers) has opened up opportunities to improve the vertical profiling of, wind, turbulent kinetic energy, water vapor, humidity and temperature in urban environments where diurnal cycles are often observed.

Keywords: Doppler lidar, Wind Profiler, Fiber Optics, Turbulence, Atmospheric Boundary Layer, Urban Meteorology

1. Introduction

The study of urban atmospheric boundary layer dynamics and turbulence by use of ground based profiling instrumentation provides valuable information that can be used for making decisions that affect many aspects of society (e.g. energy security, public health and safety, transportation, agriculture) as highlighted by the National Academies Press [1,2]. However, defining turbulence and deriving closed form physical solutions that are based on strict axiomatic and physical principles continues to challenge fundamental mathematical formalisms that rely on assumptions that are inherent in continuum mechanics and kinetic theory [3]. Such a challenge has inspired the continued development of fundamental theories that attempt to skirt the necessity of the Navier Stokes equation and the Boltzmann equation in order to formulate the principles of and to provide solutions to the time evolution of hydro dynamic systems [4]. Experiments that challenge and/or support these theories by providing precise multi sensor observations may discover the subtleties of such a complex system. To that end, the ability to experimentally characterize urban atmospheric boundary layer dynamics with instrumentation that both accounts for systematic drifts and fluctuations and is also capable of anticipating and adapting to changes that arise from the tempestuous nature of the atmosphere, provides a platform for which practical applications and fundamental research can be simultaneously explored. The design, operation and results of a fiber based coherent detection lidar system and a fiber based direct detection lidar system will be described in this report along with their relationships to other boundary layer monitoring instruments, specifically a microwave radiometer.

2. Instrument descriptions and analysis methods:

Coherent detection Doppler lidar. The system [5] consists of a 1542 nm CW laser fiber laser that is split in to two paths such that one path is used for a local oscillator and the other path is amplified by a single mode erbium doped fiber amplifier EDF and then modulated by an acousto-optic modulator, producing 200 nsec pulses at 20 kHz. These pulses are amplified further with a final amplifier and sent to an optical circulator before being launched in to the 4 inch clear aperture telescope from the single mode fiber. The aerosol back scattered light from the atmosphere is gathered by the telescope, passed through the circulator and mixed with the local oscillator with a 2x2 coupler. A 120 MHZ bandwidth balanced photodetector followed by TIA amplifiers detect the signal which is then sampled by a 400 MS/sec 12 bit ADC. These signals are processed with a FPGA that calculates gated Fourier transforms (or autocorrelations depending on the chosen mode [6]) and accumulate power spectra for further processing on a host computer using a maximum likelihood estimation method. **Systematic and adaptive processing to account for baseline drifts and background:** The spectral gain shape characteristics of the receiver system is not necessarily flat but the spectral response can be measured by operating the system with the final amplifier turned off. Depending on the required sensitivity and integration times, it pays to occasionally monitor the spectral response due systematic component drifts that are sometimes less than fraction of a dB. In addition, monitoring range gates that are far from the lidar transceiver (up to 7.5 km for a 20 kHz rep rate system) offers real time corrections to the spectral flattening process but again, depending on the sensitivity requirements and integration times, atmospheric processes can contribute to slight variations of these baseline measurements. Even though the narrow bandwidth aerosol back scatter component is dominant, it is the wide band width molecular backscatter component that influences this baseline measurement and opens up the possibility to monitor temperature profiles by appropriately accounting for these baseline drifts.

Direct detection lidar: The system runs with two channels at wavelengths of 1.545 μm (6472.5 cm-1) and at 4.55 μm (2197.8 cm-1). The 1.545 μm laser source is a 20 kHz Keopsys fiber laser with a peak power of 4 kW and pulse width of 7 ns (30 μJ/pulse). The laser source for the 4.55 μm channel is a 100 kHz Pranalytica Inc. QC laser which can deliver a peak power of 4.5 watts with a pulse width of 202 ns (0.9 μJ/pulse). Quantum-Cascade lasers offer several Watts of pulsed peak optical power, while retaining a good far field pattern as required for laser remote sensing techniques in atmospheric research. Mid-IR QC lasers produce pulsed signal at room temperature and are compact in size. The receiver consists of an f/3 10” primary mirror with a focal length of 762 mm focusing on a Vigo PVI-4TE-5 detector for the 4.55 μm channel and a Thorlabs APD110C for the 1.545 μm channel. The signal is then recorded by a 16 bit Gage digitizer with an onboard FPGA card for a maximum of 1024 hardware averages. This acquisition system has a maximum sampling rate of 200 MS/s. The dual channel IR lidar was designed to be light and compact, weighing less than 30 lbs; therefore making it portable. **Systematic and adaptive processing to account for baseline drifts and background:** The background data is considered here as the noise at the end of the signal where there is no aerosol signal; data points taken from the higher altitudes passed the PBL. To remove the background from each data set, we take the average of several data points at a high altitude and where there is no backscattered signal from aerosol or cloud and subtract it out from that data set; basically removing the DC value. The baseline for this system configuration is considered as data collected with all instruments in the system turned on, except for the laser which is turned off. The baseline gives information about the system instrumental noise including any features caused by any device. The baseline of the system is important to understand so that unusual features from instruments won’t be mistaken for signal or overpower the signal.

Microwave Radiometer: The MP-3000A incorporates two radio frequency (RF) subsystems in the same cabinet. These RF subsystems share the same antenna and antenna pointing system. The temperature profiling subsystem utilizes sky brightness temperature observations at selected frequencies between 51 and 59 GHz. Although not presented here, this instrument also measures the vertical profile of temperature, humidity and liquid water content and is being used to characterize atmospheric stability [7].

3. Coherent Lidar Co-operated with Direct Detection Lidar

Co-operating the coherent Doppler lidar system alongside the direct Doppler lidar system can expose the dynamics of the boundary layer. A particular example corresponding to a short time of operation in the early evening (between about 5 pm and 6:40 pm) on August 25, 2015 is shown in Fig. 1.

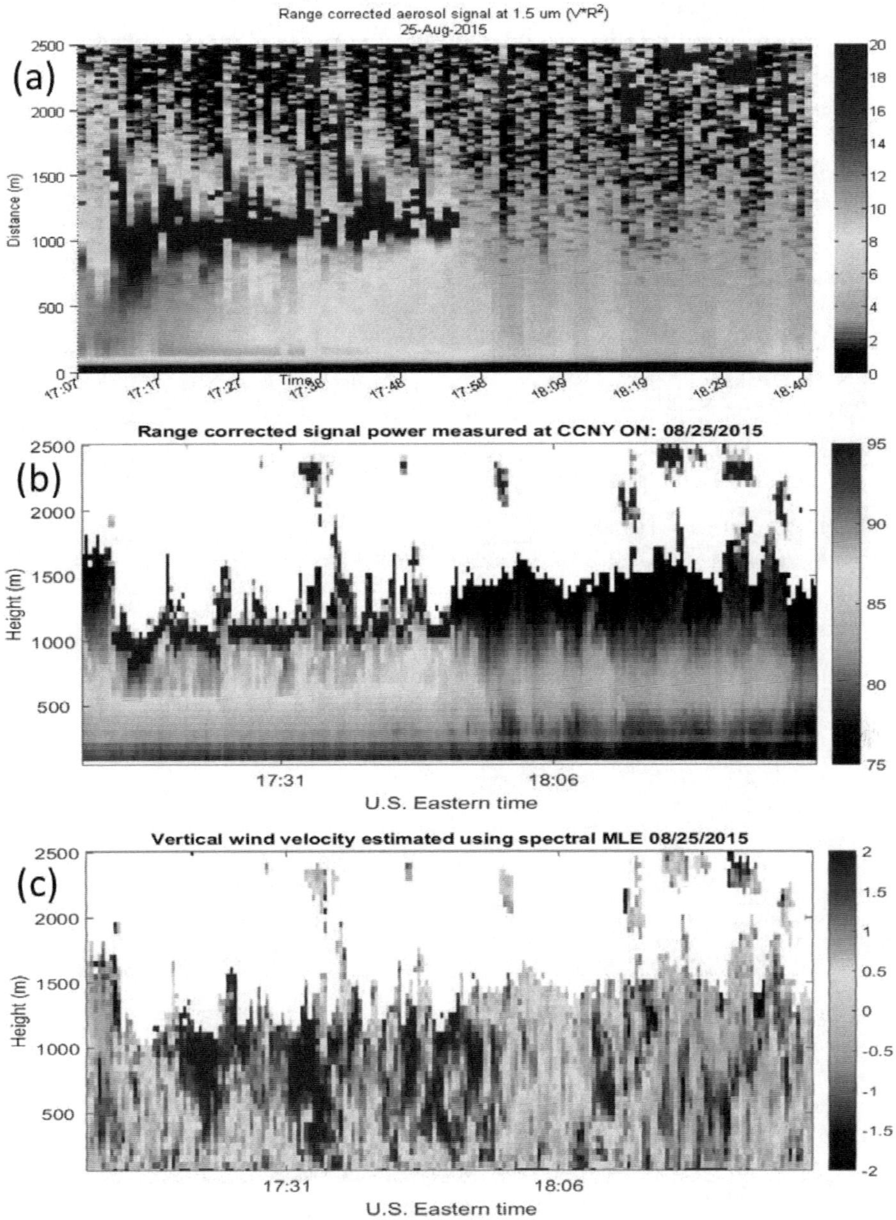

Figure 1. Vertical profile of the normalized range corrected signal for the direct detection (a) and coherent detection lidar and the vertical velocity component (c) in m/s on 8/25/2015 in upper Manhatten.

During this particular event, a dense cloud cover was associated with a strong updraft in the earlier half of the period and then as the clouds cleared out in the latter half of the time period. In the later part of the event, a cyclic behavior of aerosol concentration and clouds is observed by both lidars. A slight unexplained discrepancy of the vertical distribution of the aerosol concentration is observed when comparing both lidars in the later part of the event.

4. Coherent Lidar Co-operated with Microwave Radiometer

Diurnal patterns of atmospheric stability are being investigated with the suite of instruments that make up the NYCMetNet [2, 7]. An example of the use of the Doppler lidar in co-operation with the microwave radiometer is shown in Fig 2. These plots represent a period of about 39 hour starting at about 9 am in the morning on July 2nd, 2015. On these two days, a clear diurnal pattern of changes in the thermal gradient is observed by the microwave radiometer. The Doppler lidar observes a remarkable pattern that is coincident with this thermal gradient pattern that shows strong turbulent fluctuations occurring during periods in which the thermal gradient changes.

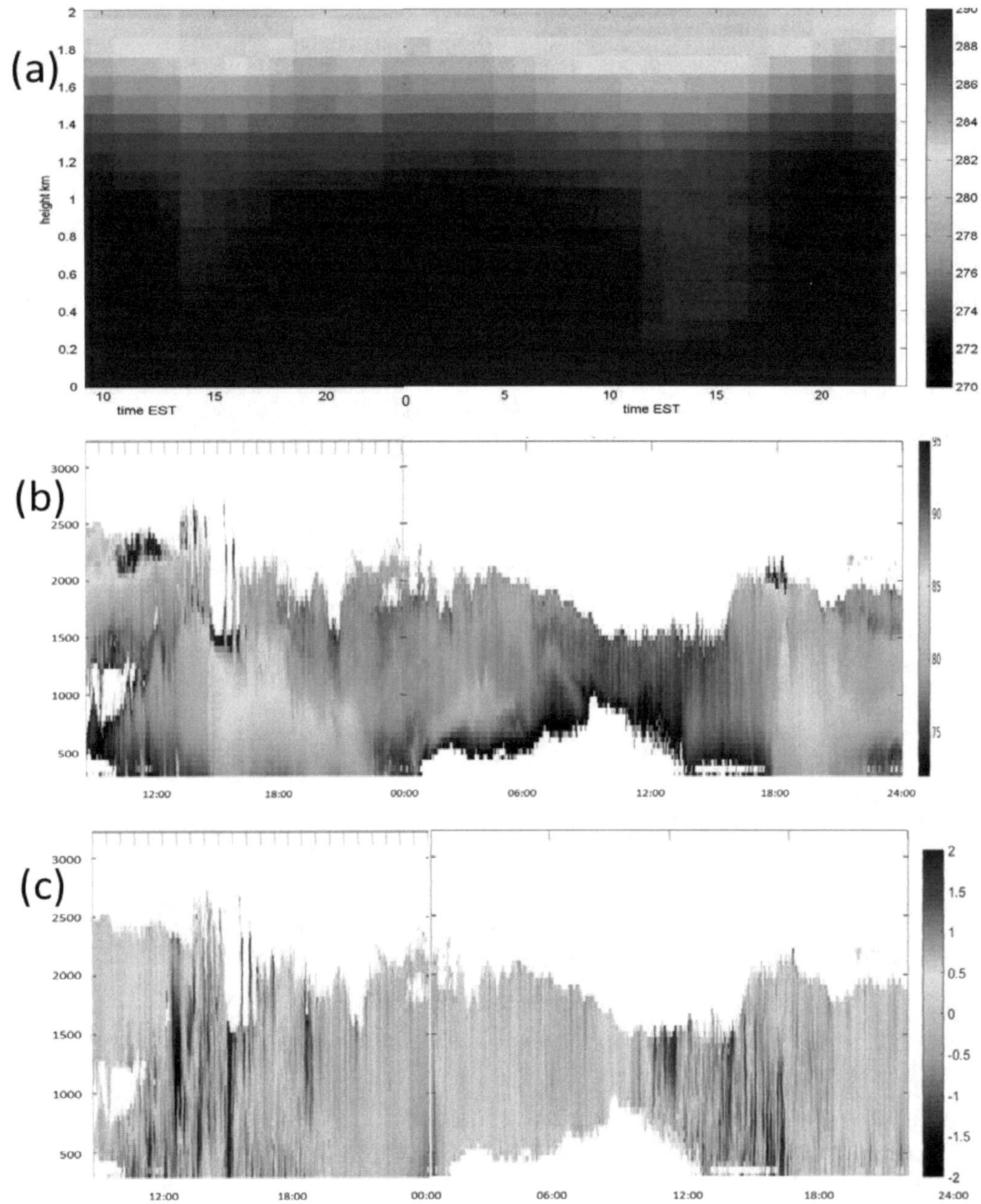

Figure 2. (a) Microwave radiometer temperature profuile, (b) Range corrected normalized Doppler lidar signal and (c) vertical velocity (m/s) during July 2nd and July 3rd, 2015.

[1] National Research Council. *Observing Weather and Climate from the Ground Up: A Nationwide Network of Networks*. Washington, DC: The National Academies Press, 2009. doi:10.17226/12540.

[2] Arend, M., 2012, NYCMetNet Graphic, in Urban Meteorology: Forecasting, Monitoring, and Meeting Users' Needs, Board on Atmospheric Sciences and Climate, National Academy of Sciences, NRC, National Academies Press, Washington. pg. 54, http://www.nap.edu/openbook.php?record_id=13328&page=54

[3] Gorban A.N.; Karlin, I. "Hilbert's 6th Problem: Exact and Approximate Hydrodynamic Manifolds for Kinetic Equations" Bull. Amer. Math. Soc. 51 (2014), 187-246

[4] Muriel, A. (2015). Time evolution equations for hydrodynamic variables with arbitrary initial data. Results in Physics.

[5] Abdelazim, S., Santoro, D., Arend, M., Moshary F., and Ahmed, S., "Development and Operational Analysis of an All-Fiber Coherent Doppler Lidar System for Wind Sensing and Aerosol Profiling," *IEEE TRANSACTIONS ON GEOSCIENCE AND REMOTE SENSING,* vol. 73, no. 12, pp. 6495 - 6506, 2015.

[6] Arend, M., Abdelazim, S., Lopez, M., and Moshary, F., (2013) "A comparison of two embedded programming techniques for high rep rate coherent Doppler lidars," Proc. SPIE 8731, Laser Radar Technology and Applications XVIII, 87310E (28 May 2013); doi: 10.1117/12.2016018

[7] Melecio-Vázquez, D., González-Cruz, J., Arend, M., Han, Z., , Dempsey, M., , Booth. B., Gutierrez, E.,, "New York Metro-Area Boundary Layer Catalogue: Boundary Layer Height and Stability Conditions from Long-Term Observations", 9th International Conference on the Urban Climate, 2015, Toulouse, France

Flash Camera Options for Coherent Imaging

By

Dr. Paul McManamon
Exciting Technology LLC & University of Dayton

Introduction:
We are coming into a time when flash imaging is available for coherent lidar applications. Over the last 20 years we have developed various flash camera options.[1] Each flash imaging camera option has benefits and drawbacks. Most of these detectors however were not developed for coherent imaging. Historically for coherent imaging scientists wanted a strong local oscillator. More recently the ability to measure Doppler shift, and the ability to measure the field, including phase, have been important aspects of coherent imaging.[2] These recent applications will be significantly enabled by flash imaging. Measuring Doppler shift point by point on a bridge, or on an engine, or on the ground, could have some value, but if you measure it in a flash image then you can instantaneously see the vibration spatial modes across the object being imaged. Flash imaging will enable many important applications associated with area vibration measurements. Another important application will be multiple input, multiple output, MIMO, lidar imaging. An array of 32 x32 format, or more, cameras behind multiple apertures could capture the field in high resolution.[3] If for example we have a hex 19 set of receive apertures we would have 5 apertures across the largest dimension, and if we use multiple transmitters separated across approximately the width of the receive array, and use 32 x 32 format cameras, we can capture coherent images as large as about 300 x 300.

Cameras we might consider include Geiger Mode APDs, GMAPDs, Linear Mode APDs, LMAPDs, pin diodes, and framing cameras. Spatial heterodyne coherent imaging can use low bandwidth framing cameras. GMAPDs, LMAPDs, and pin diodes can be used for temporal heterodyne. They have fast enough time response to measure range based upon the time it takes light to get to an object and return. Pin diodes may require a strong LO. GMAPDs will require a weak LO, and LMAPDs could require anywhere from a strong to a weak LO, depending on camera sensitivity.

Geiger Mode APDs for Coherent Imaging

Existing Geiger Mode APDs, GMAPDs, are framing cameras at up to 186 Khz for the 32 x 32, and up to 105 Khz for the 32 x 128 camera, but a GMAPD camera available by the end of the year will provide asynchronous read out. Each detector will fire and be independently reset as soon as possible. The dead time will be 400 nsec to 1 μsec. Ideally it will be 400 nsec, but to be safe we will count on no more than 1 μsec. That means each detector can continuously respond at a 1-2.5 Mhz rate. This FPA will have 32 x 32 detectors. As we group detectors together it will be possible to respond at a higher rates, but with fewer effective detectors. For example a 4 x 4 super pixel array of detectors could respond at a 16-40 Mhz rate. The full detector array could respond at .9 Ghz, limited by the read out electronics, not the dead time per detector. If it was limited by detector dead time then its response would be 1-2.5 Mhz. Then it would however be acting as a single super pixel.

Gieger mode APDs are ideal both because of sensitivity, resulting in only needing a low power local oscillator, LO, and because they inherently capture a “full waveform”. They have a simple digital read out circuit. The main drawbacks with GMAPDs for temporal heterodyne coherent imaging are background noise/backscatter and narrow dynamic range. Usually background noise/ backscatter is not an issue with coherent imaging, but it will be for GMAPDs. A narrow filter will be required, and applications with high background or backscatter, and applications with a highly variable scene, will be problematic. A 1 nm filter, which is very narrow, is 126 Ghz at a carrier wavelength of 1550 nm. With a 100 Mhz to maybe 2 or 3 Ghz detector we normally would not bother with a filter, but for GMAPDs we have to worry about photon blocking

With these cameras we have to use a low power local oscillator to do temporal heterodyne,[4] with the LO and the return signal about the same amplitude. The beat between them modulates the probability of an avalanche. A disadvantage of the weak LO approach is the signal amplitude, and that the LO need to be approximately matched. GMAPD coherent lidar will have a narrow dynamic range. A method will need to be set up to make sure the LO matches the return signal in amplitude. This could be an issue for scenes with significant differences in reflectivity. Often foliage has a higher reflectivity then manmade objects. A weak LO does not increase the sensitivity of the detector, but in the case of the GMAPD the cameras are already very sensitive.

We can obtain a Princeton Lightwave 32 x 32 framing camera with some defective pixels for $75 K. The new ITAR restricted 32 x 32 asynchronous read out camera will cost $225K when it is available. In terms of my desired FPA for coherent flash imaging once we have the asynchronous read out 32 x 32 the next step would be to increase that to 128 x128. In addition to working to reduce dead time that would be a near ideal GMAPD for flash imaging. While it is possible with a limited read out capability windowing a 128x128 down to 32 x 32 will be useful, we would then run into dead time

Pin Diode, or Linear Mode APDs, LMAPDs, for Coherent Imaging

As an alternative to a GMAPD camera we can use a pin diode with no amplification or a linear mode APD, LMAPD. There are 2 basic types of LMAPDs. There are HgCdTe LMAPDs, which have k=0. k is the ratio of holes to electrons generated during the avalanche. With k=0 the excess noise generated by an FPA is much less then with a value of k above zero, and avalanche breakdown does occur. HgCdTe cameras have low excess noise, about F=1.3, as a result of k=0. This is actually lower than the McIntyre theory, which would place the excess noise factor about 2. Excess noise is noise added due to the amplification process. When you only amplify the # of electrons, not the holes, you can keep excess noise low. The disadvantages of k=0 APDs are they need a physically larger cooler than a TE cooler because they operate near 100 deg K, and they are not commercial available, so cost more. On the positive side they can have a gain of 1000 or more, so are sensitive and use a lower power LO.

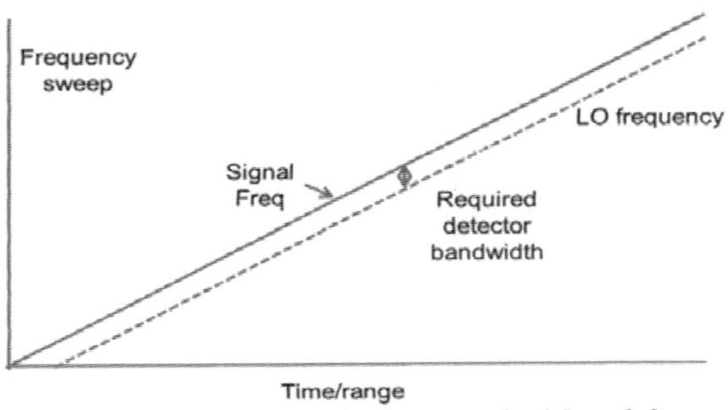

Figure 1: Stretch Processing Sweeps the LO and the transmitter in sync

One of the issues with LMAPDs is you need to develop a fast ROIC to read out the signal and record it behind each detector. While you can do better than that it is likely you might have on the order of 100 Mhz bandwidth. In that case you might want to do stretch processing, as shown in Figure 1 in order to have high range resolution.

InGaAs LMAPDs for Coherent Imaging: I plan on liking these FPAs once they are available with a high enough frame rate to sample phase well enough for multiple applications, but they are not there yet. They should be relatively low cost, and have good enough sensitivity to reduce the required LO power, maybe not to the level of a GMAPD, but quite a bit, and they should not have the dynamic range issue associated with GMAPDs

Voxtel and ASC have InGaAs LMAPDs as commercial products. Voxtel has cameras with k~.2, and is developing multi-stage cameras with k~.02. The k~.2 cameras can have gain of 5-20, whereas the k~.02 cameras can have gain of about 75, or even more, before the excess noise becomes unmanageable. For a temporal heterodyne lidar the extra sensitivity is not a significant issue, so we will only consider the lower gain Voxtel cameras, not the multi-stage cameras. Higher gain, and more sensitivity may mean the ability to use a lower power LO. Voxtel does have some cameras that are effectively AC coupled. If we need a high LO power, due to limited sensitivity, then we will want AC coupling.

One benefit of LMAPDs is you can capture a full scene on a single pulse. Also the full 3D image can be read out simply, but the disadvantage is we need a complex read out circuit. This can limit the read out rates. Each pixel needs significant electronics under it. Ideally we can have a full waveform sample in each detector element, but often a LMAPD camera only has the ability to capture one, or a limited #, of samples in each angle/angle pixel. The VX 806 only captures 3 samples in each detector. It costs $54K per camera. The VX 819 provides 24 samples in range that can be separated by 2 nsec to 16 nsec per sample. It has a 128 x 128 format, a 100 Mhz bandwidth, a 94 hertz frame rate, a jitter of < 100 psec, and a 50 μm pitch. If we window it down to a 32 x 32 format it has a frame rate of 990 hertz, and for a 16 x 16 format a frame rate of 2075 hertz. We can see from figure 2 that is all we want to do is sample a single sine wave 24 samples is not bad, so long as they are separated appropriately. Figure 3 shows sampling a single beat frequency, but also sampling a more complex waveform, the sum of 4 frequencies. We see as the waveform gets complex 24 samples is not providing good insight into the underlying waveform. Figure 4 then shows an attempt to detect pseudo random codes using only 24 sample. In this case we take a chip length of 10 nsec, and 3 nsec sampling. With 24 samples and 3 nsec sampling we only have a 72 nsec period over which to take samples.

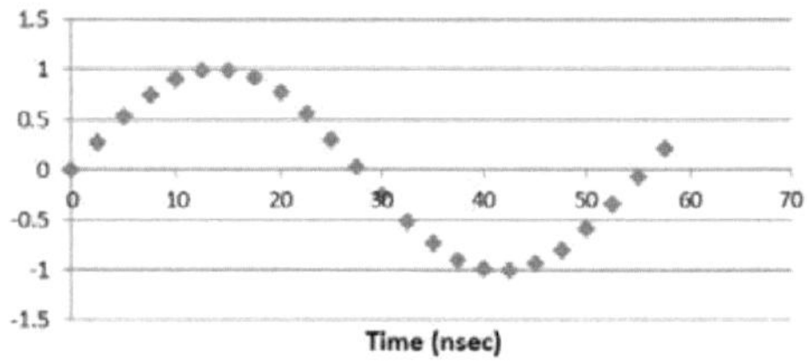

Figure 2: 24 samples @ 2.5 nsec with 18 Mhz beat freq

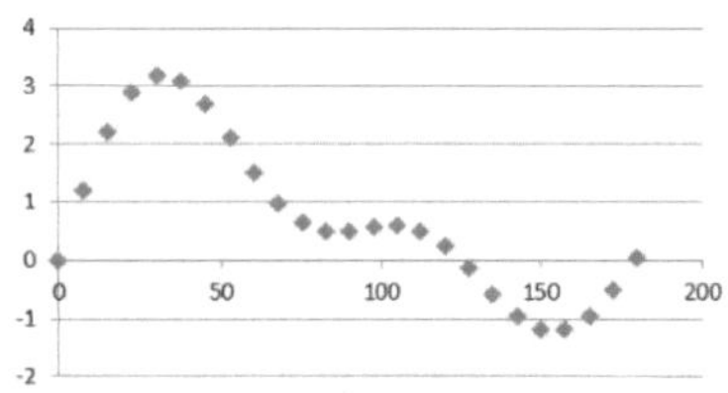

Figure 3a: Sum of 4 sine waves, 11, 7, 5, and 3 Mhz,

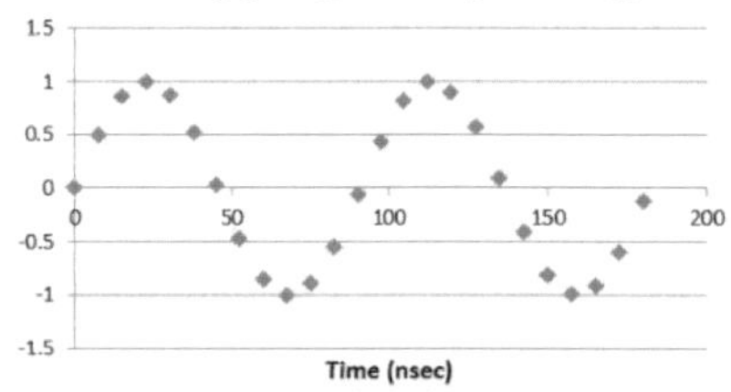

Figure 3b: 11 Mhz single sine wave

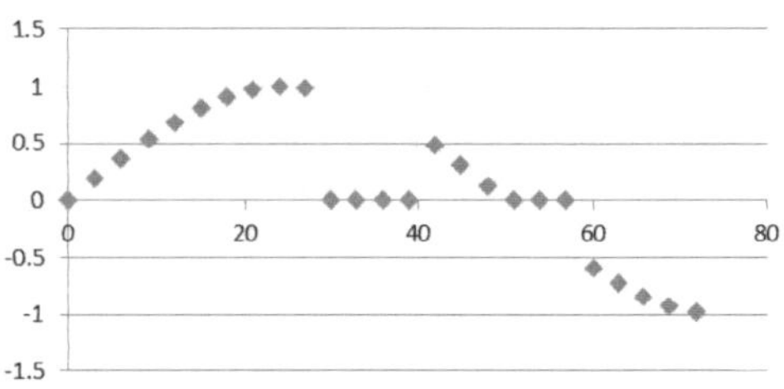

Fig 4: 10 nsec chip length, 3 nsec samples, and 10 Mhz beat frequency

We can see 24 samples is not sufficient. My ideal for a LMAPD would be at least 50 samples, and high frame rate, at least 10 Khz. We could have a continuous sample rate as high as we can, possibly 1- 10 Mhz. If we had either of these in a 128 x128 format with a single stage of InGaAs APD this would be a nearly idea coherent FPA. It would eliminate the dynamic range issue of GMAPDs. While it would require more LO power it should not be prohibitive.

HgCdTe LMAPDs for Coherent Imaging:

Raytheon and DRS have HgCdTe LMAPD cameras, but neither have commercial FPA cameras, so each FPA camera purchased would be a program with the provider. DRS was awarded a DARPA LRT contract for a camera suitable for both direct detection and coherent detection. The LRT program is basically complete, but the results have not been publically released. Many of the considerations would be similar to the InGaAs APDs for flash heterodyne imaging, but the array would be more sensitive, more expensive, and would need a 100 degree cooler. Otherwise many of the parameters would be similar. A lower power LO than the LMAPD InGaAs cameras could be used, due to increased sensitivity.

Low bandwidth Framing Cameras for Spatial Heterodyne Coherent Imaging

Spatial heterodyne does not require high bandwidth detectors capable of responding on a time period that allows speed of light based range measurement. Instead the camera merely needs to capture a spatial image. Multiple cameras are available, from Sensors unlimited, FLIR systems, and others. Voxtel has had a recent effort with AFRL to develop some cameras specifically for this application.

Summary:

GMAPDs are available now for use in flash coherent temporal imaging, and they are moderately priced. For situations where we do not have significant background, or backscatter, and where the target is not highly variable in reflectivity they are a good choice, and will get better when the asynchronous camera becomes available. They also have Ghz bandwidth, so can easily provide high range resolution. LMAPDs will be better for cases with high background or backscatter levels, or for cases with highly variable reflectivity, but will require LFM stretch processing to obtain high range resolution. HgCdTe cameras are not available commercially, but you should be able to buy them with high enough sample rates to do flash coherent imaging right. We should be able to use low power LOs with HgCdTe LMAPDs if desired. No one has yet paid to develop the ROICs to sample often enough with InGaAs LMADS detectors, but these will be attractive options once available. At this time limited flash coherent imaging situations could be implemented with InGaAs flash coherent imaging. They are cheaper than the HgCdTe LMAPD cameras now, and are likely to be less expensive when they have appropriate ROICs. I plan on liking the InGaAs LMAPD cameras when they become available with enough sampling.

---

[1] PF McManamon, P Banks, J Beck, AS Huntington, EA Watson, "A comparison flash lidar detector options", Proc. SPIE 9832, Laser Radar Technology and Applications XXI, 983202 (May 13, 2016); doi:10.1117/12.2229068; http://dx.doi.org/10.1117/12.2229068

[2] PF McManamon, "Perspectives on the Future of Coherent Ladar", 17th Coherent Laser radar Conference, CLRC, 2013, Barcelona.

[3] JR. Kraczek, PF. McManamon, and EA. Watson, "High resolution non-iterative aperture synthesis," Opt. Express 24, 6229-6239 (2016)

[4] L. A. Jiang and J. X. Luu, "Heterodyne detection with a weak local oscillator," Appl. Opt. 47(10), 1486–1503 (2008)

High-Power Highly Linear Photodiodes for High Dynamic Range LADARs

Shubhashish Datta and Abhay Joshi
Discovery Semiconductors, Inc.
119 Silvia Street, Ewing, New Jersey 08628, USA
sdatta@discoverysemi.com

Abstract: High power, highly linear photodiodes enhance the overall dynamic range of LADAR systems in two ways: faithfully transferring optical return signal into RF domain with high coherent gain and minimal non-linear distortions, and generating low-phase photonic microwave clocks. Large power handling capability of the photodiodes also reduces the requirement of signal amplification by RF amplifiers, which further improves the dynamic range. We present a 10 GHz bandwidth InGaAs p-i-n photodiode that generates broadband linear RF signal with peak-to-peak output amplitude up to 4 V and power-to-phase conversion factor <4 rad/W. The photodiode's performance is reported with pulsed stimulus, for repetition rates varying from 1 GHz to 10 GHz, as well as continuous wave signals. At higher power levels, these photodiodes produce compressed signals up to 6 V peak-to-peak output. In the compressed regime the power-to-phase conversion factor approaches zero for selected operating conditions, which is useful for generating precision clocks.

Keywords: highly linear photodiode, high power photodiode, high dynamic range, low phase noise, photonic clock.

1. Introduction

Coherent laser detection and ranging systems (LADAR) systems can significantly benefit from utilizing high power, highly linear photodiodes (HLPD) in both signal and clock paths, as shown in Fig. 1. Such photodiodes not only generate minimal non-linear inter-modulation distortions, but also improve the coherent gain through increased optical local oscillator power levels. The consequent reduction or elimination of RF amplification in the system further improves the noise figure and dynamic range of the system [1].

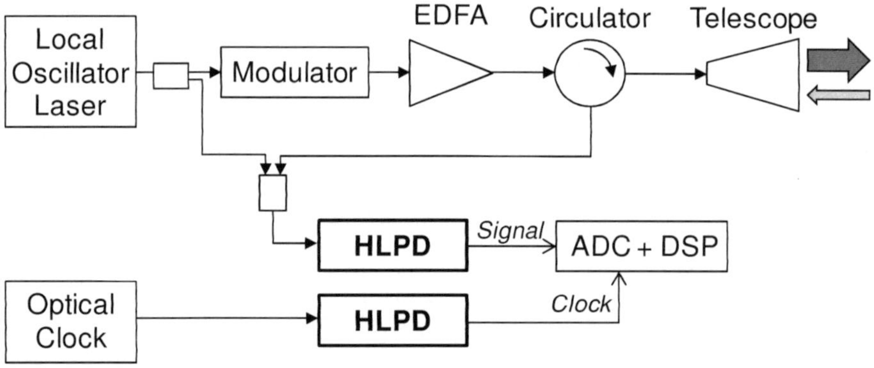

Figure 1. Block diagram of a coherent laser radar that incorporates high power, highly linear photodiodes (HLPD) for providing both signal and clock to the back-end electronics.

The overall dynamic range may also be limited by the clock jitter in the digitizer circuits. Feasibility of generating optical pulses with frequency instability of the order of 10^{-18} has made photonically generated clocks an attractive alternative to traditional microwave clock sources, especially in distributed systems with multiple telescope apertures [2, 3]. Highly linear photodiodes having negligible power-to-phase conversion (PPC) are needed to faithfully transfer the precision optical clock into the RF domain [4-7].

We present a 10 GHz bandwidth InGaAs p-i-n photodiode that generates broadband linear RF signal with peak-to-peak output amplitude up to 4 V, i.e. +16 dBm CW RF power, and PPC <4 rad/W. The photodiode's performance is reported with pulsed stimulus, for repetition rates varying from 1 GHz to 10 GHz, as well as continuous wave signals that satisfy the diverse requirements of LADAR systems.

2. Device Description

A top-illuminated dual-depletion region photodiode with optimized illumination profile was used for this work [1, 4]. The photodiode's RF output did not contain any internal resistive termination to maximize the transfer of RF power to the external 50 Ω load. A photodiode's power handling and linearity, which are limited by the collapse of applied electric field due to photo-generated space charge, increase monotonically with its reverse bias. The combination of high operating bias and the high photocurrent levels can correspond up to 1 W of power dissipation. The consequent heat generation in the InGaAs/InP photodiode chip can significantly increase its temperature and lead to thermally induced device failure. The photodiode chip was integrated with a thermo-electric cooler (TEC) and temperature sensor and assembled in a compact 8-pin microwave package, as shown in Fig. 2a, to extract the heat from the photodiode chip and ensure long-term reliable operation. The TEC and the temperature sensor were electrically isolated from the photodiode chip to minimize noise, crosstalk, and possibility of ground loops. The packaged photodiode module demonstrated a responsivity of 0.65 A/W at 1550 nm wavelength and a -3 dB bandwidth of 10 GHz, as shown in Fig. 2b.

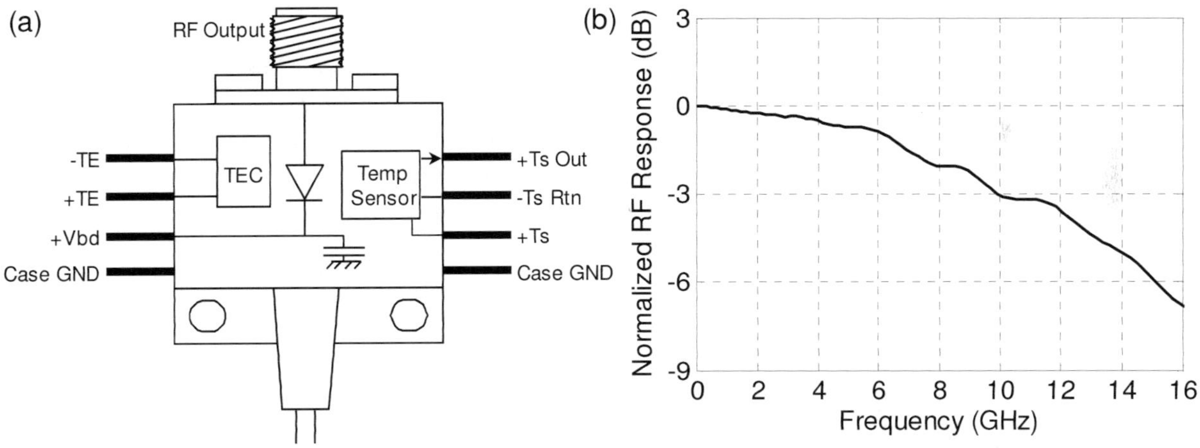

Figure 2. (a) Schematic and (b) RF response of open-terminated photodiode integrated with a thermo-electric cooler and a temperature sensor in a compact microwave package.

3. Amplitude and Phase Linearity with Pulsed Stimulus

The nonlinear transfer function of a photodiode manifests itself as amplitude compression as well as temporal distortions arising from RF pulse broadening at high optical power levels. These distortions were quantified by using the impulse response test setup shown in Fig. 3. This setup utilized a 1550 nm wavelength mode locked laser that emits 2.5 ps wide optical pulses. The optical pulse repetition rate of the laser was defined by its trigger frequency and was varied from 1 GHz to 10 GHz. The laser output was amplified using an Erbium Doped Fiber Amplifier (EDFA) and fed to the photodiode module through a variable optical attenuator (VOA). The integrated TEC of the photodiode module was driven to maintain the photodiode chip at a constant temperature of 15 °C. The module's case temperature was kept below 30 °C with appropriate heat sinking. The RF response was recorded at different reverse bias and average optical power levels using a 50 GHz sampling oscilloscope.

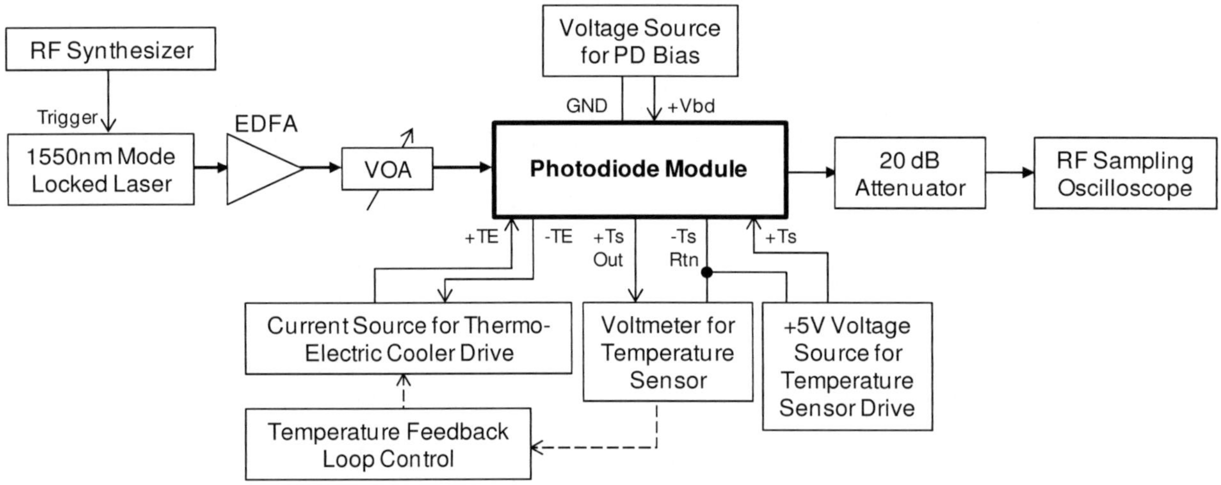

Figure 3. Test setup for characterizing the linearity of the photodiode module with pulsed stimulus.

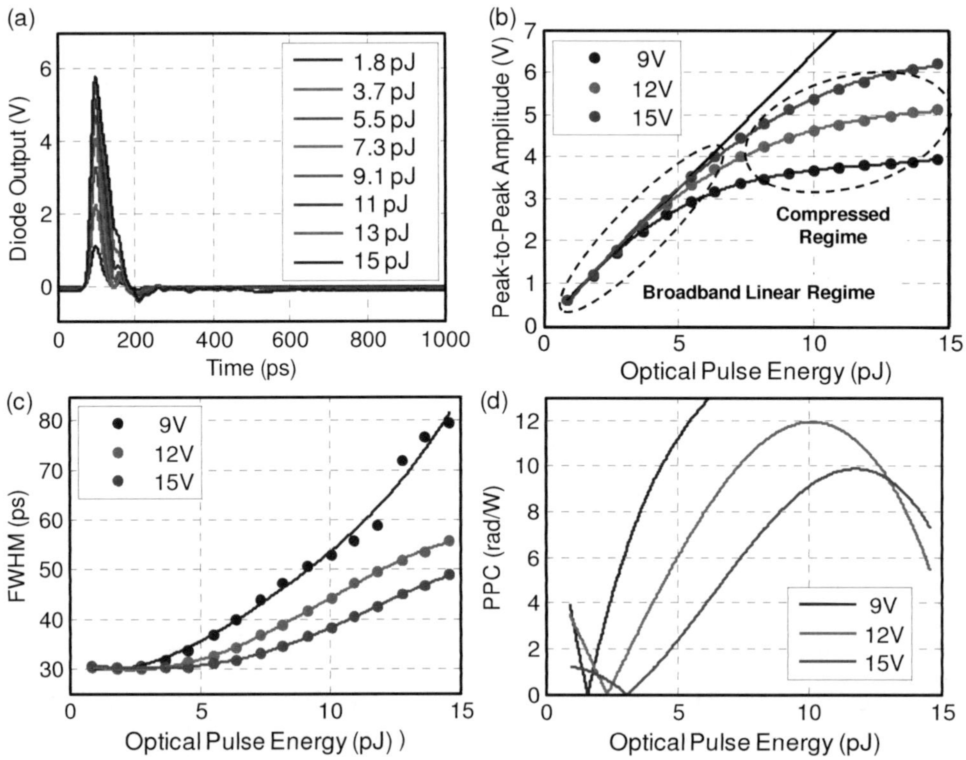

Figure 4. Impulse response of photodiode at 15 V reverse bias for various optical pulse energy levels at 1 GHz pulse repetition rate. (b) Peak-to-peak RF output amplitude, (c) full-width half maximum of the photodiode's output pulse, and (d) power-to-phase conversion of the photodiode at various reverse biases.

The RF impulse response results of the photodiode module at 1 GHz pulse repetition rate are summarized in Fig. 4. In the broadband linear regime, the photodiode's RF output amplitude scales linearly with the input optical pulse energy with negligible change in RF pulse shape. This regime can be extended to higher optical pulse energy levels by increasing the photodiode's reverse bias. The results shown in Figs. 4b and 4c displays a linear amplitude response and minimal pulse broadening up to 4 V peak-to-peak output at 15 V reverse bias. The phase nonlinearity, characterized by the power-to-phase conversion, was computed from the RF impulse response waveforms and was found to be <4 rad/W in this operating regime (see Fig. 4d).

While the broadband linear regime is ideal for detecting the optical return signal in a LADAR, the compressed regime may be preferable for generating low-phase noise clocks to trigger the digitizer. Photonic clock generation involves illuminating a photodiode with a high-power optical pulse train and filtering out a desired harmonic of the fundamental pulse repetition rate to extract a continuous wave RF clock. A photodiode's phase nonlinearity may vanish for specific sets of frequency, photodiode bias, and optical power levels in the compressed domain [6]. The photodiode's phase nonlinearity, expressed as picosecond per fractional input optical power, and the frequency dependent null points are shown in Fig. 5 at a reduced bias of 9 V.

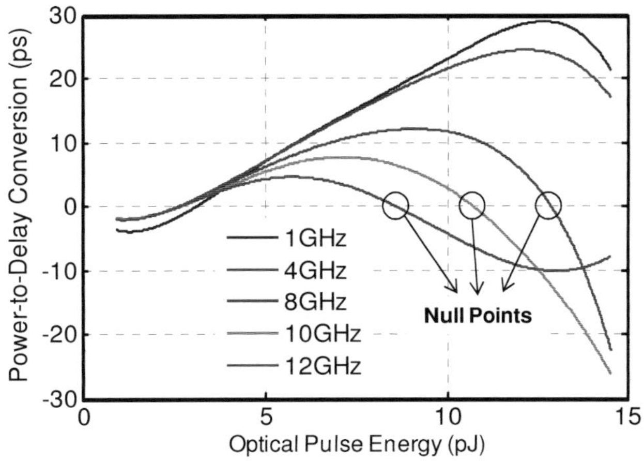

Figure 5. Power-to-delay conversion at 9 V bias illustrating the existence of frequency dependent null points in the compressed regime.

The second source of RF phase noise, namely shot noise, solely depends on the RF power of the filtered clock harmonic. As shown in Fig. 6, the peak-to-peak output amplitude of the photodiode is independent of the pulse repetition rate in both broadband linear and compressed regime, as long as the fundamental frequency is well within the -3 dB bandwidth of the photodiode. In other words, the RF amplitude at the filtered harmonic frequency scales linearly with the repetition rate. Therefore, increasing the pulse repetition rate allows generating a targeted clock harmonic power at a lower reverse bias, and improves the reliability of the photodiode.

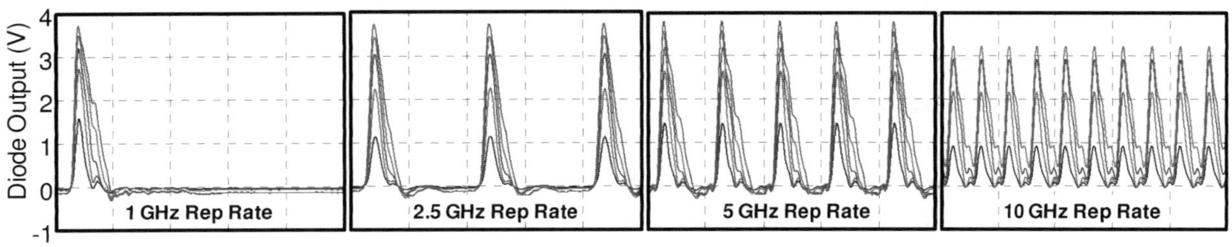

Figure 6. Impulse response of photodiode at 9 V reverse bias for different optical pulse repetition rates.

4. Power Handling with Continuous Wave Stimulus

Suppressing a photodiode's amplitude & phase nonlinearity simultaneously results in high power handling capability. The power handling test setup utilizes a Mach-Zehnder Modulator (MZM) to impose a sinusoidal RF modulation with ~100% modulation depth on a 1550 nm wavelength CW laser. The modulator output is amplified using an EDFA and fed to the photodiode module through a variable optical attenuator. The photodiode's output power is measured at different optical power levels by using an RF power meter. As shown in Fig. 7, RF output power of +16 dBm (4 Vpp) is achievable at 11 V photodiode reverse bias. Such signal level is sufficient for maximizing the effective number of bits (ENOBs) of typical digitizer circuits without requiring any RF amplification.

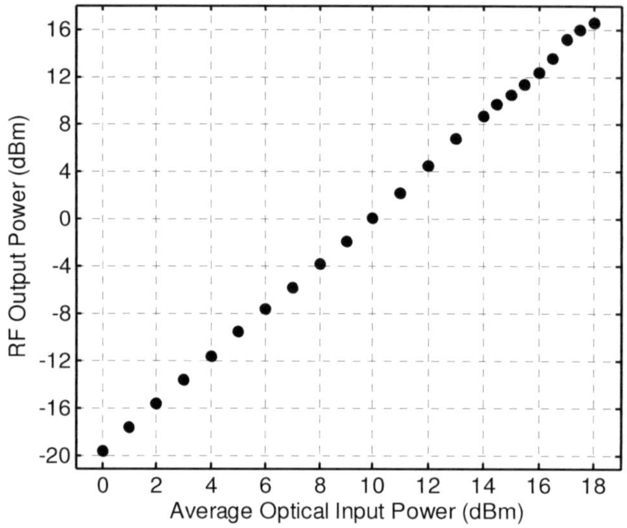

Figure 7. RF output power of the photodiode module at ~100% modulation depth as a function of average optical input power at 11 V reverse bias.

5. Conclusion

In summary, we have demonstrated a 10 GHz bandwidth high power, highly linear photodiode in a thermo-electrically cooled module that can reliably generate broadband linear RF signal with peak-to-peak output amplitude up to 4 V (+16 dBm CW RF power) with power-to-phase conversion factor <4 rad/W. The same device can be used in a compressed regime to photonically generate clocks having extremely low phase noise. These photodiodes can be incorporated in both signal and clock paths of the LADAR systems to increase their dynamic range.

6. References

[1] A. Joshi, S. Datta, and D. Becker, "GRIN Lens Coupled Top-Illuminated Highly Linear InGaAs Photodiodes," IEEE PTL **20**, 1500-1502 (2008).

[2] E. Ivanov, S. Diddams, and L. Hollberg, "Study of the excess noise associated with demodulation of ultra-short infrared pulses," IEEE Trans.Ultrason., Ferroelectr. Freq. Control **52**, 1068–1074 (2005).

[3] G. C. Valley, "Photonic analog-to-digital converters," Optics Express **15**, 1955-1982 (2007).

[4] A. Joshi and S. Datta, "Dual InGaAs Photodiodes having High Phase Linearity for Precise Timing Applications," IEEE PTL **21**, 1360-1362 (2009).

[5] J. Taylor, S. Datta, A. Hati, C. Nelson, F. Quinlan, A. Joshi, and S. A. Diddams, "Characterization of power-to-phase conversion in high-speed P-I-N photodiodes," IEEE Photonics J. **3**, 139-151 (2011).

[6] W. Zhang, S. Seidelin, A. Joshi, S. Datta, G. Santarelli, and Y. Le Coq, "Dual photodetector system for low phase noise microwave generation with femtosecond lasers," Optics Lett. **39**, 1204-1207 (2014).

[7] E. Portuondo-Campa, G. Buchs, S. Kundermann, L. Balet, and S. Lecomte, "Ultra-low phase-noise microwave generation using a diode-pumped solid-state laser based frequency comb and a polarization-maintaining pulse interleaver," Optics Express **23**, 32441-32451 (2015).

Acknowledgement

This work was supported by the DARPA PULSE program (PμreComb project). Authors thank Dr. Matthias Lezius and Dr. Ronald Holzworth from Menlo Systems, GmbH, Dr. Yann Le Coq from Observetoire de Paris, CNRS, and Dr. Giorgio Santarelli from Bordeaux University for their valuable contributions.

Velocity Rate Uncertainty and Dark Count Rate Influences on Time of Flight Measurement

Patrick Perkins
Lockheed Martin Advanced Technology Center
patrick.perkins@lmco.com

Statement of Problem

- Range to the target and the range rate of the target are known with some precision
- Lack of precise knowledge requires a search algorithm which looks over the uncertainty in range and range rate
- Low probability of detecting a true target return requires one use a correlation algorithm (usual maximum entropy search)
- The number of possible vectors can be very large
- This is a classic binomial integration problem(require M returns along a range and range rate vector as a condition for detection)
- Use slowly varying algebraic derivation to derive receiver operating characteristic (ROC) over a wide parameter space

Definition of Terms

- true range {R}; time delay $\{t_{est}\}$ is {2xR/c} = time of flight {TOF}
- time of flight: time for pulse from XCVR to be transmitted and received
- range estimate $\{R_{est}\}$; $\{t_{est}\}$ = $\{2xR_{est}/c\}$
- laser pulse width $\{t_{pulse}\}$
- set of initial range bins $\{R_{bins}\}$
- dark count rate {DCR} in count/sec
- white count rate (WCR) in counts/sec
  (photon count rate x probability of single pulse detection ≈ 0.25;
  100 photons/sec = WCR of 25 counts/sec Poisson average)
- energy required $\{E_1\}$, on average, to yield a single counted event

Link Budget Example; E^1_{Joule}

- Range = 15000 km = 15 Mm; (speed of light = 300 Mm/s)
- TOF = 100 ms >> $\{t_{pulse}\}$ (<200 ns pulse stretched fiber laser)
- ε_{Joule} = link return in units of counts/J; use dB in m^2 for convenience
  - Range = 15 Mm; R^{-2} = -143.5 dB
  - Target cross section, Ω $\{m^2\}$ = ρ x Area = 0.5 m^2 = -3 dB
  - Full angle Gaussian beam divergence, Θ_{half} = 1.5 μR; power gain of 115 dB
  - Receiver area, $(A_{rcvr}\}$ = 1 m^2 = 0 dB
  - System thruput $\{\eta\}$ = -12 dB, includes probability of detection
  - Photons/Joule = Φ_{Joule} = 5.03 x 10^{18} x λ [microns] = 187 dB at 1 micron
  - $\eta\ \Omega\ A_{rcvr}\ \{\Pi/2\ \Theta_{half}^{2}\}\ R^{-4}\ \Phi_{joule}$ = { -12 -3 + 0 + 115 – 287 + 187 = 0 }
- Return 1 count for 1 Joule of output energy, on average
  E^1_{Joule} = 1 (How convenient!)

Simple Model Without Binomial Integration

- Pick a value of total WC's to determine the ROC; use $\{N_{true} = 4\}$
- Nominal laser output 10 mJ at 10 kHz, pulse stretched fiber laser
- Need 400 pulses to output 4J
- $K_{int,}$ number of pulses, $= (E^{ROC}_{int}/P^{avg}_{out}) \times PRF = 4/100 \times 10{,}000 = 400$
- Consider fixed target
  - No increase in TOF window due to range rate "motion" in time
  - Range uncertainty = $R_P - R_V = R_{P-V}$
  - Time uncertainty, $\{\tau_{P-V}\} = 2 \times R_{P-V}/C$
  - Total time gate $\{T = k_{int} \times \tau_{P-V}\}$
  - For 15 km range uncertainty, $\tau_{P-V} = 100\ \mu s$
- $SNR_{simple} \cong N_{true}/DC^{1/2} = N_{true}/(DCR \times k_{int} \times \tau_{P-V})^{1/2}$;
  $= Ntrue \times [P_{out}/(E^{ROC}_{int} \times DCR \times \tau_{P-V} \times PRF]^{1/2}$;
  $= [P_{out}/(E^{1}_{int} \times DCR \times \tau_{P-V} \times PRF]^{1/2}$
  Usual inverse root dependence in DCR and PRF

Does not show vector field increase in noise due to range and range rate uncertainty!

Adding Range Rate Uncertainty

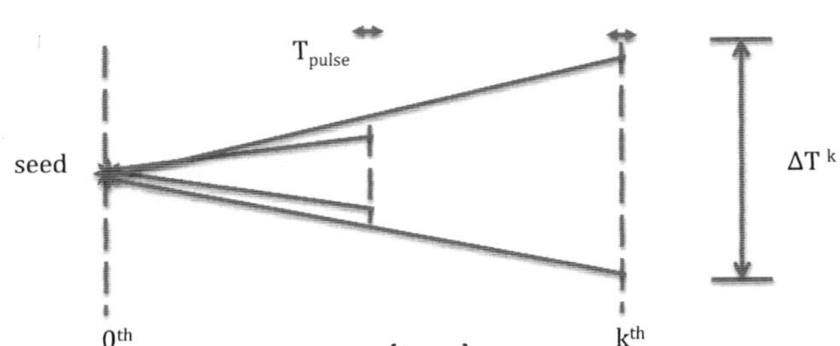

$\{t_{pulse}\}$

A seed is defined as a range uncertainty element: $C \times t_{pulse}$. Total number of seeds covers total range uncertainty. This is the usual multi hypothesis type of algorithm.

$\{k_{int}\}$ is still set by the ROC; however, the time window must grow to accommodate the change in range. For a given number of pulses, the total time growth of the acceptance window is $\{\Delta T^{k} = k_{int}/PRF \times 2\delta_V/C\}$

As the required output energy is reduced, the number of pulses integrated and the range rate uncertainty time window are linearly reduced. Hence, there is a square dependence on the value of $\{E^{1}_{int}\}$.

Estimating Increased Window Time

- ΔT^{k} $= (E^{ROC}_{int} / P_{out}) \times (2\delta_V / C)$;
- N^{k}_{lines} $= (E^{ROC}_{int} / P_{out}) \times (2\delta_V/C) / \tau_{pulse}$ {divide by the pulse width}.
- The number of points per line and thus the total time window for all points along all lines is as follows for a given seed:
- N^{points}_{line} $= k_{int} = (E^{ROC}_{int}/P_{out}) \times PRF$;
- N^{points}_{seed} $= (E^{ROC}_{int}/P_{out})^{2} \times PRF \times (2\delta_V / C) / \tau_{pulse}$;
- ΔT^{total}_{seed} $= (E^{ROC}_{int} / P_{out})^{2} (PRF \times 2\delta_V/C)$ [units of s] .

Note: each seed has the same dependency

Simple Range Rate Dependencies

Note that as we reduce the number of lines as we increase the laser pulse width or the sample time. We now calculate the noise at each "point" along the projected velocity vector which is simply {DCR x τ_{pulse}}. Thus, the total noise in the velocity estimator to first order does not have pulse width dependence. The number of points is reduced as you increase the laser pulse width but the time gate is linearly increased as well. The result is that the total number of DC's is pulse width independent.

$$DC^{points}_{seed} = (E^{ROC}int / P_{out})^{2} \times [DCR \times PRF \times 2\delta_V/C].$$

This is a unit less quantity; the first term has the units of S^2; the second term the units of S^{-2}. Let's make a sample calculation when we expect a value of unity for the variance. The first term is 4J required with an 100W output or {1/625 s^2}. We estimate the DCR and PRF as 5 kHz and 10 kHz. Thus, prior to evaluating the "Doppler" term, we have a numerical estimate of 80,000 noise counts x {$2\delta_V/C$}.

Use a value of 125 ppm for the velocity uncertainty and we would expect 10 noise counts per seed. Increasing the laser pulse width inversely reduces the number of range bin seeds which helps considerably in the tracking process. It does not change the velocity search along a given vector but does reduce the total number of vectors.

If we consider the variance as the root of the number of DC's, we recover the root dependencies.

Probability and ROC

- How many DC's along a single line?
- 400 pulses x 200 nS x 1000 Hz (DCR) = 0.08 DC's per kHz
- Sufficiently small we can approximate Poissonian probability function
- P_{FA} is the Poisson probability {DC< N_{true}}
- $P_{single\ track}$ [DC's < N_{true}] < $DC^{Ntrue} / N_{true}!$

The following graph shows the validity of this expansion by comparing the simple exponential and factorial model with the actual Poisson distribution as the expectation value is decreased in factors of 2 from unity. Consider this an upper bound.

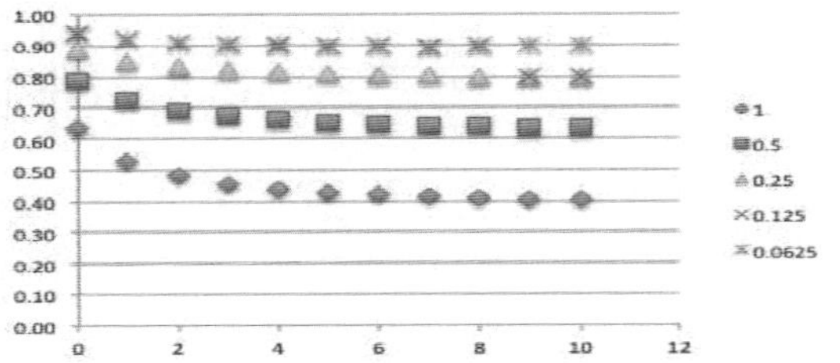

Driving Toward Binomial Integration

The total probability that an erroneous vector will be named is the single track probability multiplied by the total number of possible vectors or

$$P_{error} < [(k_{int}\, \tau_{pulse}\, DCR)^{Ntrue} / N_{true}!]\, [(E^{ROC}_{int}/P_{out})(2\delta_V/C) / \tau_{pulse}].$$

We inject the number of WC's by defining [$E^{ROC}_{int} \cong WC\, E^1_{int}$] where the superscript {1} denotes the amount of energy required to return, on average, unity WC's. Recall that {$k_{int} = (E^{ROC}_{int}/P_{out}) \times PRF$}, using n instead of N_{true},

$$P^n_{error} < (2\delta_V/C)\, PRF^n\, WC^{n+1} (E^1_{int}/P_{out})^{n+1} DCR^n \tau_{pulse}^{n-1} / n! \;;$$
$$P^n_{error} < (2\delta_V/C)\, \tau_{pulse}^{n-1} (PRF\, DCR)^n\, WC^{n+1} (E^1_{int}/P_{out})^{n+1} / n! \quad .$$

Using values of 5 kHz for PRF, 1000 Hz for DCR, as well as (1/100 sec) for the energy/power ratio, a value of 4 for WC's, and 10^{-4} for the relative velocity uncertainty,

$$P^1_{error} < (10^{-4})\, (200 \times 10^{-9})^{1-1} (5 \times 10^3 \times 1000)^1 \times\ 4^{1+1} \times (1/100)^2 = 0.8$$

which has the units of [$s^{n-1}\, s^{-2n}\, s^{n+1}$] and is correctly dimensionless.

We could not expect the algorithm to select the correct velocity vector with that much noise. At this point, we examine a 90% detection probability for the system and use binomial integration, requiring M detects out of N WC's for a true detection.

WC's for a given ROC

- We can readily generate the number of WC's required for a given selection criterion. The ROC is determined in the following way:
- Set the criterion. If you select {3}, you require three detections that fall on a straight line in velocity space where straight means that detections are within the laser pulse window.
- Recursively solve the Poisson probability function such that the probability of detecting Ntrue from WC is greater than your threshold probability of 5% or as you choose.
- Solve the error equation for the DCR that also yields an error probability of 5% or your threshold level of error.

WC Expectation Values

Criterion	Missed % 2.5	5	10	20	40
3	7.20	6.3	5.30	4.30	3.10
4	8.75	7.75	6.65	5.50	4.20
5	10.25	9.15	8.00	6.70	5.25
6	11.70	10.5	9.25	7.90	6.30
7	13.05	11.85	10.50	9.10	7.35

Example Calculation

We are using a PRF of 10 kHz, a pulse width of 200 nS and require 3 points on the velocity track. With a DCR of 1000 Hz, the probability of a DC induced error is 5%.

$(E1/P_{out})$	1.25E-02	[s]
WC	6.3	
$(2\delta_V/C)$	2.00E-04	
PRF	1.00E+04	[s-1]
DCR	1.00E+03	[s-1]
τ_{pulse}	2.00E-07	[s]
time unity return	1.25E-02	[s]
Ntrue	3	
Perror	5.1%	
kint	125.0	

WC	Ntrue≥	DCR
6.3	3	1000
7.75	4	1720
9.15	5	2420
10.5	6	3070
11.85	7	3640
13.15	8	4160

If we use a 4-criterion, we need to integrate for (7.75/6.3) = 125% longer. We can tolerate a DCR of 1720 Hz. The table summarizes a ROC table generated from these example values assuming a 5% error value. With a little more algebra, we can solve for DCR as a direct function of the ROC parameters for a given probability. Alternatively, we can generate a ROC where we use WC as an adjustable parameter, DCR fixed, and we generate error probabilities for a different value of N_{true} for each family of curves.

Scaling with PRF

It is interesting to determine how this scales with laser PRF. If the laser output power is peak power constrained but not gain constrained, the error equation is simplified. The product of [PRF x $\tau_{pulse} \cong Y_{laser}$], which is dimensionless, can be considered constant. As an example, {Y_{laser} = 10 kHz x 200 nS = 2 x 10^{-3}}. We rewrite the governing error equation, peak power limited, as

$$P_{DC}{}^{n}{}_{error} < (2\delta_V/C)\ WC^{n+1}\ (E^1{}_{int}/P_{out})^{n+1}\ Y_{laser}{}^{n-1}\ DCR^n\ PRF\ /n!$$

This quantity is dimensionless: [$s^{n+1}\ s^{-n}\ s^{-1}$]. From this, it is clear for the peak power constrained laser pulse energy assumption, the probability of detecting a spurious velocity track is proportional to PRF but not a function of laser pulse width. This is for a single seed. We have to multiply this by the number of seeds to look at the entire problem.

Thus,

$$\tau_{pulse} \cong Y_{laser}/PRF$$

$$N_{seeds} = \{2\ \delta_R/C\}\ /\ \tau_{pulse} = PRF\ \{2\ \delta_R/C\}\ /\ Y_{laser}.$$

The net result is a PRF^2 dependency in the line error. Noting the nearly exponential nature of the error, if you have 100 seeds, you would need natural log (100) = 4.8 more WC's to handle the seed field, any which could contribute to the error signal.

This process converges most quickly when the PRF is as low as possible within the laser constraint equation.

Approximating the ROC

We can approximate [WC] as a function of the decision criterion, n ranging from 3 to 8 as :

$$WC\ (P_{det} < 5\%) \approx \log_2(n^4) + (n-3)^3/128 .$$

One can generate readily a ROC of high utility using a simple approximation fit. Log's work quite well as you would expect from other expansions of the binomial and Poisson distributions.

5% ROC

WC	Ntrue≥	approx	relative error
6.30	3	6.34	0.6%
7.75	4	8.01	3.3%
9.15	5	9.35	2.2%
10.50	6	10.55	0.5%
11.85	7	11.73	-1.0%
13.15	8	12.98	-1.3%

Coherent Doppler Lidar for Measuring Velocity and Altitude of Space and Arial Vehicles

Farzin Amzajerdian(a), Diego F. Pierrottet(b), Glenn D. Hines(a), Larry Petway(a), and Bruce W. Barnes(a)

(a) NASA Langley Research Center, Hampton VA 23681
(b) Coherent Applications, Inc., Hampton VA, 23666
f.amzajerdian@nasa.gov

ABSTRACT: A coherent Doppler lidar has been developed to support future NASA missions to planetary bodies. The lidar transmits three laser beams and measures line-of-sight range and velocity along each beam using a frequency modulated continuous wave (FMCW) technique. Accurate altitude and velocity vector data, derived from the line-of-sight measurements, enables the landing vehicle to precisely navigate from several kilometers above the ground to the designated location and execute a gentle touchdown. The same lidar sensor can also benefit terrestrial applications that cannot rely on GPS or require surface-relative altitude and velocity data.

Keywords: Coherent Laser Radar, Doppler Lidar, Precision Navigation, GPS-deprived Navigation

1. Introduction

Past robotic and manned planetary landing missions relied on radars for ground-relative velocity vector and altitude data during their descent phase starting at several kilometers above the ground. The Navigation Doppler Lidar (NDL), built and demonstrated by NASA Langley Research Center, presents a viable alternative to obsolete radar sensors. The NDL offers several critical advantages compared with radars, including significantly higher precision and reduced size, weight, and power. In addition, the laser-based NDL sensor does not suffer from measurement perturbation from terrain features or signal ambiguity from transmitted side lobes, and is far less susceptible to signal clutter, such as returns from the lander structure or jettisoned components [1]. The higher quality data provided by the NDL will enable a more precise navigation towards the designated landing site and a well-controlled touchdown (greater stability and lower impact loads) that translate to lower fuel reserve and smaller leg span thus further reducing the vehicle mass. Therefore, the NDL can potentially reduce the overall cost and risk of landing missions and enable new capabilities for planetary exploration missions including missions to the Moon, Mars, asteroids, and Jupiter moons [2].

The NDL can also benefit terrestrial applications such as aircraft navigation without reliance on external satellite signals. Conventional aircraft Guidance, Navigation, and Control (GN&C) systems combine the Inertial Measurement Unit (IMU) data with the signals from a Global Positioning System (GPS) to determine the vehicle position and velocity vector. An IMU has an excellent response to rapid motions but suffers from an accumulated error over time (drift) while GPS can provide accurate long-term data. However, the GPS signal can be blocked or jammed by intentional or unintentional interference causing significant deviation in the navigation solution.

2. Lidar System Description

Fig. 1(a) illustrates the NDL system design. The lidar uses a frequency modulated continuous wave (FMCW) technique and optical homodyne detection to obtain both range and velocity data. A relatively low power, single frequency laser operating at an eye safe wavelength of 1.55 micron is used as the master oscillator. The frequency of this laser is modulated linearly with time. A portion of the laser power is amplified to be transmitted and the rest is used as the local oscillator (LO) for optical homodyne detection. The lidar transmits three laser beams into three fixed directions relative to each other, and the return signals are directed to three corresponding photo-receivers. The digitized outputs of the three photo-receivers are processed by a Fast Fourier Transform (FFT) algorithm to extract line-of-sight (LOS) velocity and range data. The platform vector velocity is determined from the LOS velocities measured along the three laser beams by using a priori pointing knowledge. Using all three simultaneous LOS range measurements allows determination of the vehicle altitude relative to the local ground without the need for vehicle attitude angle data from a separate sensor [3]. The use of three beams to compute altitude also reduces the effect of terrain features such as boulders and craters when compared to a single beam radar or lidar altimeter.

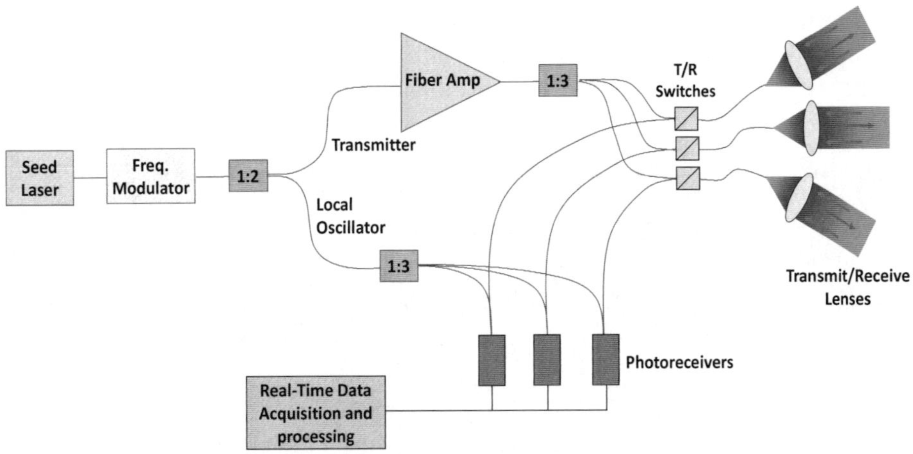

Figure 1. Doppler lidar system diagram.

Fig. 2 shows the prototype NDL, we refer to as generation 2 (GEN 2) unit, developed for a series of flight tests to demonstrate the capabilities of the NDL as a GN&C sensor. The prototype lidar consists of an electronics chassis and an optical head that houses three fiber-coupled lenses. The optical head is mounted rigidly on the vehicle with a clear field-of-view to the ground, and connected to the electronic chassis through a long fiber optic cable carrying the transmitted beams to the lenses and directing the collected signals from the same lenses to the receivers. The electronic chassis contains all the lidar components, including transmitter laser, receiver, real-time processor, system controller, and power supply unit. This prototype system is capable of measuring vehicle velocity and altitude with 0.2 cm/s and 30 cm resolution, respectively. The GEN 3 NDL currently under development will extend the NDL operational envelope increasing its maximum velocity from 70 m/s to 200 m/s and its maximum range from 2.5 km to over 4 km in order to meet the needs of a wide range of landing scenarios. The design upgrades being incorporated into the GEN 3 NDL will also result in about 40% reduction in size and mass compared with the GEN 2 instrument.

Figure 2. Prototype Doppler lidar system consisting of an electronic chassis and an optical head.

3. **Flight Tests and Results**

The capabilities of the Doppler lidar were evaluated and its performance characterized during different stages of its development through extensive laboratory experiments, dynamic testing on a swinging platform from the NASA LaRC gantry (a 240-foot high structure) and on a moving truck, and three helicopter flight test campaigns [3,4]. These tests led to the completion of the GEN 2 prototype unit and its demonstration onboard a rocket-propelled flight-test vehicle referred to as Morpheus (Fig. 3). The flight tests also included a 3-D imaging flash lidar and a long range laser altimeter that we developed under the Autonomous Landing and Hazard Avoidance Technology (ALHAT) project along with the NDL [2].

The demonstration flights were conducted in 2014 at the NASA Kennedy Space Center Shuttle Landing Facility. A 100 m x 100 m hazard field was constructed specifically for these flights that simulates a challenging lunar terrain consisting of realistic hazard features (rocks piles and craters) and designated landing areas. In this flight test campaign, the flash lidar identified the best safe landing site and reported its coordinates to the vehicle GN&C system. The data from the NDL was then used by the GN&C system to navigate and land the vehicle precisely at the selected location, avoiding the hazardous rocks and craters (Fig. 3b).

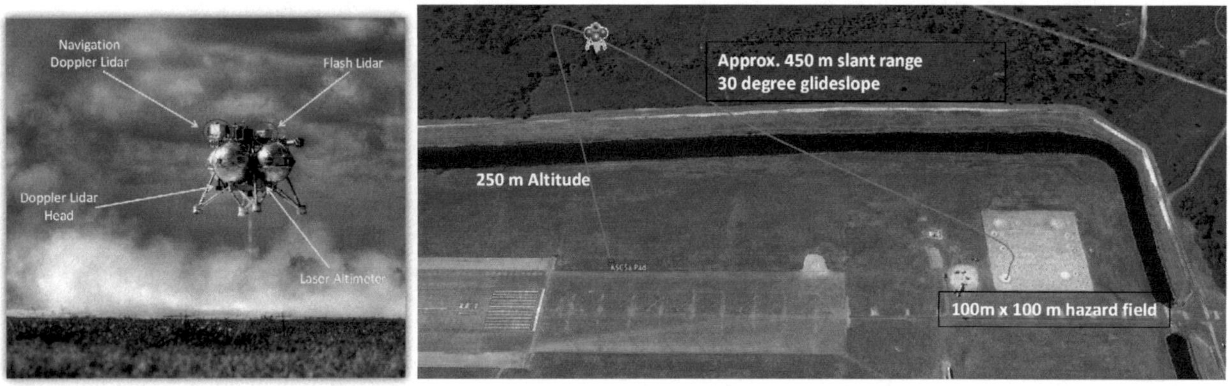

(a) (b)

Figure 3. Closed-loop flight demonstration using rocket-propelled Morpheus vehicle. a) Doppler lidar along with 3-D flash lidar and long-range laser altimeter integrated into Morpheus; b) Navigating and landing in the hazard field using the Doppler lidar data.

Fig. 4 shows the NDL data from the last flight of a series of six flights onboard the Morpheus vehicle. The red curves on the left show the NDL LOS velocity for each of the three beams over the duration of the flight. The blue curves are the velocity estimates, projected along the lidar beams, from the vehicle navigation system (using GPS and IMU data) showing excellent agreement between them. The resolution of LOS velocity measurement is 2 mm/sec limited by the FFT processing algorithm. The NDL velocity precision, defined as random noise about its mean, was measured to be 1.7 cm/sec 1-sigma, dominated by the vehicle vibration. The velocity accuracy (bias) was estimated analytically to be about 1 cm/sec. The NDL velocity precision and accuracy demonstrated in the Morpheus flights are about an order of magnitude better than those required for precision and/or well-controlled soft landings. Fig 4 (right) provides the NDL altitude data for the same flight, showing the three LOS measurements of range to ground. One of the beams (blue curve) looking along the flight path measuring a longer distance while the other two beams (green and red) looking to the sides but still tilted forward have their measured plots almost overlap. From these three LOS range data, the vehicle altitude relative to local ground is calculated in real-time without attitude data from the IMU.

The plots of Fig. 4 show some data dropouts at beginning of the flight and the last few seconds of the flight due to the dense dust cloud created by the engine during takeoff and landing (Fig. 5). The loss of lidar data in dust plume was expected and the ALHAT landing system was designed to dead-reckon to a soft landing by utilizing the precision vector vertical velocity provided by the NDL prior to the creation of dust plume during the final stage of descent.

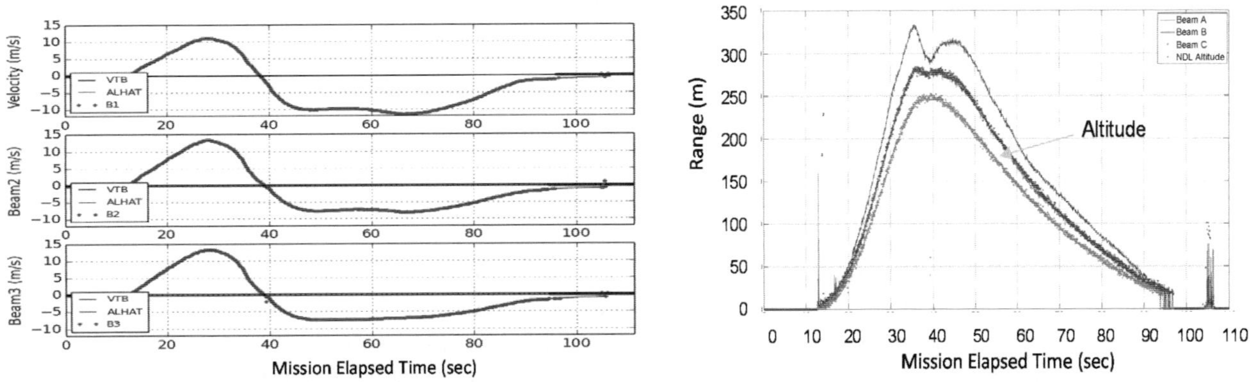

Figure 4. Morpheus flight test data: LOS velocity (left) and range (right).

Figure 5. Dust clouds created by the Morpheus engine during takeoff and landing.

4. Conclusion

The Navigation Doppler Lidar is expected to play a critical role in NASA's future planetary exploration missions because of its ability to provide the necessary data for precision navigation and executing well-controlled landings on solar system bodies. Compared to radars, the NDL offers more than an order of magnitude higher precision velocity and altitude data without concerns of measurement ambiguities or target clutter while significantly reducing the required mass, size, and power. The viability of this technology for future missions was demonstrated aboard a rocket-propelled free-flyer vehicle. The data from the NDL was used by an autonomous GN&C system to navigate and land the vehicle precisely at the selected site location surrounded by hazardous rock piles and craters. On a path to spaceflight units, we are currently developing the next generation NDL with an extended operational envelope and reduced size, mass, and power.

5. References

[1] Pollard, B. D., and Chen, C. W., "A Radar Terminal Descent Sensor for the Mars Science Laboratory Mission," IEEE Aerospace Conference, paper no.1597 (2008)

[2] Farzin Amzajerdian, Diego Pierrottet, Larry Petway, Glenn Hines, Vincent Roback and Robert Reisse, "Lidar Sensors for Autonomous Landing and Hazard Avoidance," Proc. of AIAA Space and Astronautics Forum and Exposition, 10.2514/6.2013-5312 (2013)

[3] Diego Pierrottet, Farzin Amzajerdian, Larry Petway, Glenn Hines, and Bruce Barnes, "Field Demonstration of a Precision Navigation Lidar System for Space Vehicles," AIAA GN&C Conference, 10.2514/6.2013-4717 (2013)

[4] Diego Pierrottet, Farzin Amzajerdian, Larry Petway, Bruce Barnes, George Lockard, and Glenn Hines, "Navigation Doppler Lidar Sensor for Precision Altitude and Vector Velocity Measurements Flight Test Results," Proceeding SPIE Vol. 8044, (2011).

Laser Doppler sensing in acoustic detection of buried landmines

Vyacheslav Aranchuk, James Sabatier, Ina Aranchuk, and Richard Burgett
University of Mississippi
145 Hill Drive, University, MS 38655
aranchuk@olemiss.edu

Abstract: Acoustic detection of buried landmines employs low frequency elastic waves excited in the ground and a laser Doppler vibrometer (LDV) for vibration mapping of the ground surface. The technique has shown excellent performance in field tests with few false alarms or missed targets. A critical issue in acoustic landmine detection is the speed of ground vibration measurement. The speed of a moving LDV beam is limited by two fundamental factors: the speckle noise and the required spatial and frequency resolutions of the ground vibration measurements. This paper discusses the methods of speckle noise mitigation and time multiplexing of multi-beam LDV channels that allow increasing the speed of ground vibration measurements.

Keywords: laser Doppler vibrometer, landmine detection, acoustic, laser-acoustic sensing.

1. Introduction

Laser-acoustic techniques that employ low frequency elastic waves in the ground have been successfully used for detecting buried landmines [1-3]. The method consists of excitation of the ground with elastic waves in the frequency range from about 50 Hz to 1000 Hz, and obtaining a vibration map of the ground surface using a non-contact vibration sensor. Airborne sound created by loudspeakers, or seismic waves created by mechanical shakers, can be used to excite the ground vibration. The interaction of a buried landmine with the elastic waves causes the landmine to vibrate. Due to the mechanical resonances of the landmine and the higher mechanical compliance of the landmine compared to the nearby soil the vibration amplitude of the ground surface above a landmine is higher than the vibration amplitude of the surrounding area. A LDV is used to measure the vibration of the ground in many points to create a vibration image of the ground surface. The presence of a buried landmine can be detected by an amplitude anomaly in the vibration image. LDV-based acoustic landmine detection has demonstrated a high probability of detection with very low false alarm rates in field tests. A critical issue in acoustic landmine detection is the speed of ground vibration measurement. Using a single beam point-by-point scanning LDV in landmine detection results in a long measurement time. To reduce the measurement time a Multi-Beam LDV (MB-LDV) [3] has been developed and used for landmine detection. The MB-LDV provides parallel measurement of vibration in 16 points arranged in a linear array and can create a vibration image of the ground by scanning the beams. The speed of moving beams is limited by two fundamental factors: the speckle noise and the required spatial and frequency resolutions of the ground vibration measurements. This paper describes the methods of speckle noise mitigation and time multiplexing of MB-LDV channels that allow increasing the speed of ground vibration measurements.

2. Ground Vibration Imaging Using MB-LDV

The layout of the MB-LDV system used for landmine detection is shown in Figure 1(a). 16 laser beams are focused onto the ground along a line and can scan the ground in the direction perpendicular to the line of the beams. The back scattered light is optically mixed with reference beams on 16 photodetectors creating 16 frequency modulated signals with the carrier frequency 100 kHz. The frequency deviation is proportional to the velocity of the ground. The frequency modulated signals are demodulated in the 16 channel Phase-Locked Loop (PLL) frequency demodulator. The outputs of the PLL demodulator are proportional to the vibration velocity of the object at the point of measurement. The PLL output signals are then simultaneously digitized with a 16 channel A/D card in a computer, and the velocity spectrum of each beam is calculated in the software. A vibration image of the object can be created at any selected frequency band by scanning the beams in the transverse direction. Figure 1(b) shows an example of a vibration image of a buried landmine.

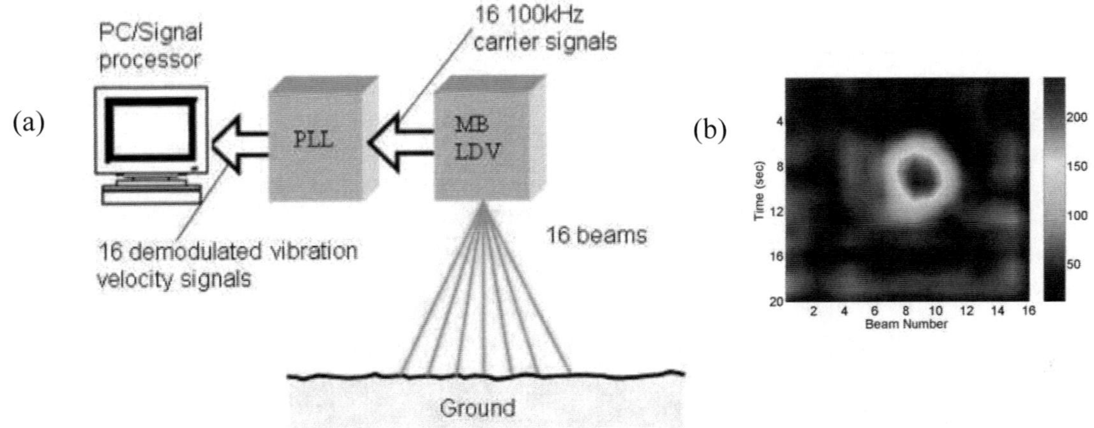

Figure 1. (a) Setup of scanning MB-LDV for acoustic landmine detection, (b) Vibration image of a buried landmine.

3. Speckle Noise Mitigation in a Continuously Scanning LDV

Scanning a laser beam across a target introduces noise in the vibrometer output due to dynamic speckles. When the laser beam moves across the target, the intensity and phase of speckle field change in a random way. This results in random fluctuations of the amplitude and phase of the Doppler signal. Dynamic speckles also cause spikes in the Doppler signal. Spikes results from dropouts in the Doppler signal due to low intensity of speckle field (dark speckle), and also from phase discontinuities in the vicinity of wavefront dislocations of the speckle field [4].

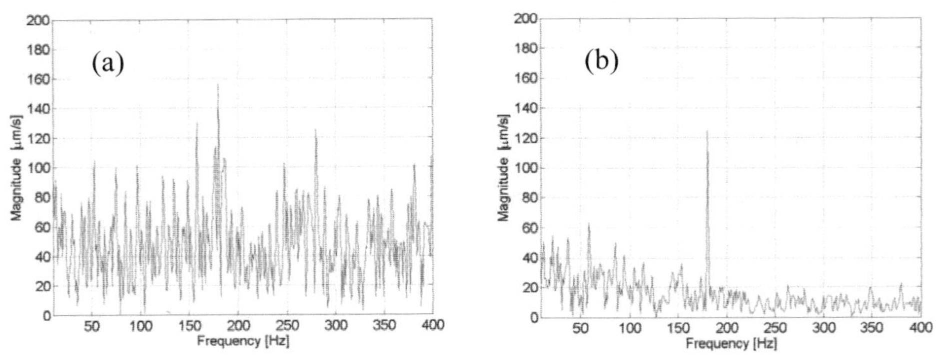

Figure 2. Spectrum of a continuously-scanning LDV velocity signal. (a) signal contains spikes; (b) spikes removed from the signal.

Normally the phase singularities coincide with dark speckles. Spikes alongside with random phase fluctuations of the Doppler signal result in speckle noise in the demodulated vibration signal [5]. The spike noise has a broadband energy spectrum, that makes filtering not efficient. The speckle noise can be reduced by removing spikes from the LDV signals.

We developed a method for spike detection and removal based on wavelet transform. The spikes in a LDV velocity signal are detected by their first level detail coefficients. After the locations of spikes are determined, those regions are replaced with interpolated values. Figure 2 shows and example of speckle noise reduction in a continuously scanning LDV signal. Figure 2 (a) shows a spectrum of a velocity signal of a continuously scanning LDV beam over a buried object excited with 180Hz single tone. Figure 2 (b) shows a spectrum of the same signal after removing spikes. One can see that removing spikes from the LDV signal allowed reduction of noise by approximately 10dB. Figure 3 shows an example of improving a vibration image of a buried landmine by removing spikes in signals of continuously scanning MB-LDV. The example shows that the removing spikes from a scanning LDV signals can significantly enhance the contrast of a vibration image of a buried object.

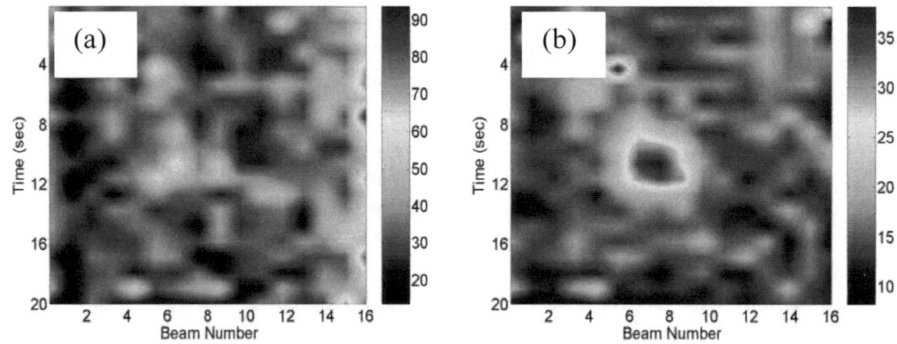

Figure 3. Velocity image of buried antitank mine before (a) and after (b) the wavelet threshold method of speckle noise reduction was applied.

4. Time-Multiplexed Multi-Beam Laser Vibrometry

Besides speckle noise, there is another fundamental limitation on speed of a continuously scanning or moving LDV, imposed by the required spatial and frequency resolutions of the ground vibration measurement. The maximum speed of a moving laser beam of the LDV is related to the required sensor spatial and frequency resolution through the expression [6]

$$V = s \cdot \Delta f \qquad (1)$$

where V is the speed of beam, s and Δf is the spatial and frequency resolution of the vibration measurement respectively. From expression (1) the beam must move over the target area of length s (spatial resolution cell) during the time T=1/Δf. Moving with a higher speed will worsen the spatial or frequency resolution, or both.

We developed a method of continuously measuring the ground vibration with the moving MB-LDV that allows one to overcome that speed limitation [7,8]. The method employs time division multiplexing (TDM) of laser beams of a row in the direction of motion of the platform. In this case the MB-LDV is moving along a linear array of N laser beams. With the proposed method, the speed of motion of the MB-LDV can be increased N times without worsening the spatial and frequency resolutions. The principle is shown in Figure 4(a). Only four beams are shown for simplicity. The distance between beams is equal to the required spatial resolution s. The beams move in the down track direction and measure the vibration of each space segment (spatial resolution cell) sequentially. The beams move N times faster than a single beam LDV. The duration t of a time signal produced by each beam during its motion over each space segment s is N times shorter than the required time T. Next, the time domain signals of each beam passing over a certain space segment s are combined together to obtain a time segment of required duration corresponding to that space segment. Then the spectrum of vibration is calculated for each combined time segment. The speed of beams V_N is N times higher than the speed of the single beam LDV defined by (1).

$$V_N = N \cdot V = N \cdot s \cdot \Delta f \tag{2}$$

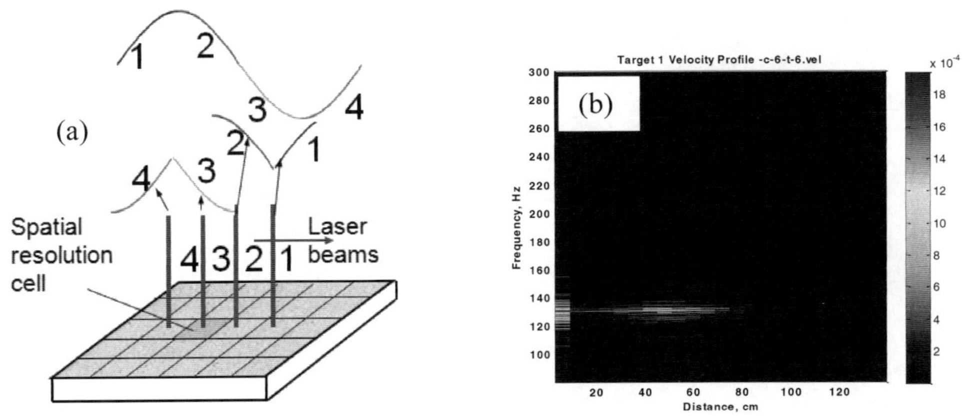

Figure 4. Principle of time-multiplexed laser vibrometry (a) and a vibration velocity profile of a buried plastic mine measured at 0.73 m/s speed.

The proposed concept of TDM of laser beams has been verified experimentally. The 16 beam MB LDV was used to obtain a velocity profile of the ground above a buried mine at a continuous motion. The MB LDV was moving along the line of beams over a buried mine. The vibration of the ground was created by shakers. The velocity profile of the ground surface was created by using the TDM method of 16 beams. Figure 4(b) shows an example of a vibration velocity profile in frequency space of a buried plastic landmine at 0.73 m/s speed of MB-LDV.

5. Summary

Methods for increasing the speed of ground vibration imaging by multi-beam LDV in acoustic landmine detection have been developed. The method of spikes removal in LDV signals allows reduction of speckle noise and increasing the speed of laser beams. The method of time-division multiplexing of multi-beam LDV channels allows increasing the speed of scanning laser beams without worsening the spatial and frequency resolutions of vibration measurement.

6. Acknowledgements

This work was supported by the US Army Research Office and the US Army Communications-Electronics Research, Development, and Engineering Center, Night Vision and Electronic Sensors Directorate.

7. References

[1] J.M. Sabatier and N. Xiang, "An Investigation of Acoustic-to-Seismic Coupling to Detect Buried Antitank Mines", IEEE Transactions on Geoscience and Remote Sensing, **39**, 1146-1154 (2001)

[2] N. Xiang and J.M. Sabatier, "An Experimental Study on Antipersonnel Landmine Detection using Acoustic-to-Seismic Coupling", J. Acoust. Soc. Am., **113**, 1333-1341 (2003).

[3] V. Aranchuk, A. Lal, C. Hess and J.M. Sabatier, "Multi-beam laser Doppler vibrometer for landmine detection" Opt. Eng. **45**, 104302-1-104302-10 (2006).

[4] V. Aranchuk, A.K. Lal, C.F. Hess, J.M., Sabatier, R.D. Burgett, I. Aranchuk, and W.T. Mayo "Speckle noise in a continuously scanning multi-beam laser Doppler vibrometer for acoustic landmine detection", Proceedings of the SPIE, Vol. 6217, Orlando, April 2006.

[5] V. Aranchuk, J.M. Sabatier, A.K. Lal, C.F. Hess, R.D. Burgett, M. O'Neill, "Multi-beam laser Doppler vibrometry for acoustic landmine detection using airborne and mechanically coupled vibration", Proceedings of the SPIE, Vol. 5794, p. 624-631, Orlando, March 2005.

[6] Xiang, N. and Sabatier, J.M., "Moving Speed of Linear Acoustic Landmine Detection System", Proceedings of the SPIE, Vol. 5794, p. 675-682 (2005).

[7] R. Burgett, V. Aranchuk, J. Sabatier, S. Bishop, "Demultiplexing multiple-beam laser Doppler Vibrometry for continuous scanning," Proceedings of the SPIE, 7303, 73030I-1, (2009)

[8] R. Burgett, V. Aranchuk, and I. Aranchuk, "Experimental investigation of buried landmine detection using time division multiplexing of multi-beam laser Doppler vibrometer channels", Proceedings of the SPIE, Vol. 8357, 83570H-1, Orlando, April 2012.

Remote Acoustic Detection Using a Coherent Laser Radar

Gabriel Lombardi, Jerry Butman, and David Rodham
Phase Coherence, Inc., 2908 Oregon Ct., I-10, Torrance, CA 90503
glombardi@phasecoherence.com

Abstract: A coherent lidar was used to detect sound remotely in an unseeded wind tunnel. The system is able to reconstruct acoustic temporal waveforms by detecting the motion of natural aerosols. The acoustic motions were measured in the presence of much larger motions caused by the ambient fluid-dynamic turbulence. Unlike conventional microphones, remote acoustic sensing is immune to wind-induced self-noise and avoids disturbing the aerodynamic flow. By forming a virtual microphone array it is possible to make the lidar system directional, thereby rejecting acoustic reflections from wind tunnel walls. The system employs a continuous-wave, single-frequency, 1.55 μm fiber laser in a bistatic configuration and a heterodyne receiver with a 200 MHz intermediate frequency. The acoustic waveform was impulsive, characteristic of acoustic signatures of helicopters. There is close agreement between the lidar and conventional microphone signals.

Keywords: acoustics, virtual microphone, aerosol scattering, heterodyne detection

1. Introduction

There is longstanding interest in measuring the acoustic emissions of rotorcraft in flight [1], and in wind tunnels [2,3]. The logistical and empirical difficulties of previous methods that relied on conventional microphones are circumvented by a laser virtual microphone. A laser sensor mounted on an aircraft avoids the need to use another aircraft with a microphone flying in formation, as in ref. 1, or a ground array of microphones, which can only measure the acoustic field below the plane of the rotor.

2. Experiment

Figure 1 is a schematic diagram of the optical layout. The master oscillator is a continuous-wave, 125-mW fiber laser operating at 1.55 μm wavelength. The oscillator beam is sampled and shifted by 200 MHz by an acousto-optic modulator to form the local oscillator (LO). The remainder is amplified and focused at the probe volume. Light scattered from the aerosols is mixed with the local oscillator on the InGaAs photodetector with 1.5 GHz bandwidth. The bistatic arrangement restricts the probe volume of the sensor to a region much shorter than the acoustic wavelengths of interest. The crossing region of the transmitted and back-propagated LO beams defines a probe of 25 cm in length (FWHM) at a range of ~5 m. The lidar system measures the acoustic acceleration of aerosols by processing the Doppler spectrum of the scattered light.

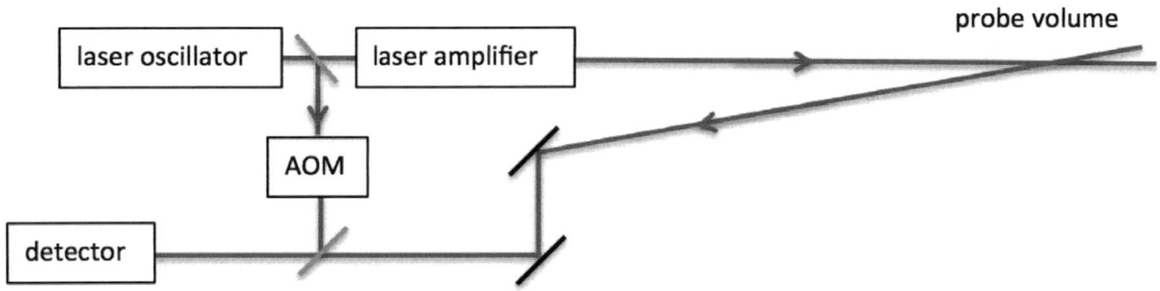

Figure 1. Optical schematic diagram.

The sensor was tested in Caltech's Lucas Wind Tunnel (Fig. 2). It is a closed-return tunnel capable of speeds up to 60 m/s with a 1.3 m x 1.8 m x 7.5 m test section. The nominal test section static pressure is 98.7 kPa. The sensor was assembled on an optical breadboard under the wind tunnel. The optical transmit/receive beams were introduced into the tunnel using a mirror attached to a steel crossbar bolted to the outer frame of the tunnel. The laser beam entered the tunnel in the gap between the test section and the tunnel return. Since the mirror was downstream of the test section it did not disturb the flow in the test section. A 15" speaker was installed in the wall of the test section.

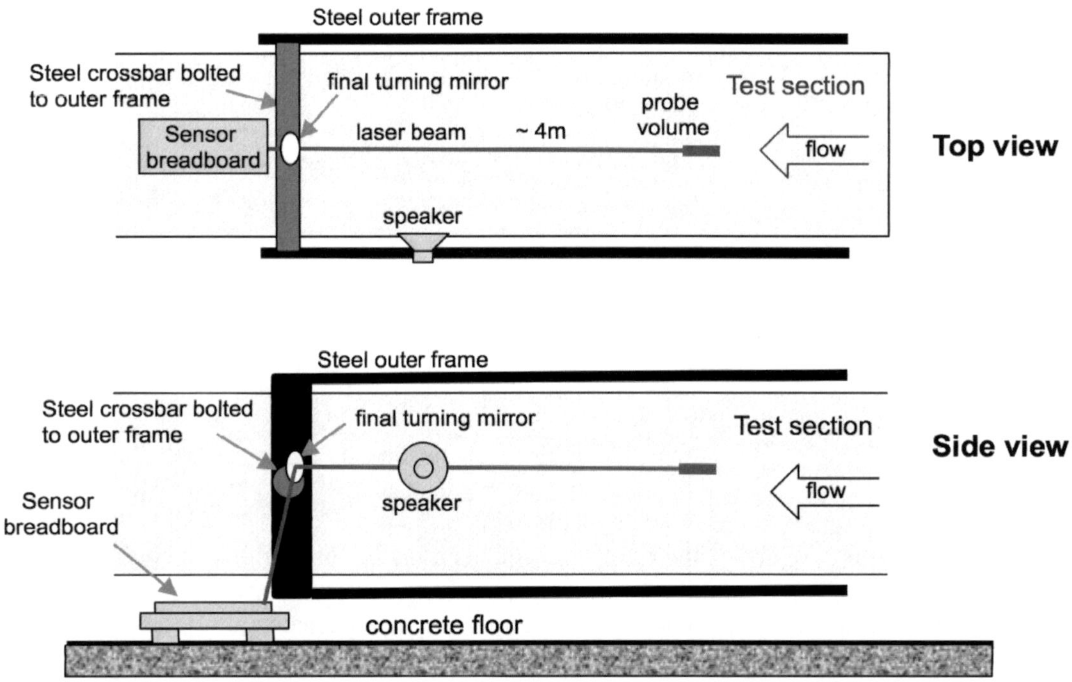

Figure 2. Schematic diagram of the installation of the sensor in the wind tunnel.

The cross section of the wind tunnel measures 1.3 x 1.8 m, which results in a reverberant environment, as the walls are not acoustically treated. Since the laser sensor measures acoustic motion *along* the beam direction, the microphone measurements must be configured to measure this motion to the exclusion of acoustic motions in other directions.

The pressure was measured with a B&K 2260 Investigator sound analyzer at two positions along the laser beam axis. Subtracting the two pressure time series and dividing by the microphone spacing results in an approximate measurement of the pressure gradient:

$$\frac{\partial p}{\partial x} \approx \frac{p_2 - p_1}{x_2 - x_1} \qquad (1)$$

The acoustic motion along the laser beam axis is related to the gradient in pressure by Newton's law:

$$-\frac{\partial p}{\partial x} = \rho \frac{\partial u_x}{\partial t}, \qquad (2)$$

where ρ is the density of air and u_x is the acoustic velocity component along the beam axis. The microphone pressure gradient was compared with the signal extracted by the laser, which is related to the particle acceleration.

The laser sensor relies on scattering from ambient particles in the flow. Natural air normally contains sufficient numbers of particles to enable the sensor to extract signals with a limited amount of averaging. Since the Lucas Tunnel is closed, the concentration of particles is much lower than typical natural air. Consequently, averaging of the acoustic signals over many repetitions was required to obtain signals with acceptable signal-to-noise ratios. Light seeding of the tunnel with water droplets at densities comparable to clean outdoor values results in good signals with less averaging. The measured particle densities are tabulated below.

Table 1. Particle Densities

particle diameter (μm)	density (particles/cm^3)	
	no seeding	light seeding
0.7	0.18	0.80
1.0	0.10	0.28
2.0	0.045	0.035

Figure 3(a) shows a comparison of the laser and microphone signals without seeding, averaging 200 pulses at 15 m/s wind speed; Fig. 3(b) shows the comparable data with light seeding and only averaging 50 pulses. The pressure gradient measured by the microphone (Eqn. 1) is plotted as a function of time and compared with the pressure gradient calculated from the particle acceleration measured with the laser sensor (Eqn. 2).

Both laser signals agree well with the microphone: the correlation between laser signal and microphone signal is 0.84 in the unseeded case and 0.92 in the seeded case. There is more noise in the unseeded case, suggesting more averaging was required. The measurements were repeated at 25 m/s wind speed resulting in a correlation of 0.59 for both unseeded and seeded cases.

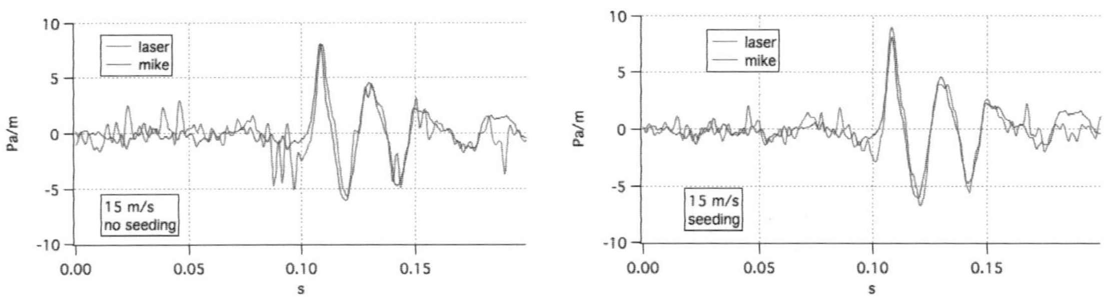

(a) no seeding (200 averages) (b) light seeding (50 averages)

Figure 3. Comparison of microphone and laser sensor signals.

In the far field of the source, the pressure time series can be computed from the time integral of particle acceleration since pressure is related to acoustic velocity by the following relation:

$$p(t) = \rho c u(t) = \rho c \int \frac{\partial u_x}{\partial t'} dt' \quad (3)$$

3. Acknowledgements

The authors are grateful for the expert mechanical design of David Windisch and helpful discussions with Ben Sim and Fred Schmitz on the aeroacoustics of helicopters. The authors appreciate the cooperation and assistance of Stephanie Rider of Caltech's Lucas Wind Tunnel. This work was supported by the Army Small Business Innovation Research (SBIR) program.

4. References

[1] F.H. Schmitz and Y.H. Yu, "Helicopter Impulsive Noise: Theoretical and Experimental Status," NASA Technical Memorandum 84390 (1983).

[2] Ben Sim, *et al.*, "Reduced In-Plane Low Frequency Helicopter Noise of an Active Flap Rotor," 65th American Helicopter Society International Annual Forum (2009).

[3] N. L. Barbely, *et al.*, "Acoustics Reflections of Full-Scale Rotor Noise Measurements in NFAC 40- by 80-Foot Wind Tunnel," American Helicopter Society Specialists' Conference (2012).

LASER DOPPLER VIBROMETRY ON ROTATING WIND TURBINE BLADES

P Lutzmann (a), B Goehler (a), C Scherer-Kloeckling (a), N Scherer-Negenborn (a), S Brunner (a), F van Putten (a) and C A Hill (b)
(a) Fraunhofer Institute of Optronics, System Technologies and Image Exploitation IOSB
Gutleuthausstraße 1, 76275 Ettlingen, Germany
(b) Malvern Lidar Consultants
2 Windsor Close, Malvern Link, United Kingdom
peter.lutzmann@iosb.fraunhofer.de

Abstract: We report a new 1.5 μm laser vibrometry system (based on a precise image tracker) that measures vibrations of rotating blades of wind turbines at ranges up to several hundred metres. After successful tests with a wind turbine scale model, measurements on real wind turbines were recently made and first results will be presented.

Keywords: Laser Vibrometry, Tracking System, Wind Turbine, Wind Power Plant

1. Introduction

The use of wind turbines, and therefore the need to monitor and analyse their performance, are growing steadily. Turbines tend to vibrate strongly, and laser Doppler vibrometry can usefully supplement the existing on-board sensors for monitoring turbine health. Its applications include condition monitoring, fault diagnostics, sound emission inspection, and also validation of turbine simulation models. Early fault detection will protect against catastrophic conditions and sudden breakdowns.

Laser vibrometry allows non-contact measurement of the vibrations of a wind turbine from a distant sensor on the ground [1-3]. For example the vibration characteristics of the whole blade surface can be determined with no need for built-in sensors or attached marks. Desired measurement distances (given the heights of modern wind turbines) are ~ 300 m or more, and 1.5 μm laser sources can satisfy the eye safety requirements.

Wind turbines with large moving blades are difficult targets. Commercial laser Doppler vibrometers (LDVs) are suited to making scans of static objects, or of spinning objects viewed from a point on their spin axis. But we wished to design and develop a system for measurement of the vibration characteristics of rotating turbine blades that move through large angles of view.

2. General System Description

The system has two main parts: a SWIR image-based tracker and an in-house-developed LDV. A fixed camera is mounted at the base of a pan/tilt unit (PTU) that carries the LDV (Figure 1). The camera captures images of the wind turbine and sends these to software that processes the images and builds a model of the rotary motion. With the help of this model, the pan and tilt head is positioned so that the laser beam automatically follows the rotating turbine blades. We pre-define a collection of *measurement points* (particular points on the blade surface) which the beam illuminates in a known sequence. Various scanning strategies are possible, but in this paper we consider a single laser beam that illuminates a single turbine blade for as long as we wish, before we turn attention to another blade; and we re-use the same measurement points for each blade. To achieve synchronisation (i.e. define a reference phase allowing us to trigger the phase of the time signal at any scanned point), we make separate measurements of one reference point with a second LDV. Such a reference may also be provided by an accelerometer fixed on a specific position of the windmill.

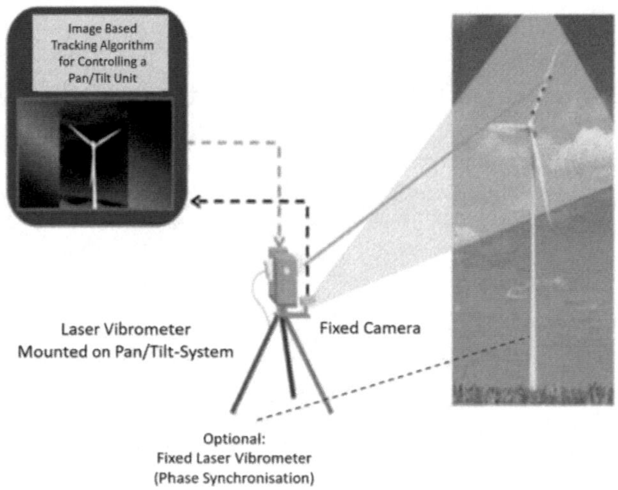

Figure 1. Principal system configuration.

For these wind turbine measurements a new 1.5 μm LDV using a polarisation diversity technique [4] was designed (Figure 2 and Table 1).

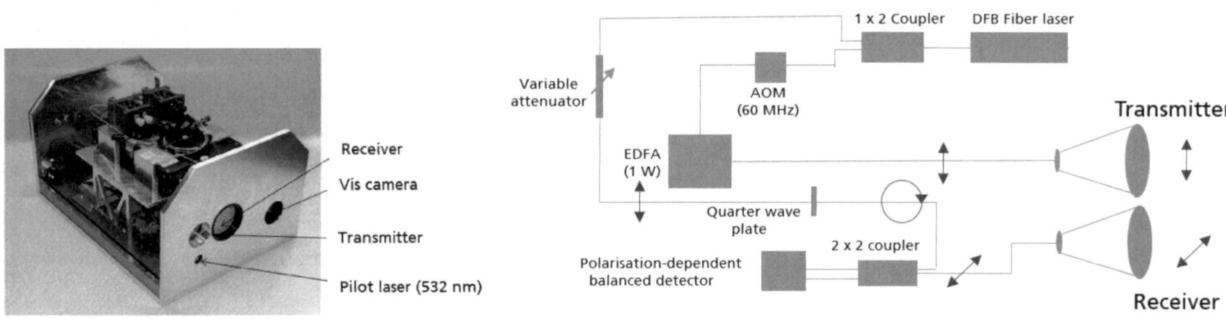

Figure 2. Experimental 1.5 μm laser Doppler vibrometer using polarisation diversity.

Table 1. Parameters of laser Doppler vibrometer

Wavelength	1.56 μm
Output power	up to 1W
Macro Doppler shift (max.)	+/- 60 MHz
Laser divergence	100 μrad
Laser safety class	1M (200 mW), 4 (1 W)

The system has a user interface developed from previous IOSB software. The user can define onscreen the desired set of measurement points on the wind turbine blade. These points are approached radially from the inside to the outside during the experiment, and coloured according to their processing state (Figure 3).

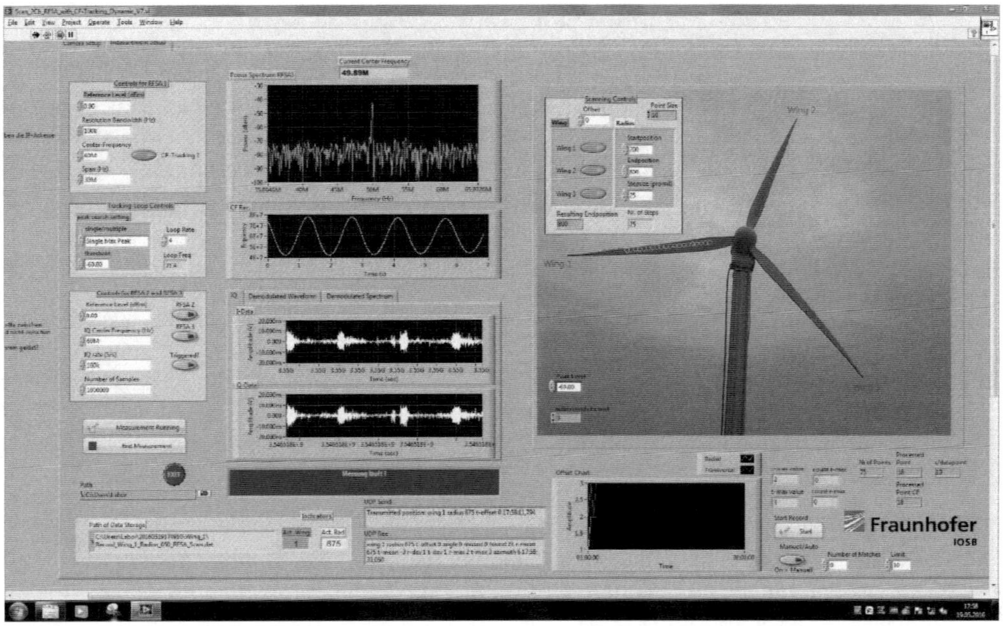

Figure 3. User interface with parameter settings, data acquisition, display and visualisation of the measurement points.

3. Measurements on Dynamic Structures of Wind Turbines

After some test measurements on our outdoor wind turbine scale model, we recorded data for a medium-size wind turbine (Vestas V90) with a rated power of 2.0 MW, a hub height of about 95 m and a rotor diameter of 90 m. The measuring system (LDV on PTU along with the fixed camera) was placed about 335 m from the base point of the wind turbine. Table 2 summarises some important parameters of the turbines, and the consequently expected line-of-sight (LOS) velocities and macro Doppler shifts. Two different data sets are always recorded: the frequency locked loop (FLL) signal related to the macro Doppler shift and the I&Q data of the frequency bandpassed IF signal. Figure 4 displays the estimated and measured macro Doppler shifts for our wind turbine model (left) and the measured wind turbine Vestas V90 (right) during 10 s time duration. The positions for signal pickup are at 20 % from the blade tip to the spinner. The macro Doppler shift variations over time of the real turbine blade are expected to be a combination of the scanning/tracking geometry, the slow mast movement and the blade bending modes. The red curve represents only the scanning/tracking, with the assumption that the blades remain in a fixed plane as they rotate; the other factors will need more detailed attention.

Figure 5 displays, with colour-coded amplitude, the first three vibration modes of the outdoor wind turbine scale model extracted from the demodulated IF signals. First a stationary blade supported on only one end (cantilever) was measured in the laboratory (22 scanning points). Then the same blade was measured when rotating on the outdoor scale model (25 scanning points, but only a part of the whole blade was scanned). In both cases the turbine was excited by a shaker at chosen frequencies, and for phase recognition the data acquisition was synchronised on the excitation frequencies of the shaker. The behaviour of the 1st vibrational mode (lower part left) is not clear.

Table 2. Estimated macro Doppler shifts

Symbol	Parameter	Model wind turbine	Real wind turbine (Vestas V90 – 2.0)	
h_0	Sensor height	1.4 m	1.4 m	
d	Rotor diameter	2 m	90 m	
h	Spinner height	4.15 m	95 m	
R	Range (measuring system – base point of WTG)	7.5 m	250 m	500 m
α_r	Angle between rotor plane normal and horizontal	0°	5°	
T	Revolution period (typ.)	5.1 s	6.2 s	
LOS_{velo}	LOS velocity (max.)	0.43 m/s	15.3 m/s	8.1 m/s
Δf_{macro}	Macro Doppler shift (max.)	+/- 558 kHz	+/- 19.9 MHz	+/- 10.6 MHz

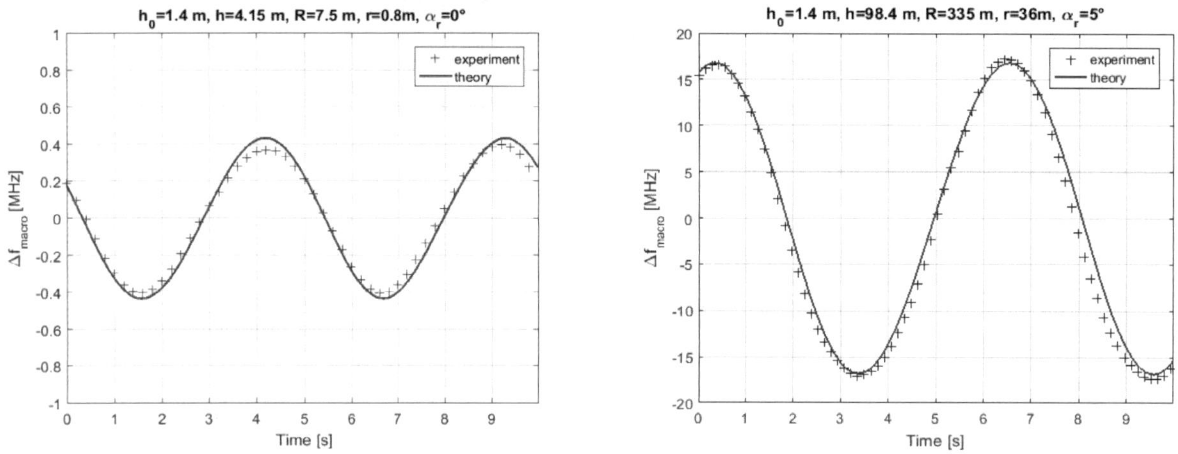

Figure 4. Theoretically estimated (red) and measured (blue) macro Doppler shifts for our wind turbine model (left) and the real wind turbine Vestas V90 (right) during 10 s time duration.

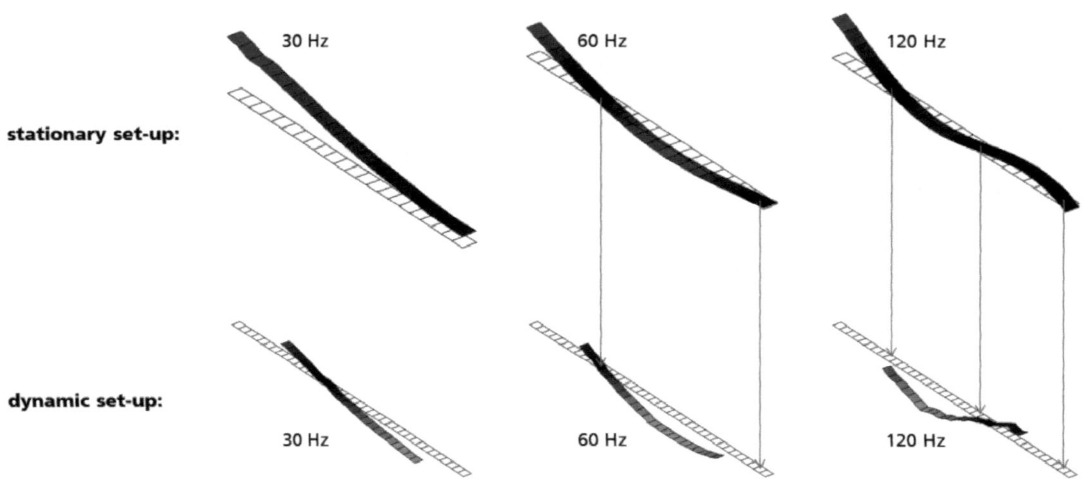

Figure 5. The first three blade vibrational modes of our wind turbine scale model (stationary and during rotation) measured with the laser Doppler vibrometer.

4. ACKNOWLEDGEMENT

The authors thank R. Ebert and I. Kaufmann at Fraunhofer IOSB for their valuable discussions and contributions, and especially F. Willutzki for his tireless experimental assistance.

5. References

[1] P. Lutzmann, B. Göhler, F. van Putten and C. A. Hill, "Laser vibration sensing: overview and applications", Proc. SPIE 8186, Electro-Optical Remote Sensing, Photonic Technologies, and Applications V, 818602 (2011).

[2] "Laser Vibrometers Make Non-contact Vibration Measurements on Wind Power Plants", Polytec InFocus 2/2008, www.polytec.com/infocus.

[3] R. Ebert, P. Lutzmann, C. Scherer, N. Scherer-Negenborn, B. Göhler, and F. van Putten, "Laser Vibrometry for Wind Turbines Inspection", in *Advanced Solid State Lasers*, OSA Technical Digest, paper ATh3A.3 (2014)

[4] A. Dräbenstedt, "Diversity Combining in Laser Doppler Vibrometry for Improved Signal Reliability", AVIELA 2014, AIP Conf. Proc.1600, 263-273.

Non-Contact Laser Ultrasound (NCLUS) for Medical Imaging and Diagnosis

Jonathan Fincke (MIT) and Robert Haupt (MIT Lincoln Lab)

CLRC

June 30, 2016

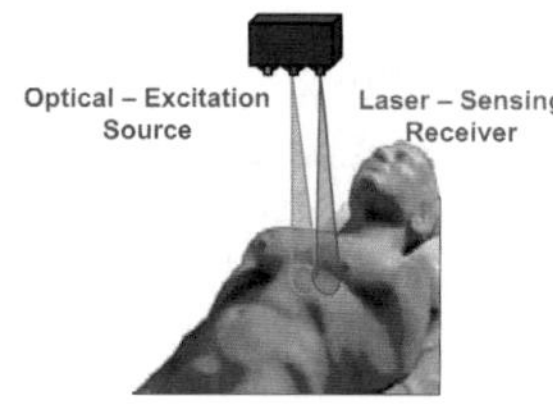

LINCOLN LABORATORY
MASSACHUSETTS INSTITUTE OF TECHNOLOGY

This material is based upon work supported by the Assistant Secretary of Defense for Research and Engineering under Air Force Contract No. FA8721-05-C-0002 and/or FA8702-15-D-0001. Any opinions, findings and conclusions or recommendations expressed in this material are those of the author(s) and do not necessarily reflect the views of ASD(R&E).

Potential of Non-Contact Laser Ultrasound (NCLUS)

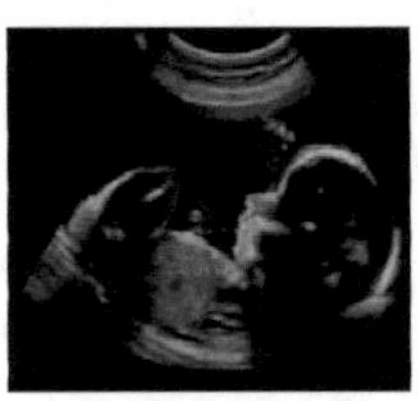

Medical Imaging

- High Resolution
- Mitigate Operator Variability
- Tumor Progression
- Elastography

First Responders

- Internal Injuries and Bleeding
- Organ Damage
- Image Through Burned Skin

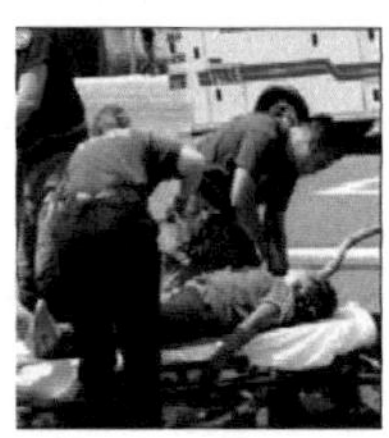

Sports Field Medicine

- Concussions
- Musculoskeletal Injuries
- Traumatized Areas

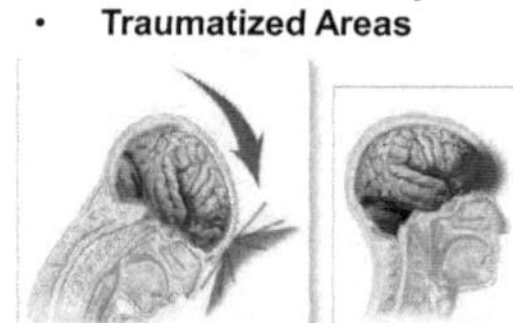

Surgical Assessment

- Open Body Imaging
- Surgical Guidance and Feedback
- Significant Standoff

Medical needs warrant invention and development of *contact-free* internal imaging technologies

State-of-Art Medical Imaging Tools

	PROS	CONS
Magnetic Resonance Imaging (MRI) 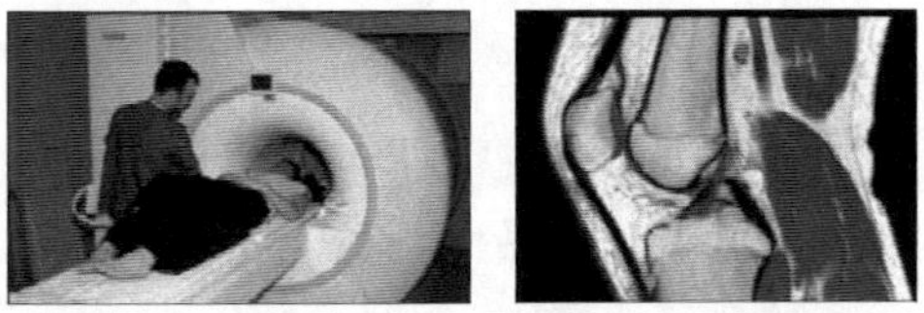	• High resolution • Safe • Fixed reference gantry – enables time image progression monitoring	• Large, expensive, in-hospital • Danger from metal debris
Computerized Tomography (CAT Scan) 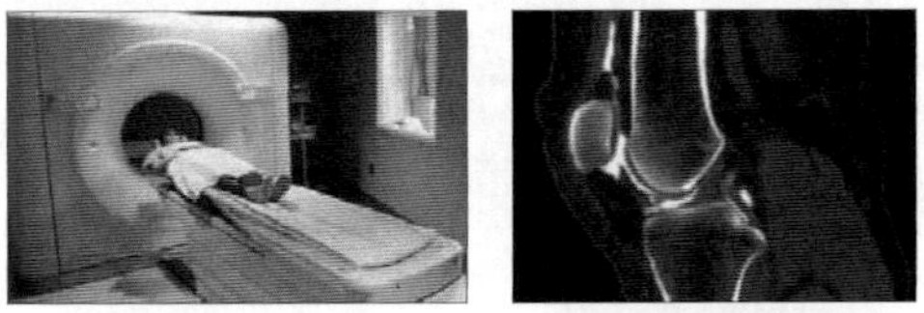	• High resolution • Fixed reference gantry – enables time image progression monitoring	• Large, expensive, in-hospital • Weak on tissue contrasts • Radiation risk
Ultrasound  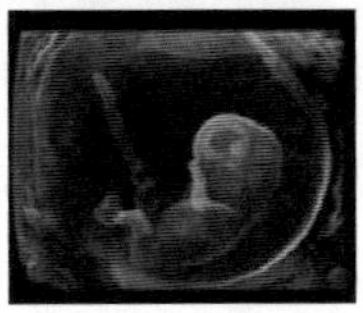	• High resolution • Portable, Inexpensive • Safe • In-hospital and field-forward	• Image distortion from *inter-observer variability* • No fixed reference • Impractical for time progression imaging in many applications

NCLUS Concept and Advantages

Standoff Laser Ultrasound System Concept
Optical 'Tri-Corder'

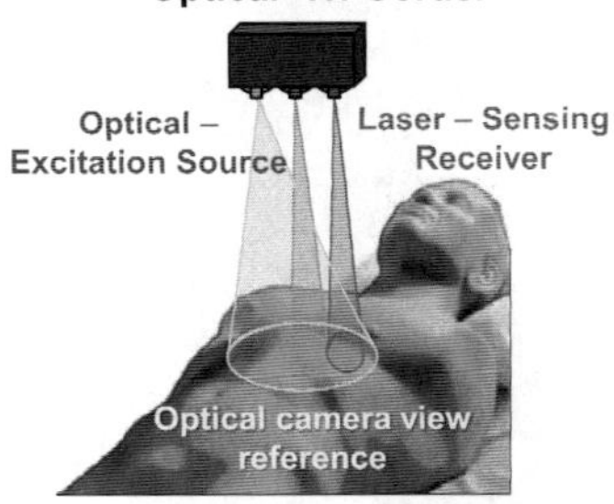

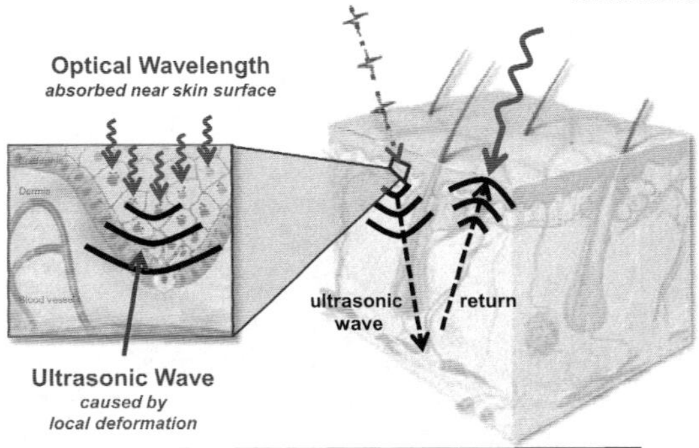

Benefits over Contact Ultrasound

- Potential to mitigate *inter-operator variability*
- Inch to 10 meter standoff
- Minimal interference in emergency and surgical settings
- Applicable to burned skin, traumatized areas, open surgical regions
- No repetitive strain
- Reduces infection risk

Capabilities in Medicine

- Anatomical Imaging
- Elastography: in-vivo tissue/bone property mapping
- Simultaneous measurement of compressional and shear waves

LINCOLN LABORATORY
MASSACHUSETTS INSTITUTE OF TECHNOLOGY

NCLUS Demonstration System

Optical Sources
(ultrasound generation)

Continuum Panther – Q switched Laser

pulse 7 nS
wavelength 215 - 2550 nm

BKtel– Q switched Fiber Laser

pulse 300 pS - 10 nS
wavelength 1550 nm

Lincoln Biomedical Laser Doppler Vibrometer (LDV)
(ultrasound measurement)

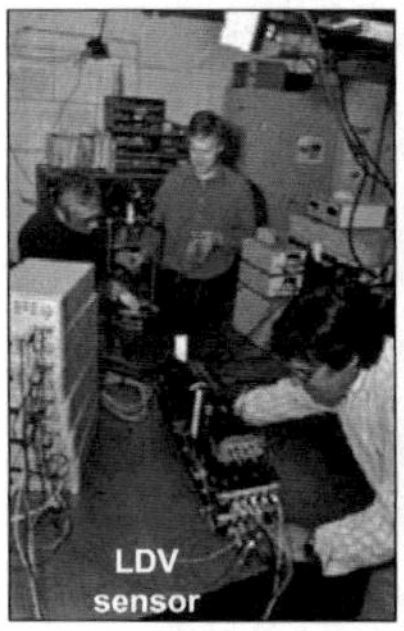

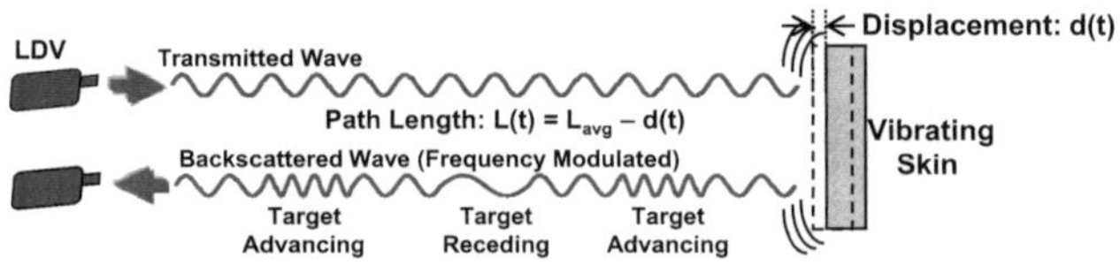

MIT LL Biomedical Laser Doppler Vibrometer

Monostatic Laser Doppler Vibrometer

Transmit – Receive Optics

Lens System for Monostatic Beam

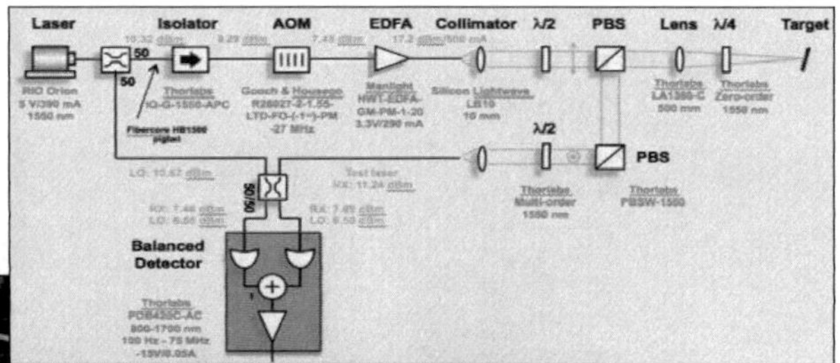

Medical Imaging Requirements

- BW: 0.1 – 10 MHz
- Spot Size: ~ 0.1-2 mm
- NEVV: 1-10 μm/sec/rtHz
- Eye Safe: 1550 nm

MIT LL developing custom standoff LDV sensor for optical ultrasound that meets eye-safety and needs for medical ultrasound imaging

Non-Contact Laser Ultrasonic Measurement

Direct Transmission Through Beef Sample

Laboratory Setup

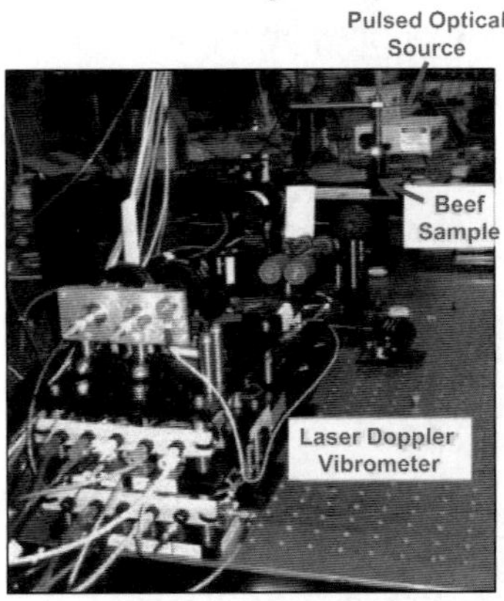

Measurement Geometry

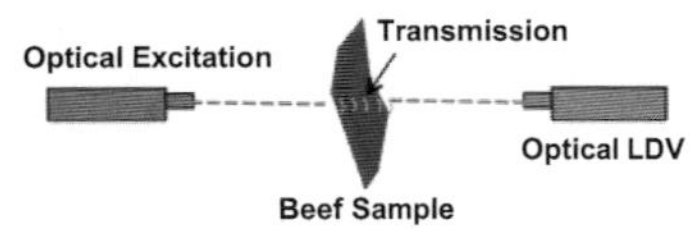

Biomedical Laser Vibrometer Measurement

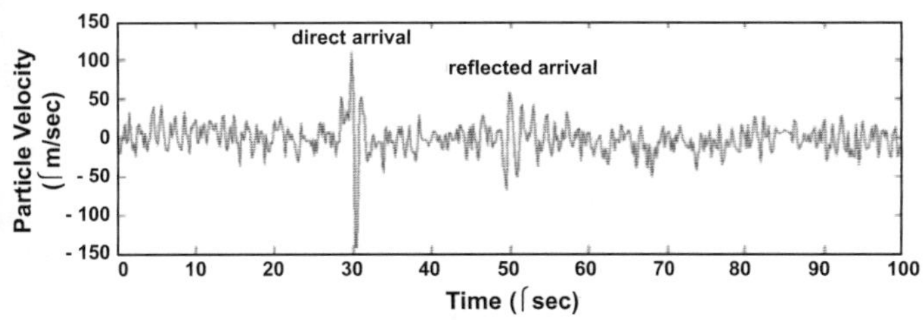

- Total Non-Contact Laser Ultrasound demonstrated using COTs optical excitation and custom MIT LL LDV without sample surface preparation
- Currently refining LDV design to yield optimal ultrasonic return

NCLUS – In-lab 2D Scanning Study System

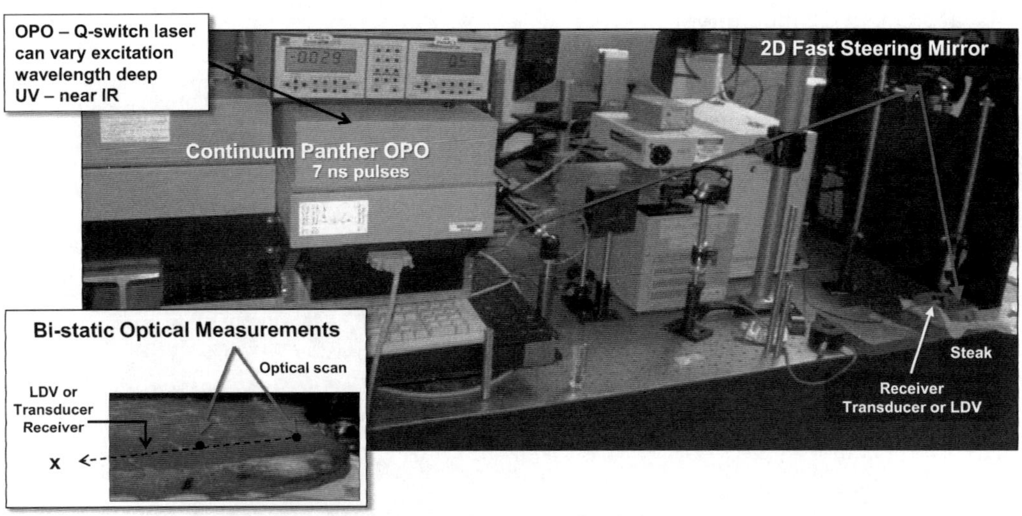

- Rapid scan excitation laser across sample in x and y
- US sensing measured with LDV or transducer at single location

2D Image - Off-end Scan Sonogram

NCLUS 2D Scan

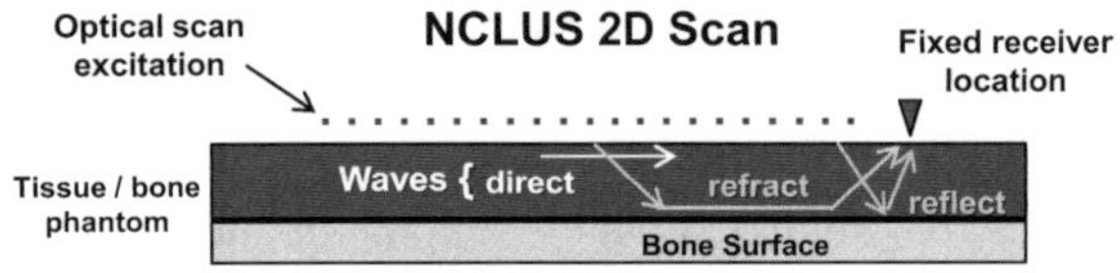

Sonogram 'Events'

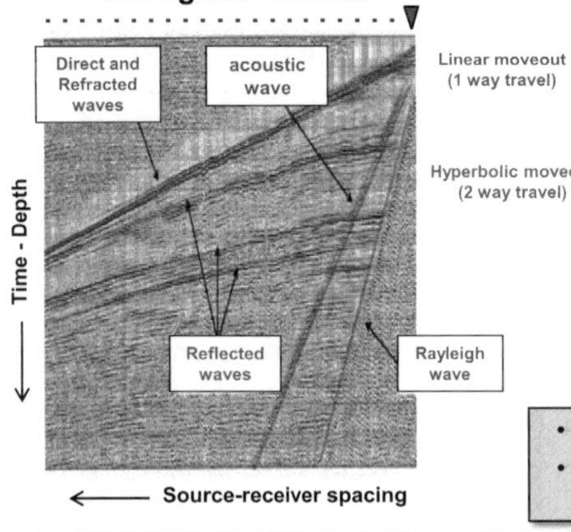

Ultrasonic Wave Types and Particle Motion

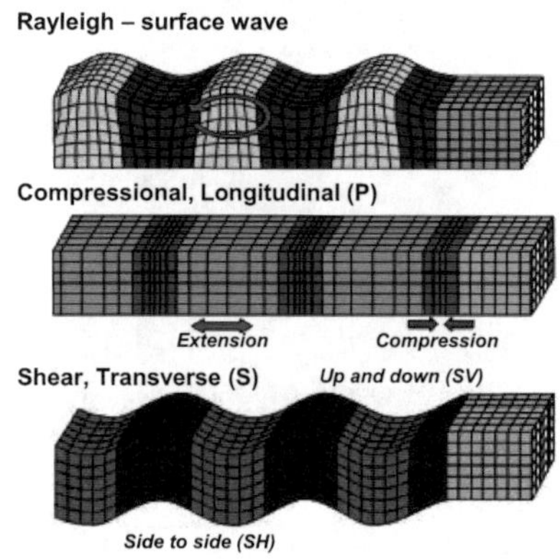

- Wave speed determined by linear moveout slope
- Wave type determined by speed and particle motion direction

Bone Phantom Ultrasonic Wave Analysis

Measurement Configuration

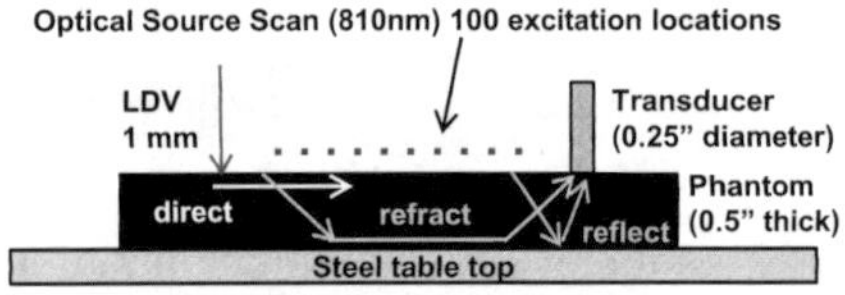

Ultrasonic Waves

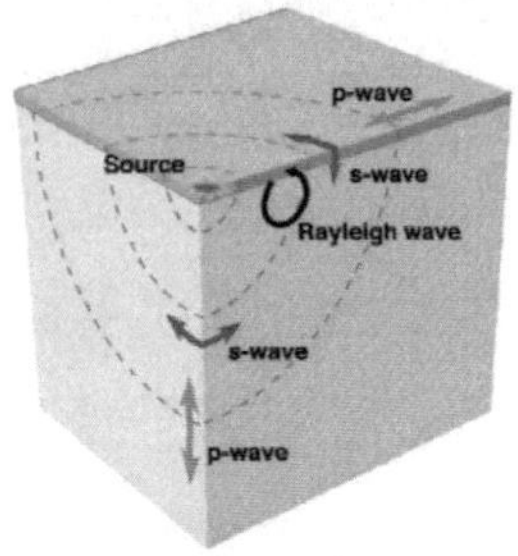

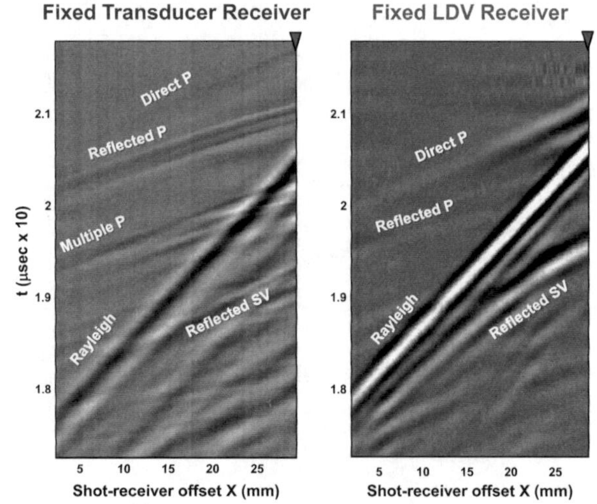

Sonogram shot records rich in ultrasonic wave information – P, S, Rayleigh waves observed

Potential Using Full Suite of Ultrasonic Waves

Compressional Wave Imaging

Compressional waves propagate in tissue and bone

- Standard for anatomical imaging in the body
- Also measures Doppler for blood flow

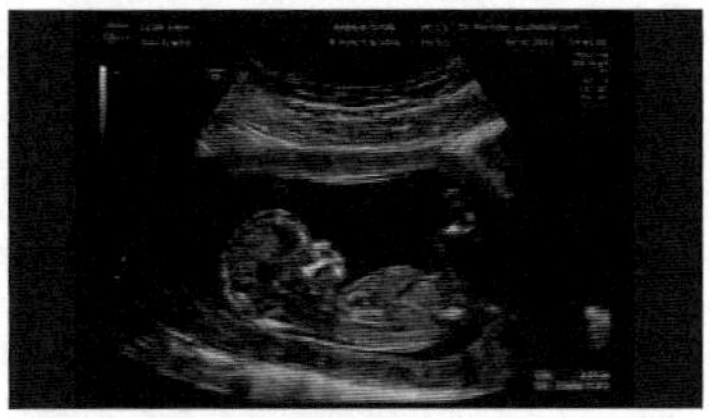

Shear Wave Dispersion

Shear-waves disperse in coagulated blood

- Detection of Hematomas
- Fluid viscosity increases due to blood coagulation
- Application for TBI, Internal Bleeding, Organ Disease

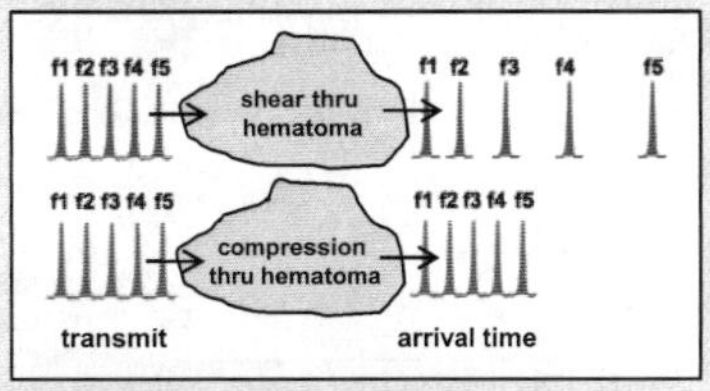

Elastography

Measure compressional and shear waves, also surface and guided waves

- Determine tissue and bone properties in-situ
- Cancerous tumor detection, osteoporosis, stress fracture detection, neuromuscular disease progression

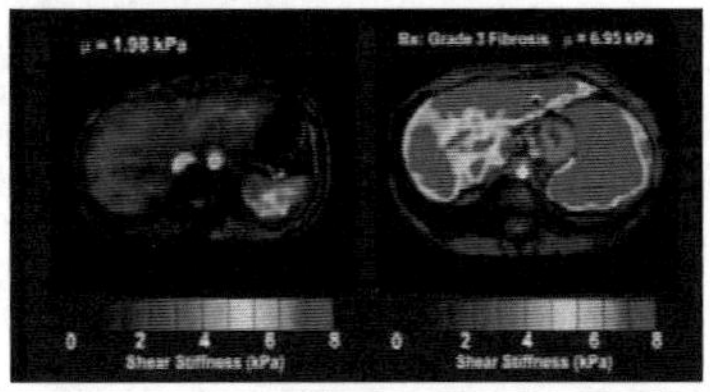

NCLUS Muscle Tissue Ultrasonic Wave Sonogram

Measurement Configuration in tissue sample

- Optical Excitation Scan – 100 locations
- Receiver – 1 location

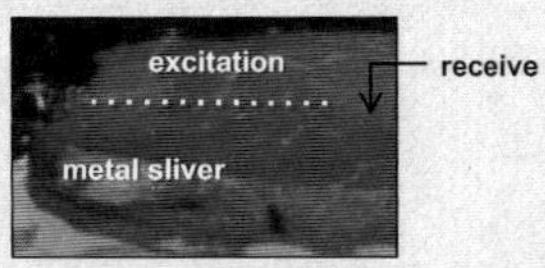

Optical Scan / Transducer Receiver

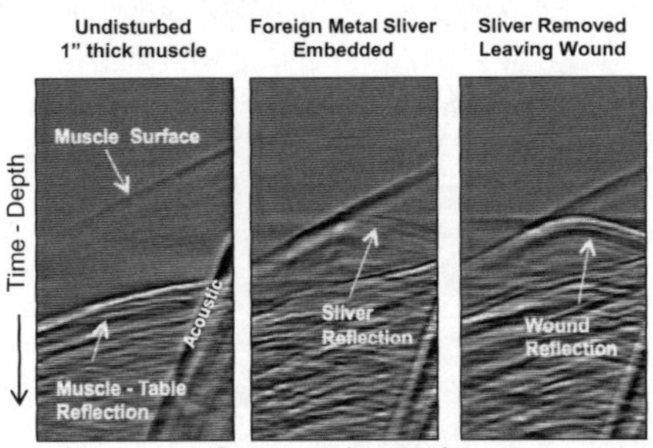

Optical Scan / LDV Receiver

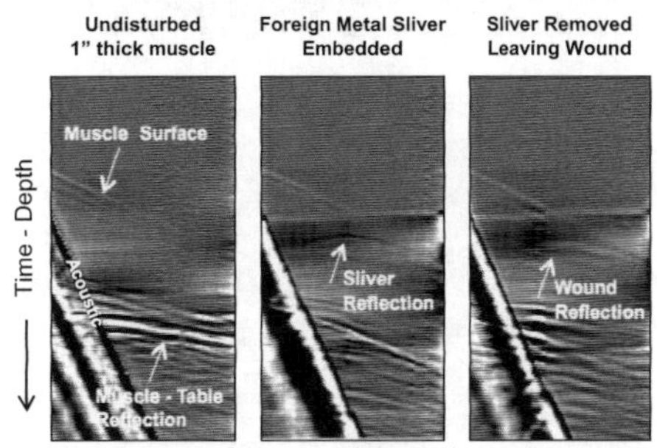

- **Optical generation of ultrasound produces useful images when measured with LDV or transducers**
- **Total optical scan and measurement made from <u>1 meter standoff</u> resolves 1-mm object**

NCLUS 3D - Anatomical Imaging

1 mm rods embedded in 1.5" thick steak

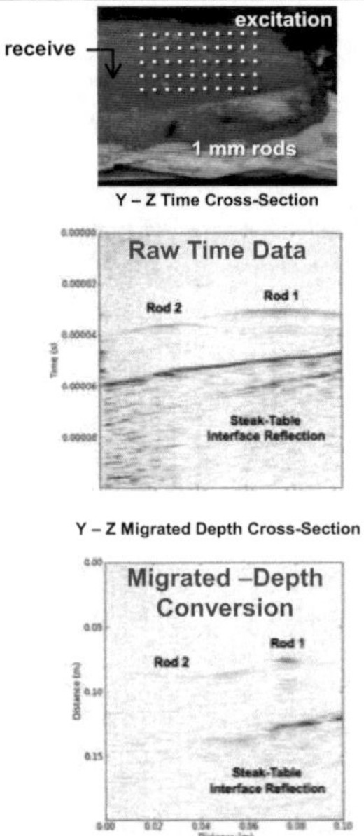

2D Horizontal (x-y) Slices In Depth across Rod 1

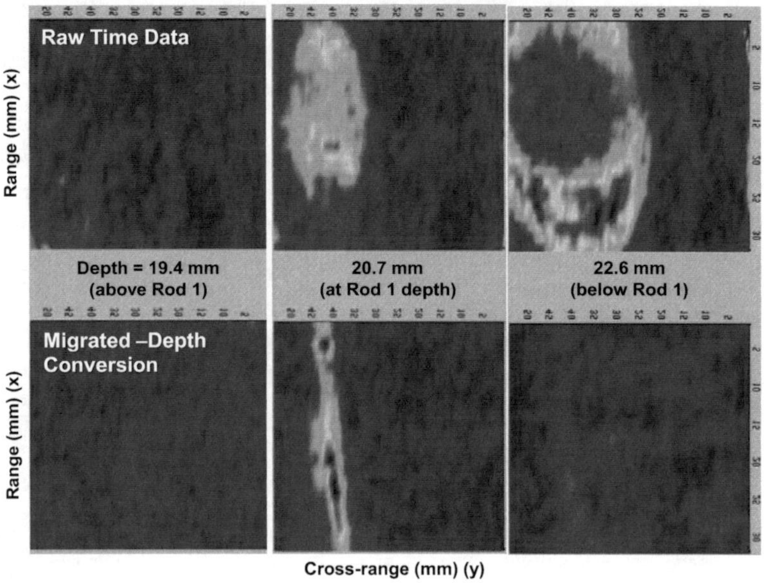

EYE & SKIN SAFE

Effects of Optical Excitation Wavelength on Ultrasound Power

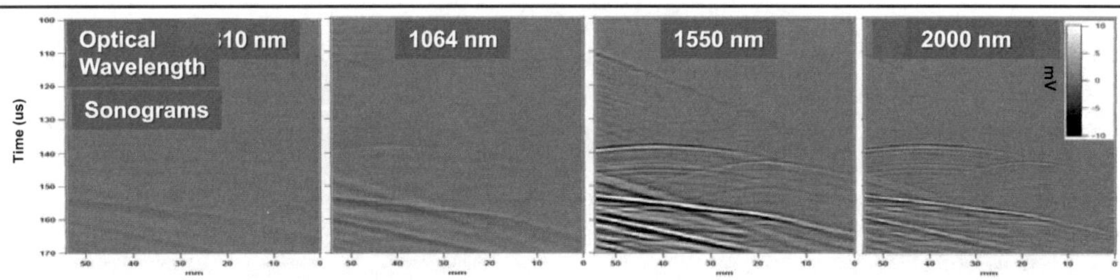

Optical Coupling In Tissue

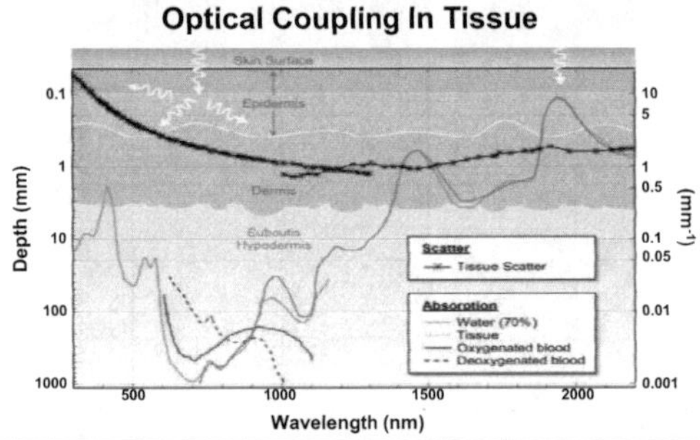

Ultrasonic Return vs Optical Excitation Coupling

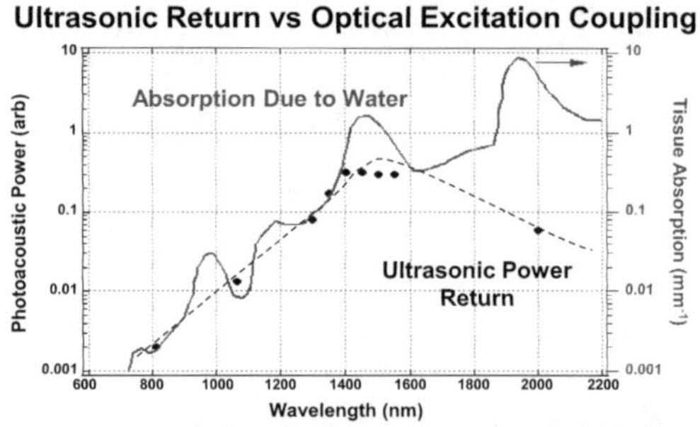

- 1550 nm light creates the largest eye-safe photo-acoustic yield and highest acoustic SNR
- 2000 nm exhibits drop which may be attributed to ultrasonic attenuation in tissue

Effects of Excitation Laser Spot Size on Acoustic Directivity

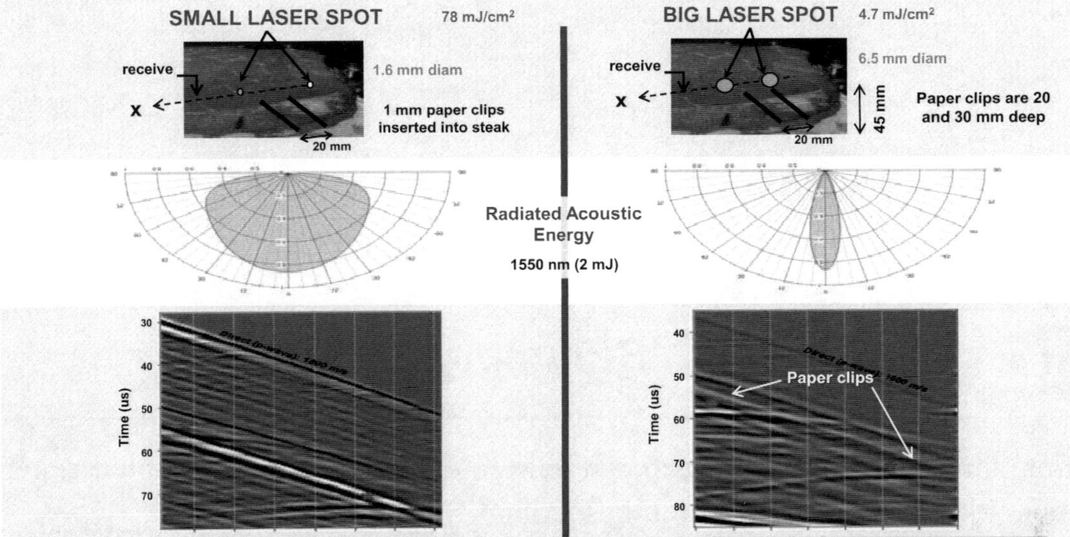

- Larger excitation laser spot size sharpens acoustic directivity, improves down-looking SNR, and minimizes 'out-of-plane' scattering while reducing optical power well within safety limits
- Smaller spot size – larger acoustic beam beneficial for generating compression and shear

NCLUS System Development Plan

Near Term 1-2 years

Standoff Laser Ultrasound System (stand-mounted)

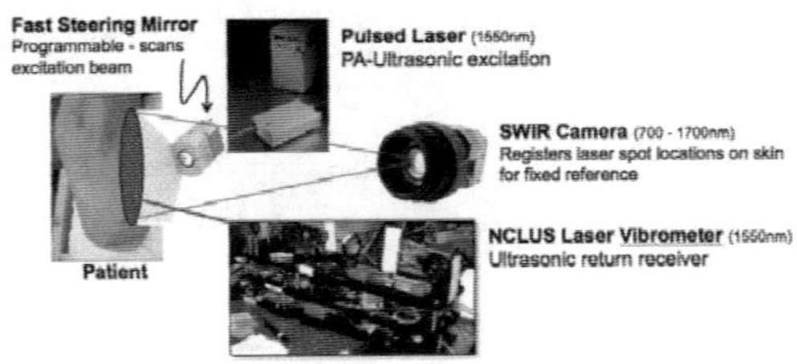

Tomographic Imaging System (In Progress)

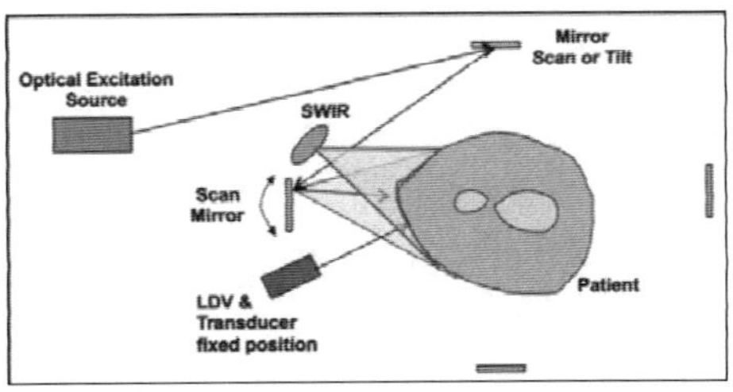

Longer Term 5 years

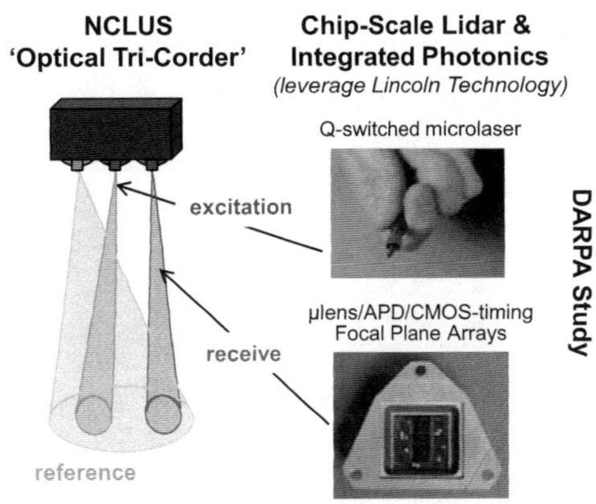

Integrated photonics and chip-scale lidar technologies enable motion compensation and miniaturization for hand-held system

Summary

- **Demonstrated NCLUS approach can generate measureable ultrasonic signals and images in bio-tissue useful for medical applications**
  - Photo-acoustic conversion generates far-field ultrasonic waves
  - Useful optical excitation possible using skin / eye safe power levels
  - Non-contact LDV capable of measuring optically induced ultrasound signal
- **Scanning optical excitation yields 2D, 3D ultrasonic images in tissue and bone**
  - Optical source can generate full suite of ultrasonic waves
  - Able to resolve 1-mm metal rod in tissue mass
- **Currently adapting NCLUS technology to specific medical applications**
  - Tomographic imaging – elastography program underway for prosthetic fitting
  - Exploring system for bone health – stress fracture detection and monitoring
- **NCLUS system planned for rapid and longer term developments**
  - Stand-mounted and hand-held field forward

NCLUS - 17
RH 02/01/2016

LINCOLN LABORATORY
MASSACHUSETTS INSTITUTE OF TECHNOLOGY

FMCW Differential Synthetic Aperture Ladar for Turbulence Mitigation

Zeb W. Barber (a), Jason R. Dahl, and Christopher Ross Blaszczyk
(a) Montana State University, Spectrum Lab
PO Box 173510 Bozeman, MT 59717
barber@spectrum.montana.edu

Abstract: Synthetic Aperture (SA) imaging, including holographic aperture ladar (HAL), synthetic aperture ladar (SAL), and combinations thereof; are promising solutions for long range imaging applications. One of the major difficulties with real-world SA imaging is coherently processing the image information in the presence of atmospheric turbulence. Differential SAL imaging was proposed and patented in 2005 as a technique to reduce the sensitivity of synthetic aperture imaging ladar to line-of-sight motion errors and shown to reduce sensitivity to dynamic turbulence near the target. We will present experimental laboratory demonstrations of high range resolution DSAL with comparisons of performance to standard SAL processing in the presence of localized dynamic turbulence. Our DSAL receiver is based on imaging the receive aperture and LO onto quad-cell detectors that measure the ladar signal in each quadrant of the aperture separately. We will also discuss how differential techniques can mitigate atmospheric turbulence with other SA imaging techniques.

Keywords: Coherent Laser Radar, Synthetic Aperture Imaging

1. Introduction

By exploiting the relative motions of the transmitter (Tx), receiver (Rx), and/or target Synthetic Aperture Ladar (SAL) imaging techniques have the ability to provide image resolution beyond the standard diffraction limited resolution of the physical optical aperture[1]. Two key requirements for SAL imaging are: a coherent laser radar system that provides range resolution commensurate with the desired image resolution, and robust techniques to correct and compensate for the inevitable phase errors that arise during the aperture/object motion. Our high resolution (< 0.5 cm) frequency modulated continuous wave (FMCW) ladar systems[2], [3], allow us to study SAL imaging at short ranges in a laboratory environment. This has the advantage of eliminating many engineering and fundamental challenges found in long-distance SAL imaging such as high power lasers, beam steering and pointing stability, and uncontrollable atmospheric turbulence, allowing us to focus on the imaging techniques.

Despite eliminating many challenges, controlling aperture motion and phase errors in the ladar system to much better than the optical wavelength is impractical so one still needs to utilize data based phase error compensation. We have found that the phase gradient autofocus algorithm (PGA), which was developed for radar imaging, is very successful at compensating phase errors for most SAL imaging situations even when the pulse-to-pulse common mode phase error exceeds $\pm\pi$. The success of the PGA algorithm is based on its fantastic ability to provide optimal estimates of the common mode piston phase error for high clutter and/or low SNR situations, even including low light levels where the average image brightness is on the order of a few photons per pixel[4]. Combining our high range resolution FMCW ladar sources and straightforward use of the PGA algorithm we have successfully investigated many SAL imaging modalities with table-top experiments including: stripmap modes, spotlight modes, bistatic modes, interferometric SAL, etc. [5].

For real-world SAL imaging scenarios atmospheric turbulence presents challenges different than with other imaging methods. In general, atmospheric turbulence causes no blurring in range dimension. (However, for FMCW ladars that utilize long pulses ($\gg 10$ μs), range blurring can be observed for atmospheres with high Greenwood frequencies due to the Doppler effect.) Thus, the effects of the turbulence on SAL imaging are mainly observed in the cross-range dimension. One advantage of SAL is that due to the ability to correct the phase using PGA or other methods, important scaling of the atmospheric coherence diameter, r_0, is to the real-aperture as opposed to the full synthetic aperture size. In terms of thin phase screens at different locations, a phase screen located near the Tx/Rx optics generates mainly common mode pulse-to-pulse phase errors and are well corrected by the PGA algorithm as long as the r_0 is larger than the real aperture. This applies even if the atmospheric coherence time is smaller than the total SAL collection time. A thin phase screen near the target that is static over the total SAL collection time merely amounts to an added phase distortion of the image, which has little effect on the intensity image. However, if the phase screen near the target is not static then the phase evolution for different areas of the target will not be common mode and the PGA estimate will be corrupted and insufficient to compensate all areas of the target image simultaneously. This is roughly equivalent to anisoplanatic errors. For a turbulent phase screen in between the target and the Tx/Rx optics there will be combinations of common mode and anisoplanatic errors.

Differential SAL (DSAL) is a hardware based technique to compensate pulse-to-pulse phase errors that was proposed and patented by Stappaerts & Scharlemann in 2005[6], [7]. The basic concept behind DSAL is to measure the derivative of the received ladar signal phase across real aperture rather than the actual field phase. The benefit is that this derivative is insensitive to common mode phase fluctuations caused by relative motion between the aperture and the object. The derivative can then be numerically integrated across the synthetic aperture dimension to recover the full phase evolution up to an overall phase. In the Stappaerts and Scharlemann paper they outline a 1D scheme and algorithm that calls for dividing the Rx aperture, d, into two subapertures and separately measuring the phase in the left and right halves for each SA step of $d/4$. In the paper, it is shown that for steps of $d/4$ the field in one subaperture is identical to that of the other in the previous step (i.e. one subaperture lags the other by one step). This means the differential phase, $\Delta\varphi_i = \varphi_{r_i} - \varphi_{l_i}$, between the left and right halves can simply be cumulatively summed to generate a recovered phase evolution, $\tilde{\varphi}_i$, rather than having to scale the phase according to the step size. This phase is then combined with the field amplitude from one subaperture to generate a recovered field measurement, which is then processed with the standard SAL processing.

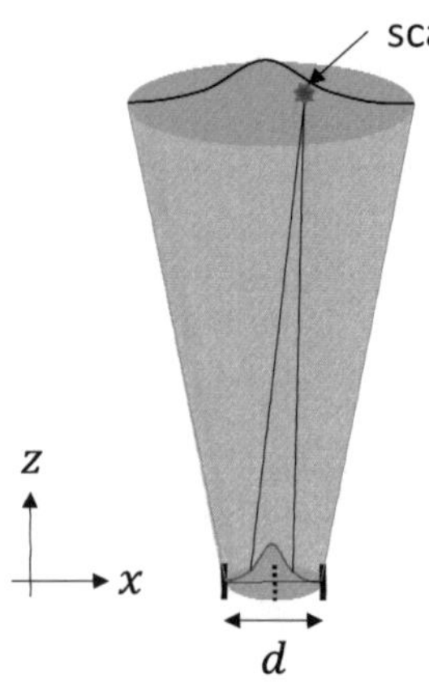

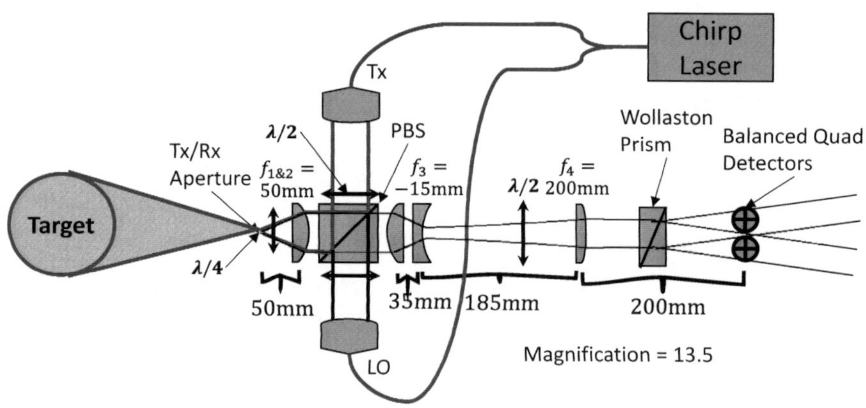

Figure 1. (Left) Differential SAL (DSAL) concept diagram. (Right) DSAL receiver design.

It is clear that the DSAL method is insensitive to piston phase fluctuations due to atmospheric turbulence, however Ref [6] makes a claim: "DSAL, unlike SAL, is not affected by turbulence changes near the target." This claim is what motivated our interest in investigating the DSAL technique. If true the DSAL would have a distinct advantage over SAL + PGA phase compensation for long rang SAL imaging applications. We report here our construction and testing of a high resolution laboratory DSAL imaging system including testing of performance in comparison to SAL + PGA for different turbulence conditions.

2. DSAL Design and Experimental Results

The design goal of our DSAL system (see Figure 1), was a monostatic system that would have reconfigurable Tx/Rx apertures and beams and a convenient method of separating the measurements in the subapertures. To accomplish a reconfigurable Tx/Rx aperture, the system uses a lens to focus the Tx beam, collimated out of the fiber coupled chirp source, to create a "virtual" Tx aperture. For the experiments shown here a 50 mm focusing lens is used to create a ~35 μm spot. This provides a sufficiently large illumination spot at the target ~20 cm so that good sized (greater than 100 x 100) SAL images could be formed with our ~2 mm resolution FMCW ladar system. The subaperture formation is accomplished by use of a quad-cell detector as the receiver, which allows us to divide the aperture into quadrants. This detector has a diameter of 1 mm, which for our short range measurements is much too large to sample the field in the aperture plane, so the optical design provides a magnification of ~13.5 for a 50 mm focusing lens. The Rx aperture is defined both by the image of the quadcell detector and the soft "virtual" Rx aperture defined by the LO beam. The LO and Rx mixing is accomplished using balanced polarization based mixing and the balance is achieved by photocurrent subtraction with a second quad-cell detector. The quad-cell detector circuit is a Hobb's type auto-balancing detector and generates four balanced outputs – one for each quadrant. The four outputs are digitized with an 8 channel, 12 bit, 80 MS/s digitizer from PicoTechnology. The DSAL Tx/Rx optics and detector have been constructed using optical cage hardware on an optical breadboard that is then mounted onto a computer controlled motorized linear stage to provide aperture motion. For our short distances only small synthetic apertures < 1 cm are required to achieve cross-range resolution commensurate with the ladar range resolution.

The target for these investigations was homemade using 3M Diamond retro-reflecting tape (for high return signal) on a black background in a pattern of triangles and bars. Placed at a distance of 5 to 8 m. Atmospheric turbulence was applied by placing a space heater below the propagation path. This generates very strong turbulence at an estimated level of $C_n^2 \leq 10^{-10}$. Both the DSAL and SAL+PGA processing start from the range compressed data $S_q(r_p, x_j)$, where the subscripts j, p, q refer to SA aperture domain, the image domains, and the quadrant of the detector, respectively. For the SAL+PGA processing the PGA algorithm is implemented starting with an estimated PSF window function that spans the whole image and slowly decreases by 10% until the phase error estimate converges to less than $\pi/10$. The SAL+PGA image quality is nearly identical using a single detector or by summing the signals from each detector before applying PGA. The DSAL processing starts with $S_q(r_p, x_j)$ for each quadrant and makes an estimate of the field from the right and left half detectors as:

$$\exp\{i\varphi(r_p, x_j)\} = \prod_{k=1}^{j} \exp\left\{\left(i v_x \delta_x \angle\left[\left(S_1(r_p, x_k) + S_4(r_p, x_k)\right)\left(S_2(r_p, x_k) + S_3(r_p, x_k)\right)^*\right]\right)\right\}, \quad (1)$$

where the δ_x is the SA step size, v_x is a scaling factor for the step size relative to the size of the Rx aperture (nominally $4/d$ for the DSAL collection defined in Ref. [6]). The product accomplishes the integration of the differential phase across the synthetic aperture. This is then multiplied by the sum of the field amplitudes as $S_{DSAL} = \left(\sum_q |S_q(r_p, x_j)|\right) \exp\{i\varphi(r_p, x_j)\}$, and then compressed in the cross-range dimension with the proper quadratic phase compensation for the collection geometry.

Figure 2 compares the resulting DSAL and SAL+PGA images for different placements of the space heater (and no heater). From these images we make several observations: First, the DSAL images show significant errors where the image is wide. We believe that this is due to the limited magnification of the Rx aperture onto the quadrature detector, which tends to low pass filter the estimate of the differential phase in the aperture plane, corrupting the phase estimate for the high cross-range frequencies. Higher magnification or use of a hard aperture stop at the Tx/Rx aperture plane could provide improvement. Second, with no turbulence the sharpness of SAL+PGA processed image is sharper than that of the DSAL image, pointing toward a better estimate of the common mode phase errors. This effect was dependent on the image brightness, indicating that the differential phase estimate is relatively sensitive to signal noise including shot-noise. Third, the cross-range position of the SAL+PGA images is not stable. We have found that the PGA algorithm tends to shift the image in cross-range as this does not affect the width of the average PSF, which is what the PGA tries to optimize. Fourth, the DSAL processing tends to degrade more gracefully in the presence of turbulence particularly when the turbulence is nearer to the target. The SAL+PGA processing degrades by reducing the image contrast, whereas the DSAL processing losses resolution and tends to converge toward the auto-correlation function.

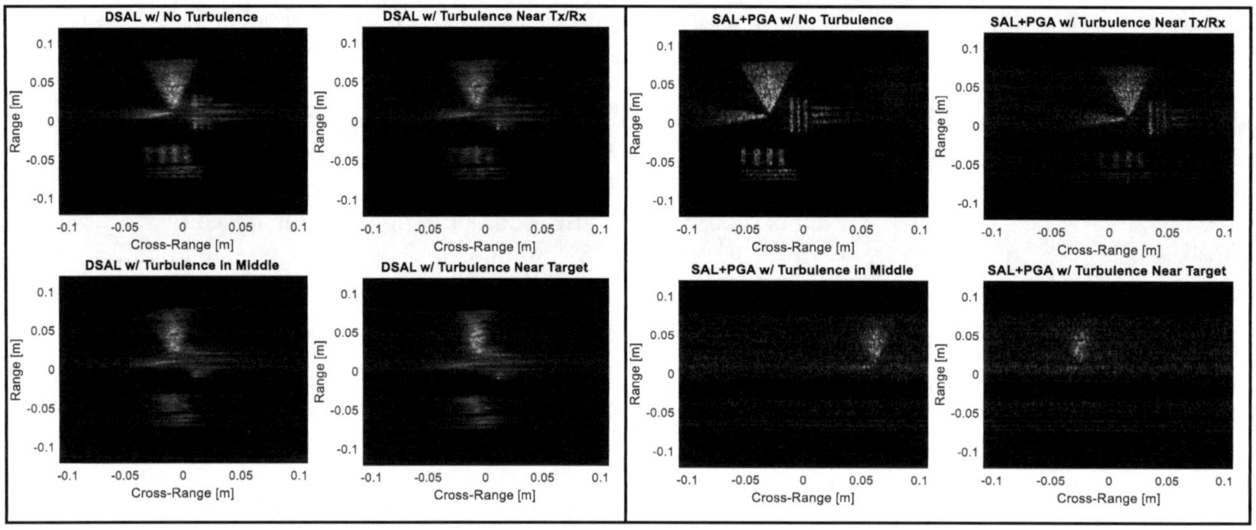

Figure 2. Comparison of DSAL and PGA+SAL for different locations of turbulence.

3. Discussion

While the experimental evidence here shows that DSAL appears more robust to turbulence near the target than SAL+PGA, turbulence near the target has a much larger effect on the DSAL than turbulence near the Tx/Rx. Further investigation shows that for targets with a single point scatterer per range line, DSAL does provide immunity from turbulence near the target as separate estimate of the piston phase is made for each range. However, fundamentally the presence of multiple scatterers in the cross-range direction with uncorrelated turbulence (i.e. separation $> r_0$) mixes these phase errors in the differential phase estimates leading to cross-range blurring. Despite this lack of immunity, the DSAL method is still attractive as it is much less processing intensive than PGA and thus merits further research.

4. References

[1] B. W. Krause, J. Buck, C. Ryan, D. Hwang, P. Kondratko, A. Malm, A. Gleason, and S. Ashby, "Synthetic aperture ladar flight demonstration," in *2011 Conference on Lasers and Electro-Optics (CLEO)*, 2011, pp. 1–2.

[2] P. A. Roos, R. R. Reibel, T. Berg, B. Kaylor, Z. W. Barber, and W. R. Babbitt, "Ultrabroadband optical chirp linearization for precision metrology applications," *Opt. Lett.*, vol. 34, no. 23, p. 3692, Nov. 2009.

[3] N. Satyan, A. Vasilyev, G. Rakuljic, V. Leyva, and Amnon Yariv, "Precise control of broadband frequency chirps using optoelectronic feedback," *Opt. Express*, vol. 17, 2009.

[4] Z. W. Barber and J. R. Dahl, "Synthetic aperture ladar imaging demonstrations and information at very low return levels," *Appl. Opt.*, vol. 53, no. 24, pp. 5531–5537, Aug. 2014.

[5] S. Crouch and Z. W. Barber, "Laboratory demonstrations of interferometric and spotlight synthetic aperture ladar techniques," *Opt. Express*, vol. 20, no. 22, pp. 24237–24246, Oct. 2012.

[6] E. A. Stappaerts and E. T. Scharlemann, "Differential synthetic aperture ladar," *Opt. Lett.*, vol. 30, no. 18, pp. 2385–2387, Sep. 2005.

[7] E. A. Stappaerts, "Differential optical synthetic aperture radar," US6879279 B2, 12-Apr-2005.

Synthetic aperture digital holography

Digital holography is a 2D angle-angle coherent imaging method. Objects are illuminated with narrowband laser light while a receiver collects the scattered light and mixes it with a coherent reference beam to form a holographic interference pattern. The holograms can be recorded with a standard focal plane array and replayed numerically with a computer. The resulting complex-valued images represent the optical field scattered by the object. Spatial resolution is typically limited by the receiver aperture diameter. Various synthetic aperture techniques, however, can be used to obtain finer resolution. We will show examples based on (i) object motion, (ii) collecting data with an array of transmitters, and (iii) combining data from an array of receivers.

Demonstration of Range & Doppler Compensated Holographic Ladar

Jason Stafford[a], Piotr Kondratko[b], Brian Krause[b], Benjamin Dapore[a], Nathan Seldomridge[b], Paul Suni[b], David Rabb[a]
(a) Air Force Research Laboratory Sensors Directorate
(b) Lockheed Martin Coherent Technologies

Abstract: Holographic ladar systems rely on the capture of temporally stable optical fringe patterns resulting from interference between the local oscillator (LO) beam and signal light imaged from a target. For pulsed systems, fringe visibility is maximized when the LO is temporally matched with the arrival time and duration of the signal, and when there is no gross relative motion between the sensor and target. In this demonstration, both range and velocity of a moving target were measured with a co-aligned high pulse rate laser range finder. Temporal matching was achieved by pulsing the LO to overlap the range-dependent signal arrival. Gross Doppler was compensated by using an acousto-optic modulator to impose a frequency shift onto the LO and transmitter (TX) that corresponded to the measured velocity. Range offset was compensated from ~200 m to >700 m and Doppler compensation was demonstrated from stand-still to full speed of the test vehicle (~24 m/s).

Keywords: Range and Doppler compensation, digital holography, holographic imaging, coherent ladar

1. Introduction

Holographic ladar systems rely on the capture of temporally stable optical fringe patterns resulting from interference between the local oscillator (LO) beam and signal light imaged from a target. For pulsed systems, fringe visibility is maximized when the LO is temporally matched with the arrival time and duration of the signal, and when there is no gross relative motion between the sensor and target. Temporal mismatching causes system efficiency degradation as the entire signal duration is not mixed with the LO beam. Additional degradation is caused by the fact that the LO is producing shot-noise on the camera during signal duration. Relative system to target motion, such as reflecting light off a moving target, causes temporal motion of the fringe phase. Unless compensated this effect again causes reduction of fringe visibility over the pulse duration. This work demonstrates a digital holography system that compensated for both effects of temporal signal to LO alignment and relative Doppler motion.

Both range and velocity are measured with a co-aligned high pulse rate laser range finder. Range data is captured directly, while velocity is calculated as range-rate, i.e. the rate at which the range is changing over time. Temporal matching can then be achieved by calculating the range-dependent arrival time of signal photons and ensuring the LO is on only when the signal is present at the receiver. Gross Doppler compensation is achieved by filtering and estimating velocity and imposing equivalent Doppler frequency shifts into a tunable acousto-optic modulators on the LO and TX light paths.

2. Theory and Performance Predictions

The system efficiency η in the presence of temporal mismatch (τ) or Doppler frequencies f_D can be calculated from the cross-ambiguity function $\mathrm{X}(\tau,f_D)$ as $\eta = |\mathrm{X}(\tau, f_D)|^2$, where $\mathrm{X}(\tau, f_D) = \int_{-\infty}^{\infty} E_S(t)E_{LO}^*(t-\tau)e^{i2\pi f_D t}\,dt$. $E_S(t)$ and $E_{LO}(t)$ correspond to the normalized electric field at time t of the signal and LO beams, respectively. In the case of a unity amplitude rectangular signal of duration t_p mixing with an identical LO pulse, with no Doppler shift, this reduces to $\eta = \left[1 - \left(\tau/t_p\right)\right]$, i.e. an efficiency loss linear with time offset. In coherent detection scenarios the effective loss is somewhat higher as the receiver integrates shot noise even during the non-overlapped time.

Similarly, in the case of temporally matched pulses in the presence of a Doppler shift the efficiency takes the form $\eta = \mathrm{sinc}^2(f_D t_p)$.

When the pulse duration is short compared with a Doppler cycle the efficiency loss is low. When the pulse duration equals a full Doppler cycle the efficiency is zero; physically this means that the first half of the pulse integrates positive contributions while the second half integrates negative contributions due to the sign change of the coherent mixing, leading to a complete cancellation of the positive contribution.

Radiometric calculations were conducted using the following key design parameters listed in Table 1.

Table 1: Key Design Parameters

Parameter	Value
Transmitted peak power (P)	114 mW
Wavelength (λ)	1545 nm
Pulse width (t_p)	300 ns
Illuminated spot diameter on target (2ω)	30 cm
Target reflectivity (ρ/Ω)	64 sr^{-1}
System efficiency (η)	35%
One-way atmospheric transmission (T)	96%

Predicted CNR was estimated from the equation

$$CNR = \eta \frac{\lambda^3}{hc} T^2 \left(\frac{\rho}{\Omega}\right) \frac{P t_p}{\pi \omega^2}. \tag{1}$$

Implicit in the calculations is that $C_n^2 < 9.3.10^{-13}$ $m^{-2/3}$ in order to maintain a ~30 cm illumination spot diameter at the target. The system was estimated to achieve CNR spanning 8 to 24 dB depending on selected target reflectivity and by choosing pulse duration between 100 and 300 ns pulse width.

3. Experiment

Figure 1 illustrates the proposed layout of the DH optical system. Key hardware components are an 11" Celestron telescope, and a FLIR SC2500 320x256 pixel InGaAs camera.

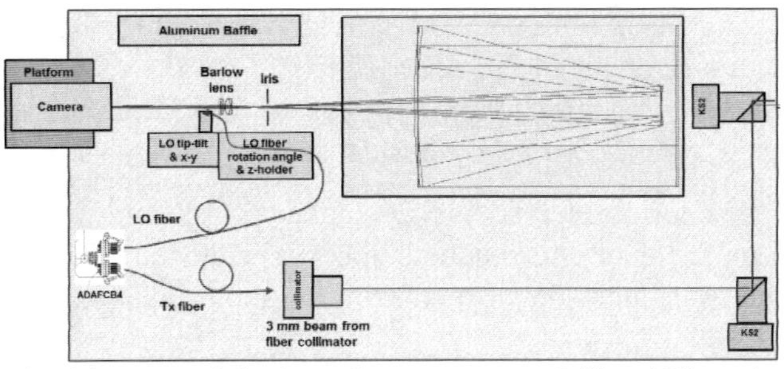

Figure 1. Physical layout of designed system on a 24" x 48" optical breadboard

Figure 2 shows the functional diagram of the source and control system as was implemented. The transmit portion begins with a CW seed laser, which is pre-amplified and split into two paths using a polarization maintaining (PM) 50/50 fiber splitter. Following the splitter, the bottom leg in the figure becomes the LO path while the upper leg becomes the target illumination leg (TX). The two paths are routed through their respective acousto-optic frequency shifters (AOFS). These components adjust the frequency of the input light according to the measured target Doppler. Each AOFS is operated at 200 MHz center frequency at zero Doppler and is capable of ±50 MHz frequency shift. The amount of shift is controlled by a CW voltage that originates from software driven PXI controller with analog output (AO) voltage. Due to the dual frequency shifter implementation (on LO and TX legs), the determined target Doppler is evenly divided

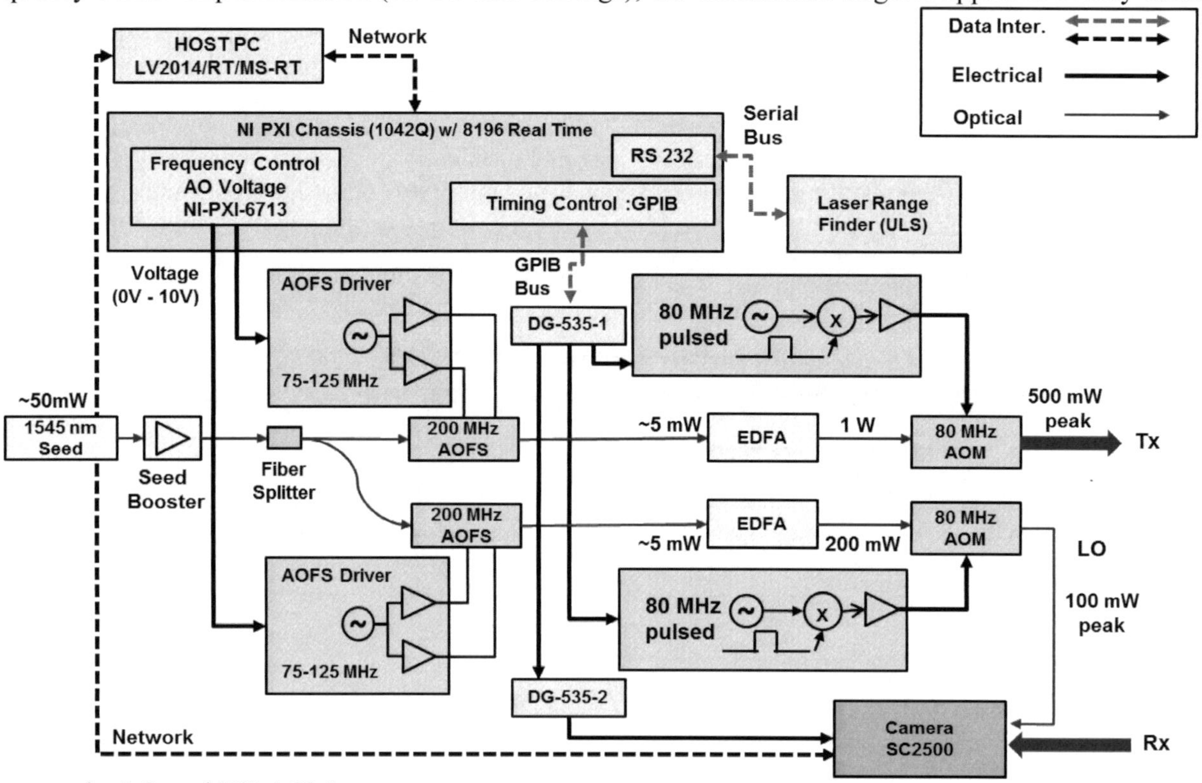

between the LO and TX AOMs.

Figure 2: Functional diagram of range and Doppler compensation system

Following the Doppler-compensation AOMs, the two paths are amplified with respective erbium doped fiber amplifier (EDFA). Each leg following the EDFA has a fixed frequency (80 MHz) AOM that carves out pulses from the CW laser beams. The pulse carving must be performed after the CW amplifiers to prevent possible damage to the EDFAs.

Timing of the fixed frequency AOMs is achieved by control system commanded by the DG535 digital delay generator. This enables correct alignment of the delay of the LO pulse relative to the TX pulse in order to ensure temporal overlap of the two signals. The timing control circuit also triggers the camera to capture digital holography data in synchronicity with the return signal.

The laser range finder, through a serial interface, reports target range and intensity information to the real-time controller. A host computer that interfaced to the real-time controller using a standard network interface served as a graphical user interface with control, data monitoring, and data logging.

The real-time controller was designed to perform three time critical tasks: acquire range, calculate Doppler, and estimate the movement of the target. The state-machine architecture included a thread that received the velocity data and calculated the frequency offsets for the LO and TX optical paths. In addition, it used a Kalman filter to improve the real-time performance of the compensation.

4. Test Results

The field campaign consisted of static and moving target acquisitions. The test scenarios included driving a car at approximately 5, 10, 13, 16, and 24 m/s. The test also included non-moving target data collection at various fixed ranges. The system performance results are plotted in Figure 3.

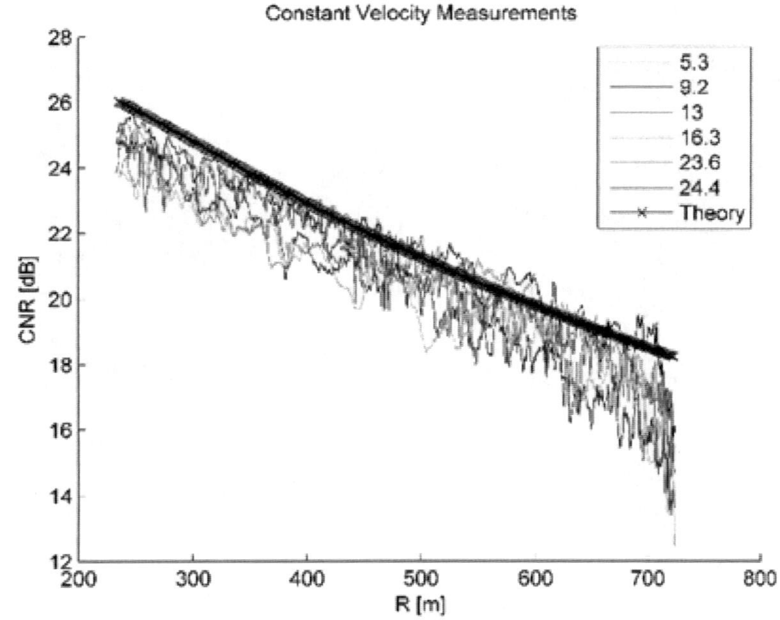

Figure 3. CNR vs. range for moving and non-moving target

The theory line of Fig. 3 includes the output of Eq. 1 as well as numerical modeled effects of the sensor modulation transfer function and physical optics effects such as range dependent vignetting. No visible evidence of CNR loss due to range and Doppler ambiguity was observed when comparing the static to moving target.

A rectangular LO and signal pulse filter overlap efficiency function is evaluated to be

$$\eta_z(f_d, t_d) = \frac{T^2}{T_u T_v} sinc^2(f_d T), \tag{2}$$

where

$$T = \begin{cases} T_v & t_d \leq (T_u - T_v)/2 \\ (T_u - T_v)/2 - t_d & \frac{T_u - T_v}{2} < t_d \leq (T_u - T_v)/2. \\ 0 & (T_u - T_v)/2 < t_d \end{cases} \tag{3}$$

T_u and T_v are the LO and signal rectangular pulse widths, respectively, and t_d and f_d are the time and frequency parameters tailored by range and Doppler offsets. The efficiency solution assumes $T_u \geq T_v$ and for the reason that the theory is reciprocal in u and v, a symmetric expression applies when $T_v \geq T_u$. This function is maximized when $T_u = T_v$ and this specific condition was implemented for the range and Doppler ambiguity measurement.

A final system demonstration consisted of mapping-out the system range and Doppler ambiguity function for a stationary target by sweeping the pulse and Doppler offsets using the software of the tracking system. The range offset was swept from -350 ns to 350 ns at 25 ns interval while the velocity offset was swept from -5 m/s to 5 m/s at 0.2 m/s interval.

Figure 4 shows the measured range and Doppler ambiguity function where residual gross range offset is evident. This is due to uncompensated physical parameters of the system such as mismatched optical path lengths in the separate LO and TX legs. For comparison, the theoretical model adapted from Eq. (2) is presented in the right of Figure 4. The theory includes an exponential rise/fall time based on the AOM model used in the experiment. The experiment amplitude dependence on range and Doppler offset shows good similarity with the model.

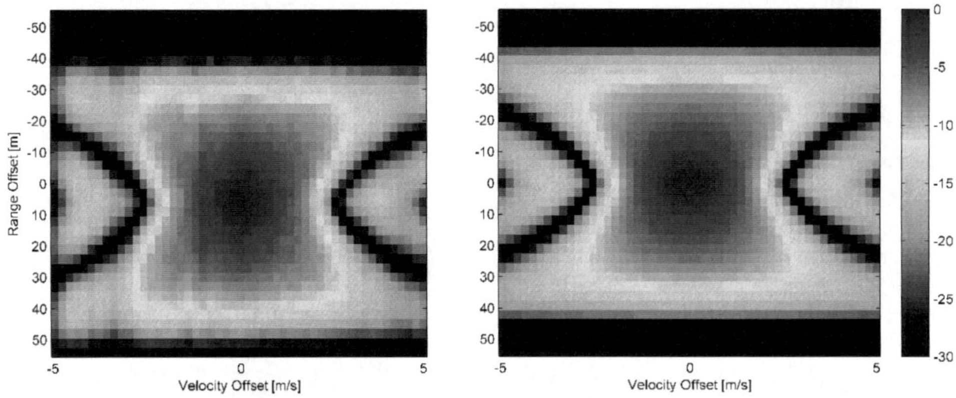

Figure 4. (left) Measured CNR vs. range and Doppler offset. (right) Theoretical CNR vs. range and Doppler offset obtained from Eq. (4). CNR is displayed in dBs.

5. Conclusion

This work summarized the hardware design, system implementation, and demonstration of range and Doppler compensation subsystem to be used with a holographic ladar system built at AFRL. The primary objective of the program was to support AFRL/RYMM with a demonstration that frequency shifting and pulse range positioning technique could be used to compensate for range and Doppler effects while a target mounted to a vehicle was driven down the runway at Wright-Patterson AFB in Dayton, OH. LMCT developed and delivered the software, and participated in field tests of the developed system. The field demonstrations showed that range could be compensated from ~200 m to >700 m and that Doppler compensation was feasible from stand-still to full speed of the test vehicle (~24 m/s).

Future work includes range and Doppler compensation subsystem development for multiple receiver and multiple transmitter digital holography systems operating from ground and air platforms.

The team is also grateful for additional system analysis from John Novotny at LMCT and for logistics and field support from Steve Erisman, Dirk Adams, Bruce Smotherman (Leidos) and Jeff Widiker (MZA) at WPAFB.

Coherent Adaptive Optical System

This paper discusses an adaptive optical system in which coherent images are processed to determine wavefront error and the error is corrected by applying the inverse to a deformable mirror. Coherent imaging is performed by flood illuminating the target with coherent light and using digital holographic detection to record a complex-valued, coherent image. Wavefront error corresponding to the atmosphere is imparted by using a calibrated phase screen located in the pupil on the return path. The wavefront error is determined by using an optimization routine that determines the phase error that maximizes image sharpness. The inverse of the error is then applied to a deformable mirror to improve the image quality. In this paper we report the results of laboratory experiments. Performance of the method is quantified by measuring the Strehl ratio before and after image correction.

Deep-Turbulence Simulation in a Scaled-Laboratory Environment Using Five Phase-Only Spatial Light Modulators

Mark F. Spencer(a), Robert A. Raynor(a), Troy A. Rhoadarmer(b), and Dan K. Marker(a)
(a) Air Force Research Laboratory, Directed Energy Directorate (AFRL/RD)
3550 Aberdeen Avenue SE Kirtland AFB NM 87117
(b) Guidestar Optical Systems, Inc.
234 Peppler Drive Longmont CO 80504
Lead Author e-mail address: mark.spencer.6@us.af.mil

Abstract: The presence of distributed-volume or "deep" turbulence presents unique challenges for beam-control applications which look to sense and correct for disturbances found along the laser-propagation path. This study uses five spatially distributed phase-only reflective spatial light modulators (SLMs) to accurately model deep-turbulence effects. In practice, we can match the Fresnel numbers for tactical engagement scenarios using optical trombones and relays placed in between the SLMs. Similar to computational wave-optic simulations, we can also command repeatable high-spatial-resolution phase screens to the SLMs with the proper statistics (i.e., Kolmogorov, von Karman, etc.).

Keywords: Deep turbulence, Wavefront sensing, Digital holography, Pupil-plane recording geometry, Branch points and cuts, Atmospheric turbulence characterization, and Spatial heterodyne interferometry

1. Introduction

Coherent-light propagation through deep turbulence causes scintillation, which manifests as non-uniform, time-varying irradiance coupling between the object and receiver planes. The Rytov number (also referred to as the log-amplitude variance) gives a measure for the strength of scintillation experienced. As the scintillation becomes severe (i.e., for Rytov numbers greater than ~0.25), this coupling gives rise to branch points in both the coherent light transmitted to the object as well as the coherent light received from the object. These branch points add a rotational component to the phase function that traditional-least-squares reconstruction algorithms cannot account for. As such, the rotational component is often referred to as the hidden phase (thanks to the foundational work of Fried [1]). The existence of branch points leads to unavoidable 2π phase discontinuities in the phase function. Because of inter-actuator coupling, continuous-face sheet deformable mirrors (DMs) are unable to fully compensate for the branch cuts. Thus, in the presence of moderately deep turbulence (i.e., for Rytov numbers greater than ~0.5), the corresponding branch-point problem tends to be the "Achilles' heel" to current beam-control solutions [2].

To accurately simulate deep-turbulence conditions in a scaled-laboratory environment, AFRL/RD teamed with Guidestar Optical Systems, Inc. to develop an atmospheric turbulence simulator (ATS). As shown in Fig. 1, the developed ATS uses five spatially distributed phase-only reflective spatial light modulators (SLMs). In practice, we can match the Fresnel numbers for tactical engagement scenarios using optical trombones and relays placed in between the SLMs. Similar to computational wave-optic simulations [3, Chapter 9], we can also command repeatable high-spatial-resolution phase screens to the SLMs with the proper statistics (i.e., Kolmogorov, von Karman, etc.). Because the framerates for commercial-off-the-shelf (COTS) SLMs are on the order of 150 Hz for visible light, this laboratory setup is appropriate for scaled-time demonstrations, where we develop the reconstruction algorithms in software, and demonstrate closed-loop performance at approximately 1-10 Hz with affordable COTS hardware for the wavefront sensor (WFS) and DM. Since deep turbulence conditions can provide Greenwood frequencies on the order of 1 kHz, this scaled-time laboratory setup does not allow for real-time demonstrations; however, it does provide a flexible test bed in which to test novel beam-control solutions.

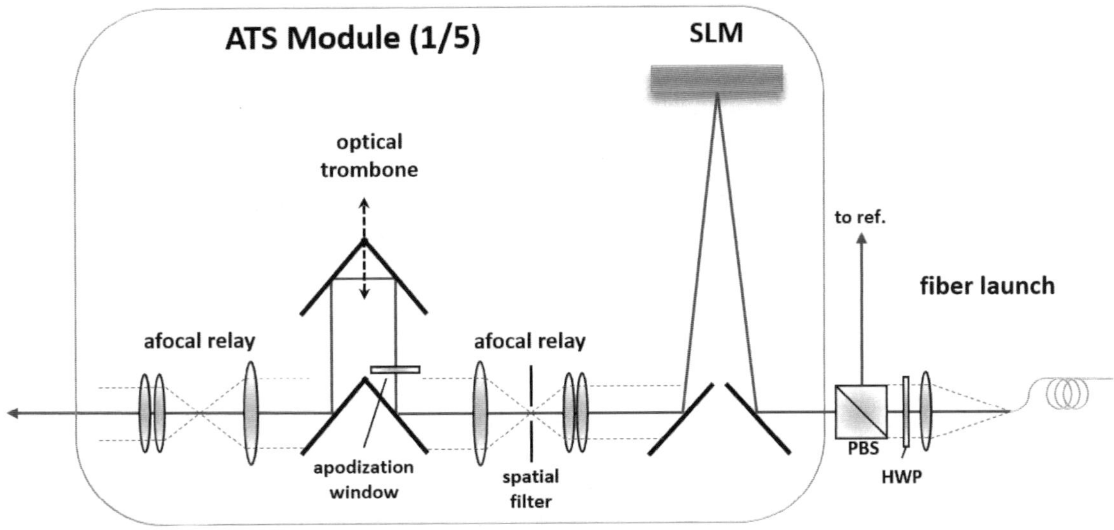

(a)

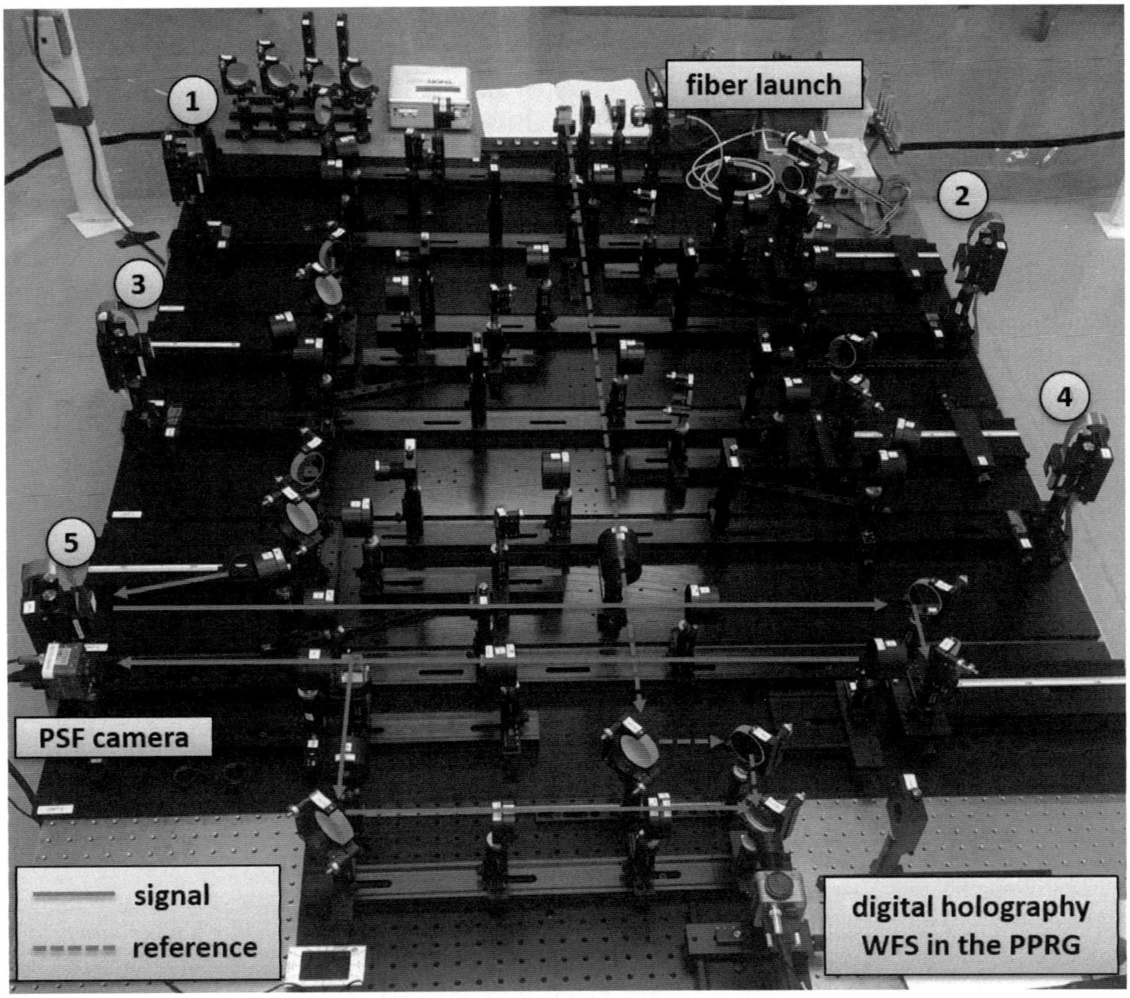

(b)

Figure 1. The atmospheric turbulence simulator (ATS) within the Phasor Laboratory at AFRL/RDL uses five modules in series with spatial light modulators (SLMs) to simulate deep-turbulence effects.

2. Demonstration

Included with the ATS is a digital holography (DH) WFS in the pupil-plane recording geometry (PPRG). This instrument allows for the characterization of the simulated deep-turbulence effects and the demonstration of various beam-control concepts. For example, Fig. 2 shows snapshots of the developed ATS GUI for simulated turbulence conditions where $D/r_0 = 4$. Note that we can command repeatable high-spatial-resolution phase screens to the SLMs contained within the ATS and can also calculate the least-squares (LS) estimated phase from the DH WFS in the PPRG. Specifically, in Fig. 2a, the 5th SLM is commanded to flat so that the DH WFS is operating in an open-loop configuration, whereas in Fig. 2b, the 5th SLM is commanded to a phase correction based on a leaky integrator control law. In the latter configuration, the residual wavefront error is nearly nulled. This result is indicative of an adaptive-optics system operating in null-seeking control loop or a closed-loop configuration.

In this particular demonstration [cf. Fig. 2], we positioned the optical trombones of the ATS, so that all of the SLMs were conjugate to each other and the pupil of the DH WFS. In practice, we can use the ATS GUI to calculate the appropriate positions of the optical trombones, so that we can distribute the SLMs all along the propagation path of the collimated single-mode fiber launch. This key feature is what allows us to match the Fresnel numbers for tactical engagement scenarios in a scaled-laboratory environment.

3. Future work

For all intents and purposes, the leading WFS architectures for beam-control applications include the Shack-Hartmann (SH) WFS, the self-referencing interferometer (SRI) WFS, and the DH WFS. This is because they each offer an appropriate amount of functionality within the engineering trade space. With respect to the SH WFS, direct detection through a lenslet array offers both light efficiency and an estimate of the phase function through slope measurements. Traditional-least-squares reconstruction algorithms is what provides this estimate; however, in the presence of branch points and the associated branch cuts, these algorithms fall short. Branch-point-tolerant reconstruction algorithms for the SH WFS do exist [4], but these algorithms need to be tested in hardware to fully quantify performance. On the other hand, interferometric WFSs, such as the SRI WFS and the DH WFS, provide access to an estimate of the amplitude and the wrapped phase (i.e., the complex optical field). This wrapped-phase estimate directly contains information about the branch points and the associated branch cuts; however, in commanding a DM through traditional-least-squares reconstruction algorithms, one does not exploit this information. Branch-point-tolerant reconstruction algorithms do exist which exploit the wrapped-phase estimate [5], but once again, these algorithms need to be tested in hardware to fully quantify performance. Furthermore, the SNR gains in using coherent detection with DH versus direct detection with the less-light-efficient (compared to the SH WFS) SRI also needs to be quantified in hardware.

Future work will take on all of these hardware demonstrations using the flexible laboratory test bed described above. Such a head-to-head comparison of existing beam-control technology will not only inform future applications of interim capabilities (with respect to the deep-turbulence problem defined above), but it will also lead to real-time hardware demonstrations.

4. References

[1] D. L. Fried, "Branch point problem in adaptive optics," JOSA A **15**, 2759-2768 (1998).

[2] P. Merrittt, *Beam Control for Laser Systems* (DEPS, 2012).

[3] J. D. Schmidt, Numerical Simulation of Optical Wave Propagation with Examples in MATLAB (SPIE Press, 2011).

[4] J. J. Kim *et al.*, "Adaptive Optics Control for Strong Turbulence Using Iterative Wavefront Reconstruction," Proc. DEPS (2015).

[5] M. J. Steinbock *et al.*, "LSPV+7, a branch-point-tolerant reconstructor for strong turbulence adaptive optics," App. Opt. **53**, 3821-3831 (2014).

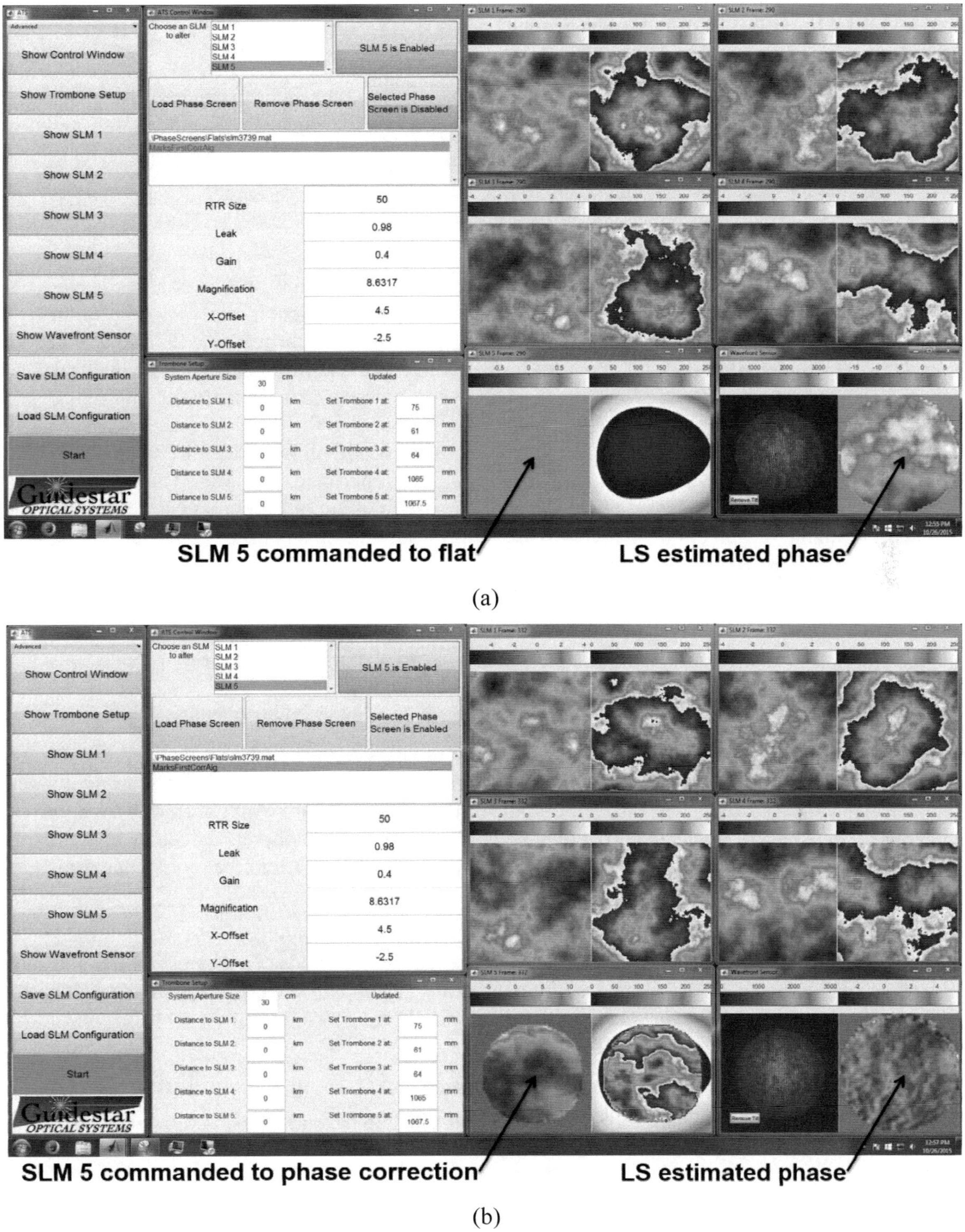

Figure 2. Open- and closed-loop demonstrations using the atmospheric turbulence simulator (ATS) GUI.

The views expressed in this paper are those of the authors and do not necessarily reflect the official policy or position of the Air Force, the Department of Defense, or the U.S. Government.

Digital Holographic Characterization of Atmospheric Wavefront Perturbation

Stephen Crouch[a], Zeb W. Barber[b], Jason Dahl[b] and Randy R. Reibel[a]
(a) Blackmore Sensors and Analytics, Inc., 3991 Valley Commons Dr., Bozeman, MT 59718
(b) The Spectrum Lab and Department of Physics, Montana State University, Bozeman, MT 59717
crouch@blackmoreinc.com

Abstract: Atmospheric turbulence is a fundamental limiter of long-range coherent ladar aperture synthesis imaging. We demonstrate a novel approach to high resolution measurement of wavefront perturbations caused by atmospheric turbulence. The approach features a simple optical design, minimal processing, and the ability to use diffuse surfaces as the wavefront characterization target. By deriving a local oscillator from the impinging beam, digital holography is used. Inspired by phase gradient autofocus, coherent processing techniques are used to extract the common mode phase gradient from a set of digital holographic images, each with a unique atmospheric realization. The common mode phase gradient is then subtracted from the phase gradient of each image to reveal the phase gradient of each atmospheric wavefront perturbation. This is used to reconstruct the perturbation. Experimental and algorithmic considerations as well as the potential for the technique to support turbulence agnostic coherent aperture synthesis are discussed.

Keywords: Coherent Laser Radar, Atmospheric Sensing, Wavefront Reconstruction

1. Introduction

Coherent laser radar aperture synthesis offers a pathway to cross-range resolution beyond the diffraction limit of physical optics. Specific schemes such as synthetic aperture ladar (SAL), holographic aperture ladar (HAL), and 3D variants have all been demonstrated. However, atmospheric turbulence introduces perturbations to the backscattered speckle field which destroy the spatial coherence of sequentially captured data and practically limit the applicability of such approaches to within the coherence time of the atmosphere.

The deleterious effects of atmospheric turbulence on coherent aperture synthesis are well studied.[1] In the digital holography/HAL field, simulation typically proceeds via the split-step beam propagation method which supports the insertion of phase screens along the propagation path with representative statistics. Such methods are also a starting point for attempts to correct for atmospheric turbulence whereby a corrective phase screen can be computed and applied.[2]

An *in situ* method to measure phase aspects of a propagated laser beam imaging a diffuse target would be a powerful tool in the effort to understand and correct atmospheric turbulence in coherent imaging scenarios. We present a method for the measurement of atmospheric turbulence induced phase perturbations to a wavefront. The approach relies on the analysis of digital holographic images, works with diffuse surfaces, and utilizes modest computational resources. We believe this approach will support the study, characterization and removal of unwanted atmospheric effects in coherent laser radar imagery.

2. Imaging Scenario

Consider the experimental scenario of Figure 1 where a 793nm CW laser beam with 15mW of optical power illuminates a diffuse target along an optical path including turbulence induced by an electric space heater. A local oscillator is run, via fiber, down to the target to enable digital holographic imaging of the spot on the target. A Point Grey USB 3.0 camera array records the speckle field at 110Hz frame rate and a processing station executes the processing of the digital holograms. A short exposure time helps to "freeze out" the speckle field which is evolving due to the turbulence induced by the space heater. We seek to derive information about the wavefront from this set of digital holographic images.

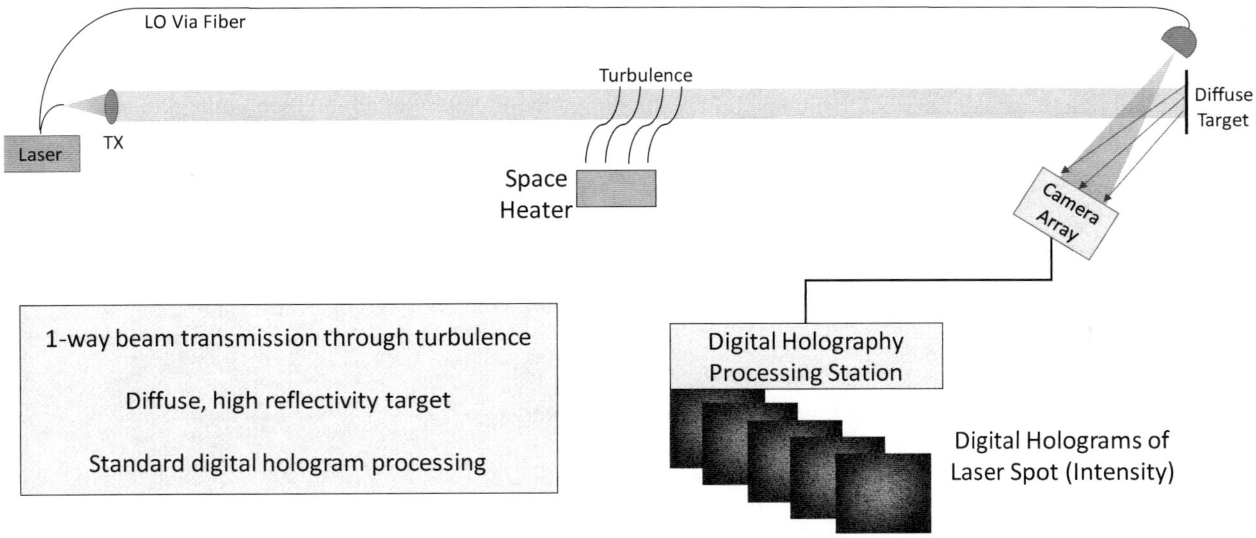

Figure 1. The experimental layout is illustrated in the schematic.

3. Theory and Algorithmic Approach

As a first step, consider the digital interference (i.e. phase differencing) of sequentially collected frames on the camera. This process is depicted in Figure 2. As the aberrations, divergence, and diffuse speckle pattern seen by the camera are constant, the phase difference observed by this digital interference is attributed to the changing atmospheric conditions. As a control, cases with no space heater present (no turbulence) were observed and generated essentially flat phase differences (not shown in this paper).

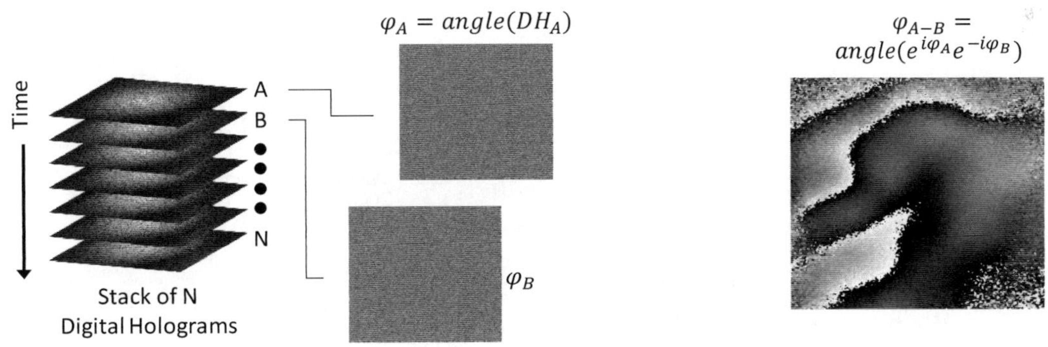

Figure 2. (Left) A set of digital holograms is collected. Pairs of digital holograms can be extracted and digitally interfered. (Right) The result of pairwise interference of digital holograms with changing atmospheric conditions reveals structure in the phase difference due to the turbulence.

The differential measurement alone is not an insightful measurement as an infinite combination of atmospheric conditions could give rise to the observed wavefront difference. However, the differential measurement described demonstrates potential conditions for the extraction of more useful information. Inspired by Warren, Ghighlia, et al.[3] we formulated a gradient based approach to extracting the atmospheric wavefront perturbation. We define the wavefront perturbation as the difference between a given frame's wavefront and the average wavefront over a set of beams. Through careful experimental control, we argue that this perturbation is only due to atmospheric turbulence. The average wavefront includes beam divergence and aberration. The digital hologram of the diffuse target also picks up a random speckle phase which is also common mode.

Our algorithm proceeds as in Figure 3. A set of several digital holograms is collected over time, each with a unique atmospheric realization. The phase gradients of each image are computed and then averaged over the set to extract the common mode aspects of the phase gradient. These are assumed to correspond to persistent features in the phase such as beam divergence, aberration, and random speckle from the diffuse target.

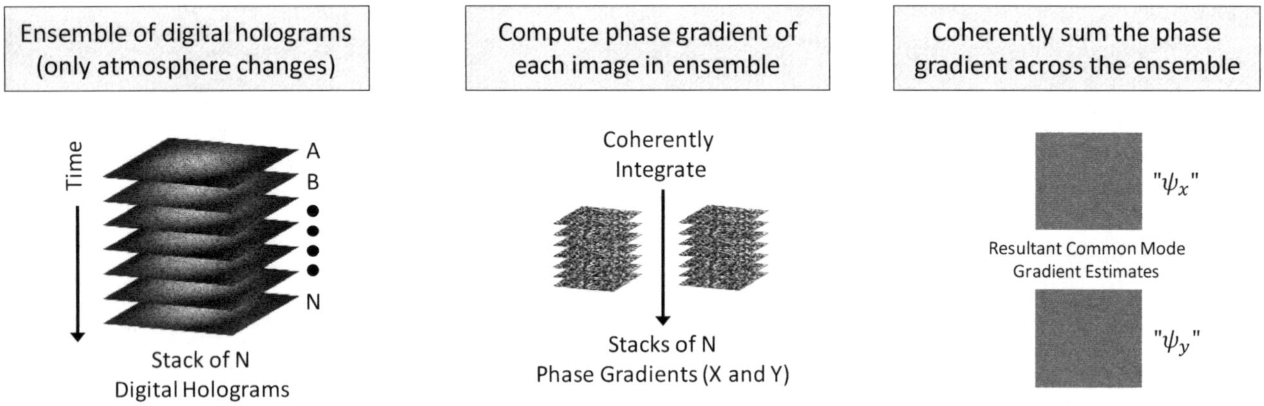

Figure 3. (Left) A stack of digital holograms is collected under changing atmospheric conditions. (Center) The gradient is computed and averaged over the set of digital holograms. (Right) The result is an estimate of the common mode aspects of the phase gradient.

Next we subtract the estimated common mode phase gradient from the phase gradient of each image in the set as in Figure 4. The residual phase gradient corresponds to the atmospheric perturbation. This gradient is ideal for input into any general purpose algorithm designed to reconstruct a function from gradients of the function. We chose to use an open source algorithm and software for convenience and were happy with the results.[4]

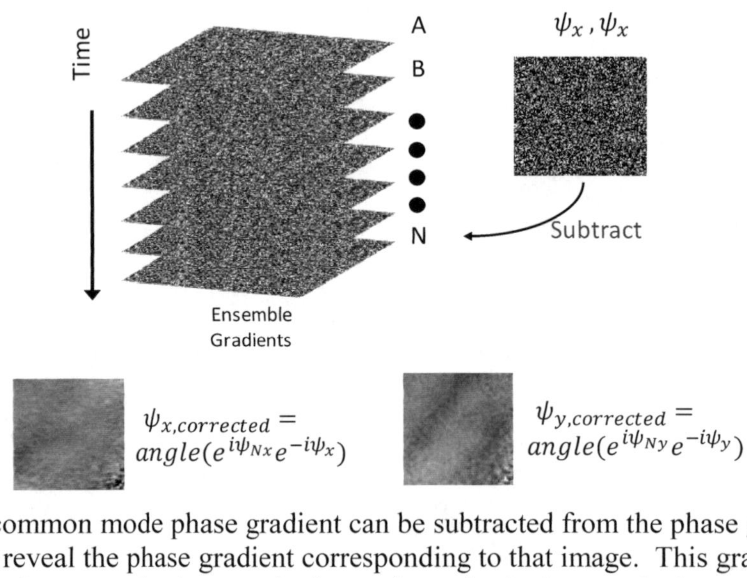

Figure 4. The common mode phase gradient can be subtracted from the phase gradient for each individual image to reveal the phase gradient corresponding to that image. This gradient corresponds to the atmospheric perturbation at that point in time on the beam.

As a final note, we modified the above algorithm to process sub-regions of the original camera array in parallel. This allowed the atmospheric perturbation gradient estimates to be coherently averaged after common mode gradient removal to mitigate speckle effects. This approach is valid as the atmospheric perturbation information is globally encoded in the speckle field sampled by the camera array. This approach trades in some spatial resolution for overall stability to good effect. We tested the number of speckle realizations and found that breaking up the camera array into 20 sub-regions produced a good tradeoff.

4. Experimental Results

The results of our approach were verified by comparing the phase difference of sequential reconstructed wavefront perturbations with phase differences of the same pair of sequential holograms. The phase difference should be identical up to a global constant phase. In Figure 5 we observe this self-consistency. A series of movies of the reconstructed wavefront will be presented in the oral presentation.

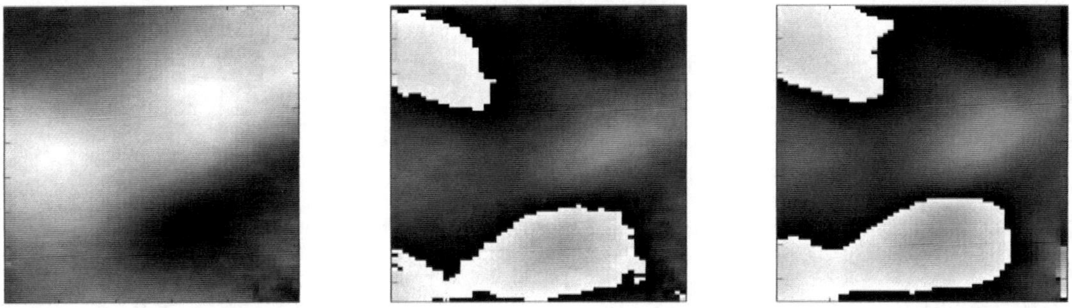

Figure 5. (Left) Reconstructed wavefront (-5pi to 5pi). (Center) Phase difference between reconstructed wavefront and the previous reconstructed wavefront in the image series (-pi to pi). (Right) Phase difference between the unprocessed digital hologram and the previous digital hologram (-pi to pi, same pair as center). Note the clear similarity between the two approaches. The important aspect is that the image at center is from actual derived wavefronts.

5. Conclusion

We demonstrated a novel wavefront characterization tool to measure atmospheric turbulence wavefront distortion. The approach relies on the static phase contribution of all factors except the changing turbulence. This contrivance could be overcome by use of speckle field tracking and appropriate speckle field registration as a pre-processing step. The computationally efficiency and overall effectiveness of the approach in extracting useful phase information for an *in situ* diffuse imaging scenario should underscore the potential of the approach. Next steps include transition to longer range imaging scenarios, larger beam diameters, and exploration of the potential for image correction. We gratefully acknowledge support from AFRL under contract number FA8650-15-C-1871.

6. References

[1] "Laser Beam Propagation through Random Media, Second Edition | (2005) | Andrews | Publications | Spie." [Online]. Available: http://spie.org/Publications/Book/626196. [Accessed: 16-May-2016].

[2] A. E. Tippie and J. R. Fienup, "Phase-error correction for multiple planes using a sharpness metric," Optics Letters, vol. 34, no. 5, p. 701, Mar. 2009.

[3] D. W. Warner, D. C. Ghiglia, A. Fitzgerrell, and J. Beaver, "Two-dimensional phase gradient autofocus," 2000, vol. 4123, pp. 162–173.

[4] I.S. Sevcenco, P.J. Hampton, P. Agathoklis, "A wavelet based method for image reconstruction from gradient data with applications", Multidimensional Systems and Signal Processing, November 2013

Robustness of Joint-Plane Phase Retrieval in Generalized Two-Path Interferometry

Wesley E. Farriss(a), James R. Fienup(a), Tanya Malhotra(b), and A. Nick Vamivakas(a)
(a) The Institute of Optics, University of Rochester
Rochester, NY, 14627, USA
(b) Department of Physics and Astronomy, University of Rochester
Rochester, NY, 14627, USA
wfarriss@ur.rochester.edu

Abstract: A technique called Generalized Optical Interferometry (GOI) has been developed that allows the user to quickly recover the modal amplitude coefficient information of coherent field distributions. We built on this research by developing a technique that, in simulation, quickly recovers the phase information from intensity mesurements given the amplitude coefficients.

Keywords: Phase Retrieval, Coherent Optical Processing, Fractional Fourier Transform

1. Introduction

Many techniques exist, such as temporal or spatial heterodyning, that enables one to retain the phase and amplitude of a coherently illuminated scene. However, many of these applications require the use of a local oscillator, suffer from phase ambiguities, or require time consuming post-processing that makes the system difficult to use when attempting to characterize a scene in real time. Improving on these techniques, a technique called generalized optical interferometry (GOI) has been developed [1] that allows for the expeditious identification and sorting of field modes present in a coherent optical field.

2. Generalized Optical Interferometry

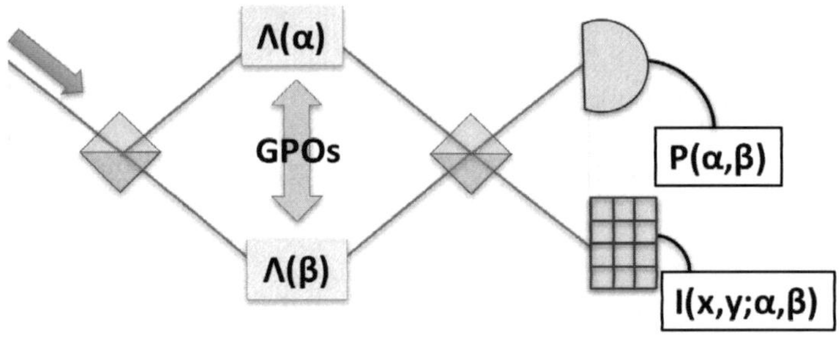

Figure 1: Generalized Mach-Zehnder interferometer employing generalized phase operators (GPOs).

Consider an optical field incident upon a generalized Mach-Zehnder interferometer (MZI), shown in Figure 1, where the field is represented as a superposition of weighted Hermite-Gaussian modes,

$$G(x, y) = \sum_{m,n} c_{mn} HG_{mn}(x, y), \tag{1}$$

with complex-valued weights $c_{mn} = |c_{mn}|e^{i\phi_{mn}}$ for the mn-th mode. The MZI has a generalized cylindrical lens (GPOs in Figure 1) in either arm that confers a known phase to each term of the field such that the output field, in the arm of the interferometer without a soft reflection at the final beamsplitter, is a superposition of

$$G_\alpha(x,y) = \Lambda(\alpha)\left\{\frac{1}{2}\sum_{m,n} c_{mn}HG_{mn}(x,y)\right\} = \frac{1}{2}\sum_{m,n} c_{mn}e^{im\pi\alpha}HG_{mn}(x,y) \tag{2}$$

and

$$G_\beta(x,y) = \Lambda(\beta)\left\{\frac{1}{2}\sum_{m,n} c_{mn}HG_{mn}(x,y)\right\} = \frac{1}{2}\sum_{m,n} c_{mn}e^{in\pi\beta}HG_{mn}(x,y). \tag{3}$$

Where α and β are the orders of the fractional Fourier transform (fFT) used to confer the phase to each term in the superposition. When the interference of these two arms is recorded by a bucket detector, shown in the top right of Figure 1, the resulting interference term is

$$P_{\mathrm{OUT},1}(\alpha,\beta) = \frac{1}{2}\sum_{m,n}|c_{mn}|^2(1+\cos(m\pi\alpha - n\pi\beta))\sum_{x,y}HG_{mn}(x,y). \tag{4}$$

Collecting many of these interference terms for a range of (α, β) allows one to define a function, $P_{\mathrm{OUT},1}(\alpha,\beta)$, which can then be Fourier transformed to yield

$$\tilde{P}(m',n') = \frac{1}{2}\sum_{m,n}|c_{mn}|^2\left[\sum_{x,y}HG^2_{mn}(x,y)\right]\left\{\delta(m',n') + \frac{1}{2}\left[\delta\left(m'-\frac{m}{2},n'+\frac{n}{2}\right)+\delta\left(m'+\frac{m}{2},n'-\frac{n}{2}\right)\right]\right\}. \tag{5}$$

From (5), we see that the modal coefficient amplitude value, $|c_{mn}|$, can be determined for each HG mode order that is present in the original field [2].

3. GOI Phase Retrieval

Now we desire to find the phases of the complex weighting coefficients. Since only the intensity of the field incident on the photodetector can be measured, we must find a way to determine the phase of the field using these intensity measurements and system constraints. In order to do this, we employ the method of nonlinear optimization-based phase retrieval. This employs an error metric reduction algorithm that, when successful, iteratively converges to a global minimum. The ϕ_{mn} values at this global minimum are the phase values associated with the modes of the field incident on the system.

In normal GOI operation, as described above, the bucket detector does not require spatial distribution information in order to determine the magnitude of the amplitude weighting coefficients. This is not the case with a nonlinear optimization approach to phase retrieval. In designing the error metric which we wish to minimize, it was necessary to retain spatial distribution information. This requires that at least one output port of the MZI be devoted to an array detector, as shown in the bottom right of Figure 1. Our error metric is

$$E = \sum_{planes}\left\{\sum_{x,y}\left[\underbrace{\left|\sum_{mn}|c_{mn}|e^{i\phi_{mn}}\left(e^{im\pi\alpha}+e^{in\pi\beta}\right)HG_{mn}(x,y)\right|^2}_{\text{Estimated Intensity}} - \underbrace{I_{REF}(x,y)}_{\text{Measured Intensity}}\right]^2\right\}. \tag{6}$$

where $|c_{mn}|$ is the amplitude of the weighting coefficient that we recovered using GOI and ϕ_{mn} is the phase value that we are trying to recover. Note, in the case where there is only one plane, there is the potential for the error metric to converge to an incorrect global minimum with modal phase values that lead to reconstructing the field $G^*(x,y)$ instead of the correct modal phase values that yield the field $G(x,y)$. This is known as the twin image problem. Results for single-plane GOI phase retrieval are covered in [3] and are plagued by these twin images.

4. Monte Carlo Simulation

In order to correct the twin image problem and introduce a greater degree of information diversity to the phase retrieval process, we optimized over a pair of fFT planes in this work. We first desired to see if trends existed with regard to which α, β planes are preferential for two-plane phase retrieval. So we performed a Monte Carlo run where we surveyed the performance of two-plane retrievals with different combinations of fFT planes. In order to limit this search space, we chose cases where $\alpha = \beta$, intentionally removing a degree of freedom and greatly reducing the overall simulation time. We consider this the "naive two-plane retrieval" approach since we do not yet know which fFT planes are best suited for phase retrieval. The parameterization of the Monte Carlo simulation is described in Table 1. We can see from Figure 2 that there does exist a strong preference for two-plane retrievals where plane-one α, β is between 0.0 and 0.2 and plane-two (α, β) is between 0.6 and 0.8 for optimizations consisting of up to 4th-order HG modes (e.g. where the set $\{HG_{mn}\}$ contains all HG modes where $m + n \leq 4$). This trend is consistent for 2nd through 6th-order mode sets. It is also of note to mention that, as hoped-for, the addition of a second plane to our optimization completely eliminated the twin image problem.

Table 1: Monte Carlo Parameterization

Parameter	Representation	Unique Parameter Values
α, β	fFT planes from [0,1] where $\alpha = \beta$	40
$\{HG_{mn}\}$	HG modes present in incident field	5
$\lvert c_{mn} \rvert, \phi_{mn}$	Random phase and amplitude reference values	20
$\vec{\phi}_{init}$	Random starting phase values fed to optimizer	50
Total Optimizations in Monte Carlo Simulation		200, 000

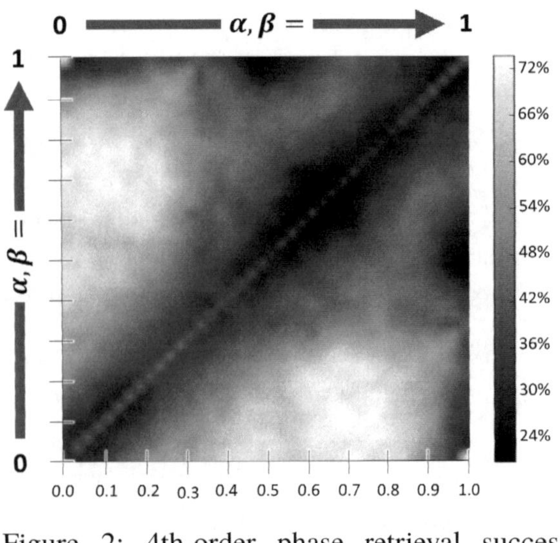

Figure 2: 4th-order phase retrieval success heatmap.

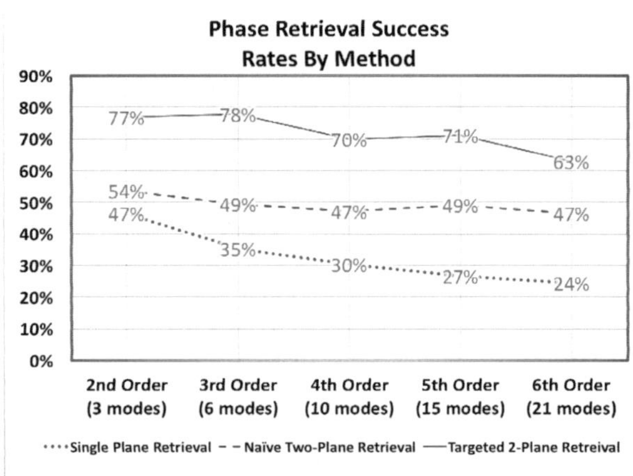

Figure 3: Successful retrieval rates by order.

After identifying the fFT values that yielded the highest rate of successful retrieval in the Monte Carlo run, a Monte Carlo simulation consisting of 1000 retrievals was run where one plane had α, β values restricted to values between 0.1 and 0.2 and the other plane with values restricted to between 0.7 and 0.8. The $|c_{mn}|$, ϕ_{mn}, and $\vec{\phi}_{init}$(the starting guess for phase values fed to the optimizer) values are randomized for each optimization. The success rates (defined as each coefficient's retrieved phase value having a RMSE ≤ 0.07 waves) are shown by HG mode order in Figure 3 labeled as the "targeted 2-plane retrievals."

5. Conclusion

In this work, we successfully implemented a two-plane phase retrieval approach in order to retrieve the modal phase values associated with the amplitude coefficients recovered from an arbitrary coherent field incident on a generalized optical interferometer. The targeted two-plane approach to phase retrieval yielded much better success rates than the naive (random) two-plane approach. Both of these techniques were much more successful than a single-plane phase retrieval approach. In the future, additional planes will be added to the optimization in hopes of further increasing retrieval success rates. Additionally, optimizations will be conducted that include various noise realizations to test the robustness of the phase retrieval technique with respect to noise.

References

[1] A. F. Abouraddy, T. M. Yarnall, and B. E. A. Saleh, "Generalized optical interferometry for modal analysis in arbitrary degrees of freedom," Opt. Lett. **37**, 2889–2891 (2012).

[2] A. F. Abouraddy, T. M. Yarnall, and B. E. Saleh, "Angular and radial mode analyzer for optical beams," Optics letters **36**, 4683–4685 (2011).

[3] W. E. Farriss, T. M. Malhotra, N. A. Vamivakas, and J. R. Fienup, "Phase retrieval in generalized two-path interferometry," in Computational Optical Sensing and Imaging, (Optical Society of America, 2016), pp. CT4C–3.

Range Dependent Turbulence Characterization by Co-operating Coherent Doppler Lidar with Direct Detection Lidar

Sameh Abdelazim(a), David Santoro(b), Mark Arend(b), Sam Ahmed(b), and Fred Moshary(b)

(a) Fairleigh Dickinson University(FDU)
1000 River Rd. M107
Teaneck NJ, 07666
(b)The City College of New York (CCNY)
Lead Author e-mail address: samehabdel@hotmail.com

Abstract: The backscattered signal power of a coherent Doppler Lidar (CDL) system that is used for wind sensing was validated against a direct detection Lidar system. In coherent detection, the received signal power depends on the overlap function of the backscattered and local oscillator fields. This overlap function is dependent on the loss of coherence of the backscattered field, which is influenced by refractive index variations of the atmosphere due to turbulence. A direct comparison of the backscattered signal power of the CDL with that of the direct detection Lidar requires that the effect of coherence loss and the overlap function as function of range is accounted for. In this study, we report on the CDL wind measurements and we present the analysis of the range dependent refractive index variations of the CDL by appropriately fitting the backscattered signal power with direct detection signal power measurements.

Keywords: Coherent Doppler Lidar, Wind Sensing, Direct Detection.

1. Introduction

Coherent Doppler Lidar (CDL) has been widely adopted in applications such as measuring atmospheric wind velocity, turbulence, aerosol concentration, cloud height and velocity, and detection of atmospheric constituents and pollutants. A CDL system for wind sensing was developed and operated at the Remote Sensing Laboratory at the City College of New York (CCNY). In our system, a 1.5μm polarized maintained (PM) fiber laser is used for its eye-safety, affordability, and availability where it is widely used in the telecommunication industry. The PM fiber optics ensures that the polarization state of the local oscillator remains aligned with that of the transmitted field. The system is capable of measuring vertical wind velocity for up to 3km. System's characteristics and main components were presented in previous papers [1-3].

In this paper, we examine the effect of range on signal to noise ratio (SNR) of backscattered signals of the CDL system. In section two, the system configuration is presented and system's main components are described. The effect of range on SNR of backscattered signals is presented in section three. In section four, wind measurement results are presented and SNR of CDL is compared with that of direct detection in vertical pointing.

2. System's Description

The system configuration is shown in Fig. 1 and consists of the following components: i) Laser source (ii) Accousto-optic modulator (AOM) (iii) Fiber amplifier (iv) Optical circulator (v) Optical antenna (vi) Balanced detector, and (vii) Signal processor. Optical components are connected with PM optical fibers. The laser source has two outputs: a low power seed laser that is used as a local oscillator (LO), and a high power output (0.5W) that is modulated, pulsed, and frequency shifted using an AOM. An RF source drives the AOM resulting in a 200 ns optical pulse with a 20 kHz pulse repetition rate (PRR) and a frequency shift of 84 MHz. These laser pulses are amplified by an erbium doped fiber amplifier (EDFA) then transmitted from port 1 to port 2 of the optical circulator.

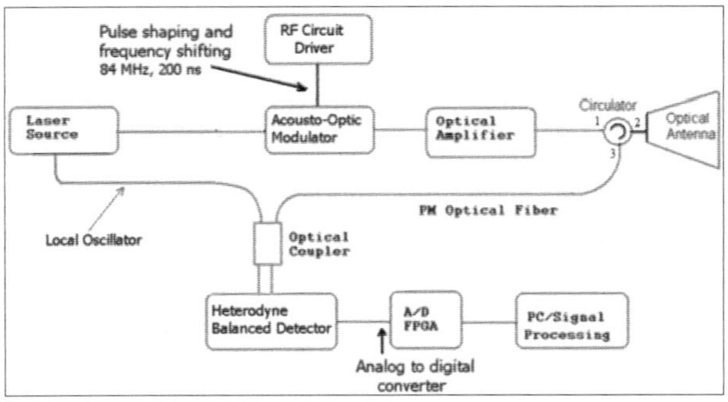

Fig. 1. Coherent Doppler lidar system configuration.

Laser pulses are transmitted into the atmosphere through a lens whereas backscattered signals are received back into the same lens and then transmitted from the optical circulator's port 2 to port 3. Backscattered and LO signals are optically combined using an optical coupler and heterodyne detected using a balanced photo detector. The RF electrical signals from the detector are acquired at a 400 MHz sampling rate using an analog to digital converter (ADC). Digital data is then streamed to a host PC for further processing.

3. The CDL Backscattered Signals Range Dependence

In this section, we present the range dependence on SNR of the CDL heterodyne detection using a monostatic configuration, and we compare analytical and experimental results. Monostatic configuration was believed to have an improved performance due to the correlation of the transmitted and back scattered fields. This correlation is the result of wave-front tilts self correction in a monostatic configuration [4-6]. The SNR range dependence of a CLR monostatic system is evaluated by using the concept of back projected local oscillator (BPLO), which is the imaginary local oscillator field distribution projected at the target side of the receiver aperture, receiver lens, originating from the detector [4,7,8]. Frehlich *et al.* [4] derived an equation that describes SNR as a function of range assuming a Gaussian Lidar system i.e., transmitter and LO fields are deterministic, detector response function is uniform, and the detector collects all LO and backscattered power incident on the receiver aperture. The SNR was then found by calculating the overlap integral between the BPLO and the backscattered fields on the receiver plane assuming a distributed aerosol target. To take into account the effects of refractive turbulence on CDL performance, different techniques of wave propagation in random medium were used [9]. Analysis shows that the SNR is proportional to the product of direct detection power and heterodyne efficiency. The calculation of received power and SNR requires mutual coherence function of the backscattered field incident on the receiver. As for natural aerosol targets, backscattered field at each aerosol particle has a random phase, and the mutual coherence function of the total backscattered field is the integration of all mutual coherence functions from each aerosol particle. The SNR range dependence [5] is expressed as:

$$SNR(L) = \frac{\eta_D(L)\lambda E\beta K^{2L/1000}\pi D^2}{8hBL^2} \tag{1}$$

where η_D is the system efficiency given by:

$$\eta_D(L) = \frac{\eta_{total}}{\left\{1+\left(1-\frac{L}{L_F}\right)^2\left[\frac{\pi(A_C D)^2}{4\lambda L}\right]^2+\left(\frac{A_C D}{2S_o(L)}\right)^2\right\}} \tag{2}$$

The system efficiency factor describes the loss of the SNR due to a mismatch between the LO and backscattered fields as a result of loss of coherence of the backscattered field. The loss of coherence is caused by: a) incoherent aerosol targets, which causes its field phase-front curvature and LO to mismatch (second term in the denominator), and b) propagation through the atmospheric refractive turbulence, which also causes an expansion of the transmitted beam resulting a larger incoherent image at the target (third term in the denominator). Figure 2 shows the simulated wideband SNR range dependence. The parameters used are listed in Table 1.

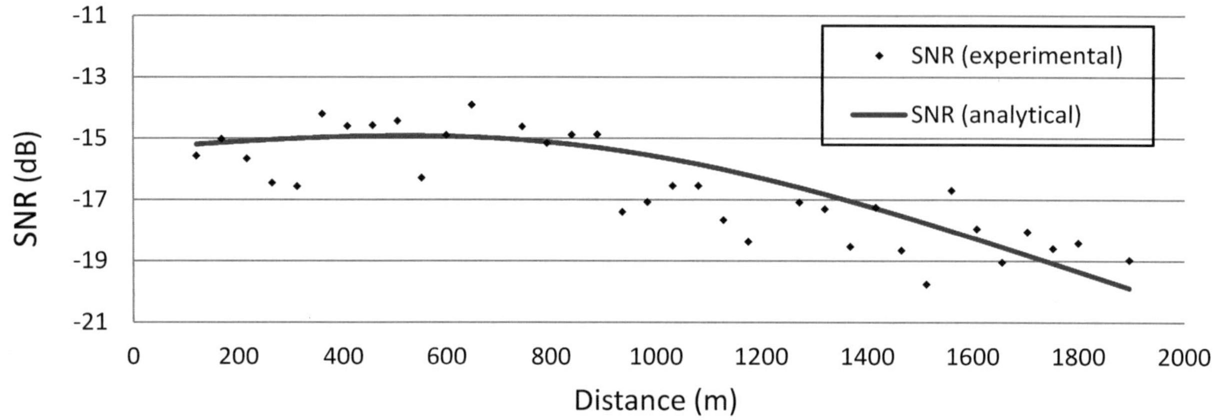

Fig. 2. Range dependence of wideband SNR of Doppler lidar's backscattered signals.

Table 1. Parameters corresponding to analytical estimation of wideband SNR range dependence

Parameter	Description	Value	Parameter	Description	Value
L	Range (m)		L_F	Focal Range of	
B	Bandwidth	100 MHz		Optical Antenna	5 km
λ	Wave length	1545.2 µm	A_c	Correction Factor	0.76
E	Pulse Energy	7 µJ		*This value was calculated*	
D	Effective aperture Diameter	0.1 m		*based on truncation ratio* given in Ref. [10]	
τ	Pulse width	200 ns	Cn^2	Refractive Index	
β	atmospheric backscatter			Structure Constant	$2x10^{-14}m^{-2/3}$
	coefficient	$8.3x10^{-7}$ /m/sr	η_{total}	Total system efficiency	-6 dB
K	one way atmospheric		$S_o(L)$	Transverse coherent	
	transmittance	0.95 /km		length	$\sim (1.1\ kw^2 L\ Cn^2)^{-2/3}$
			kw	Wave number	$2\pi/\lambda$

4. Wind Measurement Results

To obtain wind measurements, the instrument was installed and operated in a research vehicle that is located on the campus of the City College of New York, located in upper Manhattan, New York (latitude: 40°49'N, longitude: 73°56'W). Laser pulses are transmitted into the atmosphere through an opening in the vehicle's roof, which also allowed for the collection of the backscattered signals. Received signals are pre-processed in real time which is accomplished by programming the FPGA to calculate and accumulate the autocorrelation of backscattered signals from 10,000 laser pulses. Backscattered signals power is estimated by calculating the FFT of the accumulated autocorrelation. These calculations are carried out by a host computer after streaming the autocorrelation data from the FPGA. Wind velocities are calculated by estimating the Doppler frequency shift of the backscattered signals. Figure 3 (a) and (b) show vertical profiles of wind velocity and the SNR of backscattered signal, respectively, measured over a period of four hours (14:00-18:00 U.S. eastern daylight time (EDT)) on July 12th, 2012. To be able to compare backscattered signals of the CDL with that of the direct detection, CDL's backscattered signals' power are range corrected according to the inverse range dependence shown in (2). Figure 4(a) and (b) show the range corrected CDL backscattered signals power and the 1µm direct detection lidar, respectively, which was also operated at the remote sensing laboratory of the City College of New York during the same time period. Both graphs show a good agreement of signal intensity profiles and cloud patterns at approximately 14:15, 15:00 and 15:20. It is also noticed that signal power increased significantly at a height of approximately 2000 m at 14:15 and 15:20 due to clouds at that height. Both lidars also show a gradual increase of aerosol signal as a function of time.

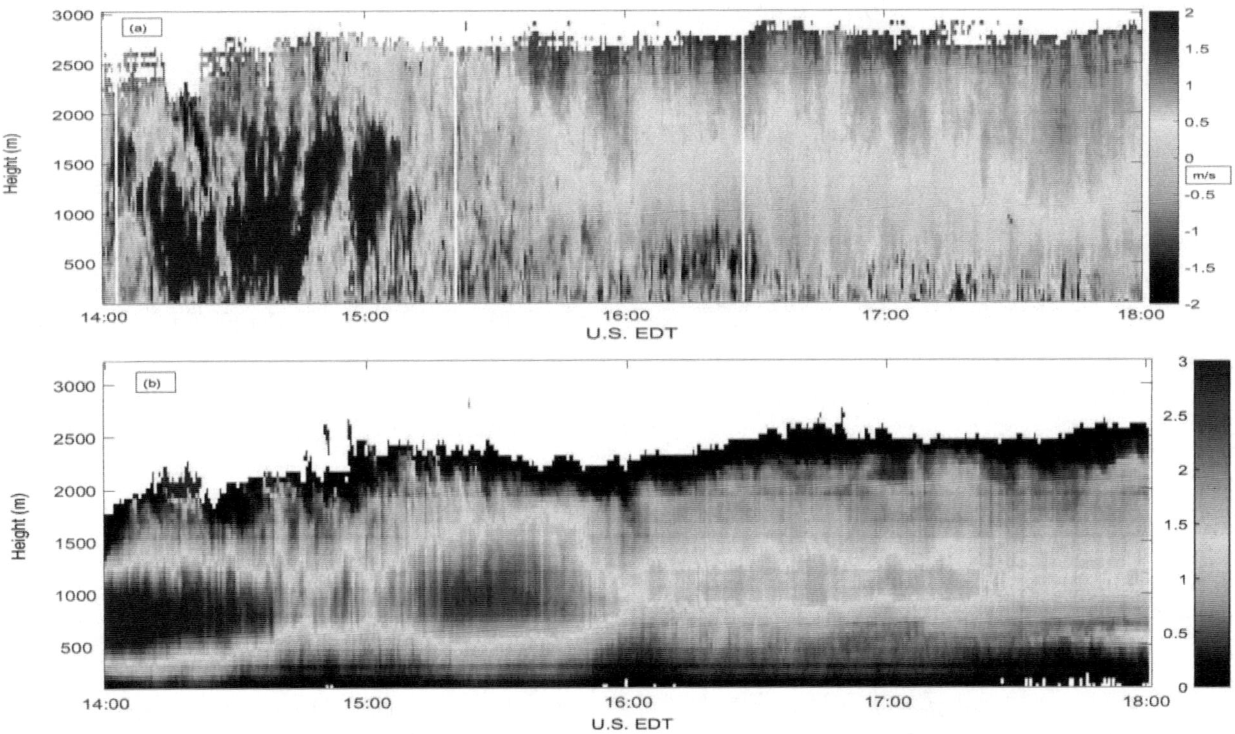

Fig. 3. Vertical wind velocity (a) and SNR(dB) of received signals (b) vs. height and time measured at the CCNY Remote Sensing Laboratory on July 12th, 2012 from 14:00-18:00 U.S. EDT.

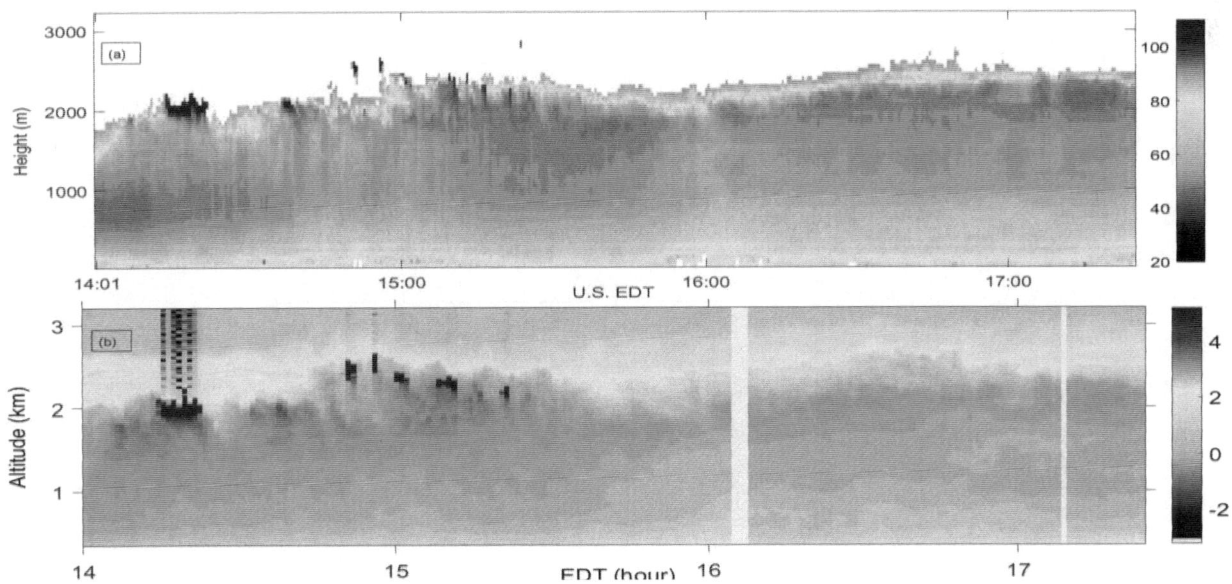

Fig. 5. Range corrected backscattered signal power (a) and the 1 μm direct detection lidar signal power (b) vs. height and time. Both profiles show a good agreement around 14:35, 15:60, and 16:15, where clouds' patterns are observed at the same heights. Aerosols concentration profiles also show a good agreement in the two measurements.

CONCLUSION

In conclusion, the turbulence and range effects on the CDL backscattered signals were corrected for which allowed to compare signals power with these of a direct detection lidar. Both lidars show a strong agreement of aerosol profiles and cloud pattern which validates measurements of the newly developed CDL instrument. More future work can be done to analytically compare backscattered signals power from both lidars.

REFERENCES:

[1] S. Abdelazim, D. Santoro, M. Arend, A. Moshary and S. Ahmed, "All-fiber Coherent Doppler LIDAR for Wind Sensing," in *15th Coherent Laser Radar Conference*, Toulouse, France, 2009.

[2] S. Abdelazim, D. Santoro, M. Arend, F. Moshary and S. Ahmed, "Wind velocity estimate and signal to noise ratio analysis of an all fiber coherent Doppler Lidar system," in *16th Coherent Laser Radar Conference*, Long Beach, CA, 2011.

[3] S. Abdelazim, D. Santoro, M. Arend, F. Moshary and S. Ahmed, "Development and Operational Analysis of an All-Fiber Coherent Doppler Lidar System for Wind Sensing and Aerosol Profiling," *IEEE TRANSACTIONS ON GEOSCIENCE AND REMOTE SENSING,* vol. 73, no. 12, pp. 6495 - 6506, 2015.

[4] M. J. Kavaya and F. G. Rod, "Coherent laser radar performance for general atmospheric refractive turbulence," *Appl. Opt.,* vol. 30, pp. 5325-5352, 1991.

[5] S. F. Clifford and S. Wandzura, "Monostatic heterodyne lidar performance: the effect of the turbulent atmosphere," *Appl. Opt.,* vol. 20, pp. 514-516, 1981.

[6] S. M. Wandzura, "Meaning of quadratic structure functions," *J. Opt. Soc. Am.,* vol. 70, pp. 745-747, 1980.

[7] M. J. Kavaya, R. T. Menzies, D. A. Haner, U. P. Oppenheim and P. H. Flamant, "Target reflectance measurements for calibration of lidar atmospheric backscatter," *Appl. Opt.,* vol. 22, p. 2619–2628, 1983.

[8] Y. Zhao, M. J. Post and R. M. Hardesty, "Receiving efficiency of monostatic pulsed coherent lidars. 2: Applications," *Applied Optics,* vol. 29, pp. 4120-4132, 1990.

[9] D. L. Fried, "Optical heterodyne detection of an atmospherically distorted signal wave front," *IEEE,* vol. 55, pp. 57-66, 1967.

[10] S. Kameyama, T. Ando, K. Asaka, Y. Hirano and S. Wadaka, "Performance of discrete-Fourier-transform-based velocity estimators for a wind sensing coherent Doppler lidar system in the Kolmogorov turbulence regime," *IEEE Transanction on Geoscience and Remote Sensing,* vol. 47, no. 10, pp. 3560-3569, 2009.

NASA ESTO Lidar Technologies Investment Strategy: 2016 Decadal Update

Azita Valinia(a), George J. Komar(a), David M. Tratt(b), William T. Lotshaw(b), Kevin M. Gaab(b)
(a) NASA Earth Science Technology Office
8800 Greenbelt Road, Greenbelt, MD 20771, USA
(b) The Aerospace Corporation
P.O. Box 92957, Los Angeles, CA 90009-2957, USA
Azita.Valinia@nasa.gov

Abstract: The NASA Earth Science Technology Office (ESTO) recently updated its investment strategy in the area of lidar technologies as it pertains to NASA's Earth Science measurement goals in the next decade. The last ESTO lidar strategy was documented in 2006. The current (2016) report assesses the state-of-the-art in lidar technologies a decade later. Lidar technology maturation in the past decade has been evaluated, and the ESTO investment strategy is updated and laid out in this report according to current NASA Earth science measurement needs and new emerging technologies.

Keywords: Lidar, Laser Radar, Technology Development, Earth Sciences.

1. Introduction

This study summarizes the 2016 state-of-the-art in lidar technology as it pertains to Earth science and discusses needed capabilities for achieving NASA's Earth science measurement goals. It updates the last Earth Science Technology Office (ESTO) lidar investment strategy, documented a decade ago [1], which laid out the scientific basis and key technology developments needed to achieve NASA's Earth science goals.

The overall space-based lidar applications landscape is illustrated in Figure 1. From this figure it can be seen that up to the present time comparatively little of the total technology trade space can claim actual space heritage, leaving considerable scope for further development and exploitation.

However, the analogous situation for airborne ("suborbital" in NASA parlance) lidar, depicted in Figure 2, indicates that a substantial reservoir of experience and heritage is available in that domain to draw on for seeding future development of space-based implementations. Note that Figure 2 applies the modified TRL definitions that have been formulated for the suborbital domain [2].

In the realm of lidar-specific technologies, progress in the last decade has been mixed. Some emerging laser materials (e.g., Cr:ZnSe) and improvements in nonlinear optical (NLO) materials have expanded options for wavelength generation both in the near-UV and SWIR/MWIR, while dramatic improvements in pump laser-diode electrical efficiency have significantly improved the wall-plug efficiency (WPE) of both bulk solid-state and fiber-based lasers.

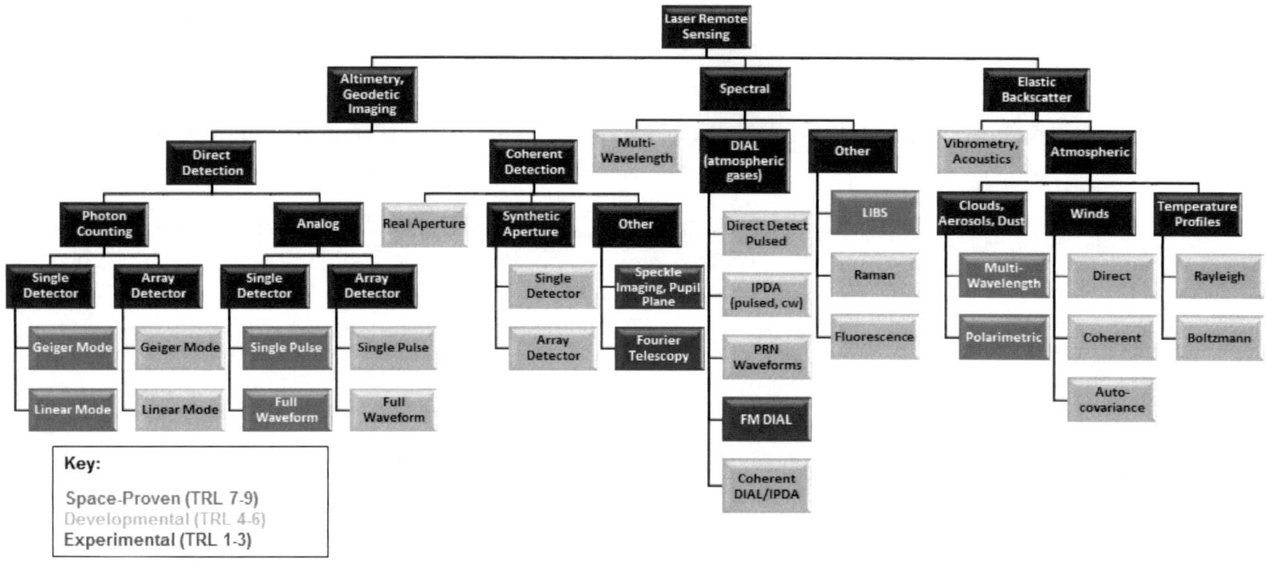

Figure 1. Cross-sector taxonomy of space-based lidar applications and associated sensor options. Adapted and expanded from [3].

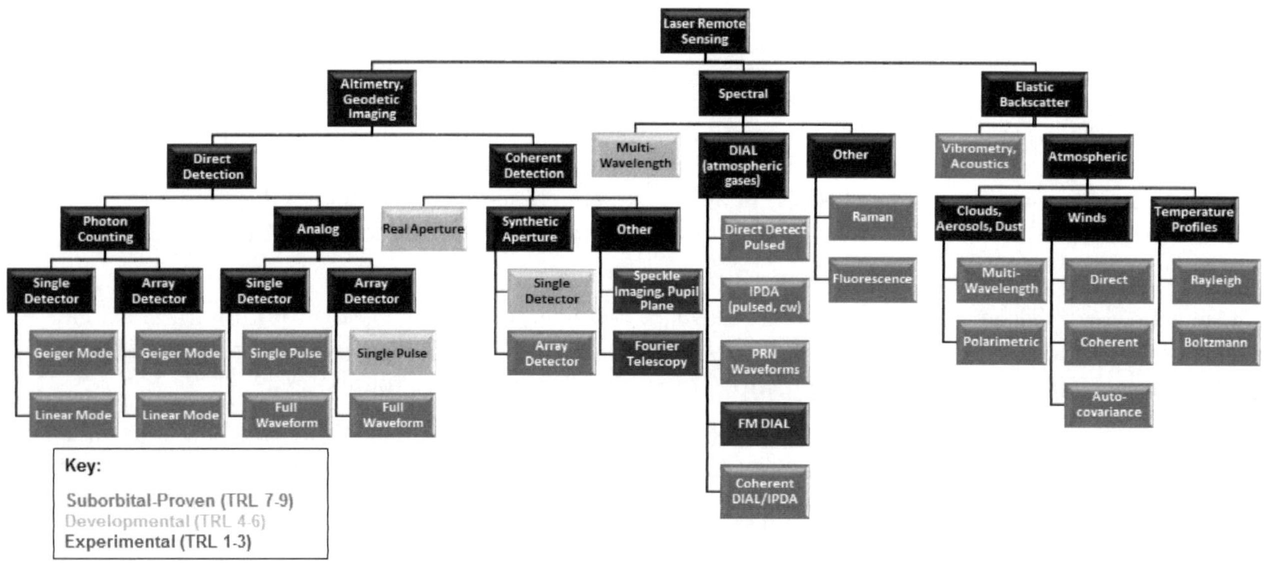

Figure 2. Cross-sector taxonomy of suborbital lidar applications and associated sensor options. Adapted and expanded from [3].

2. General Observations

An especially important consequence of laser technology development over the past decade is that fiber-laser average power capability now rivals that of traditional bulk solid-state systems, which is a distinct advantage in that all-fiber architectures are both compact, immune to misalignment, and typically exhibit higher WPE than conventional bulk solid-state lasers. The significance of these developments is that previously the restricted performance envelope of fiber-based lasers had ruled them out of consideration for measurement applications requiring high average power or moderate (i.e., ~mJ) pulse energy.

Developments of the past decade merit a re-evaluation in some of these scenarios. For instance, high pulse repetition frequency (PRF) transmitters have generally been regarded as inconsistent with the typical laser altimetry CONOPS (Concept of Operations) because of a perceived tendency for ranging ambiguity when there are multiple pulses in contention. However, the waveform agility of telecom-heritage signal laser diodes enables novel temporal waveforms that would permit disambiguation of range/altimetry measurements in such cases, and moreover would do so with the corollary SWaP (size, weight, and power) benefits of fiber lasers, as well as the additional advantages named above.

While the relief offered to laser performance requirements by improved detectors has long been recognized, technological investment has remained heavily biased toward laser development. A consistent theme expressed across all measurement scenarios was the need for improved detector performance, particularly radiation-hardened multi-element architectures with high quantum efficiency, low noise, low timing jitter, and low afterpulsing. Improved materials growth and device fabrication and processing techniques, particularly for complex band-engineered materials, could increase detector yield as well as improve device dark count rates, afterpulsing performance, and non-uniformity, which will be necessary for the new generation of array detectors. The astronomy and astrophysics communities pursue major detector development programs that could also be leveraged in this regard. A summary of scientific measurements and associated technology needs (without prioritization of technology development) is shown in Figure 3.

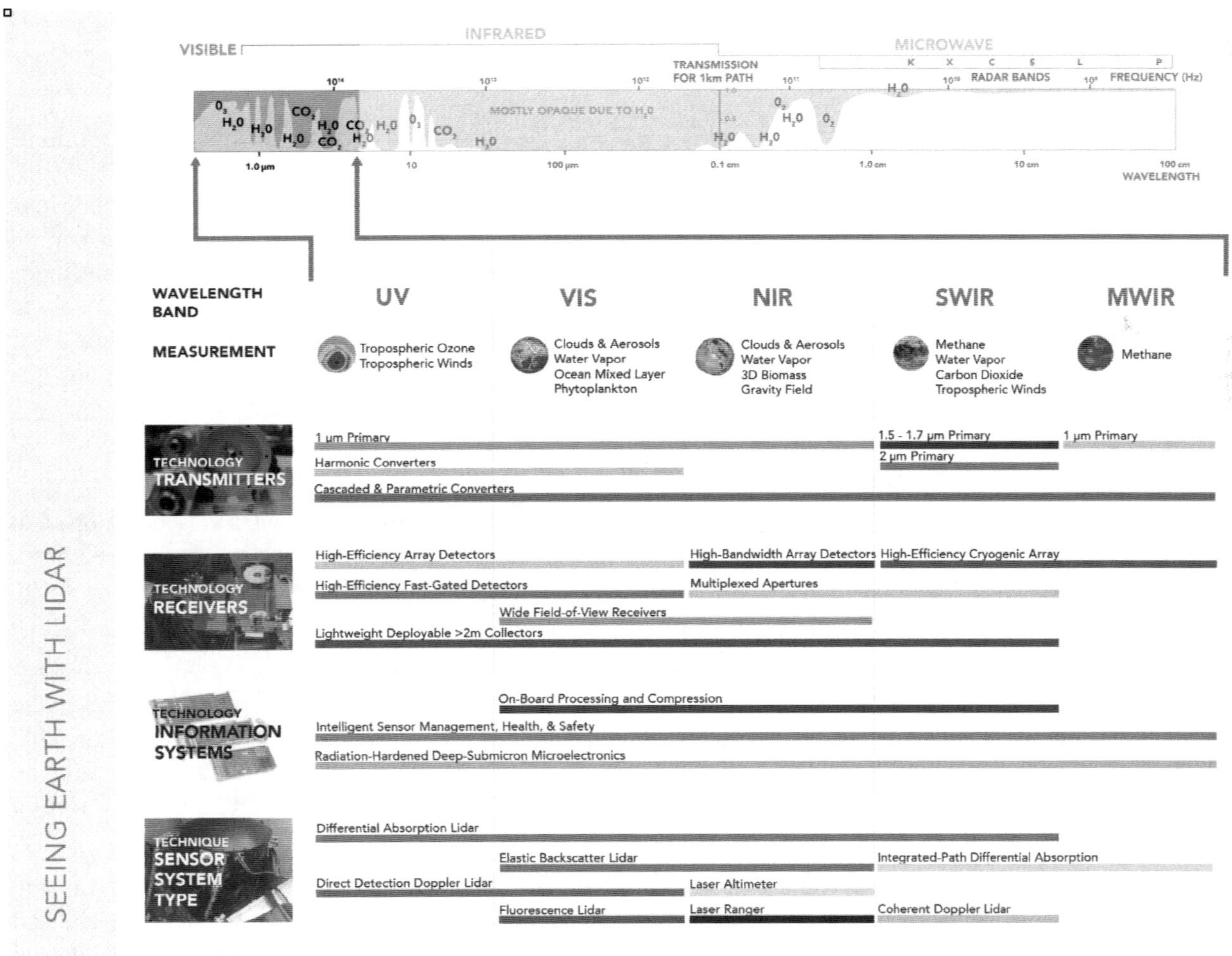

Figure 3. Summary of Earth science lidar applications and associated top-level technology needs.

Of the laser technologies covered in the 2006 report and this update, solid-state systems operating at 1 μm and lidars using harmonics thereof are by far the most mature and closest to insertion once the arduous task of space qualification is accomplished. The laser technologies required for direct detection UV Doppler wind measurements, and NIR/Vis/UV atmospheric aerosol/cloud/ecosystem measurements, have one remaining obstacle which should be within reach: improving the damage resistance and reliability of harmonic generation components. This task principally requires improved contamination control and more robust anti- and high-reflection coatings at UV wavelengths. Fiber-laser and fiber/bulk solid-state analogs of high-PRF, moderate energy (≤1 mJ) bulk solid-state systems are also rapidly approaching the critical TRL6 benchmark and could displace the bulk solid-state technology entirely in a few years. It is instructive to note that the NFIRE (Near-Field InfraRed Experiment) space-based lasercomm experiment [4] has been operational for 9 years, using relatively primitive fiber amplifier components.

As the analysis progressed it became evident that a number of technology areas identified as important in the 2006 report [1] had not advanced significantly in the ensuing decade and on that basis are being carried forward into the current report. Based on community inputs to this 2016 update [5; Appendix 3A], 1570-nm sources for ASCENDS, 2-μm sources for coherent winds, and even 1064/532/355-nm sources for aerosol/clouds/ecosystem measurements appear to have shown little TRL advancement when compared to the equivalent entries in the 2006 report [1; Appendix 5A]. The technology enterprise should consider re-prioritization of these efforts once the current Decadal Survey panel has communicated its recommended science priorities. For this reason, the current update avoids assignment of priorities to either the measurement objectives listed or the associated technology requirements.

3. Recommendations

It is important to note that the 2016 survey of lidar technologies was conducted against the background of a radical retooling of the space sensing arena occasioned by an explosion of SmallSat and/or hosted payload concepts that have evolved in response to an increasingly cost-constrained environment. SmallSats, especially the U-class concepts currently in vogue, demand a greater degree of attention to miniaturization and efficiency than has heretofore been necessary. Hence, in addition to the conventional lidar technologies that dominated the 2006 survey, the current analysis also advocates a number of technologies such as integrated photonic circuitry and deep-submicron microelectronic architectures that, while non-lidar specific, nevertheless offer considerable advantages (in some cases enabling) to lidar measurement concepts intended to be compatible with SmallSat/U-class buses. In this respect, the emergence of innovative manufacturing techniques in the last decade offers pathways to the creation of, for instance, structural elements and large-area reflectors that are lightweighted in ways not feasible through conventional means.

It is the recommendation of the report that the Earth science technology portfolio be actively partitioned to create a more symbiotic balance between emerging technologies and the ongoing development of more mature technologies. Emerging technologies such as integrated photonics, high-PRF fiber lasers, array detectors, and tunable NLO (nonlinear optical) schemes are some areas that might be leveraged under such a redirected program.

It is further recommended that provisions for classified technology development proposal appendices be instituted, analogous to the policy implemented by the NASA Earth Venture program. This would provide a mechanism whereby technological advances developed by the national security community could be leveraged by proposers in an environment where ESTO could be assured that the technologies in question are truly viable.

Several critical technology areas (notably NLO materials and associated optical coatings, and also detectors) continue to suffer from a significant shortfall in domestic capability, with many system and component technologies being dominated by non-U.S. vendors. This presents challenges to U.S.-based mission planners due to the prohibition on explicitly advising or guiding foreign technology development imposed by ITAR/EAR regulations. It is therefore recommended that these areas of need be brought to the attention of the Committee on National Security Systems (CNSS) Supply Chain Risk Management (SCRM). At the time of this writing, the SCRM was engaged in reviewing changes to CNSS 505 in order to address the full spectrum of SCRM policy across the entire U.S. Government. The updated document was scheduled for release in the April/May 2016 timeframe.

Finally, systems engineering should be more effectively employed as an arbitrator between evolving technology options, by enabling parametric trades between aperture size, detector efficiency, laser power, waveform diversity, etc. that could circumvent technological hurdles. To be successful, this approach requires robust, high-fidelity modeling and simulation capabilities, in both the environmental and sensor performance domains, which will require strengthening and further development of concurrent engineering tools. A significant body of knowledge relating to model-based system engineering (MBSE) exists within the defense community, where specialized analyses are routinely conducted within a generalized MBSE construct.

The MBSE paradigm offers an approach for independently arbitrating a number of questions prevailing within the lidar community. For example, three decades of effort have thus far failed to produce a viable solution for a perennial high-priority measurement, namely 3-D tropospheric winds. This particular question has been so resistant to resolution that instead of converging on an optimum approach the number of candidate options has instead expanded in recent years. The search for a technological pathway to the ASCENDS (Active Sensing of CO_2 Emissions over Nights, Days, and Seasons) mission currently threatens to follow a similar trajectory, with at least three options under concurrent investigation and an absence of concerted pressure to converge on an optimal approach. Another question that could be addressed by a rigorous MBSE analysis would be whether the global topography mission is most efficiently mounted using a single platform or a distributed architecture involving SmallSat constellations. Each of the analyses identified above would help to resolve long-running uncertainties, enabling NASA to more effectively target available resources.

4. Acknowledgements

In the preparation of the 2016 report [5], ESTO actively solicited and received input from the community. Written inputs by the community were submitted through ESTO's white paper input site. ESTO also organized three workshops with subject matter experts at NASA Goddard Space Flight Center, NASA Langley Research Center, and NASA Jet Propulsion Laboratory. ESTO also convened a virtual community forum to gather additional input from the community at large.

5. References

[1] ESTO, *Working Group Report: Lidar Technologies*, J. Neff and A. Valinia, eds. (NASA Earth Science Technology Office, 2006), esto.nasa.gov/files/LWGReport2006.pdf.

[2] NASA, *Airborne Technology Readiness Levels*, airbornescience.nasa.gov/sites/default/files/documents/TRL%20Levels.pdf.

[3] NRC, *Laser Radar: Progress and Opportunities in Active Electro-Optical Sensing* (National Academies Press, Washington, DC, 2014), www.nap.edu/catalog/18733.html.

[4] R. A. Fields, D. A. Kozlowski, H. T. Yura, R. L. Wong, J. M. Wicker, C. T. Lunde, M. Gregory, B. K. Wandernoth, F. F. Heine, and J. J. Luna, "5.625 Gbps bidirectional laser communications measurements between the NFIRE satellite and an optical ground station," *Proc. SPIE*, **8184**, 81840D (2011), doi:10.1117/12.894662.

[5] ESTO, *2016 NASA Earth Science Technology Office (ESTO) Lidar Technologies Review*, A. Valinia, D. Tratt, and D. Mayo, eds. (NASA Earth Science Technology Office, 2016), esto.nasa.gov/LidarStrategies/Lidar_TechStrategy_%202016.pdf.

ESA's ADM-AEOLUS Wind Lidar Mission – Status and Development

Roland Meynart, Anders Elfving, Denny Wernham and Anne Grete Straume
European Space Agency (ESA/ESTEC), Keplerlaan 1, 2200AG Noordwijk, The Netherlands
Roland.Meynart@esa.int

Abstract: The European Space Agency (ESA) is developing a direct detection Doppler Wind Lidar for measuring wind profiles from space. The pulsed UV Lidar instrument, ALADIN, will deliver horizontally projected single line-of-sight wind profiles from its molecular and particle channels. The development of the ADM-Aeolus mission has reached a major milestone with the integration of the full instrument and its functional and performance tests in April 2016. A 6-month life test of the spare UV laser transmitter is being performed with all relevant performance parameters adequate and stable at present (more than half of the required test duration). Launch readiness is expected in 4th quarter of 2017.

Keywords: Direct Detection, Doppler wind lidar, UV, high spectral resolution, line-of-sight wind profiles, backscatter and extinction profiles

1. Introduction

The primary objectives of ADM-Aeolus [1] is to provide global observations of line-of-sight wind profiles in clear air and particle rich air (aerosol layers and transparent clouds) down to the ground or top of optically dense clouds, for the improvement of Numerical Weather Predictions (NWP) and climate model parameterization. Aeolus observational data will be delivered in near-real time (NRT, e.g. within 3 hours) and quasi-real time for regions close to the data downlink station (QRT, e.g. within 30 minutes) for direct processing and ingestion into operational numerical weather prediction (NWP) models. From observation impact experiments, it was demonstrated that both the accuracy and spatial distribution of the wind observations are critical for the improvement of weather forecasts, whereas the provision of a single horizontal wind component instead of full vector information was of lower criticality. Therefore, a single viewing geometry had been adopted, avoiding the need for a complex scanning mechanism. A subset of the Aeolus observation requirements described in [2] are listed in Table 1.

Table 1. Subset of the Aeolus Observational Requirements

Requirements	Planetary Boundary Layer	Troposphere	Stratosphere
Vertical domain	0 - 2 km	2 - 16 km	16 - 20 km
Vertical resolution	0.5 km	1 km	2 km
Coverage	Global		
Horizontal accumulation length	3 km (20 pulses)		
Horizontal integration length	< 100 km		
Random error	1 m/s	2.5 m/s	3 m/s
Systematic error	0.7 m/s		
Observational dataset length	3 years		

2. Space Segment and Payload

The Aeolus spacecraft will fly in a sun-synchronous dusk-dawn polar orbit, with a 6 pm local ascending node crossing time, an inclination of approximately 97°, and a mean orbital height of approximately 400 km. A lower altitude of 320 km is being considered to benefit from the low solar activity during the mission lifetime. During nominal operation, the spacecraft will be tilted by 35° with respect to the orbit plane, while the instrument will view the atmosphere in the cross-track, anti-sun direction, as illustrated in Figure 1. A quasi-global coverage is achieved daily (with around 16 orbits) and the repeat cycle is 7 days (109 orbits). The satellite will also be periodically oriented to nadir for calibration purposes.

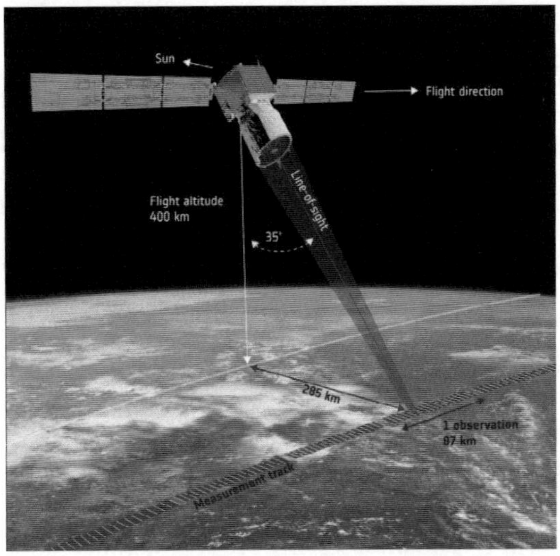

Figure 1. Aeolus orbit, pointing and sampling characteristics

Aeolus will embark a single payload, the ALADIN high spectral resolution Doppler wind lidar, which comprises a laser transmitter, a 1.5 m diameter Cassegrain afocal telescope, an optical bench assembly and the instrument control electronics. The laser transmitter is based on a diode-pumped, frequency tripled Nd:YAG laser, comprising two seeding Reference Laser Heads (RLH) and two Power Laser Heads (PLH) in cold redundancy. Each laser head can be switched to the transmit path by means of a flip-flop mechanism. A chopper mechanism is used to isolate the receiver input from the transmit path during pulse emission. The laser transmitter will be operated at e pulse repetition frequency of 50 Hz and a nominal laser output pulse energy of 80 mJ. The telescope, used in a monostatic configuration, is based on all silicon carbide structure (primary, secondary mirrors and tripod legs) resulting in a low mass (75 kg) and high overall stiffness. Its thermal re-focusing capability will allow adjustment of the focal spot while maintaining the overall telescope wavefront error within 350 nm. The transmit/receive optics use a passive diplexer/polarizer to separate emitted and received signals, and a narrowband interference filter for rejecting the broadband background signal.

The backscattered signal is analyzed in two separate spectrometers, allowing independent recording of the aerosol (Mie) and molecular (Rayleigh) components. The Mie receiver, based on the fringe imaging technique, uses a Fizeau interferometer, whereas the Rayleigh receiver, based on the double edge technique, uses two Fabry-Perot interferometers, implemented sequentially for an improved optical efficiency. Both receivers are equipped with identical detection units (e.g. accumulation charge-coupled devices ACCD of 16x16 pixels), providing on-chip accumulation over a configurable number of laser pulses. With typically 20 accumulations per readout, 35 independent signal acquisitions will be needed in order to form observations that can provide the wind velocity profiles with the required random error. The vertical sampling will be controlled by a programmable range gating that can be set individually for both receivers. In total, 24 Mie and 24 Rayleigh samples will be available. With a range bin resolution between 250 m and 2 km, backscattered signals will be acquired in both channels, covering typically in overall height interval between 0 and 30 km. The instrument control electronics comprise the Detection Electronics Units (controlling the ACCD readout and post-processing), the Transmitter Laser Electronics and the ALADIN Control and Data Management Unit which will provide the overall synchronization of laser emitter and detection chain as well as all data exchange between the instrument and the platform.

3. Ground Segment and Data Products

The Aeolus Ground Segment will perform all tasks related to the commanding and monitoring of the spacecraft, as well as the acquisition, processing and dissemination of science data. Its two main components are the Flight Operations Segment (FOS) and the Payload Data Ground Segment (PDGS).

The FOS will include the S-band station located in Kiruna (Sweden), for spacecraft tracking, telemetry reception and commanding tasks, as well as the Flight Operations Control Centre (FOCC) located at ESA/ESOC in Darmstadt (Germany), in charge of spacecraft monitoring, telemetry acquisition, flight dynamics analysis and telecommand data uplink to the spacecraft throughout the mission. The PDGS will be in charge of the science data reception via X-band and of various processing, archiving and product dissemination tasks. It will include the X-band acquisition station located in Svalbard (Norway), the Aeolus Processing Facility (APF) located in Tromso (Norway) for the processing and dissemination of the Level 1B and Level 2A products, and the Level 2 Processing Facility (L2/Met PF) hosted by the European Centre for Medium Range Weather Forecast (ECMWF) in Reading (UK).

The primary data product of the mission will be the Level 1B data set, comprising calibrated wind velocity observations for both Mie and Rayleigh channels, with various additional annotation parameters. The observation horizontal integration length is approximately 90 km, with less than 1% data gap between successive observations. The different values provided in Table 1 correspond to the horizontal integration length that needs to be considered in order to meet the wind velocity random error requirement. The Level 1B products will be globally delivered to a number of meteorological service centres within 3 hours after sensing (NRT service) and for selected regions within 30 minutes after sensing (QRT service).

Higher level products will include information on clouds and aerosols optical properties (Level 2A), as well as consolidated horizontal line-of-sight wind observations (Level 2B), after temperature/pressure corrections and scene classification of the measurements within one observation. The assimilation of Level 2B data in the ECMWF operational forecast model will provide the so-called Aeolus assisted wind products (Level 2C). A further detailed description of Aeolus wind retrievals and data delivery can be found in Tan et al. 2008 [3]. For the Level 2A processing and products, a detailed description is given in Flamant et al. 2008 [4]. A summary overview of all products is given in Table 2.

Table 2. Aeolus Data products

Product	Contents	Typical size per orbit
Level 1B	Engineering calibrated wind velocity data (preliminary one component wind observations), including viewing geometry, scene geolocation and ground echo data	~87.5 Mbytes
Level 2A	Supplementary data product for cloud and aerosol optical properties (layer backscatter and extinction coefficient, backscatter-to-extinction ratio,...), including viewing geometry, scene geolocation data and error quantifiers	~20 Mbytes
Level 2B	Consolidated geolocated wind observations after atmospheric corrections and scene classification, including additional geophysical parameters and error quantifiers	~42 Mbytes
Level 2C	Aeolus assisted wind data, result of NWP assimilation processing, including vertical wind vector profiles (u & v components) and supplementary geophysical parameters	~46 Mbytes

4. Recent achievements and future prospects

During the Aeolus development phase, a number of technical challenges for the Aeolus system have appeared and have been tackled. These include laser diode performance, optical mounting stability, laser induced damage on the IR and UV coatings, laser-induced contamination (LIC) in vacuum, and long-term UV energy drift. To mitigate these risks, the laser housing is maintained at a low pressure of 0.6 mbar.

The two flight laser transmitters have been delivered, after successful qualification including mechanical, thermal vacuum, EMC test and burn-in during 4 weeks (> 100 Mshots). The third (spare) laser is undergoing a long-duration endure test of 6 months (780 Mshots). Up to 13 June, the laser has run for 135 days, corresponding to 587 Mshots. The degradation measured by the laser UV photodiode is lower than 4 %. A higher degradation is observed in the external elements of the test equipment because of LIC effects in the vacuum chamber.

The two lasers have been integrated in the instrument and full-instrument tests have been performed in ambient conditions. In particular, a dedicated optical test equipment was developed to characterize the outgoing laser beam and generate synthetic atmospheric echoes which can be modulated in shape, amplitude and frequency. Detailed correlation of test results with predicted performance is being analysed. Initial results show that random errors extrapolated from test are within 5% of expectations for the Mie and Rayleigh channels. The response slopes in both channels have been verified. A short endurance test on the emission path of the instrument showed good stability.

The next steps will be the delivery of the instrument to the satellite prime contractor. The integrated spacecraft will be transported to test facilities end of 2016. Mechanical and thermal vacuum tests are planned for first half 2017. In particular, mechanical tests will cover sine, acoustic and shocks tests. Later thermal vacuum test, including full performance in vacuum. Flight readiness is expected in 4th quarter 2017.

5. Summary

The development of the Aeolus mission is getting close to completion after about 15 years of development challenges, during which invaluable experience has been gained. The ambitious mission and instrument concept led to a difficult development requiring time-consuming iterations in critical elements, particularly the laser. This careful step-by-step development recently culminated in the integration of the instrument and the testing of its performance in ambient conditions. The instrument will soon be integrated on the satellite and all satellite-level testing, including instrument in thermal vacuum, will be performed during the 1st half of 2017, to be ready for a launch in the 4th quarter of 2017.

The development took much more time than initially anticipated, but the mission remains unique and eagerly expected by user communities anticipating break-through in weather forecast and climate research.

6. References

[1] European Space Agency (ESA), *ADM-Aeolus Science Report*, ESA SP-1311 available at www.esa.int/esaLP/LPadmaeolus.html (2008).

[2] European Space Agency (ESA), ADM-Aeolus Mission Requirements Document, ESA reference AE-RP-ESA-SY-001 v2.0, soon available at www.esa.int/esaLP/LPadmaeolus.html (2016).

[3] D.G.H Tan, E. Andersson, J. de Kloe, G.-J. Marseille, A. Stoffelen, P. Poli, M.-L. Denneulin, A. Dabas, D. Huber, O. Reitebuch, P. Flamant, O. Le Rille and H. Nett, "The ADM-Aeolus Wind Retrieval Algorithms," Tellus, **60A**, 191-205 (2008).

[4] Flamant P., J. Cuesta, M.-L. Denneulin, A. Dabas and D. Huber: ADM-Aeolus retrieval algorithms for aerosol and cloud product, Tellus, **60A**, pp. 273-286 (2008).

Airborne wind lidar observations over the North Atlantic in preparation for the ADM-Aeolus validation

Oliver Reitebuch(a), Christian Lemmerz(a), Uwe Marksteiner(a), Stephan Rahm(a), Andreas Schäfler(a), Benjamin Witschas(a), Dave Emmitt(b), Steve Greco(b), Michael J. Kavaya(c), Bruce Gentry(d), Ryan R. Neely III (e), Dirk Schüttemeyer(f)

(a) DLR, Institute of Atmospheric Physics, Oberpfaffenhofen, Germany
(b) Simpson Weather Associates SWA, Charlottesville, USA
(c)NASA Langley Research Center, Hampton, USA
(d)NASA Goddard Space Flight Center, Greenbelt, USA
(e) University Leeds, National Centre for Atmospheric Science, Leeds, United Kingdom
(f) ESA ESTEC, Noordwijk, The Netherlands
Oliver.Reitebuch@DLR.de

Abstract: The first space-borne wind lidar mission ADM-Aeolus from ESA is currently scheduled for launch by mid-2017. Aeolus carries the direct-detection Doppler lidar ALADIN that operates at an ultraviolet wavelength of 355 nm and makes use of two types of spectrometers to measure frequency shifts from molecular and aerosol backscatter. For the preparation of the Aeolus validation, an airborne field experiment was performed during 3 weeks in May 2015 with the DLR Falcon and the NASA DC-8 aircraft. For the first time 4 wind lidars were deployed during an airborne campaign including two coherent and two direct-detection wind lidars at a wavelength of 2-µm and 355 nm. A total of 7 coordinated flights of the Falcon and DC-8 yielded an extensive dataset of wind lidar observations in the North Atlantic region around Iceland and Greenland.

Keywords: ADM-Aeolus, Airborne Wind Lidar, Coherent Detection, Direct Detection

1. Introduction

Measurements of winds throughout the atmosphere are crucial for both numerical weather prediction (NWP) and climate studies. Nevertheless observations of height profiles of the global wind field are still pending and profile measurements of wind are prioritized by World Meteorological Organization (WMO) expert teams for global NWP. The European Space Agency (ESA) is currently implementing a Doppler wind lidar mission named Atmospheric Dynamics Mission ADM-Aeolus [1]. It is considered as a technology demonstrator for future operational wind lidar missions. Aeolus will provide profiles of one component of the horizontal wind vector along the laser line-of-sight (LOS) from ground up to the lower stratosphere (20-30 km) with 0.25 km to 2 km vertical resolution and a precision of 1 m/s to 3 m/s depending on altitude. A wind profile will be obtained from horizontal averaging over 90 km along track. The launch of the satellite is currently planned for mid-2017.

The lidar ALADIN (Atmospheric LAser Doppler INstrument) is based on a direct-detection Doppler wind lidar (DWL) operating at 354.9 nm [2]. The optical receiver consists of two spectrometers to determine the Doppler shift from the spectrally broad Rayleigh-Brillouin molecular backscatter and the spectrally narrow Mie backscatter from aerosols and cloud particles.

In order to assess the performance of the Doppler lidar ALADIN and to optimize the retrieval algorithms with atmospheric signals, an airborne prototype – the ALADIN Airborne Demonstrator A2D – was developed [3,4]. The A2D was the first airborne direct-detection Doppler lidar with its maiden flight on the DLR Falcon aircraft in 2005. Three airborne campaigns with a coherent-detection wind lidar and the direct-detection wind lidar A2D were performed for pre-launch validation of Aeolus from 2007-2009 [5-7].

In preparation for the Aeolus validation, an airborne field experiment was performed during 3 weeks in May 2015 with the DLR Falcon and the NASA DC-8 aircraft. For the first time 4 wind lidars were deployed during an airborne campaign including two coherent and two direct-detection wind lidars at wavelengths of 2-µm and 355 nm. A total of 7 coordinated flights of the Falcon and DC-8 yielded an extensive dataset of wind lidar observations in the North Atlantic region around Iceland and Greenland.

2. Objectives for the airborne campaign from 2015

The objectives for this campaign in 2015 were derived from results, experience and lessons learnt from the previous ADM pre-launch airborne campaign from 2009:

1. Confirm and document the technical performance of the A2D lidar and its suitability for the foreseen calibration/validation (Cal/Val) of ADM-Aeolus.
2. Extend datasets on response calibrations over favourable areas for Aeolus calibrations, e.g. ice or land with high surface albedo in nadir-pointing mode.
3. Extend datasets on Rayleigh and Mie wind observations. This shall include measurements in highly variable atmospheric conditions (vert./hor.) w.r.t. wind and clouds
4. Rehearsal for airborne Cal/Val activity after launch with focus on coordination with other aircrafts and ground validation sites.
5. Extend datasets on Rayleigh and Mie wind observations for variable aerosol conditions, e.g. low to high backscatter and different depolarization characteristics from aerosol.
6. Extend datasets on response calibration during less favourable conditions (cloud contamination or strongly varying ground albedo conditions, PBL snow drift conditions).
7. Demonstrate the ADM-Aeolus capabilities in resolving the vertical structure of the atmosphere and compare measurements to output from numerical weather prediction models.
8. Perform satellite underpasses for CALIPSO, ASCAT, TDS-1, or other existing satellite sensors.

3. Airborne and ground-based wind lidar instruments

Both the DLR Falcon and NASA DC-8 aircraft were equipped with a coherent and direct-detection wind lidar operating at wavelengths of 2-µm resp. 355 nm. The payload of the DLR Falcon aircraft consisted of the A2D [2-4] and the 2-µm Doppler wind lidar (DWL) [8-11]. The NASA DC-8 was equipped with the DAWN (Doppler Aerosol Wind) [12], TWiLiTE (Tropospheric Wind Lidar Technology Experiment) [13] and a dropsonde unit from Yankee Environmental Systems [14]. The main properties of the 4 different wind lidars A2D, 2-µm DWL, DAWN and TWiLiTE are summarized in Table 1.

In addition to the airborne instruments, a ground-based wind lidar was deployed at the Greenland Summit Station (72.58°N, 38.48 W, 3216 m ASL) specifically for this campaign. This station releases 2 radiosondes per day and is equipped with an aerosol lidar from the MPL (micro-pulse lidar) network [15]. The NCAS (National Centre for Atmospheric Science) Doppler Aerosol lidar (manufacturer Halo Photonics) operating at a wavelength of 1.55 µm collected data continuously at the Summit station from May 1, 2015 to June 27, 2015. The objective was to characterize the backscatter and wind conditions close to the surface (e.g. blowing snow, diamond dust), which is of relevance specifically during response calibrations for the ALADIN.

Table 1. Operating parameters of the 4 airborne wind lidars in May 2015

	DLR Falcon		NASA DC-8	
parameter	**A2D**	**DWL**	**TWiLiTE**	**DAWN**
wavelength	354.9 nm	2022.5 nm	354.7 nm	2053.5 nm
pulse energy	50-60 mJ	1-2 mJ	25 mJ	100 mJ (nominal 250 mJ)
pulse length	20 ns	400 ns	15 ns	180 ns
repetition rate	50 Hz	500 Hz	200 Hz	5 Hz (nominal 10 Hz)
telescope Ø	20 cm	10.8 cm	32 cm	15 cm
vertical resolution	300 m - 2.4 km	100 m	200 m	156 m
temporal resolution	14 s (+4s data transfer) per LOS	1 s per LOS	30 s per LOS	4 s per LOS
scanning	no, fixed LOS with 20°	double wedge with conical scan and fixed LOS (vertical)	conical scan with 45°	single wedge with 30.1 °
precision	1.5 m/s (Mie) 2.5 m/s (Rayleigh)	< 1 m/s (speed)	2 m/s	< 1 m/s (speed)

4. Flight Tracks

Both aircrafts were operated from Keflavik, Iceland from May 11 to May 28, 2015 with a total of about 35 flight hours for the DLR Falcon aircraft and 50 flight hours for the NASA DC-8 (Fig. 1). A number of 7 coordinated flights could be achieved. As the endurance of the Falcon aircraft is limited to about 4 hours, the DC-8 could fly more extended tracks up to 8 hours. A total of 101 dropsondes were deployed from the DC-8 measuring profiles of the horizontal wind vector, pressure, temperature and humidity. With a coordinated flight pattern the DC-8 could provide valuable information for the A2D calibration in nadir-viewing geometry with additional wind, temperature and pressures soundings. One flight of the DLR Falcon was targeted towards the Greenland summit with overpasses of the ground-based wind lidar.

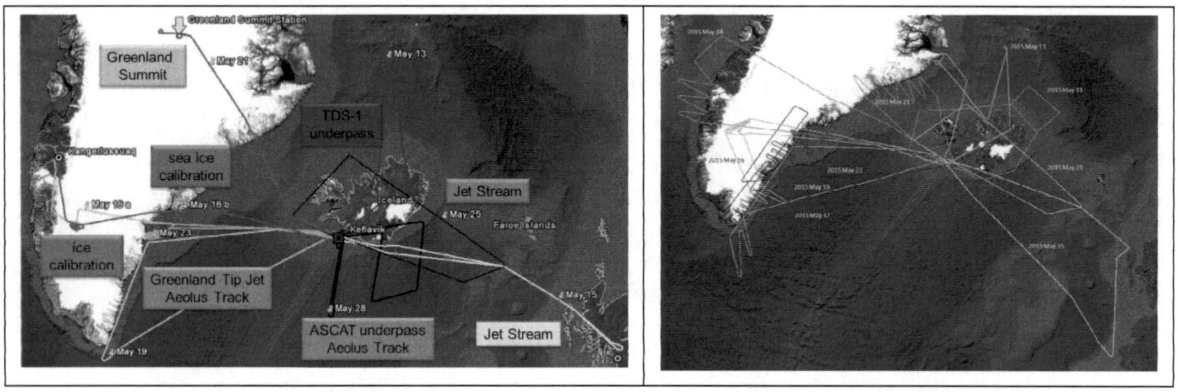

Figure 1. Flight tracks of the DLR Falcon from Keflavik, Iceland in May 2015 with the corresponding objective of the flight (left) and the track of the NASA DC-8 (right).

5. Conclusion and Outlook

The extensive dataset from 4 wind lidars, dropsondes, ground-based instruments including the wind lidar on the Greenland Summit Station and numerical weather prediction model results are currently analyzed. The objectives of the airborne campaign could be met and strategies for coordinated flights with 2 aircrafts were successfully proven. This forms the basis for future coordinated airborne validation campaigns for ADM-Aeolus after its launch.

6. Acknowledgements

The airborne campaign was funded by NASA, ESA and DLR.

7. References

[1] European Space Agency ESA, "ADM-Aeolus Science Report", ESA SP-1311, pp. 121 (2008).

[2] Reitebuch, O., "The space-borne wind lidar mission ADM-Aeolus." in *Atmospheric Physics – Background, Methods, Trends.* U. Schumann ed. (Springer Series on Research Topics in Aerospace), pp. 815-827 (2012).

[3] Reitebuch O., C. Lemmerz, E. Nagel, U. Paffrath, Y. Durand, M. Endemann, F. Fabre, M. Chaloupy, "The Airborne Demonstrator for the Direct-Detection Doppler Wind Lidar ALADIN on ADM-Aeolus. Part I: Instrument Design and Comparison to Satellite Instrument.", J. Atmos. Ocean. Tech., **26**, 2501-2515 (2009).

[4] Paffrath U., C. Lemmerz, O. Reitebuch, B. Witschas, I. Nikolaus, V. Freudenthaler, "The Airborne Demonstrator for the Direct-Detection Doppler Wind Lidar ALADIN on ADM-Aeolus. Part II: Simulations and Rayleigh Receiver Radiometric Performance." J. Atmos. Ocean. Tech., **26**, 2516-2530 (2009).

[5] Marksteiner, U., O. Reitebuch, S. Rahm, I. Nikolaus, C. Lemmerz, B. Witschas, "Airborne direct-detection and coherent wind lidar measurements along the east coast of Greenland in 2009 supporting ESA´s Aeolus mission." in Proc. SPIE Remote Sensing **8182**, Prague, Czech Republic, pp. 81820J-1 (2011).

[6] Reitebuch, O., C. Lemmerz, U. Marksteiner, S. Rahm, B. Witschas, "Airborne lidar observations supporting the ADM-Aeolus mission for global wind profiling." in Reviewed and Revised Papers of the 26th Int. Laser Radar Conference, Porto Heli, Greece, pp. S5O-01 (2012).

[7] Li, Z., C. Lemmerz, U. Paffrath, O. Reitebuch, B. Witschas, "Airborne Doppler lidar Investigation of Sea Surface Reflectance at a 355-nm Ultraviolet Wavelength." J. Atmos. Oceanic Tech., **27**, 693-704 (2010).

[8] Reitebuch, O., "Wind lidar for atmospheric research." in *Atmospheric Physics – Background, Methods, Trends.* U. Schumann ed. (Springer Series on Research Topics in Aerospace), pp. 487-507 (2012).

[9] Weissmann M., R. Busen, A. Dörnbrack, S. Rahm, O. Reitebuch, "Targeted Observations with an Airborne Wind Lidar." J. Atmos. Ocean. Tech., **22**, 1706-1719 (2005).

[10] Chouza F., O. Reitebuch, M. Jähn, S. Rahm, B. Weinzierl, "Vertical wind retrieved by airborne lidar and analysis of island induced gravity waves in combination with numerical models and in-situ particle measurements." Atmos. Chem. Phys., **16**, 4675-4692 (2016).

[11] Chouza, F., O. Reitebuch, S. Groß, S. Rahm, V. Freudenthaler, C. Toledano, B. Weinzierl, "Retrieval of aerosol backscatter and extinction from airborne coherent Doppler wind lidar measurements." Atmos. Meas. Tech., **8**, 2909-2926 (2015).

[12] Kavaya, M. J., J. Y. Beyon, G. J. Koch, M. Petros, P. J. Petzar, U. N. Singh, B. C. Trieu, J. Yu, "The Doppler Aerosol Wind (DAWN) Airborne, Wind-Profiling Coherent-Detection Lidar System: Overview and Preliminary Flight Results." J. Atmos. Oceanic Tech., **31**, 826-842 (2014).

[13] Gentry B., H. Chen, J. Cervantes, R. Machan, D. Reed, R. Cargo, C. Marx, and P. Jordan. "Airborne Testing of the TWiLiTE Direct Detection Doppler Lidar." Proc. 16th Coherent Laser Radar Conference, Long Beach, California, USA (2011).

[14] Yankee Environmental System: http://www.yesinc.com/news/research.html

[15] Shupe M. D., D. D. Turner, Von P. Walden, R. Bennartz, M. P. Cadeddu, B. B. Castellani, Ch. J. Cox, D. R. Hudak, M. S. Kulie, N. B. Miller, R. R. Neely III , W. D. Neff, P. M. Rowe "High and Dry: New Observations of Tropospheric and Cloud Properties above the Greenland Ice Sheet." Bull. Am. Meteor. Soc., **2**, 169-186 (2013).

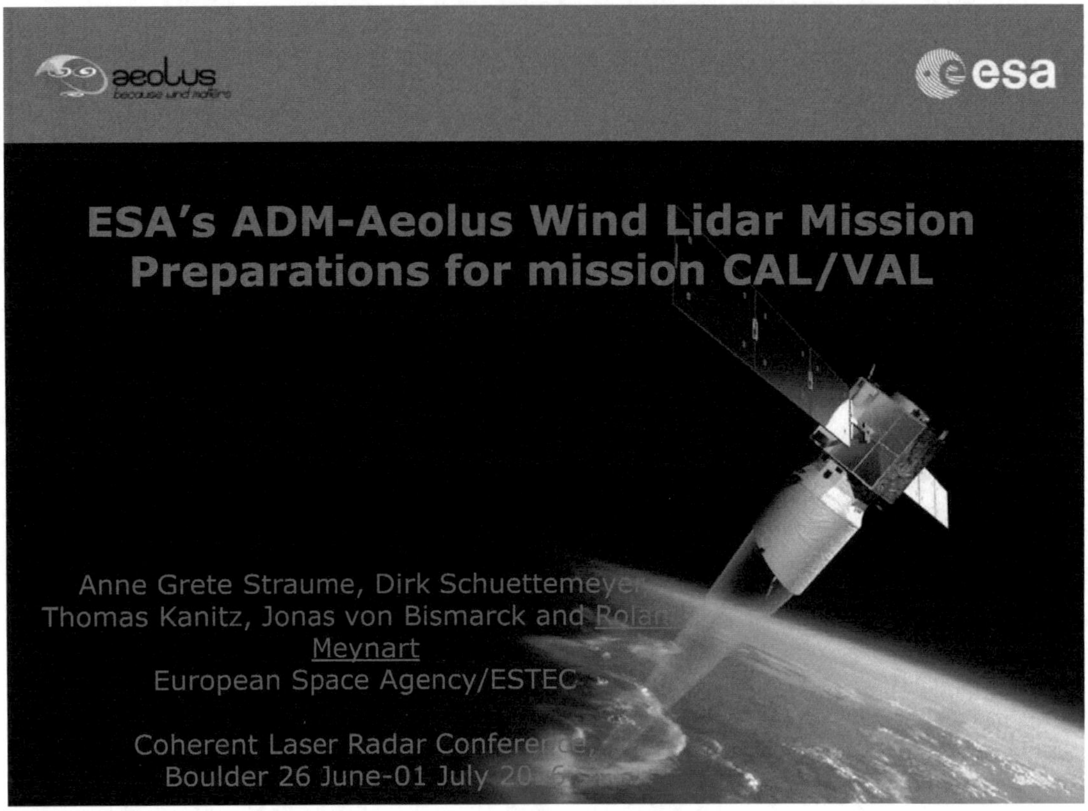
aeolus
esa
ESA's ADM-Aeolus Wind Lidar Mission
Preparations for mission CAL/VAL
Anne Grete Straume, Dirk Schuettemeye
Thomas Kanitz, Jonas von Bismarck and
Meynart
European Space Agency/ESTEC
Coherent Laser Radar Confere
Boulder 26 June-01 July

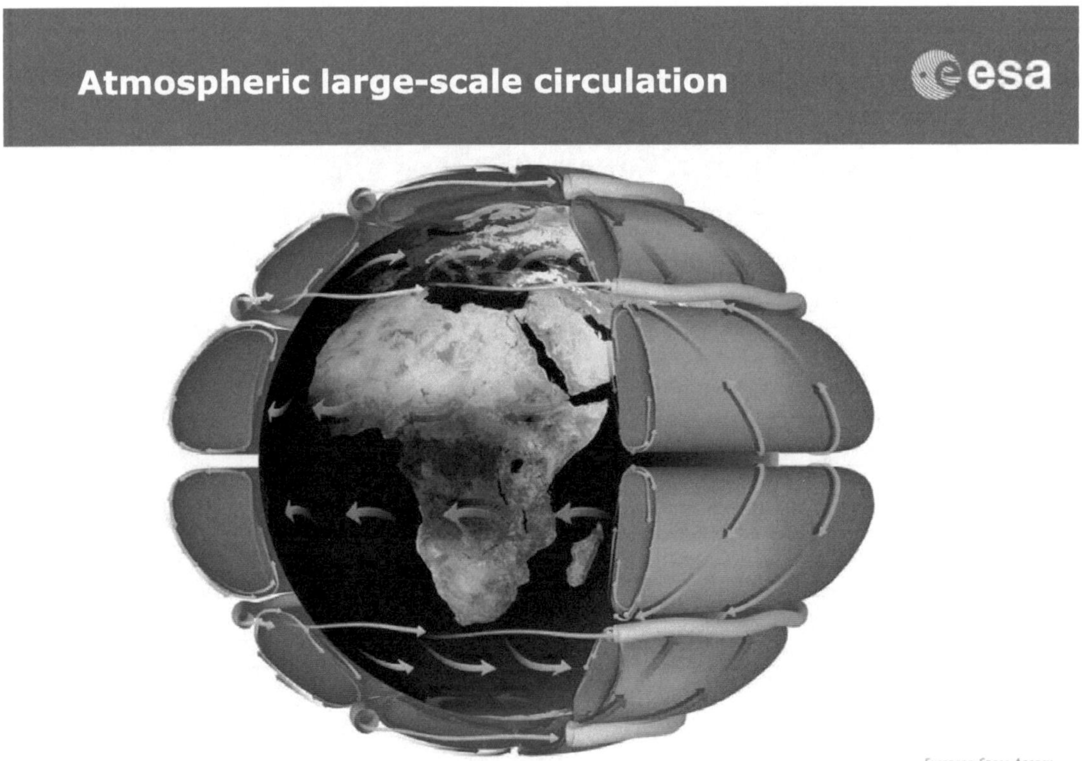
Atmospheric large-scale circulation
esa
European Space Agency

WMO Workshop Sedona, May 2012
Assessment Global Observing System Impact

esa

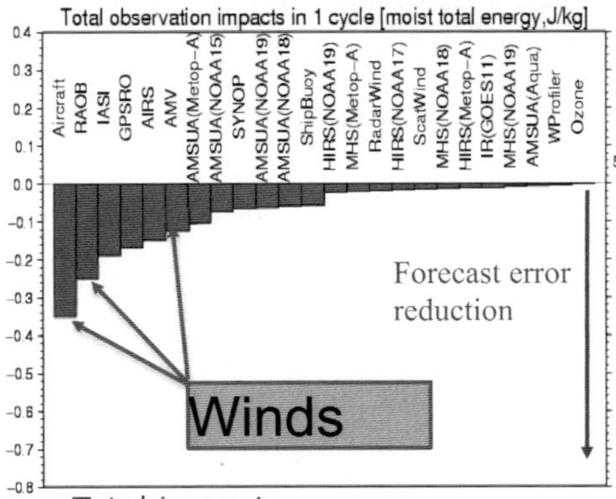

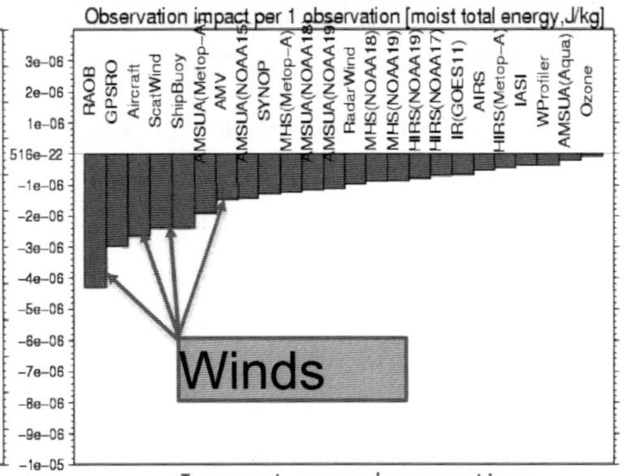

Courtesy L.P. Riishojgaard

All observation types have positive **forecast impact** on average

Total impact: 1) aircraft, 2) AMSU-A, 3) radiosonde, 4) IASI, 5) GPSRO
Impact per observation: 1) radiosonde, 2) GPSRO, 3) aircraft, 4) scatterometer wind, 5) marine surface observation

European Space Agency

Differences in forecast reanalysis data

esa

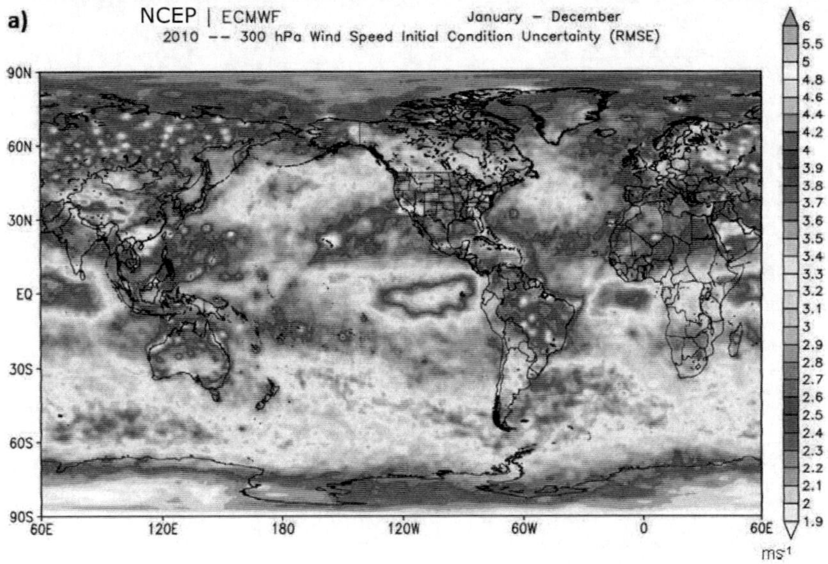

Baker et al., 2014

European Space Agency

Examples - Importance of winds for climate

esa

1. Atmospheric reanalyses for **climate model verification** need more wind observations

2. **Grand Challenges of World Climate Research Programme** are

   a. Understanding the role of dynamically driven cloud circulation interactions for **climate sensitivity**

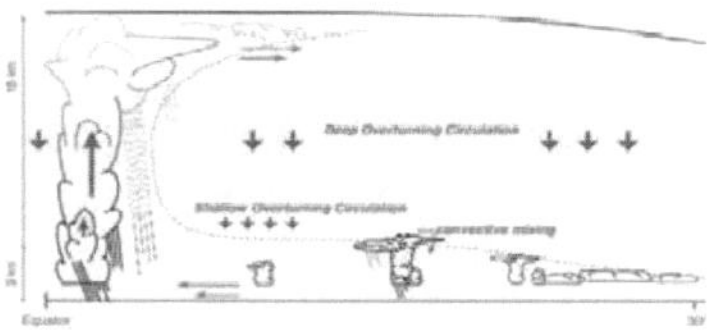

Courtesy S. Bony, B. Stevens

   b. Understanding Upper Troposphere and Lower Stratosphere (UTLS) dynamics and its impact on **climate variability**

3. Tropical **ozone** distribution is strongly impacted by UTLS dynamics (e.g. convection, gravity waves, planetary waves)

European Space Agency

ADM-Aeolus Mission Objectives

esa

Scientific objectives

- To improve the quality of weather forecasts;
- To advance our understanding of atmospheric dynamics and climate processes;

Explorer objectives

- Demonstrate space-based Doppler Wind LIDARs potential for operational use.

Observation means:

- Provide global measurements of horizontal wind profiles in the troposphere and lower stratosphere

Payload

- ALADIN: Atmospheric LAser Doppler INstrument

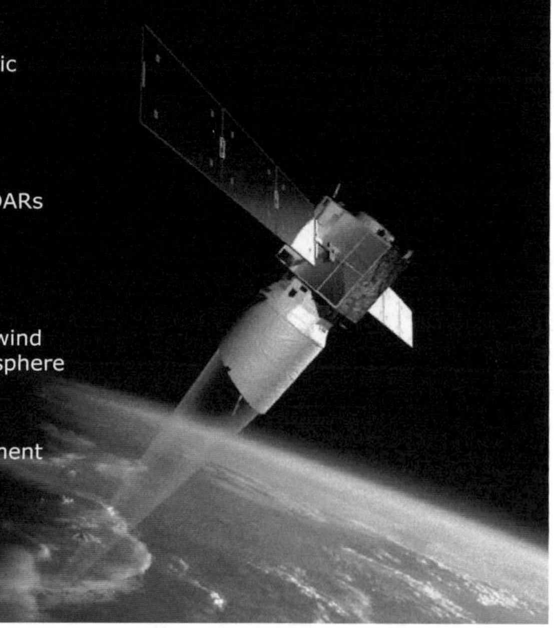

ADM-Aeolus Measurement Principle

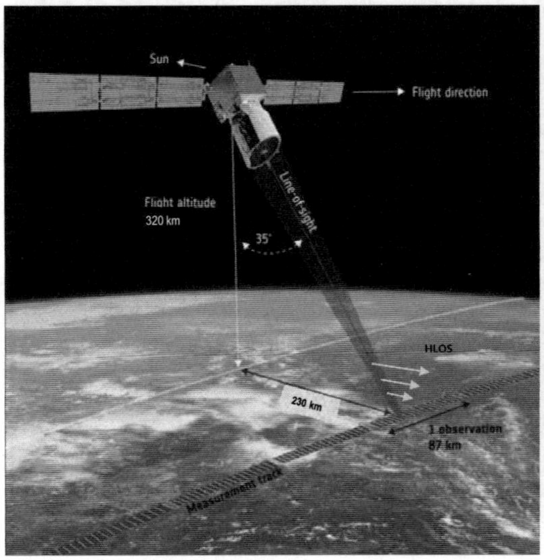

- Direct detection UV Doppler wind Lidar operating at 355 nm and 50 Hz PRF in continuous mode, with 2 receiver channels:
  - Mie receiver (aerosol & cloud backscatter)
  - Rayleigh receiver (molecular backscatter)
- The line-of-sight is pointing 35° from nadir to derive horizontal wind component
- The line-of-sight is pointing orthogonal to the ground track velocity vector to avoid contribution from the satellite velocity
- Spacecraft regularly pointed to nadir for calibration

European Space Agency

Data Processing

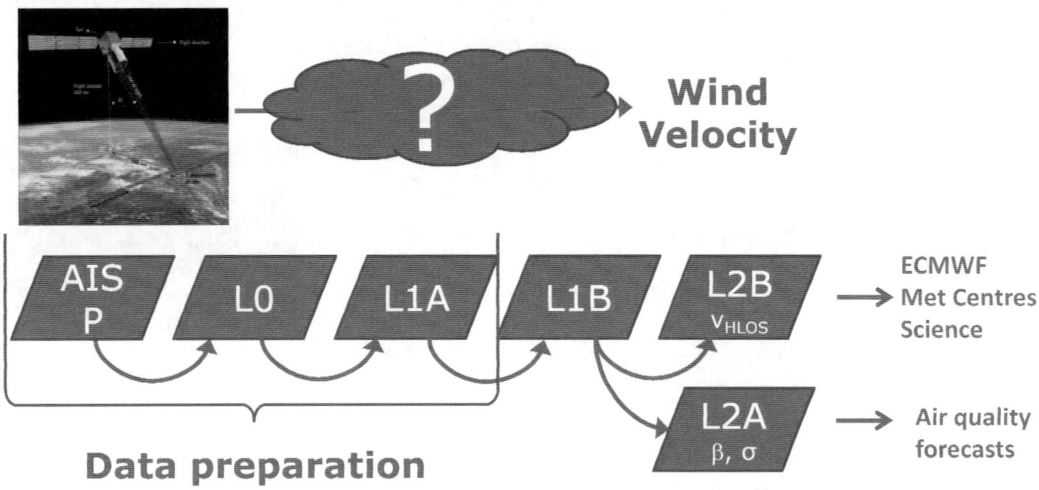

European Space Agency

Aeolus: Product Summary

esa

Product	Content	Size/Orbit
Level 0	Raw 'science' time-ordered source packets: ▪ including unprocessed instrument and platform telemetry	~60 Mbytes
Level 1B	Engineering geo-located and calibrated wind velocity data: ▪ preliminary one component HLOS wind velocity profiles, ▪ including viewing geometry, scene geo-location and ground echo data	~87.5 Mbytes
Level 2A	Supplementary data product for cloud and aerosol optical properties: ▪ aerosol/cloud backscatter and extinction coefficient, top and base heights, optical depth, feature finder and scene classification... ▪ including viewing geometry, scene geo-location data and error quantifiers	~20 Mbytes
Level 2B	Consolidated geo-located wind observations: ▪ after atmospheric corrections and scene classification ▪ including additional geophysical parameters and error quantifiers	~42 Mbytes
Level 2C	Aeolus assisted wind data: ▪ vertical wind vector profiles (u & v components), result of NWP assimilation processing	~46 Mbytes

European Space Agency

Mission products

esa

1. Primary product (L2b):

Horizontally projected LOS (HLOS) wind profiles

- Approximately zonal at dawn/dusk (6 am/pm)
- ~85 km observation from 3 km subsamples – scene classified
- From surface to ~30 km in 24 vertical layers
- Random errors: 1-2(PBL), 2(Trop), 3-5 (Strat) m/s
- Bias requirements: 0.7 m/s
- **L2c product**: assimilated wind vectors (ECMWF)

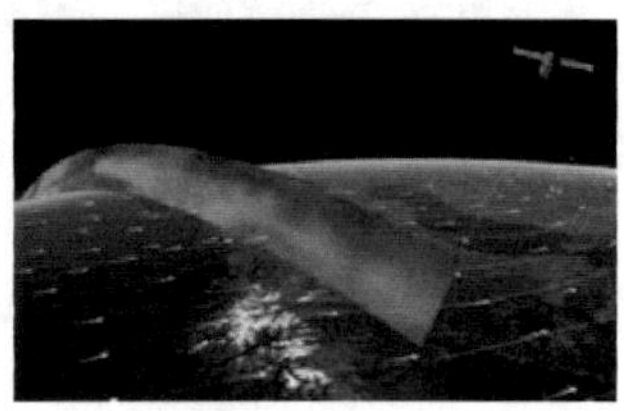

2. Spin-off product (L2a):

Optical properties profiles

- co-polar β, σ, lidar ratio
- <85 km observation averages from 3 km subsamples

From this one can deduce:

- Cloud/aerosol cover/stratification
- Cloud/aerosol top heights
- Cloud/aerosol base height (optically thin)

European Space Agency

Data processing and distribution

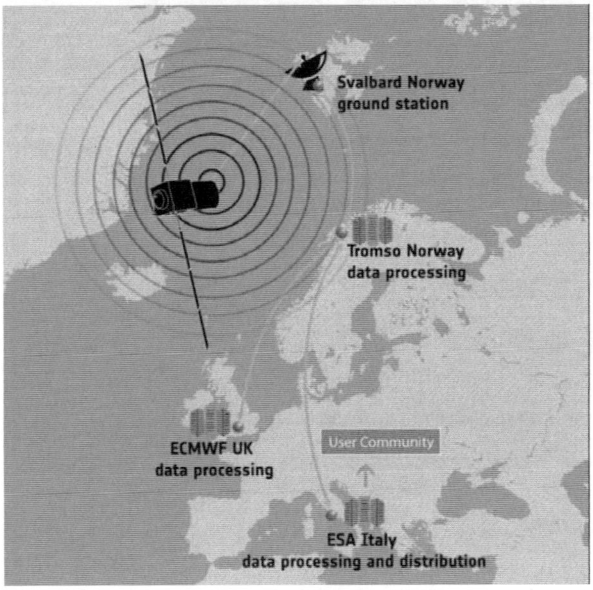

European Space Agency

Data access portal

http://aeolus-ref-addf.eo.esa.int/addf/

European Space Agency

ADM-Aeolus: Observational Requirements

Requirement ID			Observation Requirements PBL	Troposphere	Stratosphere
MR-85	Vertical Domain	[km]	0-2	2-16	16-20 (30)*
MR-60	Vertical Resolution	[km]	0.5	1.0	2.0
MR-80	Horizontal Domain		Global		
MR-70	Number of Profiles (sampling)	[hour^{-1}]	>100		
MR-150	Minimum horizontal track data availability	[%]	95		
MR-75	Temporal sampling	[hour]	12		
MR-50	Horizontal observation size	[km]	15 (goal) – 100 (threshold)		
MR-50	Horizontal measurement size	[km]	3 km		
MR-110	Precision (HLOS Component)	[m/s]	1	2.5	3 (3-5)*
MR-100	Systematic error (HLOS component)	[m/s]	0.7		
MR-90&95	Dynamic Range, HLOS	[m/s]	±100 (150)**		
MR-120	Error Correlation (per 100 km and between adjacent vertical bins)		< 0.1		
MR-130	Probability of Gross Error	[%]	5		
MR-140	Timeliness	[hour]	3		
MR-160	Length of Observation Dataset	[yr]	3		

*: Desirable range

European Space Agency

Examples of ADM-Aeolus error sources

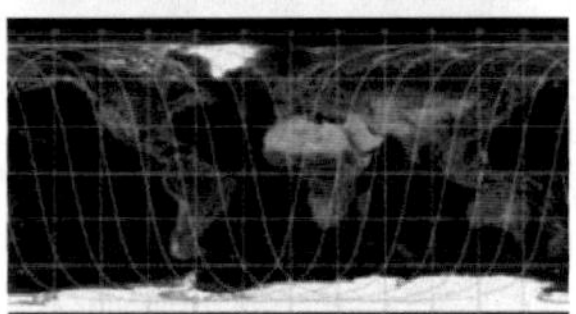

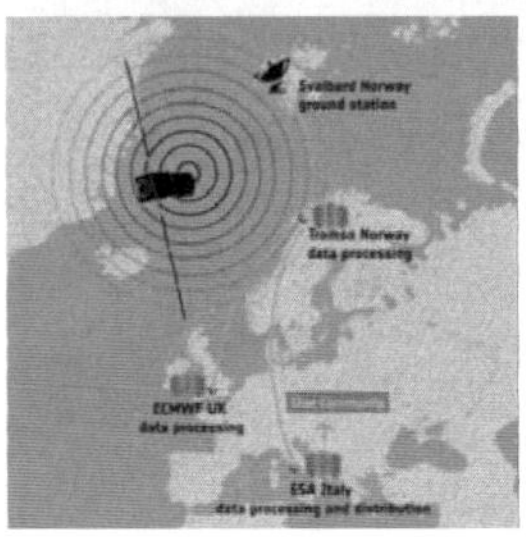

1. **Instrument errors**
   a. Instrument alignment and transmission
   b. Spectrometer imperfections
   c. Instrument degradation and laser stability, ...
2. **Satellite / orbit related errors**
   a. Harmonic biases from thermal variability
   b. Range dependent biases
   c. Pointing stability, ...
3. **L1 (and lower) processing errors**
   a. Calibration
   b. Signal processing and QC
   c. EQ, ...
4. **L2 processing errors**
   a. *A-priori* T and p (ECMWF)
   b. Calibration, signal processing and QC ...
   c. EQ, ...

European Space Agency

Examples of spatially varying error sources

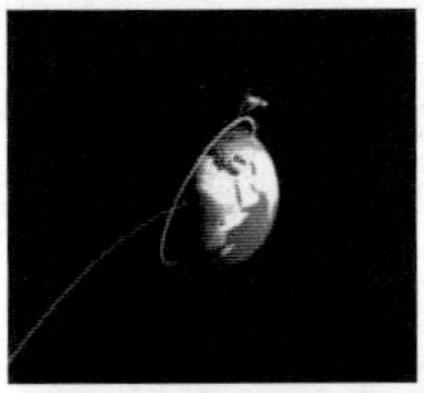

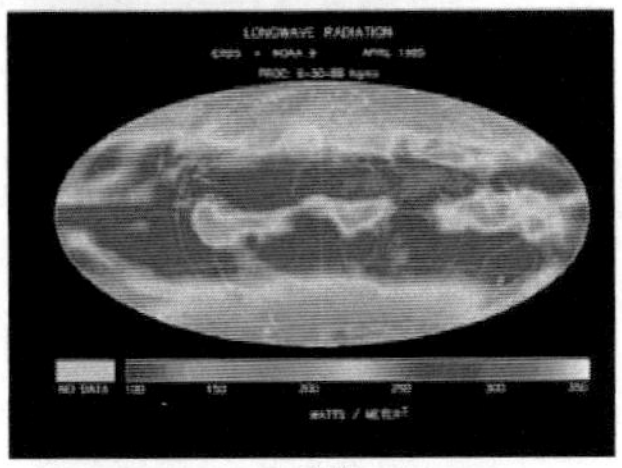

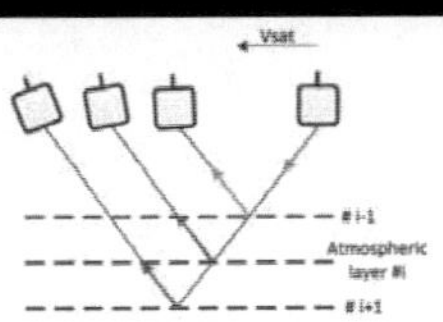

1. **Harmonic** variations in instrument alignment over an orbit lead to **wind biases**:
   a. **Thermo-elastic** effects from changes in the solar aspect angle
   b. **Thermo-elastic** effects from changes in shortwave and thermal fluxes from Earth
   c. Satellite altitude varies through orbit (harmonic **range-dependent** biases)

   Bias correction implemented using ground returns and error fitting through harmonic functions
2. Satellite movement along circular orbit cause variable backscatter angle on telescope as function of range (time)
   - **Range Dependent wind bias correction scheme implemented**
3. Regional T and p accuracy variations

European Space Agency

Examples of time varying error sources

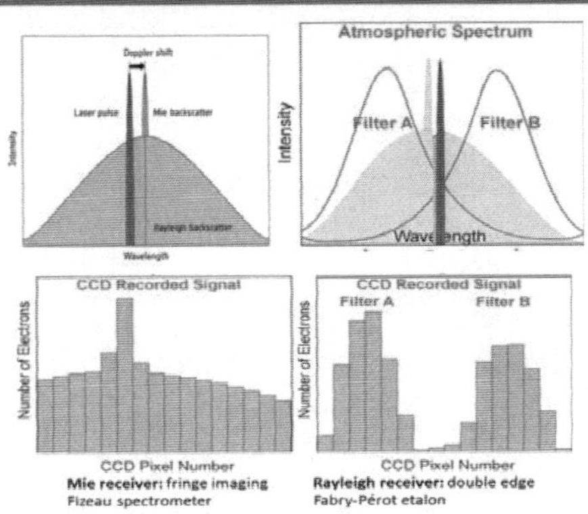

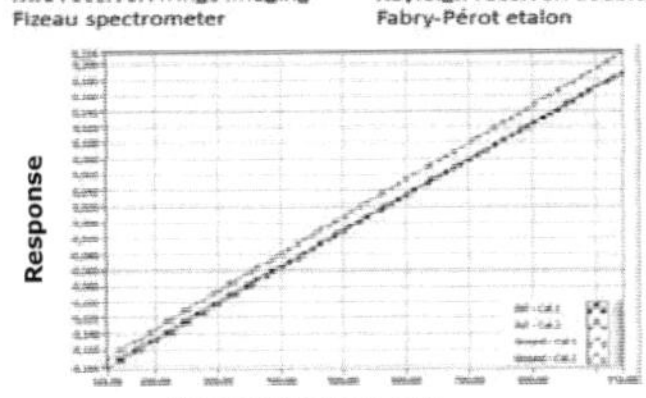

1. Regular receiver **response calibrations** (weekly) to detect and correct short-term instrument (alignment) drifts
   a. Satellite point to nadir
   b. Laser frequency scanned in 25 MHz steps.
2. **Laser** frequency and pulse energy **monitoring**

European Space Agency

ADM-Aeolus CAL/VAL needs

1. Characterization, calibration and validation needed on instrument, satellite and product levels to **verify Mission Requirements**
   a. Industry, ESA, algorithm core teams, CAL/VAL teams

2. Verification and validation needs addressed by **CAL/VAL teams**:
   a. Verification and validation on **several product levels** (L0, L1b, calibration files, L2a, L2b, L2c) looking at selected scenes
   b. NWP monitoring (i.e. comp. L2 HLOS and NWP model wind)
   c. Validation by comparison to **collocated observations** with similar and different instrumentation
      – **Airborne** (short-term, well collocated), **ground-based** (long-term, less frequent collocations)
   d. Short and long term calibration and validation (minutes, hours, days, weeks, seasons, lifetime)
   e. Appropriate **geographical coverage**
   f. Comparison with **independent retrieval algorithms**

17 ADM-Aeolus CAL/VAL Proposals – all selected after review

Activity Schedule

ID	PI Name and institute location	Topic	Method	Pre-Launch	Phase 1	Phase E2	Remarks
5156	DABAS Alain, FR	W, A	RO, AC, GC				
5166	Apituley Arnoud, NL	W, A, C	GC				
5177	Hardesty Robert Michael, US	W, A, C	RO, AC, GC, M, S				
5186	Baumgarten Gerd, DE	W, A	RO, GC, M				
5188	Apituley Arnoud, NL	W, A, C	RO, GC				
5190	Stoffelen Ad, NL	W, A	M, A				
5192	Schyberg Harald, NO	W, A, C	RO, M				linked to 5186
26989	Gausa Michael, NO	W, A, C	AC, GC				
27329	Reitebuch Oliver, DE	W, A	AC, GC				
27389	Stebel Kerstin, NO	W, A	RO, GC, S				
27409	Amiridis Vassilis, GR	A, C	RO, GC				
27411	Wu Songhua, CHI	W, A, C	GC				
27449	Zagar Nedjeljka, SLO	W	M				
27529	Forsythe Mary, UK	W, A	AC, M, S				
27589	Ishii Shoken, JA	W	GC				
27590	Joe Paul, CA	W, A, C	RO, GC, M, S				
28295	Kushner Paul, CA	W	M				

W = Wind
A = Aerosol
C = Clouds

RO = Routine Operations
AC = Airborne Campaigns
GC = Ground Based Campaigns
M = Model Studies
S = Other satellite obs

A = Alternative L2 products

funding secured
funding partly secured
no secured funding
unknown

Coordinated national effort

Multinational effort

ADM-Aeolus CAL/VAL Implementation Plan

esa

Table of contents:

European Space Agency

Geographical coverage CAL/VAL proposals

esa

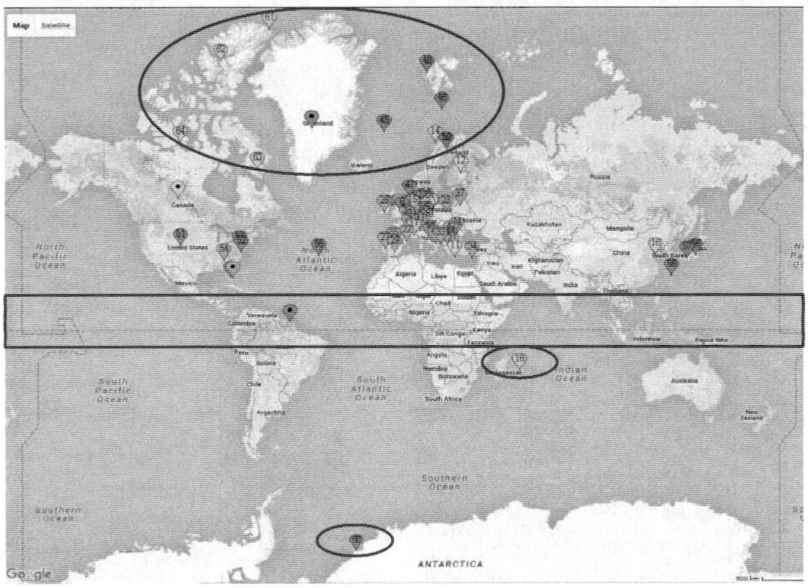

European Space Agency

Temporal coverage CAL/VAL Proposals

1. Most proposals foresee CAL/VAL **throughout phases E1 and E2**
2. Most have **limited resources**, hence **campaigns are limited in number and time-span**
3. Manpower and hardware maintenance for **long-term ground-based monitoring needs attention**
4. Iterations with teams to look for **possibilities to expand and coordinate activities**
   - Piggy-backing on campaigns for other missions (e.g. S5p, S1, S2, S3, ...)
   - Year of Polar Prediction (YOPP, 2018 -2019)
   - Tropical campaigns
   - ...

European Space Agency

Examples proposed Aeolus CAL/VAL Activities

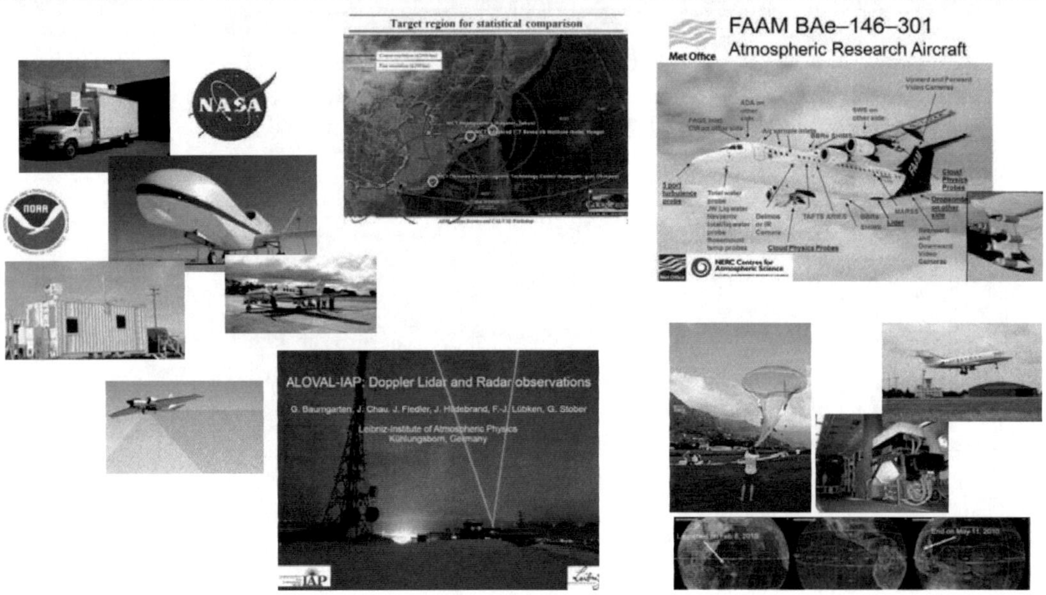

European Space Agency

WindVal pre-launch campaign – May 2015

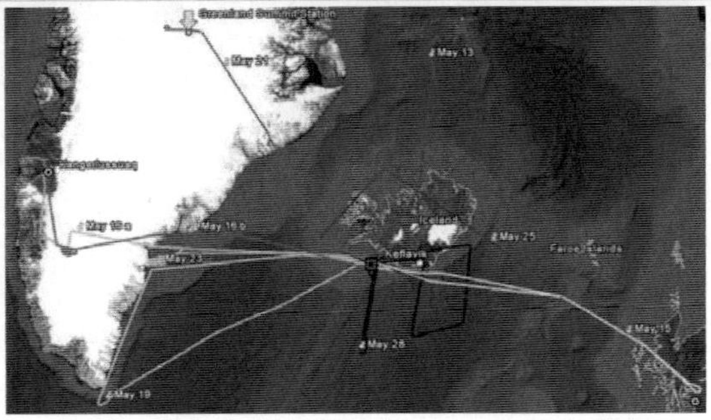

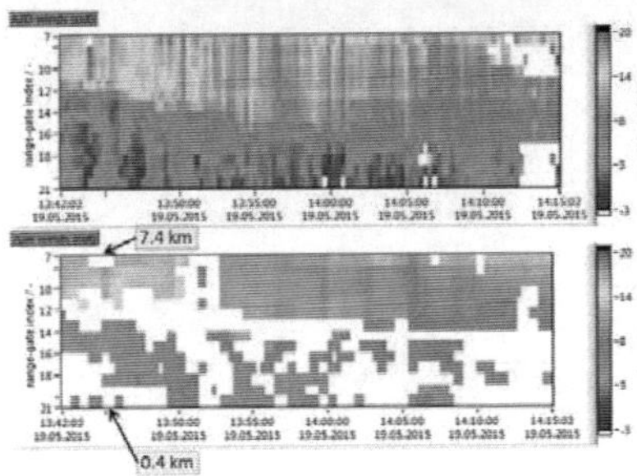

Statistical Results
corr. coeff. r = 0.89
N points = 765
slope = 1.28
std. dev. = 2.2 m/s
avg. bias = -0.17 m/s

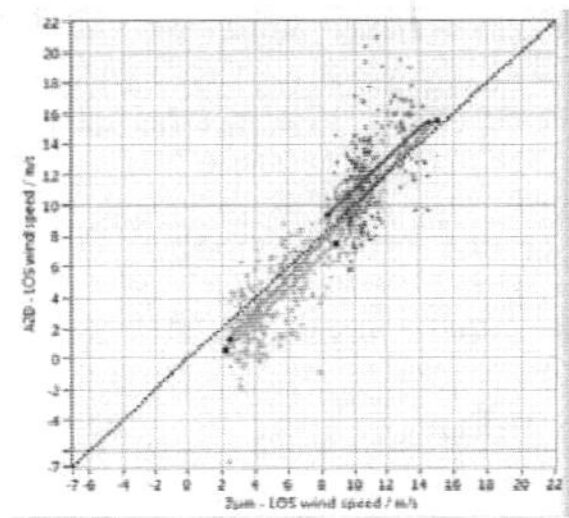

Credits U. Marksteiner, DLR

European Space Agency

ADM-Aeolus CAL/VAL Schedule

1. ADM-Aeolus Science and CAL/VAL Workshop held in February 2015
   - Instrument, processing, science and CAL/VAL Plans presented
2. Draft CAL/VAL Implementation Plan reviewed by PIs and being updated
3. CAL/VAL Coordination & Rehearsal Workshop planned for Q1 2017
4. ADM-Aeolus launch readiness 4th QRT 2017
5. Phase E1 CAL/VAL Workshop at L+3 months
6. Regular workshops throughout phase E2

European Space Agency

Concluding remarks

esa

1. ADM-Aeolus selected in response to identified deficiency in the Global Observing System w.r.t. global coverage of direct wind profile observations
2. ADM-Aeolus will serve Numerical Weather Prediction, Air Quality Forecasting and Climate Modelling (improved parameterization)
3. 17 (inter-) national CAL/VAL teams are getting ready to validate and exploit ADM-Aeolus data
4. CAL/VAL Implementation Plan drafted and reviewed
   - Coordination and further expansion of activities on-going
   - National funding confirmation sought by end 2016
   - Pre-launch campaigns -> Key for rehearsal and lessons learnt
5. ADM-Aeolus launch readiness: 4th quarter 2017
6. ADM-Aeolus L1 and L2 data availability to science community expected 3-5 months after launch

European Space Agency

aeolus

esa

Visit us @

www.esa.int/The_Living_Planet_Programme/ADM-Aeolus

www.ecmwf.int/en/research/projects/aeolus

Thank you for your attention

The ATHENA-OAWL Venture Tech Instrument

Sara C. Tucker (a), R. Michael Hardesty (b)(c) Sunil Baidar (b)(c), and Carl Weimer (a)
(a) Ball Aerospace and Technologies Corp.
1600 Commerce St., Boulder, CO 80303
(b)Cooperative Institute for Research in Environmental Sciences, University of Colorado Boulder
(c) NOAA Earth System Research Laboratory, Boulder, CO
stucker@ball.com

Abstract: The Green Optical Autocovariance Wind Lidar (GrOAWL) instrument is built to serve as an airborne demonstrator for the ATHENA-OAWL (Atmospheric Transport, Hurricanes and Extratropical Numerical weather prediction using the OAWL) mission concept for space-based wind profile measurements. The 532 nm wavelength Doppler wind lidar system is currently configured for flight aboard the NASA WB-57 aircraft. The system can make two simultaneous wind measurements along orthogonal lines of sight (to capture u and v components of the wind field). We provide an overview of the system design, architecture and preliminary performance results from May 2016 flight tests out of NASA Johnson Space Center at Ellington Field.

Keywords: Doppler wind lidar, airborne lidar, space-borne lidar demonstrator,

1. Introduction

The Green Optical Autocovariance Wind Lidar (Green OAWL = GrOAWL) is a Doppler wind lidar operating at the 532 nm wavelength. The system was developed at Ball Aerospace with funding provided by the NASA Earth Science Venture Technology program, managed by the NASA Earth Science Technology Office (ESTO). The effort is in support of the Atmospheric Transport, Hurricanes and Extratropical Numerical weather prediction using the OAWL (ATHENA-OAWL) mission concept, which aims to put a two-look Doppler Wind Lidar demonstrator on the International Space Station. The ATHENA-OAWL Venture Tech (AOVT) objectives are to build a robust, two-look, 532 nm version of the OAWL lidar system, demonstrate the instrument performance in aircraft flights (on the NASA-WB-57), validate the measurements, and scale the airborne system performance to that for a space-based mission. The verification and validation of the instrument performance, based on measurements and modeling of aerosol presence, is discussed in a separate paper at this conference (Baidar et al., CLRC 2016). Here we briefly describe the instrument and present preliminary results from ground and aircraft testing.

2. Instrument Description

The GrOAWL instrument has to two line-of-sight (LOS) lidar looks with two Nd:YAG lasers to transmit (with interleaved pulses) and two telescopes (<12" diameter) to receive. Both LOS looks are pointed 45 degrees off nadir, with one pointed at 45 degrees azimuth from aircraft forward (the "FWD" look), and the other pointed 135 degrees azimuth from forward (the "AFT" look). Both of the looks couple into the Ball-built, field-widened, quadrature-Mach-Zehnder interferometer receiver using polarization so there is no mechanical switching. The polarization approach enables the depolarization signals to be captured for use in aerosol characterization. Each transmit path includes a variable attenuator subsystem to control 532 nm output levels, allowing 532 nm output to increase from < 200 μJ to 2.5 mJ per pulse as altitude is increased during flight, and a two-axis boresight mechanism to ensure that overlap can be maintained under varying thermal conditions experienced in airborne flights.

The GrOAWL mechanical design/build effort focused on airborne-specific system designs to ensure successful system operation in high altitude (low pressure), high vibration environment. This included a vibration isolation layer underneath the instrument and kinematic mounting of the optical bench and interferometer on that isolation layer. Two floor panels in the WB-57 pressurized pallet were replaced with custom panels containing the GrOAWL windows and external air-fluid heat exchangers. The system electronics (lasers and payload control chassis) were all cooled using fluid loops running through these pallet floors.

The GrOAWL payload control and data acquisition system consists of a custom, six-channel, FPGA-based data acquisition board and two FPGA-based auxiliary data and system control boards, all running on a custom, ruggedized, conduction-cooled, payload-control chassis with a single board computer running Linux. The payload software is written in C++ with an ethernet-connected user interface built using COSMOS (Ruby) for remote command, control, and telemetry. The GrOAWL detectors are Hamamatsu multi-pixel photon-counting (MPPC), Geiger mode APDs, four per wavelength in the interferometer, and one per wavelength for depolarization. The data acquisition boards control the detector voltage and temperatures, sample the detector signals with variable sample gate resolution (1.1 to 34.3 m between samples), and calculate real-time wind retrievals for quick look applications. Custom, aircraft-grade harnesses, cabling, and power control circuitry provide aircraft power to the previously described subsystems and to various heaters, fans, telemetry sensors, etc. throughout the pallet. A dedicated GPS/IMU is installed on the optical bench for pointing/orientation and platform motion knowledge.

The GrOAWL system is built to allow for operation at the 355 nm wavelength, achieved via an additional wavelength output on both of the lasers, dual-wavelength reflective coatings, additional interferometer and depolarization detectors, and an additional data acquisition board, all added under the ESTO-funded HAWC-OAWL instrument incubator program (IIP).

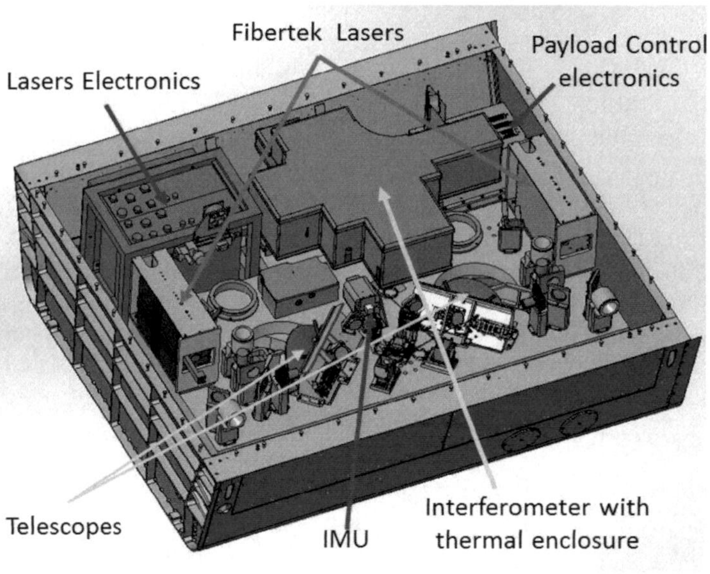

Figure 1. Left: Model image of the GrOAWL AOVT instrument as installed the WB-57 pressurized pallet.

3. Preliminary Results

The forward path of the GrOAWL transceiver system was integrated and tested in a rooftop laboratory at Ball Aerospace. A large mirror placed underneath the optical bench was used to point the beam westward over the Boulder foothills at a 30 degree elevation angle. Example data from the forward path is provided in the left panels of Figure 2. The final AFT transmit and receive path alignments were completed by mid-April after delivery of the second laser. The right panels of Figure 2 contain images of example ground-test data from the AFT look. The laboratory setup only allowed for atmospheric returns from one look at a time. Noisy data in the closest 2 km in the image, particularly in the 355 data, are due to detector saturation. The data, processed with 2 s accumulation and 43 m LOS range gates, show about 2-3 km worth of cloud returns atop a blustery aerosol boundary layer.

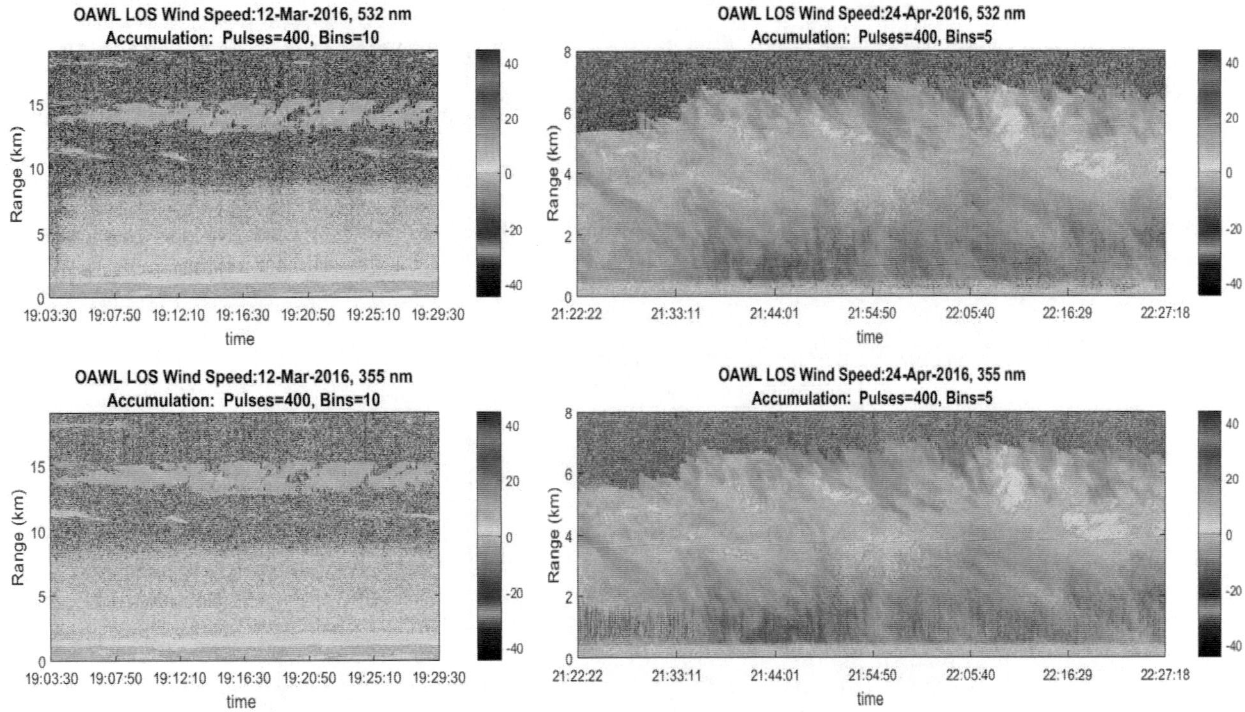

Figure 2. *Preliminary Data.* Left: Ground-based 532nm LOS wind data taken using the FWD look of the GrOAWL system. Right: Ground-based LOS wind data taken using the AFT look. Top row: 532 nm winds. Bottom row: 355 nm winds. Range scales are different on the two plots. Color scales indicate LOS wind speeds.

On May 5, the GrOAWL system, by then installed in the NASA WB-57 pallet, was shipped to NASA Johnson Space Center, Ellington Field. A series of aircraft flight tests took place starting May 10 through the end of June. On the later flights, an autonomous dropsonde system built by Yankee Environmental Systems dropped multiple radiosondes per flight leg for comparison and validation.

Two-look, 532 nm wavelength data from a flight performed on June 17 is provided in Figure 3. The data were acquired with the attenuator set to 1.5 mJ per pulse of 532 nm output. The processing was performed with 10 seconds of accumulation and ~170 meter range gates (~120 m altitude bins). Please see the accompanying paper by Baidar et al. in this conference for comparison of airborne GrOAWL data to the corresponding dropsondes.

4. Conclusions

The AOVT effort has upgraded the OAWL system to include two wavelengths, two looks, a high speed data acquisition system, interferometer fiber-coupling, and all the required hardware to fly the system in the NASA WB-57 pallet. The system has demonstrated ground-based and two-look airborne-based measurements, currently being validated against dropsondes. The in-depth processing, analysis, and validation effort for the GrOAWL system data is currently under way. The system will return to Boulder in July 2016 for additional ground testing with a focus on aerosol measurement validation.

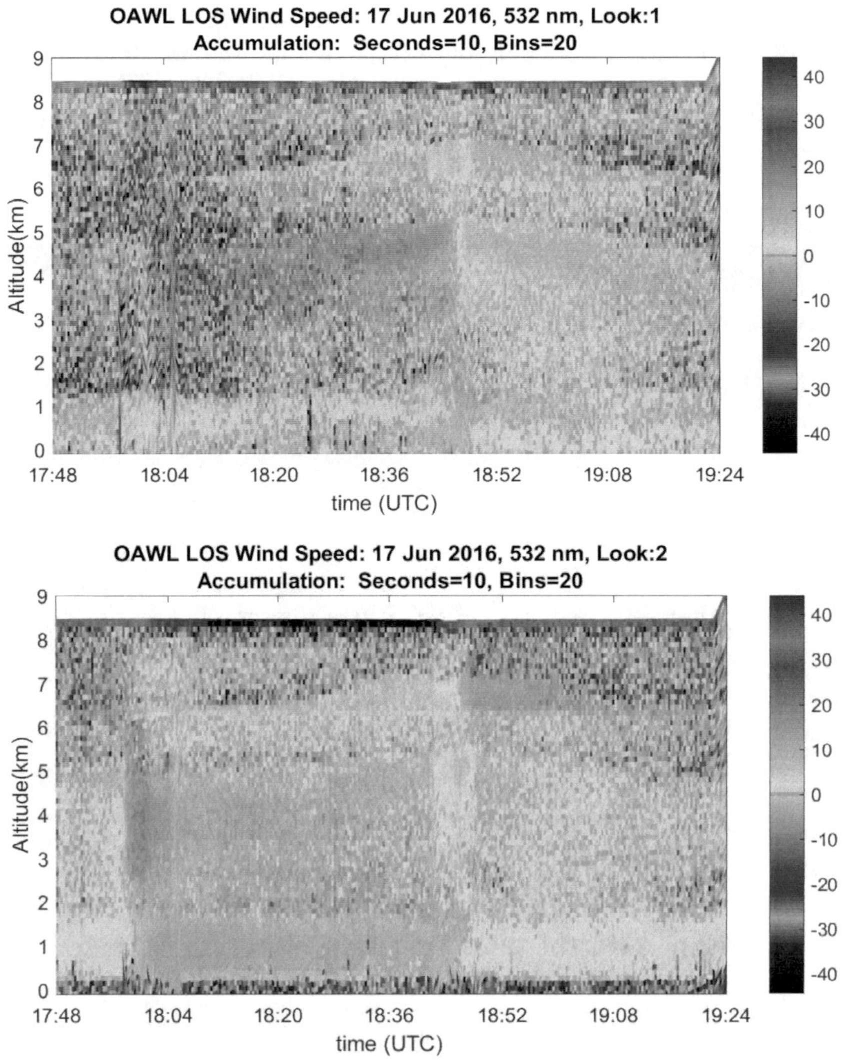

Figure 3. Dual look LOS wind data acquired over the Gulf of Mexico. Top: Look 1 is the forward facing look. Bottom: Look 2 is the aft facing look.

5. Acknowledgements

The authors wish to acknowledge the efforts of the GrOAWL hardware team at Ball Aerospace, including Rachel Narciso, Mike Adkins, Glenn Taudien, Jeff Applegate, Noah Siegel, Mike Conde, Tom Bellino, Paul Kaptchen, and Dave Taylor. We also wish to thank the pilots, engineers, and especially the maintenance crew of the NASA WB-57 aircraft who helped to make the demonstration flights possible.

Preliminary Results from the ATHENA-OAWL Venture Tech Airborne Mission

Sunil Baidar (a, b), Sara Tucker (c), Mike Hardesty (a, b)
(a) Cooperative Institute for Research in Environmental Sciences, University of Colorado Boulder, Boulder, CO
(b) NOAA Earth System Research Laboratory, Boulder, CO
(c) Ball Aerospace & Technologies Corp., Boulder, CO

Sunil.baidar@noaa.gov

Abstract: The Atmospheric Transport, Hurricanes and Extratropical Numerical weather prediction using the Optical Autocovariance Wind Lidar (ATHENA-OAWL) is a mission concept proposed as an Earth Venture mission for space based wind profile measurements. An Airborne demonstrator for the ATHENA-OAWL system, is planned for deployment aboard the NASA WB-57 aircraft in May/June 2016. The instrument makes simultaneous measurements at two azimuthally orthogonal line-of-sight to provide u and v components of the horizontal winds. The goals of this deployment are following: (1) Validate and assess the wind measuring capability of the instrument, (2) Evaluate the instrument sensitivity and efficiency, (3) Assess the effects of different atmospheric conditions, and (4) Scale the performance to that of future space mission. Here we will present the validation efforts and preliminary results from this deployment.

Keywords: Doppler wind lidar, airborne, space, validation

1. Introduction (11 Point Ariel Font)

Three dimensional wind measurement is considered as the final frontier that needs to be crossed to significantly improve the current numerical weather prediction models [1]. Currently there are no global wind profile measurements from the space. ATHENA-OAWL is a mission concept proposed as an Earth Venture mission for space based wind profile measurement using a Doppler wind lidar.

An airborne demonstrator for the ATHENA-OAWL system has been built at Ball Aerospace & Technologies Corp. The OAWL instrument makes simultaneous measurements at two azimuthally orthogonal line-of-sight (LOS) to provide u and v components of the horizontal winds at 355 nm and 532 nm. Details about the instrument can be found in Tucker et al. [2]. It was deployed aboard the NASA WB-57 aircraft during May-June 2016 to demonstrate the wind measuring capability of the instrument. A total of 10 flights were performed over the Gulf of Mexico. Due to the new laser safety regulations, validation flights were limited to flight restricted area over the Gulf. The first 5 flights were designated as engineering test flights while the last 5 flights were considered as the validation flights. The High Definition Sounding System (HDSS) from Yankee Environmental Systems were aboard the aircraft for the validation flights and deployed dropsondes which measure wind profiles. Figure 1 shows the WB-57 flight tracks over the Gulf of Mexico during the OAWL validation campaign.

2. Validation Data

High Definition Sounding System (HDSS)

The HDSS is an automated system deploying the eXpendable Digital Dropsonde (XDD) which measures wind along with pressure temperature and humidity profiles and skin sea surface temperature (SST) [3]. The XDD measures horizontal wind velocity at 4 Hz. Horizontal wind velocity measured by the XDD deployed from various high altitude aircrafts have been extensively compared with operational radiosondes and traditional RD-94 dropsondes and showed very good agreement [3]. The HDSS was deployed aboard the NASA WB-57 along with the OAWL system for the 5 validation flights.

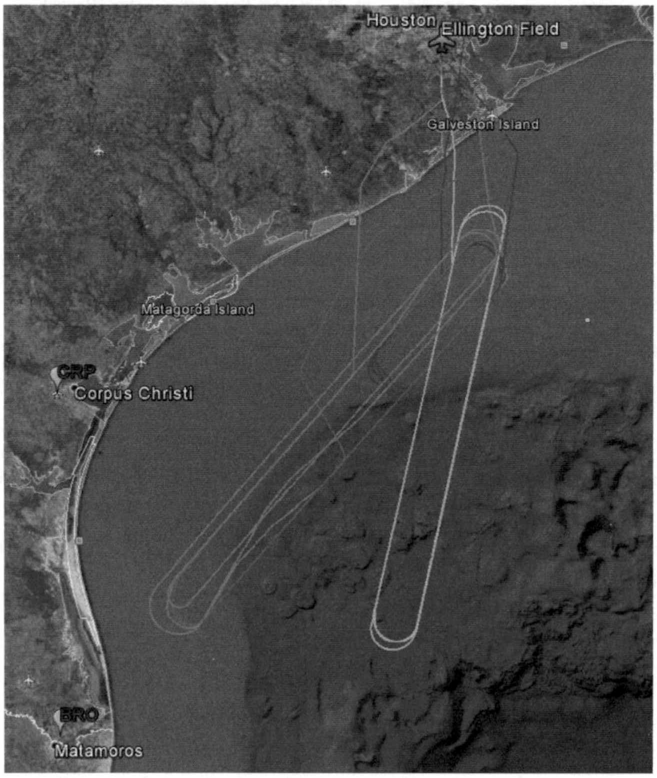

Figure 1. NASA WB-57 flight tracks during the AOVT flight campaign. NWS Corpus Christi and Brownsville office locations are marked with balloons.

Radiosondes

The National Weather Service's (NWS) Corpus Christi office launched additional radiosondes during the AOVT flight days. These radiosonde launches were coordinated with the AOVT flight times.

High Resolution Rapid Refresh (HRRR)

The HRRR is a real-time 3-km resolution, hourly updated, cloud-resolving, convection-allowing atmospheric forecast model developed at NOAA [4]. It is initialized by 3 km grids with 3 km radar data assimilated every 15 minutes. The 3 km spatial resolution for HRRR is comparable to the OAWL measurements at 10 s time resolution aboard the NASA WB-57 aircraft. Thus, the 0th hour HRRR forecast acts as a transfer standard for regular radar/radiosonde measurements to the OAWL study area.

Goddard Earth Observing System Model, Version 5 (GEOS-5)

The GEOS-5 is an atmospheric model developed in the GMAO to support NASA's earth science research. It provides 3 hourly forecast every 6 hours at a spatial resolution of 0.25 x 0.3125 degrees. The model forecast includes aerosol extinction. We use the GEOS-5 aerosol forecast to assess the atmospheric conditions during the flights (closest forecast hour from the closest model run). It will also be used for the performance modeling of the OAWL instrument. Aerosol extinction and backscatter from CALIPSO will be used (when available) to convert GEOS-5 aerosol extinction profiles to backscatter profiles, needed for the performance modelling. Aerosol optical depth (AOD) measured by Aeronet station at Houston, TX will be used to evaluate the GEOS-5 aerosol output.

3. Preliminary Results:

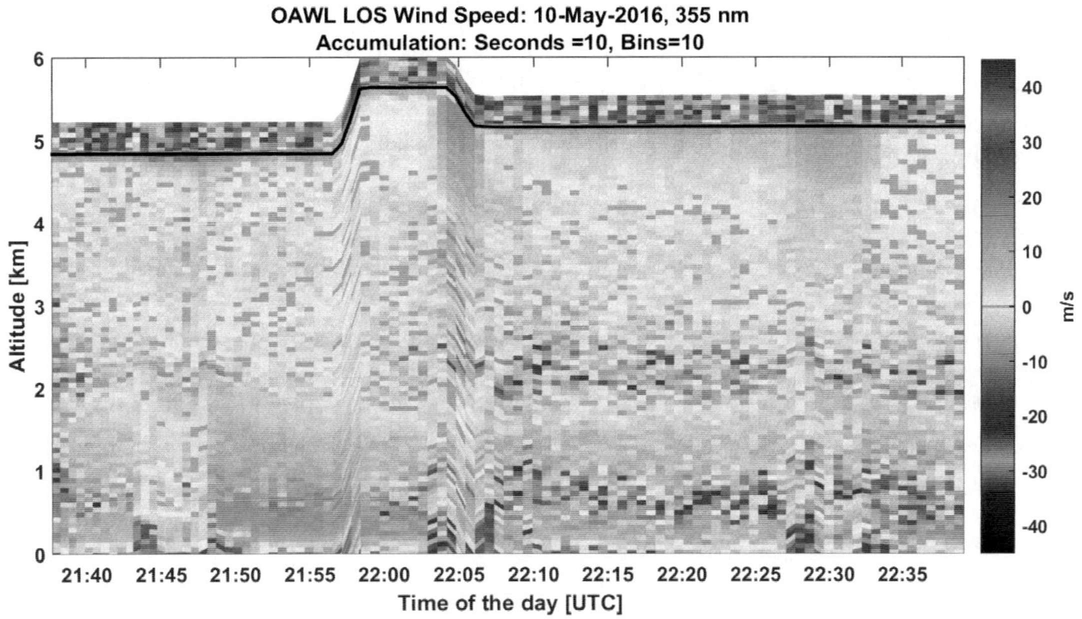

Figure 2: LOS wind speed measured by the AFT look of the OAWL instrument at 355 nm during flight #1 on May 10, 2016 (Preliminary data).

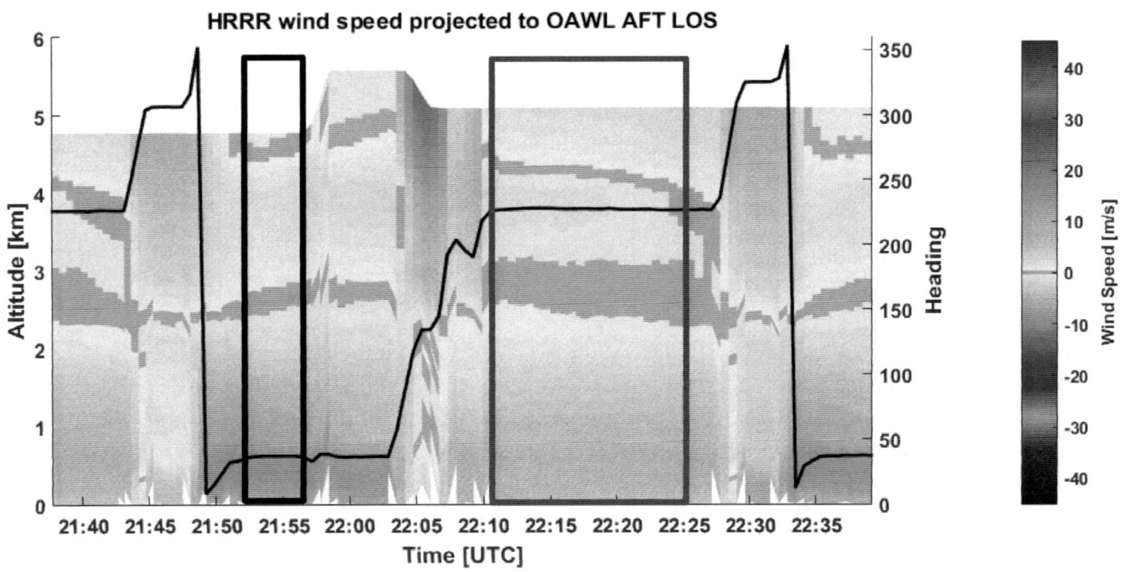

Figure 3. Projected LOS wind speed for OAWL AFT LOS using HRRR 0 hour forecast for 22 Z on May 10, 2016. The black line indicates the aircraft heading at the time of the OAWL data acquisition. The black and red boxes in the bottom panel indicate flight segment 1 and 2 respectively that is used for further analysis.

Figure 2 shows line of sight (LOS) velocity measured by the OAWL AFT look at 355 nm during flight #1 (preliminary data). The OAWL LOS velocity estimate from 532 nm agrees with the 355 nm signal but is more noisy for this flight. The HRRR wind forecast for 0 hour (22Z model run) projected to the OAWL LOS (attitude corrected) for the same time period is shown in Figure 3. The good agreement between the measurement and model indicate that the OAWL measurement generally captured the overall wind conditions over the study area. Note that while the HRRR captures the spatial variability over the study area, temporal variability in the OAWL data might not be well captured by the model and we do not temporally interpolate the model data.

The mean wind speed profile from OAWL measurements computed from the AFT look at 355 nm and projected to the horizontal and HRRR forecast for two flight segments at constant altitude and heading (see Figure 3 for details) are shown in Fig. 4. Figure 4 also shows the difference between the measurement and model. The agreement between the two is very good with differences below 2-3 m/s for most of the profile. There is also no evidence for bias in the OAWL measurements. While the model does not represent the ground truth at the time of the OAWL measurements, the good agreement does provide some validity to the measurements. Note that due to SNR, OAWL data between 500 and 900 m for segment 2 is not included in the comparison.

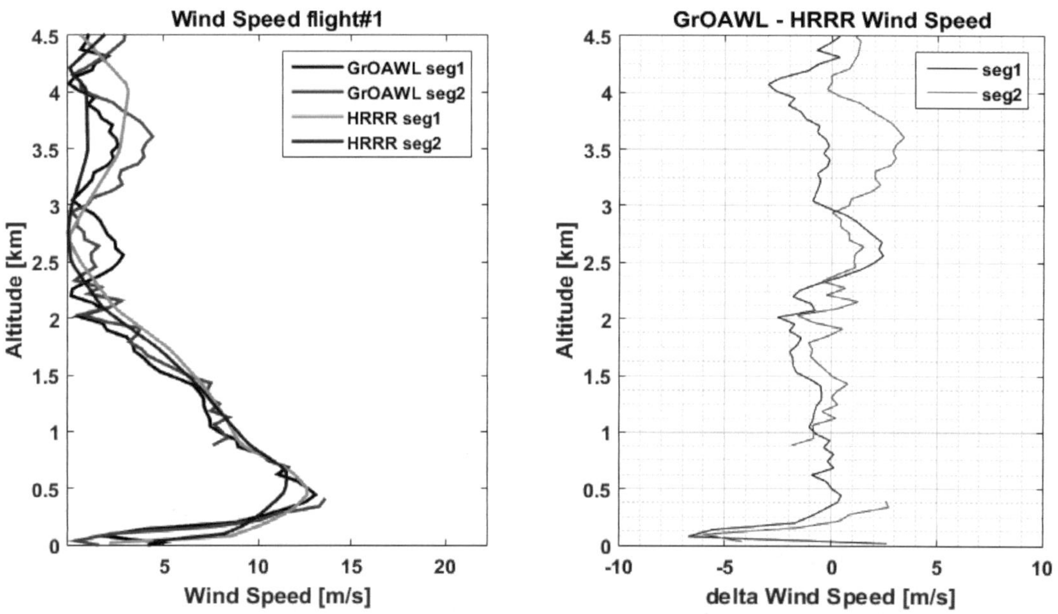

Figure 4: Mean horizontal projection of wind speed profile for OAWL (black and red) computed from AFT look at 355 nm only and HRRR (green and blue) for two flight segments at constant altitude and heading. The flight segments are marked by boxes in Figure 3. The right panel shows difference in wind speed between OAWL and HRRR for the two segments (Preliminary data).

Prior to comparison with the OAWL measurements, the performance of the model is evaluated using available radiosonde data from Corpus Christi and Brownsville, TX. Figure 5 shows comparison between the Corpus Christi 0Z radiosonde (launched at 23Z) and HRRR 0 hour forecast at the time and location of the radiosonde launch, indicating good agreement and providing confidence in the model estimates of winds along the OAWL flight path. We have arranged for additional radiosonde launches from Corpus Christi for times when the aircraft is scheduled to be offshore of Corpus Christi. These radiosondes, along with HDSS dropsondes from the aircraft will provide additional data for evaluating the suitability of the HRRR winds as validation data for periods when radiosondes and dropsondes data are not available.

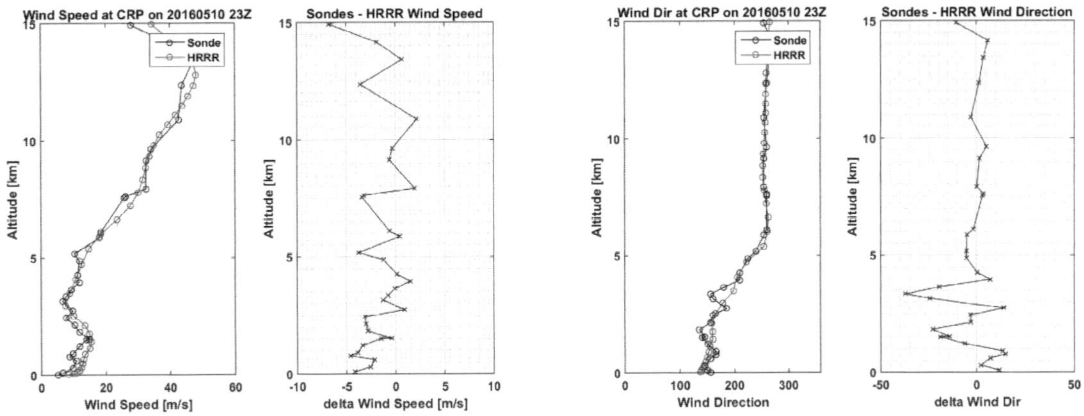

Figure 5: Comparison of wind speed (top) and direction (bottom) between Corpus Christi, TX 0Z radiosonde (launched at 23 Z) and HRRR 0 hour forecast for 23 Z at the radiosonde launch site on May 10, 2016. HRRR data were interpolated to the radiosonde altitude. The right panels show difference between the radiosonde and model data.

4. Summary:

Preliminary comparisons of OAWL radial velocity estimates at both 355 nm and 532 nm with winds estimated by the NOAA HRRR model along the aircraft track show good qualitative agreement. The OAWL signal at 355 nm is less noisy due to a stronger signal, but both estimates agree well with each other and with the model estimate. The model wind estimate from the area around Corpus Christi also agrees well with the Corpus Christi radiosonde, providing some measure of confidence in the HRRR output. We are encouraged by this result and anticipate improved comparisons for later flights as instrument issues are addressed and sensitivity is improved. In addition, OAWL data will be compared with HDSS dropsondes launched from the aircraft during the validation flights.

5. References

[1] W. E. Baker, and Coauthors, "Lidar-measured wind profiles: The missing link in the global observing system," BAMS, 95, 543-564 (2014).

[2] S. Tucker, and Coauthors, "GrOAWL: The ATHENA-OAWL Venture Tech Instrument," in 18th Coherent Laser Radar Conference and the Lidar Working Group on Space Based Winds, (2016).

[3] P. Black, L. Harrison, M. Beaubien, R. Bluth, R. Woods, A. Penny, R. Smith, and J. Doyle, "High Definition Sounding System (HDSS) for atmospheric profiling," JTECH, in press (2016).

[4] S. Benjamin, and Coauthors, "A North American Hourly Assimilation and Model Forecast Cycle: The Rapid Refresh," MWR, 144, 1669-1694 (2016).

Recent Progress on UV Lasers for Airborne and Space-Based Applications

Floyd Hovis, Michael Albert, Fran Fitzpatrick, Kent Puffenburger, Tom Schum, Joe Rudd, Slava Litvinovitch, and Darrell Jones
Fibertek, Inc, 13605 Dulles Technology Drive, Herndon, VA 20171
fhovis@fibertek.com

Abstract: We have recently been developing two single-frequency UV laser systems for airborne and space-based applications. One is a 200 Hz, 35 mJ laser system for the Optical Autocovariance Wind Lidar being built by Ball Aerospace for airborne wind measurements. The other is an ESTO funded project intended to advance the TRL of space-based UV lasers to 6. It is designed to provide a 355 nm output of 100 mJ/pulse at 150 Hz. This paper discusses the design and recent testing of these two laser systems.

Keywords: UV lasers, single-frequency lasers, space-based lasers, TRL 6 lasers, diode-pumped lasers

1. UV Lifetime Demonstrator

A 15 W, 50-200 Hz UV laser with a lifetime in excess of 1 billion shots is an enabling technology for a number of potential space-based lidar missions that have been identified as priorities in the NRC Earth Science Decadal Survey. Examples of these missions include the following.

1. Aerosol/Cloud/Ecosystems (ACE) – This mission will be an expanded scope follow-on to the highly successful CALIPSO cloud and aerosol lidar mission. Researchers at NASA Langley [1], and at NASA GSFC [2], have been developing three wavelength (1064 nm, 532 nm, and 355 nm) High Spectral Resolution Lidar (HSRL) systems as candidate technologies for the ACE mission.
2. 3-D Winds – Space-based measurements of tropospheric winds with global coverage have been identified as a key mission for both weather and climate modeling. 355 nm airborne demonstrators for this mission include a direct detection wind lidar that was built at GSFC [3], and an Optical Auto-Covariance Wind Lidar (OAWL) being developed at Ball Aerospace [4].
3. Global Atmospheric Composition Mission (GACM) – A scaled up version of the 355 nm pumped Ozone DIAL system being developed at NASA Langley [1, 5] is a strong contender for the GACM mission requirements for global ozone measurements.

The design of a 355 nm UV Lifetime Demonstrator (UVLD) we built to advance the TRL for space-based UV lasers is shown in Figures 1 and 2. It uses a master oscillator/power amplifier (MOPA) approach that incorporates diode-pumped Nd:YAG slabs as the gain media. The key are features derived from previous Phase 2 SBIRs as well as the ICESat-2 laser transmitters [6].

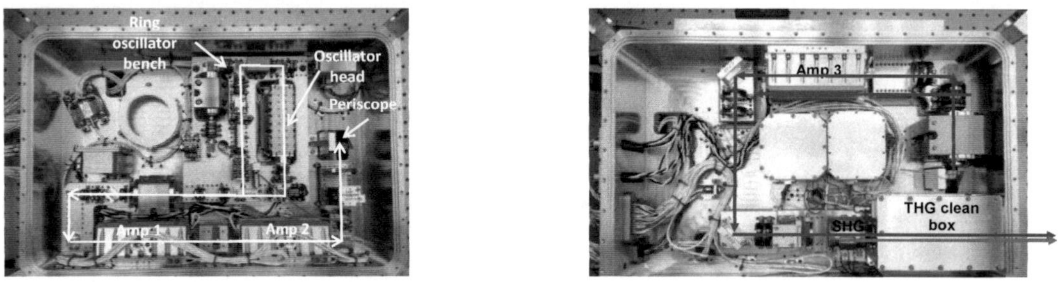

Figure 1. UVLD oscillator/pre-amplifier (l) and power amp/nonlinear converter(r) compartments

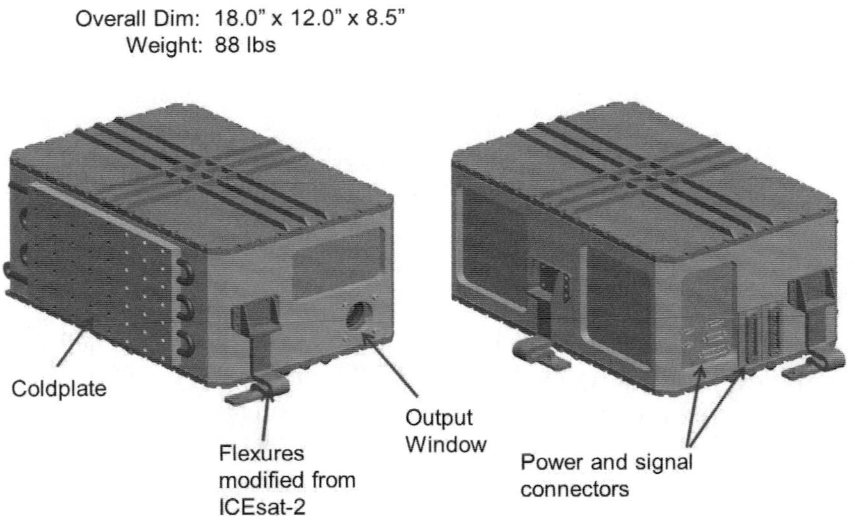

Figure 2. Dimensions, weights and interfaces of the UVLD laser optics module

The overall dimensions, weight, and external interfaces (thermal, optical, mechanical, and electrical) of the laser optics module are illustrated schematically in Figure 2. The cooling is pure conductive to a single interface. The cold plate connected to the single interface shown in Figure 6 could be easily replaced by a heat pipe interface for a flight system. The flexure mounting design was derived from the flight-qualified ICESat-2 design and analyzed to show that it would survive the same vibration testing regimen to which the ICESat-2 lasers were tested.

The UVLD laser has been built and tested through the second harmonic generation stage. The performance at various stages of the optical train is given in Table 1. All of these performance parameters meet or exceed the original performance goals.

Table 1. Performance of the UV Lifetime Demonstrator

Parameter	Goal	Demonstrated
Repetition rate (Hz)	150	150
Oscillator energy (mJ)	≥ 25	34
Oscillator beam quality (M^2)	≤ 1.5	1.3
Oscillator linewidth (MHz)	≤ 100	< 70
Preamplifier energy (mJ)	≥ 150	> 200
Preamplifier beam quality (M^2)	≤ 1.8	1.5
Power amp energy (mJ)	≥ 250	275
Power amp beam quality (M^2)	≤ 2.0	1.9
532 nm energy (mJ)	≥ 135	165
532 nm beam quality (M^2)	≤ 3	2.2
355 nm energy (mJ)	≥100	TBD
355 nm beam quality (M^2)	≤ 4	TBD

The UVLD is now undergoing a series of lifetime tests in preparation for vibration and thermal/vacuum testing that will raise the TRL to 6. The life tests include the following.

1. A 4 month, 532 nm only lifetest of the UVLD laser to assess the 532 nm lifetime. All optics except the LBO tripler were installed in the output optical train of the laser. The purpose of this test was to verify the LBO doubler coating and the cleanliness of the 1064 nm laser transmitter.

a. This test had completed with 1.3 billion shots as of April 2016.
b. Total power was down 9%
c. 532 nm power was down 19 %.
d. There was no damage to any optics
e. The power loss has been determined to be primarily due to a drop in the oscillator power.
f. The oscillator is being reconfigured to run with a lower drive current and longer pulsewidth to reduce the decay rate for the remaining tests

2. A 4 month, half-power 355 nm life test of the laser transmitter for initial UV lifetime assessment will be initiated after the oscillator operating conditions are updated.
3. A 4 month, full power 355 nm life test of the full UVLD laser transmitter for final UV lifetime assessment will be initiated after the half power UV test. This test will not provide validation of our approach for a full 3 year mission but will provide trend data on any UV degradation that may occur.

After the life testing is completed we will execute TVAC and random vibration testing. The TVAC profiles will be chosen to meet the requirements of the GSFC General Environmental Verification Standard (document # GSFC-STD-7000). The profiles for the initial random vibration testing will be chosen to envelope the actual flight requirements for the CALIPSO, ICESat-1 and ICESat-2 missions.

2. Laser Transmitter for the Optical Autocovariance Wind Lidar

Ball Aerospace and Technologies Corporation was funded by the NASA Earth Science Technology Office to build an upgraded version of their original Optical Autocovariance Wind as part of the ATHENA-OAWL Venture Technology program [7]. As part of that program, Fibertek was funded to design and build and upgraded version of the original OAWL laser that would meet the < 30 MHz linewidth requirement for both the 532 nm and 355 nm outputs and still provide 355 nm pulse energies of >30 mJ at 200 Hz. Our updated design, shown schematically in Figure 4, accomplishes this goal by the addition of a second amplifier.

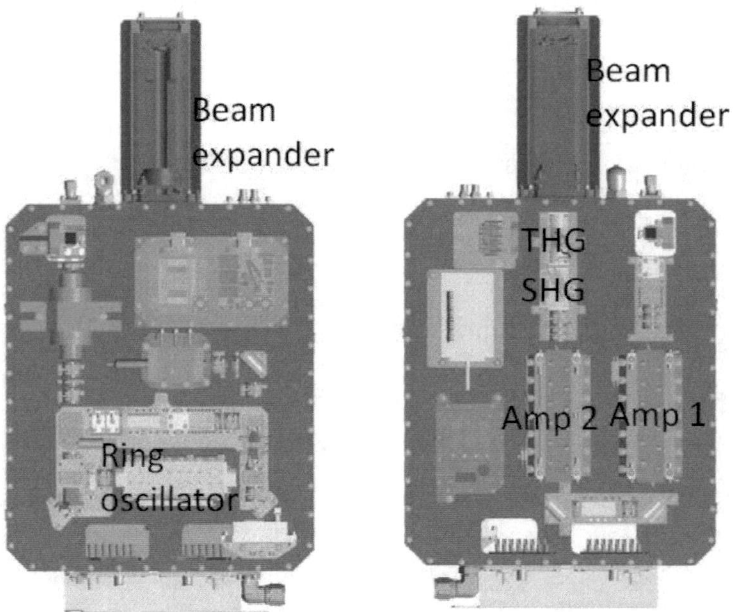

Figure 4. ATHENA OAWL oscillator (left) and amplifier (right) compartments

Performance testing of the laser, summarized in Table 2, shows that it met or exceeded all of the requirements except spectral purity, which is still quite high at 5,000:1.

Table 2. Performance of the ATHENA-OAWL Venture Tech Transmitter

Parameter	Specification	Measured Performance
Pump source	808 nm laser diodes	808 nm laser diodes
Cooling	Conductive	Conductive
Repetition rate	200 Hz	200 Hz
Seeding	Ramp & fire injection seeding	Ramp & fire injection seeding
Seeding eff.	>99% seeded and meeting spectral purity	>99.99% seeded
Mode beating	Intensities increased <1.5X when not fully seeded	No unseeded pulses observed
532 nm spectral purity	>10,000:1	>5,000:1 (1104 I2 line)
Pulse energies	30 mJ @ 355 nm 20 mJ @ 532 nm 20 mJ @ 1064 nm	35 mJ @ 355 nm 24 mJ @ 532 nm 41 mJ @ 1064 nm
Linewidth	< 30 MHz @ 355 nm and 532 nm	532 nm – 26-28 MHz 355 nm – 26-28 MHz
Energy stability	± 10% from average (3σ)	532 nm - ± 2.6% (3σ) 355 nm - ± 1.7% (3σ)
Pulse width	>15 ns @ 355 nm and 532 nm Goal of > 20 ns, not to exceed 100 ns	532 nm - 28 ns 355 nm - 33 ns
Beam quality	532 nm - < 1.4 mm-mrad 355 nm - < 1.4 mm-mrad	532 nm - 1.14 mm-mrad in X, 1.13 mm-mrad in Y 355 nm – 1.21 mm-mrad in X, 1.05 mm-mrad in Y

3. Acknowledgements

This work was supported by funding from the NASA Earth Science Technology Office. We would in particular like to thank Keith Murray and Parminder Ghuman for their help in the concept development phase of the UVLD project as well as their continued support and guidance during its execution.

4. References

[1] Hair, J. W, Hostetler, C. A., Cook, A. L., Harper, D. B., Ferrare, Mack, T. L. Welch, W, Luis Ramos Izquierdo, L. R., and Hovis, F. E. "Airborne High Spectral Resolution Lidar for Profiling Aerosol Optical Properties," Appl. Opt. 47, 6734-6753 (2008).

[2] Yorks, J. E., McGill, M. J., Scott, V. S., Wake, S. W., Kupchock, A., Hlavka, D. L., Hart, W. D., and Patrick A. Selmer, P. A., "2014: The Airborne Cloud–Aerosol Transport System: Overview and Description of the Instrument and Retrieval Algorithms," *J. Atmos. Oceanic Technol.*, **31**, 2482–2497 (2014).

[3] Gentry, B., McGill, M., Schwemmer, G., Hardesty, M., Brewer, A., Wilkerson, T., Atlas, R., Sirota, M., Lindemann, S., and Hovis, F., "Development of an airborne molecular direct detection Doppler lidar for tropospheric wind profiling," Proc. SPIE 6681, (2007).

[4] Grund, C. J., Howell, J., Pierce, R., and Stephen, M., "Optical autocovariance direct detection lidar for simultaneous wind, aerosol, and chemistry profiling from ground, air, and space platforms," Proc. SPIE 7312, (2007).

[5] Richter, D. A., Browell, E. V., Butler, C. F. and Higdon, N. S., "Advanced airborne UV DIAL system for stratospheric and tropospheric ozone and aerosol measurements," Advances in atmospheric remote sensing with lidar, 395-398, Springer, Berlin and Heidelberg, (1997).

[6] Sawruk, N. W., Burns, P. M., Edwards, R. E., Wysocki, T., VanTuijl, A., Litvinovitch, V., Sullivan, E., and Hovis, F., E., "ICESat-2 laser technology readiness level evolution," Proc. SPIE 9342, (2015).

[7] Tucker, S.C, Weimer, C., Adkins, M., Delker, T., Gleeson, D., Kaptchen, P., Good, B., Kaplan, M., Applegate, J., and Taudien, G., "Optical Autocovariance Wind Lidar (OAWL): aircraft test-flight history and current plans", Proc. SPIE 9612, (2015).

Developments Towards a Space-based Wind Lidar for the International Space Station

Carl Weimer & Sara Tucker
Ball Aerospace & Technologies Corporation

Mike Hardesty
CIRES

4/15/2016

What Is ATHENA-OAWL (A-OAWL)?

- Earth Venture Instrument – 2 (EVI-2) Proposal to NASA in 2013
  - Not Selected for space mission – Category 3
  - Was selected for Earth Venture Risk Reduction Funding ("Venture Tech") to advance its Technology Readiness
- Was Led by PI Lars Peter Riishojgaard University of Maryland (now WMO)
  - Now led by Mike Hardesty (CU/CIRES)
- Ball Aerospace is the Instrument Provider – Doppler Wind Lidar based on the OAWL technique
- Focused Science Mission
  - Tropospheric dual Line of Sight Winds plus aerosols
- Earth Venture Instrument is Cost Constrained – Design to Cost
  - ≤ $94 M with 25% reserves
  - Uses International Space Station (ISS) and its Mission Operations, and TDRSS downlink
  - Met the WMO requirement for < 3 m/s precision, < 0.5 m/s bias
- Earth Venture is for NASA Class C (Medium to Low Complexity)
  - Leverage Heritage Designs from CALIPSO and other Instruments
  - One Year Lifetime

Progress Against Plan

- Upgrade existing OAWL instrument to match the ATHENA-OAWL two-look, two laser configuration
  - New aircraft testing on the WB-57 adding in additional balloon and drop sonde comparisons for wind validation for different atmospheric conditions (Eight flights completed, approximately 45 dropsondes – Sara's talk)
  - Will also include comparisons with AERONET, HRRR, etc for aerosol calibration (In process – Sunil's talk))

- Complete qualification for space environment of key new technologies
  - Green (532 nm) only lifetime testing of the HEUVD laser at Fibertek (Complete - Floyd's talk)
  - Perform thermal/vacuum testing of the new athermal interferometer (In fabrication – below)

- Parallel Effort – HAWC-OAWL (PI Sara Tucker) is funded by NASA ESTO to develop a dual-wavelength HSRL/Wind version of OAWL for atmospheric transport and "Chemical Weather" (In process)

Athermal Interferometer in Development Being Built to Aerospace standards

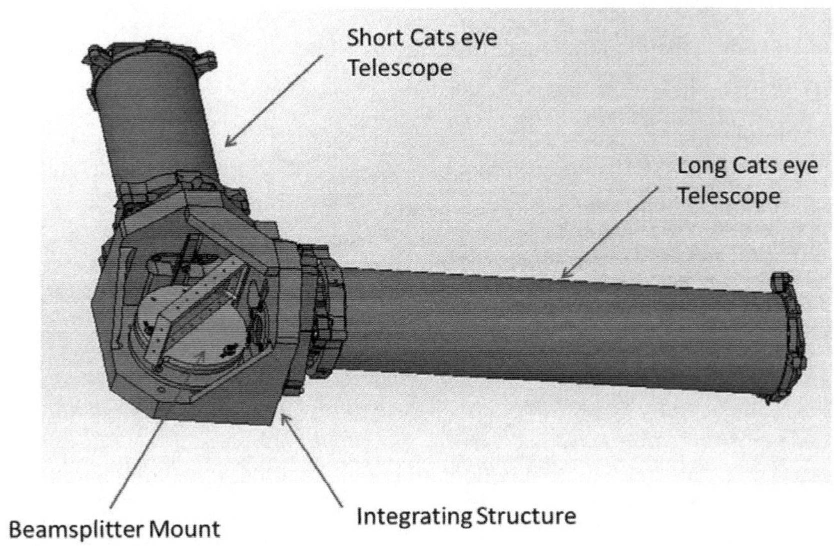

4

6/30/2016

Structural Model and Analyses are complete – Includes evaluation of modes and deformations

Ensuring that we survive launch – Beam splitter example – colors give magnitude of deformation during launch loads

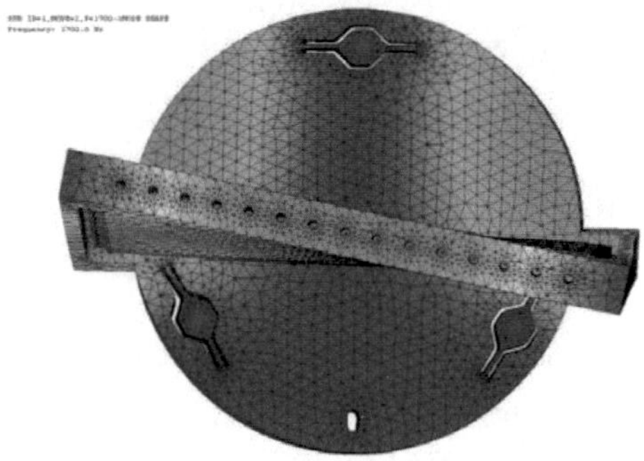

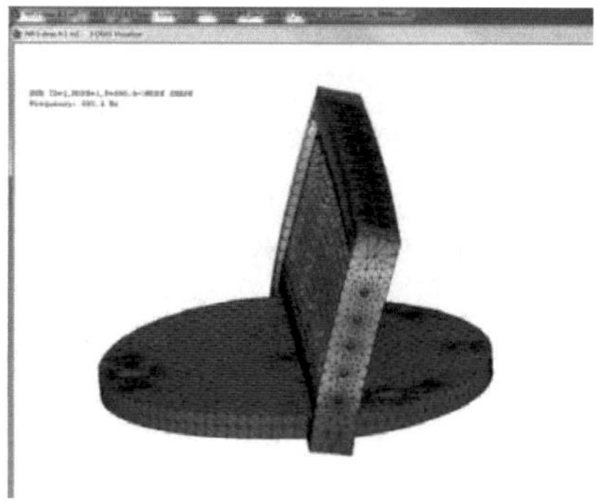

Page 5

Thermal deformation study complete

- Structural-thermal modelling used to verify athermal design will ensure interferometer alignments for ISS environment

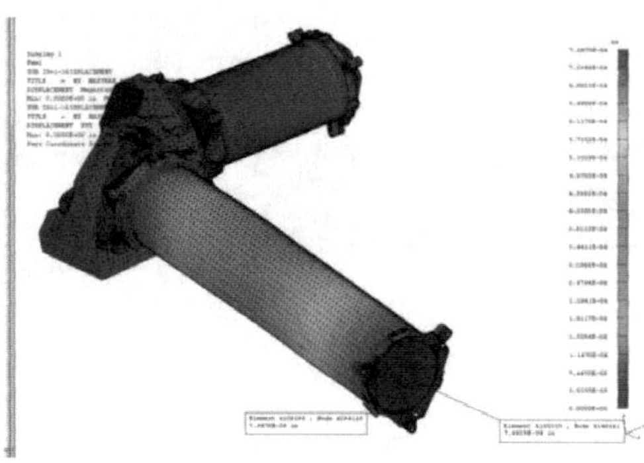

6

6/30/2016

Overall Lidar System – Start from CALIPSO Heritage

Design and Simplify

- EV-I Constraints
- Deployment to ISS
- Simplify from Heritage
- Design to Cost

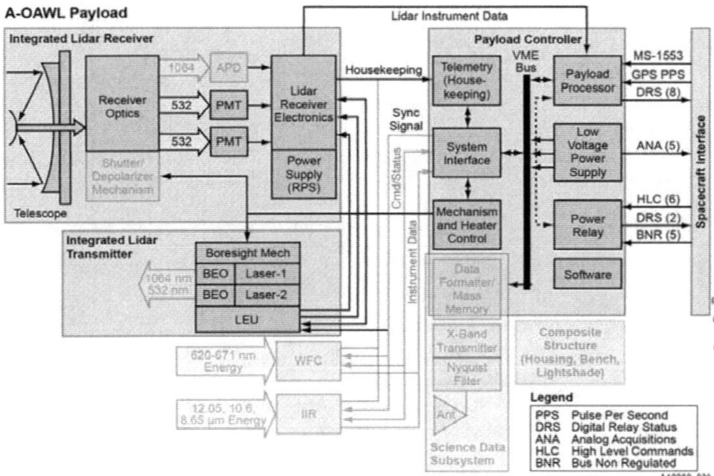

Update Design for New Application and new platform – Winds from ISS

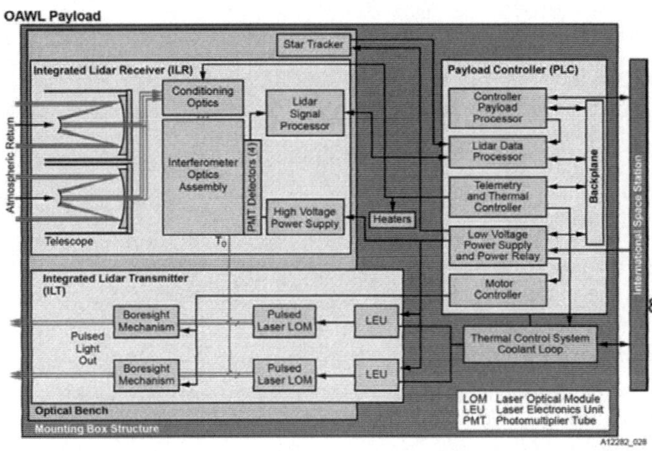

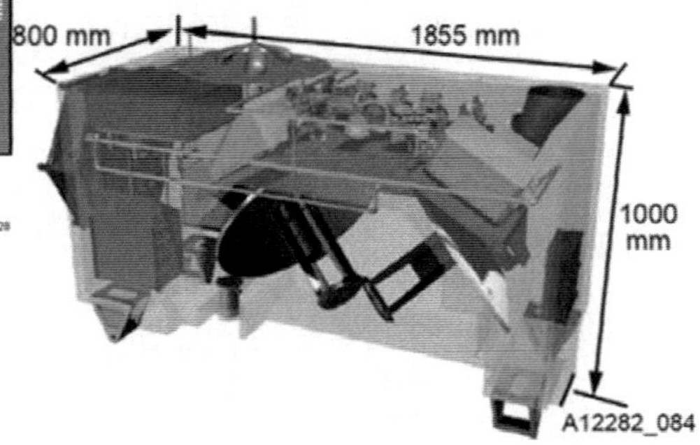

6/30/2016

CALIPSO Laser Performance – 10 Years on Orbit

- Second Laser Performance Shown. - both 1064 nm and 532 nm
- Slow energy drop is due to degradation in the pump diodes
- Expect to operate through 2017 (12 year lifetime, 3 Year Mission)
- ATHENA-OAWL will be 532 nm only with same laser eye-safety margins

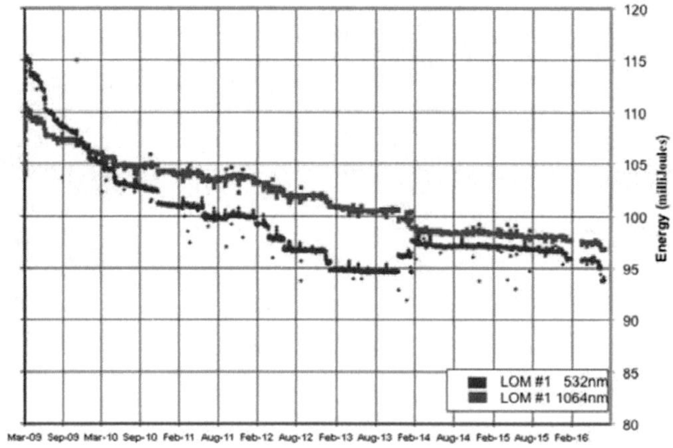

Vibration Comparison - Operational

- Core engineering principle is Design and Test "as flown" - i.e. for the launch and operation environment
  - Requires detailed knowledge of the environment
  - Requires the funding for the engineering and test facilities
  - Note - Launch vibe is off this scale

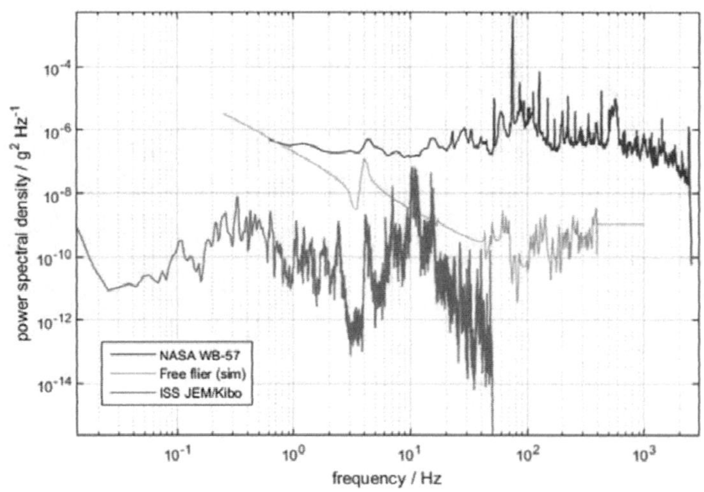

Temperature Comparison – WB vs CALIPSO Optical Benches (both passive)

- CALIPSO has a gradient but variations are < 1 C
- WB – 57 bench depends on tarmac time, flight profile, and conops

Two WB Flights

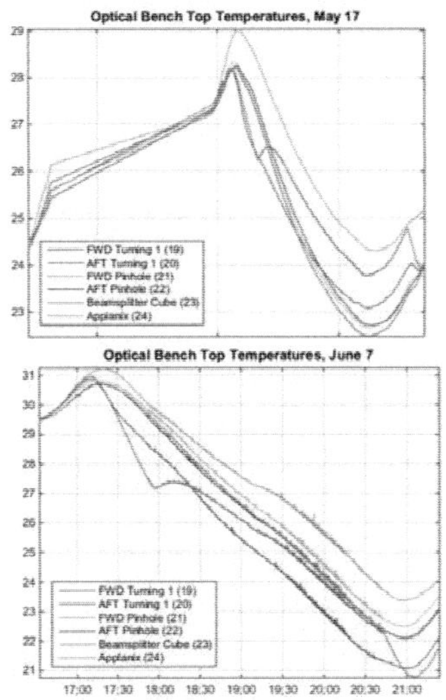

CALIPSO

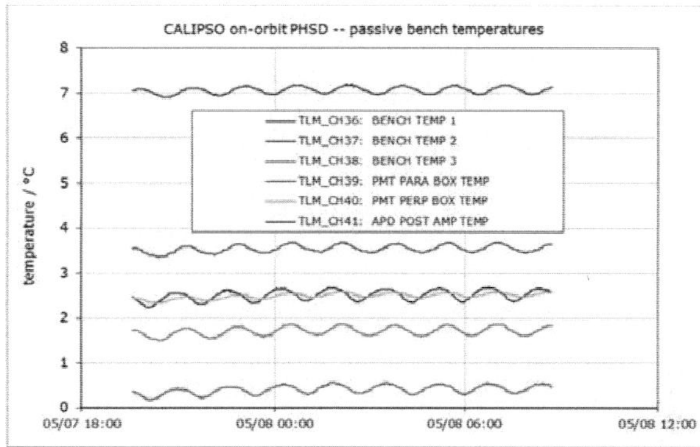

Lidar Receiver Electronics Path to Space

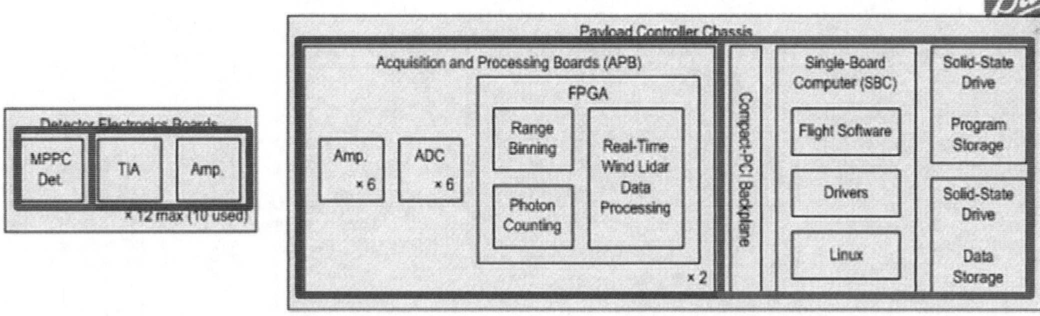

- Designed/Built on AOVT and have space-qualified equivalents (below)
- Detector replaced by qualified PMT - Heritage
- Replaced by an update of Ball's Common Instrument Controller Electronics now qualified for TEMPO

Board	Function	HAWC/AOVT Part	Space Part
Detector	TIA	AD8001	AD8001S
Detector & APB	Amplifier	AD8139	AD8138S
APB	High-Speed ADC	ADC14155	ADC14155QML-SP
APB	FPGA	XC5VFX130T	XQR5VFX130

Conclusions

- ATHENA-OAWL can act as a Pathfinder towards the full 3D-Winds mission
  - Demonstrate the science capability with immediate (< 1 hour) data availability to Numerical Weather Models
  - Validate the laser and receiver performance in the space environment
- Through the NASA Venture Technology program, significant risk reduction to the proposed effort is now occurring
- The effort will be bid again to the Earth Venture – Instrument call, which will likely be the last time ISS will be available for EV missions due to the planned 2024 end date of ISS

Impact of Doppler Wind Lidar Data on Hurricane Prediction

R. Atlas[a], G.D. Emmitt[b], L. Bucci[c], K. Ryan[c], and J.A. Zhang[c]
[a]NOAA-Atlantic Oceanographic and Meteorological Laboratory
4301 Rickenbacker Causeway, Miami, FL 33149
[b]Simpson Weather Associates, Charlottesville, VA
[c]NOAA-AOML and University of Miami, Cooperative Institute for Marine and Atmospheric Sciences
R. Atlas email: robert.atlas@noaa.gov

Abstract: One of the most important applications of a space-based Doppler Wind Lidar (DWL) would be to improve atmospheric analyses and weather forecasting. Since the mid-1980s, Observing System Simulation Experiments (OSSEs) have been conducted to evaluate the potential impact of space-based DWL data on numerical weather prediction (NWP). All of these OSSEs have shown significant beneficial impact on global analyses and forecasts. In more recent years, a limited number of OSSEs have been conducted to evaluate the potential impact of DWL data on hurricane forecasting and to also evaluate the impact of real airborne DWL observations. These latest studies suggest that DWL can complement existing hurricane observations effectively and should contribute to improved hurricane track and intensity forecasting.

Keywords: DWL, OSSE, OSE, simulation experiments, hurricanes

1. Introduction

Winds are among the most important variables in the atmosphere. They transport all the other variables of the atmosphere and govern the exchanges of mass, energy, and momentum between the atmosphere and the underlying ocean and land surfaces. There is a substantial opportunity to improve numerical weather prediction (NWP) by better observing the global wind field. Currently, winds make up a very small fraction of the observations that are used in data assimilation systems. Many of the winds that are available are created by tracking features in the cloud or water vapor field. These atmospheric motion vectors are very valuable, but they are an indirect measurement and have inherent height uncertainties that make their use somewhat problematic. In contrast, Doppler Wind Lidars (DWLs) directly and very accurately measure the line-of-sight wind by observing the Doppler shift in the lidar signal returned by a volume of atmospheric scatterers. Baker et al. [1] provide an excellent description of the need for a DWL, a review of previous impact studies that used both simulated satellite and real-world aircraft-based data, and an overview of instrument concepts and their supporting technologies. Impact experiments with real data, termed Observing System Experiments (OSEs), are conducted with and without one observing system to quantify the impact of that observing system. Similar experiments with simulated data are termed Observing System Simulation Experiments (OSSEs). In OSSEs a long forecast is taken to be the ''truth'' or nature run.

The present study complements previous space-based DWL OSSEs by examining the impact of DWL observations on hurricanes and by beginning to evaluate the impact of having an existing DWL on NOAA's Hurricane Hunter aircraft. The objectives of the OSSEs for hurricanes are to (1) evaluate the potential impact of proposed observing systems on hurricane track and intensity prediction, (2) evaluate trade-offs in the design and configuration of these observing systems, (3) optimize sampling strategies for current and future airborne and space-borne observing systems, and (4) evaluate and improve data assimilation and vortex initialization methodology for hurricane prediction.

2. Methodology

The methodology currently used for OSSEs is described in detail by Atlas [2] and consists of the following elements:

(1) A long atmospheric model integration using a very high resolution "state of the art" numerical model to provide a complete record of the assumed "true" state of the atmosphere (referred to as the "nature run" or "reference atmosphere"). Nature runs may be generated by either global or regional models or by embedding a regional model within a global nature.

(2) Simulated conventional and space-based observations from the nature run. These observations are simulated with realistic coverages and accuracies.

(3) Control and experimental data assimilation cycles, with and without the specific observing systems that are being evaluated.

(4) Forecasts produced from the Control and Experimental assimilations.

For the OSSE to be credible, it is essential that each of the components of the OSSE system be evaluated for realism and that the limitations of the system be defined. An important component of the OSSE that improves the interpretation of results is validation against a corresponding OSE. In this regard, the accuracy of analyses and forecasts and the impact of already existing observing systems in simulation is compared with the corresponding accuracies and data impacts in the real world. Ideally, both the simulated and real results should be similar. Under these conditions no calibration is necessary, and the OSSE results may be interpreted directly. If this is not the case, calibration of the OSSE results can be attempted by determining the constant of proportionality between the OSE and OSSE impact.

3. Examples from OSSEs to Assess DWL Data

An extensive series of OSSEs has been conducted since the mid-1980s to evaluate the potential impact of space-based DWL on NWP. All of these OSSEs have shown significant beneficial impact resulting from the assimilation of DWL data. Additional OSSEs evaluated trade-offs in orbit altitude, laser power, coverage, and accuracy. Figure 1 presents two examples from the first global OSSEs to address hurricane

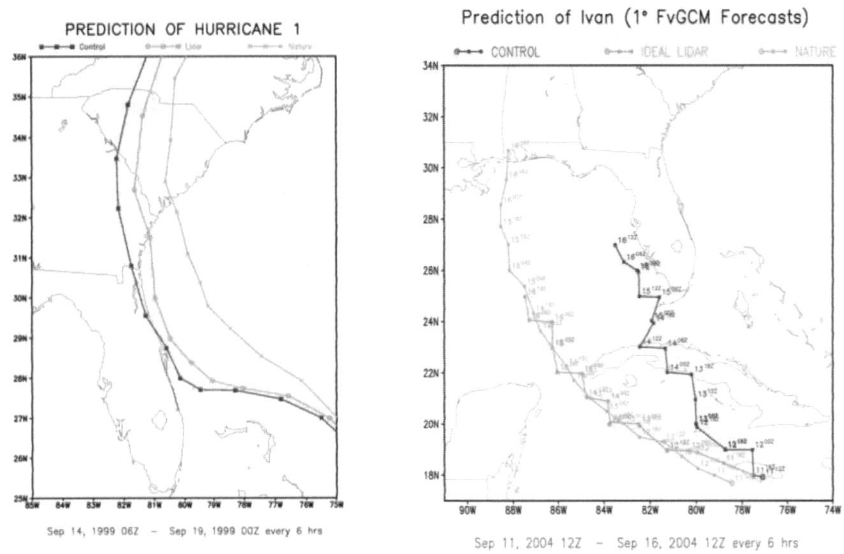

Figure 1. Illustrations of the potential impact of lidar winds in two early global OSSEs. Green (easternmost track): actual track from nature run. Red (westernmost track): forecast beginning 63 hours before landfall with all currently used data. Blue (middle track): improved forecast for same time period with simulated DWL data added.

forecasting. Here a significant impact on hurricane track prediction was observed. No similar negative impacts on hurricane track occurred in these experiments.

Figure 2 shows one example from a recent OSSE using a WRF 1-km resolution nature run embedded in an ECMWF global nature run. In this case, global assimilation of DWL data resulted in both improved hurricane track and intensity forecasts. Regional assimilation of DWL data in this case improved the intensity forecast substantially further, but did not improve the track forecast.

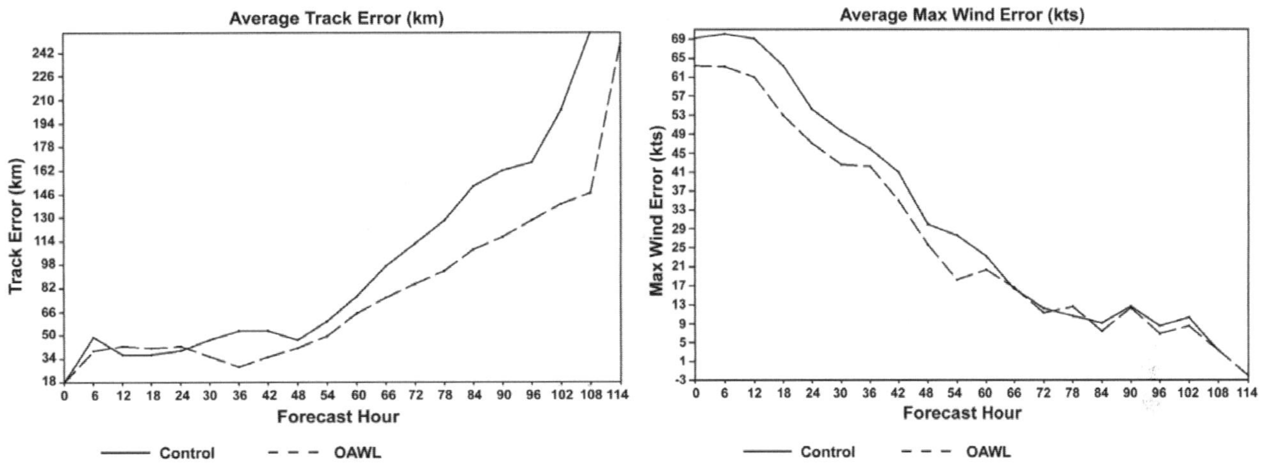

Figure 2. Impact of an Optical Autocovariance Wind Lidar (OAWL) on track and intensity forecasts in this case.

4. Current Work on Airborne DWL

An airborne DWL was flown for the first time in 2015 on the NOAA P3 Orion Hurricane Hunter aircraft into Atlantic Tropical Storms Danny and Erika. While technical challenges limited the operator's ability to use the DWL, good data were collected on the afternoon flight on August 26, 2015 into Tropical Storm Erika. The scanner was pointed down and forward (30° off nadir), sweeping out a curtain of data below the aircraft. The nearest DWL wind profiles were compared to winds from dropsondes throughout the flight. Profiles from both instruments showed qualitatively similar speed and structures in various regions of the storm. An exact replication of the dropsonde wind profiles is not expected, given that the DWL wind profiles represent a 1-km area average of the winds beneath the plane.

An impact study of the DWL observations was performed using the Hurricane Weather Research and Forecasting model. The experiment setup compared a "Control" which assimilated all observations typically available (tail Doppler radar, dropsondes, flight level, stepped frequency microwave radiometer, and satellite retrievals) to "Control+DWL" which added thinned DWL line-of-sight wind profiles. A comparison of the assimilated observations revealed that the DWL provided better coverage of the wind field, particularly on the western side of the storm which lacked deep convection. The DWL also provided wind measurements much closer to the surface (within 25 m) when compared to the tail Doppler radar observations (only to within 250-500 m). The DWL data provided the largest impact on the analysis wind field in the western portion of Erika (Figure 3). Boundary layer wind speed increased by as much as 8 kts in these regions. A smaller impact was also observed in the areas with good tail Doppler radar coverage, where a slight decrease in wind speed occurred. Unfortunately for this particular storm and time, there was no significant impact on the storm track and intensity forecast. The DWL is expected to be available for the 2016 hurricane field program, and future model impact studies will be performed after data collection.

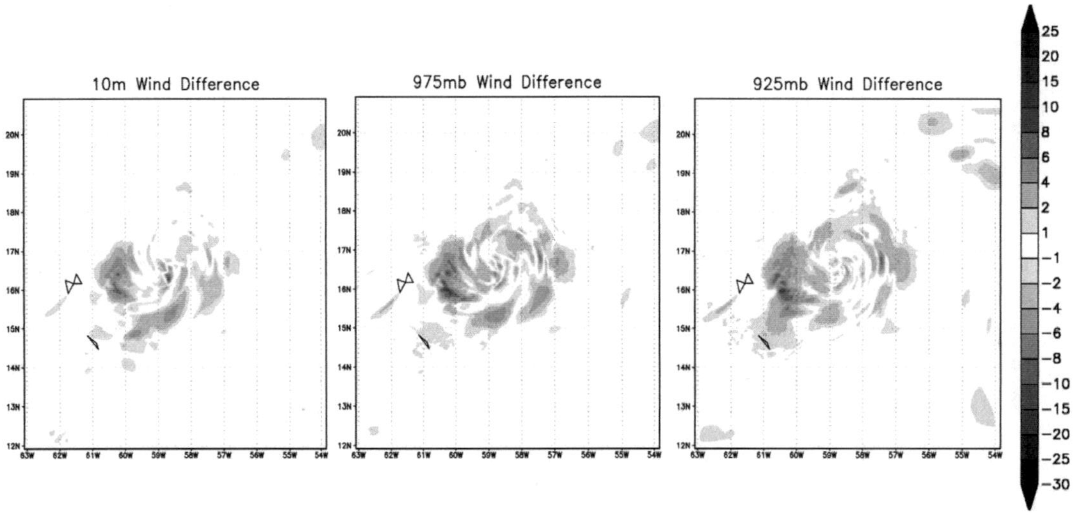

Figure 3. Difference in the analysis of the wind speeds (kts) at 10 meters, 975 mb, and 925 mb between the Control+DWL and Control experiments.

5. References

[1] W.E. Baker, R. Atlas, C. Cardinali, A. Clement, G.D. Emmitt, B.M. Gentry, R.M. Hardesty, E. Kallen, M.J. Kavaya, R. Langland, M. Masutani, W. McCarty, R.B. Pierce, Z. Pu, L.P. Riishojgaard, J. Ryan, S. Tucker, M. Weissmann, and J.G. Yoe, "Lidar-measured wind profiles: The missing link in the global observing system," Bull. Amer. Meteor. Soc. **95**, 543-564 (2014).

[2] R. Atlas, "Atmospheric observations and experiments to assess their usefulness in data assimilation," J. Meteor. Soc. Japan **75**, 111-130 (1997).

Satellite coherent Doppler wind lidar performance simulation based on CALIOP measurements

Dong Wu, Pei Zhang, Suzhen Yu
College of Information Science and Engineering, Ocean University of China,
238 Songling Road, Qingdao, 266100, China

Abstract: A computer simulation tool using MATLAB has been developed based on the coherent Doppler lidar theory. The measurement performance of a satellite coherent Doppler wind lidar is computer simulated using the CALIOP measurements instead of aerosol model. Frehlich's two-parameter model is used to characterize the performance of the velocity estimates. The accuracy of radial wind velocity good estimates and the fraction of good estimates, depending on backscattered signals from aerosols, generally decrease with altitude. The simulation results demonstrated that a global wind profiling of the lower troposphere from space is feasible using a coherent Doppler wind lidar with achievable system design, appropriate performance setting and parameter selection.

Keywords: CALIOP, coherent Doppler wind lidar, performance simulation

1. Introduction

Global measurements of wind profiles are urgently needed for many meteorological studies. A spaceborne Doppler lidar is considered to be the observation system capable of such measurements in the troposphere. As early as the 1980's, a space-based coherent Doppler lidar system (Windsat) was proposed[1,2]. In the US, a hybrid lidar concept was selected for future spaceborne wind lidar system. Both a coherent lidar using heterodyne detection and an incoherent lidar using direct detection will be used for simultaneous wind measurements. The coherent Doppler lidar measures particulate scattering signals from aerosols which is suitable for lower altitude wind measurements.

The performance simulation of a spaceborne coherent Doppler lidar is important and requires correct modeling of the realistic characterization of aerosols and clouds. In most of the performance simulations of spaceborne Doppler lidar, the assumptions of ideal atmospheres are usually used. The performance of coherent Doppler lidar measurements has been simulated and evaluated for a modeled atmosphere with invariant aerosol backscatter [3,4] or varying aerosol backscatter [5,6]. The Doppler Lidar Simulation Model (DLSM) can simulate both coherent and incoherent Doppler wind lidar using modeled aerosol backscatter profiles [7,8]. A global aerosol backscatter distribution from CALIPSO lidar Level 2 aerosol profile data was used to simulate and assess the performance of wind speed measurements of a coherent Doppler wind lidar (CDWL) instead of the aerosol model [9].

The Cloud-Aerosol Lidar with Orthogonal Polarization (CALIOP) onboard the Cloud-Aerosol Lidar and Infrared Pathfinder Satellite Observation (CALIPSO) satellite has continuous worked for more than ten years. It has been providing a large amount of global cloud and aerosol measurement data with high vertical resolution [10,11]. In this study, the CALIOP Level 1064 nm attenuated backscatter profiles are used to simulate and assess the performance of wind speed measurements of a coherent Doppler wind lidar in cloud-free conditions based on the coherent detection theories.

2. Methodology

We follow mainly the coherent Doppler lidar theory summarized in [12]. The performance of the lidar velocity estimates is characterized by two parameters, the fraction of the bad estimates b and the RMS error of the good estimates g, as a function of coherent photoelectrons Φ_1:

$$b(\Phi_1) = \exp\left[-\left(\frac{\Phi_1}{b_0}\right)^{\alpha}\right], \tag{1}$$

$$g(\Phi_1) = w_{\upsilon,eff}\left\{\chi\left[1+\left(\frac{\Phi_1}{g_0}\right)^{\gamma}\right]^{-\delta} + \mu\right\}. \tag{2}$$

The coefficients in the above equations generally vary depending on the variations of the wind field, laser frequency stability, and transmitter and receiver geometries. Here, $\alpha = 1.364$, $b_0 = 11.42$, $\chi = 1.325$, $g_0 = 9747$, $\gamma = 0.9667$, $\delta = 209.2$, and $\mu = 0.04397$. $w_{\upsilon,\text{eff}}$ is the total effective spectral width in velocity space, and is related to the effective spectral width w_{eff} by $w_{\upsilon,\text{eff}} = \lambda\ w_{\text{eff}}/2$. λ is the laser wavelength. $w_{\upsilon,\text{eff}}$ is given by

$$w_{v,eff}^2 = s_{vr}^2 + s_{shr}^2 + w_v^2 + \sigma_{vLO}^2 \quad . \tag{3}$$

Following [12], $w_{\upsilon,\text{eff}}$=1.281 m/s, including the contributions from turbulence $s^2_{\text{vr}} = 0.5759$ (m/s)^2, wind shear $s^2_{\text{shr}} = 0.6592$ (m/s)^2, local laser frequency fluctuation $\sigma_{\text{vLO}} = 0.5$ m/s, and pulsed laser spectral widening $w_v = 0.3935$ m/s.

The number of received coherent photoelectrons Φ_1 can be estimated using

$$\Phi_1(R) = \frac{\eta_Q \beta(R) T^2(R) c E A_r \eta_H t_g}{2h\nu R^2}, \tag{4}$$

Where, R is the range probed by the leading edge of the pulse at time t, η_Q is the quantum efficiency, $\beta(R)$ is the backscatter coefficient, $T^2(R)$ the two-way atmospheric transmittance between the lidar and the atmosphere at R, c the speed of light, E the energy in each laser pulse, A_r the effective area of the receiving telescope, t_g the time interval of each range gate, and $t_g = Mt_s$, where t_s is the sampling interval and M is the number of complex lidar data samples in each range gate. $h = 6.626\times10^{-34}$ (J) is Planck constant, ν is the frequency of the laser. η_H is the heterodyne efficiency, defined as $\eta_H = C(R)/D(R)$, where $C(R)$ and $D(R)$ are the dimensionless coherent and incoherent responsivity, respectively. Both C(R) and D(R) can be expressed as a series that includes two physical representations of low-spatial-frequency (lf) behavior and high-spatial-frequency (hf) behavior [13], and the first order terms are given by

$$C_0(R) = C_{0,\text{lf}}(R) + \frac{1}{1+\left[\frac{k\rho_0^2(R)}{R}\right]^2} C_{0,\text{hf}}(R), \tag{5}$$

$$D_0(R) = D_{0,\text{lf}}(R) + \frac{1}{1+\left[\frac{k\rho_0^2(R)}{R}\right]^2} D_{0,\text{hf}}(R), \tag{6}$$

where

$$\rho_0(R) = \frac{1}{\left[Hk^2\int_0^R C_n^2 (1 - z/R)^{5/3} dz\right]^{3/5}} \tag{7}$$

is the transverse-field coherence length, $k = 2\pi/\lambda$ (rad m^{-1}), $H = 2.914383$, and C_n^2 is the refractive index structure constant. The impact of the atmospheric refractive turbulence on the heterodyne efficiency is small for the space-based measurements[9].

To calculate the number of received coherent photoelectrons Φ_1, in [9], the CALIOP Level 2 nighttime aerosol profile product, i.e., aerosol backscatter coefficients at 532 nm β_{532} with resolution of 60 m vertically and 5 km horizontally are used in the simulation. Then, the backscatter coefficients at 2.1 μm are derived from backscatter coefficients at 532 nm using a wavelength conversion function presented by Srivastava et al [14]. Different with that, here, we will focus our simulation on a 1064 nm CDWL measurement. The level 1 attenuated backscatter at 1064 nm can be directly used for the calculation of Φ_1 by using

$$\beta'_{1064nm}(R) = \beta_{1064nm}(R)T^2(R). \quad (8)$$

3. Simulation and results

The CALIOP level 1 data gives a set of calibrated attenuated backscatter profiles at 1064 nm with a vertical resolution of 60 m from -0.5 km to 20.2 km and 180 m between 20.2 km and 30.1 km[11]. The latest CALIOP Version 4.00 level 1 products are released in November 2014. The comparison shows that, the relative deviations of the attenuated backscatters between CALIOP level 1 Version 4.00 and Version 3.01 products for clouds and aerosols tend to positive values, and the changes are more obvious at nighttime than those at daytime for both clouds and aerosols. The mean relative deviation of 1064 nm attenuated backscatters for aerosol is 6.94% at daytime, and 10.92% at nighttime[16]. In this study, two months（Jul. and Nov. 2011） of CALIOP Version 4.00 L1B nighttime products are used for the calculation of the number of received coherent photoelectrons Φ_1 and the corresponding level 2 vertical feature mask (VFM) products are used for cloud-free data selection.

For data selection, the cloud-free range bins are defined as the bins that have the Feature Type of "clear air" and "aerosol" , but the cloud-free bins underneath a cloud bin are not included because the presence of clouds can attenuate the laser beam and consequently reduce the lidar signals backscattered from the air below the clouds. And, only the attenuated backscatters at 1064 nm less than 0.03 and greater than -0.02 are selected for the simulation. Latitude and longitude zonal-vertical distributions of mean cloud-free attenuated backscatters at 1064 nm are shown in Fig. 1.

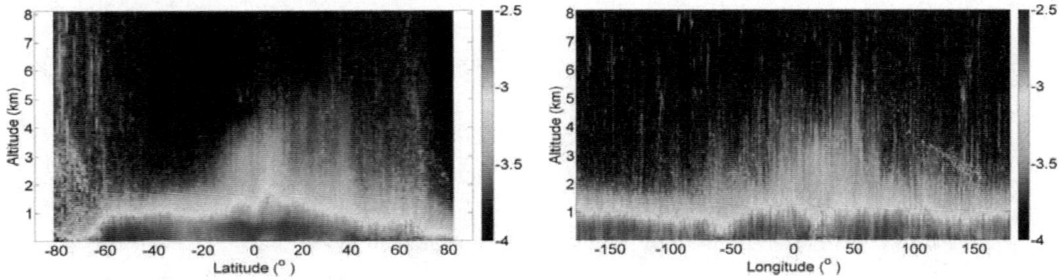

Fig. 1. Zonal-vertical distributions of mean attenuated backscatters at 1064 nm (log scale in km^{-1} sr^{-1})

A computer simulation tool using MATLAB has been developed based on the heterodyne detection theories mentioned above. The parameters of the spaceborne monostatic CDWL system are summarized in Table 1.

Table 1. System parameters of a space-based monostatic CDWL

Platform height = 410 km	Viewing angle = 45°
Laser wavelength λ = 1064 nm	Laser pulse energy E = 250 mJ
Radius of Gaussian-distributed laser beam and local oscillator $\sigma_L = \sigma_{LO}$ = 35 cm	Radius of receiver lens σ_R = 50 cm
Focal length of the transceiver F = 578 km	Detector quantum efficiency η_Q = 0.8
Gate interval t_g = 7.5 μs	Sampling interval t_s = 0.05 μs
Range-gate length R_g = 1.125km	Vertical resolution Z_g = 0.795 km
Effective spectral width, $w_{\upsilon,eff}$ = 1.281 m s^{-1}	Normalized spectral width Ω = 18.05

Based on the vertical distributions of mean attenuated backscatters at 1064 nm from CALIOP level 1 data shown in Fig. 1, the spaceborne CDWL given in Table 1 is simulated. The main parameters and conditions follow [9] and [12]. The refractive index structure constant C_n^2 measured in clear-air conditions in winter at nighttime [17] is used for the η_H calculation. Fig. 2 gives simulated latitude and longitude zonal-vertical distributions of received number of coherent photoelectrons Φ_1. It shows a strong similarity with Fig. 1 because a CDWL uses aerosol as a tracer of wind. The received coherent photoelectron number can reach several thousands in the boundary layer less than1 km where most of the atmospheric aerosol is distributed, and decreases with altitude because the aerosol loading decreases with altitude. In most area shown in Fig.2, the received coherent photoelectron number is larger than 100.

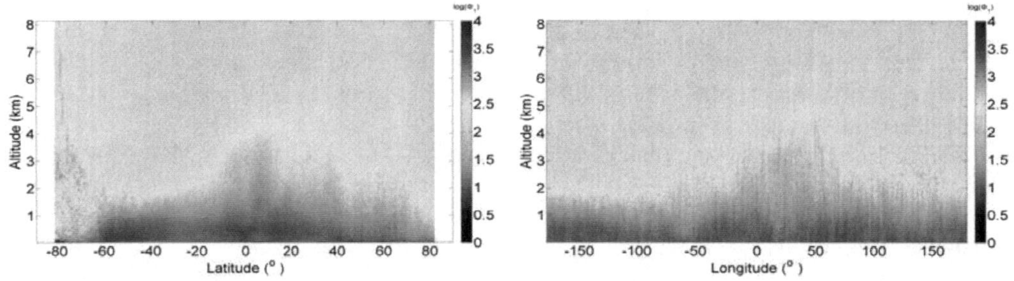

Fig. 2. Simulated zonal-vertical distributions of received number of coherent photoelectrons Φ_1

The latitude and longitude zonal-vertical distributions of the calculated fraction of bad estimates b and radial velocity RMS error of good velocity estimates g are presented in Fig. 3 and Fig. 4, respectively. Fig. 3 shows that b is less than 0.1 in most of the atmospheric aerosol is distributed. The altitudes of b = 0.1 where a wind measurement with a faction of 10% bad estimates decreases as approaching the two poles where the aerosol loading is small. It is seen that the accuracy of radial wind velocity good estimates g increases as Φ_1 decreases (Fig. 4 vs. Fig. 1), and can reach an altitude of 2 km with radial velocity RMS error less than 0.3 m/s except in the areas of the two poles.

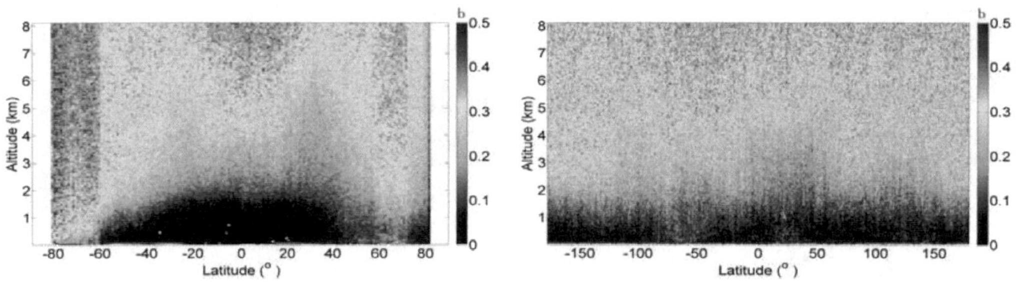

Fig. 3. Zonal-vertical distributions of the calculated fraction of bad estimates *b*

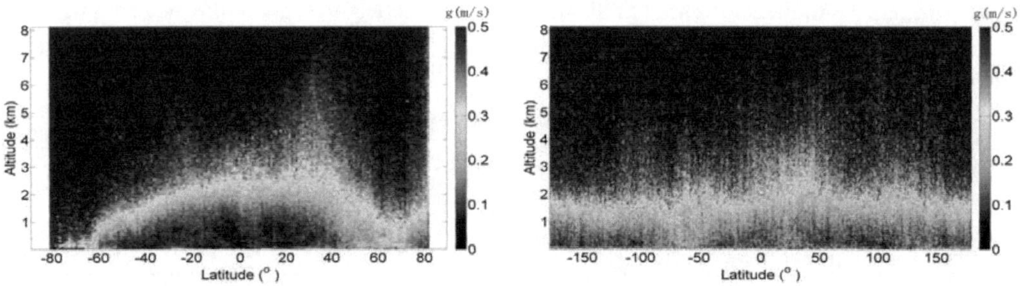

Fig. 4. Zonal-vertical distributions of RMS error of good velocity estimates g in m/s

4. Conclusions

The single-shot measurements of a 1064 nm CDWL in cloud- free conditions are simulated using latitude and longitude zonal-vertical distributions of mean attenuated backscatters at 1064 nm from two months （Jul. and Nov. 2011） of CALIOP Version 4.00 level 1 nighttime profile products. The corresponding feature types from CALIOP level 2 vertical feature mask (VFM) products are used for cloud-free data selection.

The simulation results show that the distributions of calculated fraction of bad estimates b and radial velocity RMS error of good velocity estimates g show strong similar patterns with the distribution of attenuated backscatters at 1064 nm because a CDWL uses aerosol as a tracer of wind. The altitude of accuracy of radial wind velocity good estimates g less than 0.3 m/s can reach an altitude of 2 km except in the areas of the two poles.

5. Acknowledgements

This work is supported by the National Natural Science Foundations of China (Grant No.41376180). The authors acknowledge the Atmospheric Science Data Center (ASDC) at the NASA Langley Research Center for providing the CALIPSO data used in this paper.

6. References

[1] Huffaker RM, Lawrence TR, Post MJ, Priestley JT, Hall FF, Richter RA, et al, "Feasibility studies for a global wind measuring satellite system (Windsat): Analysis of simulated performance," Appl Opt 23, 2523-2536 (1984).

[2] Menzies RT, "Doppler lidar atmospheric wind sensors: A comparative performance evaluation for global measurement applications from earth orbit," Appl Opt 25, 2546-2553 (1986).

[3] Frehlich RG, Yadlowsky MJ, "Performance of mean frequency estimators for Doppler radar and lidar," J Atmos Oceanic Technol, 11, 1217-1230 (1994).

[4] Lottman BT, Frehlich RG, "Evaluation of coherent Doppler lidar velocity estimators in non-stationary regimes," Appl Opt36, 7906-7918 (1997).

[5] Frehlich RG, "Simulation of coherent Doppler lidar performance for space-based platforms," J Appl Meteor 39(2), 245-262 (2000).

[6] Frehlich RG, "Errors for space-based Doppler lidar wind measurements: Definition, performance, and verification," J Atmos Oceanic Technol18,1749-1772 (2001).

[7] Wood S, Emmitt GD,Greco S, "DLSM: A coherent and direct detection lidar simulation model for simulating space-based and aircraft-based lidar winds," In:Gary W. Kamerman, Upendra N. Singh, Christian Werner,Vasyl V, Molebny, Editors. Laser Radar Technology and Applications V. Proceedings of SPIE 4035, 2-12 (2000).

[8] The Community Doppler Lidar Simulation Model (DLSM). Available from:

http://www.swa.com/10-services/environment-laser-division/365-dlsm-version-4-4

[9] Wu D, Tang J, Liu Z, Hu Y, "Simulation of coherent Doppler wind lidar measurement from space based on CALIPSO lidar global aerosol observations," J Quant Spectrosc Radiat Transfer122, 79-86 (2013).

[10] Winker DM, Hunt WH, McGill MJ, "Initial performance assessment of CALIOP," Geophys Res Lett 34, 228-262 (2007).

[11] Winker DM, Pelon J, Coakley Jr JA, Ackerman SA, Charlson RJ, Colarco PR, et al, "The CALIPSO mission: a global 3D view of aerosols and clouds," Bull Am Meteorol Soc 91, 1211-1229 (2010).

[12] Frehlich R, "Velocity error for coherent Doppler lidar with pulse accumulation," J Atmos Oceanic Technol 21, 905-920 (2004).

[13] Frehlich RG, Kavaya MJ, "Coherent laser radar performance for general atmospheric refractive turbulence," Appl Opt 30(36), 5325–5352 (1991).

[14] Srivastava V, Rothermel J, Clarke AD, Spinhirne JD, Menzies RT, Cutten DR, et al, "Wavelength dependence of backscatter by use of aerosol microphysics and lidar data sets: application to 2.1-μm wavelength for space-based and airborne lidars," Appl Opt 40(27), 4759–4769 (2001).

[15] Kacenelenbogen M, Vaughan M A, Redemann J, et al, " An accuracy assessment of the CALIOP/CALIPSO version 2/version 3 daytime aerosol extinction product based on a detailed multi-sensor, multi-platform case study," Atmos Chem Phys 11(11), 3981-4000 (2011).

[16] Zhang T, Wu D, "Differences between attenuated backscatters obtained from CALIOP version 3 and latest version 4 products for clouds and aerosols", Laser & Optoelectronics Progress, 53, 060102 (2016).

[17] Fairall CW, Frish AS. "Diurnal and annual variation in mean profiles of C_n^2," NOAA Technical Memorandum ERL WPL-195. National Oceanic and Atmospheric Administration, Boulder, Co. (1991).

Recent results from feasibility study of space-based Doppler Wind Lidar in Japan

Kozo Okamoto (a)(b), Shoken Ishii (b), Philippe Baron (b), Takuji Kubota (c), Yohei Satoh (c),Daisuke Sakaizawa (c), Toshiyuki Ishibashi (a), Taichu Y. Tanaka (a), Koji Yamashita (d), Kyoka Gamo (e), Satoshi Ochiai (b), Motoaki Yasui (b), Riko Oki (c), Masaki Satoh (f), and Toshiki Iwasaki (g)

(a) Meteorological Research Institute, Japan Meteorological Agency
1-1 Nagamine, Tsukuba, Ibaraki 305-0052, Japan
(b) National Institute of Information and Communications Technology, Koganei, Japan
(c) Japan Aerospace Exploration Agency, Tsukuba, Japan
(d) Japan Meteorological Agency, Chiyoda, Japan
(e) Fujitsu FIP Corporation, Koto, Japan
(f) Atmosphere and Ocean Research Institute, The University of Tokyo, Kashiwa, Japan
(g) Graduate School of Science, Tohoku University, Sendai, Japan

Abstract: Global wind profiling is important to improve initial conditions for numerical weather prediction or general circulation model. A working group for a future space-based DWL mission is studying a future space-based coherent DWL. NICT developed an end-to-end comprehensive simulator for wind measurement from space called ISOSIM-L (Integrated Satellite Observation SIMulator for a space-based coherent Doppler Lidar) in order to study measurement performances of a space-based Doppler lidar. Retrieved LOS wind data simulated by the ISOSIM-L are used for an Observing System Simulation Experiment (OSSE) system to investigate potential impacts on the numerical weather prediction. In the paper, we present recent results from feasibility study of space-based Doppler Wind Lidar with using the ISOSM-L and OSSE.

1. Introduction

Improvements of numerical weather prediction (NWP) is important for severe weather-related disaster prevention. Global wind profile observation is crucial to significantly improve the initial conditions essential for NWP, and various meteorological studies. Wind is one of the fundamental meteorological variables describing the atmospheric state, but current space-borne observing systems are biased to water-vapor- and temperature-related measurements in comparison with wind measurements (Baker et al. 2014). The World Meteorological Organization (WMO) Integrated Global Observing system technical report (WMO, 2012) states, "Development of satellite-based wind profiling systems remains a priority for the future global observing system.". Wind profiles are provided mainly by radiosonde networks and also by aircraft measurements. The radiosonde measurement is mainly performed over populated regions in the northern hemisphere (NH) but not in the southern hemisphere (SH). The number of weather stations observing the upper atmosphere has been decreasing. A lack of wind observations over oceans, SH, and other sparse areas causes non-uniform errors in NWP and subsequent analysis. Space-based wind profiling system with high vertical resolution, low bias, and high precision is necessary to fill the gap of current observations. The European Space Agency is planning to launch the first space-based Doppler Wind Lidar named ADM-Aeolus for obtaining global wind profiles (Stoffelen et al. 2005). The current target year of the launch is 2017. It will provide profiles of line-of-sight (LOS) wind speed.

In light of these circumstances, a working group for a future space-based DWL mission was organized in Japan in 2011 to discuss a space-based coherent DWL (CDWL) for vector wind measurement. The National Institute of Information and Communications Technology developed an end-to-end comprehensive simulator for wind measurement from space called ISOSIM-L (Integrated Satellite

Observation SIMulator for a space-based coherent Doppler Lidar) in order to study measurement performances of a space-based Doppler lidar (Ishii et al., 2016). ISOSIM-L uses a pseudo-truth atmospheric field created from Sensitivity Observing System Experiment (SOSE) (Marseille et al., 2008) and aerosol field computes backscattered signal, and then retrieves a line of sight (LOS) wind speed. Retrieved line-of-sight wind data simulated by the ISOSIM-L are used for an Observing System Simulation Experiment (OSSE) system based on the SOSE (hereafter, SOSE-OSSE, Ishibashi 2014) to quantitatively assess potential impacts on NWP. Numerical simulation flow from the ISOSIM-L to the SOSE-OSSE is shown in Fig.1. Recent results from feasibility study will be presented in this paper.

2. Lidar simulator

The ISOSIM-L is an end-to-end comprehensive simulator for wind measurement from space. It has been developed at NICT. It simulates each shot and each range gate backscattered power, signal-to-noise ratio (SNR), line-of-sight (LOS) wind speed, and LOS wind speed error. First objective in the development of the ISOSIM-L is to study performances of a space-based CDWL. Trade-off studies are very important to realize a space-based mission. Second objective is to evaluate the random error, sampling produced by laser beam and the configuration of the receiver, and bias in a non-turbulent atmosphere and in a turbulent atmosphere. Third objective is to collaborate with other universities and research institutes to combine results simulated using the ISOSIM-L with SOSE-OSSE. An example of down-looking observation geometry using two telescopes for measuring two orthogonal components of the horizontal winds in the same horizontal air slab is show in Fig. 2. Retrieval simulations have been conducted using ISOSIM-L for 1 month during 1-31 August, 2010. The percentage of good quality estimates is 40% at an altitude of <8 km. The percentage of good quality estimates at 8-20 km in the NH and SH is 20-50% and 10 %, respectively (Ishii et al., 2016).

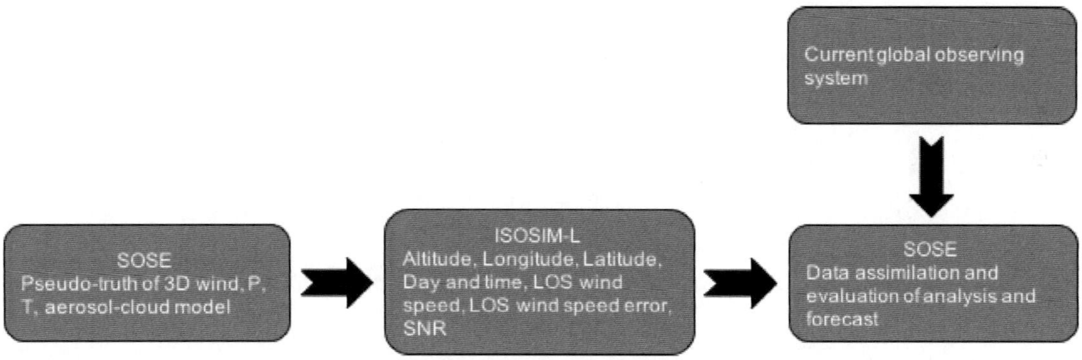

Figure 1. Numerical simulation flow from space-borne CDWL lidar simulator to

3. Potential impact on NWP

The SOSE-OSSE system is developed at the Meteorological Research Institute (MRI) using the global NWP system of Japan Meteorological Agency (JMA 2013). Pseudo-truth atmospheric field created by SOSE is used for ISOSIM-L simulations described in section 3. Preliminary results of one-month assimilation experiments using the SOSE-OSSE on polar orbit and low-inclination angle orbit showed positive impacts on short-range forecasts on wind speed at pressures of 850 and 250 hPa. We are conducting the assimilation experiments to perform robust impact studies.

4. Summary

A full-fledged lidar simulator was developed to study performances of a space-based CDWL. It is used for the feasibility and trade-off studies of the future space-based CDWL mission. The SOSE-OSSE is a useful tool to quantitatively assess potential impacts on NWP. Assimilation experiments are conducting at MRI. We will implement the simulations of space-based CDWL lidar and assimilation experiments in different seasons to investigate robust impacts.

5. Acknowledgements

A part of this research is supported by JSPS KAKENHI under Grant Numbers 15K06129 and 15K05293. The authors wish to thank the working group for a future Japanese space-based CDWL for supporting the research activity of the working group.

6. References

[1] Baker et al., "Lidar-Measured Wind Profiles: The Missing Link in the Global Observing System," *Bull. Amer. Metor. Soc.* **95**, 543-564 (2014).

[2] Marseille et al., "Sensitivity observing system experiment (SOSE): a new effective NWP-based tool in designing the global observing system," *Tellus A* **60**, 216-233 (2008).

[3] Stoffelen et al. "The atmospheric dynamics mission for global wind measurement," *Bull. Amer. Meteor. Soc.* **86**, 73-87 (2005).

[4] WMO integrated global observing system; final report of the fifth WMO workshop on the impact of various observing systems on numerical weather prediction. *WMO Tech. Rep.* 2012-1, 6 (2012).

[5] Ishibashi, "Observing system simulation experiments with multiple methods," *Proceedings of SPIE* **9265**, 926508; (2014).

[6] Ishii et al., "Measurement performance assessment of future space-borne Doppler wind lidar," *SOLA* **12**, 55-59 (2016).

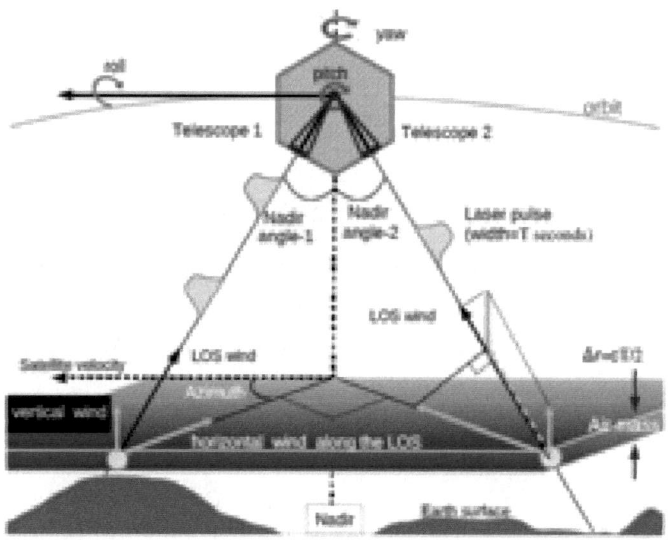

Figure 2. Down-looking observation geometry using two telescopes

AUTHOR INDEX

AUTHOR INDEX

AUTHOR INDEX

Cooperative Institute for Research in Environmental Sciences (CIRES)
University of Colorado Boulder
216 UCB
Boulder, CO 80309
USA

ISBN 978-1-5108-2854-4
9 781510 828544

CURRAN ASSOCIATES INC.
proceedings.com